International
Dictionary of Literary Awards

by

Jane Clapp

The Scarecrow Press, Inc.
New York   1963

Table of Contents

Sources And Use of
International Dictionary of Literary Awards

The International Dictionary of Literary Awards is a selected list of
major literary honors granted internationally and in countries other than
the United States, Canada, and the United Kingdom. Each literary
award is briefly described, and a list of winning authors and titles
of winning works is usually given. Most of the awards are currently granted, but a few famous literary honors no longer presented (such as the Kleist Prize, the Stalin Prize) are included.

In listing winners of prizes, emphasis is on the authors honored
during the last five years, with a selective list of winning writers
since the end of World War II. For some awards (such as the
Nobel Prize for Literature, Japan Academy of Arts Prizes, Bancarella Prize, Nadal Prize, Planeta Prize) complete lists of prize-
winners are given.

Most of the information about the literary awards was obtained
through correspondence and questionnaire from learned societies,
educational institutions, libraries, official cultural representatives,
awarding agencies, and other private and public groups in the countries where formal encouragement of good writing is given.

Appreciation is expressed to the many individuals and groups
who gave descriptions of awards and lists of winners, and who
designated most significant literary honors.

The section "Literary Awards by Country" mentions major awards,
gives some additional literary honors not in the Dictionary list,
shows major sources of information, and lists the prizes granted
as mentioned in the Dictionary list.

The index includes names of literary awards, winning authors, awarding and sponsoring agencies, and awards offered specifically for one form of writing (as, Children's and Young People's Literary Awards, Journalism, Novel, Poetry, Short Story and Novella).

The International Dictionary of Literary Awards should bring to the attention of publishers, librarians, students of literature and culture, and general readers, the names of many authors who are honored in their own country, but are less well-known in other lands and languages.

Authors Distinguished By Three Or More Literary Honors

Authors winning three or more of the literary awards listed or mentioned in the International Dictionary of Literary Awards are listed below. The nationality of each writer is indicated by the following code:

Ar	Argentina	J	Japan
Au	Australia	L	Lithuania
Aus	Austria	M	Mexico
B	Belgium	N	Netherlands
Bo	Bolivia	NZ	New Zealand
Br	Brazil	No	Norway
Bu	Bulgaria	P	Philippines
C	Chile	Pa	Paraguay
Cz	Czechoslovakia	Po	Poland
D	Denmark	Pr	Puerto Rico
F	Finland	R	Rumania
Fr	France	S	Spain
G	Germany	Sw	Sweden
GE	East Germany	Swi	Switzerland
Gr	Greece	UK	United Kingdom
H	Hungary	USA	United States of America
I	Iceland	USSR	Union of Soviet Socialist
Ir	Ireland		Republics
Is	Israel	V	Venezuela
It	Italy	Y	Yugoslavia

Because the awards are a selection of a large number of literary honors granted, because winning authors usually are those given prizes during the last few years, and because the numbers of awards listed for different countries vary widely and many different types of prizes are included, comparisons of merit between authors and between countries are not meaningful.

Authors Winning Three Literary Awards

Kjeld Abell (D)
Elio Filippo Accrocca (It)
Leopold Ahlsen (G)
Dámaso Alonso (S)
José María Álvarez Blázquez (S)
Alfred Andersch (G)
Stefan Andres (G)

Hugo Argüelles Cano (M)
Marcel Arland (Fr)
Wystan Hugh Auden (UK---USA)
Colette Audry (Fr)
Albert Ayguesparse (B)
Rudolf Bayr (Au)
Hervé Bazin (Fr)

7

Jacinto Benavente (S)
Mihai Beniuc (R)
Richard Benz (G)
Georges Bernanos (Fr)
Giuseppe Berto (It)
Carlo Betocchi (It)
Ugo Betti (It)
Richard Billinger (G)
Thorkild Bjørnvig (D)
Anna Blaman (N)
Robert Bourget-Pailleron (Fr)
Felix Braun (Aus)
Mattias Braun (G)
Gregorio C. Brilliantes (P)
Italo Calvino (It)
Emilio Carballido (M)
Francis Carco (Fr)
Maurice Carême (Fr)
Emilio Carilla (Ar)
Hans Carossa (G)
José Luis Castillo Puche (S)
Camillo-José Cela (S)
Winston Churchill (UK)
Eduard Claudius (GE)
Josef Cohen (N)
Francisco Coloane (C)
Giorgio Croce (It)
Alexis Curvers (B)
Pierre Daninos (Fr)
Miguel Delibes (S)
Hernán Díaz Arrieta ('Alone") (C)
Samuel Eichenbaum (Ar)
Josep María Espinás (S)
Gonzalo Fernández de la Mora (S)
Vera Ferra-Mikura (Aus)
Luis Leopoldo Franco (Ar)
Leonhard Frank (G---GE)
Franz Fühmann (GE)
Rómulo Gallegos (V)
Manuel Gálvez (Ar)
José García Nieto (S)
André Gide (Fr)
Natalia Ginzberg (It)
José María Gironella (S)
Alberto Girri (Ar)
Fyodor V. Gladkov (USSR)
Jurgis Gliauda (L---USA)
Luis de Goytisolo (S)
Guillaume van der Graft (N)
João Guimarães Rosa (Br)
Rudolf Hagelstange (G)
Gerhart Hauptmann (G)
Harald Hauser (GE)
Finn Havrevold (No)

Fritz Hochwälder (Aus)
Hans-Egon Holthusen (G)
Luc Hommel (B)
Veikko Huovinen (F)
Aldous Huxley (UK)
Masuji Ibuse (J)
Gyula Illyés (H)
Frank Jaeger (D)
Yves Jamiaque (Fr)
Karl Jaspers (G)
Ernst Jünger (G)
Vjekoslav Kaleb (Y)
Hermann Kasack (G)
Rudolf Kassner (Aus)
Nikos Kazantzakis (Gr)
Martin Kessel (G)
Erwin Guido Kolbenheyer (G)
Tom Kristensen (D)
Kirsi Kunnas (F)
Czeslaw Kuriata (F)
Enrique Lafourcade (C)
C.-F. Landry (Swi)
Othmar Franz Lang (Aus)
Armand Laroux (Fr)
Halldór Kiljan Laxness (I)
Cora Ria Leeman (B)
Gertrud von Le Fort (G)
Charles Le Quintrec (Fr)
Alexander Lernet-Holenia (Aus)
Kelvin Lindemann (D)
Astrid Lindgren (SW)
Willy-August Linnemann (D)
Teodoro M. Locsin (P)
Anna Lo Monaco Aprile (It)
Luis López Anglada (S)
Hans Lorbeer (GE)
Armen Lubin (Fr)
Juha Mannerkorpi (F)
Michel Manoll (Fr)
Gianna Manzini (It)
Gabriel Marcel (Fr)
Leopoldo Marechal (Ar)
Rene Marqués (Pr)
Harry Martinsson (Sw)
John Masefield (UK)
Georg Maurer (GE)
José Ramón Medina (V)
Max Mell (Aus)
Martti Merenmaa (F)
Agnes Miegel (G)
Eugenio Montale (It)
Rafael Montesinos (S)
Rafael Morales (S)
Paul Mousset (Fr)

Saisei Murou (J)
Saneatsu Mushanokoji (J)
Franz Nabl (Aus)
Enrique Nácher (S)
Pablo Neruda (C)
Martin Andersen Nexö (D---GE)
Viteslav Nezval (Cz)
Ramón Nieto (S)
André Obey (Fr)
Pedro Miguel Obligado (Ar)
Mimei Ogawa (J)
Poul Ørum (D)
Miguel Otero Silva (V)
Aldo Palazzeschi (It)
Miron Radu Paraschivescu (R)
Enrico Pea (It)
Edouard Pea (Fr)
Ernst Penzoldt (G)
Jan Petersen (GE)
Hannes Pétursson (I)
Heinz Piontek (G)
Franz Pühringer (Aus)
Henri Queffélec (Fr)
Sigismund von Radecki (G)
Aristo Radevski (Bu)
Gerard Kornelis van het Reve (N)
Afonso Reyes (M)
Alain Robbe-Grillet (Fr)
Manuel Rojas Sepulveda (C)
Romain Rolland (Fr)
Ward Ruyslinck (B)
Max Rychner (G)
Robert Sabatier (Fr)
Mikhail Sadoveanu (R)
Carlos Sahagún (S)
Antoine de Saint-Exupéry (Fr)

José Salas Guiror (S)
Fernando Santiván (C)
Wilhelm Schäfer (G)
Edzaard Schaper (Fr)
Reinhold Schneider (G)
Rudolf Alexander Schröder (G)
Bernhard Seeger (G)
George Bernard Shaw (Ir---UK)
Edith Sitwell (UK)
Erwin Strittmatter (GE)
Jules Supervielle (Fr)
A.A. Surov (USSR)
Michio (also Michi) Takeyama (J)
Marko Tapio (Fr)
Evert Taube (Sw)
Oskar Jan Tauschinski (Aus)
Bonaventura Tecchi (It)
Henri Thomas (Fr)
Niculae Tic (R)
Rodolfo Usigli (M)
Roger Vailland (Fr)
István Vas (H)
José Manuel Vergara (C)
Jan Veulemans (B)
Alan J. Villiers (Au)
Martino Vitali (It)
Hendrik de Vries (N)
Victor E. Van Vriesland (N)
Georg von der Vring (G)
Franz Werfel (Aus)
Thornton Wilder (U.S.A.)
Liliane Wouters (B)
S. Yishar (also Yizhar) (Is)
Maurice Zermatten (B)
Leopold Ziegler (G)
Hedda Zinner (GE)

Authors Winning Four Literary Awards

Giovan Battista Angioletti (It)
Riccardo Bacchelli (It)
Giorgio Bassani (It)
Carlo Bernari (It)
Jorge Luis Borges (Ar)
Henri Bosco (Fr)
Marta Brunet y Caraves (C)
Antonio Buero Vallejo (S)
Hermann Burte (G)
Michel Butor (Fr)
Juan Antonio Cabezas (S)
Remco Campert (N)
Arturo Capdevila (Ar)
Libera Carlier (B)
Étienne Cattin (Fr)
Paul Cazin (Fr)
Sidonie Gabrielle Colette (Fr)
Carmen Conde (S)
Antoon Coolen (N)

André Dhôtel (Fr)
Gerardo Diego Cendoya (S)
Maurice Duggan (NZ)
Luis Durand (C)
Jean Dutourd (Fr)
Ilya Ehrenburg (USSR)
Diego Fabbri (It)
Gerhard Fritsch (Aus)

Gerd Gaiser (G)
Romain Gary (Fr)
Jean Giono (Fr)
Jean Giraudoux (Fr)
Nestor V.M. Gonzales (P)
Andrei Goulyashki (Bu)
Corrado Govoni (It)
Javier del Granada (Bo)
Günter Grass (G)
Massimo Grillandi (It)

Jean Guehenno (Fr)
René Guillot (Fr)
Fritz Habeck (Aus)
Matti Hälli (F)
Helvi Hämäläinen (F)
Martin A. Hansen (D)
Helmut Hauptmann (GE)
William Heinesen (D)
Ernest Hemingway (USA)
Philippe Hériat (Fr)
Adriaan Roland Holst (N)
Yasushi Inoue (J)
Slavko Janevski (Y)
Joseph Kessel (Fr)
Annette Kolb (G)
Jacques de Lacretelle (Fr)
Carmen Laforêt (S)
Mihajlo Lalic (Y)
Horst Lange (G---GE)
Christine Lavant (Aus)
Wilhelm Lehmann (G)
Väinö Linna (F)
Osman Lins (Br)
Torcuato Luca de Tena (S)
Pierre Mac Orlan (Fr)
André Malraux (Fr)
Eeva-Liisa Manner (F)
Félicien Marceau (Fr)
Hans Marchwitza (GE)
Ezequiel Martínez Estrada (Ar)
Hakucho Masamune (J)
Miguel Mihura (S)
Yukio Mishima (J)

Gabriela Mistral (C)
Mauro Musiacchio (It)
Cees Nooteboom (N)
Shohei Ooka (J)
Jacob Paludan (D)
Nino Palumbo (It)
Ramón Pérez de Ayala (S)
Mario Praz (It)
Pandelis Prevelakis (Gr)
Salvatore Quasimodo (It)
Raquel de Queiros (Br)
Augusto Roa Bastos (Pa)
Emmanuel Roblès (Fr)
Jules Romains (Fr)
Bertrand Russell (UK)
Umberto Saba (It)
Michel de Saint-Pierre (Fr)
Haruo Sato (J)
Ton Satomi (J)
Jens August Schade (D)
Oda Schaefer (G)
Ernst Schnabel (G)
Mikhail Sholokhov (USSR)
Daniel Sueiro (S)
Junichiro Tanizaki (J)
Henri Troyat (Fr)
Kerima P. Tuvera (P)
Fritz Unruh (G)
Bernardo Verbitsky (Ar)
Benno Voelkner (GE)
Eiji Yoshikawa (J)
Herbert Zand (Aus)
Arnold Zweig (GE)

Authors Winning Five Literary Awards

Jorge Amado (Br)
Ivo Andric (Y)
Vicente Barbieri (Ar)
André Billy (Fr)
Alain Bosquet (Fr)
Bertolt Brecht (GE)
Carl Jacob Burckhardt (Swi)
Henry Daniel-Rops (Fr)
Oskar Davico (Y)
Heimito von Doderer (Aus)
Carlo Emilio Gadda (It)
Jorge Guillén (S)
Hermann Hesse (G---Swi)
Theodor Heuss (G)
Yasunari Kawabata (J)
Aleeksandr Korneichuk (USSR)
Selma Lagerlöff (Sw)
Per Lange (D)

Thomas Mann (G---USA)
Giuseppe Marotta (It)
François Mauriac (Fr)
Ramon Menéndez Pidal (S)
Harry Mulisch (N)
Conrado Nalé Roxlo (Ar)
Pier Paalo Pasolini (It)
Saint-John Perse (pen name of Aléx-
    is Saint-Léger Léger) (Fr)
Marie Pujmanova (Cz)
Beinvenido N. Santos (P)
Jean-Paul Sartre (Fr)
Camillo Sbarbaro (It)
Hans Hartvig Seedorff (D)
Konstantin M. Simonov (USSR)
Knud Soenderby (D)
Johannes Wulff (D)
Juan Antonio de Zunzunegui (S)

Authors Winning Six Literary Awards

Georg Britting (G)
Karl Bruckner (Aus)
Christine Busta (Aus)
Dino Buzzati Traverso (It)
Vicenzo Cardarelli (It)
Günter Eich (G)
Nick Joaquin Y Marques (P)
Friedrich Georg Jünger (G)
Erich Kästner (G)
Leonid Leonov (USSR)
Eduardo Mallea (Ar)

Ana María Matute (S)
Manuel Mujica Láinez (Ar)
Marie Noël (Fr)
Vasco Pratolini (It)
Jules Roy (Fr)
Albert Schweitzer (Fr)
Anna Seghers (G---GE)
Giuseppe Ungaretti (It)
Simon Vestdijk (N)
Carl Zuckmayer (G)

Authors Winning Seven Literary Awards

Ilse Aichinger (Aus---G)
Kurt Bartel ('Kuba'') (GE)
Knuth Becker (D)
H. C. Branner (D)
Martin Buber (G---Is)

Branko Copic (Y)
Isak Dinesen (D)
T. S. Eliot (USA---UK)
Max Frisch (Swi)
Pär Fabian Lagerkvist (Sw)

Authors Winning Eight Literary Awards

Carlo Cassola (It)   Friedrich Dürrenmatt (Swi)

Authors Winning Nine Literary Awards

Ludwig Renn (GE)

Authors Winning Eleven Literary Awards

Heinrich Böll (G)

Alphabetical List of Prizes

AE MEMORIAL PRIZE (Ireland)
This award, administered by the Irish Academy of Letters (c/o Abbey Theatre, Pearse Street, Dublin), is one of several literary honors granted by the Academy.   1.

Emil AARESTRUP PRIZE (Denmark)
Established December 4, 1950 to commemorate the 150th anniversary of the birth of the Danish lyric poet, Carl Ludwig Emil Aarestrup, this prize consists of a medal and 2,500 D. Kr. Authors honored by this annual prize include: Aage Berntsen, Thorkild Bjørnvig, Tove Ditlevsen, Otto Gelsted, Frank Jaeger, Hans Hartvig, Seedorff-Pedersen, Sigfred Pedersen, Halfdan Rasmussen, Jens August Schade, Ole Wivel, and-- in 1962--Erik Knudsen.   2.

Estanislao ABARCA PRIZE (Spain)
This 50,000 pts prize for a novel, established in 1951 and offered under the auspices of the Banco de Santander, was won in 1957 by Manuel Arce with "Pintado sobre el vacio."   3.

ABINGDON AWARD (International--U.S.A.)
This publisher's literary prize of $12,500 ($10,000 outright prize and $2,500 royalty advance), awarded from time to time since 1947 by the Abingdon Press (201 Eighth Avenue, South, Nashville 3, Tennessee), honors a book which will "accomplish the greatest good for the Chris-

tian faith and Christian living among all people." All writers are eligible to compete for the award, without any limit as to nationality, race or creed. The fifth award, given in 1959 to Jaroslav Pelikan (U.S.A.) for "The Riddle of Roman Catholicism," is the latest prize, and no additional awards are planned at present (1962).   4.

ACADEMIA BRASILEIRA DE LETRAS (Brazil)
The Brazilian Academy (Avenida Presidente Wilson 203, Rio de Janeiro) includes among its members outstanding writers of Brazil and annually awards a number of prizes for the best Brazilian writing (currently the MACHADO DE ASSIS PRIZE of Cr$200.000 to the writer who has made the most outstanding contribution to literature through his entire works, including those published in the three years preceding the award; Claudio de SOUSA PRIZE, Cr$110.000 for the best unpublished and unproduced play; Julia LOPES DE ALMEIDA PRIZE, Cr$7.200 for the best unpublished or published work by a woman writer, preferably a novel or collection of novellas; and five or more prizes of Cr$50.000 each for books in various literary forms, unpublished or published during the two years preceding award--Olavo BILAC PRIZE for poetry; Afonso ARINOS PRIZE for short stories and novel; Silvio ROMERO PRIZE for literary criticism and history; Artur AZEVEDO PRIZE for a historical or critical work on the theatre, or a translation

13

of a theatrical work; José
VERISSIMO PRIZE for a scholarly essay; COELHO NETO
PRIZE for novel; Joaquim
NABUCO PRIZE for social history, politics, memoirs; João
REBEIRO PRIZE for philology,
ethnography, and folklore;
RAMOS PAZ PRIZE for young
writers of works of literary
history and criticism; Francisco ALVES PRIZE for monographs on set subjects--in
1962, three prizes of Cr $10.000
each on Primary Education in
Brazil; Portuguese Language).

Academy members include
Alvaro Lins, literary critic
(1956); José Lins do Régo
(1956), who in his acceptance
speech, conventionally given in
praise of a deceased predecessor, stated that his predecessor
had not produced anything re-
motely resembling literature;
Olegario Mariano Carneiro da
Cunha (1958); Afonso Arinos
(1958); Aurelio Buarque de
Holanda (1961); Jorge Amado
(1961).   5.

ACADEMIA MÉXICANA DE LA
LENGUA (Mexico)
Members of the Mexican
Academy of Letters include
Celestino Gortostiza, dramatist;
and José Luis Martínez, critic.
Alfonso Reyes, an honorary
member since 1928, was presi-
dent of the Academy from 1957
until his death.   6.

ACADÉMIE DES INSCRIPTIONS
ET BELLES-LETTRES PRIZES
(France)
One of the sections of the
Institut de France, this Academy
(Alfred Merlin, Permanent
Secretary, 23 quai de Conti,
Paris 7e), includes among its
members a group of 12 "As-
sociés Étrangers," foreign authors
who are distinguished writers or
scholars, such as Ramon Menendez

Pidal of Spain, and Henry Gri-
goire, Byzantine scholar, of
Brussels. Of the approximately
fifty prizes the Academy offers
for scholarly writing in such fields
as history, linguistics, archaeolo-
by, two are listed in the International Dictionary of Literary Awards:
GILES PRIZE; SAINTOUR PRIZE.
                                  7.

ACADÉMIE FRANÇAISE GRAND
PRIX DE LITTÉRATURE (France)
This annual prize for prose
or poetry is one of the richest
awards given by the French
Academy, with a premium that
reached 100.000 francs in 1955-
1959. Offered since 1912 for the
entire literary output of an author,
rather than for a single book,
the award--granted for writing of
"inspiration élevée et d'une forme
remarquable"--includes among
winners, honored for their
"Entire Work" unless otherwise
noted:
    1912 André Lafon. L'élève
    Gilles
    1913 Romain Rolland. Jean-
    Christophe
    1915 Emile Nolly
    1916 M. Masson
    1917 Francis Jammes
    1918 Gérard d'Houville
    1919 J. and J. Tharaud
    1920 Edmond Jaloux
    1921 Mme de Noailles. Les
    innocentes
    1922 Pierre Lasserre
    1923 François Porche
    1924 A. Bonnard. En Chine
    1925 Général Mangin
    1926 Gilbert de Voisins.
    Mauclair
    1927 Joseph de Pesquidoux.
    Sur la glèbe
    1928 Jean-Louis Vaudoyer
    1929 Henri Massis
    1930 Mme Pailleron
    1931 Raymond Escholier
    1932 Franc-Nohain
    1933 Henri Duvernois. A
    l'ombre d'une femme, and

his other work
1934 Henry de Montherlant.
  Les célibataires
1935 André Suarès
1936 Pierre Camo
1937 Maurice Magre
1938 Tristan Derème
1939 Jacques Boulenger
1940 Edmond Pilon
1941 Gabriel Faure
1942 Jean Schlumberger
1943 Jean Prévost
1944 André Billy
1945 Jean Paulhan
1946 Henri Daniel-Rops
1947 Mario Meunier
1948 Gabriel Marcel
1949 Maurice Levaillant
1950 Henri Martineau
1952 Marcel Arland
1953 Marcel Brion
1954 Jean Guitton
1955 Jules Supervielle
1956 Henry Clouard
1958 Jules Roy
1959 Thierry Maulnier
1960 Mme Simone
1961 Jacques Maritain
1962 Luc Estang   8.

ACADÉMIE FRANÇAISE GRAND
PRIX DU ROMAN (France)
   One of the famous literary
prizes of France, and the best
known of the French Academy
prizes is this annual award for
a novel by a young writer for a
work of "inspiration élevée."
Recipients of the Prix du Roman,
honored each year toward the
end of Spring for a single work
or for their entire literary output, include:
   1915 Paul Acker. Entire
   work, including Les De-
   moiselles Bertram
   1916 Avesnes. L'île heureuse
   1917 Charles Geniaux. La
   passion d'Armelle Louanais
   1918 Camille Mayran. Gotton
   Connixloo
   1919 Pierre Benoît. L'Atlantide
   1920 André Corthis. Pour moi
   seule

1921 Pierre Villetard.
  Monsieur Bille dans la
  tourmente
1922 Francis Carco. L'homme
  traqué
1923 Alphons de Chateaubriant.
  La Brière
1924 Emile Henriot. Aricie
  Brun ou les Vertus bourgeoises
1925 François Duhourcau. L'
  enfant de la victoire
1926 François Mauriac. Le
  désert de l'amour
1927 Joseph Kessel. Les
  captifs
1928 Jean Balde. Reine d'
  Arbieu
1929 André Demaison. Le livre
  des bêtes qu'on appelle
  sauvages
1930 Jacques de Lacretelle.
  Entire work
1931 Henry Pourrat. Entire
  work, including La tour du
  Levant
1932 Jacques Chardonne. Entire work
1933 Roger Chauviré. Mlle de
  Bois-Dauphin
1934 Paule Régnier. L'abbaye
  d'Evolaine
1935 Albert Touchard. Entire
  work
1936 Georges Bernanos. Journal d'un curé de campagne
1937 Guy de Pourtalès. La
  pêche miraculeuse
1938 Jean de la Varende. Le
  Centaure de Dieu
1939 Antoine de Saint-Exupéry.
  Terre des hommes, and his
  other work
1940 Edouard Peisson. Le
  voyage d'Edgar, and his other
  work
1941 Robert Bourget-Pailleron.
  Entire work
1942 Jean Blanzat. L'orage du
  matin
1943 J. H. Louwick. Danse
  pour ton ombre
1944 Pierre Lagarde. Val-
  maurie
1945 Marc Blancpain. Le

solitaire
1946 Jean Orieux. Fontagre
1947 Philippe Hériat. Famille
Boussardel
1949 Yves Gandon. Ginèvre
(for 1948); Yvonne Pagniez.
Evasion 1944
1950 Joseph Jolinon. Les
provinciaux
1951 Bernard Barbey. Chevaux
abandonnés sur le champ de
bataille
1952 Henry Castillou. Le feu
de l'Etna
1953 Jean Hougron. La nuit
indochinoise
1954 Paul Mousset. La chasse
royale; Pierre Moinot. Neige
sur un amour nippon
1955 Michel de Saint-Pierre.
Les Aristocrates
1956 Paul Guth. Le naïf
locataire
1957 Jacques de Bourbon-
Busset. Le silence et la
joie
1958 Henri Queffélec. Un
royaume sous la mer
1959 Gabriel d'Aubarède.
La foi de notre enfance
1960 Christian Murciaux.
Notre-Dame des Désemparés
1961 Pham Van Ky. Perdre
la demeure
1962 Michel Mohrt. La prison
maritime   9.

ACADÉMIE FRANÇAISE PRIZE
FOR A BOOK WRITTEN IN
FRENCH BY A FOREIGNER
(International-France)
Recent winners of this prize
of the French Academy, granted
annually to several foreign writ-
ers include:
1957 Princesse Marthe
Bibesco (Rumania)
1958 Francisco Garcia
Calderón (Peru); Franz Hel-
lens (pseud of Franz van
Ermengen) (Belgium); S.E.
Jaime Torres-Bodet (Mexico)
1959 Jean Price-Mars;
Muhammad Hamidullah;

Christine Arnothy
1960 Mme Andree Chedib;
Paul Toupin;   Maurice
Zermatten (Switzerland);
Luc Hommel (Belgium).
Marguerite d'York (Medal).
                                10.

ACADÉMIE FRANÇAISE PRIZES
(France)
The French Academy (Maurice
Genevoix, Permanent Secretary,
23 quai de Conti, Paris 7e),
best known of the learned societies, is one of the five sections
of the Institut de France, founded
officially in 1635 by Louis XIII.
Authors who are and have been
members of the Academy, and
so one of the "Forty Immortals,"
are as famous as those who have
never been elected to the Academy.
Currently among the members,
whose "green fever" has led them
to actively seek election, (with
year of election) are: François
Mauriac (1933); Georges Duhamel
(1935); André Maurois (1938);
Marcel Pagnol (1946); Jules
Romains (1946); Jean Cocteau
(1955); Henri Daniel-Rops (1955);
Jean Rostand (1959); Henri
Troyat; Marcel Achard (1959);
Henry de Montherlant; René Huyghe (1960). Of the some 135 separate prizes awarded each year by
the Academy, those listed in the
International Dictionary of Literary Awards are: Broquette-Gonin
Grand Prize; Durchon-Louvet
Prize; Gobert Prize; Langlois
Prize; Académie Française Prize
for a Work Written in French by
a Foreigner; Académie Française
Grand Prix de Littérature; Académie Française Grand Prix du
Roman.
The Académie Française PRIX
D'ACADÉMIE of the Institut de
France, with a monetary premium
and the title "Lauréat de l'Institut,"
has honored a number of writers
each year, including:
1944 André Dhôtel

1948 Marcel Brion; Henri
Clouard
1949 Maurice Carème; Marie
Noël
1952 Lo Celso; Marguerite
Yourcenar
1953 Henri Queffélec; Em-
manuel Roblès
1955 Guy Chastel
1956 Gaston Picard
1958 Paul Cazin
The Grand Prix de Poésie in
1962 was presented to Marie
Noël for her entire literary
work.   11.

ACADÉMIE INTERNATIONALE DU TOURISME PRIZE (International--Monaco)

The International Academy of
Tourism (2 A boulevard des
Moulins, Monte Carlo) established this award in 1951 as an
annual competition on the theme
or subject of tourism. Writers
of any nationality may enter the
contest for the prize of 500
francs, medal engraved with a
likeness of Prince Rainier III
of Monaco, and a month's stay
at the Paris Hotel in Monaco.
Among winners of the award,
presented in August or September each year, are:
1952 De Meyer (Belgium)
1953 Mainil (Belgium)
1955 Thomas Hammerton
(United Kingdom)
1956 Alcide Spaggiari (Italy)
1961 A. Gavlin   12.

ACADEMY OF THIRTEEN PRIZE (France)

Granted since 1955 to an
author of a spiritual work (prose
or poetry) appearing during the
year, this award--"Prix le
Boisson"--(166 rue de la Burgone,
Niort, Deux-Sevres) of 16 bottles of a famous vintage wine
has been won by such authors
as:
1959 Pierre Daninos.
Vacances à tous prix.

1960 Jean l'Anselme. Au bout
du quai
1961 Paul Baredenon
1962 not awarded   13.

ACENTO PRIZE (Spain)

This award of the Revista
"Acento" (Quevedo 8, Madrid) is
offered for writing in three categories: Short Novel (12,000
pts); Poetry (10,000 pts); and
Short Stories (6,000 pts).   14.

ADAMJEE PRIZE FOR LITERATURE (Pakistan)

"Among the richest literary
awards in Southeast Asian Countries," is this annual Adamjee
Prize established in 1960 and
distributed through the House of
Adamjee (Karachi), and administered by the Pakistan Writers'
Guild (20 Hotel Excelsior, In-
verarity Road, Karachi). Two
prizes of Rs 10,000 each, awarded on October 27 each year, are
granted for the best literary book
written in the two official languages of Pakistan: Urdu and
Bengali; and published between
August of the previous year and
July of the year of competition.
"Creative original writings"
(Poetry, Novel, Short Story,
Drama, Non-Fiction, Literary
Criticism, Travelogue, Biography)
by citizens of Pakistan are entered in competition by sending
five copies of the eligible book to
the Pakistan Writers' Guild before
July 31, accompanied by the
prescribed entry form. A Panel
of Judges, composed of distinguished scholars and authors,
determines the winners. The
1960 and 1961 awards were divided equally among four works:
1960 Urdu--Ghulam Abbas.
Jare-ki-Chandni (collected
short stories); Shaukat
Siddiqi (also Siddiqui). Khuda-
ki-Basti (novel)
Bengali--Abdul Sattar. Kabi-
Da (dramatized biography of

the poet, Nazru Islam);
Rawshan Yazdahi (also)
Roshan Izdani). Khataman-
Nabiyeen (poem in East Pakis-
tan village dialect on the
life of the Holy Prophet).
1961 Urdu--Jamila Hashmi.
Talash-e-Baharan (novel);
Abdul Samad Khan. Iqbal
Aur Khushhal (criticism)
Bengali--Rashid Karim.
Parush (novel);
Abdul Razzaq. Kanya Ku-
mari (novel)   15.

Jane ADDAMS CHILDREN'S
BOOK AWARD (International--
U.S.A.)
    Established in 1953 to "en-
courage publication of books
for children which are of literary merit and contain constructive themes," this annual award,
an honor prize to recognize and
commend authors and publishers
for such books, consists of an
Award Certificate for the author,
and Award Seals to be used on
the book jacket for the publisher. The literary honor is offered to "a writer of any country" by the United States Section of the Women's International League for Peace and Freedom (Mrs. Trevor Teele, Chairman, 306 N. Aurora Street, Ithaca, New York), as one of its
several projects relating to
children, and named in honor
of Jane Addams, a league
founder. Publishers submit
books published during the year
by December 1 for consideration by the Award Committee,
and the top ten or fifteen books
from which the winner is chosen
are included in an annual list:
"Books for Youth Which Build
For Peace," and represented in a
permanent book exhibit at the
International Friendship Center (306 N. Aurora Street,
Ithaca, New York).
    Winners of the Award, with
books demonstrating a basic
"faith in people," include:

International Literary Awards
1956 Arna Bontemps. Story of
    the Negro.
1957 Margot Benary-Isbert
    (Germany). Blue mystery
1961 Shirley Arora. What
    then, Raman?
1962 Aimee Sommerfelt. The
    Road to Agra   16.

ADELAIDE FESTIVAL OF ARTS
AWARDS (Australia)
    Since 1959 prizes have been
granted annually by the Lord
Mayor, Adelaide, South Australia,
at the biennial Adelaide Festival
of Arts in March. The newspaper literary contest, THE
ADVERTISER LITERARY COM-
PETITION, established in 1962,
is also a feature of the Festival.
                            17.

ADONAIS PRIZE (Spain)
    Designated "the most coveted
poetry prize in Spain," by an
authority on Spanish literary a-
wards, José Sanchez, this 5,000
pts award was established in 1943
by Ediciones Rialp (Preciados
35, Madrid). Offering a main
prize, as well as a second and
third prizes ('Accesit del Premio
Adonais"), prize-winning works
are published in the "Adonais Collection," the series of the publisher comparable to the Yale
Series of Younger Poets in bringing new poets to public attention.
Among the 150 winners (issued
in paper-bound books that intro-
duce unknown young poets, many
of whom have won subsequent
literary prizes through such
publication), recent first prize
winners include:
    1954 José Angel Valente. A
        modo de esperanza
    1955 Javier de Bengoechea.
        Hombre en forma de elegia
    1956 Maria Elvira Lacaci.
        Humana voz
    1957 Carlos Sahagún. Profecias
        del aqua
    1958 Rafael Soto. La Agorera
    1959 Francisco Brines. Las
        Brasas

1960 Mariano Roldán. Hombre
nuevo
1961 Luis Feria. Conciencia
1962 Jesús Hilario Tundidor.
Junta a mi silencio   18.

THE ADVERTISER LITERARY COMPETITION (Australia)

Awarding agency of this ₤A
2,000 literary prize is Advertiser Newspapers Ltd (Box 392,
G.P.O., Adelaide, South Australia). Established in 1962 as
a feature of the biennial Adelaide
Festival of Arts, the prize consists of cash awards for a book
(Fiction, History, Biography,
or Travel)--₤A1,300 with second
and third prizes of ₤A400 and
₤A100); a short story--₤A100,
with second and third prizes;
and a poem--₤A40, with a
second prize. Established "to
encourage Australian writers to
produce original, unpublished
works on any subject, as well as
to induce writers in other countries to produce work on an Australian subject or with an Australian background," the winners
of the competition are determined by a jury which includes
two university teachers of
English literature--one a special-
ist in Australian literature--and
a member of The Advertiser
literary staff.
Winners in 1962 are:
Book--Douglas Lockwood. I,
the aboriginal (biography
of an Australian native)
Short Story--Hal Porter.
First love   19.

AEDOS PRIZE (Spain)

A "Santa Lucia Prize," and
one of the several literary a-
wards of the Barcelona publisher, Editorial Aedos (Consejo de
Ciento 391), this annual honor
for the best biography brings
25,000 pts for the best biography written in Castilian, and a
similar amount for the best
biography written in Catalan.
Editorial Aedos also grants
an award for writing in agriculture and animal husbandry:
PREMIO AGRICOLA AEDOS of
25,000 pts.
Winners of the biography prizes,
announced on Santa Lucia Day,
December 13, are:
Castilian--
1951 H.R. Romero Flores.
Biografia de Sancho Panza
1952 Pedro Voltes. El arch-
iduque Carlos de Austria
1953 Diego Sevilla Andrés.
Antonio Maura
1954 Antonio J. Onieva. Bajeza
y Grandeza de Dostoiewski
1955 Antonio Gallego Morell.
Vida y poesia de Gerardo
Diego
1956 Carmen Bravo. Vida de
Bettina Bretano
1957 José Cruset. San Juan
de Dios
1958 Bernardo Vollarrazo.
Miguel de Unamuno
1959 Antonio Oliver Belmas.
Este otro Rubén Darío
1960 Román Oyarzun. Vide de
Ramon Cabrera
1961 Elvíra Martín. Tres
mujeres Gallegas

Catalan--
1953 A Galí. Rafael D'Amat
y De Cortada
1954 J. de Camps y Arboix.
Verntallat, Cabdill del re-
mences
1955 Juan Reglá. Felip II y
Catalunya
1957 P. Prat Ubach. Juan
Junceda
1958 Rafael Tasis. Joan I
1959 J.M. Corredor. Joan
Maragall
1960 Jordi Ventira. Alfons el
Cast
1961 Romuald M. Diaz i
Carbonell. Dom Bonaventura
Ubach   20.

AFRICA PRIZES (Spain)
Two types of annual awards
have been offered since 1945
by Direccion General de Plazas
y Provincias--Africanas (Instituto de Estudios Africanos,
Castellana 5, Madrid) for writings submitted in competition by
December 1:
Literature--25,000 pts for
unpublished works on a set
theme announced each year
(1962 contest: "Estudio geo-
grafico de las Provincias y
Plazas espanolas en Africa").
Recent winners:
1959 Diego Sevilla Andrés.
Africa en la Politica Es-
pañola de Siglo XIX
1960 Luis Pericot Garcia,
and Miguel Tarradell Mateu.
Manual de Prehistoria Afri-
cana
Journalism--Six prizes, from
5,000 pts first prize to 500 pts
sixth prize, to be granted to the
authors of the six major collections of articles "dedicated to
interpreting the accomplish-
ments of Spain in Africa and
stimulating international interest
in the subject of Spanish Africa."
First prize winners include:
1959 Domingo Manfredi Cano
1960 José M. Fernandez
Gaytán; Estaban Calle
Iturrino
1961 Salvador López de la
Torre   21.

AFRIKAANS CHILDREN'S BOOK
AWARD (South Africa)
In 1961 the South African Library Association (c/o Transvaal
Provincial Library Service, 433
Pretorious Street, Pretoria,
Transvaal) instituted a gold
medal to be granted from time
to time "for the best original
Afrikaans children's book of the
year." The first award, presented on the recommendation
of the Committee of Selection,
was granted at an Annual Con-

ference of the South African Library Association in Grahams-
town in September 1961 to W.O.
Kühne, for "Huppel verjaar," which
was illustrated by Dorothy Hill
Kühne.   22.

AFRIKAANS P.E.N. CENTRE
PRIZE (South Africa)
This award for Afrikaans
writers (white South Africans of
European descent), granted every
five years by the Afrikaanse
Skrywerskking (P.O. Box Hillbrow 1719, Johannesburg) "to the
most promising young writer in
the past five years," brought
a prize of R 100 for the period
1950-1955 to H.S. van Blerk.
                         23.

AFRICAN GRAND PRIZE FOR
LITERATURE IN FRENCH (Africa--
France--Grand Prix Littéraire
d'Afrique Noire d'Expression
Française)
This prize of Association
Nationale des Écrivains de la
Mer et de l'Outre Mer (41 rue de
la Bienfaisance, Paris 8e) was
won in 1961 by Aké Loba (Ivory
Coast) with "Kocoumba, l'étudiant
noir."   24.

AFRICAN PRESS COMBINE
PRIZE (South Africa)
An award of L 100 offered for
prose literature and dramatic
works by the Afrikaanse Pers
Boekhandel(P.O. Box 845,
Johannesburg), also designated
the "SOUTH AFRICAN LITERARY
AWARD," was shared in 1947 by
E. Webster with "Ceremony of
innocence," and D. Rooke with
"A grove of fever trees."
More recent awards of A.P.B.
Booksellers (Afrikaanse Pers
Boekhandel) are:
    AFRIKAANSE PERS-BOEK-
    HANDEL YOUTH NOVEL
    AWARD (R 800)
    1961 Chris Barnard. Boela
    van die Blouwater

AFRIKAANSE PERS-BOEK-
HANDEL LITERARY AWARD
1962 (2 2nd prizes of R300
each) Uys Krige. Die name-
lose muse (essays); Chris
Barnard. Man in die Mid-
del (novel).   25.

ADAI PRIZE (Lithuania)
A literary prize of the Aidai
Lithuanian Culture Magazine
(910 Willoughby Avenue, Brooklyn,
New York) granted each year for
the best writing by Lithuanians.
26.

AKUTAGAWA PRIZE (Japan)
This Japanese prize,"con-
sidered the most helpful to
launch hopeful aspirants on a
writing career," was created in
1935 in honor of the novelist
Ryunosuke Akutagawa (1892-
1927, author of such internationally famous works as "In a
grove," "Rashomon," "Hell
screen,")by his friend Hiroshi
(Kan) Kikuchi (1888-1948),
founder of the publishing company
Bungei Shunjusha, in which the
awarding group--Japanese Society
for the Promotion of Literature
(Bungaku Shinkokai)--is located.
A jury, "most of whom are
leading novelists in contemporary
Japan," awards the prize each
six months to one or two unknown
writers of promise, prize-winning
works being "selected chiefly
from works appearing in coterie
magazines and others."
Among the more than forty
prize-winners are:
1935 Tatsuzo Ishikawa. Sobo
(The ordinary people)
1936 Jun Ishikawa. Fugen
(Fugen, a Buddhist Saint of
Knowledge)
1937 Kazuo Ozaki. Nonki
Megane (An Easy-going
man's spectacles)
1938 Yoshihide Nakayama.
Atsumono Zaki (Long curly-
petalled chrysanthemums)

1949 Yasushi Inoue. Togye
(Bull fights)
1951 Yoshie Hotta. Hiroba
No Kodoku (Solitude fell in
the plaza)
1952 Kiyoharu Matsumoto.
Aru "Ogura Nikki" Den (A
commentary on the "Ogura
Diary")
1955 Shusaku Endo. Shiroi
Hito (A white man)
Shintaro Ishiwara. Taiyo No
Kisetsu (The season of the
sun)
1957 Itaru Kikumura. Iwoto
(Iwo Jima Island)
Takeshi (Ken) Kaiko. Hadaka
no Osama (The naked king--
short stories)
1958 Kenzaburo Ooe. Shiiku
(The catch)
1959 Shiro Shiba. Santo
1960 Morio Kito. Yoru to
Kiri no Sumi de; Tetsuro
Miura. Shinobugawa
1961 Koichiro Uno. Kujiragami
27.

Pedro Antonio de ALARCÓN
PRIZE (Spain)
This 50,000 pts novel prize,
offered by Editorial Colenda (Cea
Bermudez 45, Madrid), includes
among its recent recipients:
1956 Francisco Ferrari Billoch.
La sombra detrás del cora-
zón
1957 Roberto Otaegui Echevar-
ria. Donde se pone el sol.
Preludio a lo conquista de un
nuevo mundo
1959 Virgilio Rodriguez Macas
(Guatemala). Nebrura
1961 J. Antonio Cabezas. La
Máscara del Alma   28.

Leopoldo ALAS PRIZE (Spain)
A short story prize of 10,000
pts, an annual award of Editorial
Roca (Laforja 138, Barcelona),
established in 1955 to honor an
outstanding collection of literary
stories written in Spain or in
Latin America, includes among

recent winners:
  1956 Jorge Ferrer-Vidal.
  Sobre la piel del mundo
  Luis de Goytisolo. El sol
  en las Afueras
  1957 Ramón Nieto. Los des-
  terrados
  1958 Mario Vargas Llosa.
  Los jefes (short stories)
  1960 Pedro Espinosa Bravo.
  El viejo de las Naranjas
  1962 Felipe Mellizo. Los
  redimidos   29.

Duke of ALBA PRIZE (Spain)
  Each nine years the Real
Academia Española (Felipe IV,
4, Madrid) awards this 25,000
pts prize for an original, unpublished work in Spanish literary
history or language--especially
for regional linguistics.   30.

ALBACETE PRIZE (Spain)
  The Diputacion Provincial de
Albacete awards this prize for a
Novel (25,000 pts); Poetry
(5,000 pts); and Journalism
(5,000 pts).   31.

ALBERDI AND SARMIENTO
AMERICAN FRIENDSHIP PRIZE
(Latin America--Argentina)
  Offered by the Buenos Aires
newspaper, "La Prensa" (Av. de
Mayo 567-75), this annual award,
consisting of a silver plaque and
25,000 pesos, is granted by a
board of distinguished judges "to
reward, honor, and make known
those who have worked and are
working for the ideals of the A-
mericas and of democracy, and
who keep alert the conscience of
America." Among recent winners
are Germán Arciniegas (Colombia);
Rómulo Gallegos (Venezuela); and
Efraim Cardozo (Paraguay). 32.

Juan ALCOVER PRIZE (Spain)
  One of the literary awards of
Ayuntamiento de Palma de Mallorca, this 10,000 pts prize is
offered for a poem or a collection of poems in Castilian or
in Majorca dialect (mallorquina).
In 1961 the prize winner was
Jaime Vidal with "A dos viatges
per mar."   33.

ALERCE PRIZE (Chile)
  Awarded by the Sociedad de
Escritores de Chile (Agustinas
925, Santiago), this prize has
been granted since 1959 for the
best work entered in competition.
Categories of competition, as
established each year, may include: Short Story and Poetry;
Novel; Tales, Poetry, Drama
and Essay.   34.

ALGERIAN GRAND PRIZE FOR
LITERATURE (Grand Prix Littéraire de L'Algérie)
  A government prize that is
offered annually (Gouvernement
général de l'Algérie, Direction
de l'Intérieur et des Beaux-Arts,
Alger) for the best literary work
or scientific or historical writing
by a French resident of Algiers
who is not over thirty-five years
of age and has lived in Algeria
for five years, or has written on
a subject "specifically Algerian."
  Recent winners of the 2.000
NF prize, granted since 1921,
which must be applied for before
October 15, include:
  1937 Paul Achard
  1941 Mohammed Sifi
  1942 Emmanuel Roblès; Edmond
  Brua
  1955 Marcel Moussy. Arcole ou
  la terre promise; Le sang
  chaud
  1956 Max Marchand. L'étrange
  mari
  1958 Paul Passager. Ouargla
  1960 Ervan Marec. Entire
  work
  1961 Jean Noel. Isabelle Eber-
  hardt   35.

ALL NATIONS PRIZE NOVEL
COMPETITION (International--
thirteen countries)

An outstanding example of
international cooperation among
publishers in offering a literary
prize, this competition, granting
approximately $20,000 for an
unpublished novel, was held twice:

First Contest--1935-1936,
with associated publishers in 13
countries (England, France,
Canada, Germany, Hungary,
Denmark, Sweden, United States,
Spain, Italy, Holland, Norway,
Czechoslovakia) publishing the
winning book simultaneously.
The winner of this contest was
also a U.S. Literary Guild
Selection and considered for a
motion picture by Warner
Brothers-First National Studios.

Second Contest--1939-1940,
with associated publishers in 10
countries (England, France, Germany, Hungary, Sweden, Poland,
United States, Italy, Holland,
Czechoslovakia).

Judges in each of the participating countries selected the one
manuscript (minimum of 50,000
words) "most suitable for book
publication," from entries in
that country for consideration by
an international jury (First con-
test--Carl Van Doren, Hugh Wal-
pole, John Bojer, Rudolph C.
Binding, Gaston Rageot; Second
contest--Frank Swinnerton,
Gaston Rageot, John Beecroft).

The U.S.A. publisher participating was Farrar & Rinehart
(which became Rinehart & Company in 1946, and merged early
in 1960 with Holt and Winston to
become Holt, Rinehart and
Winston), and a separate American prize was offered if the U.S.
A. entry did not win the international award.

Contest winners were:
1936 Jolan Foldes. Street
of the fishing cat
Runners-up: J. McIntyre
(U.S.A.) Steps going down;
C. Berg (Sweden). Blue dra-
goons.

1939 Robert Henriques.
No arms, no armor
Runners-up: J. Selby (U.S.
A.). Sam; Kozik (Czecho-
slovakia). The Great
Debureau; P. Mikhali (France).
The young concubine   36.

Alphonse ALLAIS PRIZE (France)
First granted in 1952, this
annual award for a humorous
book or novel (Ralph Messac,
Secretary, 21 bis, rue de Paradis,
Paris 10e) includes among the
prize winners--a gold louis presented during Mardi Gras--such
works as:
1952 Pierre Melon. Les moines
de Saint-Bernardin
1954 Louis Velle. Ma petite
femme
1956 Alexandre Breffort.
Contes du grand-père Zig
1957 Jean-Paul Lacroix. Com-
ment ne pas réussir
1958 Gus. Toutes folles de
moi
1960 Jean Portelle. Le monde
dans ma poche en quatre-
vingt-dix-huit jours
1961 Emile Noel. Fleurs de
méninges   37.

Fialho de ALMEIDA PRIZE
(Portugal)
A recent winner of this literary
award for a short story or a
novella was Manuela de Azevedo in
1954 with "Filhos do Diabo." 38.

ALMENNA BOKAFELAGSO PRIZE
(Iceland--Bokmenntaverolaun
Almenna bokafelagsins)
This prize of the publisher,
Almenna bokafelagio (Tjarnargata
16, Reykjavik) has been won by:
1958 Loftur Guðmundsson.
Gangrimlahjólið (The tread-
mill)
1959 Hannes Pétursson. Í
sumardölum (In the valley of
summer--poems)   39.

ALPI APUANE-PEA PRIZE
(Italy)
   Granted by Amministrazione
Prov. di Massacarrar for poetry
and prose writing, this prize of
the Apuan Alps region, offering
premiums of L 500.000 has been
won by such authors as:
   Poetry--1958 Luciano Lera.
   Donna
   1959 Ugo Renna. I p'iu lontani
   toni;Roberto Micheloni.
   Questa mia eta
Stories--1959 Eriberto Storti.
   I bianchi giardini del sol
1962 Beppe Fenoglio. Na il m.
   o amore e Paco   40.

ALVAREZ QUINTERO PRIZE
(Spain)
   A 5,000 pts biennial award of
the Real Academia Española (Fe-
lipe IV, 4, Madrid) presented
alternately for Novel or Col-
lected Short Stories; and for
Drama, offered the 1960 Drama
Prize for the best play by a
Spanish writer produced during
the period 1956-1959. The 1957
prize-winner was Pedro de
Lorenzo with "Una conciencia de
Alquiler;" and in 1962 Mercedes
Ballesteros de la Torre received
the prize for her novel, "Taller."
                              41.

ALVARO PRIZE (Italy)
   Among the recent winners of
this literary prize for a novel
are:
   1959 Teresa Carpinteri. La
   Signora di Belfronte
   1960 G. Manna. Le Terrazze
                              42.

Francisco ALVES PRIZE (Brazil)
   One of several literary honors
granted periodically by the Academia Brasileira de Letras
(Avenida Presidente Wilson 203,
Rio de Janeiro), this prize was
offered in 1962 for two monographs on specified subjects
(Best Means of Conducting Pri-

mary Education in Brazil; The
Portuguese Language), with
several prizes (ranging from
Cr$3.000 to Cr$10.000) in each
subject. Unpublished works or
those published between 1957-
1961 are eligible to compete in
the 1962 contest. Scholars
awarded the 1962 prize are: Jairo
Dias de Carvelho for "A Lingua
Portuguesa no Ensino Medio;"
and Hilda Reis Capucci for "Culto
e Ensino da Nossa Lingua." 43.

AMBASSADORS' PRIZE (France--
Prix des Ambassadeurs)
   This prose prize of 1.000 NF
was founded in 1948 as an annual
award, granted toward the end of
each June by a jury of 24 French
and foreign diplomats accredited
to France (M.J.-P. Dorian,
Secrétariat, 16 boulevard Haussmann, Paris). Recipients of the
literary honor, designating a novel
or other book which most clearly
expresses the French spirit, are:
   1948 Antoine de Saint-Exupéry.
   Citadelle
   1949 Henri Bosco. Malicroix.
   1950 Simone Weil. Entire
   work, especially L'attente de
   Dieu
   1951 René Laporte. Un air de
   jeunesse
   1952 André Billy. Sainte-Beuve
   1953 Jean Guehenno. Jean-
   Jacques Rousseau
   1954 P.H. Simon. Les hommes
   ne veulent pas mourir
   1955 Marcel Brion. Schumann
   et l'âme romantique
   1956 Jacques Chastenet. Winston Churchill et l'Angleterre
   du xxe siècle
   1957 Raymond Picard. La car-
   rière de Racine
   1958 Joseph Kessel. Le lion
                              44.

AMERICALEE LITERARY CON-
TEST (Latin America--Argentina)
   Publisher's contest, conducted
by Editorial Americalee (calle

Tucuman 353, Buenos Aires), offers as a biennial prize 20,000 Argentine pesos for the best writing to "promote study and knowledge of Latin American social problems through frank discussion and presentation of ideas by writers and students of the subject, without political, religious or ideological barriers." Any citizen of Latin American countries, or resident of at least five years, is eligible to submit essays in competition (writings of 35,000 to 100,000 words). The first of the biennial contests closed April 30, 1961.   45.

AMERICAN ACADEMY OF ARTS AND LETTERS AWARD OF MERIT MEDAL (International--- U.S.A.)

The fifty members of the American Academy of Arts and Letters, who as a prerequisite to membership in the Academy are writers and artists who have been honored with membership in the National Institute of Arts and Letters (633 West 155th Street, New York 32), established this international cultural award in 1940. The Award of Merit Medal, consisting of a medal and a monetary premium (originally $500, then increased to $1,000, and most recently $1,500), is granted for outstanding achievement in a specified cultural area--rotating awards to: Novel, Poetry, Drama, Painting, Sculpture. Presented each year in April at a joint ceremony of the Academy and the Institute of Arts and Letters, the medal has recognized the outstanding literary achievement of such distinguished writers as:

1945 Wystan Hugh Auden (United Kingdom)---U.S.A.)
1949 Thomas Mann (Germany-- U.S.A.)
1950 St. John Perse (France)

1955 Jorge Guillén (Spain)
1959 Aldous Huxley (United Kingdom)
1960 Hilda Doolittle (H.D.) (United Kingdom)

From time to time, the Academy and the Institute, in joint activity, elect distinguished foreign artists, writers, and composers as "Honorary Corresponding Member." Among such cultural leaders (a maximum of fifty) honored with such membership, created "in order to establish cultural ties with other countries," are representatives from France: André Gide, Colette, Jean Cocteau; Denmark: Isak Dinesen; Italy: Benedetto Croce; Germany: Gerhart Hauptmann; Austria: Franz Werfel; Chile: Gabriela Mistral; Norway: Sigrid Undset; and the United Kingdom: H. G. Wells, George Bernard Shaw.   46.

AMICI DEL LIBRO PRIZE (Italy)

Offered by Associazione Amici del Libro d'Italia, this prize for a monograph about Porrino carries a premium of L 500.000, and a second prize of L 100.000.
                                           47.

AMICI DI VENEZIA PRIZE (Italy)

A journalism award of L 1.000.000 offered by the International Center of the Friends of Venice (Centro Internazionale Amici di Venezia).   48.

AMITIÉS FRANÇAISES PRIZE (International--France)

This "Friends of France" award of the Société des Poètes Français (15 rue Plumet, Paris 15e) is one of the many literary honors offered by the Société. Granted each December to a non-French poet writing poetry in French, foreign authors honored by award are:
1954 Lionello Fiumi (Italy)
1955 T. S. Eliot (United

Kingdom)
1956 Pär Lagerkvist (Sweden)
1957 Jaime Thorres-Bodet
(Mexico)
1958 Ribeiro Couto (Brazil)
1959 Kojiro Serizawa (Japan).
J'irai mourir à Paris
1960 Victor Van Vriesland
(Netherlands). La vent se
couche
1961 Léopold Sédar Senghor
(Republic of Senegal)   49.

AMITIÉS LATINES PRIZE
(International--France)

One of several literary awards generally termed "PRIX DE LA FRANCE LATINE" (8 impasse Truillot, Paris 9e), this prize is offered to honor a work by a writer of France or a Latin country, concerning the cultural interrelation of the Latin countries of Europe and America, and upholding Latin culture in literature and the visual arts. Among recipients of the 500 NF award are:

1958 Marcel Jardonnet.
Michel de l'hospital, poète
et écrivain néo-latin
1959 Paul Gache. L'Idée
latine de Roger Barthe
1961 Marion Coulon.
L'autonomie culturelle en
Belgique; Raymond Barbeau.
J'ai choisi l'indépendance
                  50.

AMSTERDAM PRIZES (Netherlands)

At the end of each year, the city of Amsterdam presents literature prizes in five areas of writing--Drama, Novel, Poetry (since 1946), Essays (since 1947), and Novella (since 1949); also in Short Story. These prizes, consisting of a scroll and a monetary premium (varying from 125 to 3.000 florins, depending upon the type of writing and whether the prize is divided among several writers) are directed to promoting literature by honoring and increasing the distribution of works by outstanding authors. The Amsterdam Arts Council, a group of "50 persons who represent different facets of the Amsterdam artistic life," acts in an advisory capacity to the Burgomaster and Alderman of Amsterdam, recommending each year what prizes will be offered and how the Committees of Judges are to be constituted. In the first years of the prizes, instituted in 1945, "free contributions" were encouraged so that any author might submit his work for consideration; today, and for some years past, the Committees of Judges consider works published during a specified period and make recommendations from these published works for awards. Also, in later years authors have been commissioned by the city of Amsterdam (Gemeente Amsterdam, Town Hall, O. Z. Voorburgwal 197-199, Amsterdam--C) to write works in "special fields of literature."

Among prize-winners are:
Drama (500 to 2.000 fl). All commissioned works except 1945.
1945 G. Gonggrijp. Hier is London
1953 A. J. Herzberg. Herodes
1954 Ed. Hoornik. De zeewolf
E. E. de Jong-Keesing. Drie tegen Een
H. Tiemeijer. Angst
1955 Jan de Hartog. De Vredesduif
Theo Vesseur. Kiezen of delen
1956 Josepha Mendels. Breng de bessen, Berthe
J. W. Hostra. De lachende derde
Cees Nooteboom. De swanen van de Thames
1957 Harry Mulisch. Tanchelijn
1959 G. K. van het Reve. Moorlandshuis
A. Morriën. De jacht
1960 J. Wolkers. De Babel
Essay (250 to 2.500 fl). Com-

missioned works
1951 Elisabeth de Roos. Mis-
verstand, mythe en Amsterdam
H. A. Gomperts. De
Mirakels van Amsterdam
A.J. Herzberg. Der. E-
manuel Boekman
Jacob van der Ster. De
Alderministe onder de Rijmers
1955 J. C. Brandt Corstius.
De nieuwe beweging
1958 Helène Wagenaar-Nolthen-
ius. Muziek in de Kentering
1960 R. W. D. Oxenaar.
Jacoba van Heemskerck
Novel (usually 2.000 and since
1954 3.000 fl). All commissioned works except 1946
1946 Simon Vestdijk. Pas-
torale 1943
1947 Dola de Jong. En de
akker is de Wereld
1948 Annie Romein-Verschoor.
Vaderland in de verte
1949 Anne Blaman. Eenzaam
avontuur
1954 J. B. Charles. Volg
het spoor teruq
1956 Anna Blaman. Op leven
en dood
1960 Simon Vestdijk. De
Ziener
Novella (1.000 and recently
1.500 or 2.000 fl)
1949 J. Cohen. De tocht van
de dronken man
1953 A. Alberts. "Groen," in
De Eilanden
1955 R. Blijstra. Een schot in
de bergen
Inez van Dullemen. Het
Verzuim
Marie-Sophie Nathusius. De
partner
1957 Maurits Dekker. Op
zwart stramien
1959 Remco Campert. De
jongen met het mes; Vincent
Mahieu. Tjies
Poetry (1.000 fl as a single prize,'
shared prize or separate prizes)
1957 Jan Hanlo. Niet
ongelijk

Maurits Mok. Stormen en
Stilten (collected poems)
Guillaume van der Graft.
Woorden van brood
1958 Gabriel Smit. De Stoel,
in Ik geloof
Gerrit Kouwenaar. De mensen
zijn geen goden, in De ondoor
dringbare landkaart
1959 Jan Hanlo. Verzamelde
gedichten (collected poems)
Mischa de Vreede. Een jong
meisje droomt
Sybren Polet. Vleselijke stad
1960 Paul Rodenko. Stilte,
woedende trompet (collected
poems)
Cees Nooteboom. Ibizencer
gedicht
Chr. J. van Geel. Een
zomerdag
Short Story (750 fl)
1960 Margo Minco. Het huis
hirnaast   51.

José de ANCHIETA PRIZE (Brazil)
This award, named for the
Jesuit missionary Father José de
Anchieta (1553-1597) whose Indian
grammar and historical writings
hold a significant place in Portuguese American colonial literature,
was granted as a result of a contest held in connection with the
fourth centenary celebration of
the city of São Paulo. The winning work was a novel, "Os
escopioes" (The Scorpions) by
Gastão de Holanda.   52.

ANCKER PRIZE (Denmark)
Established in 1947 by the
money willed by writer Ancker
at his death, this award (one-
fourth of the annual income of the
endowment) is given to authors as
a grant to widen their horizon by
travel. Winners of the travel-
grant include Martin Andersen Nexö
(1917), and Solberg, author of
People of the Sea" (1920).   53.

Hans Christian ANDERSEN
INTERNATIONAL AWARD (In-
ternational)

Established in 1953, this biennial prize for books for young
people brings an honorary award
(a medal and a diploma) to the
winning author. The prize,
awarded by the International
Board of Books for Young People (Engl. Viertel Strasse 20,
Zurich, Switzerland), honors a
"living author who has made a
lasting contribution to good
juvenile literature by the outstanding value of his or her
works," and who has had the
most outstanding book, preferably
fiction, published during the two
years preceding year of award.

National juries from each of
the 18 countries participating
in the award of this literary
honor select one candidate for
the Award for final decision by
the international jury, and three
candidates for the "Honour List
Books" (12 books), and the
"Runner-Up Books" (15 books).
Many of the candidates have won
high national honors for children's
literature with their competing
books. In 1960, the lists included national award winners
from France (Prix Enfance du
Monde); Austria (Austrian State
Prize for Children's Book;
Vienna Children's and Youth Book
Prize); Germany (German Youth
Book Prize--Young People and
Children Categories; and Norway
(Damm Prize).

Since 1956, date of the first
award, prize winners are:
   1956 Eleanor Farjeon (United
      Kingdom). The little book-
      room
   1958 Astrid Lindgren (Sweden)
      Entire work, including
      Rasmus Paloffen (Rasmus
      and the vagabond)
   1960 Erich Kästner (Germany)
      Entire work, including his
      recent autobiography for

young people, Als ich ein
kleiner junge war.
   1962 Meindert de Jong   54.

Hans Christian ANDERSEN PRIZE
(Denmark)

Established April 2, 1955 to
commemorate the 150th anniversary of the birth of Hans Christian Andersen, this prize is a-
warded each year on his birthday.
The prize of 5.000 D Kr is offered by Nyt Nordisk Forlag
through an award committee, consisting of the Minister for Cultural Affairs (Chairman), the
head of Copenhagen University,
and the chairman of the Danish
Authors' Association (Committee
address: The Ministry of Cultural Affairs, Copenhagen K).

   Winners include:
   1955 Karen Blixen (pseud:
      Isak Dinesen)
   1958 Helge Topsoe-Jensen
   1959 Hans Brix
   1960 H. C. Branner
   1961 Frank Jaeger
   1962 Poul Rubow   55.

ANDORRA INTERNATIONAL CUL-
TURAL CONTEST (International--
Andorra--Curs Internacional de
Cultura d'Andorra)

This literary prize is awarded
each fall in Andorra, one of the
"miniature" countries of Europe,
to the winner of a competition on
a set theme--geography, history,
traditions, economics, art.
Works in Catalan, Occita, Spanish
and French are eligible for award.
                              56.

Anselmo de ANDRADE PRIZE
(Portugal)

One of numerous literary
prizes of S.N.I. (Secretariado
Nacional da Informação), this
8.000 $ award is offered for an
essay in political science or
economics.
   Recent winners include:
   1952 Lúcio Craveiro da Silva.

A idade do social
1954 Adérito Sedas Nunes.
Situação e problemas do
corporativismo
1956 Henrique Martins de
Carvalho. O pacto do
Atlântico
1958 José Duarte Amaral. O
desenvolvimento económico
do país e a posição da
agricultura   57.

ANISFIELD-WOLF SATURDAY
REVIEW AWARDS (International--
U.S.A.)
Since 1935 these awards,
administered by the "Saturday
Review" (25 W. 45th Street, New
York 36), have been granted annually for the book or books
dealing "most creditably with
social or group relations." Initiated in 1934 by Mrs. Anisfield
Wolf, to honor the donor's
father, Cleveland philanthropist
John Anisfield, who died in 1929,
the name of Eugene Wolf, Mrs.
Wolf's husband was added to the
awards in 1944, following his
death. The first prizes were
given for published scholarly
books in the field of race relations, and in 1942 a second award
was added for a published book
of creative literature concerning
racial problems--in such literary
forms as Fiction, Drama, Poetry,
Biography, Autobiography.
Among the winners are such
authors as:
1936 Julian Huxley (United
Kingdom), and A.C. Haddon.
We Europeans
1948 Alan Paton (South Africa).
Cry the beloved country
1950 Henry Gibbs (United
Kingdom). Twilight in South
Africa
1952 Han Suyin (Malaya). A
many-splendored thing
1956 Gilberto Freyre (Brazil).
The masters and the slaves
(English translation title of
Casa Grande e Senzala)

1960 E. R. Braithwaite
(British Guiana). To Sir,
with love   58.

ANTIRACISM PRIZE (France--
Prix Antiraciste)
Offered by the organization
L.I.C.A. (Ligue internationale
contre le racisme et l'antisémit-
isme, 40 rue de Paradis, Paris),
this annual prize of 1.000 NF is
given for the best work, or best
two works, in a variety of factual
and imaginative writing: Philosophy, sociology, ethnography,
ethics, history, novel, drama,
journalism, novella, short story,
criticism, motion picture scenario.
Recipients include:
1957 René Cathal A. Rouge le
soir
1958 Trévor Huddleston. Qui
est mon prochain   59.

ANTWERP PRIZES (Belgium)
Among the most numerous an-
nual literary awards for Belgian
works in Flemish are those prizes
of the Province of Antwerp.
Prizes are offered for Fiction,
Nonfiction, First Works, Entire
Literary Work, Manuscripts of
unpublished works, Children's
Books, Young People's Books,
and writing in a variety of literary
forms: Novel, Drama, Poetry,
Prose, Essay.
Recent winners are such well-
known, established authors and
new young writers as:
Children's Book
1956 Erik Suls. Het boek van
Lew de Boere Kat
Aster Berkhof. Paavo de Lap
1957 Cor Ria Leeman. Jan
Klaassen
Marie de Vleeschouwer-Ver-
braeken. Een ui'l vloog over
1958 Albert van Nerum. Reint-
jes-reeks
1959 A. de Knop and J. Piere-
ault. Indiantje
Drama
1956 Piet Sterckx. De

verdwaalde plant
1957 Tone Brulin. Nu het dorp
niet meer bestaat
1958 Paul Hardy. Pavil joen op
Heidebergen

Essay
1957 Victor Leemans. Sören
Kierkegaard
1959 Aug. Keersmaekers. De
dichter Gilliam van Nieu-
welandt en de Senecaans-
classieke tragedie in de
Zuidlijke Nederlanden
1960 Rene Verbeeck. Hendrik
Marsman

Fiction
1956 Piet van Aken. Klinkaart

First Work
1956 Luc ter Elst. Afscheid
van he paradijs
1957 Albert van Hoeck. Mijn
vrouw was een negerin
1958 José de Ceulaer. De
mens in het werk van Tim-
mermans
1959 Jo de Meester. Bergen
en builen
1960 Libera Carlier. De
Zondagsslepers

Manuscripts
1956 Diana Donceele. Avond-
mosaiek
1958 Jan Veulemans. Klaaske
mijn zoon
1959 Jan Christiaens. Een
vredesduif braden (drama)

Nonfiction
1956 Korneel Goosens. David
Vinckboons
1957 N. Wildiers. Terrein-
vereffening

Novel
1959 Yvonne de Man. Een
vrouw met name Suzanna
1960 Paul Lebeau. Xantippe

Poetry
1956 Karel Vertommen.
Vluchtig schoon
1957 Paul Verbruggen. Heer
in knecht
1958 Gaston Durnez. Rijmenam
1959 Johan van Mechelen. De
ring
1960 Frans de Wilde. Voor de

stilte

Prose
1957 Hubert Lampo. De duivel
en de maagd
1958 Ward Ruyslinck. De
ontaarde slapers

Works
1956 Eug. de Bock
1957 Anton van de Velde
1958 Maria de Lannoy
1959 F. van der Mueren
1960 Frank van der Wyngaert

Youth Book
1958 P. E. Ferklaveren. De
papierraper van Tientsin
1959 Leen van Marcke. De
zon brecht door   60.

Guillaume APOLLINAIRE PRIZE
(France)

This award for poetry in the
tradition of Guillaume Apollinaire
(1880-1918), French avant garde
poet and interpreter of cubism
and surrealism, is presented annually on January 7. The 50 NF
prize gives recognition to a work
of classical or modern poetry by
a poet under forty years of age.
Winning poetry collections, published within the two years preceding the year of award, include
works of:
1947 Hervé Bazin. Jour
1948 Rouben Melik. Passeurs
d'horizon
1951 Paul Gilson. Entire work,
in particular Ballades pour
fantômes
1952 Alain Bosquet. Langue
morte
1956 Robert Sabatier. Les fêtes
solaires
1958 Jean Rousselot. Agrégation
de temps
1959 Luc Berimont. L'herbe à
tonnerre
Pierre Seghers. Entire work
1960 Marcel Béalu; Vincent
Monteiro
1961 Gisèle Lombard-Mauroy.
Terres de hêtres; Jean Breton.
Clair de soleil
1962 Jane Kieffer. Cette sauvage

lumière 61.

Graça ARANHA PRIZE (Brazil)
A novel award of the P.E.N.
Club do Brasil (Avenida Pecanha
26, Rio de Janeiro), this prize,
named for the author Graça
Aranha (1868-1931), who cham-
pioned modernism and wrote
"Chanaan" (Canaan), considered
by some critics the "most
representative Brazilian novel,"
was won by Jorge Amado in
1936 with "Mar morto" (Sea of
the dead). Rachel Queiroz won
the PREMIO DE ROMANCE DE
GRAÇA ARANHA with "O Quinze"
(1930), first of a trilogy. 62.

ÅRETS KRITIKERPRIS (Denmark)
The Danish Publishers' Association (Dansk Forlaeggerforening,
Nyropsgadeig, Copenhagen V)
offers this prize each year, which
is also designated the DANISH
CRITICS LITERARY PRIZE
(Deense Literaire Kritiek Prize).
Winners of the 1.000 D Kr award
since its establishment in 1957
are:
  1957 Karen Blixen (pseudonym
    Isak Dinesen); Per Lange
  1958 Poul Ørum. Lyksalighe-
    dens Ø; Frank Jaeger
  1959 Willy-August Linnemann;
    Willy Sorensen
  1961 Cecil Bodiker. Øjet (The
    eye)
  1962 Albert Dam. Syv skil-
    derier (Seven pictures) 63.

ARGENTINE AUTHORS SOCIETY
LITERARY PRIZES
The Sociedad General de
Autores de la Argentina (Argen-
tores) has conducted literary
competitions and awarded prizes
for outstanding contributions to
literature, such as:
  Concurso Nacional de la
    Sociedad General de Autores
    de la Argentina--won in
    1946 by Abelardo Arias with
    "La viña estéril" (motion
    picture script)
    Medalla do Oro--granted in 1955
    to Pedro Miguel Obligado, for
    "El grito sagrado" 63a.

ARGENTINE NATIONAL PRIZE
National government awards
for outstanding works in science
and literature were established
by law in 1913, and have been
administered by various agencies
(1933-1944: Comision Nacional
de Cultura, with 12 members--
scholars and men of letters;
1955-1959; Direccion Nacional de
Cultura, del Ministerio de Educacion; 1959-Present: Direccion
General de Cultura, del Ministerio
de Educacion y Justica (Av. Alvear
1690, Buenos Aires). The literary awards, first called PREMIO
NACIONAL EN LETRAS, offered
three prizes (10,000 to 30,000
pesos) and were divided into two
literary classes during the early
years of award (1933-1936): (1)
History, Archaeology, and Philology; (2) Philosophy, Criticism, and Essays.
In 1940 there was considerable
revision of prize rules so that
three prizes (8,000 to 20,000
pesos) were offered in nine areas
of science and literature, rotating
awards during a three year
period, resulting in prizes for
literature given for: Works of
Imagination in Prose; Works of
Philosophy, Criticism (literary,
social, customs); Poetry. Six
regional literary awards were
also established in 1940.
After several further modifica-
tions, the areas of prize awards
and the amounts of awards are at
present:
  Premios Nacionales a la Pro-
    duccion Cientifica y Literaria-
    Annual cultural awards for
    imaginative and factual writ-
    ing that include triennial prizes
    for literature (First Prize--
    110,000 pesos; Second Prize
    --70,000 pesos; Third Prize

--35,000 pesos) in the following forms--
Prose: publications during
1960-1962; 1963-1965
Poetry: publications during
1961-1963; 1964-1966
Premios "Inciacion"--Annual
"first book" prizes offering
8,000 pesos each in three
classes of writing (Prose,
Poetry, Essay) to young
authors under 30 years of
age who have not previously
published a book in the genre
of their competition entry
Premios a la Produccion
Regional--Cultural prize of
10,000 pesos offered in each
of 8 specified geographic
regions of Argentina, with
an annual rotation of three
subject fields: Ethnology,
Archaeology, and History;
Folklore and Literature;
Science
Premios a la Produccion
Teatral--Triennial drama
prize (40,000; 25,000; and
15,000 pesos) for the best
produced play in each of
three classes: Drama, Comedy, Musical Work
Winners of the Argentine National Prize for literature (variously termed GRAN PREMIO
NACIONAL DE LITERATURE;
PREMIO NACIONAL DE CUL-
TURA; LOS PREMIOS NACION-
ALES) include the early winners
Pablo Groussac; Calixto Oyuela;
Roberto J. Payró; José Ingeni-
eros; and
1920 Arturo Capdevila
1921 Ricardo Rojas. La literature argentina (4 vol, later
in 1924-1925 expanded to 8
vol)
1922 Arturo Capdevila
1924 Leopoldo Lugone;
Delfina Bunge de Galvez
1925 Hugo Wast (pseud of
Gustavo Martínez Zuviría).
Desierto de piedra (Stone
Desert)

1929 Ezequiel Martinez
Estrada. Humoresca
1930 Carmelo Meliton Bonet.
El realismo literario
Carlos Buenaventura Quiroga
1932 Manuel Gálvez. El General Quiroga
1933 Pedro Miguel Obligado--
prose
1938 Juan Pablo Echaque--
imaginative prose
1940 Leopoldo Marechal
1941 Luis Leopoldo Franco
Pablo Rojas Paz. El patio
de la noche (short stories)
1942 Eduardo Acevedo Diaz.
Cancha larga (novel)
Conrado Nalé Roxlo. El
grillo; Claro desvelo
1943 Rafael Alberto Arrieta.
Don Gregorio Beeche
1944 Sixto Pondal Rios, and
Carlos A. Olvari. Los
Maridos engañan (drama)
Francisco Luis Bernárdez.
La ciudad sin Laura
1945 Eduardo Mallea
2nd prize--Juan Oscar
Ponferrada. El carnaval del
diablo (drama)
1946 Vicente Barbieri. Anillo
de sal (poetry)
1947 Conrado Nalé Roxlo. El
pacto de Cristina; El Cuervo
de arca
1948 Ernesto L. Castro. Desde
el fondo de la tierra
1949 Emilia Carilla. El gon-
gorismo en America (phi-
losophy; criticism and essay)
1950 Fermin Estrella Gutierrez
1953 Leopoldo Marechal
1954 Pablo Palant. La dicha
impía (drama)
1956 Francesco Romero. Teoría
del hombre
Vincente Barbieri. El Ballarín
(poetry)
Salvador Canals Frau. Las
civilizaciones pre-hispánicas
de América y prehistoria de
América
Gustavo Levene. Mariano
Moreno (drama)

Conrado Nalé Roxlo. Las puertas del Purgatorio (stories)
Teodoro Hunziker. Las especies de Cuscuta (Convulvulaceae) de Argentina y Uruguay
1957 Jorge Luis Borges. El Aleph
Manuel Mujica Láinez. Los ídolos; Los viajeros (novel series)
H.A. Murena. La Fatalidad de los cuerpos
Guillermo Furlong. Nacimiento y desarrolo de la filosofia en el Rio de la Plata
Conrado Nalé Roxlo. Judith y las rosas (drama); Samuel Eichelbaum. Dos brases (drama)
1959 Bernardo Canal Feijóo. Constitución y revolución
Julio E. Payro. Historia grafica del arte universal
Segundo V. Linares Quintara. Tratado de la ciencia del derecho constitucional Argentino y comparado (6 vol)
Poetry: Ricardo E. Molinari; José Pedroni; Alberto Girri
1960 Alberto Girri. La Condicion necessaria (poetry)
Horacio Jorge Becco. Diálogo del hombre y de la llanura
3rd prize Manuel Peyrou. El estruendo de las rosas
64.

ARGENTINE WRITERS' SOCIETY PRIZES

The GRAN PREMIO DE HONOR and the FAJA DE HONOR awarded by La Sociedad Argentina de Escritores (Calle Mexico 564, Buenos Aires) are two of several literary prizes of Argentina's national organization of professional writers (see other prizes of the group: Bianchi Essay Prize; Moreno Poetry Competition; Rojas Paz Prize for Stories). Recipients of the "Faja de Honor", respected national literary honor which is assigned by professional writers and critics for an author's "international contribution to literature" include: Juan Carlos Ghiano, and
1943 Roberto Ledesma. Tiempo sin ceniza
Maria de Vallarino. Puebla en la niebla
1944 Leon Benaros. El rostro inmarcesible
1945 (?) Vicente Barbieri. El rio distante--relatos de una infancia
1946 Maria de Vallarino. La sombra iluminada
1947 Bernardo Verbitsky. En esos anos
1947 (?) Ernesto Sabato. Uno y el universo
1948 Luis Leopoldo Franco
1949 Fermin Estrella Gutierrez. Sonetos de la soledad del hombre
Dardo Enrique Cuneo. Sarmiento y Unamuno
Manuel Mujica Laínez. Aqui vivieron
1950 Margarita Abella Caprile. La mire con lagrimas
1953 Max Dickmann. Los habitantes de la noche
1954 Adolfo Bioy Casares. El sueno de los heroes
Ann Mercedes Perez (Venezuela). Cielo Derrumbado (collected poems)
Among recipients of the "Gran Premio de Honor" of the Argentine Writers' Society are:
1945 Jorge Luis Borges
1946 Eduardo Mallea
1947 (?) Ezequiel Martinez Estrada
1949 Arturo Capdevila
1950 Victoria Ocampo
1952 Werner Bock. Writings, including literary history
1954 Enrique J. Banchs
1957 Manuel Mujica Láinez
1958 Roberto Fernando Giusti
1959 Norah Lange
Other authors honored by the

Argentine Writers' Society
Prizes include Alberto Salas,
given the "First Prize" in 1950
for "Las armas de la conquista"
(The weapons of the conquest);
and Agustín Cuzzani, granted
the Gold Medal in 1956 for his
play, 'El centro forward murió
al amanecer" (The center forward died at dawn).   65.

Afonso ARINOS PRIZE (Brazil)
One of five Cr$50,000 liter-
ary prizes currently offered by
Academia Brasileira de Letras
(Avenida Presidente Wilson 203,
Rio de Janeiro), this award for
fiction--unpublished or published
during the two year period
preceding the year of award--
may be granted for stories or
novellas (conto e novela).
Winning authors include:
1956 Waldemar Pequeno, and
A. Accioly Neto
1957 José Condé. Os diasan-
tigos (tales)
1959 Harry Laus. Os in-
coerentes
1961 Nelson de Faria. Tiziu
66.

ARK PRIZE OF THE VRIJE
WOORD (Belgium)
Recent prize winners of this
Flemish language award offered
in Belgium have included:
1957 Albert Bonyridder.
Dood hout
1958 Ivo Michiels. Het
afscheid
1959 Libera Carlier. Action
Station Go
1960 Ward Ruyslinck   67.

ARNHEM CULTURAL PRIZE
(Netherlands)
In this prize the literary a-
wards are granted every five
years, as they rotate with annual
awards in four other arts: Singing and Music; Sculpture; Architecture; Painting. Established in
1950 with a monetary premium of

£100 and an illuminated certificate, the prize is awarded by a
jury (12 Koningsplein, Arnhem),
which evaluates achievements of
the five-year period preceding
award to determine the prize
winner. Only residents of the
province of Gelderland, of which
Arnhem is the capital, are eligible. Literary awards, granted
for an author's entire work, have
been presented to:
1950 Guillaume van der Graft
1955 Maria Dermoût
1960 Henriëtte de Beaufort
68.

Carlos ARNICHES PRIZE (Spain)
Founded in 1955, this 50,000
pts prize of Ayuntamiento de
Alicante is offered for an original,
unpublished play in Castilian--"of
normal stage length," and on any
theme.
Among winning playwrights are:
1956 Alfonso Paso Gil. Los
probecitos
1960 A. Corniero Suárez. Algo
extrano in casa de los Bran-
nigan   69.

ASAHI CULTURAL PRIZES
(Japan)
This general cultural award of
the Asahi Newspaper Publishing
Company includes prizes for literature. Established in 1929
as an annual cultural prize, including honors for authors, the
prize has been won by such
Japanese writers as:
1949 Jun-ichiro Tanizaki.
Sasame-Yuki (Light snow)
1954 Daisetsu Suzuki. Introduction of Japanese Buddhist
thought to foreign cultures;
and Suzuki Daisetsu Senshu
(Selected works)
1955 Eiji Yoshikawa. Shin
Heike Monogatari (New tales
of Heike)
1956 Kikan Ikeda. Genji Monogatari (Tales of Genji, with
commentary, 8 vol)   70.

ATAÇ CRITICS PRIZE (Turkey--
Ataç Eleştirme Armağani)
Established in 1957 by the
daughter of Meral Tolluoğlu, to
commemorate his death in that
year, this award of 500 TL has
been awarded to Mehmet Fuad.
71.

ATENEA PRIZE (Chile)
Awarded annually since 1929
by the Universidad de Concepción "to the major works of
imaginative writing published in
Chile during the preceding year,"
this E 500 prize is determined
by a jury whose members include
the Rector of the University of
Concepción, and the Director
of the review, "Atenea."
The Premios "Atenea," which
are awarded for scientific as
well as for literary achievement,
consist of a monetary premium
and a Diploma of Honor, and the
prizes--one for the best scientific and one for the best literary
work--are presented in a formal
ceremony presided over by the
Rector of the University of
Concepción. Authors awarded
the Premio Literario "Atenea,"
for work in various literary forms
--Novel, Story, Poetry, Drama,
Comedy, Theatrical Work, or
Essay--include:
  1929 Manuel Rojas Sepulveda.
    El Delincuente (short
    stories)
  1930 Eugenio González. Más
    Afuera
    Alberto Ried. Hiriundo
    Alberto Romero. La Viuda
    del Conventillo
  1931 Joaquín Edwards Bello.
    Valparaíso la Ciudad del
    Viento
  1932 Luis Durand. Campesinos
  1933 Ernesto Montenegro.
    Cuentos de mi Tio Ventura
  1934 Domingo Melfi. Pacifico-
    Atlántico
  1935 Augusto D'Halmar. Entire
    literary work

1936 Guillermo Koenengkampf.
  Geografía Santa
1937 Mariano Latorre Court.
  Hombres y Zorros
1939 Chela Reyes. Puertas
  Verdes y Caminos Blancos
1940 Hernán Díaz Arrieta.
  Don Alberto Blest Gana
  Benjamín Subercaseaux. Chile
  o una Loca Geografía
1941 Daniel de la Vega Uribe.
  La Sonrisa con Lágrimas
1942 Rafael Maluenda. Armiño
  Negro
  Reinaldo Lomboy. Ranquil
1943 Marta Brunet y Caraves.
  Aguas Abajo
1944 Oscar Castro. La Sombra
  en las Cumbres
1945 Luz de Vianna. No Sirve
  la Luna Blanca
1946 Fernando Santiván. El
  Bosque Emprende su Marche
1947 Maria Flora Yáñez. Vis-
  ione de Infancia
  Luis Meléndez. El Unicornio,
  La Paloma y la Serpiente
1948 Eduardo Barrios Hudtwalcker. Gran Señor y Rajadiablos
1949 Luis Durand. Frontera
1950 Benjamín Subercaseaux.
  Jemmy Button
1951 Daniel Belmar. Coiron
  "Literario Extraordinario"--
  Antonio Romera. Historia de
  la Pintura en Chile
1952 Emilio Rodríguez. La
  Emancipación y el Fraile de
  la Buena Muerte
1953 Luis Oyarzún. El Pensa-
  miento de Lastarria
1954 Juan Marín. El Egipto de
  los Faraones
1955 Fernando Santiván. Memorias de un Tolstoiano
1956 José Manuel Vergara.
  Daniel y los Leones Dorados
1957 Efraín Barquero. La
  Compañera (poetry)
1958 Fernando Alegría. Caba-
  llo de Copas
1959 Luis Merino Reyes. Ultima Llama (novel)
1960 Jorge Millas. Estudios

sobre la Historia Espiritual
de Occidente
1961 Roque Esteban Scarpa.
Thomas Mann, Una Per-
sonalidad en una Obra   72.

ATENEO ARENYS PRIZE (Inter-national--Spain)

Offering 40,000 pts for an
unpublished novel (90 to 180
double-spaced sheets in length)
in any Romance language by a
writer of any nationality, this
prize of Ateneo Arenys (José
Anselmo Clavé 22, Arenys de
Mar) will be granted for the
first time in 1962.   73.

ATENEO DE CARACAS PRIZE (Venezuela)

Ateneo de Caracas, Venezuelan
cultural group, offers this prize
each year for the best Venezuelan
drama. Winner of the first award
was Ida Gramcko for the three-
act comedy, "La Rubiera."   74.

ATENEO DE MADRID PRIZE (Spain)

A cooperative prize of the
Ateneo de Madrid and the Editora
Nacional (Av. José Antonio 62,
Madrid 13), granted since 1955
by a jury consisting of a literary
critic, a book trade representative and a novelist, this award of
20,000 pts has been won by:
1955 María Beneyto. La in-
vasión
1956 Luis Ponce de León
75.

ATENEO DE VALLADOLID PRIZES (Spain)

Each year this prize for a short
novel (novela corta) has been
presented on December 29, date
of a regional celebration, by the
organization, Ateneo de Valladolid
(Juan de Juni 1, Valladolid). In
addition to a monetary premium
of 40,000 pts (ranging from year
to year from 30,000 to 50,000
pts), the prize-winning work is
published. The first four winning books were issued by Editorial Gerper (Calle Heroes de
Teruel, Valladolid), and the fifth
winner in 1961 was published by
Editorial Biz (a branch of Cierre
S.A., Paseo del Pintor Rosales
8, Madrid).

Winners since the first competition in 1957, who entered the contest by submitting two copies of
the competing manuscript before
September 30 of the year of a-
ward, are:
1957 Jorge Cela. Blanquito,
péon de brea
1958 Miguel Buñuel. Narciso
bajo las aguas
1959 Fernando Gutiérrez. La
muerte Supitaña
1960 Carlos Rivero. Mañana
empieza el alba
1961 Máximo Regidor Garrote.
El pan muerto   76.

ATENEO ESPAÑOL DE MÉXICO AWARD (Mexico)

This scholarly prize of Ateneo
Español de México was granted
in 1956 to Javier Malagón for his
work on the Spanish juridical
literature of the 16th and 17th
centuries in New Spain (La literatura jurídica española del siglo
de oro en la Nueva España).
77.

ATHENS ACADEMY AWARDS (Greece)

Included in the continuing
periodic cultural awards of the
Athens Academy, granted for outstanding service to art, are prizes
for literature, given annually to
"literary works which comply with
the high standards set by the
Academy." The literary prize of
the Academy is granted "to a
Greek author living in Greece or
elsewhere who, by his past work
in general, and by a book published during the past four years
in particular, contributed more
than any other author, to the pro-

gress of literature in Greece."
The prize for authors (Class of
Belles Lettres and Fine Arts),
to be next awarded March 25,
1963 is for: Prose--25,000 Dr
premium for novel or short story
collection; Poetry--25,000 Dr
premium for an anthology of poetry. A total of 23 prizes will
be awarded by the Academy in
1963, many of the honors for
works in specialized subjects,
such as biography, economics,
history, or science.

Among literary prizes is the
GREEK NATIONAL ACADEMY
SILVER MEDAL, which was
given to William Faulkner, the
U.S.A. Nobel Prize winning
author, in 1957; and the ATHENS
ACADEMY AWARD, granted to
two cultural periodicals in 1960;
"Ipirotiki Estia" (Epirotic Hearth,
29 October Street, 60 Jannina,
Greece)--a monthly review; and
"Cretan Chronicle" (Hirakleion,
Crete)--a quarterly scientific
publication.

Among the scholarly prizes
currently awarded by the Academy are the Nicolas KAROLOS
PRIZES--Drs 20,000 for the best
original, unpublished study on the
icon script in the three monas-
teries of Athens; and Drs 15,000
for the best original, unpublished
study relating to the defense of
Hellenic national interest in
Macedonia; the Miltides STA-
MOULIS PRIZE--Drs 10,000 for
the best original study of the
raids against the Byzantine
Empire up to the fall of Con-
stantinople; the Alexander
SKOUZES PRIZE--Drs 45,000
for writing on a historical subject pertaining to the wars against
Greece until World War I.

Awards called ACADEMY OF
ATHENS PRIZE are also granted
for various forms of literary
work: Drs 25,000 for the best
one-act drama; two premiums of
Drs 50,000 each for the best

bibliography of Greek works from
1853-1897, and from 1897-1960.78.

ATHENS POETRY PRIZE (Inter-
national--Italy)
The third contest for the
GRAN PREMIO INTERNAZIONALE
DI POESIA "CITTA DI ATENE"
is being held in 1962 (Fondatore
del Premio, Giorgio Croce,
Casella postale 4120, Rome) to
give public recognition to the
best poem submitted by a poet
of any nationality honoring Greece,
by "exalting the eternal values of
the Land of Aeschylus, Homer
and Sappho."										79.

ATICA PRIZE (Portugal)
A prize of 5.000$ is offered
by Editorial Atica (Rua das
Chagas, 25, Lisbon) for unpublished short stories, novellas, or
novels.											80.

ATLANTIC COUNCIL PRIZE
(Europe--France)
Awarded for political science
writing, this prize, given for the
first time in 1959 for works
published from January 1, 1957
to December 1, 1958, was offered
for a work concerning the defense
of the Atlantic Community, and
for a work dealing with the under-
lying principles and values of cooperation (political, military,
economic, social or cultural)
within the Community.

Winner of the 7.000 NF prize
in 1959 was Claude Delmas with
articles on the Atlantic Alliance
appearing in the publication "Combat." Also in 1959, an Atlantic
Community Awards Competition of
the British Section was won by
Margaret Ball with her book,
"NATO and the European Union,"
who shared the £ 500 award with
her publisher, Stevens & Son,
London.											81.

ATLANTIC FICTION AND NON-
FICTION CONTESTS (International

---U.S.A.)

These publisher's prizes are offered by Atlantic Monthly Press (8 Arlington Street, Boston 16, Massachusetts) in association with Little, Brown and Company, for unpublished manuscripts, generally biennially, and each brings a premium of $5,000 ($2,500 outright prize, and $2,500 royalty advance) to the winner, and publication of the winning work in the United States and Canada.

The Nonfiction Contest, first award 1929, is open to an author of any nationality or citizenship, and the manuscript (70,000 to 175,000 words) must be in English, and may be submitted in translation. The prize, awarded to a "work of distinction" in areas including the social sciences, biography or autobiography, travel, history, race relations or integration, has been won by such authors as:

1959 George Paloczi-Horvath (Hungary). The undefeated

The Fiction Contest, first award 1927, is also open to authors of any nationality or citizenship, and the manuscript--"a novel that is both original and distinctive"--must be in English, and may be submitted in translation. Winners include:

1927 Mazo de la Roche (Canada). Jalna (prize of $10,000)
1932 Ann Bridge (United Kingdom). Peking Picnic
1940 Nina Federova (pseud of Antonina Federovna Riasanovsky) (USSR-USA). The family   82.

József ATTILA PRIZE (Hungary)

Established in 1952 by a decision of the Hungarian Council of Ministers, this annual prize offers a diploma, a medal, a monetary premium, and the right to use the title, "József Attila-dijas" (József Attila Prize-Winner). Writers are selected for this honor "upon suggestion of the pertinent professional federations, the National Council of Trade Unions, jointly with the Federation of Young Communists," by the Hungarian Minister of Culture, and the "remarkable literary compositions" so honored are primarily "outstanding socialist-realistic works of young authors."

The prize, distributed on April 4, anniversary of the Liberation of Hungary, are made public in the government's Official Gazette ('Magyar Közlöny"), and are awarded in three groups: First Prize--10,000 Forints; Second Prize--7,000 Forints; Third Prize--5,000 Forints.

Among First Prize winners are:

1952 Gábor Devecseri; Tibor Méray; László Németh; Sándor Rideg; Lajos Tamási
1953 Tibor Barabás; Béla Gádor; Zsuzsa Thury; István Békeffy; Gábor Thurzó; Endre Gáspár; Péter Földes; Lehel Szeberényi
1954 Lajos Aprily; Ferenc Karinthy; Péter Nagy; Imre Sarkadi; István Simon; Lörinc Szabo
1955 Ferenc Jankovics; István Örkeny; Sándor Sásdi; Tibor Tardos
1956 Anna Balázs; Géza Képes; István Vas; Zseni Varnai
1957 Jozsef Langyel; Gábor Goda; Sándor Tatay
1958 Zoltán Keszthelyi (poetry); János Földeák (poetry); György Dezö
1959 Lajos Mesterházy; György Szántó; József Nádass
1960 Gábor Goda; László Boka; Gábor Tolnai (criticism)
1961 Ferenc Kis (poetry); Sándor Tatay; István Vas (poetry)   83.

AUDACE PRIZE (Belgium)
Recent winners of this French
-language novel award, offered
by the Belgian literary review,
"Audace," include Marcel Thiry,
Marie-Paul Thierry, Albert
Kies, and
1957 Raoul Thiry. Simul
1958 André Villers. L'arche
de Nöel   84.

AUDITORIUM PRIZES (Italy)
Writing on the subject of
"Animals" is honored by these
literature awards of the review
"Auditorium" (casella postale
230, Rome), which were estab-
lished in the form of competi-
tions for verse or prose writing.
First Prize winners include:
1959 Lucia Salvatore (poetry);
Italo Vignati (prose);
Antonio Deidda (Premi dell'
Ente Nazionale Protezione
Animali)   85.

AUSTRALIAN CHILDREN'S BOOK
OF THE YEAR
Since 1946 an Australian Chil-
dren's Book of the Year has been
selected during Children's Book
Week by Book Societies and
Councils in Australia. With the
formation of the Australian
Children's Book Council in 1959,
the award has been determined
by this nation-wide organization.
Prior to 1959, the Children's
Book of the Year was an award
of the Australian Book Society
(1946-1949), New South Wales
Children's Book Council (1951-
1956), and joint prize of two
Australian states--New South
Wales and Victorian Children's
Book Council (1957-1958).
Recipients of this high honor
for a writer of books for children
and young people are:
1946 Leslie Rees. Karrawingi
the emu
1948 Frank Hurley. Shackle-
ton's argonauts
1949 Alan Villiers. Whalers

of the midnight sun
1951 Ruth C. Williams. Verity
of Sydney Town
1952 Eve Pownall. The Australia Book
1953 Joan Phipson. Good
luck to the rider
J.H., and W.D. Martin.
Aircraft of to-day and to-
morrow
1954 K. Langloh Parker.
Australian legendary tales
1955 Norman B. Tindall, and
H.A. Lindsay. The first
walkabout
1956 Patricia Wrightson. The
crooked snake
Peggy Barnard. With and the
magic nut
1957 Enid Moodie-Heddle, ed.
The boomerang book of
legendary tales
1958 Nan Chauncy. Tiger in
bush
1959 Nan Chauncy. Devil's
hill
John Gunn. Sea menace
1960 Kylie Tennant. All the
proud tribesmen
1961 Nan Chauncy. Tangara
1962 L. F. Evers. The
Racketty Street gang
Joan Woodberry. Rafferty
rides a winner   86.

AUSTRALIAN COMMONWEALTH
LITERARY FUND
In each year since 1908, a
number of government Fellowships
(currently £1,000 a year) have
been awarded to writers 'who
have proved their ability in the
field of creative literature, to
enable them to devote their time
for a period to a project they
specify." Applications for the
Fellowship--giving details of past
work and of the project to be
pursued--are submitted to the
Advisory Board of the Commonwealth Literary Fund, an independent body of "six experts in
the various fields of literature."
The actual awards, based on the

recommendations of the Advisory
Board, are made by the Committee of the Commonwealth
Literary Fund (with the Prime
Minister of Australia as chairman, and leaders of the two
major parties of Australia in the
Commonwealth Parliament as
members).

The Commonwealth Literary
Fund also sponsors lectures;
underwrites two literary magazines, and the publication of
literary works; and grants pen-
sions "to writers who have gained
a nation-wide reputation for their
work in the field of creative literature." Other special occasion
awards of the Commonwealth include that of 1927 in celebration
of Australia's 150th Anniversary
--when Xavier Herbert's novel
"Capricornia" was named "Best
Australian Novel of the Year."

Winners of six and 12 month
Fellowships, granted in 1962,
were Judith Wright, Dal Stivens,
W. E. Harney, Max Harris,
David Martins, D. R. Stuart.
87.

AUSTRALIAN JOURNALISTS' CLUB AWARDS

Varying from year to year in
the category of work honored,
these cultural prizes are awarded
for Literature, and also for the
Visual and Performing Arts.
Future literary awards planned
are those in 1963: £1,000 for
the best play by an Australian
or resident of Australia; and in
1965; £1,000 for the best biography of an Australian by an
Australian or resident of Australia. Australian writers have
previously been recognized
with £500 prizes for:
   1959 Best Television Play:
   Phillip Mann. The sergeant
   from Lone Pine; J. V.
   Warner. World without end
   1961 Best Stage Play: Hal
   Porter. The tower

Robert Amos. When the
grave diggers come   88.

AUSTRALIAN LITERATURE SOCIETY OF MELBOURNE MEDAL

Annually a gold medal is
bestowed on the author of the
published fiction work which may
be considered the "most meritorious literature in any calendar
year."

Winners of the medal include
Eleanor Dark, William Baylebridge, and such early winners
as:
   1929 Henry Handel Richardson
   (pseud of Mrs. J.G. Robertson). Ultima Thule
   1931 F. D. Davison. Red
   Heifer
   1932 Mann. Flesh in armour
   1936 Miles Franklin. All that
   swagger
   1937 Mackenzie. The young
   desire it   89.

AUSTRALIAN NATIVES ASSOCIATION PRIZE

The Australian Natives Association (28 Elizabeth Street, Melbourne) annually grants this award
of 110 guineas for the best original, unpublished short story by
an Australian resident, in a contest conducted by the Victorian
Board of Directors. Ten guineas
of the first prize is a publication
fee for inclusion of the winning
story in the Association's quarterly Journal, "Anapress."

Winners, announced at the Association Conferences, held each
year in March, for the first two
competitions are:
   1961 Griffith Watkins. Four
   entries
   1962 A. C. Eadie. Two
   entries: The green panther;
   End of the road   90.

AUSTRALIAN POETRY SOCIETY COMPETITION

A prize of £50 was offered by

the Poetry Society of Australia
for "an unpublished poem on an
Australian subject of less than
250 lines." Competitors for
the prize, donated by Dr. Grace
Perry, editor of the Society's
magazine, "The Poetry Magazine," sent entries by
December 31, 1962 to: Editor,
The Poetry Magazine, Box 21,
Royal Exchange Post Office,
New South Wales, Australia.
91.

AUSTRIAN LEAGUE FOR THE
UNITED NATIONS DRAMA PRIZE
(Dramenpreis der Österreich-
ischen Liga für die UN)
    In 1956 this award of the
League (Boesendorfer Strasse
9, Vienna) was granted to Kurt
Becsi.   92.

Drama
    1951 Franz Püthringer; Harald
        Zusanek
    1955 Günter Buxbaum; Franz
        Karl Franchy, Kurt Klinger;
        Anny Tichy
Novel
    1952 Ilse Aichinger; Fritz
        Habeck; Herbert Zand
    1957 Gerhard Fritsch; Hannelor
        Valencak.
Short Stories
    1953 Marlen Haushofer; Ernst
        Vasovec
    1958 Herbert Eisenreich;
        Ernst Kein
Radio Play
    1954 Werner Reimerschmid;
        Franz Hiesel; Oskar Zemme
        (shared prize)
    1959 Rudolf Bayr; Eduard
        Koenig   93.

AUSTRIAN STATE FÖRDERUNGS
PRIZE
    Since 1950 this general cul-
tural award of the Austrian
Ministry of Education (Bundesministerium für Unterricht,
Minoritenplatz 5, Vienna 1),
has been granted each year--
with a certificate and a premium of S10.000--for Literature, as well as for Music and
Painting. The Literature prize,
designed to promote younger
writers and to encourage new
talent, is determined by a committee upon application, and is
presented to the winner during
the week before Christmas.
    Winners of the award, granted
on a rotating basis in the successive categories of: Poetry,
Drama, Novel, Short Stories,
Radio Play, are:
Poetry
    1950 Christine Busta; Franz
        Kiessling
    1956 Rudolf Felmayer;
        Gerhard Fritsch; Johann
        Gunert; Christine Lavant
    1961 Christine Busta;
        Christine Lavant; Karl Wawra

AUSTRIAN STATE GRAND PRIZE
(Grösser Österreichischer Staatspreis; Staatspreise der Republik Österreich)
    Two national prizes of this
name have been awarded in Austria for outstanding contributions
to Austrian literature. In the
first period of award (1934-1937),
the winners were:
    1934 Karl Heinrich Waggerl.
        Das jahr des herrn
    1935 Josef Friedrich Perkonig.
        Mensch wie du und ich
    1936 Josef Wenter
    1937 Heinrich Suso Waldeck
    During these years an encour-
agement to young authors prize
(Förderungspreise) was also
granted under the name "GRÖSSER
ÖSTERREICHISCHER STAATS-
PREIS to: Ernst Sheibelreiter
(1935); Maria Grengg (1936);
Johannes Freumbichler, Erich
August Mayer (1937).
    In 1938, the year of the begin-
ning of the occupation of Austria
in World War II, these literary
prizes ceased. The government
prize was reestablished in 1950-
1953 as ÖSTERREICHISCHER

STAATSPREIS (Würdigungspreis)   94.
and designated KUNSTPREIS
DER REPUBLIK ÖSTERREICH   AUSTRIAN STATE PRIZE FOR
from 1954-1957. Since 1958   CHILDREN'S BOOK (Österreichis-
the award has again been called   cher Staatspreis für Kinderbuch)
GRÖSSER ÖSTERREICHISCHER   Established in 1956 by the
STAATSPREIS.   Austrian Ministry of Education
     This literary honor, a "Prix   (Bundesministerium für Unter-
d'estime," given to an already es-   richt, Minoritenplatz 5, Vienna
tablished writer for distinguished   1) as an annual award of S 10,000
creative work, may be granted   (together with a S 5,000 prize for
authors of Austrian extraction   the illustrator of a prize-winning
as well as to those writers   children's book) this official
who are Austrian citizens. Of-   recognition of the best Austrian
fered since 1950, by the Aus-   writing for children has been given
trian Ministry of Education   for the best book by a living Aus-
(Bundesministerium für Unter-   trian author issued by an Austrian
richt, Minoritenplatz 5, Vienna   publisher during the preceding
1) as an annual award presented   three years:
during the week before Christ-   1956 Lilli Koenig. Gringole
mas, the prize has been deter-   1958 Mira Lobe
mined from 1954 to the present by   1959 Christine Busta. Die
the Kunstsenat--a body advising   Sternenmühle
the government on art--Litera-   1960 Kurt Eigl; and for Klein-
ture, Music and Painting.   kinderbücher: Helmut Leiter
     Recipients of this high official   1961 Käthe Recheis   95.
Austrian honor (which includes
a certificate, a premium of S   AUSTRIAN STATE PRIZE FOR
50,000 and membership in the   YOUNG PEOPLE'S LITERATURE
Kunstsenat) and of the Sonder-   (Österreichischer Staatspreis für
preis (Special Prize) awarded   Jugendliteratur)
from time to time are: Since 1955 this S 10,000 annual
     1950 Josef Leitgeb   award of the Austrian Ministry of
     1951 Felix Braun   Education (Bundesministerium für
     1952 Marina Weid   Unterricht, Minoritenplatz 5,
     1953 Rudolf Henz; and as a   Vienna 1) has been granted for
        Sonderpreis: Rudolf Kassner   an outstanding book for young peo-
     1954 Max Mell   ple (together with a S 5,000 prize
     1955 Franz Theodor Csokor   for the illustrator of a prize-
     1956 Franz Nabl   winning young people's book) to:
     1957 Heimito von Doderer;   1955 Irene Stemmer. Prinz
        Franz Karl Ginzkey   Seifenblase und andere mär-
     1958 Imma Bodmershof   schenhaften Geschichten
     1959 Carl Zuckmayer; and as   Gerhart Stappen and Otto
        a Sonderpreis: Ludwig   Huber Servus, Pinguin
        Ficker   1956 Karl Bruckner. Der
     1960 Martin Buber (Israel),   Weltmeister; Auguste Lechner.
        as a Sonderpreis   Das Licht aus Monsalvat
     1961 Albert Paris Gütersloh;   1957 Oskar Jan Tauschinski.
        Alexander Lernet-Holenia   Wer ist diese Frau?
        (awarded as a special prize   1958 Franz Braumann
        to authors such as these,   1959 Gerhart Ellert (pseud of
        whose occupation is not   Gertrud Schmirger)
        "writing" in the strict sense)   1961 Karl Bruckner; Othmar

Franz Lang   96.

AUSTRIAN STATE SPECIAL PRIZE (Sonderpreis des Öster-reichischen Staatspreises)

This special award of the Austrian Ministry of Education (Bundesministerium für Unter-richt, Minoritenplatz 5, Vienna 1), has been granted from time to time to such authors as Thornton Wilder, American novelist and playwright, who received the Sonderpreis for his drama in 1959. Other such Sonderpreis winners (see Aus-trian State Grand Prize) are Rudolf Kassner, Ludwig Ficker, and Martin Buber.   97.

Maulana AZAD PRIZES (India)

Directed to increasing cul-tural understanding in India, this prize is presented annually by the Indian Council for Cultural Relations (Azad Bhavan, Indra-prastha Estate, New Delhi 1) in two categories:

For the best essay in English by a citizen of India or Pakistan
(1) on Islam by a non-Muslim;
(2) on Hinduism by a Muslim.

The prizes, named for Maulana Azad, Oriental scholar and Na-tional Moslem leader active in India's independence--Abul Kalam Azad (1888-1958)--who attained the Muslim title of re-spect, "Maulana," equivalent to the English 'Reverend', before he was 24 years old, are a-warded when the endowment fund reaches Rs 60,000. This prize endowment fund is created from 50 per cent of the income from the sale of Maulana Azad's book, "India wins freedom."

In 1962-1963 an Azad Prize (in the form of a free round trip to India) was offered to an Italian educator, writer, journal-ist or artist.   98.

Arthur AZEVEDO PRIZE (Brazil)

One of several Cr$50,000 literary prizes of the Academia Brasiliera de Letras (Avenida Presidente Wilson 203, Rio de Janeiro), this award is granted for dramatic works--unpublished or published during the two years preceding the year of award. Types of writing eligible are plays; and works related to drama: history of the theatre; criticism and essays interpreting dramatic works; translations of poetical classical and neo-classi-cal works into Portuguese.

Among the winners are:
1956 Isaac Gondim Filho
1957 Acioli Neto. Helen fouchou a porta (play)
1959 Guilherme de Figueiredo. Xântias
1961 Bandeira Duarte. As Três Máscaras   99.

BAALBECK ARAB DRAMA PRIZE (Lebanon)

Established and to be awarded for the first time in 1962, this prize of 3.000 LP is offered by the Committee of the Baalbeck Festivals "for the best Arab Theatre played in Lebanon."   100.

Leo B. BAECK PRIZE (Germany)

Zentralrat der Juden in Deutschland founded this prize in 1957 "for humanitarian work in word and deed." Included among recent winners of the 3000 DM annual award are: Ernst Ludwig, Eleonore Sterling, Schalom Ben-Chorin.   101.

Lode BAEKELMANS PRIZE (Belgium)

This Flemish language award of the Belgian Royal Academy of Flemish Science, Letters and Arts has been granted such writ-ers as Libera Carlier for "Duel met de Tanker;"A. van Hageland for "De magische zee."   102.

BAGUTTA PRIZE (Italy)

Since January 14, 1921, date of the first award, this Milanese prize--"the oldest and still one of the most significant of all literary prizes in Italy" (Golino, p. 45)--has been presented annually for the "best book of the year." Named for the Via Bagutta, the street on which the Tuscan inn is located, that was the scene in which the group of 11 young writers, critics and journalists who established the prize customarily met, the monetary value of the award has increased from an initial L 5.000 to the present L 100.000. The premium, however, has always been small compared with the amount of prestige of the prize and the general professional and financial returns accruing to the author receiving the award.

The Bagutta jury, composed of writers, critics and journalists (Fondazione Bagutta, via Bagutta 14, Milan), acting with "good judgment and great independence" has granted the award to authors writing in many literary forms, and to established writers as well as to young authors who have never previously written a published book. Areas of writing which have been honored by the Bagutta Prize include: Novel, Poetry, First Book, Woman Writer, Bagutta d'Argento-Verri, Bagutta-Agnesi, Opera Prima-Borletti, Bagutta-Fracchia, Vent-anni dopo, Tre signore, and Journalism.

"Opera Prima" winners include:

1956 Nicco Tucci. Il segreto (short stories)
1960 Mario Bonfantini. Il salto nel buio

Other Bagutta Prizes have honored:

1927 Giovan Battista Angioletti. Il giorno del Giudizio
1928 Giovanni Comisso. Gente di mare
1929 Vicenzo Cardarilli. Il sole a picco
1930 Gino Rocca. Gli ultimi furono i primi
1931 Giovanni Titta Rosa. Il varco nel muro
1932 Leonida Repaci. I fratelli Rupe
1933 Raul Radice. Vita comica di Corinna
1934 Carlo Emilio Gadda. Il castello di Udine
1935 Enrico Sacchetti. Vita di artista: L. Andreotti
1936 Silvio Negro. Vaticano minore
1938 BAGUTTA-TRIPOLI divided between Renzo Martinelli and Corrado Testa
1940 BAGUTTA-TRIPOLI divided between Luigi Barzini and Vittorio G. Rossi
1947 Pier Antonio Quarantotti Gambini. L'onda dell'incrociatore
1949 Giulio Confalonieri. Prigionia di un artista: Vita di Cherubini
1950 Vitaliano Brancati. Il bell'Antonio
1951 Indro Montanelli. Pantheon minore
1952 Francesco Serantini. L'osteria del gatto parlante
1953 Leonardo Borgese. Primo amore
1954 Giuseppe Marotta. Coraggio, guardiano
1955 Alfonso Gatto. La forza degli occhi
1956 Giuseppe Lanza. Rosso sul lago
1957 Pier Angelo Soldino. Sole e bandiere
1958 Renzo Montano. A passo d' uomo
1959 Italo Calvino. Racconti
1960 Enrico Emanuelli. Uno di New York
Poetry--Antonio Barolini.

Elegie di Croton
BAGUTTA D'ARGENTO-
VERRI--Bonaventura Tecchi.
Gli egoisti
TRES SIGNORE (for a
woman writer)--Giovanna
Zangrandi. Campo rosso
1961 Giorgio Vigolo. Notti
romane
1962 Giuseppi Dessi'. Il
disertore
VENT 'ANNI DEL BAGUTTA
--1959 Romano Bilenchi.
Racconti   103.

Hans BAIMLER MEDAL (Ger-
many, East)
This literary honor of East
Germany has been awarded such
writers as Ludwig Renn.   104.

Jaime BALMES PRIZE (Spain)
One of the national journalism
prizes of Spain (others are the
Franco and Rivera Prizes)
established in 1956 to give
public recognition to outstanding
editors of Spanish newspapers.
Recipient of the honor in 1960
was Juan Pujol, editor of
"Madrid."   105.

BALZAC PRIZE (Germany)
A literary award of the
Mainz Academy of Science and
Literature (Mainzer Akademie der
Wissenschaften und der Literatur,
Geschwinter-Scholl Strasse 2,
Mainz) which was granted only
once--in 1952, the year the
prize was established. The
premium of 3000 DM was given
to Erwin M. Schneider.   106.

BALZAN FOUNDATION PRIZES
(International)
In March 1962 the Fonds
Balzan was formally established
in Bern, Switzerland. This
organization, "similar in scope
and purpose to the Nobel Foundation," will award an annual
prize in each of three humanitarian and cultural fields: Peace

and Humanity; Literature, Philosophy or the Arts; Science--
Physics, Chemistry, Engineering
or Medicine.
The Fonds Balzan, which will
administer the funds and pay all
awards, operates under the supervision of the Swiss Federal Department of the Interior. The
Foundation "PREMI," another
administrative unit of the Fonds
Balzan, located in Italy, will select recipients of the prizes,
who will be "chosen without regard to nationality, race, color
or creed."
The Awards Committee (Foundation "PREMI') is composed of
the world's most distinguished
scholars and authors, with wide
representation of countries:
U.S.A., Czechoslovakia, Argentina, Germany, Poland, Switzerland, U.S.S.R., and France. The
major representative for literature is the noted French author,
member of the Académie Française, François Mauriac (Science,
September 7, 1962, p. 740).
                                      107.

Eugenio BALZAN PRIZE (Italy)
An award recently established
by the memorial foundation for
the Italian journalist, Eugenio
Balzan (Fondazione Internazionale
Balzan, corso Porta Nuova 3/a,
Milan).   108.

BANCARELLA PRIZE (Italy)
This "Barrow-Prix" of Italy's
itinerant book peddlers is a
"best-seller" award with no attempt at literary evaluation of
the winning book or selection of
the prize-winner by a jury of experts. The Bancarella prize is
offered each year for the "book
that during the year has sold the
greatest number of copies on the
bancarelle"--the push-carts or
stands of Italy's book peddlers,
most of whom come from Pontre-
moli in northern Tuscany, and

who are considered to control
the book market in provincial
Italy. Initiated by two organizations (Unione Librai Pontremol-
esi and Associazone Nazionale
delle Bancarelle) in 1952, additional prizes have been added
to the original PREMIO BAN-
CARELLA: BANCARELLINO,
granted for books for children
and young people; BANCARELLA-
SPINTA, awarded since 1957 to
a young author.

Among award winners (with
a guarantee of 2,000 copies of
the winning work purchased for
distribution to libraries and
various Italian institutions) are:
   1953 Ernest Hemingway (USA).
   Il vecchio e il mare
   1954 Giovannino Guareschi
   (Italy). Don Camillo e il
   suo gregge
   1955 Herve Le Boteri
   (France). Lo spretato
   1956 Han Suyin (Malaya).
   L'amore e una cosa
   meravigliosa
   1957 Werner Keller (Germany)
   La Bibbia aveva ragione
   1958 Boris Pasternak (U.S.S.
   R.). Il dottor Zivago
   1959 Heinrich Gerlach (Germany). L'Armata dradita
   1960 Bonaventura Tecchi
   (Italy). Gli egoisti
   Additional awards to: Mario
   Soldati, La messa dei vil-
   leggianti; Carlo Cassola, Il
   taglio del bosco; Karen
   Blixsen (Denmark), La mia
   Africa
   1961 André Schwarz-Bart
   (France). L'ultimo dei
   giusti
   Additional awards to: Gerald
   Green, L'ultimo uomo ar-
   rabbiato; Carlo Cassola, La
   ragazza di Bube; Richard
   Powell, Vacanze matte; Dino
   Buzzati, Il Grande Ritratto
   1962 Cornelius Ryan. Il giorno
   piu lungo dell'anno
BANCARELLA-SPINTA

   1957 Mario Luzi. Onore al
   vero
   1958 Maria Teresa Nessi. Sabato sera
BANCARELLINO
   1958 Dino Beretta and Roberto
   Costa. L'uomo e la nave
   1959 Cesare Dei. Il libro di
   Madur   109.

BANCO NACIONAL DE MÉXICO
NATIONAL ECONOMICS PRIZE
(Mexico)
   This PREMIO ANUAL DE
ECONOMÍA BANCO NACIONAL
DE MÉXICO has been offered each
year since 1951 for the best work in
the field of economics, published
or written during the year.
Sponsored by Banco Nacional de
México (Isabel La Catolica 44,
Mexico, D.F.), the prize
(50,000 pesos first prize, with
second and third prizes and
honorable mentions) is granted
for the best work on a problem of
major importance in the economics of Mexico, written or published in Mexico during the preceding year, and submitted in
competition by January 15. In
the event no study or essay submitted in the contest is considered
worthy of the first prize, the
prize money is presented to the
National University of Mexico for
use in improving instruction in
economics--as, purchasing
specialized books in economics,
creating a fund for study grants
to students in economics.
   Winners of the prize include:
   1951 Alfredo Navarret, Jr.
   Estabilidad de cambios el
   ciclo y el desarrolo económico
   1952 Gonzaolo Robles. La in-
   dustrialización de México y
   la conservación de sus recursos
   1953 Cristobal Lara Beautell.
   La industria de energía
   eléctrica
   1954 Guadalupe Rivera de

López Malo. Estudio sobre
las relaciones obrero-patron-
ales
1955 Francisco R. Calderón.
Historia moderna de México
--La vida económica
1956 Armando González Santos.
La agricultura. Estruc-
tura y utilizacion de los
recursos
1959 Jésus Silva Herzog. El
agrarismo mexicano y la
reforma agraria   110.

Carmem Dolores BARBOSA
PRIZE (Brazil)
This Cr $100. 000 award of-
fered in São Paulo (Rua General
Jardim, 51-3º) for the best
"Brazilian creative literary work
of the year" has been granted
such authors of Brazilian "best
sellers" as:
1955 Cornelio Pena. A
menina morta.
1956 Orígenes Lessa. Rua de
sol
1957 João Guimarães Rosa.
Grande Sertão: Veredas
                             111.

Rui BARBOSA PRIZE (Inter-
national: United Kingdom; Brazil)
The British government grants
this £350 literary award each
five years to a Brazilian writer
for a work on England. The
award, established by a cultural
agreement between the United
Kingdom and Brazil, is matched
by a comparable Brazilian
Prize (Robert SOUTHEY PRIZE),
which is given to a British author
for a work on a Brazilian subject.
First awards were granted in
1957 to: Gustavo de Sá Lessa,
A experiéncia inglesa e suas
licões; and Charles R. Boxer,
Salvador de Sá, the struggle
for Brazil and Angola.   112.

Ole BANG PRIZE (Norway)
One of the endowments ad-

ministered by the Board of the
Norwegian Association of Writers,
this prize brings 1. 000 N Kr to
the winning author.   113.

BARCELONA DRAMA CRITICS
PRIZE (Spain)
Granted for the best play presented during the Barcelona
drama season at the Calderón
Theatre in Barcelona, this prize
has recently been won by:
1958-1959 Miguel Mihura
1960-1961 A. Buero Vallejo
                             114.

BARCELONA PRIZES (Spain)
Among the Spanish literary
awards with the greatest national
prestige are these annual prizes
of the city of Barcelona, offered
for works submitted to Negociado
de Bellas Artes y Museos,
Ayuntamiento de Barcelona.
Prizes are offered for works
written or published during the
contest year (currently December
1 to October 15 of the subsequent
year) in a number of categories
of writing: Novel; Drama; Poetry
in Castilian and in Catalan:
Journalism; Essay; Scientific Research; Law. The monetary
premium for each award is
50, 000 pts, except for the two
classes of Poetry, where the
prize is 30, 000 pts in each class.
The Barcelona Prizes, an-
nounced each January 26, the anniversary of the city holiday,
"Liberacion de la Ciudad," have
recently been awarded:
Novel--
1959 Carlos Roca. El asesino
de César
1960 Julio Manegat. Lo Feria
Vacia
1962 Andrés Bosch Villata.
Homenaje privado
Drama--
1959 Eduardo Criado. Cuando
las Nubes Cambian de Nariz
1960 Francisco Bargadá. La
espuma y la nada

1962 Noel Clarasó. El Rio
  Croce
Poetry-- Castilian
1959 Jésus Tomé. Esta
  tristera que traigo
1960 José Cruset. La In-
  finita Manera
1962 José Jurado Morales.
  Sombras anilladas
  --Catalan
1959 C. Fages de Climent.
  Sonets
1960 Juan Arús. El vas transparent
1962 Olegario Huguet Ferré.
  Ales d'Argila
Journalism--
1959 Luis Marsillach. Forty-
  eight articles: "La vida se
  cuenta," in "Hoja del Lunes"
1960 Avelino Artis   115.

BAROJA PRIZE (Spain)
  This award of 100,000 pts is
granted under the patronage of
"Paneles de Son Armadans,"
Palma de Majorca.   116.

Joáo de BARROS PRIZE
  (Portugal)
  One of several awards offered
by the Portuguese government
department, Agencia Geral do
Ultramar, this prize of 15.000$
for historical writing is granted
each year to promote new writing by Portuguese citizens, on
subjects dealing with overseas
topics. In 1957 the prize was
given to L. Ferrand de Almeida
for his work, "A diplomaia
portuguesa e os limites meri-
dionais do Brasil." Most recent
winners are: Alexandre Marques
Lobato (1960), "A expansáo
portuguesa em Moçambique de
1948 a 1930;" and Jofre Ribeiro
do Amaral Nogueira (1961),
"Angola, na epoca pombalina..."
                            117.

Jakub BART-CISINSKI PRIZE
(Germany, East)
  The East German Ministry

for Culture (Minister für Kultur,
DDR) first granted this award on
August 19, 1956, the centennial
of the birth of the National Poet
Jakub Bart-Cisinski (National-
dichter). Planned as a biennial
literary prize, in two groups with
two classes each (1--to a person,
5,000 and 3,000 DM; 2--to an
organization (kollektive), 8,000
and 5,000 DM), the award has
been given for a fundamental contribution to "sorbischen cultural
life" to such writers as:
  1956 Milavs Krjecmar.
    Sorbische literaturhistorische;
    Martin Nowak-Neumann. Sor-
    bisches Volkstheater, Bautzen
  1958 Paul Nedo
  1959 Alfred Mietzsoke; Jurij
    Brezan. First sorbisches
    Drama: "Marja Jancowa"
                            118.

BASEL ARTS PRIZE (Switzerland--
Kunstpreises der Stadt Basel)
  This prize, one of over fifty
cultural, arts, and literature
honors offered by Swiss cities
and communities, is awarded in
rotation in four cultural areas:
Painting; Literature; Musical
Composition; Sculpture. Writers,
who are residents of Basel or
especially associated with Basel,
honored with the 10,000 franc
premium since the prizes were
established in 1948 include:
  1950 Siegfried Lang, poet
  1961 Carl Jacob Burckhardt,
    writer   119.

BASEL LIONS CLUB PRIZE
(Switzerland)
  A general cultural award for
the encouragement of young
artists, this 2,000 franc prize
established in 1954 was given for
achievement in writing in 1957
to the poet and playwright
Herbert Meier.   120.

BASEL LITERATURE PRIZE
(Switzerland)

In 1960 the Basel Literature Prize was granted to Rudolf Frank for his book, "Spielzeit meines Lebens."   121.

"BASTIAN" PRIZE (Norway)

A statuette and 2.000 N Kr are granted in this award of the Norwegian Association of Trans- lators. Nominations for the prize are made by a jury of three members of the Associa- tion, appointed at the Associa- tion's year-end meeting. The prize, which must be awarded an Association member, is granted for an outstanding translation published in book form during the preceding year.   122.

BAYERISCHE AKADEMIE DER SCHÖNEN KÜNSTE LITERATURE PRIZE AND AWARD OF HONOR (Germany)

Literary honors, granted by the Bavarian Academy of Fine Arts, Munich, include two prizes:

Literature Prize--awarded since 1950 for outstanding con- tributions to literature

Award of Honor--granted since 1952, with or as an alternate award to the Literature Prize, as an encouragement award for new authors and as a recognition award for the achieve- ment of established authors

Winners of these annual literary honors, ranging in mone- tary premium from 500 to 5,000 DM--in 1961, 4000 DM--include:

Literature Prize
1950 Friedrich Georg Jünger
1951 Günter Eich
1953 Marieluise Fleisser
1955 Gerd Gaiser; Martha Saalfeld
1957 Alfred Döblin; Sigismund von Radecki
1959 Agnes Miegel
1960 Otto Flake
1961 Ilse Aichinger; Joachim

Maas
Award of Honor
1952 Oda Schaefer; Inge Westpfahl
1954 Friedrich Märker
1956 Emil Barth; Peter Gan; Eberhard Meckel; Ludwig von Pigenot; Elfriede Skalberg
1957 Friedrich Alfred Schmid- Noerr; Regina Ullmann
1958 Heinrich Böll; Theodor Kramer; Horst Lange; Benno von Mechow; Heinz Piontek
1960 Martin van Katte
1961 Ernst Günther Bleisch
123.

Pierre BAYLE PRIZE (Nether- lands)

Also known as the NETHER- LANDS CRITICS PRIZE, awarded by the Rotterdamse Kunststichting annually since 1956, this "spring" prize is given in April or June. The award consists of a medal and fl 1.250 "for him or her, who has performed his or her task of mediating criticism about arts during a series of years in a systematic constructive way on a literary level and in an author- ity commanding manner."

Among the critics honored are:
1956 J. J. Vriend--architec- tural criticism
1957 L. J. Jordaan--film criticism
1959 W. Paap--music criticism
1960 H.A. Gomperts--theatre criticism
1961 Jos de Gruyter--plastic arts criticism   124.

Johannes Robert BECHER PRIZE (Germany, East)

To commemorate and further the literary work of Johannes Becher, East German writer most famous as the author of the East German National Anthem, who died in 1958, this official government prize of the Minister- rat is awarded biennially for Ger-

man lyric poetry. A student
grant is also awarded (Johannes-
Robert-Becher Stipendium für
Stendenten der Germanistik).
The 20,000 DM Becher Prize,
first given on May 22, 1961,
honored Georg Maurer and Uwe
Berger.   125.

Gustavo Adolfo BECQUER PRIZE
(Spain)
   Offered by the Ministry of
Information and Tourism, this
prize was won in 1960 by Manuel
Montero with his poem, "Tiempo
del Hombre."   126.

August BEERNHAERT PRIZE
(Belgium)
   One of a number of French
language awards of the Belgian
Royal Academy of French
Language and Literature, the
Beernhaert Prize was established in 1925 for award each four
years for "the most outstanding
work of a Belgian author writing
in any form or on any subject."
To compete for the prize--
current value: 20,000 Fr--manu-
scripts must be submitted at
least two years in advance of the
award date for consideration by
a jury of three Academy members and two professors of the
history of French Literature.
   Most recent prize-winners
are:
      1953 O. P. Gilbert. Les
      portes de la solitude (novel)
      1957 Fernand Crommelynck.
      Tome I, of his Théâtre
      complet
      1961 Marie-Thérèse Bodart.
      L'autre   127.

BELGIAN CATHOLIC WRITERS
PRIZE
   Honoring writers in the two
official languages of Belgium
(French and Flemish), the prize
has been presented to such
Belgian authors as:
   French--

1957 Jean Stienon du Pré. Un
   cri perdu
1958 Jean Stienon du Pré.
   Altérable Délice
1960 Marcel Lobet. J.K.
   Huysmans ou le témoin
   écorché
Flemish--
1957 Victor Leemans. Kierkegaard
1959 Theo Bogaerts, Jr.
   Kunsten illusie
1960 Leo van Puyvelde. Antoon
   Van Dyck   128.

BELGIAN GOVERNMENT PRIZES
FOR LITERATURE
   Offered in the two official
languages of Belgium: French
and Flemish, this government
literary honor is an annual award,
given in turn to writing in the
form of: Prose, Drama, Poetry.
   Among recent recipients of
this official government recognition of an author's work are:
   French--
1957 Prose: Alexis Curvers.
   Tempo di Roma (novel)
1958 Drama: Claude Spaak.
   Le pain blanc
1959 Poetry: Georges Norge.
   Les oignons
1960 Prose:

   Flemish--
1957 Prose: Marnix Gijsen. Er
   gebourt nooit iets
1958 Drama: Piet Sterckx. Slak-
   ken en naalden
1959 Poetry: Gaston Burssens.
   Adieu
1960 Prose: Johan Daisne. De
   neusvleugel der Muze   129.

BELGIAN GRAND PRIZE
   One of the significant literary
honors awarded in Belgium, this
quinquennial award was granted
most recently (1960) to Marie
Gevers, to honor her entire
literary work.   130.

BELGIAN PRIZE FOR COLONI-
AL LITERATURE (Prijs voor
Koloniale Letterkunde)
In 1957 this triennial award
was given to Marcel Coole, for
his book "Kaluna."   131.

BELGIAN TRANSLATION PRIZE
Recent winners of this
Flemish language award are:
1957 Jan Keuleers. De
     zoveelste illusie
1958 Libera Carlier. Action
     Station Go   132.

V.G. BELINSKY PRIZE
(U.S.S.R.)
Named for the famous Russian
literary critic, Vissarion Gri-
gorievich Belinsky (1811-1848),
whose writings "form the foundation of Russian literary criticism,"
this literary honor granted by
the USSR Academy of Sciences,
Division of Literature and Language (Volhonka, No. 18/2,
Moscow), is awarded for the
"best scientific works in the
field of literary criticism, and
in the theory and history of
literature."
Established December 10,
1947, as two annual awards
(25,000 rubles; 15,000 rubles),
after some years (on June 23,
1956) the prize was combined into
one award (20,000 rubles) to be
granted triennially. Names of
proposed candidates for the prize
are considered by a special commission, and the selection of the
winner is subject to approval
by the Presidium of the USSR
Academy of Sciences.
Recipients of the prize include:
1950 V.S. Spirdonov. His
     "Scientific Comments" to the
     6 volume edition of the com-
     plete works of Belinsky, and
     the preparation for publica-
     tion of a 13-volume edition
     of Belinsky's writings.
Mrs. V.S. Nechayeva. V.G.

Belinsky--the beginning of
his life career and literary
activity
1951 Collective award to the
     workers of "Literary Heri-
     tage" Magazine for preparing
     a 3-volume edition dedicated
     to V. G. Belinsky (A.S.
     Yegolin, Belchikov, Silber-
     shtein, Makashin)
N.I. Mordovchenko. Belinsky
     and the Russian literature of
     his time (posthumous award)
1958 Divided prize: Mrs. K.
     D. Murotova. M. Gorki in
     his fight for development of
     Soviet literature; L.N.
     Novichenko. Poetry and
     revolution
1961 U. G. Oxman. Detailed
     description of the creative
     activity of V.G. Belinsky
                              133.

BELLMANN PRIZE (Sweden--Bell-
manspriset)
One of the major literary honors of Sweden is this 30,000
kroner annual prize granted by
Svenska Akademien (Swedish
Academy, Börshuset, Stockholm
C) to a "poet or ballad writer"
from funds derived in operation
of the 18th century restaurant,
"Gildene Freden," in Stockholm's
old town. The restaurant was
willed the Academy by the Swedish
painter Anders Zorn, who died in
1919.
One of the recipients of the
prize, named to commemorate
Karl Mikael Bellmann (1740-
1795), the Swedish Gustavian
ballad writer most famous for his
drinking and love songs, is Evert
Taube.   134.

Andrés BELLO PRIZE (Venezuela)
Named for the Venezuelan
philologist and poet Andrés Bello
(1781-1865), this Bs15.000 biennial award of the Venezuelan Min-
isteria de Educacion (Direccion
General de Cultura y Bellas Artes,

Caracas) is awarded to a Venezuelan writer or to an author
with five years' residence in the
country, for a major work on
Andrés Bello.
  Recipients include:
  1955 Edoardo Crema
  1959 Louell Dunham. Manual
  Diaz Rodríguez: Vida y obra
                              135.

BELO HORIZONTE PRIZE
(Brazil)
  One of a number of city and
regional literary and cultural
honors granted in Brazil, this
prize in 1959, granted by the
city of Belo Horizonte, capital
of Minas Gerais State, was
awarded to João Camilia de
Oliveira Torres for his essay,
"Democracia Coroada."   136.

BENSON MEDAL (International--
United Kingdom)
  This prize, one of several
literary honors granted by the
Royal Society of Literature of
the United Kingdom 1) Hyde
Park Gardens, London W 2)
was established in 1917 "to be
awarded to authors in respect
of meritorious works in Poetry,
Fiction, History, and Biography,
and Belles Lettres."
  Among the distinguished
writers honored with the Silver
Medal for their entire literary
work are:
  1917 Gabrielle d'Annunzio
       (Italy)
       Benito Perez Galdos (Spain)
       Maurice Parres (France)
  Since 1917, the award has
been granted writers of the U-
nited Kingdom, including Lytton
Strachey (1923), Edith Sitwell
(1934), E.M. Forster (1938),
and John Galsworthy (1940).
Three Gold Medals have also
been awarded in the Benson A-
ward: George Bernard Shaw;
Rudyard Kipling; Thomas Hardy.
                              137.

BERGAMO E PROVINCIA PRIZE
(Italy)
  A poetry prize established in
1958 as an annual award is
given in two sections:
  L 250.000--5 unpublished
     lyrics;
  L 150.000--poems on a set
     theme, varying from year to
     year, as recently: poem
     inspired by the rivers and
     lakes of Bergamo
  Recipients of the prize, who
submitted winning works to
Segretaria del Premio (Via
Duca degli Abruzzi 8, Bergamo),
include:
  1958 Emanuele Mandara,
       Martino Vitali--divided prize
       Domenico Cara, Cario Pol-
       leschi, C. Bendinelli--shared
       prize for poems on set theme
  1961 Luciano Luisi
       Tiberi Petroni (poems on set
       theme)   138.

BERLIN DRAMA PRIZE (Germany)
  Awarded for the "best play"
each year by the Union for
Christian-Jewish Cooperation
(Gesammte für christlischen-jud-
ischen Zusammenarbeit), the
Berlin Drama Prize in 1956
brought a premium of 2000 DM
to Friedrich Kolander.   139.

BERLIN PRESS GOLDEN PLAQUE
(Germany)
  The "Goldene Plakette für
Berliner Presse," a journalism
award granted to "commemorate
the battle of the West Berlin
Press for the freedom of their
city," was presented in 1959 to
Walter Wegner, Vorsitzender des
Presseverbandes Berlin.   140.

BERN LITERATURE PRIZE
(Switzerland)
  The Canton of Bern grants
this prize each year to young and
old writers with the purpose of
encouraging outstanding writing
in the Canton. Presented by

Erziehundirektion des Kantons Bern, with the advice of the Kommission zur Förderung des bernischen Schrifttums, the award--granted since 1930--may consist of a monetary premium of from 500 to 2,000 francs, and --as an alternate or combination award--purchase of the winning author's works by institutions such as libraries, schools, hospitals.

Among recent recipients of the prize is Friedrich Dürrenmatt, whose play, "Das Versprechen"(The Pledge) was honored in 1960.   141.

BERTELSMANN PRIZES (Germany)

The several awards offered by the publisher, C. Bertelsmann Verlag (Eickhoffstrasse 14/16, Gütersloh, West Germany) include outright grants of monetary premiums, royalty advances, or purchase of winning work. In the novel prize (Romanpreis, Novellenpreis) winners include:
   1954 Christine Brückner, Erich Landgrebe, Ernst Khuon, Johannes Weidenheim
   1955 Leopold Sievers, Erich Landgrebe, Maria Müller-Gögler.

A poetry prize (Lyrikpreis der "Neuen deutschen Hefte") offered in 1956 was won by Christine Busta, Christine Lavant, and Doris Mühringer. The two best works in the 2000 DM competition of 1959 (Bertelsmann-Erzähler-Wettbewerb) were Jeannie Ebner with "Königstiger;" and Werner Wilk with "Heilriegel."

The Carl Bertelsmann Publishing Company Foundation (Stiftung des Carl Bertelsmann Verlages), which is endowed with 50.000 DM "for the encouragement of young authors," included among the 1959 awards grants to: Erich Junge; Jörg Steiner

(Switzerland); and Karl E. Trautmannsdorf.   142.

BIALIK PRIZE (Israel)

Referred to by some critics as "the highest literary award in Israel," the Bialik Prize, named for the famous Hebrew poet, Chaim Nahman Bialik (1873-1934), has included among recent winners: Moshe Shamir (1958), with "The king of flesh and blood;" and the poet Yaakov Fichman, with "Pe'at Sadeh."   143.

Alfredo A. BIANCHI ESSAY PRIZE (Argentina)

A scholarly award of the Sociedad Argentina de Escritores (Calle Mexico 564) the Bianchi Essay Prize was granted in 1961 to Adolfo Fernández de Obieta for "Experiencias con el tiempo en el arte contemporáneo" (Experiments with time in contemporary art).   144.

BIELEFELD CULTURAL PRIZE (Germany)

Since 1956 an annual award of 3000 DM has been granted by the Westphalian city of Bielefeld for outstanding works in Art, Science and Technology by persons who were born in Bielefeld or who have worked in that area. Writers winning the prize include: Else Buddenberg (1957), and Gustav Engel (1961).   145.

BIJENKORF PRIZE (Netherlands--Bijenkorf-Boekenweekprijs)

The recipients of this prize, since its establishment in 1956, include:
   1957 Harry Mulisch. Het zwarte licht (novel)
   1958 Herman van den Bergh. Entire work
   1960 Aya Zikken. De Atlasvlinder (novel)   146.

Carl BLECHEN PRIZE (Germany, East)

Established by the council of
the district of Cottbus (Rat des
Bezirkes Cottbus) in 1956 to
commemorate the 800-year anniversary of Cottbus on October 7
of that year, the prize is a
general cultural award for art
and literature, granted for a
single work or for the entire
work of an artist who lives in
the district or whose work concerns it.

Literary awards include those
to Herbert Scuria (1956), and
Bodo Krautz (1958).   147.

Steen Steensen BLICHER PRIZE (Denmark)

The Danish lyric poet Steen
Blicher (1782-1848) is commemorated by the prize which
is given to painters, actors
and other artists in addition
to writers. Authors who have
won the award include: Hans
Brix, H. P. Hansen, and--in
1961--Hans Povlsen.   148.

BODENSEE LITERATURE PRIZE (Germany)

The "Lake Constance" Literature Prize of the city of Überlingen (Burgermeisteramt, Überlingen, Bodensee) has been a-
warded annually since 1954.
Winners of the 1000 DM premium
include:

1954 Wolfram von den Steinen
     (Switzerland). Notker
     der Dichter und seine geistige
     Welt
1955 Friedrich Georg Jünger.
     Lyric writing
1956 Leopold Ziegler. Entire
     work in philosophy
1957 Richard Beitl (Austria).
     Entire work in folk art
     and literature
1958 Mary Lavater-Sloman
     (Austria). Einsamkeit, life
     and work of Anette von
     Droste-Hülshoff
1959 Wilhelm Boeck. Joseph
     Anton Feuchtmayer

1960 Johannes Duft (Switzer-
     land). For his work in St.
     Gall
1961 Albert Knoepfli (Switzer-
     land). Kunstgeschichte des
     Bodenseeraumes, monograph
     on painter Carl Roesch
                             149.

Simon BOLIVAR PRIZE (Inter-national--Italy)

This L 400.000 poetry award,
offered by the monthly literary
review "Ausonia" (via di Malizia
48, Siena, Italy), has been won
by such authors of Europe and
the Americas as:

1956 George Libbrecht (Belgium);
     Carmen Conde (Spain); with
     special mention for Luis
     Beltrán Guerrero (Venezuela)
     for his book "Secretos en
     Fuga;" and honorable mention
     to José Ramón Medina (Vene-
     zuela); Alcides Pinto (Brazil);
     and Ruth Silva (Portugal).
1957 Ribeiro Couto (Brazil).
     Jeux de l'apprenti animalier
                             150.

BOLIVIAN GRAND NATIONAL PRIZE FOR LITERATURE (Gran Premio Nacional de Literatura)

In 1951 this high state award
in recognition of literary achievement was granted Fernando Diez
de Medina for his book "Nayjama."
                             151.

BOLIVIAN NATIONAL NOVEL CONTEST

Parts of the celebration of the
fourth centennial of the city of La
Paz in 1948 was a Concurso
Nacional de Novelas. The con-
test prize was given Nazario
Pardo Valle for "Trópico del
Norte."   152.

BOLIVIAN SOCIETY OF WRITERS AND ARTISTS PRIZE

First prize winners of the
Sociedad Escritores y Artistas
de Bolivia award include Humberto

Guzman Arze, who received the cultural honor for his work, "Siringa."   153.

BOND VAN NEDERLANDSE PRIZE (Netherlands)
Offered by Vereeniging van Nederlandse--Toneeluitgevers, this prize for stage plays has been granted to such writers as H.A. Keuls (1957), for "Plant age Tamarinde."   154.

Albert BONNIERS FUND AND GRANTS (Sweden).
Oldest and most important of the literary prize-granting Swedish foundations which are connected with publishing houses and newspapers, is that of Albert Bonniers Forlag (Sveavagen 56, Stockholm), with the Albert Bonnier Fund for Swedish Authors (established in 1901 and distributing about 20,000 kroner each year). In addition, a new Fund, which was established in 1937 in celebration of the centenary of the publishing house, now distributes 26,000 kroner each year to authors, and 11,000 kroner to journalists and illustrators.
Travelling and working grants of 12,000 kroner a year are also offered Swedish writers by the Bonnier company, as is a 3,000 kroner prize for authors of books for children and young people.   155.

A. BOON PRIZE (Belgium)
One of the awards of the Davids Fund is the Boon Prize, recently granted (1959) to Jules van Ackere, for "Zingend steen. Wandelingen in en om Italie's historische gebouwen."   156.

Giuseppe BORGIA PRIZE (Italy)
A prize of L 500.000 given by Fondazione Dott. Giuseppe Borgia and administered by Accademia Nazionale dei Lincei

(via della Lungara 10, Rome), has offered since 1958 a rich premium to the young author (under 35 years of age) of a scientific or a literary work.
Recipients include:
1958 Philology and Linguistics --Cesare Segre. For various works on Italian prose writing of the 13th and 14th centuries, particularly for the edition of "Bestaire d' amours."
1960 History--Giuseppe Alberigo. "I vescuvi italiani al Concilio di Trento (1545-1547)," and other writings on the history of the Council of Trent   157.

BORLETTI PRIZE (Italy)
The Senator Borletti Prize "for a first work of fiction" was granted in 1962 to Angela Bianchini for her three novellas, "Lungo Equinozio" (Long Equinox).
158.

Augusto BORSELLI PRIZE (Italy)
Since 1959 the Dino De Laurentis (Piazza SS Giovanni e Paolo 8, Rome) has awarded its L 1.000. 000 prize for a novel published during the contest year which is judged most suitable for adaptation in motion pictures. Six copies of the book may be entered in competition before April 30 each year.
Recipients of the award in 1960 were Carlo Bernari, with "Amore amaro;" Giovanni Arpino, with "La suora giovane;" and C.M. Franzaro, who was given a gold medal for his book about Oscar Wilde.   159.

Juan BOSCÁN PRIZE (Spain)
The Boscán Prize and the Adonais Prize are the two most important poetry awards given in Spain (according to the authority on Spanish prizes, José Sanchez). The Boscán Prize is awarded an-

nually by the Barcelona Institute
of Hispanic Studies (Instituto
de Estudios Hispanicos de Barcelona, Calle de Valencia 231,
Barcelona) to the "best Spanish
and Hispano-American poets
writing in Castilian." The monetary value of the prize (originally 5,000 pts, and more
recently 7,000 pts) is small
compared with the prestige of
the award. Deadline for entries
each year is May 1, with the
winners announced in June.
Recent laureates are:
1958 José Manuel Caballero
Bonald. Obras muertas
1959 Rafael Santos Torroella.
Cerrada noche
1960 Carlos Sahagún (His-
pano-American). Como si
hubiera muerto un nino
1961 J. Corredor Matheos.
Poemas para un nuevo
1962 Eduardo Zepeda
(Nicaragua). A mano
alzada   160.

BOSNIA AND HERZEGOVINA
WRITERS SOCIETY PRIZES
(Yugoslavia-Udruzenje knijizevnika
Bosne i Hercegovine)
One of a number of literary
honors offered by Writers'
Societies in the Provinces of
Yugoslavia, this award has
been given:
1953 Camila Sijaric. Ram-
Bulja (Ram-Bulja) (col-
lected short stories)
1954 Dusan Durovic. Zdrijelo
(The defile) (collected short
stories)
Sukrija Pandzo. Razgovori
(Conversations) (collected
poems)   161.

Ernest BOUVIER-PARVILIEZ
PRIZE (Belgium)
Established in 1925 as an
award of the Belgian Royal
Academy of French Language
and Literature, this prize is
granted every four years for the

entire work of a Belgian writer
in French, whose published writings evidence sustained and exceptional literary contributions
over a period of years.
Recent recipients of the 5,000
fr premium include:
1925 Charles Delchevalerie
1929 Auguste Vierset
1933 Maurice Gauchez
1941 Arsene Soreil
1945 Charles Conardy
1949 Paul Champagne
1953 Yvonne Herman
1957 Nelly Kristink
1961 Georges Guérin   162.

BRABANT PRIZE (Belgium)
Annually awarded for prose
writing in Flemish, and--less
frequently--for prose writing in
French, this cultural honor given
by Brabant, province of central
Belgium in which Brussels is
located, has been won by such
writers as:
1957 Jean Mogin. La reine de
neuf jours
1958 Bernard Kemp. Het
laatste spel
1959 Ary Delen. Geschiedenis
van de Grafische Kunst
Fanny Leys. Ontwijding
1960 Albert Bontrieder.
Bagatelle hangende Vis   163.

Afonso de BRAGANÇA PRIZE
(Portugal)
A journalism prize offered each
year by Secretariado Nacional da
Informação and bringing 6.000$
to winners in the last several
years:
1957 Francisco de Paula Dutra
Faria. O Tribunal de Haia,
articles published in Voz pelo
1958 Artur Maciel. Romeiro
na Espanha
1959 Ferreira da Costa. O
Quanza corre para o Noroeste
1960 João Falcato. Reporta-
gens sobre Angola, published
in Diário de Noticias and
Comercio de Luanda

1961 Rodriguez Júnion. A
Costa do Malabar   164.

BRAIBANTI PRIZE (Italy)
Under the auspices of the
Minister of Agriculture, this
award for literature and journalism was established in 1955 by
the review "Molini d'Italia"
(Piazzi Campo Marzio 3, Rome).
The premium of L 1.000.000,
offered for writing that discusses
and illustrates the origin of
milled food products, was won
in 1957 by Giovanni Artieri.
165.

BRAND-VAN GENT PRIZE
(Netherlands)
The novel "Ik dom niet
terug" of Jos. Panhuysen won
this Dutch literary honor in
1960.   166.

BRANKO'S PRIZE (Yugoslavia--
Brankova Nagrada)
Offered by the People's Committee of Stremski Karlovci to
young poets of Yugoslavia, this
poetry prize has been won by
such collections of poems as
those by:
1953 Vasko Popa. Koa (The
crust)
1954 Gordana Todorovic.
Pesme (Poems)
1955 Aleksandr Tismi.
Naseljeni svet (The populated
world)   167.

BRASILIA PRIZE (International--
Brazil)
This international poetry
prize, offered by the city of
Brasilia, the interior capital
of Brazil, to commemorate its
founding and to attest Italo-
Brazilian friendship, is granted
to poets writing in Italian,
Spanish, French, or Portuguese.
Prize-winners of 1962 include
European and Latin American
poets:
First three prizes--Floro di

Zenzo; Idillio Dell'Era (Italy)
Marie Thérèse Laethem
(France)
Medal "Amicizia Italo-Brasil-
iana"--Anderson Braga-Horta
(Brazil)
Guillermo Flores Avendano
(Guatemala)
Certificate "Lauro al merito
litterario"--Caio Gracco
Maranhao (Brazil)
Ariel Canzani (Argentina)
168.

BRAZIL "DISCOVER-THE-AUTHOR"
PRIZE (Prêmios Revelação de
Autor)
The purpose of these awards is
to "assist in the completion of a
serious work" by an author who
is writing a novel or poetry. The
two prizes of Cr$200.000 each
are granted to allow an author
to finish a novel (award by
Câmara Brasileira do Livro, Av
Ipiranga 1.267, São Paulo); and
a work of poetry (award by
Sindicate Nacional dos Editôres
de Livros, Av. Rio Branco 138,
Rio de Janeiro).   169.

BRAZIL THEATRE PRIZE (Latin-
America--Brazil)
Established in 1958 by Divisae
Cultural do Ministerio das Rela-
coes Exteriores, this Latin A-
merican "Prêmio Brasil" is given
in recognition of the "best
theatrical work of Pan American
authorship." "Theatre authorities
in each country of Latin America
forward the dramatic work selected as best in their country to
Rio de Janeiro," where the final
judging takes place.   170.

BRAZILIAN CULTURAL PRIZE
OF THE ITALIAN CONSULATE
The Italian Consulate in
Brazil awarded this "Premio Cul-
tura" in 1960 to the Italian-
Brazilian poet Mauro Musciac-
chio for his work, "Um Pássaro
que se Chama Sabía."   171.

BRAZILIAN DRAMA CRITICS AS-
SOCIATION PRIZE
   In addition to medals presented to directors and pro-
ducers for outstanding contribution to Brazilian drama, the
A.B.C.T. (Associação Brasileira
de Críticos Teatrais) gives a
medal to the author of the best
play of the season in Rio de Janeiro, and a special diploma
to the most promising new playwright.
   In 1959 the medal was given
playwright Gianfrancesco Guarn-
ieri for 'Éles não usam black-
tie;" and the "Discovery Diploma"
to Cleber Ribeiro Fernandes
for "A Torre de Marfim." 172.

BRAZILIAN NATIONAL FEDERA-
TION OF INDUSTRY PRIZE
   This literary award of the
C.N.I. (Confederação Nacional de
Indústria, Av. Calogeras 15, Rio
de Janeiro) was granted in
1959 to Miécio Táti, for the
essay, "O Rio de Janaero na
obra de Machado de Assis."
                              173.

BRAZILIAN NATIONAL PRIZES
   Among the several literary
awards of the Brazilian national
government agency, Instituto
Nacional do Livro (Rua Araujo,
Porto Alegre, Rio de Janeiro),
a division of the Ministerio da
Educacion y Saude, are literary
prizes granted for works published during the preceding
year: Novel, Story, Poetry,
Memoirs, Scholarly Writing,
Essay, Criticism.   These prizes
have been referred to as:
"Premio Nacional;" Premios do
Instituto Nacional do Livro;"
"Premio Edgar Cavalheiro;"
"Premio Instituto Nacional do
Livro."
   Among recent recipients of
the eight annual awards, which
are presented on September 29,
in commemoration of the anniversary of Brazil's famous poet,
Machado de Assis (1839-1908)
are:
   1958 Marly de Oliveira. Cêrco
      de Primavera (poetry)
      Lígia Almansur Haddad
      Valdomiro Autran Dourado.
      Novo histórias contadas em
      grupos de tres
      J. M. Moreira Campos.
      Portas Fechadas
      G. W. Sassi. Amigo Velho
   1959 Homero Homem. Calen-
      dário de Marinheiro; Paulo
      Mendes Campos. Domingo
      azul do mar (poetry)
      Jorge Amado. Gabriela,
      cravo e canela (novel)
      Lígia Fagundes Teles. His-
      torias de Desencontro (short
      stories)
      Bernardino José de Sousa. O
      Ciclo de Carro de Boi (essays)
      Raquel de Queirós. A Beata
      Maria do Egito; Jorge de
      Andrade. Vereda da Salvação
      (drama)
      Edy Lima. A farsa da Esôpô-
      sa Perfeita; Francisco
      Pereira da Silva. Cristo
      Proclamado ('outro de teatro')
                              174.

BRAZILIAN PRIZE (Prêmio
Brasiliana)
   A publisher's prize, established
in 1956 by the Companhia Editora
Nacional (Rua dos Gusmoes 639,
São Paulo) to celebrate the 30th
anniversary of the publishing
house, this prize offered Cr
$50.000 for any new unpublished
work on a Brazilian subject,
suitable for publication in the
Companhia Editora Nacional
series, "Brasiliana."
   In 1959, the award which is
administered by Sociedade Paulista
de Escritores, was granted to
Alceu Maynard de Araojo for
"Medicina Rustica."   175.

BRAZILIAN WRITERS' UNION OF
SÃO PAULO PRIZES

These "Prêmios da U.B.E."
(União Brasileira da Escritores
de São Paulo, Rua 24 de Maio
250-13º) comprise a number of
literary prizes given each year
by the Paulist Society of Writers.
Among the honors for writers
are:

RENATO CRESPI PRADO PRIZES
and FÁBIO PRADO PRIZES--
Cr$50.000 awarded in rota-
tion for the best writing in the
category of: Novel, Short
Stories, Drama, Motion Picture
Writing, Poetry, Essay, and
Brazilian Studies.

Recipients of the award,
given each January 15 for a
work of the previous year, include:
1954 Osman Lins. O visitante
     Aluslo Jorge Andrade Franco.
     O telescópio (play)
     Luis Canabrava. Sangue de
     Rosaura (stories)
1955 Fernando Pessoa Fer-
     reira. Os instrumento do
     tempo (poetry)
     Oraci Nogueira. Ralacões
     raciais num municipio
     Paulista Itapetininga
     (Brazilian studies)
1956 Edda Martins. Messias
     (novel)
     Nataniel Dantas. Veias
     desatadas (stories)
     Maria Inês Barros de Al-
     meida. O Diabocospe ver-
     nelho (play)
1957 Brito Broca (A vida
     literario no Brasil--1900
     (literary study)
     Francisco Martins. Volta à
     Serra Misteriosa (children's
     book)
     Armando Ferrari. Etienne de
     la Bóetie no quadro politico
     do Século XVI (history)
1958 José de Barros Pinto. A
     Jangada (The lifeboat) (novel)
1959 Mario da Silva Brito;
     Edith Pimentel Pinto;
     Arthur Neves; Jannart

Ribeiro Moutinho
Moacir C. Lopes. Maria de
cada Porto
ÁLVERES DE AZEVEDO PRIZES
--Cr$35.000 for writing in
various literary forms.
Winners in 1959 were: Jamil
Almansur Haddad (essay);
and Lígia Fagundes Teles
(poetry).

Currently announced annual
awards, each with a premium of
Cr$50.000 except the Müller
Prize with a premium of Cr$
20.000 are:
RENATA CRESPI PRADO PRIZES
--Poetry; Children's Literature;
Stories;Drama
FABIO PRADO PRIZES--Essays
or Brazilian Studies; Essays or
General Studies; Novels; Motion
Picture Writing
HERMAN MÜLLER CARIOBA
PRIZE--Children's Plays

Three copies of works entered
in competition must be submitted
during the contest period (January 1 to January 15 of the following year) and both unpublished
and published (during the contest
year or the preceding year) are
eligible. For the Müller Prize,
Children's Plays published or
presented during the award year--
November 1 to October 31 of the
following year--are eligible. The
Renata Crespi Prado "Concurso de
Teatro" considers only plays that
have been neither published nor
presented.   176.

BREMEN LITERATURE PRIZE
(Germany)
The "Literaturpreis der Freien
Hansestadt Bremen," awarded an-
nually since 1954 on January 26,
the birthday of the Bremen poet
Rudolf Alexander Schröder,
carries a premium in recent years
ranging from 6000 to 8000 DM.
Beginning in 1962 the Schröder
Stiftung Literaturpreis will be
offered in place of the Bremen

Literature Prize.
Among winning authors are:
1954 Heinrich Schmidt-
Barrien
1955 Ilse Aichinger; Herbert
Meyer
1956 Ernst Jünger
1957 Ingeborg Bachmann.
Anrufung des grossen Baren
(collected poems); Gerd
Oelschlägel
1958 Paul Celan
1959 Rolf Schroers
1960 Günter Grass. Die
Blechtrommel (The tin
drum) (novel)
RUDOLF ALEXANDER SCHRÖDER
-PREIS
1962 Siegfried Lenz. Zeit der
Schuldlosen (play); Herbert
Heckmann. Benjamin und
seine Väter (novel)
177.

BRENNER PRIZE (Israel)
A literary honor of the
Palestinian Authors' Association
that includes among its winners
David Maletz (1950) for his
book in Hebrew, "Maagalot,"
Young hearts. S. Yizhar also
received a Brenner Prize in
1950 for his story, "Shayara
Shel Hatsot" (The midnight con-
voy).   178.

BRENTANO PRIZE (International
--France)
In 1929 when this prize offered 25,000 fr to the author of
the winning novel, it was the
"richest international literary
prize with the exception of the
Nobel Prize."
The prize winner, with the
"best novel published in France
during the year" (March 1,
1928 to March 30, 1929) was
the French author Jean Giono,
with "Colline" (translated title,
Hill of destiny).   179.

BIBLIOTECA BREVE PRIZE
(Spain)
One of Spain's richest and
most recently established prizes
for the novel, this publishers'
award of Editorial Seix Barral
(Provenza 219, Barcelona) is an
annual prize (currently 100,000
pts and originally 75,000 pts)
granted for the best unpublished
novel in Castilian submitted in
competition.
The monetary premium of the
prize is a royalty advance of 10
percent royalty on the published
price of the first edition of
10,000 copies, and, in addition,
the winning novel automatically
becomes an entry in the group of
Spanish novels considered for
Spain's nomination for the international Formentor Prize,
offered by a group of publishers of which Seix Barral is
the cooperating Spanish publisher.
Closing date for novels to be submitted for the Biblioteca Breve
Prize is March 1, and the winner
is announced in May. Recipients
include:
1958 Luis Goytisolo. Las
Afueras
1959 Juan Garcia Hortelano.
Nuevas Armistades;also high
in competition: Carlo Droguett
(Chile). Eloy
1960 Not awarded for "lack of
a majority vote of the jury"--
three highest competitors:
Juan Marsé. Encerrados
con un solo jugeuete; Ana
Mairena. Los Extraordinarios;
Daniel Sueiro. La Criba
1961 José Manuel Caballero
Bonald. Dos Dias de Sep-
tiembre
1962 Mario Vargas Llosa. Los
impostores   180.

John BRINCKMANN PRIZE
(Germany, East)
Founded in 1957 for outstanding contributions to Low German literature and drama,

this award of the Council of the District of Rostock (Rad des Bezirkes Rostock) has been granted such German writers as:

1957 Peter E. Erichson
1959 Dr. Kuba (pseud of Kurt Bartel). Klaus Störtebecker (play)
1960 Frits Meyer   181.

Paula BRITO PRIZE (Brazil)

Granted by the Biblioteca Municipal (1 Distrito Federal, Rio de Janeiro), these library prizes are offered for the best works in nine types of writing, with one award for the "entire work" of an author. João Guimarães Rosa won an award in 1957 with Grande Sertao: Veredas; and winners in 1959 were:

Poetry--Homero Homem. Calendário-Marinheiro
Novel--Jorge Amado. Gabriela, cravo e canela
Essay--Barbosa Lima Sobrinho. A Língua Portuguésa e a Unidade do Brasil
Drama--Raquel de Queirós. A Beata Maria do Egito
Criticism--Adonias Filho. Modernos Ficcionistias Brasileiros
Chronicle--Rubem Braga. 100 crônicas escholhidas
History (História carioca)-- Nelson Costa. O Rio de Ontem e de Hoje
Bibliography--J. Galante de Sousa. Fontes para o Estudio de Machado de Assis
Memoirs--Eduardo Porica. Diemsões-I
Entire Work--Otavio Tarquinia de Sousa   182.

BROQUETTE-GONIN GRAND PRIZE (France)

One of the literary honors of the Académie Française, this annual prize is granted to an author of a philosophical, polit-ical or literary work, which is considered capable of inspiring a "love for the true, the beautiful and the good."

Laureates of the prize, with writings judged of high philosophic worth, include:

1946 Maurice Rat. Entire work
1949 Bernard Guyon. Works on Balzac
1950 Emile Magne. Works
1951 Jean Alazard. Ingres et l'ingrisme
1952 Henri Terrasse. Histoire du Maroc
1954 Jacques Duron
1955 Maurice Allem. Entire work
1956 Renée Huyghe. Dialogue avec le visible
1958 Tran-Minh-Tiet. Histoire des persécutions au Viet-nam
1960 André Ducasse. Jacques Meyer, and Gabriel Perreux. Vie et mort des Français (1914-1918)
1961 André Rousseaux. Entire work
1962 André George. Entire work.   183.

BROSS PRIZE (International-- U.S.A.)

First granted in 1880, the award in 1940 was the 15th prize, and since that date the $7,500 premium "for the best book or treatise on the relationship of science and the Christian religion" has been decennial. William Bross, Lt. Governor of the state of Illinois during the Civil War, founded the prize in memory of his son, Nathaniel Bross, and the award is administered by Lake Forest College (Lake Forest, Illinois) of which William Bross was a Trustee.

The scope of the writing eligible for the prize "is so comprehensive that any phase of science, of literature, of human history, and of modern life that may throw light upon the Christian religion, or upon any phase of the same..." is considered a fitting theme for the unpublished manuscripts entered in competition. Works by foreign authors are eligible, but they must be presented in English translation, and winners through 1960 have been citizens of the United Kingdom or of the U.S.A.   184.

BRUSSELS COLONIAL FAIR PRIZE (Africa--Belgium--Prix Littéraire de la Foire Coloniale de Bruxelles)

Two of the awards made to African writers at the Colonial Fair in Brussels (1948-1949) were presented to Paul Lomami-Tshibamba (Congo) for "Ngando" (The crocodile); and J. Saverio Naigiziki (Ruanda-Urundi) for "Escapade Ruandaise. Journal d'un clerc en sa Trentième Année."   185.

BUAZZELLI PRIZE (Italy)

In 1960 this novel award was granted to the two writers: Giovanni Arpino, for "La suora giovane" (The young nun); and Carlo Bernari, for "Amore amaro" (Bitter love).   186.

Georg BÜCHNER PRIZE (Germany)

One of the oldest of established German literary honors, this prize was originally given (1923-1933) as a state prize of Hesse, in commemoration of the Darmstadt poet, Georg Büchner (1813-1837). For a ten year period (1933-1944) the Büchner Prize was replaced by a cultural award of the City of Darmstadt, but in 1951 the Büchner Prize was reestablished as a joint literary award of the German Academy for Language and Literature (Deutsche Akademie für Sprache und Dichtung, Alexandraweg 26, Darmstadt), and the

two cooperating government agencies, who finance the award: the State of Hesse (Staatsministerium) and the City of Darmstadt (Magistrat).

The prize, with a premium of 7000 DM (more than double the initial premium of 3000 DM) is awarded each year on October 17, the birthday of poet Büchner--a city holiday in Darmstadt--to German poets and prose writers (especially younger authors). Recipients include:

    1923 Adam Karillon
         Alfred Bock
    1925 Wilhelm Michel
    1927 Kasimir Edschmid
    1929 Carl Zuckmayer
    1930 Nikolaus Schwarzkopf
    1932 Albert H. Rausch
    1945 Hans Schiebelhuth
    1947 Anna Seghers
    1950 Elisabeth Langgässer
    1951 Gottfried Benn
    1953 Ernst Kreuder
    1954 Martin Kessel
    1955 Marie Luise Kaschnitz
    1956 Karl Krolow
    1957 Erich Kästner
    1958 Max Frisch (Switzerland--
         first award to a non-German)
    1959 Günter Eich
    1960 Paul Celan
    1961 Hans Erich Nossack
    1962 Wolfgang Koeppen   187.

BUENOS AIRES DRAMA PRIZE (Argentina)

A literary award for an Argentine playwright (variously designated "Premio Municipal de Teatro;" "Premio Municipal--Pieza Teatral;" "Premio Nacional de Drama") has been given such dramatists as:

    1930 Samuel Eichelbaum
    1937 Horacio Rega Molina. La
         posada del león
    1953 Antonio Pages Larraya.
         Santos vega el Payador
                                    188.

BUENOS AIRES INSTITUCIÓN
CULTURAL ESPAÑOLA MEDAL
(Argentina)
The Medalla de Oro of the
Buenos Aires cultural group has
been awarded such writers as:
1936 Manuel Mujica Láinez.
La pureza de Don Quijote
1937 Enrique Larreta.
Orillas del Ebro
1948 Emilio Carilla. Cervantes
in Argentina.   189.

BUENOS AIRES LITERARY
PRIZE (Argentina)
In 1959 this literary honor
awarded by the Province of
Buenos Aires was granted:
Rodolfo Falcioni for "El hombre
olividado" (The forgotten man);
and Hellen Ferro for "Los
testigos."   190.

BUENOS AIRES LITERARY
PRIZES (Argentina--Premios
Municipales de Literatura)
Since 1920 the cultural awards
of the city of Buenos Aires
(Municipalidad de la Ciudad de
Buenos Aires, Secretaria de
Cultura y Accion Social) have
included a prize for literature,
as well as for visual art, drama
and music. · Granted for the best
work published during the year
in the city, three literary prizes
($50.000; $30.000; and $20.000)
are given for prose and poetry.
Recently--since 1957--the prose
prize has been awarded in two
categories of writing: Works of
Imagination or Fiction (Novels,
Stories, "Relatos"); and Essays
(including Biography and Criticism). Also, since 1957, an
annual prize of $15.000 is given
for unpublished poetry.
The Jury of Awards, comprising
representatives of the city of
Buenos Aires, and of the Academia Argentina de Letras, and
of the Sociedad Argentina de
Escritores, has granted the
prizes (a diploma and a mone-

tary premium) to such authors
of works given the First Prize
as:
Poetry--
1920 Alfonsina Storni. Lan-
guidez
1921 Pedro Miguel Obligado.
El ala de sombra
1922 Arturo Vázquez Cey.
Aguas serenas
1923 Fernán Félix de Amador.
La copa de David
1924 Arturo Marasso. Poemas
y coloquios
1925 Fernández Moreno. Aldea
española
1926 Rafael Alberto Arrieta.
Estío serrano
1927 Ezequiel Martínez Estrada
Argentina
1928 Rafael Jijena Sanchez.
Achalay
1929 Leopoldo Marechal. Odas
para el hombre y la mujer
1930 César Tiempo. Libro
para la pausa del sábado
1931 Eugenio Julio Iglesias.
Ruta y soledad
1932 Eduardo Keller. Poemas
para el ángel
1933 Ricardo E. Molinari.
Hostería de la Rose y el
Clavel
1934 Amado Villar. Marimorena
1935 Francisco Luis Bernárdez.
El buque
1936 Luis Cané. Romancero del
Río de la Plata
1937 Carlos Mastronardi. Con-
ocimiento de la noche
1938 Margarita Abella Caprile.
50 poesías
1939 Arturo Cambours Ocampo.
Poemas para la vigilia del
hombre
1940 César Fernández Moreno.
Galo ciego
1942 Vicente Barbieri. La
columna y el viento
1943 José M. Castiñeira de
Dios. Del ímpetu dichoso
1944 León Benarós. El rostro
inmarcesible
1945 Miguel D. Etchebarne.

Lejaniá
1946 Mario Binetti. La lumbre dormida
1948 Enrique Lavié. Memoria di mi soledad
1953 Miguel A. Etcheverrigaraway. El canto y el Reino
1954/56 Alberto Girri. Examen de nuestra causa
1957 Osvaldo Horacio Dondo. Oda menor a la poesía
Carmen Blanco Amores. Torre de silencio (unpublished)
1958 Juan Carlos La Madrid. Hombre aumado
César Magini. Relato del sobreviviente (unpublished)
1959 Luis Franco. Constela ción
José Isaacson. Amor y amar
1960 César Rosales. Vengo a dar testimonio
Joaquín G. Giannuzzi. Contemporáneo del mundo

Prose--
1920 Manuel Gálvez. Nacha Regules
1921 Héctor Olivera Lavié. El caminante
1922 Arturo Cancela. Tres relatos porteños
1923 Arturo Capdevila. Del libre albedrío
1924 Roberto F. Giusti. Crítica y polémica
1925 Victor Juan Guillot. El alma en el pozo
1926 Nicholás Coronado. Nuevas críticas negativas
1927 Aníbal Ponce. La vejez de Sarmiento
1928 Roberto Gache. Paris, glosario argentino
1929 Sara de Etcheverría. El constructor del silencio
1930 Enrique Méndez Calzada. Pro y contra
1931 Alfonso Corti. François Villon
1932 Eduardo Acevedo Díaz. Ramón Hazaña
1933 Ignacio B. Anzoátegui. Georgina Arnhem y yo

1934 Enrique Corbellini. Cántico y forma
1935 Eduardo Mallea. Nocturno europeo
1936 José María Monner Sanz. El teatro de Pirandello
Ernesto Palacio. El espiritu y la letra
Lorenzo A. Stanchina. Endemoniados
1937 Carlos Alberto Erro. Diálogo existencial
Julio Irazusta. Actores y espectadores
Norah Lange. Cuadernos de infancia
1938 Armando Cascella. La cuadrilla volante
Bruno Jacovella. Confortantes y prodigiosas aventuras del poeta J.E. Malanik
Luis Emilio Soto. Crítica y estimación
1939 Luis María Albamonte. La paloma de la punalada
Augusto Mario Delfino. Fin de siglo
Homero H. Guglielmini. Temas existenciales
1940 Adolfo Bioy Cesares. La Invención de Morel
Guillermo Guerrero Estrella. Donde se empina la Cruz del Sur
Enrique Wernicke. Hans Grillo
1942 Abelardo Arias. Alamos talados
Sigfrido A. Radaelli. Ejercicios
Isidoro Sagtíes. Banco inglés
1943 Sylvina Bullrich Palenque. La redoma del primer ángel
Pilar de Lusarreta. Cinco dandys porteños
Manuel Mujica Láinez. Vida de Aniceto el Gallo
1944 Arturo Cerretani. El bruto
Héctor I. Eandi. Hombres capaces
Manuel Peyrou. La esposa dormida
1945 Ernesto Sábato. Uno y el

Universo
Estela Canto. El muro de
mármol
Nené Devoy. En run rincón
de la Boca
1946 Julio Ellena de la Sota.
Persecución de Gladys
1948 Alberto A. Iglesias.
Tierra de hombres
1953 Rodolfo J. Walsh. Vari-
aciones en rojo
1954-1956 Carlos Mastronardi.
Valéry o la infinitud del
método
HH.A. Murena. El pecado
original de América
Luisa Mercedes Levinson.
Concierto en mí (com-
partido)
Boris David Viñas. Cayo
sobre su rostro (compartido)
1957 Bernardo Verbitsky.
Villa Miseria también es A-
mérica
1958 C. Córdova Iturburu.
Pintura argentina del siglo
XX
1959 Luisa Mercedes Levinson.
La pálida rosa del Soho
(imaginative prose)
Alfredo de la Guardia. El
verdadero Byron; Rosa
Franco.
Origen de lo erótico en la
poesiá femenina americana
(unpublished) (essay)
1960 Augusto Roa Bastos.
Hijo de hombre; Carlos
A. Velazco. Buenos Aires,
tú, él y yo (unpublished)
(fiction)
Jaime Alcalay. Clásicos
modernos; Sigfrido Radaelli.
El hombre y la historia
(unpublished) (essay) 191.

Emil BUHRIL FOUNDATION
AWARD (Switzerland)
Established in 1943 in Zurich,
this prize has been awarded to
over 30 writers.   192.

BULGARIAN WRITERS' UNION
PRIZES

The prizes of the Bulgarian
Writers' Union, established in
1960, are "awarded by a jury
appointed by the Union's secre-
tariat," with the purpose of the
prizes described as: "to encourage the writers who have
written good literary works during the year, and give them
public recognition."
The prizes, consisting of a
monetary premium, of "First
Prize;" "Second Prize," have
been awarded in the last several
years to:
1960--
Kamen Kalchev. The weaver's
family
H. Radevski. They are still
living
2nd prize Chelkash. Unwelcome
guests
Balga Dimitrova. Till to-
morrow
Andrei Goulyashki. Counter-
Reconnaissance
Kroum Grigorov. Tancho of
Gorotsvet
Mladen Issayev. Clear distances
Lamar. The wisdom of the
years
Pavel Matev. With the people's
faith
Dimiter Methodiev. Song of
communism
Dimiter Panteleyev. The
mower comes from the fields
Peter Pondev. Elin Pelin
Ivan Rouzh. In the jungles of
literature
Lozan Strelkov. The gold re-
serve
Lyubomir Tenev. Drama and
stage
1961 Vesselin Hanchev. Lyrics
Valerii Petrov. In mild autumn
G.D. Goshkin. Questions and
books of socialist realism
2nd prize Ivan Davidkov. The
Dnieper flows beneath my
window
Maria Groubeschlieva. Joys
and sorrows
Efrem Karamfilov. Shadows

of the past
Alexander Mouratov. A light
saved
Bogomil Rainov. As only we
can die   193.

BUNDESVERBAND DER DEUTSCHEN INDUSTRIE PRIZE (Germany)

Considered more an honorary
cultural award than a literature
prize, these annual grants of the
German industrial association
are given in varying amounts
(usually 2500 to 5000 DM, some
for 10,000 DM) usually to
older established writers, and
also to younger "rising generation" authors (as the Förderungspreis awarded Karl Horst in
1952).

Over 50 German authors have
received these grants, which
may be given more than once to
a writer, including such well-
known German literary figures
as: Ilse Aichinger, Ingeborg
Bachmann, Richard Benz, Hein-
rich Böll, Georg Britting,
Heimito von Doderer, Günter
Eich, Albrecht Fabri, Peter
Gan, Hans Hennecke, Hans-Egon
Holthusen, Karl August Horst,
Ernst Jünger, Friedrich Georg
Jünger, Erhart Kästner, Annette
Kolb, Karl Krolow, Horst Lange,
Jürgen Rausch, Max Rychner,
Friedrich Sieburg, Hermann
Stresau, Kyra Stomberg, Leopold
Ziegler.   194.

BUNGAKUKAI SHINJIN PRIZE (Japan-New Japanese Literature Society Prize)

A semi-annual award established in 1955 by the literary magazine, "Bungakukai," which is
awarded the author winning a
literary contest. First winner
of the prize was Shintaro Ishiwara, who received the prize
for his book "Taiyo no Kisetsu"
(Season of the sun), a work which
also won the Akutagawa Prize.

195.

BURMESE UNESCO COMMISSION LITERARY AWARD

Granted each year for the
best writings in various areas of
science and the arts and designed
to "encourage the writing of
instructional and cultural works,"
this prize of 1,850 Burmese
Kyats is offered by the UNESCO
Commission (New Secretaria,
Merchant Street, Rangoon).

Recent recipients of the
prizes are:
Simple Science 1959 U Awain.
General science for standards
I, II, and IV
U Kyaw Ngwe, and K. S. San
Ban. General science for
standards VI, VII
1960 Theikpan Ba Htwe. "Law-
peta"--Biluchaung's Hydro-
electric water power scheme
Economic and Social Development
1959 Ludu U Hla. Hlaung-
Jine-Twin-Hma-Nget-Ngai-
Myar (Birds in the cage)
Culture 1960 U Min Naing.
Pyidaungsu-Aka-Padetha
(Various dances of the Union
of Burma)
International Understanding 1959
Tet Toe (pseud of U On Pe).
Indonesia, Ceylon, Japan
Central Knowledge 1960 Natmauk
Phone Kyaw. Minhla Fort
Translations (or Adaptations) of
Simple Classics
1959 Yawai Tun. Sakuntala (an
Indian drama by Kalidasa)
1960 Thakin Ba Thaung. Kaba-
Patle-Yet-Shitse (Jules Verne,
"Around the world in eighty
days")   196.

Robert BURNS FELLOWSHIP IN LITERATURE (New Zealand)

With the purpose "to encourage
and promote imaginative New
Zealand literature," the annual
Robert Burns Fellowship was
established in 1958 by privately
subscribed funds in order "to

commemorate the bi-centenary of
the birth of Robert Burns and
to perpetuate appreciation of the
valuable services rendered to
the early settlement of Otago by
the Burns family."

A one-year grant, with provision for extension to a second
year, the Fellowship is open to
New Zealand writers of imaginative literature, preferably candidates under 40 years of age.
The Fellow, who is attached
to the English Department of
the University of Otago, receives
the equivalent of a lecturer's
salary ($L250$ to $L1700$), and--
as a condition of the award--
resides in Dunedin during the
University year and devotes
major time to the pursuit of his
own literary work or studies.

Applications addressed to:
Registrar, University of Otago,
P.O. Box 56, Dunedin, New
Zealand, must be received by
October 31 to be considered for
the subsequent year's award.

Among Fellowship winners
are:

1959 Ian Cross--publications include: The God boy; The
backward sex; After Anzac
day

1960 M. Duggan--publications
include: Immanuel's land;
Falter Tom and Water boy;
Miss Bratby's career (novel
draft, 1960)

1961 R.A.K. Mason, described
as the "foremost living New
Zealand poet"--publications
include: No new thing; This
dark will lighten; China
197.

Maria Moors CABOT PRIZE
(Latin America--U.S.A.)

Since 1939 the Cabot prizes
in journalism "have been awarded
to 99 journalists from 20 countries of the Americas for their
roles in advancing inter-American friendship." One of the

Western hemisphere's major
academic and professional honors,
the prizes were endowed in 1938
by Godfrey Lowell Cabot of Boston as a memorial to his wife.
The winners, selected each year
by the Trustees of Columbia University from the recommendations
of the Dean of the Faculty of
Journalism, each receive a gold
medal, a premium of $1,000, and
travel expenses to New York City
where the awards are presented,
in a ceremony in the rotunda of
Low Memorial Library on Columbia University campus.

Among the distinguished re-
cipients of this tribute to the free
and intelligent press, in its
recognition of the "contributions
of journalists to the advancement
of peaceful relationships among
the American peoples," are:
Miguel Lanz Duret (Mexico);
Pedro G. Beltrán (Peru); David
Michel Torrino (Argentina);
Hermane Tavares de Sá, Herbert
Moses, Orlando Ribeiro Dantas
(Brazil); Rene Silva Espejo,
Alfredo Silva Carvallo (Chile);
Eduardo Cárdenas, Eduardo Santos
(Colombia); Ricardo Castro
Beeche (Costa Rica); Alejandro
Carrion (Ecuador); Juan Andres
Ramirez (Uruguay).   198.

CALDERÓN DE LA BARCA
NATIONAL PRIZE (Spain)

This 40,000 pts award of the
Spanish Ministry of Information
and Tourism, established in 1950,
is granted to the best new playwright. In addition to the monetary premium, the "new dramatist
who has never had a play produced
by professional artists" has his
winning play produced at Teatro
Nacional Maria Guerrero, in
Madrid.

Among recipients of the drama
prize are:

1954 Juan Antonio Laiglesia. La
rueda, comedia

1957 Santiago Moncada Mercadal.

Tránsito a la Madrugada
1958 Marcial Suárez Fernández.
Miércoles y jo jo; Manual Gallego Morell. Requerimiento
Notarial   199.

Manuel Avila CAMACHO PRIZE (Mexico)

A cultural award in the Sciences and the Arts established in 1947 by the Instituto Mexicano del Libro A.(sociacion) C.(ivil) (Av. San Juan de Letran 9, desp 702, Mexico, D.F.)-- a group organized in 1944 from Asociacion de Libreros y Editores Mexicanos--the Camacho Prize consists of a gold medal and a monetary premium of $15, 000.

Awarded from time to time with no specific frequency, the prize has been granted for the entire work of authors of poetry or of creative works in prose (Novels, Stories). Among recipients of this high Mexican honor, which is presented by the President of Mexico in a ceremony at the Palacio Nacional, are such literary figures as Carlos González Peña, and:
1948 Alfonso Reyes. Outstanding
     contribution in many areas
     of literature
1953 Enrique González Martínez.
     Poetry
1959 Martín Luis Guzmán. Novels
                          200.

CAMÕES PRIZE (International-- Portugal)

Named in memory of Luis Vaz de Camões, 16th century Portuguese poet and dramatist who wrote the Portuguese national epic, the "Lusiads," this biennial literary prize (alternating each year with the Ferro Prize) is offered by the Portuguese government (Secretariado Nacional da Informação, Lisbon) for a book published abroad by a foreign author. A jury of dis-

tinguished authors of Portugal selects from among competing works--books written in Portuguese, French, English, German, Spanish, or Italian and published during the two year period preceding the year of award (January 1 to December 31 of the following year)--the "best literary or scientific work on Portugal." Eligible works are submitted in six copies accompanied by a certificate attesting the time of publication and the nationality of the author before February 1, following the period of competition.

Winners of the prize--a monetary premium of 30,000 escudos and a visit to Portugal as an official guest for a fortnight to receive the award, which is presented in Lisbon during the month of May--include:
1937 Conde Gonzague de
     Reynold (Switzerland).
     Portugal
1939 John Gibbons. I gathered
     no moss
1941 Jesus Pabon. La
     Revolución Portuguesa
1943 Elaine Sanceau.
     Portugal in quest of Prester
     John
1945 Florentino Peres Embid.
     El Mudejarismo en la Arquitectura Portuguese de la
     Época Manuelina
1947 Harold V. Livermore.
     History of Portugal
1951 Alan Villiers (Australia).
     The quest of the Schooner
     Argus
1953 Sidney Welch. Portuguese and Dutch in South
     Africa
1956 Gilbert Renault (coronel
     Rémy) Les Caravelles
     du Christ
1958 Richard Pattee.
     Portugal and the Portuguese
     world
1960 Beat de Fisher.
     Dialogue Luso-Suisse
                          201.

Julius C. CAMPE PRIZE
(Germany)
     The Hamburg publisher,
Verlag Hoffmann und Campe
(Harvestehuderweg 41) (established
the Campe Prize in 1959 in
celebration of the firm's 175th
anniversary. The 60,000 DM
premium is granted in four
prizes of 15,000 DM each--
one prize each four years in
November. In 1959 the prize
offered for a novel or for a
non-fiction book was won by
Rudolf Hagelstange with his
novel, "Spielball der Götter."
                             202.

Jan CAMPERT PRIZE (Netherlands)
     One of the best-known literary
honors in the Netherlands, the
Campert Prize is awarded annually in November/December
for poetry. The award of the
Jan Campert Stichtung, instituted
in 1948 by the municipality of
The Hague, is generally given
to young writers (initially to
authors under 30 years of age,
although the age limit, increased
to 35 years, has not always
been strictly adhered to).
     Writers honored by the fl
500 premium include:
     1948 Jan G. Elburg. Klein
     ter reurspel
     1949 Michel van der Plas.
     Going my way
     1950 Hans Lodeizen. Hen in-
     nerlijk behang (posthumous
     award)
     1951 Bert Voeten. Met het oog
     op morgen
     1952 Albert Besnard. Doem en
     dorst
     1953 Nes Tergast. Werelden
     (prize of fl 1.000 refused)
     1955 Remco Campert. Men
     man en muis, and Het
     huis waarin ik woonde
     1959 Sybren Polet (pseud of S.
     Minnema). Geboorte-stad
     (Native town, poems)

     1961 Ellen Warmond (pseud of
     P.C. van Yperen). Warmte
     een woonplaats (Warmth a
     dwelling place, collection of
     poems)
     1962 Gerrit Kouwenaar. De
     Stem op do 3e etage (The
     voice at the third floor,
     collection of poems)   203.

CAPE TERCENTENARY FOUNDA-
TION MERIT AWARD (South
Africa)
     An annual cultural award, con-
sisting of an illuminated Certificate of Merit and a monetary
premium varying between £200
and £500, given to South African
writers in English and in Afrikaans
"for outstanding work done over a
period of years." Established
with an endowment by Harry and
Edward Molteno, the Award
brings "recognition to persons
who have made conspicuous contributions to the literature, art,
drama, architecture or other
arts of the Cape Province."
     The Cape Tercentenary Founda-
tion (Kaapse Drie-Eeue-Stigting,
"Teviot," Hillbrow Road, Kenil-
worth, Capetown) initiated the
cultural honor in 1952, as a part
of its activities in "the mainten-
ance of culture and the preservation of the historical objects and
natural beauties of the Province
of the Cape of Good Hope." A
special Committee appointed by
the Council of the Foundation
considers nominations for the
award, suggested by cultural
leaders and organizations in the
area.
     The Foundation also gives
literary recognition to Cape Province authors by subsidizing the
publication of "books of literary,
cultural, or historic value in
order that they may be sold at a
price within reach of the general
public."
     The Foundation Merit Award
for literature (also called the

"Van Riebeck Tercentenary Prize"
is granted every three or four
years as it rotates with Awards
in other cultural fields. Authors
receiving the honor include:
  1953 Guy Butler. The dam
    (English literature)
    Mrs. M.E. Rothman
    (Afrikaans literature)
  1956 D. J. Opperman
    (Afrikaans drama)   204.

CAPITOLINE WOLF PRIZE
(Italy--Premio Lupa Capitolina)
  A poetry award, established
in 1959 and administered by
Mauro Musciacchio (via Caulonia
9, Rome), this prize offers a
silver statue of Rome's lupa
capitolina and a premium of L
500, with a second prize of
L 200.
  Italian poets, living in Italy
or abroad, who have won the
first prize with a poem in the
Italian language on no set subject, include:
  1959 Nicola Rossi Lemeni
  1960 Nino Pino; Gaetano
    Savelli   205.

CAPRI PRIZE (Europe--Italy)
  This L 1.000.000 poetry
prize is offered each year by
Ente Provincial per il Turismo
di Napoli (via Partenope 104,
Naples) for unpublished poetry
in the French language, and is
granted in turn to a poet in
France, Belgium, and Switzerland.
  Winners of the prize, which
includes the premium and a
"siren of gold" are such poets
as:
  1958 Jean Follain. Valeur du
    pain
  1959 Pierre Emmanuel. Les
    justes, les Gourreaux
                             206.

CARACAS MUNICIPAL COUNCIL
PRIZES (Venezuela)
  Recent winners of annual

awards for poetry and prose
granted by the city of Caracas
are:
  1957 Enriqueta Aruelo
    Larriua. Mandato del Canto
    (poetry)
    Adriano Gonzáles Léon. Las
    Hogueras Mas Altas
  1961 Juan Ángel Mogollón.
    Poetry.
    Federico Brito Figueroa.
    Writings in history   207.

Giosué CARDUCCI PRIZE (Italy)
  For 12 years this poetry
prize of the city of Pietrasanta in
Tuscany (Commune di Pietrasanta
e Azienda Autonoma) has offered
a premium--currently L 500.000
--for a work of poetry, published or unpublished, written in
the Italian language by an Italian
resident in Italy or abroad.
Competing works are submitted
before May 31, and the award is
announced on July 27, anniversary of the birth of Giosué
Carducci, national poet of modern
Italy who won the Nobel prize in
1906.
  The jury of distinguished authors
and critics, such as Alberto
Moravia, has assigned the prize
to:
  1952 Mariano Suali. Indicazione
    (unpublished collection of
    poems)
  1959 Corrado Govoni. I canti
    del puro folle
  1961 Bartolo Cattafi. Qualcosa
    di preciso
  1962 Silvio Ramat. Lo svago
    della vista   208.

Conde de CARTAGENA PRIZE
(Spain)
  Established by D. Anibal
Morillo y Perez, Conde de
Cartagena, in 1929, this prize,
administered by the Real Acade-
mia Española (Felipe IV, 4,
Madrid), is granted for pub-
lished or unpublished works by
Spanish or Spanish-American

authors on specified topics in the subjects of linguistics, literary history and criticism. The next award period ends April 1, 1965.

In 1959 the competition themes (prize for first theme--20,000 pts; prize for each of the other themes--10,000 pts) were:

1. Biography and critical study of a Spanish author, a model of the language and style, from earlier than the 19th century
2. Spanish oratory of the 19th century (winner: Rafael Oliver Bertrand. "Caracteristica de la oratoria politica española...")
3. Origins of the Spanish Theatre--critico-bibliographical study from the beginnings down to Lope de Vega
4. Collection of technical works, ancient or modern, relating to one or several arts and crafts...excluding music and dancing (winner: Carlos Fernández Gómez. Vocabulario completo de las obras de Cervantes, excludio 'El Quijote")   209.

CASA DE CULTURA ECUATORIANA PRIZE (Ecuador)

In 1958 this publisher's prize of Casa de Cultura Ecuatoriana (Av. Seis de Deciembre 332, Quito) was won by Laura del Castillo (Argentina) with the novella, "Mirar el limonera y morir."   210.

CASA DE LAS AMÉRICAS PRIZE (Latin America--Cuba)

The single, continuing major literary prize offered currently in Cuba, this Concurso Literario Hispanoamericana (also designated "Premio Continental") has been held annually since 1960 for all authors of Central and South America. The prize, consisting of 1,000 pesos ($1,000 U.S.) and publication of the winning work by Casa de las Américas (G.Y. Tercera, Vedado, Havana), is awarded each January 30 in five areas of writing: Essay, Drama, Short Story, Poetry, and Novel. Authors writing in Spanish, who are citizens of Latin American countries by birth or naturalization, are eligible to compete for the prize with manuscripts that have not previously been published in any form.

Among the distinguished jurors who assign the prize are the leading Latin American authors: Miguel Angel Asturias, Fernando Benítez, Carlos Fuentes, Miguel Otero Silva, Benjamín Carrión, Luis Cardoza y Aragón, Juan José Arreola, Elvio Romero, José Bianco, Ezequiel Martínez Estrada, Nicolás Guillén, Virgilio Piñera, Alejo Carpentier.

Recipients of the prize in the first three contests are:

1960 Essay--
Ezequiel Martínez Estrada. (Argentina). Análisis funcional de la cultura
Drama-- Andrés Lizárraga (Peru). Santa Juana de América
Story--José María López Valdigón (Colombia). La Vida rota
Poetry--Jorge Enrique Adoum (Cuba). Dios trajo la sombra
Novel--José Soler Puig (Cuba). Bertillón 166
1961 Essay--
Luis Emiro Valencia (Colombia). Realidad y perspectiva de la revolución cubana
Drama--Manuel Galich López. (Guatemala). El Pescado indigesto
Story--Luis Díaz Chávez. (Honduras). Pescador sin fortuna
Poetry--Roberto Ibáñez (Uruguay). La Frontera
Novel--Dora Alonso (Cuba).

Terra inerme
1962 Essay--
Gumersindo Martínez Amengual (Cuba). Presencia de la Reforma Agraria en América
Drama--Emilio Carballido (Mexico). Un pequeño día de ira
Story--Raúl González de Cascorro (Cuba). Gente de Playa Girón
Poetry--Fayad Jamis (Cuba). Por esta libertad
Novel--Daura García (Cuba). Maestra voluntaria   211.

CASALECCHIO PRIZE (Italy)
Offered each year for poetry published in Italy, and for an unpublished poem or collection of poems, this L 100.000 premium was given in 1962 by Pro-Loco di Casalecchio di Reno (Bologna) to Domenico Cara for the published work, "Migologia familiare;" and to Walter Galli for the unpublished work, "Anniversario."   212.

Carlos **CASAVALLE PRIZE** (Argentina)
Named for the first Argentine bookseller, this government award granted each year on June 15 by Cámara Argentina del Libro (Sarmiento 528, Buenos Aires) was established in 1955 as a 25,000 pesos prize for the best book published in Spanish in Argentina in a first edition in three classes of writing (which rotate annually for the award): Novels, Stories, and Prose Narratives; Poetry and Drama; Essays, excluding purely scientific writing. Eduardo Mallea was honored with the prize in 1955.
In 1958, the Argentine federal government (Direccion General Cultura del Ministerio de Educacion) offered a 25,000 pesos Casavalle Prize to encourage the

publication and distribution of books by Argentine writers. Argentine publishers eligible for the prize were those who had published during the year works of Argentine nationals or of foreigners resident in Argentina for more than ten years.   213.

CASEMENT AWARD (Ireland)
Honoring the famous Irish patriot and statesman, Sir Roger Casement (1864-1916), this award is one of several literary prizes administered by the Irish Academy of Letters (c/o Abbey Theatre, Pearse Street, Dublin). Offered each year for poetry and drama, the ₤50 premium is given in recognition of "the best book of verse or the best play by an Irish author."   214.

Camilo **CASTELO BRANCO PRIZE** (Portugal)
Among a number of literary honors financed by Fundation Calouste Gulbenkian, this 50.000 escudo award, carrying "great prestige among Portuguese intellectuals", is granted by Sociedade Portuguesa de Escritores, with the sponsorship of Grêmio Nacional dos Editores e Livreiros, for a work of prose fiction-- Novel, Novella, Short Story. Original works by Portuguese authors which have been published during the preceding year may be submitted in competition during January of the year following publication.
The jury has selected for award, presented on November 3, the works of:
1958 José Rodrigues Miguéis. Léah e outras histórias (collection of tales)
1959 Vergilia Ferreira. Aparição
1960 Fernando Botelho. A Gata e a Fábula
1961 Maria Judite de Carvallo. As Palavras Poupadas   215.

Julio de CASTILHO PRIZE
(Portugal)
Câmara Municipal de Lisboa
offers a prize of 15.000$ for
an original work on Lisbon.
216.

Victor CATALÁ PRIZE (Spain)
One of the Santa Lucia
Prizes, this publishers' award
of 25,000 pts (originally 10,000
pts), offered by Editorial
Selecta (Ronda de San Pedro 3,
Barcelona), was established in
1953 in honor of the Catalan
writer Catalina Albert, who
write under the pen-name of
Víctor Catalá. The prize,
granted for short stories (nar-
raciones cortas) on Santa Lucia
Day (December 13), has
recognized the work of such authors writing in Catalan as:
1957 Mercé Rodereta.
Vint-i-dos contes
1959 R. Folch y Camarasa.
La sala de espera
1960 J. Baixeres. ¿Per que
no?
1961 Estanislao Torres. La
xera 217.

Mariano de CAVIA PRIZE
(Spain)
A long-established journalism
award (articulos y crónicas) of
the Madrid newspaper, ABC
(Calle de Serrano 61), this
prize has been given to over 40
writers over the period of its
establishment. Granted each
year, and by its rules of award
not capable of being divided or
withheld from presentation, the
prize has recognized outstanding
writing in newspapers or magazines by such authors as:
Ramón Pérez de Ayala, Gabriel
Miró, Francisco de Cossio,
José María Pemán, Jésus
Sáiz, Jacinto Benavente, Luis
Calvo, Julio Camba, Ramón
Serrano Suñer, Manual Aznar,
Enrique Llovet, Gonzalo

Fernández de la Mora, and
Pedro Rocamora. In 1954,
Dionisia Ridruego received the
award for his essay, "En los
70 Años de Don José Ortega y
Gasset." 218.

CAZES PRIZE (France)
In 1935 the brewer, Lipp (151
boulevard Saint-Germain, Paris)
established this annual prize of
1.000 NF for a work of originality
and literary quality by a young
writer who has not previously
won a literary prize. Named for
the proprietor of a literary cafe
(Marcillin Cazes), the prize
which is granted on the "first
day of Spring," honors various
forms of creative writing: Novel,
Essay, Poetry.
Laureates include:
1941 Olivier Sechan. Les
chemins de nulle part
(awarded in 1946)
1943 Jean Proal. Où souffle
la lombarde
1946 Jean-Louis Curtis. Les
jeunes hommes
1949 François Raynal. Marie
des solitudes
1955 Albert Vidalie. Les
bijoutiers du clair de lune
1960 Monique Lange. Les
platanes
1961 Henny Dory. La nuit de
la passion; Solange Fasquelle.
Le congrés d'Aix 219.

CEARÁ UNIVERSITY PRIZE
(Brazil--Prêmios da Universidade
do Ceará)
A literary honor awarded by
the Universidade do Ceará (Av
Visconde de Cauipe 2853, Fortaleza,
Ceará) that offers "six Cr $50.
000 monetary premiums, and
publication of the prize-winning
works by the University Press,"
(1,000 copies with 20 per cent
royalty for author). Originally
established as four prizes of Cr
$10.000 each (Novel, Poetry,
Short Story, Essay), the current

awards are offered for unpublished works in six categories: Poetry, Short Story, Novel, Literary Criticism, Social Studies, Drama. As three prizes are granted each year, the awards in one subject area or literary form are biennial.

A jury of three authorities has awarded the prize, for which Ceará born or resident authors may compete, to such writers as:

Poetry--Francisco Carvelho da Silva. Do Girassol e da Nuvem (The sunflower and the cloud)
Jairo Martins Bastos. Orpheo
Short Story--Artur Eduardo Benevides. Caminhos sem Horizonte (Paths without horizon)
Sinval Sá. A fuga (The escape)
Braga Montenegro. As viagens (The travels)
Novel--Fran Martins. A rua e o mundo (The street and the world)
Essay--Cruz Filho. O Soneto (The sonnet)   220.

CENTRAL DAILY NEWS PRIZE (China, Republic of)

Offered by the "Tapai," Taiwan newspaper, this prize was won in 1958 by Ne Ro with the short novel, "Lu Lu and I."
221.

CEPPO PRIZE (Italy)

A prose award of Accademia Pistoiese del Ceppo (via Panciatichi 5, Pistoia), the Ceppo Prize offers two monetary premiums (L 300.000 and L 50.000) and a gold and silver medal for the best "racconto" of the year, which is published in reviews, journals or magazines. Magazine stories may be entered in this national competition by being sent to the jury before December 31 of the year of

award, and the winning stories are announced between January 16 and 27 of the following year.

Since 1955, first year the competition was held, winners include:

1959 L. Bartolini; M. Pacini; B. Sablone; G. Bimbi
1961 Nino Palumbo. La gita al paese; Antonio Seccareccia. La piazza; Piero Bernardino. Il mio frak.
222.

Marques de CERRALBO PRIZE (Spain)

Each four years this literary honor is presented by the Real Academia Española (Felipe IV, 4 Madrid) for an original, unpublished work relating to Spanish language and literature. The 15,000 pts premium is awarded to writings pertaining to such questions of linguistics and literature as: Archaeology in Spanish Literature; Study of Archaic Influences on Spanish Idioms; Regional Languages of Spain; Terminology of Archaeology.
223.

Miguel de CERVANTES HISPANIC PRIZE (Spain)

Oficina de Cooperacion Intelectual and the Instituto de Cultura Hispanica established a $5,000 prize for hispanic literature, to be given to a work published during the previous year. Forms of writing considered for award were: Fiction, Poetry, Drama, Criticism, History, Essays, Chronicles.
224.

CERVANTES LITERARY COMPETITIONS (Mexico)

A biennial "Concurso Literario Cervantes," of Instituto Tecnologico y de Estudios Superiores de Monterrey (Sucursal de Correos 'J', Monterrey, N. L.), initiated with the patronage of the industrialist Carlos Prieto, offers--

in addition to several prizes for student writing--two prizes for works on Cervantes or his writings. These two awards: PREMIO MONTERREY of $15,000 and a second prize of $5,000 with possible publication of the winning works, are directed to encouraging Mexican interest in "Idioma Español" and in classical literature. Writing entered in competition must be at least 25 pages in length, and may be either unpublished or published, and must be submitted by December 24, preceding the year of award.

The prizes, presented in Monterrey on April 23 (next awards to be given April 23, 1963), were won in the first competition of 1960-1961 by: Angel Francisco Oruesagasti.

Miguel de Cervantes Saavedra (En su tiempo, en su patria y en su obra-universal)

Rutilo Riestra, and Guadalupe Rodrigues de Riestra. Ensay de Numeración por Párrafos y Guía General de El Ingenioso Hidalgo Don Quijote de la Mancha 225.

Miguel de CERVANTES NATIONAL PRIZE (Spain)

Considered by one critic "the most esteemed of the national prizes of Spain," this prize offers 25,000 pts for the best novel published during a year. Granted annually since 1950 by the Spanish Ministry of Information and Tourism, the award has been won by some of Spain's most popular writers of fiction:

1950 Enrique Larreta. Orillas del Duero; Concha Espina. Un valle en el mar

1951 Ramón Ledesma Miranda. La casa de la fama

1953 José María Gironella. Los cipreses creen en Dios

1954 Tomás Salvador. Cuerda de presos, which also received one of the Barcelona Prizes.

1955 Miguel Delibes. Diaria de un cazador

1956 Carmen Laforêt. La mujer nueva; Jorge Campos. Tiempo pasado

1957 Alejandro Nuñez Alonso. El lazo de púrpura

1958 J. L. Castillo Puche. Hicieron Partes

1959 Ana María Matute. Los Hijos Muertos

1960 Manuel Halcón. Monólogo de una Mujer Fría

1962 Bartolome Soler. Los Muertos no se Cuentan 226.

CERVANTES PRIZE (Latin America)

Created by the Third Congress of Academies of the Spanish Language, which met in Managua, Nicaragua in August 1960, the Pan-Latin America literary honor was initiated with the hope that it might "become the Nobel Prize of the Spanish language." 227.

CERVANTES SOCIETY PRIZES (Spain)

Recent winners of the annual award, presented on May 20 for a novel and a book of poetry (25,000 pts premium to each) were (1961): Novel--Torcuato Luca de Tena, "Edad Prohibida;" Poetry--Federico Muelas, "Apenas Esto." 228.

CERVIA PRIZE (Italy)

A prize of L 1.000.000 is offered by Comune e Azienda Autonoma di Soggiorno di Cervia (Segretaria del Premio "Cervia," Cervia, Ravenna) for unpublished poetry. The winning work is published by Editore Rebellato. Poetry manuscripts must be submitted by July 15 for consideration. An annual prize is also offered for journalism (L 250.000

and L 150.000); these entries
must be submitted by July 20.

In 1962, the poetry prize
was divided equally between
Elio Filippo Accrocca with
"Porta Ninfina," and Umberto
Bellintani, with "Ventatto
Poesie."   229.

CHATRIAN PRIZE (International
--France)

Offered by the weekly railroad
magazine, "La Vie du Rail" (11
rue de Milan, Paris 9e), the
Chatrian Prize recognizes outstanding writings on the subject
of railroads. The 2.000 NF
award, which is named for Alexandre Chatrian (1826-1890),
French novelist and playwright,
is presented each year on
December 25, for the year's
best book written in French,
preferably a published work,
about railroads. Works in six
classes of writing are considered
for award: Novel, Poetry,
Novella, Essay, Drama, or
Entire Literary Work.

Winners since the first award
in 1950 include:

1950 Charles Agniel. Les
    laboureurs de la nuit
1954 Étienne Cattin. Trains
    en détresse
1955 (Janet) Taylor Caldwell.
    Dynastie du Rail (Dynasty
    of Death)
1956 René Dupuy. Le roman
    du rail
1960 C. F. Landry, and
    Michel Hartmann. Magie du
    Rail
1961 Henri Vincenot. Les
    chevaliers du Chaudron
1962 Roger Guerrand.
    Mémoires du Métro.   230.

CHIANCIANO PRIZES (Italy)

Each year since 1949 several
kinds of writing (Novel, Poetry,
Journalism) have been honored
by the Chianciano prizes, which
rank with the significant literary

prizes of Italy. A Tourist Society
prize (Ufficio Premi "Chianciano,"
Enter per il Turismo, Chianciano)
for works published between July
16 and August 15 of the following
year, the premiums are L 1.000.
000 (for Novel and Poetry), and
L 500.000 (for Journalism).
Recent winners are:

1957 Giovanni Titta Rosa.
    Poesia d'una Vita
1958 Corrado Govoni. Stradario
    della Primavera
1961 Pier Paolo Pasolini. La
    religione del mio tempo
    (poetry)
    Natalia Ginzburg. La voci
    della sera (novel)
    Pietro Castro, "Ore 12,"
    Rome; Guido Farolfi, "Gior-
    nale del Mattino," Florence;
    Marco Marchini, "Tempo,"
    Rome; Ugo Reale, "Giusitizia,"
    Rome (Journalism)
1962 Andrea Zanzotto. IX
    Ecloghe; Velso Mucci. L'eta
    della terra (poetry)
    Sandro De Feo. Gli inganni
    (novel)
    Massimo Grillandi (journalism)
                              231.

CHILEAN NATIONAL PRIZE FOR
LITERATURE (Premio Nacional
de Literatura)

Most important literary award
of an official nature in Chile,
this government prize established
by national law in 1942, and revised in 1959, has been granted
each year by the National Ministry of Public Education (Ministerio
de Educacion Publica, Alameda
Bernardo O'Higgins 1371, Santiago).
The award, which gives public
recognition to a Chilean author of
prestige who has shown sustained
literary production ('un escritor
chileno cuya obra de creacion
tenga trascendencia nacional'),
is determined by a jury composed
of the Rector of the University
of Chile, and representatives of
the Ministry of Public Education,

Sociedad de Escritores de Chile, and the Academia Chilena de la Lengua.

Recipients of this high national award, which honors the entire literary work of an author with a medal and a monetary premium (currently E°5.000) are:

1942 Augusto D'Halmar (pseud of Augusto Goemine Thompson). Novelist and short story writer (1882-1950)

1943 Joaquin Edwards Bello. Novelist and journalist

1944 Mariano Latorre Court. Novelist and short story writer (1886-1955).

1945 Pablo Neruda (Neftali Ricardo Reyes Basoalto). Poet (1904-)

1946 Eduardo Barrios Hudtwalcker. Novelist (1884-)

1947 Samuel A. Lillo. Poet (1870-1958)

1948 Angel Cruchaga Santa Maria. Poet (1893-)

1949 Pedro Prado Calvo. Poet, essayist and novelist (1886-1952)

1950 José Santos González Vera. Novelist, short story writer, and essayist (1897-)

1951 Gabriela Mistral (pseud of Lucila Godoy Alcayaga). Poet (1889-1957)

1952 Fernando Santivan (pseud of Fernando Santibanez Puga) Novelist and short story writer (1886-)

1953 Daniel de la Vega Uribe. Novelist, short story writer, dramatist, and poet (1892-)

1954 Victor Domingo Silva Endeiza. Poet and novelist (1882-1960)

1955 Francisco Antonio Encina y Armenet. Historian and essayist (1874-)

1956 Max Jara (pseud of Macimiliano Jara Troncoso). Poet (1886-)

1957 Manuel Rojas Sepulveda. Novelist, short story writer, and poet (1896-)

1958 Diego Duble Urrutia (Alter Ego). Poet (1877-)

1959 Hernán Diaz Arrieta (Alone). Critic, essayist, and novelist (1891-)

1960 Julio Barrenchea Pino. Poet (1910-)

1961 Marta Brunet y Caraves. Novelist and short story writer (1903-)   232.

CHILEAN NATIONAL THEATRE PRIZE

Drama honor of the University of Chile, this prize has been granted such playwrights as Juan Guzman Cruchaga (1951) for "Maria Cenicienta" (poetic drama), and Natanael Yanez Silva (1956).   233.

CHILEAN WRITERS' ASSOCIATION PRIZES

Sociedad de Escritores de Chile offers a number of literary prizes to recognize outstanding writing in a variety of forms (see Alerce Prize, Nascimento Prize, Tierra del Fuego Prize).

Writers honored by this award of their peers, such as the Premio de Novela, presented by the national writers group (Agustinas 925, Santiago) are such authors of imaginative work as:

1933 Marta Brunet Caraves

1950 Antonio de Undurrago. Carlos Pezoa Velis (essay); Fernando Durán. Velámen (poetry)

1953 Victor Molina Neira. El polvo y el tiempó (short stories)

1955 Guillermo Atiás. El Tiempo Banal (novel)

1956 Enrique Lafourcado. Punta de Rieles (novel) Leonardo Espinoza. Puerto Engaño   234.

CHILEAN WRITERS' UNION
NOVEL CONTEST
In 1954 this novel competition of Sindicato de Escritores de Chile was won by Guillermo Atías with his book "El Tiempo Banal."   235.

CHINA ASSOCIATION OF LITERATURE AND ARTS PRIZES
(China, Republic of)
On the occasion of its tenth anniversary in 1960, the cultural association, which was organized May 4, 1951, awarded medals for literary achievement. Among the writers honored by the medal were: Chang Hsiu-ya (Essay); Shih Ts'ui-fen (Translation); Yang Nien-ts'u (Fiction); Wang Ting-chun (Criticism).
                                    236.

Castillo de CHIREL PRIZE
(Spain)
Each four years since 1916 the 4,000 pts award of the Real Academia Española (Felipe IV, 4, Madrid) has been granted for the best journalistic work published in newspapers or magazines during the four-year competition period.   237.

CHUNG HUA PRIZE FOR ART AND LITERATURE (China, Republic of)
The "China Prize for Art and Literature" of the Chinese Ministry of Education has been awarded annually on March 12 since 1955. One candidate is nominated each year for the gold medal and NT $20,000 premium in several classes of writing: Poetry, Essay, Novel, Drama (and also in other cultural fields: Music, Painting). In the literature categories the prize is also designated "China Ministry of Education Literature Award."
Prize winners include:
Poetry 1955 You-Jen Yu

1956 Han-Kuang Chen
Essay 1955 Hsueh-Ling Su
Novel 1958 Lan Wang
1959 Nankuo (pseud of Hsieh-Tsan Lin, also written Shih-ts'un Ling). The resourceful woman
1960 Chi-Yin Chen
Drama 1957 Man-Kuei Lee
1959 Ping-Ling Wang   238.

CHUO KORON SHINJIN PRIZE
(Japan)
A literary award of the magazine "Chuo Koron," granted in an annual literary contest since 1956.   239.

CHRISTIAN FICTION CONTEST
(International--U.S.A.)
The Zondervan Publishing House (1415 Lake Drive, S.E. Grand Rapids 6, Michigan) first announced this contest in 1947 to discover talent in the field of the novel. A first prize of $4,000, and several other monetary prizes, have been granted in four contests, but not further competitions are planned at this time (1962-1963).   240.

CHRISTOPHER AWARD (International--U.S.A.)
Granted each year in July by The Christophers (16 East 48th Street, New York 17), this award presented in conjunction with the Catholic Library Association, gives recognition to authors of adult, juvenile, and children's books who have "made notable contributions" during the year." Published short stories and articles from newspapers and magazines, as well as books, are considered for recognition by the award.
The prize, consisting of a bronze medallion bearing the image of St. Christopher on one side and on the other, the motto of The Christophers: "Better to light one candle than to curse the darkness," was established

"to encourage individuals in all walks of life to show a personal and practical responsibility in restoring the love and truth of Christ in the market place, especially in government, education, literature, entertainment, and labor relations."

Winners of the prize for literature, which honors a popular work suitable for the entire family and considers content as well as literary style in assigning the award, include:

1954 Heinrich Harrer (Austria) Seven years in Tibet
1955 Carlos Romulo (Philippines). Crusade in Asia
1956 George Mardikian (Armenia-U.S.A.). Song of America
1961 G. B. Stern (United Kingdom). Bernadette
1962 Jacques Maritain (France) On the use of philosophy Roland de Vaux (France.) Ancient Israel   241.

Hubert CHURCH PROSE AWARD (New Zealand)

Since 1945 this annual award of ₤50 has been offered for the best prose writing (including essays, newspaper articles, fiction, biography, or any other form of prose), written or published during the calendar year by a New Zealand writer (a native New Zealander, or any other person who has resided continuously in New Zealand during the previous five years). No application is required for the literary honor, which is administered by the P.E.N. New Zealand Centre (P.O. Box 9016, Wellington, New Zealand).

Winning novelists, biographers, essayists, short story writers, and journalists include:

1945 M. H. Holcroft. The waiting hills (essays)
1946 M. H. Holcroft. Encircling seas (essay)

1947 Lilian Keys. Thomas Arnold, biographical article in "Catholic Review," April 1947
1948 David Ballantyne. The Cunninghams (novel)
1949 J. C. Beaglehole. Chapter 6 in "Victoria University College" (history)
1950 Frank Sargeson. Up onto the roof and down again (biography)
1951 Janet Frame. The lagoon and other stories (short stories)
1952 Oliver Duff. "Sundowner" in the "New Zealand Listener" (articles)
1953/4 E. H. McCormick. The expatriate (biography)
1955 James Courage. The young have secrets (novel)
1956 Maurice Duggan. Immanuel's land (short stories)
1957 Dennis McEldowney. The world regained (autobiography)
1958 M. K. Joseph. I'll soldier no more (novel)
1959 Maurice Shadbolt. The New Zealanders (short stories)
1960 Noel Hilliard. Maori girl (novel)   242.

Bimala CHURN LAW GOLD MEDAL (India)

One of several medal awards of the Asiatic Society (1 Park Street, Calcutta 16) "for encouragement of studies in letters and the humanities," this honor is granted biennially to a person who has made "conspicuously important contributions to History, Geography, Philosophy, Religion, Ethnology, Folklore, Fine Arts and Agriculture--with special reference to India from the earliest times down to the 13th century A.D.; Bengali language, literature and philosophy."

Recently honored by the Medal are: Hem Chandra Roy Choudhuri, R.C. Majumdar, P.V. Kane, Louis Renau, S.K. Belvalkar.

243.

CIRCULO DE BELLAS ARTES PRIZE (Spain)

Two prizes of 50,000 pts each--one for poetry, one for novel--are offered by the Club America, Madrid. This literary award, administered by the Instituto de Cultura Hispanica, was granted in 1952 to the novel of Juan Antonio de Zunzunegui, "Esta Oscura Desbandada." 244.

CITTADELLA PRIZE (Italy)

Among the most significant Italian poetry prizes is this award, offered by the town of Cittadella in the province of Padua, the publisher Editore Bino Rebellato (via Garibaldi 54), and the service organization--Rotary Club di Padova e di Venezia. A premium of L 500.000 is granted in a national poetry competition for a book of poetry published during the contest year (August of the year preceding award to September 1 of the year of award).

Winners since the first prize in 1952 are such poets as:
1952 Carlo Munari
1954 Carlo Martini
1957 Angelo Barile. Sereno
1958 Nelo Risso. Civilissimo
1959 Elio Filippo Accrocca.
Ritorno a Portonaccio
Bartolo Cattafi. Le mosche del merriggio
1960 Luciano Erba
1961--special decennial competition: Biagio Marin. Solitàe 245.

CIVITATE CHRISTIANA PRIZE (Italy)

Pro Civitate Christiana (casella postale 46, Assisi) grants each year in September an award for Drama and Journalism, with a premium of L 1.000. 000 for each class of writing.

In 1961 playwright Luigi Candoni won an award with "Edipo a Iroschima;" and the journalism winner was Ferruccio Lan franchi. Giuseppe Berto won the 1962 drama prize with his play, "L' uomo e la sua morte."

246.

Denyse CLAIROUIN PRIZE (France)

A translation prize granted annually on the second Wednesday of December, the award is named for Denyse Clairouin, the translator and literary agent killed in the Resistance, who was instrumental in introducing major literary works in English to the French public through excellent translations into French.

The Clairouin Prize, an award of Les Amis de Denyse Clairouin (66 rue de Miromesnil, Paris 8e), honors the best translation of a literary work in English--exclusive of drama--into French, which has been published during the 12 months preceding the close of competition on November 1.

Translators accorded this national honor, which has been discontinued for the last few years with no current prospects for reactivation, are:
1946 Marie Canavaggia.
Nathaniel Hawthorne. La Lettre Ecarlate
1947 Pierre Leyris. T.S. Eliot. Poèmes
1948 Raimbault and Gorce. Thomas Wolfe. De la Mort au Matin
1949 Dominique Aury. Evelyn Waugh. Le Cher Disparu; and J. Hoog. Confession du Pêcheur Justifié
1950 Denise Van Moppès. Alan Paton. Pleure, O Pays Bein-Aimé
G. Belmont. Henry James. Les Ambassadeurs
1952 Henriette de Sarbois. Thornton Wilder. Les Ides

de Mars
1953 Ludmilla Savitzky. Rex
Warner. Hommes de Prière
Additional awards made for
the best translation of a French
work into English by juries in
London and New York were
granted:
1948 Rosamond Lehmann.
Jacques le Marchand. Geneviève
1950 Antonia White. Guy de
Maupassant. Une Vie
1951 Alan Pryce Jones.
Jules Supervielle. Le
Voleur d'Enfants
1952 Denise Folliot. Julien Green.
Moira
1954 Gerard Hopkins. Translation of the work of François
Mauriac
1956 Jonathan Mayne. Charles
Baudelaire. The mirror of art
247.

Luisa CLAUDIO DE SOUSA
PRIZE (Brazil)
"The best book published in
the previous year" is designated
by the award of the P.E.N.
Club do Brazil (Avenida Pecanha
26, Rio de Janeiro 13), which
has been granted for a variety
of literary works including
novels, plays, and literary history and criticism.
Among recent recipients are:
1957 Antonio Callado. A
Madona de Cedro (novel)
1958 Luís Inácio Jardim.
Isabel do Sertão
1959 Aníbal M. Machado. O
Piano (play)
1960 Alfredo Dias Gomes. A
Invasão
Santos Moraes. Terra e
Sangue   248.

"CLUB ESPAÑA" JOURNALISM
PRIZES (Mexico--Premio de
Periodismo "Club España")
Established as an annual
prize by the Club España (In-
surgentes 2390, Mexico 20,
D.F.) in 1954 as recognition
of the "best articles on a 'tema

hispánico,' " published by October
1 each year in Mexican periodicals, the prizes are also given
for the best article in Spanish on
'tema mexicano.'
Journalists honored with the
prize are:
1954 Jésus Guisa y Azevedo.
El centenario del Himno
Nacional y España
1955 Andrés Iduarte. De la
lengua y su día
1956 Miguel Lanz Duret.
México y España
1957 Jésus Guisa y Azevedo.
Los errores de un oficial
mayor
1958 José Vasconcelos. La
hispanidad
1959 Alfonso Junco. La mistad
en la verdad
1960 Antonio Uroz. Fraternidad
hispanoamericana
1961 Carlos Marín Foucher.
Nuestra deuda con España
249.

"CLUB ESPAÑA" NOVEL PRIZE
(International--Mexico)
The Premio "Club España"
de la Novela is an annual novel
award of Club España (Insurgentes
2390, Mexico 20, D.F.), which
was established in 1954 "to foster
and spread knowledge of Hispanic
values." Designed to stimulate
writing in Latin American countries, Spain and the Philippines,
the prize offers $25,000 and a
first edition of the winning book
for a manuscript in Spanish by
an author of these countries--a
novel with a main character
that is Spanish, Hispano-American, or Filipino, with some of
the action taking place in a
Spanish-speaking country.
Among the winners of this
"Concurso de Novela" are:
1954 Miguel Sáinz y López
Negrete. Cruces en el
Teocali
1956 Manuel Pomares Mon-
león. Ya no existe la luz

de esa estrella
1957 María Asunción Porta
Graell. Damas de Indias
1958 Manuel de Heredia.
Barro
1960 Hernan Robleto. La
brújula fija de Bernardo
Rodríguez   250.

COCHABAMBA SOCIETY OF
WRITERS AND ARTISTS STORY
CONTEST (Bolivia)
The Sociedad de Escritores
y Artistas de Cochabamba short
story contest (Concurso de
Cuentos) was won in 1939 by
Fernando Ramirez Velarde with
"Trópico."   251.

COELHO NETO PRIZE (Brazil)
Named for the Brazilian
novelist H.M. Coelho Neto,
this Cr $50.000 novel prize of
the Academia Brasileira de
Letras (Avenida Presidente
Wilson 203, Rio de Janeiro) is
offered for the best unpublished
work or the best book published
during the two years preceding
the year of award. Winners
include:
1956 Ondina Ferreira. Chão
de espinhos; Osman Lins.
O Visitante
1958 Antônio Olavo Pereira.
Marcoré
1960 Moacir C. Menezes.
Maria de Cada Pôrto;
Barbosa Lessa. Os Guaxos
1962 Jose Condé. Terra de
Caruaru; Herberto Sales.
Além dos Marimbus
                              252.

COFFS HARBOUR ARTS
COUNCIL PLAY AND SONG
CONTEST (Australia)
A Play and Song Contest
offers monetary premiums for
the best novel (Ŀ 100, Ŀ 30,
and Ŀ 20) and song (Ŀ 50,
Ŀ 30, Ŀ 10) submitted to the
Council   253.

ČOIBALSANG NATIONAL PRIZE
(Mongolian People's Republic)
In 1954 this national honor
was granted to Sengge for his
poem, "A Dove," about the dove
of peace.   254.

COLOGNE LITERATURE PRIZE
(Germany)
One of several cultural honors
granted by the city of Cologne
(Köln) since 1954, the Literature
Prize of 10,000 DM, which is
presented for distinguished literary production, has honored such
well-known authors of Germany
as:
1957 Erhart Kästner
1959 Heinrich Böll
1961 Annette Kolb   255.

COLOMBIAN ASSOCIATION OF
WRITERS AND ARTISTS PRIZE
Asociacion de Escritores y
Artistas de Colombia granted
their award in 1954 to Gabrial
García Márquez for "Un día
después del Sábado."   256.

COLOMBIAN PRESS PRIZES
Premios de la Prensa Colombiana prizes for journalism,
granted by Asociacion de Period-
istas de Colombia, brought a
gold medal and $2.000 in 1958
to Alberto Zalamea for the best
journalistic chronicle published in
the country during the year.
Essay themes set for subsequent
prizes include the two subjects
for 1959: José Pens Faus and
Humberto de Castro; and Carlos
Delgado Fernández.   257.

COLUMBIA-CATHERWOOD
AWARDS (International--U.S.A.)
Outstanding contributions to
international journalism are
recognized by a plaque and
$2,000 premium, which was won
in 1960 by Nicolas Chatelain of
"Figaro," Paris.   258.

COMBAT PRIZE (France)

This award offered for a published or an unpublished novel by the magazine "Combat" (18 rue du Croissant, Paris) was established in 1959 with a premium of 2,000 NF, and a second prize of a 15 day voyage to Tunis.

Prize winners include:
1960 René de Obaldia. Le Centenaire Alain Jouffroy. La vie privée (manuscript)
1961 Emile Cioran. Histoire et utopie
1962 Roger Caillois. Ponce Pilate   259.

CONDÁL PRIZE (Spain)

Alonso Alcaldo won the Condál Prize in 1960 with his literary story, "La Sentencia."
                                260.

CONDOR OF THE ANDES (Bolivia)

Highest official decoration of the Bolivian government, the plaque of the Gran Oficial de la Orden del Condor do los Andes, granted for outstanding contributions to Bolivian culture, has been awarded such major Bolivian authors as Fernandez Diez de Medina, the essayist, poet and critic who received the honor in 1953 for his intellectual work and public service.
                                261.

CONGO LITERARY PRIZE (Africa)

"About once a year," a literary prize was awarded to an African writer who won a contest originated by King Rudahigwa, Mwami of Ruanda. Among native authors winning the prize are Dieudonne Mutombo, Jean Bolikango, and the two novelists who won the Brussels Colonial Fair Prize:
1948 Paul Lomami-Tshibamba (Congo). Ngando (The crocodile)
1949 J. Saverio Naigiziki (Ruanda-Urundi). Escapade Ruandaise   262.

COOPAL PRIZE FOR TRANSLATION (Belgium)

A Flemish language award granted for translation of outstanding foreign literary works into Flemish has recently been presented to:
1958 Bert Decorte. Baudelaire. De bloemen van den boze
1960 Hugo Claus. Dylan Thomas. Onder het Melkwoud
                                263.

CORNING SCIENCE PRIZE (International--U.S.A.)

Established in 1962, as an annual award, this $10,000 prize ($7,500 outright grant, and $2,500 royalty advance) is offered by the publisher Little, Brown and Company (34 Beacon Street, Boston 6, Massachusetts) in cooperation with Corning Glass Works, for "the best book-length manuscript in the field of the natural or physical sciences for the general reader."

The contest, which is directed to "stimulating science writing and encouraging writers to undertake books on science for the general audience," calls for manuscripts that are book-length and are written originally in English on a scientific subject intended for the intelligent layman. Manuscripts for the first award must be submitted to Little, Brown and Company between April 1, 1962 and March 1, 1953, and the winner of the 1963 award will be announced on or before September 1, 1963.   264.

CORTINA-ULISSE PRIZE (Europe-Italy)

The Premio Europeo Cortina-Ulisse, a literary prize offered

for a work of popular science, is administered by the international cultural review, "Revista Ulisse," under the patronage of the city of Cortina and various learned and professional groups. Works eligible to compete for the prize must be on a prescribed subject, and must be an original work published for the first time in Europe during the last five years, by an author of any European country. While works in any European language will be considered for award, writings in other than Italian, English, French, German, or Spanish must be accompanied by a printed or typed translation into one of these languages.

The set subjects announced for each year's competition include: theoretical and philosophical works; popularization of science; art (as, the "best popular work dealing with general aesthetics, either historical or illustrative of the figurative arts"). For the next several years, winning works will be chosen from among writings (a) by foreign authors about the Italian Risorgimento; (b) on the problems of automation; (c) on the problems of communication and transport. Subject of the 1961 competition was "the problems of the new African countries, particularly in respect to the economic situation in Europe."

A work may be entered in competition by sending five copies to Editor, Revista Ulisse (Sezione Premio Europeo Cortina-Ulisse (corso d'Italia 43, Rome) by October 30. "Monographs, acts, memorials, or academic reports and works intended for school use" are not accepted in the contest. A jury, composed of members of learned societies (as Accademia Nazionale dei Lincei), editors, authors

and scholars, selects the winning work so that the prize may be awarded in August. If the winning book is by a non-Italian it may be published in Italian by an Italian publisher.

Among the winners of the prize, first awarded under the name "Cortina Prize" in 1949, which brings an indivisible premium of L 1.000.000 are:

1949 John Read (United Kingdom). A direct entry to organic chemistry

1950 Carlo Morandi (Italy.) L'idea dell'Unita politica d'Europa nel XIX e XX secolo Pierre Belperron (France). La guerre de sécession

1951 Leon Venturi (Italy). Come si comprende la pittura

1952 Ernest Baldwin (United Kingdom). Dynamic aspects of biochemistry

1953 Graham Hutton (United Kingdom). We too can prosper

1954 Edward Spranger (Germany). Pädogogische Perspektiven

1956 Luigi Preti (Italy). Le lotte agrarie nella Valle Padana

1957 Gerhard Löwenthal and Josef Hausen (Germany). Wir werden durch Atome Leben

1958 G. Elgozy (France). La France devant le Marche Commun

1960 Felice Ippolito (Italy). L'Italie e l'energia nucleare

1961 Werner Holzer (Germany). Das Nackte Antilitz Afrikas
265.

COSENZA PRIZE (Italy)
The Union of Catholic Poets and Writers (Unione dei Poeti e Scrittori Cattolici Ital., piazza Parrasio 16, Cosenza) grants this L 500.000 prize for literary criticism--anthologies of

Catholic writing; and L 200.000 for articles and lectures. Recipients of the latter award include: G. Rossino, A. Ubiali, E.M. Salvi, and M. Guidacci. In 1959 a prize of L 500.000 was won by Mario Nantelli with his collection, "Antologia di poeti cattolici ital."   266.

COSTA DO SOL PRIZE
(Portugal)

A journalism prize offered by Junta do Turismo da Costa do Sol brings the winner 5.000$ in each of two classes of articles written about the "Portuguese Sunny Coast." A prize is granted for the best article appearing in the Portuguese press, and for the best article appearing in the Foreign press.   267.

COUNCIL OF EUROPE PRIZE
(Europe)

For five years the Assembly of the Council of Europe (Place Lenotre, Strasbourg, France) awarded an annual prize, financed by the Hamburg foundation-- Freiherr vom Stein Stiftung, "for an achievement in science, literature, administration, or journalism intended to promote European unity." While not a literary prize in the strict sense, the 6.000 NF Council of Europe Research Fellowships, which are granted each year for research leading to the production of publishable works, may result in books of "European interest" in the subject areas: (a) Political, legal, economic, scientific, agricultural, social, education and youth problems connected with European integration; (b) European civilization (philosophy, history, literature and the arts.) The theses prepared during the fellowship must be at least 150 pages in length and are considered for publication by the international publisher--A.W. Sijthoff, Leyden, Netherlands.

Candidates considered for the fellowship are nationals of one of the 16 member states of the Council, although one fellowship in five is reserved for refugees. Preference in assigning fellowship grants is given to applicants under 45 years of age.   268.

Albert COUNSON PRIZE (Belgium)

First awarded in 1940 this quinquennial prize of 20.000 fr is granted by the Belgian Royal Academy of French Language and Literature for a scholarly work in the philology of the Romance languages. The prize may be granted to a foreign author, but only for a work of particular Belgian interest.

Recent winners are:
1950 Gustave Charlier. Le mouvement Romantique en Belgique (1915-1950). Tome I--La Bataille Romantique
1955 Fernand Desonay. Ronsard poète de l'amour
1960 Julia Bastin. For editing Rutebeuf's complete works (in collaboration with Edmond Faral, Institut de France).
                                269.

COURTELINE PRIZE (France)

One of approximately fifty literary awards of the Societé des Gens de Lettres (38 rue du Faubourg-Saint-Jacques, Paris 14e), this prize has been granted since 1930--biennially through 1950, and annually since that date. It is granted for the best humorous novel of the year by an author of at least 50 years of age.

Recipients of the prize, with books that demonstrate literary worth in comic observation and philosophy of society, include:
1951 Jean Dutourd. Une tête de chien
1952 Pierre Daninos. Sonia, les autres, et moi

1958 Prix du Centenaire:
  Marcel Pagnol
1960 Jacques Natanson. La
  nuit de Matignon
1961 Costa de Loverdo. Les
  tribulations du colonel
  Grey
1962 André Couteaux. Un
  monsieur de Compagnie
                            270.

COWELL AWARD (South Africa)
  An African Music Society
prize (P.O. Box 138, Roode-
poort, Transvaal, Republic of
South Africa), consisting of
records and equipment to "assist
the receiver with his work on
African music," granted in
1956 to J.H. Kwabena Nketia
of Ghana for his monograph on
the funeral dirges of the Akan
people.   271.

Archer CRAWFORD MEMORIAL
SHORT STORY AWARD
(Australia)
  Sponsored by the National
Council of Realist Writers
Groups of Australia, this prize
is open to all writers. A first
prize (₤ 20) and a second
prize (₤ 5) will be given winning stories selected from the
short stories submitted to the
'Realist Writer," during 1961-
1962.   272.

Rose Mary CRAWSHAY PRIZE
FOR ENGLISH LITERATURE
(International--United Kingdom)
  One of the literary awards
administered by the British
Academy (Burlington Gardens,
London W. 1), this ₤ 100 prize
was established in 1888 as a grant
to 'a woman of any nationality
who has written or published
within three years preceding the
date of the award an outstanding historical or critical work
on any subject connected with
English literature, preferably a
a work regarding Byron, Shelley,

or Keats." While earlier prizes
considered only works about
these three English poets, the
scope of the prize was expanded
in 1915 to include writings on
the whole field of English literature.
  Among winning authors are:
1917 Léonie Villard (France).
  Jane Austen: Sa Vie et Son
  Oeuvre
1924 Madeleine L. Cazamian.
  Le Roman et les Idées en
  Angleterre--Influence de la
  Science, 1860-1890.
1927 Alice Galimberti. L'Aedo
  d'Italia (A.C. Swinburne)
1934 Giovanna Foà. Lord
  Byron, Poeta è Carbonaro
1940 M. M. Lascelles. Jane
  Austen   273.

CREOLE FOUNDATION PRIZE
(International--Venezuela)
  A $10,000 prize (Premio
Fundacion Creole) for scientific
research is offered biennially by
the Creole Foundation (Apartado
889, Caracas; U.S.A. address:
15 W. 51st Street, New York 19),
a subsidiary corporation affiliated
with the Standard Oil Company of
New Jersey (through the Creole
Petroleum Corporation), "for the
best work on Venezuela in any
branch of the natural, physical,
or social sciences."
  Citizens of any country are
eligible to submit writings for
consideration, but the work
must be in Spanish, English,
French, German, Italian, or
Portuguese, or must be accompanied by an "adequate summary"
in one of these languages. For
the first contest, unpublished
writings or works published
within two years preceding the
year of award were submitted
by December 1959, accompanied
by a letter from a university,
academy, or other institution of
higher learning related to the
field of writing. The first award,

granted in 1961, was shared by
Dr. Miguel Layrisse, and Dr.
Johannes Wilbert, for 'El
Antigeno del Sistema Sanguineo
Diego' (The antigen of the
Diego Blood System).   274.

CROATIAN PEOPLE'S REPUBLIC PRIZES (Yugoslavia--Vlade nr Hrvatske)

The People's Republic of
Croatia, since 1945 one of the
Federated Republics of Yugo-
slavia, grants literary prizes on
the state Holiday of May 1. The
prizes are granted for various
forms of writing and for trans-
lation, and include among the
authors of national fame in
Yugoslavia honored with the
prize:
Novel
  Ivanka Vujcic-Lazovska.
  Vranjara (Vranjara)
  Josip Barkovic. Sinovi
  slobode (Sons of freedom)
  Novak Simic. Miskovici (The
  Miskovich Family)
Poetry
  Vesna Parun. Pjesme (Poems)
  Sime Vucetic. Knjigu pjesama
  (Book of poems)
Drama
  Marjan Matkovic. Drama-
  turske studije (Dramatic
  studies)
Literary Studies
  Slavko Kolar. "Most renowned
  contemporary Croatian
  humorist," Kadic p. 52
  Marin Franicevic. Pisci i
  problemi (Writer and his
  problems)
Children's Literature
  Mato Lovrak
Translation
  Jure Kastelan. Macedonian
  poems
  Dobrisa Cesarić. Pushkin
  and Goethe   275.

CROATIAN WRITERS' ASSOCIATION PRIZES (Yugoslavia-- Dustvo hrvatski knjizevnika)

Novels, poetry, and other
literary works receiving these
writers' group prizes include:
  1953 Vladimir Popovic. Lirske
  minijature (Lyric miniatures)
  Jure Franicevic Plocar.
  Stope na kamenu (Tracks on
  stone)
  1954 Marjan Matkovic. Na
  kraju puta (At the end of the
  road)
  Ervin Sinko. Optimisti (The
  optimists) (novel)
  Miroslav Feldman. Zbirku
  pesama (Collection of poetry)
        276.

CROTONE PRIZE (Italy)

Awarded each November since
1956, the L 1.000.000 prize of
the city of Crotone in southern
Italy (Commune di Crotone, Crotone, Catanzaro) was established
for "a social novel" published
during the contest year (December 1 to November 31 of the following year), and has been a-
warded for fiction and other
prose writing.
  Recipients include:
  1956 Leonida Rapaci. Un Ric-
  cone torna alla sua Terra
  1957 Gaetano Salvemini.
  Scritti sulla questiono meri-
  dionale
  1958 Ernesto De Martino
  Elemire Zolla. Eclissi Dell'
  Intellettuale (collected essays)
  1959 Pier Paolo Pasolini. Una
  vita violenta
  1960 Davide Lajolo. Il vizio
  assurdo   277.

CROUCH MEMORIAL GOLD MEDAL AWARD (Australia)

This prize, offered for the
"best novel and best book of
poems by an Australian author,"
is granted each year--alternately
for a novel and for poetry.
        278.

CULTURE FRANÇAISE PRIZE (West Indies--France)

A newly established prize, Prix de la Culture Française, for a novel by a writer from the West Indies, the award was first granted in 1960 as the French Antilles Prize (Prix de France-Antilles). The honor was established as a triennial prize with a premium of 100.000 fr directed to distinguishing the best published or unpublished novel--not experimental or of a confessional or political nature --by a writer originally from one of the French-speaking countries of the Caribbean: Haiti, Martinique, Guadeloupe, or French Guiana.

Of works submitted in the first contest--deadline June 1, 1960--that of Marie Chauvet, "Fonds de nègres," was selected as a winner. The newly established Prix de la Culture Française is an annual prize to be announced on the second Monday in May, and manuscripts competing for the award must be sent to C.E.C.F. (Centre d'Expression de la Culture Française, 1 Square Raynouard, Paris 16e).   279.

CUP FOR NEW WRITERS OF LIGHT FICTION (Japan--Oru Shinjin Hai)

The "Oru Yomimono," magazine of the Bungei Shinju Company, established this literary honor in 1952 to honor the writer of an outstanding novel published during the year. 280.

CZECHOSLOVAK NATIONAL ARTIST

A general cultural honor of the Czechoslovak government, the title "Czechoslovak National Artist" is an official national title bestowed upon Czech and Slovak writers in public recognition of "a lifetime's work which has enriched the cultural wealth of the nation."

Among the writers who have won this high honor are: Petr Bezruc, Jarmila Glazarova, Josef Hora, Janko Jesensky, Peter Jilemnicky, Frano Kral, Ivan Krasko, Mariet Majerova, S. K. Neumann, Vitizslav Nezval, Ivan Olbracht, Ludmila Podjavorinska, Marie Pujmanova, Frana Sramek, Vladislav Vancura.
281.

CZECHOSLOVAK STATE PRIZE OF KLEMENT GOTTWALD (Statni cena Klementa Gottwalda)

Since 1951 this highest Czechoslovak literary award has been presented by the President of the Czechoslovak Socialist Republic each year on May 9, Czechoslovak V-Day, in a ceremony held on the evening of the national holiday celebrated for Czechoslovak liberation.

The Czechoslovak national government has awarded a literary prize each year since 1920, and during the period of 1945-1960 the prize was called "Czechoslovak State Prize," and from 1945 to 1950 was presented each year on October 28, a holiday that marked the Day of the Nationalization of Industry, and of the establishment of the first Czechoslovak Republic in 1918. This prize was granted in all fields of literature (as well as in other areas of creative work--musical composition, motion pictures, painting, sculpture). Pre-World War II winners of the Czechoslovak State Prize included Karel and Josef Capek; Vladislav Vancura; and such writers as:

1928 Franz Werfel. Entire work
1932 Majerova. Prehada
1933 Baum. Die Schrift, die nicht log
1934 Olbracht. Nikola Subaj
1941 Maurice Hindus. To sing with the angels
1943 S. Harrison Thompson.

Czechoslovakia in European history

The state prize recognizing cultural contribution that was re-established after World War II (legal decree in "Collection of Laws, Czechoslovak Socialist Republic, June 28, 1960") is awarded in such areas as: Folklore, National Art, People's Literature. The prize (consisting of three monetary premiums ranging from 40,000 kcs to 20,000 kcs; a ribbon decoration; and the right to use the title, "Laureat of the State Prize of Klement Gottwald") is awarded "for outstanding creative works which have enriched knowledge, created artistic values, or have otherwise contributed to the socialist construction of Czechoslovakia."

Winners of this national literary honor include:

Children's and Youth Books
1954 Frantisek Hrubin. Menesuv orlof (Figurine clock of Manes); Kuratko a obili (Chicken and corn); Jrajte si s nami (Play with us)

Drama
1951 Vojtech Cach. Duchcovsky viadukt (The Duchcofsky Tunnel); Vasek Kana. Parta brusice Karhana (Kahana's party of the grinders)
Ilja Pracher. Hadaju sa o (The debate over the mind)
1952 Jaroslav Klima. Stesti nepada s Nebe (Good luck does not fall from Heaven)
Miroslav Stehlik. Jarni hromobiti (Spring thunder)
1953 Milan Jaris. Boleslav I (Boleslav I)
1960 Peter Karvas. Pulnocni mse (Midnight mass)

Drama--Motion Picture Scenario
1951 Frantisek Dvorak. Vstanou novi bojovnici (New fighters shall rise)
1952 Jan Werich. Cisaruv pekar a pedaruv cisar (The baker of the emperor and the emperor of the baker)
1953 Jiri Marek. Nad nami svita (The sky is clearing above us)
1954 Miloslav Stehlik. Nositele radu (Wearer of awards); and his dramatic adaptation of Makarenko's novel, "Flags on the Towers" (Vlajky na vezich)

Literary Criticism
1951 Ladislav Stoll. Tricet let boju za ceskou poesii (Thirty years' struggle for Czech poetry)
1957 Jan Rypka. Dejiny novoperske literatury (Glimpses into recent Persian literature); Prehled Tadzicke literatury (Introduction to the literature of the Tadz race)
Alexandr Matuska. Pre a proti (For and against)

Non-Fiction
1947 Vladislav Vancura. Obrazy z dejin naroda ceskeho (Glimpses into the history of the Czech nation) (posthumous award)
1951 Jarmila Glazarova. Leningrad Zdenek Nejedly. History of the Czech nation, Vol 1 (Dejiny Ceskeho naroda, Vol 1)
1952 Jaroslav Prusek. Sinological work contributing to "the mutual approachment of the Chinese and Czech cultures"
1953 Jan Kopecky. Sovetske zpisky (Soviet diary)
1954 Josef Horak. The Shafts
1955 Marie Majerova. Zpivajici Cina (Singing China)
Katerina Lazarova. Wasps' nest
Karel Ptacnik. Born in 1921
Vladimir Minac. On the boundary

Novel
1948 Marie Pujmanova. Hra s ohnem (Playing with fire)
1951 Alena Bernaskova. Cesta ofevrena (Open road)
Vaclav Rezac. Nastup (File-

up!)
1953 Adolf Branald, Chleb a pisne
(Bread without songs)
Marie Pujmanova. Zivot
proti Smrti (Life against
death--third part of a trilogy;
two preceding titles; People
on the crossroads; Playing
with fire)
K. F. Sedlacek. Luisiana se
probouzi (Luisiana awakens)
1954 Turek Svatopluk. Bez sefa
(Without a boss)
1955 Jan Otcenasek. Obcan Brych
(Citizen Brych)
1958 Zdenek Pluhar. Oputis-li
mne (If you should leave me)
1960 Karel Novy. Plamen z
vitr (Flame and wind)
Poetry
1948 Vladimir Holan. Poetical
work
1951 Stanislav Neumann. Piseno
Stalinu (Ballad of Stalin)
Vitezslav Nezval. Z domoviny
(Remembrance of my home);
Stalin
Marie Pujmanova. Miliony
holubicek (Millions of
pigeons); Viznani lasky
(Expression of love)
1952 Konstantin Biebl. Bez obav
(Without fear) (collected
poems) (posthumous award)
Frantisek Branislav. Nilostny
napev (love poems)
1953 Vitezslav Nezval. Kridla
(Wings)
Vojtech Mihalik. (The singing
heart)
1954 Josef Kainar. Cesky sen
(Czech dream); and puppet
play, Zlatovlaska (Goldi-
locks)
Jan Kostra.   The maple leaf
1955 Marie Pujmanova. Praha
(Prague)
Jaroslav Seifert. Maminka
(Mother)
1956 Vilem Zavada. Polni kviti
(Field flowers)
1958 Frantisek Hrubin. Mus
spev (My songs); Promena
(Transformation)

1959 Ivan Skala. Ranni vlak
nadeje (Morning train of hope)
Andrej Plavka. Liptovska pistala
(The whistle of Liptov)
1961 Stefan Zary. Ikar vecne
zivy (Eternal Icarus)
Short Stories
1951 Jiri Marek. Nad nami svita
(The sky is clearing above us)
(collected stories)
1953 Jan Drda. Krasna Tortiza
(The beautiful Tortiza)
1954 Vaclav Lacina. Mostannske
besedy (Civic society) (satiric
stories)
Translation
1951 Jiri Taufer. Translation d
Majakovskij
1955 E. A. Saudek. Translation
of Shakespeare's plays: Romeo
and Juliet; Merchant of
Venice
Works
1949 J. S. Kubin   282.

CZECHOSLOVAK WRITER PRIZE
    Annually awarded on the "Day
of the Press," September 21, by
the publishing house, The Czechoslovak Writer (Ceskoslovensky
spisovatel), this monetary award
of 10,000 kcs is granted to books
published between September 15
of the previous year and September 15 of the next year--in the field
of: Fiction; Poetry; Essay;
Criticism; Translation; and Il-
lustration.
    Prize-winning authors include:
    Jan Petrmichl. Patnact let
ceskoslovenske literatury
(Fifteen years of Czechoslovak-
ian literature)
    Milan Kundera. Umeni romanu
(The art of the novel) (essay)
    Jiri Fried. Oasova tisen
(Fearful times) (novella)
    Ivan Divis. Uzlove pismo
(Mysterious writing) (collected
poems)
    Jan Kozak.   Horky dech
(Heated breath) (novella)
                                        283.

DALMIA PEACE PRIZE (International--India)

In 1948, Seth Damkrishna Dalmia, one of India's wealthiest industrialists and publishers, offered a peace prize of $5,000 to "any person irrespective of race or religion who renders the greatest service to the promotion of human peace, and who makes the best effort for one-world government." A jury of six members from different countries designated prize winners, and also awarded a $4,000 prize for the best book on the concept of world government.
284.

Silvio D'AMICO PRIZE (Italy)

This literary prize for a work of drama criticism was established in 1955 by the Italian Drama Institute (Instituto del Dramma Italiana, via Antonio Salandra 6, Rome). The L 500.000 prize, granted biennially since 1958, honors an outstanding work of criticism--appraisal, or review, monograph, or other writing on the theater arts--which is published in book form or in periodicals during the contest period.

Recipients include:
1956 Giovanni Calendoli; Vito Pandolfi--Divided prize for works of drama criticism
1957 Achille Fiocco. Teatro italiano di ieri e di oggi
1958 Mario Apollonio. Contributions to the knowledge and evaluation of dramatic writing
1960 Nicola Chiaramonte. La situazione drammatica
1962 Federico Doglio. Studies of Italian dramatic writing 285.

DAMM PRIZE (Norway)

N. W. Damm & Son (Slottsgt 6, Oslo) grants this annual publisher's prize in the fall of the year. Eligible to compete for the award, offered since 1952, are all Norwegian authors "who are invited to submit one (or more) manuscript(s) for a book for children or young people, with no restrictions as to age group, idiom, etc."

The Dammprisen at the start was offered in collaboration "with one other publisher in each of the Scandinavian countries," and currently publishers outside Scandinavia have joined in the awards. The prize consists of an outright monetary grant and a royalty advance: Norway--kr 10,000; Sweden--kr 3,500; Denmark--kr 2,500; Finland--kr 2,500; Iceland--kr 2,500.

Among recipients of the honor designating the best work for children or young people are:
1952 Kari Ørbech. Hun som fikk navnet Loretta
1953 Sigmund Moren. Dimii far vener
1955 Finn Havrevold. Den ensomme kriger
1957 Finn Havrevold. Marens lille ugle
1959 Babbis Friis Baastad. Æresord
1960 Finn Havrevold. Grunnbrott
1962 Babbis Friis Baastad. Kjersti 286.

DANISH ACADEMY'S PRIZE

One of the richest and most recent of the literary prizes in Denmark is this award of 50.000 D kr offered by the Danish Academy (Karl Bjarnhof, Secretary, Duevej 3, Copenhagen F). Established and awarded for the first time in 1961, the initial winner was Knuth Becker. 287.

DANISH AUTHORS' COLLEAGUES' PRIZE OF HONOR (Kollegernes aerespris)

The Danish Authors' Association Board annually offers a prize

of 1.500 D kr to a colleague who
has published "a meritorious
work." Initially called "Forfat-
terforbundets hæderslegat" in
1943 when established by the
group Forfatterforbundet, the
prize was given its present name
when the founding group merged
with the Danish Authors' Association (Dansk Forfatterforening,
Ved Stranden 20, Copenhagen)
in 1946, and the prize was
continued by the combined group
from 1950 to the current award.
Among the winners are:
    1943 Martin Jensen. Vestenvind
    1944 Andrea Andreasen.
    Bobler fra dybet
    1945 Johanne Buchardt. Der
    gar ingen vej tilbage
    1946 Karen Enevold
    1947 Steen Christensen
    1948 Hilmar Wulff. Vejen til
    livet
    1949 Kelvin Lindemann.
    Gyldne Kaeder
    1950 Leck Fischer
    1951 Johannes Wulff. Mor
    ta'r til byen
    1952 Knuth Becker
    1953 Erling Kristensen
    1954 Aage Dons
    1955 Erik Aalbaek Jensen
    1956 C. Eric Soya. Blodrodt
    og blegrodt
    1957 Poul Ørun
    1958 Knud Soenderby. Gensyn
    med havet
    1959 Erik Knudsen. Udvalgte
    digte
    1960 Jan Michael Tejn.
    Drommen om virkelighed
    1961 Pinches Welner. Den
    brogede gade
    1962 Marcus Lauesen   288.

DANISH AUTHORS' LYRIC
PRIZE (Dansk forfatterfonds
lyrikerprise)
    Since 1960 this 5.000 D kr
prize has been awarded by the
board of the Danish Authors'
Fund, whose membership includes one or more representa-

tives from such professional and
scholarly groups as: authors,
professors of literature, book
dealers, librarians, and the
Danish Ministry for Cultural Affairs.
    Award winners, who receive
this honor on November 4, are:
    1960 Jens August Schade
    1961 Otto Gelsted   289.

DANISH PRIZE FOR CHILDREN'S
AND YOUTH'S BOOKS (Forfatterprisen for borneog ungdomsboger)
    "Author awards for children's
and youth's books" are granted
by the Danish Ministry of Education and financed from the
country's football pools. In
1954 the 3.000 kroner premium
was divided equally between
Alfred Johnsen, author of "Den
Gronne Flaske," and Egon
Mathiesen, author of "Mis Med
de Bla Ojne." In 1961 Thoger
Birkeland won the national prize
with "Nar Hansen Galer."   290.

DANISH STATE GRANTS TO
AUTHORS (Statsydelser til
Kunstnere og Videnskabsmaend)
    The oldest and most extensive
official and public recognition of
authors in Denmark is this
"Remuneration from the King's
Purse," with a history of award
"going back several hundred
years." Current financial grants
from the Danish national government, included as a regular ex-
pense in the national budget, are
two allowances of 12.000 D kr to
Karen Blixen, and Tom Kristensen.
    Among approximately 75 addi-
tional authors receiving state
stipends are the following Danish
authors with grants of 5.400 D kr:
Knuth Becker; Eric Bertelsen;
Karl Bjarnhof; Thorkil Bjoernvig;
H. C. Branner; Albert Dam; Aage
Dons; Sigurd Elkjaer; Gunnar
Gunnarson; Aase Hansen; William

Heinesen; Per Lange; Marcus
Lausen; Kelvin Lindemann;
Willy August Linnemann; Niels
Nilsson; Paul Ørum; Sigfred
Pederson; Hans Povlsen; Ellen
Raae; Ole Sarvig; Jens August
Schade; Hans Hartvig Seedorff;
Knud Sonderby; C. Eric Soya;
Hilmar Wulff; Johannes Wulff.
291.

Gabriele D'ANNUNZIO PRIZE
(Italy)

To stimulate writing of
books about the life and works
of Gabriele D'Annunzio (1863-
1938), Italy's famous author of
plays and novels and one of the
best-known of Italian poets,
Biblioteca Provinciale Gabriele
D'Annunzio (Palazzo del
Governo, cas post 180, Pescara)
offers a L 1.000.000 prize in an
annual competition for scholarly
work, published or unpublished, in
Italian or a foreign language
dealing with D'Annunzio. Competing works are submitted for
decision by the jury during
July each year.

Recipients of the prize are:
1957 Adelia Noferi.
L' "Alcyone" nella storia
della poesia dannunziana
Guglielmo Gatti. Vita di
Gabriele D'Annunzio
1959 Nicola Francesco
Cimmino. Poesia e poetica
in Gabriele D'Annunzio
1961 Rdy. de Cadaval 292.

Orlando DANTAS NOVEL
COMPETITION (Brazil)

The "Concurso de Romances
Orlando Dantas" is an annual
competition conducted by the
newspaper, "Diário de Notícias
(Rua Riachuelo 25, Rio de
Janeiro). In addition to the
Premio Dantas for a novel, the
paper also offers an award for
nonfiction writing.

Recent winners of the Premio
Dantas are:

1956 Geraldo Santos. Loucos,
Poetas, Amantes (Fools,
poets, lovers)
1957 Zora Seljan. Festa do
Bomfim
1958 Ferruccio Fabbri. A
estacão
1959 Luis Beltrao. Inciação a
Filosofia de Jornalismo
293.

DANTE MEDAL (International--
Italy)

A gold medal offered in the city
of Florence (Nuovo cenacolo
Fiorentino, presso Aldemaro Nannei, v dell'Orto 22, Florence) for
an outstanding contribution to
Dantean Studies is conferred upon
'a great, foreign, living Dantist,"
during a ceremony held on the
third Sunday of May each year
(the conventional date of the
poet's birth) in Palazzo Vecchio.

Foreign authors who have
received this Italian honor for
scholarly writing about Dante,
author of Italy's best-known classic of world literature, "The
Divine Comedy," include:

1957 Jorge Guillén (Spain)
1958 T.S. Eliot (U.S.A.-
United Kingdom); Camillo
Sbarbaro (Italy)
1959 André Pezard (France);
Eugenio Montale (Italy)
1960 Pierre Jean Jouve (France)
1961 Charles S. Singleton
(U.S.A.)
1962 Theophil Spoerri (Switzerland) 294.

Rubén DARÍO PRIZE (Nicaragua)

Named for the Spanish language
poet of Nicaragua, Rubén Darío
(1867-1916), this award was
granted in 1960 to Pablo Antonio
Cuadra for his book, 'El jaguar
y la luna." Another earlier
winner of the Premio Interamericano de Poesía Rubén Darío was
the Bolivian poet, Javier del
Granado. 295.

DARMSTADT "BOOK OF MAY"
(Germany)
In 1961, a prize jury granted
this city award to Arno Schmidt
for his novel, "Kaff, auch Mare
Crisium." 296.

DAVID PRIZE (Italy)
Marina di Carrara (Segre-
tario del premio nazionale di
poesia "David," cas post,
Marina di Carrara) offers an annual prize for Italian poetry--
one to three poems published or
unpublished, not exceeding 50
verses, by a poet resident in
Italy or another country. The
award was founded in 1959 by
the industrialist Ruggero Lera
and the writer Guido Piero, and
honors the prizewinner with a
reproduction in Carrara marble of
Michelangelo's "David."
Among winners of this national recognition for an outstanding
work of Italian poetry are:
1959 Lugi Fiorentino.
Transito di cicala
1960 Tonino Ledda. Pianto di
una vedova di campagna
1961 Rosellini di Marina. Il
vollo
A similar prize for prose has
been granted:
1959 G. B. Lillia. Poveraccio
1960 Mario Previtera
297.

DAVIDS FUND PRIZE FOR
COLONIAL LITERATURE (Bel-
gium)
Winner of this literary prize
in 1957 was Jos. Gijsbrechts
for "Droog siezoen." 298.

Eve DELACROIX PRIZE (France)
Galerie Deveche (19 rue Brey,
Paris 8e) has granted this
3.000 NF prize each year since
1956 to "honor a literary work,
preferably a novel of indisput-
able literary worth and with a
deep feeling for the dignity of
man and the moral responsi-

bility of the writer." Books published from January 1 of the
year preceding award to April
30 of the year of award are eligible,
and the prize is presented on May 15.
Laureates include:
1956 Georges Bordonove. Les
armes à la main
1957 Denis de Rougemont.
L'aventure occidentale de
l'homme
1958 Luis Leprince-Ringuet.
Des atomes et des hommes
1959 Jean Guehenno. Sur le
chemin des hommes
1960 Jean Larteguy. Les
Centurions
1961 André Lang. Bagage à la
consigne 299.

Carlos DE LAET PRIZE (Brazil)
A book in the form of a
chronicle or travel report is
honored by the Academia Brasileira de Letras (Avenide Presidente Wilson 203, Rio de Janeiro)
by a Cr$50.000 prize, granted
the best such work--published or
unpublished--completed during
the two years preceding award.
Recent authors honored are:
1956 Morales de los Rios
1958 Lêdo Ivo. A Cidade e os
Dias
1960 Dante Costa. Israel,
Terra Viva
1962 Luís Henrique. Môça
Sòzinha na Sala 300.

Lucien DELARUE PRIZE (France)
One of the literary honors
granted by the Syndicat des
Journalistes et Écrivains (c/o
Lucien Delarue, 2 rue d'Igli,
Oran, Algeria) the Delarue
Prize is offered to writers of
Algeria. Winners of an award,
which consists of a diploma and
a premium (60,20,10 NF) in-
clude:
1960 Mme Meyer-Meyer;
Gilbert Lévy; Louis Joly
1961 Louis Joly; René
Pericat 301.

Grazia DELEDDA PRIZE (Italy)
Grazia Deledda, the Sardinian-
born Nobel prize-winner of 1926
is honored by this prize which
is granted for an unpublished
novel or collection of stories.
Established in 1952 and offered
biennially by Ente Provinciale
per il Turismo (via Roma 114,
Nuovo) the prize consists of a
rich premium (L 2.000.000,
formerly L 1.000.000), a gold
medal, and publication of the
winning work by Casa Editrice
Mondadori, in their series "Nar-
ratori Italiani," or "Medusa degli
Italiani." Competing works must
be submitted by May 10, and the
winner is announced on August 29,
date of the holiday, Sagra del
Redentore.

Among authors winning the
prize are:
1952 Paride Rombi. Perdu
1954 Giovanna Zangrandi. I
Brusaz
1956 Nino Palumbo.
L' impiegato d' imposte
1958 Nelio Ferrando. Un
Giornale per Luca
1960 Mario Cartasegna. Un
Fiume per Confine
1962 Liliana Scalero. La
Ruinette   302.

DELTA PRIZE NOVEL AWARD
(International--U.S.A.)
This annual $5,000 ($2,500
outright grant; $2,500 royalty
advance) prize "for a work of
outstanding fiction to be published as a paperback original"
was established in 1961 primarily "to discover and encourage fresh creative talent and
bring it to wide public and
critical attention." The contest,
open to writers of every nationality, requires that the novel
entered in competition be an
unpublished work of at least
50,000 words in the English language (writings published in
magazines as serials will be

considered for award, but English
translations of novels published
in book form in their original
language are not eligible). Works
must be received by May 31,
1962 (Dell Publishing Company,
750 Third Avenue, New York 17).
Judges for the first contest (Mary
McCarthy, Leslie Fiedler, Walter
van Tilburg Clark) were to select
a winning work to be published
as a "Delta Book" by the end of
1962. As none of the works
entered in the initial contest was
considered worthy of award, the
prize in the second contest ending June 30, 1963 is increased
to $10,000, and competing manu-
scripts will be judged by the
same jury.   303.

Felix DENAYER PRIZE (Belgium)
The Belgian Royal Academy of
French Language and Literature
grants the Denayer Prize each
year for a single work or for
the entire literary output of a
Belgian writing in French. The
award has been given since 1956
to the following authors for their
"entire literary work" unless otherwise noted:
1956 Adrien Jans
1957 G. Linze
1958 Maurice Carème. Poetical
works
1959 Carlo de May. Founder
and director of the literary
magazine, "Audace"
1960 Georges Sion
1961 Albert Ayguesparse
304.

DE SARIO PRIZE (Italy)
Honoring works in many
areas of prose writing and poetry
with monetary premiums ranging
from L 700 (for a popular poetical work) to L 200.000 (for a
collection of at least 15 poems)
and L 300.000 (for a novel), this
publisher's prize is offered by
Giacomo De Sario Editore (via
Nazionale 230, Rome) for works

submitted for consideration by
July 15. First prize winners
in 1960 were: Aldo Onorati
with his poems, "Nise;" Blan-
chette Montasio with a popular
story, "Il gabbiano ferito;" and
Germano d'Ita, Nicola Fascila,
and Laura Niobe--authors of
novellas.   305.

DEUTSCHE AKADEMIE FÜR SPRACHE UND DICHTUNG TRANSLATION PRIZE (Germany)

In addition to the Georg
Büchner Prize, the German Academy for Language and Literature
(Alexandraweg 26, Darmstadt)
also offers a translation prize
(Übersetzerpreis) for the best
translation (belles lettres and
history) from a foreign language
into German.

The 3000 DM prize, which is
awarded annually on New Year's
Day, has been won by:
  1958 Edmund and Willa Muir
  1959 Benno Geiger. Transla-
    tion of Petrarch's Lyrics
  1960 E. K. Rahsin
  1961 Jakob Hegner   306.

DEUX MAGOTS PRIZE (France)

Granted for an avant-garde
book by a young writer, the
Deux Magots Prize, named for
the Café des Deux-Magots (place
Saint-Germain-des Prés, Paris)
was first awarded in 1933. The
award has been given each
January (usually on the 22nd)
for an original work--Novel,
Essay, Poetry.
  Laureates include:
  1933 Raymond Queneau. Le
    chiendent
  1935 Jacques Baron. Charbon
    de mer
  1942 Olivier Séchan. Les
    corps ont soif
  1949 Antoine Blondin. L'Eur-
    ope buissonnière
  1958 Michel Cournot.   Le
    Premier spectateur
  1960 Bernard C. Landry.

Aide-mémoire pour Cécile
1961 Bernard Jourdan. Saint
  Picoussin   307.

Denis DEVLIN MEMORIAL FOUNDATION PRIZE (Ireland)

The Irish poet, Denis Devlin
is honored by the establishment
in 1961 by this literary award
"to reward and encourage the
writing of poetry." A triennial
prize of ℒ250-300, the honor will
first be granted in the later
summer of 1964 for a book of
poetry by an Irish citizen, written
in English, and published during
the three year period--1961-1963.

Applications for the prize,
which is administered by the Irish
Arts Council (An Chomhairle
Ealaion, 70 Merrion Square,
Dublin) are made by bringing the
competing works to the attention
of the Council. Two adjudicators,
appointed by the Council, one of
whom must be an American
citizen, will determine the winning work.   308.

Hendrik DE VRIES PRIZE (Netherlands)

A biennial award of fl 1.500
and a silver medal is the prize
granted by the Gronigen town
council, who established the
literary honor on September 10,
1946 on the occasion of the 50th
birthday of the poet and painter,
Hendrik de Vries, then resident
in Gronigen. The prize is assigned by a jury of three experts
to authors "who can be considered
representative of the literary art
circle of Gronigen." Currently
proposed changes in award procedure will grant the prize every
four years, and increase the
monetary premium to fl 2.000,
half of which will be used for a
special edition of the work of the
prize-winner.

Since the first award in 1946,
granted to Hendrik de Vries for
his entire work, winners have

been:
1948 Koos Schuur. Herfst,
Hoos en Hagel (collected
poems)
and, for their "Entire Literary
Work:"
1950 W.H. Nagel (pseud of
J.B. Charles)
1952 Sjoerd Leiker
1954 Jozef Cohen
1956 Jan Boer
1958 Ab Visser
1960 H.P. Schönfeld Wichers
(pen name: Belcampo)
309.

DEWAN BAHASA DAN PUSTAKA
LITERARY COMPETITIONS (Federation of Malaya)
In accordance with one of its
stated purposes--"to develop
literary talent, particularly in
the national language (Malay)"--
the government Language and
Literature Agency (Dewan
Bahasa dan Pustaka, Peti Surat
803, Kuala Lumpur), which is
part of the national Ministry
of Education, has organized
literary competitions since 1956.
Works may be entered in competition by any citizen of the Federation of Malaya, and a jury
determines winners from among
competing works and awards
prizes consisting of monetary
premiums (ranging from M$2,500
to M$3,500); certificates; and
publication by the Dewan Bahasa
dan Pustaka--with the prize-winning authors receiving 10 per
cent royalty on the retail price
of their works.
Literary forms specified for
award include: Short Story (in
1956); Novel (in 1958 and 1962);
Short Story for Children, between
the ages of 11 and 14 years
(in 1960). Recent recipients of
the prize (which is supplemented
by second and third prizes, and
as many as 10 consolation
prizes) include:
1956 Short Story--Hassan bin

Muhammad Ali. Pelayan tua
(Elderly hospital attendant)
1958 Novel--2nd prize (highest
awarded) Hassan bin
Muhammad Ali. Musafir
(The wanderer--a story of a
convert to Islam)
1960 Short Story--Ma'aruf bin
Mahmud. Organg Churang
Terjun Ka-jurang (The corrupt and the doomed)   310.

"DIARIO DE NOTICIAS" PRIZE
(Portugal)
The newspaper prize, established in 1957 by the "Diario de
Noticias," offers a premium of
30.000 escudos "to further Portuguese Letters and Visual Arts."
The prize, which is awarded in
alternate years to Letters
(Poetry, Novel, Drama, Novella,
Criticism, History or Journalism)
and to Art (Painting, Sculpture,
Architecture or Decorative Art),
has been given such literary winners as:
1957 Fidelino de Figueiredo.
Omeda da historia (collection
of essays)
1959 Mário Beirão. For his
entire poetical works, including "O Ultimo Lusiadada"
(1913), and "Mar de Cristo"
(1957)
1961 José Régio. As Monstruosidades Vulgares (vol 4 of
the semi-autobiographical
series: A Velha Casa)
311.

Georgi DIMITROV PRIZES
(Bulgaria)
Bulgarian state prizes, established in 1949, are awarded in
three grades and carry a monetary premium and the right to
use the title: "Dimitrov Prize
Laureate." The awards, highest
official literary honor in Bulgaria,
are directed "to stressing and
popularizing those works of literature which bring something new in
subject and treatment and mark a

certain state in the individual
work in the awarded writer, as
well as in Bulgarian literature."
   The state honor gives recognition to achievement in a number
of fields of culture. In literature, winners are selected by a
jury of "distinguished literary
critics and writers" which has
awarded prizes to authors such
as:
1949 First Class--Georgi
       Karaslavov. Entire literary
       work, especially his books
       On guard; Village tales;
       The pass of youth; Tango
     Dimiter Polyanov. Entire
       literary work, especially
       selected poems (1945)
     Hristo Radevski. Entire
       literary work, especially his
       collections of poems Pulse;
       To the parts; The air was
       not enough
     Lyudmil Stoyanov. Cholera;
       Mehmed Sinap; Colonel
       Matov's silver wedding; his
       poems about Lenin, Stalin
       and the Soviet Army, and
       his articles in defence of
       peace and democracy
Second Class-Vesselin Andreev.
     Partisan songs
     Elisavetta Bagryana. Cycle of
       verses on Stalin, Georgi
       Dimitrov, and the poem,
       "To My Son"
     Gyoncho Belev. Events in the
       life of Minko Minin
     Krustyu Belev. Antifascist
       literary work
     Assen Bossev. Victors; The
       village of Tsvetna; Joins the
       grid; and Dimitrov fire
     Stoyan T. Daskalov. Paths;
       Without Boundaries; The girl
       from the pass
     Nikolai Hrelkov. Entire
       poetical work, particularly
       the poem, "Congress at Mid-
       night"
     Kroum Kyulyavkov. Antifascist
       and progressive work in
       literature

Lamar Lalyo Marinov. Soldier's
  poems and the poem, "Goran
  Gorinov"
Kiril Penev. Entire work in
  poetry
Lozan Strelkov. Reconnaissance
  (play)
Orlin Vassilev. Alarm (play)
Kroum Velkov. The village of
  Borovo (novel)
Pavel Vezhinov. The second
  battalion
Stoyan Zagorchinov. The last
  day (novel)
Kamen Zidarov. Royal clemency
  (play)
Third Class--Dimiter Chavdarov
  -Chelkash. Literary works
  of humor and satire
Andrei Goulyashki. The
  swamp (1950, play)
Mariya Grubeshlieva. Anti-
  fascist literary work
Kamen Kalchev. Work in the
  field of children's literature
Marko Marchevski. Progressive
  literary activity
Harlan Roussev. Down the
  steep slopes
Anghel Todorov. Progressive
  poetical work
1950 Second Class--Ivan Bourin.
  The Tractor-driver's spring
  (collected verses); and the
  sketch of Penyu Genchev
Nikita Fournadjiev. Great
  days (poem)
Andrei Goulyashki. Machine
  and Tractor Station (novel)
Mladen Issayev. Star of peace
  (collected poems)
Nikola Lankov. Progressive
  poetical work
Hristo Radevski. Fables
  (collected poems)
Pantelei Zarev. Bulgarian
  literature
Third Class-Bozhidar Bozhilov.
  Agitator (collected poems)
Ivan Martinov. Miners (short
  story)
Pantelei Matev. Poems of
  peace (collected poems)
Peter Slavinski. The last

assault (novel)
1951 First Class-Dimiter Dimov.
Tobacco (novel)
Second Class-Lamar Lalyo
Marinov. Dawn over the
homeland; and Constructive
years (collected poems)
Bogomil Rainov. Verses on
the Five-Year Plan (collected
poems)
Third Class--Emil Koralov.
A school for the baring; and
Septembrist (novels)
Dimiter Methodiev. Dimitrov's
Tribe (novel in verse)
Ivan Milchev. Harvest, Cam-
paign, Fighters (poems)
1953 Second Class-Kroum Gri-
gorov. Chairman of the vil-
lage council
1960 First Class--Georgi
Karaslavov. Ordinary people
(novel)
Dimiter Talev. Trilogy: The
iron candlestick; The bells
of Prespa; and St. Eliyah's
Day
Second Class--Stefan Dichev.
For freedom, parts 1 and 2
(novel)
Nikita Fournadjiev. I followed
in your wake (collected
poems)
Hristo Ganev. Song of man
(film script)
Andre Goulyashki. The village
of Vedrovo (novel)
Third-Class--Dimiter Anghelov.
For life or death (novel)
Vasselin Hanchev. Verses
in cartridge   312.

DOBLOUG ENDOWMENT PRIZE
(Sweden)
The Swedish Academy dis-
tributes this award of Swed Kr
14,000 each year on May 17.
Nominations for the prize are
made by a jury consisting of
"one representative from the
Norwegian Association of
Writers, the senior professor
of Nordic Literature at the
University of Oslo, and one

representative from the Academy
of Science."   313.

DOMINICAN REPUBLIC NATION-
AL LITERARY PRIZES
National awards presented on
"Book Day" were given Virgilia
Díaz Grullón in 1958 for his
book of essays, "Un día cualquiera,"
published in"Cuadernos Hispano-
americanos," Madrid.   314.

DOMOWINA LITERATURE PRIZE
(Germany, East)
Karl Jannack was the winner
of the literary honor in 1961,
with 'Wir, mit der roten Nelke,"
and his autobiography, "In den
Klauen des Faschismus."
                            315.

DONCEL PRIZE (Spain)
A publisher's award for children's and young people's books,
established by Editorial Doncel
(Victor Hugo 3, Madrid 4), offers
three prizes of 20.000 pts for the
best unpublished works (Novel,
Short Story, Biography) submitted
by March 7, 1962. A 20.000
pts prize is also offered for the
best children's play submitted.
In addition to the monetary
premium, the prize winning
author also receives royalties on
a minimum first edition of 5,000
copies.
Prize-winners, who receive
the award on May 30--Spain's
Young People's Day (Dia de la
Juventud)--are;
1961 Concha Castroviejo;
Rafael Morales; Carmen
Conde; Antonio Oliver
1962 Federico Muelas (Novela);
Angela C. Ionescu (Stories);
Mariano Tudela (Biography)
                            316.

DONG IN LITERARY PRIZE
(Korea)
The Sa Sang Ge Publishing
Company (2nd-ka, Chongno,
Seoul) offers a short story prize

each year in October. Competing works must be submitted by July in the year of award to qualify for the citation and monetary premium of 500,000 hwan.

Winners since 1956, date of the first award, are:

1956 Sung Hwan Kim. Babi-do
1957 Woo Whee Sun. Flame
1958 Oh Sang Won. Treason
1959 Chang Sup Son. The surplus man   317.

DONIN ZASSHI PRIZE (Japan)

A Shinshosha Publishing Company prize, established in 1954, which is granted for an "outstanding work published in Japan's numerous donin zasshi (private-circulation magazines)."   318.

DOS ESTRELLAS PRIZE (Spain)

The "Two Star Prize" is offered by the publisher, Editorial Alhambra (Caudio Coello 76, Madrid) for "a novel on a subject connected with horses." Competing works must be submitted by a specified date (1962: August 31) to Sociedad de Fomento de la Cría Caballar, Fernan flor 6, Madrid). C. Enrique Granados received the 150.000 pts prize in 1961 for his book, "Wahoo."   319.

DOUBLEDAY CATHOLIC PRIZE CONTEST (International---U.S.A.)

"To encourage authors and to stimulate interest in all fields of Catholic writing," this publisher's prize of Doubleday & Company (575 Madison Avenue, New York 22) offers three $5,000 awards (a royalty advance) for unpublished manuscripts of a minimum length of 50,000 words, written in English, by any author--"new or established, Catholic or non-Catholic." The winning manuscript, and perhaps other manuscripts submitted during the contest period (the calendar year)

will be published by Doubleday in the U.S.A. and in Canada.

Areas of award are:

Fiction--"For the best novel of Catholic interest, whose theme and treatment embody Catholic principles and values"

Biography--"For the best biography of a Catholic figure, whose life and activities constitute a significant contribution to the Catholic heritage," including an autobiography of a Catholic

Nonfiction--"For the best book of nonfiction which personifies the spirit of Catholicism as propounded in the teachings and tradition of the Church"   320.

Holger DRACHMAN PRIZE (Denmark)

Established in memory of Holger Drachman, Danish poet and prose writer (1846-1908), on October 10, 1940, this 2.000 D kr award has been granted: Carl Erik Soya; Jens August Schade; Martin A. Hansen; Sigfred Pedersen; Borge Madsen; Knud Sonderby; Johannes Wulff; William Heinesen; Eva Drachman; Agnes Henningsen; Hans Scherfig; H.C. Branner; Knuth Becker; Per Lange.   321.

DRAUGUS NOVEL AWARD (Lithuania)

As a major cultural event of the Chicago Lithuanian community, a novel prize is offered each year by the Lithuanian Roman Catholic daily newspaper, "Draugus," the only Lithuanian daily newspaper in the free world. The prize offered to a Lithuanian writer for the best novel manuscript submitted in competition is designed "to promote Lithuanian literature and to supply the newspaper with good literary material," as the manuscript winning the prize becomes the property of the paper, where it is serialized before being published in book form.

The award consists of a citation of $1,000 premium (usually donated by 'a business or professional person of a Lithuanian community in the U.S.A. or Canada"), and it is assigned by a five-member jury, which considers manuscripts entered in competition (minimum length 200 typewritten pages).

Since its establishment in 1951, the award,which is presented on a Sunday in January or February, has been won by:
1952 Jurgis Gliauda. (pseud of Jurgis Gliaudys). Namai ant smelio (the house on the sand)
1953 Jurgis Gliauda (pseud of Jurgis Gliaudys). Oro pro nobis
1954 Algirdas Landsbergis. Kelione (The journey)
1955 Ale Ruta (pseud of Elena Viktorija Nakaite-Arbaciauskiene). Trumpa diena (A short day)
1956 Birute Pukeleviciute. Astuoni lapai (Eight leaves)
1957 Paulius Jurkus. Smilgaiciu akvarele (An aquarelle of Smilgaiciai)
1958 Jeronimas Ignatonis. Ir nevesk mus i pagunda (And lead us not into temptation)
1959 Juozas Svaistas (Balciunas) Jo suzadetine (His fiancee)
1960 Jurgis Gliauda (pseud of Jurgis Gliaudys). Siksnosparniu sostas (The throne of bats)
1961 Aloyzas Baronas. Lieptai ir bedugnes (Abysses and passages)
1962 Juozas Kralikauskas. Titnago ugnis (The fire of flint)   322.

DRESDEN LITERATURE PRIZE (Germany, East)

A literary award offered by the city of Dresden, one of a number of literary and cultural prizes granted by regions and cities in East Germany, won in 1956 by Karl Otto with "Zwinger-Sonette."   323.

Heinrich **DROSTE LITERATURE PRIZE** (Germany)

In celebration of the 75th birthday of the publisher, Heinrich Droste, the Heinrich-Droste-Literaturpreis is offered by the publishing firm, Droste Verlag (Pressehaus 4, Düsseldorf 1). The premium of 50,000 DM for the best unpublished humorous novel on a contemporary theme was awarded Hugo Hartun in 1956 for his book, 'Wunderkinder."   324.

Annette von **DROSTE-HÜLSHOFF PRIZE** (Germany)

A biennial literary prize, granted by Landschaftsverband Westfalen-Lippe (Munster, Westfalen), established in 1935 as the 'Westfalischer Literaturpreis" to recognize and encourage the work of Westphalian authors writing in High and Low German. The 5000 DM literature prize (also called "Badischer Staatspreis") alternates yearly with the Conrad von Soest Prize for painting, and each third time the cultural award may be granted for a musical composition.

The literary honor, which may be granted for a single work or for the entire literary output of an author, provided the writings depict the spirit and character of Westphalia, has brought public recognition (for their entire literary work, except as otherwise indicated) to:
1935 Josefa Berens-Totenohl. Der Femhof; Frau Magdlene (novels)

1937 Maria Kahle
1939 Karl Wagenfeld
1941 Heinrich Luhmann
1943 Christine Koch
1946 Augustin Wibbelt;
 Margarethe Windhorst
1953 Paul Schallüch; Walter
 Vollmer
1957 Ernst Meister
1961 Anton Aulke   325.

DRUM PAN-AFRICAN SHORT STORY CONTEST (Africa-- South Africa)

All Negro writers in Africa are eligible for the contest sponsored by "Drum" (15 Troye Street, Johannesburg), a monthly magazine comparable to "Ebony," described as "Africa's leading magazine" with 4,000,000 non-white readers. A first prize of ₤50 is offered and five additional prizes of one guinea each for the next best stories, published in "Drum." South African and East African stories entered in the competition should be sent directly to "Drum" and Rhodesian entries to 208-209 Bryanston House, Gordon Avenue, Salisbury. Deadline for the first contest is December 15, 1962. In a previous "Drum" literary contest, when Langston Hughes was one of the judges, a prize was won by Daniel Lanadoce Themba (South Africa) for "Mob passion;" and Peter Kumalo (South Africa) also received an award.   326.

DUCA FOUNDATION PRIZE (France)

One of the richest allowances for a French writer, the Prix de la Fondation Del Duca (2 rue des Italiens, Paris), with an endowment of a million francs, is an annual award to a French writer, which permits him to complete a literary work with freedom from immediate financial considerations. Established

in 1951 and presented each year during the late spring (April to June), the prize consisting of a monetary premium of at least 10.000 NF (1.000.000 fr in 1959) has been awarded:

1952 Paul Gadenne. La plage de Scheveningen
 Felicien Marceau. L'Homme du Roi
1954 Louis Calaferte. Requiem des innocents
 Gilbert Sigaux. Les chiens enragés
1955 Jean Rousselot. Le fleur de sang
 Gaston Chéry. Les couteaux sont de la fête
1956 Maurice Guy. L'enseigne
 Alain Robbe-Grillet. Les gommes. Le voyeur
1957 Constantin Amariu. La fiancée du silence
 Martine Cadieu. La terre est tendre
 M. Revillon. Le veau d'or et les vaches maigres
1958 Charles Le Quintrec. Noces de la terre
 René Rembeauville. La boutique des regrets éternels
1959 Jacques Lanzmann. Viva castro
1960 Jean-Pierre Chabrol. Innocents de Mars
 Jacques Coudol. Le voyage d'hiver
1961 Michel Kammerer. Au bruit du soleil
 Raphaël Sorin. Serge a trois temps
 Georges Ferdinandy. L'île sous l'eau   327.

Konrad DUDEN PRIZE (Germany)

The city of Mannheim (Rathaus, E. 5) established the prize in 1960 as an award for outstanding service to contemporary German language. Planned as a biennial award, the prize was given for the first time--in 1960--to Leo Weisgerber.   328.

Rémy DUMONCEL PRIZE
(France)

A French popular novel
prize (Prix du Roman Populaire)
established in 1954 with a 5.000
NF premium to honor the best
unpublished popularly written
novel, which carries on the
great tradition of France's
roman populaire. Manuscripts
competing for the publisher's
prize offered by Editions Tal-
landier (17 rue Remy-Dumoncel,
Paris 14e) must be at least
300 pages in length and must be
submitted for consideration by
April 10.

 Laureates are:
 1954 Jean d'Astor. La sorcière
  du crépuscule
 1955 Georges Godefroy. Les
  naufrageurs
 1956 Anne-Mariel. Je me
  damnerai pour toi
 1957 Raymond Dumay. La
  moisson de sel
 1958 Saint-Bray. Inez
  de la nuit
 Denise Noel. Le miel amer
 1959 Liliane Robin. Malgré
  la trahison
 1960 Michelle Campards.
  Opération coeur perdu
 1961 Stéphane Murat. Qui
  sème la vengeance?
        329.

DURCHON-LOVET PRIZE
(France)

The Académie Française
awards from one to ten prizes
each year from the return on
the endowment of the Durchon-
Louvet Foundation, with the
prizes designated 'Grand Prix
de l'Empire," and Grand Prize
in History, in Literary History,
and in Philosophy.

Writers honored with the
award, which reached 50.000
fr in 1956, include:
 1944 (first award) Paul
  Azan. Entire work (Grand
  Prix de l'Empire)

1955 Noel Bernard. Yersin
1956 Romain Gary. Entire
 work (25.000 fr)
 André Berry. Poetic work
 (50.000 fr)
1957 Maurice Regard
1958 R. Georgin. Works in
 the French language
1960 Auguste Dupouy; Henri
 Dupuy-Mazuel
1961 Nicole Védrès
1962 Dominique Fernandez
        330.

DUTCH ACADEMY OF LETTERS
PRIZE (Netherlands)

Authors winning the award,
granted for the entire work of a
writer, include:
 1953 Adriaan van der Veen
 1955 Dola de Jong   331.

DUTCH LITERATURE PRIZE
(Netherlands; Belgium--'Grote"
Prijs der Nederlandse Letteren)

A cultural treaty between
Belgium and the Netherlands
established this literature prize
in 1956. "The most honored
literary prize in the Dutch language," the prize was instituted
upon a proposal of the Conference
of Netherlands Literature (Con-
ferentie der Nederlandse Letteren)
and is granted every third (or
fifth) year alternately to a
Flemish and a Dutch writer 'to
distinguish significant authors
writing in the Dutch language."

The prize (75.000 B Fr/
6.000 H Fl), administered by
the Minister van Openbaar Onderwijs, Brussels, and the Minister
van Onderwijs Kunsten en Wetenschappen, Amsterdam, is awarded
authors for their entire literary
work in poetry or in factual or
imaginative prose. Winners
receive the award in an impressive ceremony on October 25--
Netherlands authors are presented their honor by the King of
Belgium in Brussels, and Belgian
authors receive their prize from

the Queen of the Netherlands at
The Hague.
    Winners have been:
    1956 Herman Tierlinck
    (Belgium). Entire work,
    including the recently pub-
    lished autobiographical novel
    "Zelfportret of galgemaal"
    1959 Adriaan Roland Holst
    (Netherlands)   332.

DUTCH MASTERHIP OF LET-
TERS PRIZE (Netherlands--
Meester-prijs van de Maats-
shappij der Nederlandes)

Granted by the Society of
Netherlands Literature (Maatschappij der Nederlandse Letterkunde, Rapenburg 12, Leiden)
since 1921 to signify "mastership
in the art of writing a book,"
this fl 1.000 prize is awarded
every fifth year.
    Laureates include:
    1921 Jac. van Looy. Jaapje
    (novel)
    1925 P.C. Boutens. Zomer-
    wolken (poetry)
    1931 A. E. van Giffen. De
    hunebedden in Nederland;
    and Die Bauart der Einzel-
    graber in den Niederlanden
    (archaeology)
    1934 Henriëtte Roland Holst-
    van der Schalk. Entire
    work
    1939 Wobbe de Vries. Entire
    work in linguistics
    1950 J. S. Bartstra. Entire
    work in history
    1954 M. Schönfeld. Entire
    work in linguistics
    1959 F. L. Ganshof (Belgium)
    Entire work in history
                            333.

DUTCH NOVELLA PRIZE
(Netherlands)

Annual award of the Netherlands booksellers' trade organization, Commission for the Promotion of the Netherlands Book

(C.P.N.B.--Commissie voor de
Propaganda van het Nederlandse
Boek, of the Bevordering van de
Belangen des Boekhandels, Jan
Tooropstraat 109, Amsterdam),
granted each spring--usually March
--for the best novella. The public
is invited to guess the prize-winner's name, which is announced
during Boekenweek.

Winners of the fl 2.000 award
(increased to fl 3.000 in 1962)
are:
    1947 Antoon Coolen. De
    ontmoeting
    1948 Hella Haasse. Oeroeg
    1949 Clare Lennart. Twee
    negerpopjes
    1950 Marianne Philips. De
    Zaak Beukenoot
    1951 Olaf J. de Landell. De
    porseleintafel
    1952 Manuel van Loggem.
    Insecten in plastic
    1957 J. Presser. De nacht
    der Girondijnen
    1958 A. Defresne. Het gehucht
    1959 Hella Haasse. Dat weet
    ik zelf niet
    1960 E. de Jong-Keesing. De
    zalenman
    1961 Agaath van Ree. De
    onbekende uren   334.

DUTCH PRIZE FOR THE BEST
CHILDREN'S BOOK (Netherlands
--Prijs voor het Beste Kinder-
boek)

Since 1955 the Netherlands
booksellers trade organization,
Commission for the Promotion
of the Netherlands Book (C.P.
N.B.--Commissie voor de
Propaganda van het Nederlandse
Boek, of the Vereeniging ter
Bevordering van de Belangen des
Boekhandels, Jan Tooropstraat
109, Amsterdam) has offered a
prize for the best children's book.

Winners of the award, which
is granted in the fall of the
year--usually between September

and December--and brings fl 1.000 to the selected author-- include:

1955 A. Rutgers van der Loeff-Basenau. Lawines razen
1956 Cor Bruyn. Lasse Länta
1957 Miep Diekmann. De boten van Brakkeput
1958 Annie M. G. Schmidt. Wiplala
1959 Harriet Laurey. Sinter-klaas en de struikrovers
1960 C. E. Pothast-Gimberg. Corso het ezeltje
1961 Jan Blokker. Op zoek naar een oom   335.

DUTTON ANIMAL-BOOK AWARD
(International--U.S.A.)

This annual publisher's literary prize of E.P. Dutton & Company (201 Park Avenue South, New York 3) guarantees $7,500 to the author of the winning manuscript--"a book-length work of adult fiction or nonfiction relating to animals." The international competition is "open to new authors and to authors whose works have already been published, to authors in the United States and to foreign authors," for manuscripts in English of at least 35,000 words--narratives "in which the chief protagonist is an animal, large or small, tame or wild, native or foreign."

The first contest (May 1, 1962 to December 31, 1962) was established following the "enthusiastic critical and public reception" of Gavin Maxwell's account of two otters he owned, 'Ring of bright water." Entries must not have been published in book form, but may have been published "in serial or condensed form in a magazine, or "developed from a short story in a magazine."

The winning manuscript, selected on such considerations as "ease and effectiveness of writing, narrative interest, credibility of plot, atmosphere and scientific background," and perhaps other entries will be published by Dutton during the year following the contest period.

1963 winner: Sterling North. Rascal   336.

EAST FLANDERS PRIZE
(Belgium--Prijs van de Provincie Oost-Vlanderen)

The Belgian province of East Flanders offers this annual prize, which is one of many literary rewards and prizes granted by cities and regions (as Antwerp and Brabant) in Belgium for the work of Flemish language authors.

Winners, who may receive the award for a variety of writing (Novel, Poetry, Drama, Essay, Monograph, Youth Book), include:

1958 Gerry Hederensberg.
Triomf van de dood (poetry)
Frans Sierens. De kleurloze (play)
G. M. van der Gucht. De Madonna en de Knechtjes (youth book)
1959 G. M. van der Gucht. De Moordenaar leeft gelukkig (novel)
Valeer van Kerkhoven. Personlijke Motieven (play)
1960 M. Cordemans. Dr Laporta en De Student. (monograph)
J. L. de Belder. Sully Prudhomme of de abdicatie van het hart   337.

EAST GERMAN MINISTRY FOR CULTURE PRIZES

The Ministerium für Kultur of the D.D.R. (Deutsche Demokratische Republik) offers literary awards, among its cultural honors, in several areas of writing to bring official public recognition to established authors and to encourage new writers.

Included in the government honors for writers are:

Encouragement of Contemporary Literature (Förderung des Gegenwartsschaffens)-- A biennial prize established in 1955 as a stipend for writers. Among the number of awards (15 or 20 at each presentation) are those for:

1955 Benno Voelkner, Martin Selber, Hans Schönroch, Herbert Otto, Joachim Kupsch, Dinah Nelken, Helmut Hauptmann, Bernhard Seeger, Herbert Ziergiebel, Harald Hauser, Werner Salchow, Franz Fühmann, Uwe Berger, Kurt Buccholz, Peter Jokostra, Gerhard Wolf

1957 Karl Mundstock, Hans Grundig, Egon Günther, Werner Ilberg, Wolfgang Joho, Heiner Müller, Bernhard Seeger, Harry Thurk, Horst Beseler, Franz Kain, Hans-Günter Krack, Jupp Müller, Jan Petersen, Paul Kanut Schäfter, Wolfgang Schreyer, Werner Steinberg, Peter Jokostra, Georg Maurer

Recognition for the Best Literary Translation (Anerkennung der besten literarischen Übersetzung)--Among writers receiving the prize in 1956 were: Erich Arendt, Gunter Jarosch, Kuba, Rudolf Schaller, Eva Schumann.

Prize for Children and Youth Literature (Preis für Kinder- und Jugend-Literatur)--An annual award since 1951, with a number of recipients each year, such as Anna Jurgen, Benno Pludra, Horst Beseler, Ludwig Renn, Rudolf Kirsten, Gerhard Hardel, Helmut Hauptmann.
338.

EAST GERMAN NATIONAL PRIZE FOR LITERATURE

Highest literary prize of the D.D.R. (Deutsche Demokratische Republik) is the Nationalpreis für Literatur, one of several annual cultural prizes, offered as Nationalpreis für Kunst und Literatur, to bring official government recognition for achievement in four major fields: Science, Technology, Art, and Literature. The awards are granted for work of "high ideals and artistic worth which contributes to the cultural and democratic growth of the German Republic." Over 50 prizes may be presented each year for individual and group achievement on October 7, the national holiday celebrating the founding of the D.D.R.

Included among the recipients of this high government reward (offered in three classes-- Class I, 100.000 DM; Class II, 50.000 DM; Class III, 25.000 DM) are:

Class I
Entire work or Several Titles
1949 Heinrich Mann. Der Untertan Heinrich IV; Ein Zeitalter wird besichtigt
Johannes R. Becher
1950 Arnold Zweig
1951 Martin Andersen-Nexö (Denmark)
Anna Seghers
1952 Erich Weinert, especially Memento Stalingrad; Camaradas
1953 Lion Feuchtwanger
1955 Leonhard Frank
1961 Ludwig Renn
Walter Gorrisch, especially for the film Fünf Patronenhülesen
Novel
1959 Anna Seghers. Die Entscheidung
Poetry
1950 Johannes R. Becher. National anthem of the D.D.R.
Drama
1951 Bertolt Brecht. Mutter Courage und ihre Kinder

Class II
Entire Work or Several Titles
1950 Willi Bredel
1954 Ehm Welk
  Bodo Uhse, especially his novel, Patrioten
1955 Ludwig Renn, especially his novel, Trini
1956 Louis Fürnberg, especially the story, Bruder Namenlos und sein Lieder
1958 Otto Gotsche, especially his novel, Zwischen Nacht und Morgen
1959 Stefan Heym
  Jan Petersen
  Kuba (Kurt Bartel), especially the literary arrangements for the Rügenfestspiele
1961 Hans Lorbeer, especially Das Fegefever; Der Widerruf
  Walther Victor, for popularization of classical German literature for the general reader, and his writings for young people
Novel
1949 Bernhard Kellermann, Der 9 November
Drama
1949 Friedrich Wolf. Professor Mamlock
Other Prose
1956 Johannes von Guenther. Creative free translation of Russian works.

Class III
Entire Work or Several Titles
1949 Herbert Eulenberg
1950 Hans Marchwitza, especially his novels, Die Kumiak; Meine Jugend
1955 Alexander Abusch, especially, Schiller
1957 Benno Voelkner, especially, Die Leute von Karvenbruch
  Franz Fühmann, especially his war stories
1958 Kuba (Kurt Bartel) especially the ceremony for the 40th anniversary of the Grossen Sozialistischen Oktoberrevolution
1959 Helmut Sakowski
  Fred Reichwald

1960 Werner Eggerath, especially for the novel, Wassereinbruch
1961 Raimund Schelcher
Novel
1951 Eduard Claudius.
  Menschen an unserer Seite
  Juij Brezan. Auf dem Rain wächst Korn
1952 Maria Langner. Stahl
1953 Karl Grünberg. Brennende Ruhr
1955 Hans Marchwitza. Roheisen
  Erwin Strittmatter. Tinko
1958 Bruno Apits. Nackt unter Wölfen
Poetry
1949 Kuba (Kurt Bartel). Gedicht vom Menschen
1951 Peter Huchel. Entire lyric work
Drama
1950 Gustav von Wangenheim. Du bist der Tichtige
1953 Erwin Strittmatter. Katzgraben
  Heinar Kippnardt. Shakespeare dringend gusucht
1954 Hedda Zinner. Teufelskreis
1960 Harald Hauser. Weisses Blut
1961 Helmut Bairl
  Manfred Werkweruth. Frau Flinz
Short Story
1949 Erich Weinter. Rufe in die Nacht
1952 Erich Arendt. Trug coch die Nacht den Albatros; Berwindballade
Other Prose
1950 Stephan Hermlin. Mansfelder Oratorium
  Paul Rilla. Literary history and criticism, especially work concerning Lessing

339.

EAST GERMAN ORDER FOR SERVICE TO THE FATHERLAND

A cultural honor of the D.D.
R., offered in several degrees,
which has been awarded such
authors of the Deutsche Demo-
kratische Republik as:
Ludwig Renn (1959, Gold
Order)
Walter Gorrisch (1957, Silver
Order)
Hans Lorbeer (1958, Silver
Order)
Willi Göber (Bronze Order)
340.

EAST GERMAN PEACE MEDAL
A general cultural prize of
the D.D.R., which has been
granted citizens of the Deutsche
Demokratische Republik as the
author, Ludwig Renn.   341.

**EAST GERMAN WRITERS' AS-
SOCIATION PRIZE**
Established in 1957, this
prize of the national writers'
group, Ost-Deutscher Schrifttum,
a "Kunsterlergilde" of Esslingen,
is presented each year in
October for outstanding works by
East German writers. The award
which has increased in premium
from an initial 1500 DM to
10.000 DM (1960), has honored
such authors as:
1957 Heinz Piontek; Gerhart
Pohl
1958 Edzard Schaper
1959 August Scholtis; also
an "Encouragement Prize"
of 1000 DM to Herbert
Schmidt-Kaspar
1960 Horst Lange; also
"Encouragement Prize" of
3000 DM each to Franz
Bahl; Richard Tschon; and
the Polish novelist, Tadeusz
Nowakowski, author of
"Polonaise Allerheiligen"
342.

ECUADOR NATIONAL PRIZE
In 1935 a national literary
honor was granted to Jorge Icaza
for his novel, "En las calles"
(In the streets).   343.

Joris EEKHOUT PRIZE (Belgium)
The Flemish language prize,
granted by the Belgian Royal
Academy of Flemish Science,
Letters and the Arts, was won
in 1958 by Raf Seys for his work,
"De dichter der Rozen."   344.

**EGYPTIAN STATE AWARDS FOR
OUTSTANDING INTELLECTUAL
ACHIEVEMENT**
A gold medal and a monetary
premium of 1500 Egyptian pounds
honor the individual "who has
achieved outstanding work in the
field of science, social sciences,
literature, or the fine arts."
345.

**EGYPTIAN STATE AWARDS FOR
THE ADVANCEMENT OF SCI-
ENCE, SOCIAL SCIENCES, LIT-
ERATURE, AND THE FINE ARTS**
A periodic continuous cultural
prize, with 28 awards of 500
Egyptian pounds each, distributed
among four areas of knowledge:
Science (16 awards); Social
Sciences (3 awards); Law and
Economy (3 awards); Fine Arts
(3 awards) and Literature (3
awards). An Egyptian honored
with an award may be considered
for a subsequent award after five
years.   346.

**EIFEL-ARDENNEN LITERATURE
PRIZE** (Europe)
The organization, Europäische
Vereinigung für Eifel und Ardennen
awards the literature prize, as part
of the yearly Eifel-Ardennen Literature and Art Prizes. In literature,
the prize is granted for a literary
work that furthers the purpose of the
Vereinigung and concerns the significance of the Eifel-Ardennen area, in
the heart of the European industrial
organization. Belgian, German,
French, or Luxembourg writers
are eligible for the award,
which in 1960 was granted to
Maurice Schadeck, and in 1961

to Paul Dresse.   347.

EINAUDI PRIZES (Italy)
    The Premi Nazionali, national
cultural awards of Italy, were
established by Luigi Einaudi,
President of the Italian Republic,
and are awarded by the national
academy of Italy, Accademia
Nazionale dei Lincei, Rome.
These prizes replace the Premio
Reale, the Royal Prizes which
were formerly presented by the
King of Italy. The prize consists of four awards of L 1.000.
000 each which are granted for
the highest national achievement
in scholarly and professional
writing--two awards for humanistic
writing, and two awards for scientific works.
    First prizes granted in 1949,
year of establishment of the
award, are:
    O.M. Olivo. Bio-electric
      phenomena of the cardiac
      cell (General Prize--Mathe-
      matical and Natural Sci-
      ences)
    G.P.S. Occhialini. Nuclear
      physics research and dis-
      covery of the heavy meson
      (Physics)
    R. Mondolfo. History of
      philosophy (General Prize--
      Moral Sciences)
    C. Anti. Researches in
      ancient Greek Theatres
      (Archaeology)   348.

EISTEDDFOD POETIC COMPE-
TITION (Wales)
    The "annual congress of bards
and literati" of Wales follows
a century-old tradition, of
which the current annual meetings
in a national poetry competition
are a 19th century revival.
Competitors must submit works
entered in the contest to
Ystradgynlais Eisteddfod Committee (Cardiff). Writings
entered in competition must be
odes of specified length (300 to

350 lines), in a strict meter and
upon a specified subject, which
is announced each year.
    In 1960 no entries (Ode Sub-
jects: "Glamorgan," a Welsh
county; or "The Day of Judgment
and the End of the World") met
the high standards of the competition. John Evans, a Welsh
schoolmaster, has several times
won the national competition over
a field of entrants to have his
ode read at eisteddfod--most
recently, in 1954 with a 350 line
poem about the flooding of a
Welsh village.   349.

EL SALVADOR NATIONAL PRIZES
IN SCIENCES AND LETTERS
    The literature section of the
national government prize of
¢8.000, Premio de Letras, was
won in 1948--the first and only
time the prize has been awarded
--by Miguel Angelo Espino, with
"Hombres contra la muerte."
                              350.

EL SALVADOR NATIONAL
CULTURAL AWARDS (Certamen
Nacional de Cultura)
    All Central American writers
are eligible for the annual government awards of El Salvador,
which are granted for cultural
achievement in the arts (Painting
and Sculpture) and the sciences,
as well as in literature. Literary awards include rotating prizes
for: Novel and Poetry; Short
Story; Essay; Drama; and
Factual Writing. The prizes,
established in 1955 and presented
each year on December 14, the
anniversary of the El Salvador
Revolution of 1948, are given in
two classes: First Prize--
"Premio de Republica de El
Salvador," 8.000 colones salvadorenos (approximately $3,200),
and contract for publication of
the winning work; Second Prize
--Diploma of honor, silver medal,
4.000 colones salvadorenos, and

contract for publication of the
winning work. Unpublished works
in Spanish may be submitted
in competition (Ministerio de
Cultura, Direccion General de
Bellas Artes, San Salvador) by
the annual deadline of August 31.

The El Salvador national
prize in letters, awarded by a
jury of three authorities, has
honored such writers of El
Salvador and other countries
(nationality indicated if other
than Salvadorean) as:
Poetry 1955 Salomón de la
    Selva (Nicaragua). Evoa-
    ción de Píndaro
    1962 Isaac Felipe Azofeifa
    (Costa Rica); Alberto
    Ordóñez Arguëllo (Nicara-
    gua)
Essay 1957 Juan Felipe Toruño
    (Nicaragua). Desarrollo
    literario de El Salvador
    Rafael Antonio Tercero.
    Masferrer, una ana contra
    el huracán
Drama 1958 Walter Béneke.
    Funeral home
    Roberto Arturo Menéndez. La
    ira del cordero   351.

EMECÉ PRIZE (Latin-America--
Argentina)
    This publisher's prize for
Fiction (novels or short stories)
of Emecé Editores (Alsina 2061
Buenos Aires), first awarded
in 1954, is granted at the end
of each year for the best manuscript by a Latin American
writer, which is submitted in
competition. Recipients of the
prize, consisting of a premium
(m$n 50.000--fifty thousand
Argentine pesos) and publication
of the winning work in March-
April of the year following
award, are:
    1954 Beatriz Guido (Argentina)
        La casa del ángel
    1955 Federico Peltzer (Argen-
        tina). Tierra de nadie
    1956 Alberto Ponce de Leon

(Argentina). La quinta
1957 Giselda Zani (Uruguay).
    Por vínculos sutiles
1958 Margarita Aguirre (Chile).
    El huésped
1959 Rubén A. Benítez (Ar-
    gentina). Ladrones de luz
1960 Polo Godoy Rojo (Argen-
    tina). Campo gaucho
1961 Estela L. de Lacau
    (Argentina). Rastrojo
                            352.

ENCOUNTER PRIZE (Nigeria--
United Kingdom)
    Wole Soyinko won the prize of
the magazine, "Encounter" (25
Haymarket Street, London, S.W.
1) with his play, "A dance of the
forest," written for the Nigerian
Independence Celebration.   353.

ENCYCLOPAEDIA BRITANNICA
PRESS PRIZE (International--
U.S.A.)
    Encyclopaedia Britannica
Press, the newly established
(1962) general and educational
publishing division of the Encyclopaedia Britannica, announces
for 1962-1963 an international
competition for the "best manuscript submitted for publication
which makes the most significant
contribution to the advancement
of knowledge." Manuscripts
may be submitted in any language,
and should be "original works of
reasonable general interest aimed
at an adult audience," must be
over 25,000 words in length, and
must not have been previously
published in whole or in part.
The competition is planned as an
annual contest, with deadline for
entries August 1 each year (first
contest deadline, August, 1963),
with the winner announced and
published early in the following
year. The prize offers $10,000
as an outright grant, in addition
to all royalty and income, and
the winning work, in addition to
being published in book form by

Antonio Enes Prize** 111

1960 Jean Ollivier. Deux
oiseaux ont disparu
1961 Yvonne Meynier. Une
petite fille attendait
1962 R. Recher. Rüdi et le
chamois   356.

Antonio ENES PRIZE (Portugal)

The prize, offered for writings in journalism, or doctrinal and polemical works, is granted from time to time with no specified frequency. Among the nine prizes awarded from 1934 to 1944 are those to:

1934 Augusto da Costa.
Portugal--Vasto Império
1937 Luís de Pina. Em
Verdade Vos Diego...
1941 João Mendes. Os três,
verbos da vida
1943 José Sebastião da Silva
Dias. Escandalo da verdade
1944 Dário Martins de
Almeida. Series of articles
published in "Diário da Manhã"   355.

ENFANCE DU MONDE PRIZE
(International--France--Prix
Enfance du Monde)

This 2.000 NF international literary prize of the organization for children, C.I.E. (Centre International de l'Enfance, Château de Longchamps, Bois de Boulogne, Paris 16e), was established in 1954 as an annual award to distinguish an outstanding unpublished book for children of from 8 to 12 years of age.

The jury of distinguished writers and scholars has awarded the prize--usually presented in April or May--to such authors as:

1956 Léonce Bourliaguet.
Pouk et les loups-garous
1957 Michel-Aimé Boudouy.
Le seigneur des Hautes
Buttes
1958 René Guillot. Grischka
et son ours
1959 L.-N. Navolle. Numo
de Nazaré

ENFANTS TERRIBLES PRIZE
(France)

A novel award, established in 1961, with a 100 NF premium for a young writer, under 24 years of age, for an avante garde or "nonconformist" work of fiction. The jury of seven (c/o M. A. Payraud, 34 rue Saint-Didier, Paris), of which Jean Cocteau is president, awarded the prize in January 1962 to Nikolas Genka for his book, "Épi monstre."   357.

Camille ENGELMANN PRIZE
(Belgium)

The Belgian Royal Academy of French Language and Literature administers the prize for a literary work (Drama, Poetry, Novel), which was founded by l'Association Pour le Progrès Intellectuel et Artistique de la Wallonie with a premium to be given each year (75.000 fr). The contest is open to all authors, regardless of nationality, writing in French, and unpublished works as well as published books (released between May 1 and November 15 of the year of competition) must be submitted for consideration by December 31 (M. Pierre Martin, 2 place Saint-Aubain, Namur).

Among recent winners are:
1958 Albert Ayguesparse. Le
vin noir de Cahors
1959 Marc Blancpain. La femme
d'Arnaud vient de mourir
1961 Robert Vivier. Chronos
Reve
Liliane Wouters. Le Bois
Sec   358.

ENGHIEN-LES-BAINS GRAND
LITERARY PRIZE FOR DRAMA
(France)
   A drama prize, offered under
the patronage of "Paris-Presse,"
is granted each year by Société
des eaux d'Enghien (10 rue
Caumartin, Paris 9e), an organization that established the
award in 1951 as part of the
centennial celebration of the
commune, Enghien-les-Bains--
a town located north of Paris
in Seine-et-Oise Department and
known for its springs and baths.
Play manuscripts are entered
in competition with three
typed copies submitted by March
31, and the prize is granted in
June.
   Playwrights honored with the
First Prize of 10.000 NF
(Second and Third Prizes are
also awarded) include:
   1951 Georges Bouyx. Gauvain
   1953 Jules Roy. Le cyclone
   1954 Jeanne Waltz. Le
      portrait de Don Philippe
   1955 Claude Magnier.
      Monsieur Masure
   1956 Jacques François.
      Monsieur de France
   1957 Jacques Mauclair. L'oncle
      Otto; Gilbert Cesbron.
      L'homme seul
   1958 Max Rouquette. Le
      pastorale des voleurs
   1959 Gilbert Nery. Erica de
      Berlin
   1960 Yves Jamiaque. Les
      cochons d'Inde
   1961 Jean-Jacques Varoujean.
      Facades
   1962 Robert Beauvais.
      Quelques jours de vacances
                                    359.

ENGLISH ASSOCIATION OF
SOUTH AFRICA LITERARY
PRIZE FUND (South Africa)
   Each year since 1959 literary
competition for creative writing
has been held by the English
Association, South African

Branch (P.O. Box 81, Rondebosch,
Capetown). A prize of £50 is
offered for the best work in the
form specified for the year--such
as poetry; short story.   360.

ENTE NACIONALE PER LE
BIBLIOTECHE POPULARI E
SCOLASTICHE PRIZE (Italy)
   Granted under the direction
of the E.N.B.P.S. (the National
Society for Public and School
Libraries, via Montanelli 11,
Rome), these awards were
initiated with a literary competition in 1953, and are offered
for cultural achievement in
various areas of writing--an-
nounced from year to year. In
1959, three prizes were offered:
(1) Stories for Children--L
1.000.000; (2) Stories for Adults
--L 2.000.000; and (3) Monograph on a set subject--L 1.000.
000.
   Winners of the First Prize
include:
   Adult Stories
   1956 Michele A. Serra. A
      ciascun giorno el proprio
      affano
   1957 N. Cima. Gli uomini non
      piangono
   1959 Alfredo Baiocco. La
      vigilia e la festa (novel)
      Luigi Pompilj. Un uomo
      felice (novella)
   Children's Stories
   1953 Guglielmo Vallo.
      Trombetta d'oro
   1957 René Reggiani. Quando i
      sogni non hanno soldi
   1959 Giovanni Floris. La
      avventure di Biondomoro
                                    361.

ERASMUS AWARD (Europe--
Netherlands)
   A general cultural prize of
the European Cultural Foundation
(Fondation Europeenne de la
Culture) in Amsterdam, the
Erasmus Award is a pan-
European honor for the creative

artist whose work is most in the spirit of the "First European," Erasmus (1466?-1536), Dutch scholar of Rotterdam. The premium of 100.000 florins is awarded each year for cultural contribution in literature and the arts. In 1959 the prize was presented to Karl Jaspers and Robert Schuman, and in 1962 to P. Romano Guardini, for his entire work, including studies concerning Dante, Dostoevskii, Socrates, Rilke, and Pascal.
362.

Concha ESPINA PRIZE (Spain)
Novels and poetry are honored by the award granted each year by Ayuntamiento de Torrelavega. Prize winners, who have received a premium varying from 25.000 to 50.000 pts, include:
1955 Manuel Arce. Testamento en la Montaña (novel)
Aurora Díaz-Plaja. Lux en la sombra
1956 Ricardo Fernández de la Reguera. Bienaventurados los que Aman (Novel)
Gerardo Diego. Un nave en el Mar (poetry)   363.

Manuel ESPINOSA Y CORTINA PRIZE (Spain)
The Spanish Academy (Real Academia Espanola) offers an award of 4,000 pts for a major dramatic work by a Spanish writer. The prize, granted each five years, considers significant plays presented for the first time during the quinquennial contest period.   364.

ESSO (COLOMBIA) LITERARY PRIZE (Colombia--Premio Literario ESSO)
This annual award was granted for the first time on April 13, 1962, during a special session of the Academia Colombiana de la Lengua to mark the celebration of the "Day of the Spanish Language." The prize, consisting of Ps$25.00, and an edition of 5,000 copies of the winning work, was initiated by ESSO Colombiana (International Petroleum (Colombia) Ltd, Cra 72, # 36-45, Bogota) "to stimulate creative writing in Colombia." Eligible to compete for the award are unpublished works (by Colombian citizens) which must be sent in an original and two copies to ESSO before November 30. Literary forms considered are rotated each year (Novel, Drama, Poetry, History, and others), and in 1962 novel manuscripts (less than 100 typed pages) are called for in the "Gran Concurso Nacional de Novela."   365.

ESTACIONES LITERARY PRIZES (Mexico)
Compania Vincola de Saltillo sponsored several competitions for writers in 1957, which were administered by the literary review, 'Estaciones (Revillagigedo 108-202, Mexico, D.F.). The contests and their winners were:
Estaciones Drama Contest-- Hugo Arguelles Cano. Los prodigiosos
Estaciones Poetry Contest-- Mauricio Gómez Mayorga. Muerte en el Bosque
Estaciones Short Story Contest --Raymundo Ramos. Muerte amura llada   366.

ETNA-TAORMINA INTERNATIONAL POETRY PRIZE (International --Italy)
One of the major international prizes for poetry, this award offered by the compartment of Sicily (Assessorato Turismo, Regione Siciliana) and the Sicilian commune of Catania (E.P.T. di Catania, via Pacini) is open to all poets of Europe, Asia, United States of America, and Latin America who have had a book of poetry published during the period

of competition (most recently, 1959-1961). A jury of Italian poets, publishers and critics selects the winning book, which receives a rich premium of L 2.000.000.
Among the poets honored are:
1953 Dylan Thomas (United Kingdom, Wales). Posthumous award for his collected poems published in January 1952, a few months before his death
Salvatore Quasimodo (Italy)
1956 Jules Supervielle (France) Camillo Sbarbaro
1959 Diego Valeri (Italy); Jorge Guillén (Spain); V. Cardarelli (Italy) (PREMIO REGIONE SICILIANA)
1961 Leonardo Sinisgalli (Italy); Tristan Tzara (France), founder of the Dada group in Zurich, and early (1922) participant in Parisian avant garde poetry and "engaged" literature.   367.

EUROPEAN LITERARY PRIZE (Europe--Switzerland--Prix littéraire Européen)
Offered a single time in 1952, this award of the European Book Clubs Community, an organization of European Book Publishers' Associations and Book Clubs, was granted by Centre Européen de la Culture (Ville Moynier 122, rue de Lausanne, Geneva) for the best book entered in competition by any author, without limitation as to the nationality of the writer, language of writing, or subject of the work. National juries in each of the participating countries considered 356 manuscripts and forwarded eight (3 German, 2 Spanish, 2 Italian, 1 French) for consideration of the international jury, whose members included such world-famous writers as Salvador Madriaga, Ignazio Silone,

Elizabeth Bowen, Gottfried Benn. The premium of 10.000 swiss francs was evenly divided in 1953 between the two prize-winning works, both novels: Czeslaw Milosz (exiled Pole, writing in French), "Prise de pouvoir;" and Werner Warsinsky (German), "Kimmerische Fahrt."
368.

Johannes EWALD SCHOLARSHIP (Denmark)
An annual award of 2.000 D kr is offered in memory of Johannes Ewald (1743-1781), Danish national lyric poet and dramatist, who wrote the national festival drama of Denmark, "The Fishers," containing the Danish National Anthem: "King Christian Stood By the Lofty Mast." A special prize committee "consisting of a representative from the Ministry for Cultural Affairs (Chairman) and from the Board of the Danish Authors' Association," has granted the national literary honor to such writers as:
1954 Poul la Cour; Martin A. Hansen
1955 Ove Abildgaard; H.C. Branner
1956 Kjeld Abell; Jacob Paludan
1957 Alex Garff; Sigurd Elkjaer
1958 Johannes Wulff; Hans Hartvig Seedorff
1959 Per Lange; Karl Bjarnhof
1960 Knuth Becker; Mogens Jermiin Nissen
1961 Grethe Risbjerg Thomsen; C. E. Soya   369.

"L'EXPRESS" PRIZE (France)
Formerly called "Nouvelle Vague" Prize, this literary award is presented each year in December by the weekly paper, "L'Express" (91 Champs-Elysées, Paris) for the best novel, journalism or essay interpreting the sentiments or ideals of the generation which today is at least 35

years of age.
    Recipients of the 1.000 NF
premium include:
    1958 Christiane Rochefort.
    Le repos de guerrier
    1959 Yves Bonnefoy. Hier
    régnant désert
    1960 Claude Simon. La
    route de Flandres   370.

Max EYTH PRIZE (Germany)
    This literary reward for out-
standing technical writing, along
with several other literary
honors (Niedersachs Literaturpreis,
Literaturpreis des Kulturkreises
der Deutschen Industrie) is
granted by the V.D.I. (Vereinigung der Industrie--und Handel-
skammerodes Landes Nordrhein-
Westfalen, Goldsteinstrasse 31,
Dusseldorf).   371.

Mauricio FABRY PRIZE (Chile)
    Camara Chilena del Libro
established the annual literary
prize in memory of Mauricio
Fabry. The award is given for
the best novel or book of short
stories, written by a Chilean
writer or by a foreign author
with five years' residence in
Chile. Recipients of the Eº
250 premium are designated by a
jury, whose members include a
winner of the Chilean National
Prize, and representatives from
Academia Chilena de la Lengua,
Sociedad de Escritores de Chile,
and Camara Chilena del Libro.
Among recent winners are:
    1959 Jose Manuel Vergara.
    Daniel y los leones
    dorados
    1960 Manuel Rojas. Mejor
    que el vino
    1961 Daniel Belmar. Los
    Tuneles Dorados   372.

Sait FAIK SHORT STORY PRIZE
(Turkey--Sait Faik Hikaye
Armagani)
    Named in honor of Sait Faik,
one of the most gifted of the

"new generation" Turkish short
story writers, an annual prize
of 1.000 TL was established in
1954 by the mother of Abasiyanik.
    Recipients include:
    1955 Haldun Taner-Sebahattin
    Kudret Aksal
    1956 Tahsin Yucel. Haney
    Yasamali
    1957 Necati Cumali. Degisik
    Gozle
    1958 Orhan Kemal
    1959 Oktay Akbal. Berber Aynasi
                                373.

Matilde FALCO PRIZE (Italy)
    In 1962, the Casa Editrice
"La Bargese" (Barge, Cuneo)
divided the prize offered by their
publishing house equally among
five authors:
    Theo Parodi. Processo a Pan
    Delia Venzo. Interpretazione
    della Quinta di Beethoven
    Mario Sista. Gli eroi puzzani
    si sudore
    Carla Federica Giacomasso.
    Marcolino
    Vittorio Farneti. La corda di
    seta   374.

FANTASIA PRIZE (France)
    An annual publisher's prize
offered by Editions Magnard
(122 boulevard Saint-Germain,
Paris) brings a premium of
2.500 NF, and publication of the
winning work to the author whose
unpublished manuscript of a novel
for young people is judged the
best in competition. Among
recipients of the prize, announced
each year in October, are:
    1955 Elsie (Mme Collin-Dela-
    vaud). Mylord et le saltim-
    banque
    1956 Michele Massane. Au
    vent de fortune
    1958 L. Bourliaguet. Les
    compagnons de l'arc
    1959 Chaine et Voeltzel.
    Chat sauvage et sapin bleu
    1960 René Guillot. Le maître
    des éléphants

1961 Claude Cenac. Quatre
pattes dans l'aventure
1962 J. C. Froelich. Voyage
au pays de la Pierre Ancienne   375.

FAR NORTH QUEENSLAND PLAY
WRITING COMPETITION (Aus-
tralia)

Prizes of L50 are offered for
the best one-act play each year,
usually in February, by the Far
North Queensland Amateur Theatrical Association (P.O. Box
232, Cairns, Queensland, Australia). Original plays, of approximately three-quarters of an hour
performing time, by authors
resident in Queensland for at
least three months may be
entered in competition by submitting the manuscript in three
copies to the Association not
later than January 31.

Recipients of the First Prize
are:
1960 V. J. Moran. Find me
at the Federal
1961 Mrs. M.D. Cooper.
Coffee for sixpence
1962 J. Naish. The Maoris
                          376.

FASTENRATH PRIZE (Spain)

One of the longest-established
and best-known literary awards
in Spain, this distinguished honor
which is awarded by the Real
Academia Espanola was established in 1909 by bequest of the
famous German hispanist for
whom it is named--Johannes
Fastenrath (1839-1908). Awarded annually for five forms of
writing in rotation (Poetry, except
drama; Literary criticism; Novel
or short stories; Historical
criticism, biography, general
history, politics, history of
literature, art or custom; Dramatic works--prose or verse),
the prize consists of a monetary
premium, varying in amount
from year to year, but pre-

sently 6,000 pts.
Winners of this respected literary reward include:
Novel
1909 C. Espina de Serna.
Mariflor
1911 Leon Reyles-Camba.
Elamorde los Amores
1927 Antonio Porras. Centro
de los Almas
1941 Juan Antonio Zunzunegui.
Ay, estos hijos
1949 Carmen Laforêt. Nada
History
1947 Julián Mariás. Miguel de
Unamuno
1955 Luis G. de Valdeavellano.
Historia de España
Poetry
1956 José García Nieto. La Red
1962 Blas de Otero. Ancia
Literary Criticism
1953 Carlos Bousoño. Teoria
de la Expressión
1957 Luis Felipe Vivanco. In-
troducción a la poesía española   377.

William FAULKNER FOUNDA-
TION LATIN AMERICAN NOVEL
AWARD (Latin America--U.S.A.)

The William Faulkner Foundation (under the direction of Dr.
Arnold A. Del Greco, Associate
Professor of Romance Languages,
University of Virginia, Char-
lottesville, Virginia) offers an
honorary award (A Certificate of
Merit) in each Latin American
country participating in the award
"project" for an outstanding novel
never translated into English,
and published since World War
II. In 1962, a committee of
three qualified judges in each
participating country will designate the novel to receive the
award. "On the grounds that
youngsters are best able to evalu-
ate the work of their contemporar-
ies, none of the judges will be
older than 35 years." This
competition, The Latin American Novel Project, was under-

taken at the suggestion of William Faulkner to bring to English-speaking North America some of the "many novels of the highest literary quality written by Latin American authors in their native languages." Novels given the national Certificate of Merit in recognition of "literary distinction and achievement," are eligible for the Grand Award of the Foundation (the William Faulkner Plaque), which will be presented to the one book selected from among the national prize-winners as "a notable novel representing the best literary traditions of Latin America."

As part of the Ibero-American Novel Project, the Foundation will "use its influence to effect the translation and subsequent publication in the U.S.A. of the books nominated by the various committees, both national and international."

Winning novels, announced in 1962-1963, are:

Argentina---Eduardo Mallea. Los enemigos del alma
Bolivia---Marcelo Quiroga Santa Cruz. Los deshabitados
Brazil---Graciliano Ramos. Vidas Sêcas
Chile---José Donoso. Coronación
Costa Rica---Carlos Luis Fallas Sibaja. Marcos Ramírez
Dominican Republic. Marcio Veloz Maggiolo. El buen ladrón
Guatemala---Miguel Angel Asturias. El señor Presidente
Mexico---Emma Godoy. Erase un hombre pentafácico
Panama--Joaquín Belaño. Los forzados de Gamboa
Paraguay---A. Roa Bastos. Hijo de hombre
Peru---José María Arguedas. Los ríos profundos

Puerto Rico---René Marqués. La víspera del hombre
Uruguay---Juan Carlos Onetti. El Astillero
Venezuela---Ramón Díaz Sánchez. Cumboto
378.

FÉDÉRATION DES ARTISTES PRIZE (France)
A literary honor of the Fondation Louis Jungmann (52 rue Marquette, Nancy) established in 1961 to reward a literary work that increases knowledge of and love for the fine arts. The 5.000 NF premium was granted in 1961 to Alain Bosquet, for "Verbe et vertige;" and to Rene de Solier, for "L'art fantastique." 379.

FELTRINELLI PRIZE (Italy)
An award in literature is one of the five cultural prizes offered by Fondazione "Antonio Feltrinelli" for distinguished works in the arts and sciences, and administered by the Italian Academy (Accademia Nazionale dei Lincei, via della Lungara 10, Rome). The prize is granted for Italian and international scholarly achievement (in the fields: Moral and Historical Sciences; Physical, Mathematical, and Natural Sciences; Letters; Art; Medicine), comparable to that honored by the Nobel Prize. A jury, composed of members of leading Italian Academies and of international Academies in other countries, announces the winners on June 1, and presents the awards (L 5.000.000---Italian prize: L 20.000.000---International prize) in a solemn ceremony in a formal Academy meeting.

Literary winners of the prize, one of Italy's highest cultural honors, include:
1952 Marino Moretti. Prose works
Emilio Cecchi. Literary

essays
Ferdinando Neri. Literary
history and criticism
International Prize (L 5.000.
000)
Thomas Mann (Germany.
Entire literary work, in
particular his tetralogy,
"Joseph and his Brothers"
Ramon Menendez Pidal.
(Spain). Entire research
work in Spanish literature.
1955 Gianfranco Contini
(Spain). Works in philology
and literary history
International Prize
Leo Spitzer (Austria).
Works in philology and the
history of literature
1957 Antonio Baldini
Virgilia Giotti
Vasco Pratolini
International Prize (L 20.000.
000)
Wystan Hugh Auden (United
Kingdom)
Aldo Palazzeschi
1960 Mario Praz. Works in
philology, history, and
literary criticism
1962 Bruno Cicognani; Giuseppe
De Robertis; Carlo Emilio
Gadda; and poet Camillo
Sbarbaro
International Prize--Eugenio
Montale   380.

FÉMINA PRIZE (France)
One of the most famous and
oldest literary prizes in France,
this award is presented each
December for the "Best book of
the year," by a jury of women
writers and intellectuals.
Founded in 1904 by the review,
"Femina," the magazines "Vie
Heureuse" and "Vie Pratique"
have also participated in sponsoring the prize so that through
its history the Prix Fémina has
also been designated: "Prix
Fémina-Vie Heureuse," "Prix
Fémina-Vie Pratique."

Awarded for the best work of
imagination--prose or poetry--in
the French language published in
France during the year (up to
November 1), the prize is not
applied for, but books that merit
consideration are brought to the
attention of the jury by jury members. In several meetings from
October to December, the jury
limits the suggestions of works
considered for award, and decides
upon a single work, as the prize
is not divided.
The prize (consisting of 50 NF,
a token award, and a minor aspect of the honor when the increase in the author's prestige and
the great sales of the winning
work are considered) is presented during the Christmas season,
generally around December 1.
Laureates include:
1904 Myriam Harry. La
conquête de Jérusalem
1905 Romain Rolland. Jean-
Christophe
1906 André Corthis. Gemmes
et Moires
1907 Colette Yver. Princesses
de science
1908 Edouard Estaunié. La
vie secrète
1909 Edmond Jaloux. Le
reste est silence
1910 Marguerite Adoux.
Marie-Claire
1911 Louis de Robert. Le
roman du malade
1912 Jacques Morel. Feuilles
mortes
1913 Camille Marbo. Le
statue voilée
1917 Maurice Larrouy. L'o-
dyssée d'un transport torpillé
1918 Henri Bachelin. Le
serviteur
1919 Roland Dorgelès. Les
croix de bois
1920 Edmond Gojon. Le jardin
des dieux
1921 Raymond Escholier. Can-
tegril

1922 Jacques de Lacretelle.
Silbermann
1923 Jeanne Galzy. Les
allongés
1924 Charles Derennes. Le
bestiaire sentimental
1925 Joseph Delteil. Jeanne
d'Arc
1926 Charles Silvestre. Le
prodige du coeur
1927 Marie Le Franc. Grand-
Louis, l'innocent
1928 Dominique Dunois.
Georgette Garou
1929 Georges Bernanos. Le
joie
1930 Marc Chadourne. Cécile
de la Folie
1931 Antoine de Saint-Exupéry.
Vol de nuit
1932 Ramon Fernandez. Le
pari
1933 Geneviève Fauconnier.
Claude
1934 Robert Francis. Le
bateau refuge
1935 Claude Silve. Bénédic-
tion
1936 Louise Hervieu. Sangs
1937 Raymonde Vincent.
Campagne
1938 Félix de Chazournes.
Caroline ou le départ pour
les îles
1939 Paul Vialar. La rose
de la mer
1944 Editions de Minuit
(Collection "Sous l'oppres-
sion")
1945 Anne-Marie Monnet. Le
chemin du soleil
1946 Michel Robida. Le
temps de la longue patience
1947 Gabrielle Roy. Bonheur
d'occasion
1948 Emmanuel Roblès. Les
hauteurs de la ville
1949 Maria Le Hardouin. La
dame de coeur
1950 Serge Groussard. La
femme sans passé
1951 Anne de Tourville.
Jabadao
1952 Dominique Rolin. Le

souffle
1953 Zoë Oldenburg. La
pierre angulaire
1954 Gabriel Veraldi. La
machine humaine
1955 André Dhôtel. Le pays
ou l'on n'arrive jamais
1956 François-Régis Bastide.
Les adieux
1957 Christian Mégret. Carre-
four des solitudes
1958 Françoise Mallet-Joris
(Belgium). L'Empire
céleste
1959 Bernard Privat. Au pied
du mur
1960 Louise Bellocq. La porte
retombée
1961 Henri Thomas. Le pro-
montoire
1962 Yves Berger. Le Sud
381.

FEMINA PRIZE (Spain)
A 50,000 pts prize of the
publisher, Editorial Colenda
(Cea Bermudez 45, Madrid),
awarded for nearly 30 years,
includes among recent winners of
the novel award:
1957 Margarita Gomez
Espinosa. Por Almas
y por Mares
1961 Casanova Vicuna. La
Hija del Pintor   382.

FÉMINA-VACARESCO PRIZE
(France)
Offered by the administrators
of the Prix Fémina and determined by the same jury (Jacques
Nels, Secretary, 79 boulevard
Saint-Germain, Paris 6e), this
prize honors the work of a French
writer with the best published
book during the year (April 1
of the year preceding award to
April 1 of the year of award)
in the subject areas of: Art,
History, or Criticism.
The 5.000 fr prize, usually
presented between May 20 and
30, has been won by:
1952 Marguerite Yourcenar.

Mémoires d'Hadrien
1953 G. C. Cattaui. Marcel
Proust
1954 Antonina Vallentin. Le
drame d'Einstein
1955 Fred Berence. La
Renaissance italienne
1956 Jean-Pierre Richard.
Poésie et profondeur
1957 Claude Roger-Marx.
Les impressionnistes
1958 Jean Starobinski. Jean-
Jacques Rousseau. La
transparence et l'obstacle
1959 Maurice Lanoire. Les
lorgnettes du roman anglais
1960 Georges Piroue. Proust
et la musique du devenir
1961 Robert Aron. Les
années obscures de Jésus
1962 Alain Bosquet. Verbe et
vertige   383.

FÉNÉON PRIZE (France)
Each year on February 15
since 1949, the Fondation Fénéon
(10 place du Pantheon, Paris 5e)
has awarded literary prizes of
from 100.000 to 500.000 fr to
outstanding published works,
with no restriction as to literary
form, by French writers who
are at least 35 years of age.
The jury, which includes as
members the Rector and other
officers of the University of
Paris, has awarded prizes to
such writers as:
1949 Michel Cournot (Martinique)
1953 Mohammed Dib (Algeria).
La grande maison
1954 Albert Memmi. La
statue de sel
Alain Robbe-Grillet. Les
gommes
1957 Michel Butor. L'emploi
du temps
1959 Armand Gatti. Le
poisson noir
1961 Jean Laugier. Les Bogues
Michel Deguy. Fragments de
cadastre
Jean Thibaudeau. La

cérémonie royale   384.

FERIA DEL LIBRO PRIZE
(Spain)
A 6,000 pts award for journal-
ism (periodismo) is offered by
the Instituto Nacional del Libro
Español (Ferraz 13, Madrid 8).
                            385.

Antonio FERRO PRIZE (Inter-
national--Portugal)
This biennial journalism award
of the Portuguese government
(Secretaria do Nacional de Informação, S.N.I.) was instituted
in 1957 "to distinguish the best
report or articles on Portugal
published during the two previous
years in the Foreign Press."
Named to honor the first
director of the National Information Office, the 15.000$ award
is granted by a special committee,
which considers for the prize
articles in Portuguese, English,
Spanish, German, Italian, or
French. Articles entered in
competition must be written by
journalists who are not citizens
of Portugal, must be submitted in
six copies, and may be sent by
the author, or a third person
with the author's permission, accompanied by a letter of application for the award, before
February 1 following the two-
year period of competition.
The prize (which alternates
with the Camões Prize, is presented in Lisbon before the end of
May in the award year, and has
been granted to:
1957 Leo Magnino. Il Con-
tributo del Portogallo alla
Civiltá Occidentale, in
Revista Latina," Rome
1959 Ramón Ledesma
Miranda.
Articles published in the
Spanish press
1961 Roland Faure. Articles
published in "L'Aurore"
                            386.

G. FEXIS PRIZE (Greece)
One of the five prizes offered annually since 1950 by the group of writers and literary men known as the "Group of Twelve," and so also called "The Group of Twelve Prize," this award designates the most promising new writer of the year, whose writing talents give promise of the greatest contribution to Greek letters, with a premium of 20,000 Drachmas.
387.

FIERA LETTERARIA PRIZE
(Italy)
In 1957 this award was granted by "Fiera Letteraria" (via del Corso 303, Rome) to R. Bosi for his short story collection, "Veronica."   388.

FIESTA DEL LIBRO PRIZE
(Spain)
The Fiesta del Libro, held in Spain as a national event, includes the awarding of literary honors, and this journalism prize given by the Spanish government (Dirección General de Archivos y Bibliotecas, Ministerio de Educación Nacional, Alcalá 34, Madrid) is granted in conjunction with the Fiesta on April 23, anniversary of the death of Cervantes. Among winners of the 5,000 pts premium are: Felipe Benicio Calvo y Val, with "Amigo Libro;" Félix Merino Sánchez, with "El Libro y la Educación del Pueblo;" Luis Artigas Giménez, with "Dialogos conmigo;" and (1961) Asunción Delgado Serrano, for his essay, "Las bibliotecas públicas embalses de la cultura," which was published in "Hoy."
Also offered in a "Concurso Infantil Fiesta del Libro" by I.N.L.E. (Instituto Nacional del Libro Espanol, Ferraz 13, Madrid 8), with the patronage

of the National Minister of Education, are prizes consisting of approximately 100,000 pts worth of books. Alumnos de Centros de Enseñanza Media are eligible for the prizes, the most important of which (8,000 pts) was won in 1962 by Amparo Casado.
389.

FILA INES ED ADOLFO PRIZE
(Italy)
A literature prize, together with a prize for painting and sculpture, is offered by Fila Ines Ed Adolfo, with a premium in each category of L 2.000.000. Giacomo Debenedetti, leading Marxist literary critic, received the award in 1961 for his collected works, such as "Saggi Critici;" "16 Octobre 1943;" and "Otto ebrei."   390.

FINNISH CULTURAL FOUNDATION AWARD
Authors receiving this prize for creative work include:
1957 Tyyni Tuulio
1960 Väinö Nuorteva
Aila Meriluoto   391.

FINNISH GOVERNMENT SALARIES FOR CREATIVE WORK
National salaries are granted in Finland by the government, with the advice of a board of literary experts and other authorities in the arts. Stipends vary in amount, with such an award-winning author as Mika Toimi Waltari, one of the 12 members of the Academy of Finland, receiving a salary equivalent to the highest paid by the government, to "enable him to carry out creative work."   392.

FINNISH LITERATURE SOCIETY AWARD
A triennial prize, which has been won by:
1954 Väinö Nuorteva

Aale Tynni
1957 Martti Merenmaa
1960 Veikko Huovinen
Marko Tapio   393.

FINNISH LITERATURE UNION
PRIZE
From 1952-1962, the annual
award was presented to:
Väinö Voipio
Huugo Jalkanen
Heikki Asunta
Simo Puupponen
L. Onerva
Matti Hälli
Juha Mannerkorpi
Elina Vaara
K. M. Wallenius
Helvi Hämäläinen   394.

FINNISH STATE PRIZE FOR
LITERATURE
An official government prize
of Finland, granted annually--
usually in May--for literary works
published during the previous
year. Early winners of the national honor for authors, one of
the oldest cultural awards in
Finland, are: A. Kallas (1928)
with "Wolf's bride;" M. T.
Waltari (1937) with "From
father to son," a three-volume
historical novel.
  Among recent recipients of this
highly-regarded prize (Valtion
Kirjallisuuspalkinto) are: Jussi
Talvi, winner of the Finnish
National Play Contest in 1955,
with "Ennen Pitkaa Perjantaita;"
and
  1956 Tuomas Anhava; Gunnar
    Björling; Matti Hälli; Eeva
    Joenpelto; Helvi Jubonen;
    Martti Merenmaa; Paavo
    Rintala; Olavi Siippainen;
    Göran Stenius; Arvo Turt-
    iainen
  1957 Viljo Kojo; Kirsi Kunnas;
    Iiris Kähäri; Eeva-Liisa
    Manner; Juha Mannerkorpi;
    Ralf Parland; Solveig von
    Schoultz; Marko Tapio

1958 Anna Bondestam; Rabbe
  Enckell; Matti Hälli; Helvi
  Hämäläinen; Veijo Meri;
  Sakari Pälsi; Sirkka Selja;
  Marja-Liisa Vartio
1959 Simo Puupponen; Paavo
  Haavikko; Juha Mannerkorpi;
  Aila Meriluoto; Solveig von
  Schoultz
1960 Tito Colliander; Pentti
  Holappa; Väinö Linna; Eeva-
  Liisa Manner; Olavi Siip-
  painen
1961 Anna Bondestam; Paavo
  Haavikko; Lauri Kokkenen;
  Eeva-Liisa Manner; Veijo
  Meri; Peter Sandelin; Eino
  Salmelainen   395.

S. FISCHER DRAMA PRIZE
(Germany)
  A drama award is offered by
one of Germany's major pub-
lishers, S. Fischer-Verlag
(Zeil 65/69, P.O. Box 3489,
Frankfurt am Main), for the
best play by a German author
under 40 years of age. A First
Prize of 5000 DM and a Second
Prize of 2500 DM are presented.
                           396.

Kuno FISCHER PRIZE (Germany)
  Established in 1904 by the
University of Heidelberg and ad-
ministered by the Kuno Fischer
Prize Foundation (Kuno Fischer
Preis-Stiftung), this prize for
scholarly writing was created to
commemorate the 80th birthday
(July 23) of the philosopher Kuno
Fischer (1824-1907), famous for
his literary studies of Goethe,
Lessing, Schiller, and Shakespeare.
  The award distinguishes out-
standing works in the History of
Philosophy that appear in German
scholarly writing, and is pre-
sented before the Academic
Senate of Ruprecht-Karl University (Grabengasse 1, Heidelberg),
upon motion of the Philosophy
Faculty of Heidelberg. The

honor has been granted four
times and is to be awarded
again when the premium of the
prize (based on a capital endowment of 10.500 DM) reaches
1.000 DM. Writers who have
received the prize are:
  1914 Ernst Cassirer. Das
  Erkenntnisproblem in der
  Philosophie und Wissen-
  schaft der neueren Zeit
  1932 Hermann Glockner.
  Hegel; and Augustus Faust.
  Der Möglichkeits-gedanke.
  1942 Ernst Krieck. Völkisch-
  politische Anthropologie;
  Volkscharakter und Sen-
  dungsbewusstein
  1947 Wilhelm Nestle. Vom
  Mythos zum Logos   397.

FIUME-LEROUX PRIZE
(Europe--France--Prix Franco-
Italien Marthe Fiumi-Leroux)
  A 2.000 NF prize, "Gran
Premio Franco-Italien," established by friends of the poet
Lionello Fiumi in honor of the
memory of his wife, is granted
annually by Société des poètes
français. The award, which is
presented alternately to a French
writer-translator and critic of contemporary Italian poetry, and to
an Italian writer-translator and
critic of contemporary French
poetry, has honored such
authors as:
  1957 Eugène Bestaux
  1958 Gugliemo Lo Curzio
  1959 André Pezard
  1960 Carlo Pellegrini
  1961 Roger Clérici   398.

THE FIVE PRIZE (France--
Prix des Cinq)
  A distinguished jury (André
Maurois, Pasteur Valery-Radot,
Jean Cocteau, Yves Gandon)
awarded the literary honor (c/o
Cercle d'informations et d'études
sociales féminines, 20 cours
de l'Intendance, Bordeaux) in
1961 to Marcelle Capron, for

her writing, "Le vin du matin."
                              399.

FLEMISH PROVINCES LITERA-
TURE PRIZES (Belgium--Letter-
kundige prijs der Vlaamse
Provincien)
  Among the prizes offered by
the Flemish Provinces of Belgium
is a Grand Prize of the Flemish
Provinces (Grote Prijs der
Vlaamse Provincien), which is
offered each year for work published during the preceding five
years. Among recipients of the
Grote Prijs are
  1955-1959 P. Nuten. Madrigali
  Spirituali van Philippus
  de Monte
  1956-1960 Albert Westerlinck.
  De wereldbeschouwing van
  August Vermeylen
Other writers who have received Flemish Provinces Literary
Prizes include:
  1956 Anton van Wilderofe. Het
  land der mensen
  1957 Achilles Mussche.
  Christoffel Marlowe
  1958 Valeer van Kerkhoven. De
  bungalow (novel)
  Ernst Claes. Entire Work
  1959 Maria de Vleeschouwer-
  Verbraecken. Een uil vloog
  over (youth book)
  Cor Ria Leeman. Jan Klaasen
  (children's book)
  Lo Vermeulen. Penge de
  Pygmee (children's book)
                              400.

FLORENCE PRIZE (Italy--Premio
Firenze)
  The Premio Citta' di Firenze,
one of the best-known Italian
prizes for poetry (Segretario
Commissione Giudicatrice, Presso
Aldemaro Nannei, via dell'Orto
22, Florence), consists of a
premium (currently L 800.000)
and a gold or silver medal. The
award is presented annually in
December and designates a collection of poetry published in one

volume during the contest period
(October 1 to the following
October 1) which are judged the
best submitted in competition
(deadline: October 31.)
  Laureates include:
  1947 Giuseppe Berto. Il
  cielo é rossi
  1956 S. Giannini. Prai di
  fieno
  1958 L. Pignotti; B. Rondi
  1961 Eugenio Miccini. Dolore
  dell'assenza
  Silvio Remat.   Lo speechio
  dell'afa
The FLORENCE MEDALS,
awarded for outstanding service
to Italian Art and Culture, have
been granted to:
  Gold Medal Dante Alighieri:
  T.S. Eliot (1959); Carlo
  Betocchi (1961)
  Gold Medal: C. Sbarbaro
  (1958); Vittore Pagano
  (1961)
  Silver Medal: B. Rebellato
  (1958); Denis Mahon (Great
  Britain--1959)
  Golden Lily Award: Irving
  Stone (U.S.A.) for "The
  Agony and the Ecstasy"
                              401.

Henri La FONTAINE PRIZE
(International)
  UNESCO (Palacio Egmont,
Brussels, Belgium) offered the
$1,000 prize in 1957 to "recog-
nize the best major study on
international organization of
government" during the contest
years.   The competition, open
to writers of all nationalities,
required that a work be in the
English or the French language.
                              402.

FONTANE PRIZE (Germany)
  An official government literary award, offered by West
Berlin (Senat des Landes (West)
Berlin), the "Fontane Award" is
named in honor of the German
poet, novelist and essayist,

Theodor Fontane (1819-1898),
and together with comparable
prizes in other areas of the arts
(Painting, Architecture, Music,
Motion Pictures), is referred to
as the "Berlin Arts Prize" (Berliner Kunstpreis), offered by Der
Senator fur Volksbildung (Berlin-
Charlottenburg 9).
  These cultural prizes are
granted artists associated with
Berlin, and the 4000 DM literary
award, which is presented each
March 18 on the advice of the
Academy of Art, has honored
such German authors as:
  1949 Hermann Kasack. Die Stadt
  hiner dem Strom
  1951 Gerd Gaiser; Hans Werner Richter
  1952 Kurt Ihlenfeld
  1953 Edzard Schaper (Finland)
  1954 Albert Vigoleis Thelen
  1956 Hans Scholz
  1957 Ernst Schnabel
  1958 Günter Blöcker
  1959 Gregor von Rezzori
  1960 Uwe Johnson. Mutmas-
  sungen uber Jakob
  1961 Martin Kessel.   Entire
  work, with special mention
  of "Gegengabe"
  1962 Golo Mann.   Entire work
  as an essayist and historian
  A section of the Fontane Prize
is also awarded to encourage
young writers (Junge Generation
Prize--which see).   403.

Theodor FONTANE PRIZE
(Germany, East)
  A general cultural honor
granted since 1954, this 10.000
DM prize of the region of Potsdam (Rat des Bezirkes Potsdam)
is presented each year for Painting, Architecture, and Literature.
  In Literature, the monetary
premium and medal (since 1956
two second and third prizes have
also been awarded) have honored
authors including:
  1954 Eduard Claudius. Früchte
  aus harter Zeit

1955 Peter Huchel. Entire
work
1956 Bernhard Seeger. Sturm
aus Bambushütten
Irma Harder. Im Haus am
Wiesenweg (novel, 2nd class)
Herbert Otto. Die Lüge
(novel, 3rd class)
1957 Horst Erich Beseler.
Im Garten der Königen
(novel, 2nd class)
Rudolf Daumann (in memori-
am). Der Untergang der
Dakota (novel, 3rd class)
1958 Wolfgang Joho. Die
Wendemarke (novel)
1959 Anna and Friedrich
Schlotterbeck
Hans Marchwitza. Die
Kumiaks (novel, trilogy)
1960 Gerhard Bengsch. Manko
(television play)   404.

FONTE CIAPPAZZI PRIZE
(Italy)

A poetry award, established
by Pro-Loco di Castroreale
Terme of S.T.E.A. (Societa
Terme & Alberghi), grants five
prizes to Sicilian poets. Winner
of the first prize (L 100.000)
in 1961 was Giuseppe Cassinelli.
405.

Stiftung zur FÖRDERUNG DES
SCHRIFTTUMS PRIZE (Germany)

Established in 1950 by Friedrich Märker, President of the
writers' group, Schutzverband
Deutscher Schriftsteller, this
Munich prize awarded a premium
(1500 to 2000 DM) to young
writers of talent each year from
1951-1957. The most recent
award, in the fall of 1960 on
the 10th anniversary of the
Foundation, brought the winning
author 4000 DM.

Recipients are:
1951 Joseph Bernhardt;
Richard Billinger; Georg
Britting; Hedwig Conrad-
Martius; Alfons von

Czibulka; Marieluise Fleisser;
Leonhard Frank; Bernt von
Heiseler; Hans-Egon Holthu-
sen; Gottfried Kölwel; Walter
Kolbenhoff; Max Peinkofer;
Ernst Penzoldt; Hans Rehberg;
Luise Rinser; Eugen Roth;
Peter Scher; Hermann Stahl;
Alfons Teuber; Inge Westphal;
Barbara Zaehle
1952 Hans Braun; Otto von
Taube
1953 Mechtilde Fürstin Lich-
nowsky; Alfred von Martin
1954 Curt Hohoff; Paula
Schlier
1955 Oda Schaefer; Herman
Uhde-Bernays
1956 Friedrich Märker; Georg
von der Vring
1957 Karl Amery; Chrisoph
Meyer
1960 Siegfried von Vegesack;
Heinz Flügel; and PRIZE OF
HONOR (Ehrenpreis) to
Friedrich Märker   406.

FORMENTOR PRIZE (International)

Like the International Publishers'
Prize, this newly established annual prize, first granted in 1961,
is a rich international literary
award of $10,000 royalty advance,
which was founded in May 1960
at an international meeting of
publishers in Formentor on the
Island of Mallorca. While the
International Publishers' Prize
brings recognition to an established author of world stature,
the Formentor Prize is a "discovery" award offered for "the
best available unpublished fiction
manuscript worthy of publication
throughout the world" submitted
by the 13 participating publishers-
six founding publishers: France
(Librairie Gallimard); Spain
(Editorial Seix and Barral); Italy
(Guilia Einaudi Editori); England
(Weidenfeld & Nicholson); Germany (Ernest Rowohlt Verlag);
U.S.A. (Grove Press); and seven

additional publishers who joined
in sponsorship of the prize after
its founding: Portugal; Canada
(McClelland & Stuart); Sweden
(Bonniers Forlag); Finland
(Kustannusosakeyhtio Otava);
Denmark (Gyldendalske Boghande);
Norway (Gyldendal Norsk Forlag);
Netherlands (Meulenhoff).

All manuscripts entered in
competition are sent to the
publishers in each country for
consideration, and not directly
to the Formentor Prize Committee. Each participating
publisher then submits one or
two novel manuscripts from his
country which he has accepted
for publication during the award
period (the calendar year), and
which he judges worthy of consideration by the international
jury of publishers who pick the
winner.

The international jury, meeting at the Club des Poètes in
Formentor, judges the publishers'
entries by such criteria as "exceptional literary merit, their
manifestation by way of subject
matter, form and style of an
effort to revitalize the literary
genre (novel), and by the effect
they are likely to have on the
further development of the novel
form."

Prize winners, whose novels
are published simultaneously
in 11 languages by the publishers
in the 13 countries participating
in the award and are released
in May following the year of
award, are:
  1961 Juan Garcia Hortelano
    (Spain). Tormenta de
    Verano (Orage d'été; Som-
    mergewitter; Summer
    Storm)
  1962 Dacia Maraini (Italy).
    L'Eta del Malessere (The
    age of Malaise)
  1963 Jorge Semprun (Spain---
    France) Le grande voyage

407.

FOUR JURIES PRIZE (France--
Prix des Quatre Jurys)

This novel prize granted in
February each year was established in 1952 with a premium of
1000 NF, and selects a winner
from among the candidates for the
four major French literary honors
which are presented at the end of
the year: Goncourt, Renaudot,
Fémina, and Interallié.

Winners, chosen from those
candidates who have obtained at
least two votes for one of the
four major French awards, include:
  1953 Mouloud Mammeri. La
    colline oubliée
  1954 Félicien Marceau.
    Bergère légère
  1955 Jacques Gorbof. Les
    condamnés
  1956 Christine de Rivoyre.
    L'alouette au miroir
  1957 Michèle Perrein. La
    sensitive
  1958 Georges-Emmanuel
    Clancier. La fabrique du
    roi
  1959 Roger Grenier. Les em-
    buscades
  1960 Paul Guyot. Un été en
    Brière
  1961 Violette Jean. Eugénie
    les larmes aux yeux   408.

FRANCE-AFRICA PRIZE (Africa--
France--Prix France-Afrique)

A newly established novel
prize of Cercle Artistique et
Littéraire France-Antilles (1
square Raynouard, Paris 16e)
offers a 1.000 NF premium as a
biennial award. Eligible authors
are those submitting a published
novel or novel manuscript in
French (not confessional or
political in nature) in three copies
by August 1. Writers must be
Africans (Afrique noir) from a
country in Africa using the French
language--including Malagasy
Republic and the independent states

of the former Congo--Leopold-
ville and Brazzaville. The first
award will be granted 1961-1962.
409.

"FRANCES EXTÉRIEURES"
LITERARY PRIZE (International
--France)
In order to insure publication
and distribution of outstanding
literary works (prose or poetry)
by French writers residing outside of continental France, the
award was established in 1956
by Mouvement des Frances
extérieures (30 rue René-Bou-
langer, Paris 10e). The ini-
tiating group, Fédération nationale des écrivains et artistes
fonctionnaires, requires that
works entered in competition
concern French people or their
places of residence outside
France, and that the writings
be entered in competition by
October 31 (2 manuscript copies
of unpublished works, and six
copies of published books).
The award (which consists of
publication of the winning work
in France) has been granted:
1956 Bonneville (Canada)
1957 Emmy Guittes
1958 Emil Rainer. L'Utopie
d'une république huguenote
du marquis Henri Duquesne
et le voyage de F. Legat
1959 Ry de la Touche. Dis-
tributeurs automatiques de
fiancées et de maris parfaits
1960 L. M. Escullier. Les
choses de Dieu 410.

Francisco **FRANCO NATIONAL**
PRIZE (Spain)
An official award of the
Spanish government granted each
year by Ministerio y Director
General de Prensa for a published book that is a "Doctrinal
work on a political, social or
economic subject." In 1962,
works eligible for competition
were articles published in

Spanish newspapers or periodicals
in the Spanish-language countries,
between February 1 and October
31; to be entered in the contest,
these writings were to have been
sent before November 10, 1962
to Subdirección General de Prensa.
Recipients of the journalism
award include:
1957 Díaz de Villegas. Guerra
de liberación
1958 Gerardo Oroquieta, and
César Garcia Sánchez. De
Leningrado o Odesa
1959 Miguel Siguán. Del
Campo al Suburbio
1960 Manual Alvar. Estructura
Lingüistica de Andalucia
J. M. Solá y Solé. Las In-
scripciones subarábigas Nono-
teístas y de la Epoca Imperial
Enrique Aguinaga López
1961 Antonio Millán Puelles.
La función social en los
saberes liberales 411.

Anne **FRANK AWARDS** (Netherlands)
Offered by the Netherlands
Ministry of Education, Arts and
Sciences (Ministerie van Onderwijs, Kunsten en Wetenschappen),
the Arts Section, this annual
award is granted "as an encouragement to promising young
writers." The donation of the
award premium through the
Netherlands American Foundation
(551 Fifth Avenue, New York 17)
established the prize and continues
it through 1966. The jury,
appointed by the Director of the
Arts Section, commends the
names of writers of Dutch
nationality under 30 years of age
on January 1 of the year of the
award for the prize. These writers must have published an
original work in Dutch during the
five-year period preceding the
award. Types of works specified
for the two prizes (First Prize--
fl 2,500; Second Prize--fl 1.000)

are: 1957--novel; 1958--poetry;
1959--plays (prose or poetry);
1960--stories; 1961--essays,
literary history, criticism, or
biography; 1962--novel; 1963--
poetry; 1964--play (prose or
poetry); 1965--essays, literary
history, criticism, biography;
1966--stories.

Among the winning authors
are:
1957 Harry Mulisch; Cees
Nooteboom
1958 Remco Campert; Nico
Scheepmaker
1959 Eric Vox; Esteban Lopez
1960 Cornelis Bauer; Rutger
van Zeyst   412.

FRANKFORT-ODER ART PRIZE
(Germany, East)

The Kunstpreis des Bezirkes
Frankfurt/Oder has been awarded
such writers as Helmut Preissler, who won the award in 1960
for his entire literary work.
413.

Miles FRANKLIN LITERARY
AWARDS (Australia)

"The best Australian novel" is
designated by this Ł500 prize for
a book published during each
calendar year. The awards are
named for a well-known Australian author, who died in 1954,
creating the prizes in her will.
Closing date for submitting
works for consideration for award
(Miles Franklin Estate, The
Manager, Permanent Trustee
Company of N.S.W., Ltd, Box
4270, Sydney, N.S.W., Australia) is February 28, and
awards are generally announced
early in April.

According to the conditions
of the prize, it "shall be
awarded for the novel for the
year which must present Australian life in any of its phases,"
and--if no novel is found worthy
of the prize--plays for stage,
radio or television may be con-

sidered for the award.

Novelists honored with the
award, among the most famous,
continuing literary prizes in Australia, are:
1957 Patrick White. Voss
1958 Randolph Stow. To the
islands
1959 Vance Palmer. The big
fellow
1960 Elizabeth O'Connor. The
Irishman
1961 Patrick White. Riders
in the chariot   414.

FRATERNIDAD HISPÁNICA
PRIZE (Spain)

Founded by José Fernández
Martínez, resident of Mexico, for
a "series of articles advocating a
high degree of cordial relations
between hispanic countries" published each year, the 100,000
pts prize was awarded in 1959
to Manuel Lizcano for his articles
in "Mundo Hispanico," and
"Cuardernos Hispanoamericanos."
415.

FRATERNITÉ PRIZE (France)

Each year this literary prize
is given for a work of literature
or art (Theater, Cinema or
Painting) that best contributes to
the high ideals of equality and
fraternity among men, without
distinction as to origin, race, or
religion. The award is granted
in the Spring (Secretary, Siège
du M.R.A.P., 15 faubourg,
Montmartre, Paris) for the most
outstanding work related to the
principles of democracy.

Recipients of the 100.000 fr
premium include:
1957 Gabrielle Gildas-Andrievski.
Pas de cheval pour Hamida
Elsa Triolet. Le rendez-
vous des étrangers
1958 Theatrical production,
"Journal of Anne Frank"
1959 Jules Isaac. Jésus et
Israël
1961 Jules Roy. La guerre

d'Algérie
1962 Robert Merle. L'Ile
416.

FRIEDENSPREIS DES DEUTSCHEN
BUCHHANDELS (International--
Germany)

The 10.000 DM Freedom
Prize of the German Book Trade
(Börsenverein des Deutschen
Buchhandels, Grosser Hirsch-
graben 17/19, Frankfurt am
Main), "an outstanding mark of
literary recognition," has been
awarded annually in October at
the Frankfurt Book Fair (Frankfurter Buchmesse) since 1950.
The international honor, sponsored by the book publishers and
book sellers of West Germany,
is presented "to an author whose
works have contributed to peace
among men."

Recipients of the prize are
such world figures as:
1950 Max Tau (first award of
    prize, then designated:
    FRIEDENSPREIS DEUTSCHER
    VERLEGER)
1951 Albert Schweitzer
1952 Romano Guardini
1953 Martin Buber
1954 Carl J. Burckhardt
1955 Hermann Hesse
1956 Reinhold Schneider
1957 Thornton Wilder (U.S.A.)
1958 Karl Jaspers
1959 Theodor Heuss
1960 Victor Gollancz (United
    Kingdom)
1961 Sarvepalli Radhakrishnan
    (India)   417.

FRIEDENSPREIS DES VERBAN-
DES DER KRIEGSBESCHÄDIG-
TEN (Germany)

The 10.000 DM humanitarian
prize of the organization, Kriegsbeschädigten, Kriegshinterbliebe-
nen, und Socialrentner Deutschlands (Landesverband Bayern)
was awarded for the first time
in 1957 to Albert Schweitzer, and
again in 1960 to Theodor Heuss.

418.

FREIE DEUTSCHE GEWERK-
SCHAFTSBUNDE LITERATURE
PRIZE (Germany, East)

The FDGB (Freie Deutsche
Gewerkschaftsbunde), the state
labor union of the DDR, grants an
annual literary award, with First
and Second Prizes totalling
30.000 DM. The two areas of
writing honored are: Major
Literary Form (Grosse Form)--
Novel; Story; and Minor Literary
Form (Kleine Form)--Journalism;
Poetry; Sketches.

Recipients of the FDGB-Litera-
turpreis since the award was
established in 1955 include:
1955 Eduard Claudius. Men-
    schen an unserer Seite
2nd prize, Wolfgang Neuhaus.
    Wetterleuchten um Wadrina
Minor--Dieter Noll. Die
    Dame Perlon und anderer
    Reportagen
Jan Koplowits. Unser Kumpel
Max der Riese
Hans Gert Lange. Kumpel
Sepp Wenig
1956 Stefan Heym. Im Kopf--
    sauber
2nd prize Paul Wiens, and
Dr. K. Georg Engel. Gene-
    sung (radio play and film
    scenario)
Minor--Jürgen Lenz. Die See
    kommt dwars
Klaus Beuchler. Das Dorf
    in der Wildnis
1957 Kuba (Kurt Bartel).
    Schlösser und Katen (film
    scenario)
Minor--Valentin Rabis. Am
    seidenen Faden
1959 Hans Marchwitza. Die
    Kumiaks und ihre Kinder
Otto Gotsche. Die Fahne
    von Kriwoj Rog
Regina Hastedt. Die Tage
    mit Sepp Zach
Minor--Hasso Grabner. Wer
    verschenkt schon seinen
    Sieg; and Fünfzehn Schritte

gradaus
Jochen Koeppel. Heisse
Eisen
Jupp Müller. Im Auftrag
meiner Klasse; Auf den
Spuren unserer Siege
Walter Baumert (with others).
Die grune Mappe (television
play)
1960 Hans-Jürgen Steinmann.
Die grössere Liebe
Benno Voelkner. Die Bauern
von Karvenbruch
Günter Görlich. Die Ehrgeizi-
gen
Minor--Eva Damm, and Roland
Eisenmenger. Frau Kollegin
(short film)
Günter Glante. Tagebuch
eines Brigadiers
Günter Schabowski. Bei
Fremden im freien Afrika
Werner Barth. Gedichte
eines Maxhüttenkumpels
1961 Herbert Nachbar. Die
Hochzeit von Länneken
J. C. Schwarz. Der neue
Direktor
Paul Schmidt-Elgers. Es
begann im Sommer
Erik Neutsch. Die Regenge-
schichte
Marianne Bruns. Das ist
Diebstahl
Minor--Karl-Heinz Schleinits.
Ins Herz geblickt
Walter Baumert. Die unbek-
annte Grösse (television play)
Brigitte Reimann, and
Siegfried Peitschmann.
Sieben Scheffel Salz; Ein
Mann steht vor der Tür
(radio plays)
Helmut Preissler. Stimmen
aus den Brigaden der
socialistischen Arbeit
1962 Fritz Seipmanns. Die
Heimkehr des Joachim Ott
                                    419.

FREIHERR VOM STEIN PRIZES
(Germany)
A number of literary prizes
are among the cultural honors

awarded by the Freiherr vom
Stein Stiftung founded in 1931
(Stiftung F.V.S. zu Hamburg,
Ballindamm 6, Hamburg 1), including the Goethe Prize of Hamburg, known also as the Hansischer International Goethe Prize.
Four 1000 DM literary prizes
for the encouragement of authors
writing in Low German (Nieder-
deutscher Preis) are awarded
each two years, alternating each
year:
Hans BOTTCHER PRIZE:
Radio play in Low German--
awarded in 1960 for the first
time to Heinrich Schmidt-
Barrien for "Die Frömde Fro,"
and in 1962 to Konrad Hansen;
Klaus GROTH PRIZE:
Poetry in Low German--granted
to Hermann Claudius (1956);
Otto Tenne (1958); Carl
Bucichs (1960) for "Ut Dag
und Drom."
Additional biennial literature
awards, alternating each year are:
Fritz REUTER PRIZE: Fiction
in Low German--awarded to
Heinrich Behnken (1955);
Hans Henning Holm (1957);
Moritz Jahn (1959); Rudolf
Kinau (1962);
Fritz STAVENHAGEN PRIZE--
Drama in Low German--a
prize for a single play or a
playwright's entire work--
first award granted in 1959
to Hans Ehrke; in 1960 to
Hermann Otto for "Afsiet."
The Joost van den VONDEL
PRIZE is also sponsored by the
Foundation (Freiherr vom Stein
Stiftung). The 10,000 DM pre-
mium was awarded for the first
time in 1961, through the Rector
of the University of Münster, to
the Netherlands writer Antoon
Coolen; and to the Belgian
(Flemish) cultural philosopher
Max Lamberty.   420.

FRENCH ANTILLES GRAND
PRIZE FOR LITERATURE
(West Indies--France)

Awarded in France (M.G. Benard, 48 rue des Morillons, Paris), this 20.000 fr prize was established as an annual prize to be granted each May for writing in various forms (Novel, Historical Novel, Essay, Poetry) to honor a work in the French language on the subject of the "French Antilles," preferably by an author from that area.

Laureates, including writers from Martinique and Haiti, are:

1947 René Clarac. Bagamba David. Sur les rives du passé
1948 Raphaël Tardon. Syarken-first
1949 Mayotte Capécia. Je suis martiniquaise
1950 Auguste Joyau. Belain d'Esnambue
1951 Eugène Revert. La magie antillaise
1952 Léopold Sainville. Dominique, nègre esclave
1953 Emmanuel Flavia-Léopold Soleils caraïbes   421.

FRENCH-BELGIAN GRAND
PRIZE FOR LITERATURE
(Europe--France)

The Grand-Prix de Littérature Franco-Belge de la Mer et de L'Outre Mer, of the writers' group, Association Nationale des Écrivains de la Mer et de l'Outre Mer (31 rue de la Bienfaisance, Paris 8e), was established in 1956 with a 200.000 fr premium. Granted annually in June for a work of imagination (Novel; Story; Novella); for a work of history (History; Biography); or for a major work of factual reporting, the prize is given alternately to a French and to a Belgian author, whose writing has been published during the 12 months preceding May 1, deadline for entries for the award.

Laureates are:
1956 Jose Gers. Entire work.
1958 Pierre MacOrlan. Entire work.
1959 René-Jules Cornet   422.

FRENCH-BELGIAN LIBERTY
PRIZE (Europe--Belgium)

The Grand Prix Littéraire de la Résistance was established in 1959 with a 25.000 fr belges premium to honor the writing of a French or Belgian author, writing in French, inspired by the ideal of justice and of defense of democratic liberties. Jurors for the award, also designated "Prix France-Belge de la Liberté," consider writing in any literary form (Belgium: M. Dethier, 39 rue du Général-Bertrand, Liège; France: Hotel de Massa, 38 rue du Faubourg-Saint-Jacques, Paris). In 1959 the prize was presented to Edmond Michelet, for 'Rue de la Liberté."   423.

FRENCH CATHOLIC GRAND
PRIZE FOR LITERATURE

The Grand Prix Catholique de Littérature is granted by the Catholic writers' organization (Syndicat des Écrivains Catholiques, 11 rue Pachot-Laine, Livry-Gargan, Seine-et-Oise), and brings a premium of 1000 NF each March 24 to honor a recent book, or--on the occasion of the publication of a new work--the entire literary output of an author. A jury of distinguished men of letters, including such well-known writers as François Mauriac and Henri Daniel-Rops, has awarded the prize recently to:

1955 P. A. Lesort. Entire work
1958 Franz Weyergans. Les gens heureux
1959 Maurice Zermatten (Belgium). Entire work

1960 Jean Pelegri. Les
oliviers de la justice
1961 Lucien Guissard.
Écrits en notre temps
1962 Victor Henri Debidour.
Entire work
Claude Tresmontant. Entire
work   424.

FRENCH CRITICS PRIZE
Since 1945 the Prix des
Critiques has been awarded the
best literary work (novel or
work of prose or poetry) published during the 12 months
preceding the competition
period, closing annually on May
1. The prize was founded by
the publisher, Les Éditions du
Pavois (M. Jean Denoel, 1 bis,
rue Vaneau, Paris 7e) and is
a New Year's award, being presented on the first Monday of
the year.
Among authors honored by
this respected literary recognition are:
1945 Romain Gary. Education
européenne
1946 Agnès Chabrier. La vie
des morts
1947 Albert Camus. La peste
1948 Georges Buraud. Mas-
ques
1949 Jules Supervielle.
Oublieuse mémoire (poetry)
1951 Pieyre de Mandiargues.
Soleils des loups
1952 Georges Borgeaud. Le
Préau
1953 Pierre Gascar. Les
bêtes
1954 Françoise Sagan. Bonjour
tristesse
1955 Alain Robbe-Grillet. Le
voyeur
1956 Michel Leiris. Fourbis
1957 Micheline Maurel. Un
camp très ordinaire
1958 Yves Régnier. Le
royaume de Bénou
1959 Henri Lefebvre. La
Somme et le reste
1960 Michel Butor. Repertoire

1961 José Cabanis. Le bonheur du jour
1962 André Du Bouchet. Dans
la Chaleur Vacante   425.

FRENCH DRAMATIC AUTHORS
AND COMPOSERS SOCIETY
GRAND PRIZE (France)
The Grand Prix de la
Société des Auteurs et Compositeurs Dramatiques is a prize that
is not applied for and not granted
through a competition, but a prize
of honor presented to a playwright
or composer for his entire dramatic work.
Laureates include:
1954 Charles Vildrac
1959 André Obey
1960 Jules Romains   426.

FRENCH GRAND NATIONAL
PRIZE FOR LETTERS
The Grand Prix National des
Lettres is the highest official
French recognition of major a-
chievement by a French writer,
other than the Académie Française prizes, and was established
in 1950 by the French Minister
of National Education (Direction
générale des Arts et Lettres,
53 rue Saint-Dominique, Paris
7e). The 5.000 NF premium
selects for a government honor
a French author, who through
his entire work has made the
greatest contribution to French
letters.
Distinguished laureates, honored by presentation of France's
most significant official award
for letters--presented each
November--include:
1951 Alain
1952 Valéry-Larbaud
1953 Henri Bosco
1954 André Billy
1955 Jean Schlumberger
1956 Alexandre Arnoux
1957 Louis Martin-Chauffier
1958 Gabriel Marcel
1959 Saint-John Perse (pseud
of Aléxis Saint-Léger Léger)

1960 Marcel Arland
1961 Gaston Bachelard
1962 Pierre-Jean Jouve
427.

FRENCH GRAND LITERARY PRIZE FOR NOVELLAS

The Grand Prix Littéraire de La Nouvelle, an award of the Ville d'Evian (Jean-Pierre Dorian, 16 boulevard Haussmann, Paris), is granted each June for the year's best book of collected novellas.

Winners of the 500 NF premium are:
1953 Pierre Boulle. Contes de l'absurde
1954 Christian Murciaux. Le douzième iman
1955 Jacques Robert. Le désordre et la nuit
1956 Michel de Saint-Pierre. Dieu vous garde des femmes
1957 Jean-Jacques Gautier. Vous aurez de mes nouvelles
1958 Matthieu Galey. Les vitamines du vinaigre
1959 Georges Govy. Sang d'Espagne   428.

FRENCH GRAND NOVEL PRIZE

A "special selection jury" assessing the French novel in the first half of the 20th century, in 1950, honored 12 novels with the Grand Prix des Meilleur Romans du Demi-Siècle:

M. Barrès. La Colline inspirée
Georges Bernanos. Journal d'un curé de campagne
Anatole France. Les Dieux ont soif
André Gide. Les Faux-Monnayeurs
Jacques de LaCretelle. Silbermann
Valéry Larbaud. Fermina Marquez
André Malraux. La Condition Humaine

François Mauriac. Thérèse Desqueyroux
Marcel Proust. Un Amour de Swann
Jules Romains. La Douceur de la vie
Jean-Paul Sartre. La Nausée
Colette (one of the jury). La Vagabonde   429.

FRENCH GRAND PRIZE FOR ADVENTURE NOVELS

A mystery story prize offered by the publisher, Librairie des Champs-Élysées (2 bis, rue de Marignan, Paris 8e) brings the winning author a 500 NF premium, and publication of his winning story in the magazine, "Le Masque." The Grand Prix du Roman d'Aventure was established in 1930 and is presented each year in June. Among the writers of "roman d'aventure policier" honored by the prize are:
1938 Pierre Boileau. Le repos de Bacchus
1946 René Guillot. Les équipages de Peter Hill
1949 Henri David. Jeux de plomb
1954 Maurice Bastide. Réactions en chaine
1956 Paul Alexandre and Maurice Roland. Voir London et mourir
1957 Jacques Chabannes. L'assassin est en retard
1958 Charles Exbrayat. Vous souvenez-vous de Paco?
1959 Jacques Ouvrard. L'assassin est dans le couvent
1960 Robert Bruyez. Crime sur onde courte
1961 André Benzimra. Le couloir de la mort
1962 Pierre Caillet. Cette morte tant desirée   430.

FRENCH GRAND PRIZE FOR CHILDREN'S LITERATURE

The 5,000 NF Grand Prix de Littérature Enfantine, offered by the Association du Salon de

l'Enfance (11 rue Anatole-de-la
Forge, Paris 17e)--the exhibition hall with demonstrations of
professional, industrial, and
technical advances for "furthering the well-being of children"--
brings an award each spring on
the Sunday before Palm Sunday
to a French writer whose work
entered in competition is judged
"best" by a "Children's Jury."
The judges are students in the
age group for which the competing works are written--one year
a jury of girls, the next a jury
of boys.

A variety of literary works are
eligible for award (Novel;
Travelogue; Adventure, Historical
or Scientific Writing; Monograph
concerning illustrious men; and
similar subjects), and works
entered in competition should
be from 100 to 200 typed pages
in length, unpublished manuscripts directed to young readers
between nine and fourteen years
of age, and should be submitted
in three copies by January 31
of the year of award.

Winning works, selected by
the young people's jury, include:
    1954 Mlle. Saint-Marcoux.
    Princesse Cactus
    1955 Paul Berna. Le cheval
    sans tête
    1957 José-Marie Bouchet.
    Coeurs sauvages d'Irlande
    1958 Paul Jacques Bonzon.
    L'Éventail de Séville
    1959 Jacqueline Dumesnil.
    Les Compagnons du cerf
    d'argent
    1960 Mme. L.N.Lavolle. Les
    clés du désert
    1961 Jean Ollivier. L'aventure
    Viking
    1962 Maurice Vauthier. Faôn
    l'Héroique   431.

FRENCH GRAND PRIZE FOR
ESPIONAGE NOVELS
    The Grand Prix du Roman
d'Espionage, a 5.000 NF prize

established in 1958, is awarded
each year during the first ten
days of December for the best
novel of espionage--either a
published book or an unpublished
manuscript (c/o Agence générale
de publication, 116 rue du Bac,
Paris).

A jury of experts in the field
of espionage (including a former
préfet de police and intelligence
and O.S.S. officers) has selected
for the honor:
    1958 Jean Bruce. Panique à
    Wake
    1959 André Pujol. Opération
    totem
    1960 Michel Carnal. A
    l'ouest d'Aden
    1961 Alain Yaouanc. Mouve-
    ments vers la mort
    In 1962 this prize was re-
placed by LES PALMES D'OR
DU ROMAN D'ESPIONNAGE,
awarded by Éditions Fleuve Noir.
                            432.

FRENCH GRAND PRIZE FOR
MYSTERY STORIES
    The Grand Prix de Littérature
Policière, first awarded in 1948
under the designation "Grand
Prix du Club des Detectives,"
is presented each year in November (M. B. Endrèbe, Secretary,
19 rue Fontaine, Paris 9e) to
the writers of the two best
mystery stories published during
the year--a "roman policière"
written in French, and a "roman
policière" written in a language
other than French and translated
into French.

The award, consisting of the
honorary "Winner of the Grand
Prix de Littérature Policiére,"
has been given such mystery
stories (which are often translated
into several languages) as:
    1948 Leo Malet. Le Cinquième
    Procédé; Frances Noyes
    Hart. Le procès Bellamy
    (The Bellamy Trial)
    1956 Michel Lebrun. Pleins

feux sur Sylvie; Charles
Williams. Peaux de
bananes
1957 Frédéric Dard. Le
bourreau pleure; Patricia
Highsmith. Monsieur Ripley
1958 Fred Kassak. On n'en-
terre pas de dimanche; Ches-
ter Himes. Le reine des
pommes
1960 Paul Gérard. Deuil en
rouge; Donald Downs.
Bourreau fais ton métier
1961 Hubert Monteilhet. Les
mantes religieuses; Thomas
Sterling. Le tricheur de
Venise (The evil of the day)
1962 Pierre Forquin. Le
Procés de Diable; Suzanne
Blanc. Feu vert pour la
mort (The green stone)
                        433.

FRENCH GRAND PRIZE FOR HUMOR

The Grand Prix de L'Humour,
an award of the Académie de
L'Humour, is administered by
the Société des Auteurs et
Compositeurs Dramatiques (11
bis, rue Ballu, Paris 9e) and
is presented annually for the
best humorous writing published
during the year, preferably a
novel. Established in 1924,
and after several years of inactivity, reestablished again in
1947, the award consists of a
premium of one franc and the
title of Laureate of the award.
Among the winners are:
1951 Jean Duche. Elle et
lui
1955 Guy Verdot. Monsieur
avec enfant
1956 Paul Guimard. Faux
frères
1957 Henri Kubnik. Voyage en
Lidurie
1958 Jacques Faizant. Rue
Panse-Bougre
1959 Arlette De Pitray. Tais-
toi Adam
1960 Robert Escarpit. Pein-

ture fraîche
1961 Georges de Caunes, and
Christian Plume. Les
coulisses de la télévision
                        434.

FRENCH GRAND PRIZE FOR YOUTH LITERATURE

The Grand Prix de la Littérature pour les Jeunes was established in 1959 with a 1.000 NF
premium by the Fédération des
Associations de parents d'Élèves
des Lycées et Collèges Français
(29 rue Jean-Jacques-Rousseau,
Paris) to designate the best book
for adolescents published during
the 12 months preceding the
award. Eligible for award are
books of recreational reading
with educational and moral value,
which are inspired by the principles of classical and modern
humanism--written originally in
French or translations into French,
illustrated or not illustrated.
Books for young people honored
with the prize are:
1959 Henri Bosco. Barboche;
Paul Berna. Le Champion
1960 André Dhôtel. Le neveu
de Parencloud; Claude Campagne. Adieu mes quinze
ans
1961 Jean Guehenno. Changer
la vie; Michel Manoll. Saint-
Exupéry, prince des pilotes
1962 Lionel Terray. Les con-
quérants de l'Inutile; Yvonne
Meynier. Un Lycée pas
comme les autres   435.

FRENCH LITERARY CRITICS GRAND PRIZE

The Prix de Critique Littéraire, a 250 NF prize of the
critics' organization (Syndicate des
Critiques Littéraires, 1 rue
Renault, Saint-Mande), has been
awarded on the third Monday of
November since 1949 for the best
work of literary criticism or
literary history published during
the preceding year (up to Novem-

ber 1).

Critical writings honored with the prize include:

1952 Georges Poulet. La distance intérieure

1953 François Régis. Bastide. Saint-Simon par lui-même

1954 John Brown. Panorama de la Littérature contemporaine aux U.S.A.

1955 Robert Mallet. Une mort ambiguë

1956 Samuel S. De Sacy. Descartes par lui-même

1957 Jean Delay. La jeunesse de André Gide

1958 Dominique Aury. Lecture pour tous

1959 R. P. Blanchet. La littérature et le spirituel

1960 Michel Butor. Répertoire

1961 Henri Fluchere. Laurence Sterne, de l'homme à l'oeuvre   436.

FRENCH POETS GRAND PRIZE

One of a number of literary honors granted by the Société des Poètes Français (15 rue Plumet, Paris 15e), this 250 NF award was established in 1936 as an annual poetry prize to be granted each February. Poets recently awarded the Grand Prix des Poètes Français are:

1953 André Delacour
1954 Charles Vildrac
1955 Marie Noel
1956 Tristan Klingsor
1957 Mme Gérard d'Houville
1958 André Salmon
1959 Pascal-Bonetti
1960 Fernand Dauphin
1961 Roger Devigne
                              437.

FRENCH POPULAR NOVEL PRIZE

Novels published during the year are eligible for the 100 NF Prix du Roman Populiste (Mme Antoine Coullet-Tessier, 13 rue Gabriel-Peri, Colombes,

Seine), first granted in 1931, and reestablished as an annual award in 1939. Novelists honored with the award, which is presented in May or June, include:

1932 Jules Romains. Les hommes de bonne volonté, vol 1 and 2 (Romains accepted the honor, but refused the monetary premium, which was given 8 years later to Jean Pallu for "Ports d'escale")

1935 Henri Troyat. Faux jours

1940 Jean-Paul Sartre. La nausée

1941 Jean Rogissart. Le fer et la forêt

1942 Louis Guilloux. Le pain des rêves

1943 Marius Richard. La naissance de Phèdre

1945 Emmanuel Roblès. Travail d'hommes

1948 Armand Lanoux. La nef des fous

1949 Serge Groussard. Des gens sans importance

1950 René Fallet. Banlieue Sud-Est, Pigalle

1952 Herbert Le Porrier. Juliette au passage

1958 René Rembauville. La boutique des regrets éternels

1960 André Kédros. Le dernier voyage du "Port-Polis"

1961 Christiane Rochefort. Les petits enfants du siècle

1962 Bernard Clavel. La maison des autres   438.

FRENCH PRIZE FOR THE BEST FOREIGN BOOK (International-- France)

The Prix du Meilleur Livre Étranger is offered each year for a novel or a book of essays by a foreign writer (Secretary, rue de Grenelle 3, Paris 7e), to give public recognition to the best such foreign book published in France during the year preceding the award. New foreign authors of literary merit are brought to attention of French readers by this prize, which may be granted only to those writers who have had no more than three books published in France.

Winners of this international literary honor, presented with the award in May each year, are:

1950 Angel Asturias (Guatemala). Monsieur le président
1951 Pär Lagerkvist (Sweden). Barabbas
1952 Vasco Pratolini (Italy). Chronique des pauvres amants
1953 Robert Penn Warren (U.S.A.). Les fous du Roi
1954 Nikos Kazantzakis (Greece). Alexis Zorba
1955 Heinrich Böll (Germany). Rentrez chez vous Bogner
1956 Aléjo Carpentier (Cuba). Le partage des eaux
1957 Melnikov-Petchersky (Russia). Dans les forêts; S. N. Kramer (U.S.A.). L'histoire commence à Sumer
1958 Robert Musil (Austria). L'homme sans qualités
1959 Lawrence Durrell (United Kingdom). Justine et Balthazar
1960 Angus Wilson (United Kingdom). Les quarante ans de Mrs. Eliot
1961 Yasunari Kawabata (Japan). Pays de neige; Norman Brow. Eros et Thanatos
1962 Günter Grass (Germany). Le Tambour   439.

FRENCH YOUTH PRIZE

The Prix Jeunesse, one of the best-known of the French awards for literature for children and young people, is presented each May by the publisher, Éditions Bourrelier (55 rue Saint-Placide, Paris 6e). The prize is directed to "encouraging the best writing for young people between 7 and 14 years of age," and manuscripts--entered in competition with two copies submitted before December 15-- may deal with any subject but religion or politics, and should be approximately 250,000 words in length. The winning work, selected by an award jury with Georges Duhamel as President of Honor, is published by Editions Bourrelier, as the "Prix Jeunesse."

Laureates since the first award in 1935 include:

1937 Georges Nigremont. Jeantou, la maçon creusois
1950 René Guillot. Sama l'éléphante
1953 Louis Delluc. Le mousse de la Nina
1958 Étienne Cattin. Rat blanc et son chauffeur
1959 Simone Martin-Chauffier. L'Autre chez les corsaires
1960 Mme. Gine-Victor Leclercq. Va comme le vent
1961 Pierre Gamarra. L'aventure du serpent à plumes
1962 Magda Contino. Le mystère de l'ancre coralline   440.

FRIEDLANDPREIS DER HEIM-KEHRER (Germany)

Established and administered through the organization, Verband der Heimkehrer, Kriegsgefangenen und Vermissten Angehörigen, this annual prize, in the form of a 3000 DM encouragement premium, was granted for the first time in 1960 to Wolfgang Schwarz for his book, "Die unsichtbare Brücke."   441.

FRISIAN NOVEL PRIZE (Netherlands)

The Kristlik Fryske Folksbilbeteek Pris has been granted since 1952 by the Christian Frisian Library (Kristlik Fryske

Folksbilbeteek, Leeuwarden,
Friesland). Among the winners
with the best novels considered
are: **G. Lootsma-Smitstra**
with "Deienlike wei;" and A. A.
Van der Werf with "In hânfol
brieven fon Lipk Adema." 442.

Gustaf FRODING STIPEND
(Sweden)

The Frödingsstipendiet is an
award of the students' unions of
Sweden, administered by the
Upsala (Uppsala) Students Union
(Uppsala studentkår, Uppsala
Universitet, Uppsala), in the
form of a five-year stipend, pay-
ing 1.600 Swedish crowns each
year--with a possible extension
of one or two years beyond the
five-year grant. The prize,
established May 27, 1903, is
determined by vote of the students who are members of various
Swedish student unions, belonging
to the Swedish National Union of
Students. Swedish writers who
have won the grant by receiving
the most student votes are: Ola
Hansson, Wilhelm Ekelund,
Jarl Hemmer, Hjalmar Soder-
berg, Nils Ferlin, Harry Martinsson, Gunnar Ekelof, F. Nilsson
Piraten, Evert Taube.   443.

Andor GABOR PRIZE (Hungary)

A biennial award established
in 1958 by the widow of Andor
Gabor with a premium of 10,000
Forints to be granted each
January 20, anniversary of the
death of author Gabor, the prize,
which honors alternately an outstanding poet and a prose writer,
has been won by:

    1958 Imre Györi (poetry)
    1960 Zoltán Galabárdi (prose)
    1962 András Dioszegi (poetry)
                              444.

GAELIC LEAGUE PRIZES
(Ireland)

A number of Gaelic literary
prizes in poetry, fiction and
drama are awarded annually by
the Gaelic League (Connradh na
Gaeilge, 14 Parnell Square,
Dublin) at the League Festival
(Oireachtas) held each year since
its revival in 1939. Because of
the large number of plays entered
in the drama competition, the
Festival is now held (since 1961)
in two parts--All-Drama Festival
in May; Festival Week (Oireachtas),
with award of Literary Prizes in
October.

Designed "to discover and en-
courage new writers in Irish and
to promote the new Gaelic litera-
ture," the prizes for authors are
awarded in various categories:
Plays; Short Stories; Poems;
"Works for the Ordinary Irish
Reader;" Romantic or Historical
Novels; Biography. Major awards
are the CLUB LEABHAR COM-
PETITION (Chlub Leabhar)--
L200 for original works of
60,000 to 70,000 words; DUAIS
N COMHDHALA--L50 for original
work of 30,000 words; OIREACH-
TAS SPECIAL AWARD FOR OUT-
STANDING MERIT--awarded only
twice since 1939; SAIRSEAL
AGUS DILL PRIZE: COMHAR-
THA AN CHRAOIBHIN--an exceptional honor awarded from time
to time to an outstanding writer;
or--as BONN AN CHRAOIBHIN
(a language award)--to a person
who has given outstanding service
to the Gaelic language; AN
CHOMBAIRLE EALAION--a drama
prize (which see).

Writers honored by awards are:
Eugene Watters (Gaelic Poetry), and
    1957 Bonn an Chraoibhin--
    Padriag Mac Con Midhe
    1960 L200 premium--Eoghan Ó
    Tuairisc. D'Réir na Rúibrici
    (play--3-act comedy)
    1961 Eoghan Ó Tuairisc.
    Gradam an Oireachtais (novel)
    --granted a L200 premium,
    and the "Oireachtas Special
    Award for Outstanding Merit,"
    the second such award

granted since the revival of
the Festival in 1939   445.

Georges GARNIER PRIZE
(Belgium)

Founded as a triennial award
in 1942, this prize is granted
by the Belgian Royal Academy of
French Language and Literature
to a Belgian author, writing
in French, for a novel or
stories concerned with "aspects
and customs of the Walloon
provinces of Belgium." Novelists
receiving the 10,000 fr premium
include:
1954 Marianne Stoumon. La
Marquise
1957 Maud Frere. Vacances
secrètes
1960 Nelly Kristinck. La
Rose et le Rosier   446.

GASTALDI PRIZE (Italy)

Among the most famous and
the most important of Italian
literary honors is the Gastaldi
Prize, a publisher's award of
Editore Gastaldi (via Leopardi
22, Milan) granted in a number
of literary forms: such as
Novel, Poetry, Drama. The
total annual premium of L 1.500.
000 has been divided among as
many as 16 categories of
works: Critical Essay, Children's Books, Poetry, Drama,
Novel, Short Stories.

Writers honored include:
Children's Books (Gastaldi
Ragazzi)
1950 Riccardo Chiarelli.
La citta proibita
1954 Guido Spadini. Baffilonghi
1957 Luigi Rinaldi. La
grande battaglia
1958 Lorenzo Dojmi di Delupis.
Io e le chiocciole
1959 Angelo Mariani. Il
maestro racconta
1960 Adriana d'Gisimberti.
Ferronia citta del Cinque-
mila
1961 Lucilla Antonelli.

Piccola segretaria di papa
Poetry
1955 Fernando di Buglione.
Riflettori sull'anima
1958 Domenico Cuce. Questa
mia sera
1959 Michele Tommasino.
Vecchia citta
1960 Vito Liberio. Ho visto
morire l'estate
1961 Giuseppe Rigotti. Don
Chisciotte a riposa
Fiction (Gastaldi Narrativa; Concorso Romanzo)
1952 Edoardo Nulli. I sognatori dell'Ottagono
1953 Berto Bertu. Fortunale
1954 Guido Nanni Croce.
Sergio Coperni
1955 Giuseppe Urbani. Farisei
1956 Giuseppe Frasca. L'a-
more di Ippolito
1957 Carlo Callovini. Voli
d'aquila
1958 Gaetano Leto. Gli
allegri partigiani
1959 Antonietta Forte. Piano
inclinato
1960 Adamo Degli Occhi. Il
bianco e el nero
1961 Mario Perrone. Racconti
a Dawa
Essays (Gastaldi Saggistica;
Concurso Cultura)
1958 Giancarlo Torti. Lorenzo
Perosi; Maria Annunziata
Papini.Ricimero
1959 Ubaldo Riva. Due saggi
1960 Giovanni Acquaviva. Le
colonne d'Ercole
1961 No entries qualifying
Drama (Concurso Teatro)
1955 Edoardo Nulli. La divina
illusione
1956 Ernesto Sfriso. La
Giostra
1957 Francesco Ferrari. Il
corsaro bianco
1958 Giuseppe Frasca. L'amore
di Ippolito Nievo
1959 Cornelia Benazzoli. Un
personaggio superfluo
1960 Zeno Verga. L'incredi-
ble sfida; Mario Fratti. Il

rifiuto   447.

A GAZETA COMPETITION FOR
POETRY AND SHORT STORIES
(Brazil)
   A contest for women writers,
the Concurso Feminino de
Poesias e Contos, sponsored by
Fundação Casper Libero, of the
publication "A Gazeta" (Av.
Casper Libero 88, Sao Paulo),
offers an award to encourage
women writers throughout Brazil.
Initiated in 1950, the competition (with a First prize monetary premium of Cr $50.000 and
publication of the winning work)
has been held from time to time
for unpublished short stories and
poetry. In 1958, the premium
was increased and the contest
established as an annual event,
to alternate between Short Story
and Poetry.
   Contest winners include:
Short Story
   1950 Cecilia Prada. Ponto
      Morto (Dead Point)
   1959 Consuelo dos Reis
      Mello. Terra Bravia (Wild
      Land)
   2nd prize, Maria Lysia Correa
      de Araujo. Tres Historias
      (Three Tales)
Poetry
   1953 Lacyr Schettino. O
      Espelho da Morta (The
      Mirror of the Dead Woman)
   2nd prize, Renata Pallottini.
      Caes da serenidade (Serenity
      Embankment)
   1954 Celina Ferreira. Nave
      Incorpórea (Immaterial Ship)
   1956 Cléa Marsiglia. Canticos
      da Terra (Canticles of the
      Land)
      Lelia Coelho Frota. Alados
      Idilios (Winged Idyls)
   1957 Maria Lucia Alvim. XX
      Sonetos
   1960 Raulita Guerra Odriozola.
      Poemas de Minha Ronda
      (Poems of My Round) 448.

Reina Prinsen GEERLIGS PRIZE
(Netherlands; South Africa)
   Established by her parents
to commemorate the execution of
Reina Prinsen Geerligs by the
Germans at Oranienburg on November 23, 1943 for her part in the
underground resistance, this prize
is awarded for writing in Dutch,
Flemish and Afrikaans. The prize,
consisting of £20 and a document,
has been awarded every three
years in Holland since 1947; and
every three years in South Africa
since 1953. In South Africa,
the Geerligs Prize is presented
as part of the "commemoration of
the landing of Jan van Riebeeck at
the Cape, when the first white
settlement was founded."
   The award is directed to
recognizing promising talent and
encouraging the literary work of
young people, and authors between
20 and 30 years of age are eligible for the prize. Prize-winners
selected by the awarding agency,
Reina Prinsen Geerligs Foundation
(Koninginneweg 121, Amsterdam),
and presented the honor on November 24 include:
Netherlands (Dutch or Flemish
Language)
   1947 Simon van het Reve
      (Gerard Kornelis v.h. Reve).
      De avonden (prose)
   1948 Mies Bouthuys. Ariadne
      op Naxos (poetry)
   1949 Willem Witkampf. Het
      kanon (prose)
   1950 J. A. Blokker. Séjour
      (prose)
   1951 Harry Mulisch. Archibald
      Strohalm (novel)
   1952 Kees Stempels. De glazen
      bol (stories)
   1953 Ellen Warmond. Proeftuin
      (poetry)
      Remco Campert. Berchtesgaden
      (poetry)
   1954 Henk Meijer. Consternatie
      (stories)
   1955 W. G. Klooster. Tweemal.

Zonder het genadige einde
(two stories)
1956 Winnie Pendèl (G.W.
Hamer). Ik ga weg, tot
ziens (novel)
1959 J. Bernlef (H.J. Marsman). Kokkels (poetry)
1960 A.P. van Hoek. Duitsland
nu (play)
1961 Peter van Gestel. Vier
verhalen
1962 Steven Membrecht. Het
einde komt vanzelf
Republic of South Africa
(Afrikaans Language--plays,
prose or poetry; published or not
yet published)
1953 Ina Rousseau. Die Ver-
late Tuin (poems)
1956 Peter Blum. Steenbok
tot Poolsee (poems)
1962 Abraham H. de Vries.
Prose works, including:
Hoog teen die Heuningkrans
(1956); Verlore erwo (1958);
Vetkers en neonlig (1960)
449.

**GENERAL MOTORS HOLDEN'S
THEATRE AWARD (Australia)**

This drama prize is made in
association with the Australian
Elizabethan Theatre Trust (85
Goulburn Street, Sydney, N.S.W.)
and offers a premium (£300 and
trophy for First Prize) for the
best play or musical manuscript
submitted in competiton. Also,
the Australian Elizabethan
Theatre Trust 'will offer to
present or arrange the first
production of the prize-winning
play on the stage upon terms
and conditions negotiated." Any
citizen or resident of Australia
may compete for the award by
sending a manuscript play for
consideration (Deadline 1962:
September 30).
A MANIFOLD PLAYWRITING
AWARD of £1000 is also offered
by the Theatre Trust (239
Collins Street, Melbourne; 153
Dowling Street, East Sydney,

N.S.W.) for the best full-length
stage play--in prose or in verse,
published or unpublished--on the
subject of Australia, which is
submitted by any playwright,
Australian or foreign, by September 15, 1962.   450.

**GENEVA PRIZE (International--
Switzerland)**

Since 1944 an annual award has
been granted for cultural achieve-
ment--in successive years for:
Literature, Fine Art, Music,
and Science. The monetary premium for literature (at present
5000 fr) is presented by the
Administrative Council of the city
of Geneva upon the designation
of the prize winner by a special
sub-committee of five (including a novelist, a poet,
and a literary critic, three of
which must be members of the
Swiss Writers Association
(Association des Écrivains
suisses).

The prize was initiated to
honor a writer (novelist, historian, poet, dramatist, or essayist)
who by his entire work or a
particular writing has made an
eminent contribution to the cultural fame of Geneva. Writers
not resident in the city of Geneva
may be given the prize, as the sole
criterion for selection of the winner is the subject of the winning
work, which must be an outstanding writing about Geneva.
Laureates include:
1947 Jacques Chenevière
1951 Pierre Girard
1955 Marcel Raymond
1959 Henri de Ziegler   451.

**GENEVA WRITERS' PRIZE
(Switzerland)**

Since 1957 the Prix des Écrivains Genevois has been awarded
by the city of Geneva (Administrative Council) for an unpublished work in French. The
3.000 fr prize, presented in the

first three months of each year, is offered for a work by an author who is a native of Geneva or has specified years of residence in the city. Areas of writing honored rotate: Novel or Collection of Short Stories; Poetry; General Literature -- Essays, Critical Studies, Memoirs, Recollections. The jury of five members, including representatives of the Association des Écrivains de Genève, has selected for this literary honor:
    1957 Yvette Z'Graggen
    1958 Jean Hercourt
    1959 Henri Tanner, and Louis
      Bolle (divided equally)
    1961 Jérôme Deshusses
                 452.

GENS DE LETTRES SOCIETY PRIZES (France)

One of approximately 50 literary honors granted by the Société des Gens de Lettres (38 rue de Faubourg-Saint-Jacques, Paris 14e), an organization founded in 1838 by novelist Louis Desnoyers (1802-1868) and active primarily in questions of authors' rights, such as copyright and publication (Oxford Companion, p. 677). Two major prizes (Grands Prix) are awarded for the entire literary achievement of an author, and for a single published book of exceptional interest.

Recent winners of the 1000 NF prizes, which are announced the first week in March, are:
    1959 Jules Bertaut. Entire
      work
      Paul Tillard. L'outrage
    1960 Albert t'Serstevens.
      Entire work
      Jean Bassan. Les distractions
    1961 Raymond Las Vergnas.
      Entire work
      Robert Sabatier. La Sainte
      Farce
    1962 Catherine Paysen. Nous
      autres, les Sanchez

Marie Nöel. Entire work
                 453.

Alberto GERCHUNOFF PRIZE (Argentina)

Named in honor of the Russian-born Jewish writer of Argentina, Alberto Gerchunoff (1883-1950), this literary award of Instituto Argentino de Cultura y Informacion was granted
    1951 (?) Pablo Rojas Paz.
      Echeverria, el pastor de
      soledades
    1953 Samuel Eichelbaum;
      Manuel Mujica Láinez.
      Los Ídolos   454.

GERMAN CRITICS' PRIZE (Germany)

Since 1951 the Kritikerpreis has been awarded by the Verband der Deutschen Kritiker, Berlin, as part of the Berlin Festwoch in September or October. In addition to prizes for Music, Architecture, Dance, and Motion Pictures, there are two prizes for writers: Literature, and Drama. Recipients are:

Literature
    1951 Martin Kessel
    1952 Rudolf Hagelstange
    1953 Heinrich Böll
    1954 Arnold Hauser
    1955 Kurt Hiller
    1956 Gertrud Kolmar
    1957 Eva Rechel-Mertens
    1958 Alfred Andersch. Sansibar
      oder der letzte Grund
    1959 Theodor W. Adorno
    1960 Günter Grass
Drama
    1951 Maria Becker
    1952 Martin Held; Rudolf
      Forster
    1953 Rudolf Noelte
    1955 Leopold Rudolf
    1956 Oscar Fritz Schuh
    1957 Friedrich Maurer
    1958 Klaus Kammer
    1959 Hermann Herrey
    1960 Curt Bois   455.

GERMAN STAGE ORGANIZATION
DRAMA PRIZE (Germany)
Annual prizes of 3000 DM
are offered to three playwrights;
the Dramatikerpreis des Deutschen Bundesverein were won
in 1955 by: Ulrich Becker;
Matthias Braun, Claus Hubalek.
456.

GERMAN YOUTH BOOK PRIZE
(Germany)
The Deutscher Jugendbuch-
preis is offered each year for
books for children and young
people by the German Ministry
for Family and Youth Problems
(Bundesministerium für Familien-
und Jugendfragen, Bonn), in cooperation with the Juvenile
Writers' Association (Arbeits-
kreis für Jugendschrifttum,
Munich). Directed to encouraging the writing of good books
for children and young people,
the award--whose premium has
increased from 3000 to 5000 DM
since it was first granted in
1956--is offered in three categories: Young People's Book;
Children's Book; Children's Picture Book. Recipients include:
Young People's Book--
1956 Kurt Lütgen
1957 Meindert de Jong. Tien
Pao
1958 Marlene Reidel. Kasi-
mirs weltreise
1960 E. F. Lewis
Children's Book--
1956 Louise Fatio; Roger
Duvoisin
1957 Nicholas Kalashnikoff
1958 Heinrich Maria Danne-
borg. Jan und die Wild-
pferde
1959 Hans Peterson (Sweden)
Mathias and the Unicorn
1960 James Krüss
1961 M. Ende. Jim Knopf
und Lucas der Lokomotiv
fuhrer
Special Prize--
1956 Alberta Rommel

(Mädchenbuch)
Helga Strätling-Tölle
1958 Herbert Kaufmann.
Roter Mond und heisse Zeit
1960 Del Castillo
1961 P. Alverdes. translation
of J.F. Cooper, "Deer-
slayer"   457.

GERMAN YOUTH BOOK PRIZE
OF FRANZ SCHNEIDER PUBLISH-
ING COMPANY (Germany)
Offered by Franz Schneider
Verlag (Frankfurter Ring 150,
Munich 13), for the "beste Mäd-
chenbuch," this prize was won in
1954 by: Berte Bratt; Irene
Kordt; Rolf Ulrici; and Marlis
Zilknen.   458.

Friedrich GERSTÄCKER PRIZE
(Germany)
The City of Brunswick (Braunschweig) prize is named for the
19th century German author and
traveler, Friedrich Gerstäcker,
famous for his novels and adventure stories, and is offered biennially for a book through which
young people can experience the
whole world, in the adventurous
spirit of Gerstäcker. The prize,
consisting of a plaque and 3000
DM, has been granted:
1952 Kurt Lütgen
1954 Fritz Mühlenweg
1956 Hans Baumann
1959 Erich Wustmann. Taowaki
459.

Guido GEZELLE PRIZE (Belgium)
A recent winner of the Belgian
Royal Academy of Flemish Sci-
ences, Letters and the Arts award
is Jos de Haes (1957), with
"Gedaanten."   460.

GHANA ACADEMY OF SCIENCES
MEDALS
Instituted in November 1959 by
Prince Philip, Duke of Edinburgh,
when he visited Ghana and established the Ghana Academy of Learning (now Ghana Academy of Sciences,

P.O. Box 179, Accra), these
awards are also designated the
"Prince Philip Medals." A Gold
Medal, to be offered each year
"for the most distinguished contribution to knowledge by a
Ghanian," may be granted on the
anniversary of the inauguration
of the Academy, November 27.
The Silver Medal offered by the
Academy is granted for "the
most promising work in science"
achieved by a Ghana university
student.   461.

GHENT PRIZE (Belgium)
    The Prijs van de Stad is an
annual award for Flemish writing,
which has recently been won by:
    1958 Prosper de Smet. Aan
        de vort van het Gravensteen
    1959 Jo Verbrugghen. Ik ben
        Judas Iskarioth   462.

"GIDS" PRIZE (Netherlands)
    An award granted for one-
act plays since 1955 by the
periodical "Gids," P. V. van
Kampen & Zoon, Singel 330,
Amsterdam C.   463.

Café GIJON PRIZE (Spain)
    Named for a famous Café,
frequented by writers, this very
popular prize of 10,000 pts has
been awarded by the Revista
"Garbo" (Calle Tallers 62,
Barcelona) for the best novella
(Novela corta) by a Spanish or
a Latin American writer. Since
this award was established in
1952, winners have included:
    1952 Ana Maria Matute.
        Fiesta al noroeste
    1954 Carmen Martin Gayite.
        El Balneario
    1955 Begona Garcia Diego.
        Bodas de Plata
    1957 Daniel Sueiro. La
        Caza
    1959 José Medina Gómez.
        Cámara oscura   464.

Rosamond GILDER AWARD
(Latin America)
    The prize, granted in a con-
test for the best translations of
Latin American plays, was
granted in 1959 to: Carlos
Gorostiza, "Bridge of Rio Cam-
pana," translated by Louis Curcio;
Usigli, "Another springtime,"
translated by Wayne Waif; and--
a prize for children's play--
Arthur Soferman, "The ugly
little dwarf," translated by
Howard van Roy.   465.

GILES PRIZE (France)
    A biennial prize of the Académie
des Inscriptions et Belles-Lettres
is granted to a French writer
for a work relating to China,
Japan, or the Far-East in general.
Winners include:
    1951 Henri Deydier. Contribu-
        tion à l'étude de l'art du
        Gandhara
    1953 Charles Haguenauer.
        Morphologie du japonais
        moderne
    1955 Marcelle Lalou. Bibliog-
        raphie bouddhique, t. XXI,
        XXII, XXIII
    1957 Jacques Gernet. Les
        aspects économique du Boud-
        dhisme dans la société
        chinoise du ve et xe siècle
    1959 Kanda Kiichiro.
    1961 Maurice Durand. Tech-
        niques et panthéons des
        mediums vietnamiens et
        Imagerie populaire vietna-
        mienne   466.

Mary GILMORE PRIZE (Australia)
    An award offered by trade
unions (Secretary, Mary Gilmore
Award, Room 75, Trades Hall,
Sydney) "to encourage writing on
themes of significance to the life
and aspirations of the Australian
people," offers a medallion and
a premium for various forms of
literature. Presented on May 1
each year, the prize rotates for:
Novel (1961); Short Story and

Poetry (1962); and Children's
Book (1963).   467.

GIRAFFE PRIZE (Italy)

Granted to writers of animal
stories for children, and instituted by the Center for Promotion of Children's Books (Centro
di propaganda del Libro per
ragazzi), the prize is administered by the "La Giraffa" press
(The Zoo, Rome). Each of the
ten prizes offered consists of a
country holiday in Piedmont.
468.

Esther GLEN AWARD (New Zealand)

Granted each year by the New
Zealand Library Association to
the most distinguished children's
book by a New Zealander (citizen
or resident) published in New
Zealand during a fiscal year
(July 1 to June 30 of the following year), the award consists of
a bronze medal "suitably inscribed," and may also include a
monetary premium, according to
a prize rules amendment of 1961.
Three judges, appointed by the
Association (New Zealand Library Association, 10 Park
Street, Wellington, N. 1, New
Zealand) recommend a publication for award, and no applications are called for. The prize
is presented during Children's
Book Week, if held, or at another
suitable time--not later than the
following annual meeting of the
Association.
Winners have been:
1945 Stella Morice. The book
of Wiremu
1947 A. W. Reed. Myths and
legends of Maoriland
1951 Joan Smith. Nimble,
Rumble, and Tumble
1959 Maurice Duggan. Galter
Tom and the Water Boy
469.

GOBERT PRIZE (France)

This annual prize of Académie
Française is granted for a writing in history. It was founded
by Baron Gobert, with a "Grand
Prix" for the "most eloquent work
on the history of France," and a
second prize for "the most
meritorious approach" to the subject.
Recent recipients of the honor,
first awarded in 1944, include:
1955 Henri Fréville. L'Intendance de Bretagne (50, 000 fr)
1956 François Pietri. Entire
historical work (50, 000 fr)
1957 Rousselet. Histoire de la
magistrature française
1958 Bernadine Melchior-Bon-
net. Napoléon et la Pape
1959 Jean-François Gravier.
Paris et le désert français
1960 Marquise de Maille. Research on the Christian
origins of Bordeaux
1961 François Bluche. Les
magistrats du Parlement de
Paris, au XVIIIe siècle
1962 Pierre Grosclaude.
Malesherbes, témoin de son
temps   470.

GOETHE MEDAL (International-- Germany)

Since the reestablishment of the
Goethe Institute for the Encouragement of the German Language in
countries other than Germany
(Goethe-Instituts zur Pflege der
deutschen Sprache im Ausland) in
Munich, the medal has been
granted each year to the person
in Germany or another country
who has made the most outstanding contribution to the furthering
of the German language outside
Germany. Winners of the Gold
Medal--a Silver Medal is also
awarded--are such scholars and
writers as:
1954 D. Moe (Copenhagen)
1955 A. Lodewyck (Melbourne);
C. Lucerna (Zagreb)
1956 A. Lindquist (Goteborg,

Sweden)
1957 G. Alfero (Genoa); P.
Katara (Helsinki); K. Magnus
(Wiesbaden); J. H. Scholte
(Amsterdam); E. G. Water-
house (Sydney)
1958 G. Bohnenblust (Geneva);
M. Boucher (Paris); M.
Colleville (Paris); L. L.
Hammerich (Copenhagen);
E. Löffler (Stuttgart)
1959 G. Bianquis (Bagneux,
France); A. Rojo (Santiago,
Chile); E. Rooth (Lund,
Sweden)
1960 L. Bianchi (Bologna);
R. Foncke (Brussels);
Bonaventura Tecchi (Italy)
                                    471.

GOETHE PLAQUE (Germany)
   The Goethe-Plakette, a cultural
prize of the region of Hesse,
is offered by the Hessen Minister für Erziehung und Volksbildung in the form of a bronze
medal, granted for service to the
cultural life of Hesse (Hessen).
Established May 9, 1932, as part
of the centennial commemoration of Goethe's death, the prize
has been awarded each year for
cultural, artistic, and scientific
achievement "in the spirit of
Goethe." Recent plaques granted
in literature include:
   1955 Bernard von Brentano
   1956 Karl Friedrich Borée;
   Hermann Kasack; Fritz von
   Unruh
   1958 Werner Bock
   1960 Fritz Usinger
   The city of Frankfurt also
offers a prize called "Goethe-
Plaque" (Goethe-Plakette), which
is granted by the Magistrat of
Frankfurt am Main. This
Goethe Medal, established in 1932,
includes among recent recipients:
   1956 Peter Suhrkamp
   1957 Kasimir Edschmid;
   Benno Reifenberg; Gottfried
   Bermann Fischer; Rudolf
   Pechel

1959 Thornton Wilder (U.S.A.),
one of five awards   472.

GOETHE PRIZE (Germany)
   One of Germany's most distinguished literary honors is the
cultural prize of the city of Frankfurt am Main, birthplace of
Goethe. The award was es-
tablished in 1926 as an annual
prize to be presented each August
28, Goethe's birth date, "for
outstanding literary and humanistic
achievement." The award is not
a competitive prize that is applied
for, but is rather a high honor
which "crowns work that has already achieved general recognition." Winners are determined
by a committee of selection
of nine members--scholars, public officials, and German authors,
such as Benno Reifenberg and
Carl Zuckmayer. Since 1952
the prize is given triennially,
and the initial premium of
10.000 DM has increased to the
50.000 DM granted in 1961.
   Recipients of Germany's
highest honor for literature and
cultural achievement, which is
presented by the Lord Mayor of
Frankfurt in historic St. Paul's
Church, meeting place of Germany's first national Assembly in
1848, are:
   1927 Stefan George
   1928 Albert Schweitzer
   1929 Leopold Ziegler
   1930 Sigmund Freud
   1931 Ricarda Huch
   1932 Gerhart Hauptmann
   1933 Hermann Stehr
   1934 Hans Pfitzner
   1935 Hermann Stegemann
   1936 Georg Kolbe
   1937 Erwin Kolbenheyer
   1938 Hans Carossa
   1939 Carl Bosch
   1940 Agnes Miegel
   1941 Wilhelm Schäfer
   1942 Richard Kuhn
   1945 Max Planck

1946 Hermann Hesse
1947 Karl Jaspers
1948 Fritz von Unruh
1949 Thomas Mann
1952 Carl Zuckmayer
1955 Annette Kolb
1958 Carl Friedrich, Freiherr
von Weizsäcker
1959 Ernst Beutler
1961 Walter Gropius   473.

GOETHE PRIZE OF EAST BERLIN (Germany, East)

The Magistrat von Gross-Berlin grants the award for Science, Technology and Art, and since 1950, the prize has honored such East German authors as Jan Petersen (1950)--Entire Work; Paul Wiens (1952)--Gedichte and Lieder; Alex Wedding (1956)--Children and Youth Literature; Hedda Zinner (1959) --Entire Work.   474.

GOETHE PRIZE OF EAST GERMANY

The Goethe-Nationalpreis der DDR für Literatur is awarded German writers for outstanding literary contributions, whether they reside in Germany or in another country. Recipients of the honor include: Heinrich Mann; Carl Orff; Hirnforscher-Ehepaar Voigt; Volksliederforscher Meier.

On October 28, 1958, occasion of the celebration of the 209th anniversary of Goethe's birth, a GOETHE PREIS FÜR LEISTUNGEN AUF DEM GEBIET VON KUNST UND KULTUR was presented to Walter Friedrich, Vice-President of the German Academy of Science in East Berlin, and to Gottfried Hermann, Varieté-Direktor.   475.

GOETHE PRIZE OF HAMBURG (International--Germany)

The Hansischer Goethe-Preis, awarded since 1949 (early awards annual and beginning in 1959 biennial) by the Foundation "Freiherr vom Stein" of Hamburg, honors a person whose life and work have served to increase understanding among the peoples of the world. The Hanseatic Goethe Prize of Stiftung F.V.S. zu Hamburg (25.000 DM and a gold medal) is presented each year by the Rector of the University of Hamburg. Recipients, recognized for their distinguished achievements and contributions in the humanities, are:
1950 Carl Jacob Burckhardt
(Switzerland)
1951 Martin Buber (Israel)
1952 Edouard Spranger (Germany)
1953 Elvind Josef Berggrav
(Norway)
1954 T. S. Eliot (U.S.A.--United Kingdom)
1955 Gabriel Marcel (France)
1956 Walter Gropius (Germany--U.S.A.)
1958 Paul Tillich (Germany--U.S.A.)
1959 Theodor Heuss (Germany)
1961 Benjamin Britten (United Kingdom)   476.

GOLDEN BOOK PRIZE (Italy)

Since 1957 the Premio Libro d'Oro, a national award offered by Officio della Proprieta Letteraria Artistica e Scientifica della Presidenze del Consiglio dei Ministri (via Boncampagni 15, Rome), has honored each year a publisher whose activities have contributed the most to the elevation and diffusion of Italian culture. The award jury, composed of distinguished authors and leading publishers, has awarded the Libro d'Oro--usually given in March--to:
1957 Arnoldo Mondadori
1958 Enrico Vallecchi
1959 Valentino Bompiani
1960 Zanichelli
1961 Casa Editrice UTET
(Unione Tipografico--

Editrice Torinese)   477.

GOLDEN GOOSE-FEATHER
(Netherlands)
De Gouden Ganzeveer, prize of
the Royal Netherlands Associa-
tion of Editors (Koninklijke
Nederlandse   Uitgeversbond),
has been granted since 1955.
Among the winners is A.J.
Barnouw.   478.

GOLDEN MADONNA PRIZE
(Italy)
A national Italian award,
offered in three sections of
writing: Poetry, Narrative,
Journalism; and granted by
Premio "La Madonnina" (via Fra-
polli 22, Milan). The 1962
prize with a premium of L
500.00 is offered for collections
of short stories published from
January 1961 to September 1962,
and for unpublished poetry with
no set theme.   479.

GOLDEN QUILL PRIZE (Italy)
This high national literary
honor, offered by Officia della
Proprieta Letteraria Artistica
e Scientifica della Presidenze
del Consiglio dei Ministri (via
Boncampagni 15, Rome), annually recognizes a writer who
has made a major contribution
to Italian letters. Since 1957,
the L 5.000.000 prize has
been conferred by a jury of
distinguished authors and publishers on:
    1957 Giovanni Papini
    1958 Giuseppe Ungaretti
    1959 Emilio Cecchi
    1960 Bruno Nardi
    1961 Giacoma DeVoto   480.

GONCOURT PRIZE (France)
Awarded each year on the
first Monday in December, this
literary honor of the Académie
Goncourt (6 rue Jean-Goujon,
Paris) is among the most impor-

tant and best-known French prizes
for authors. The Académie Goncourt, composed of ten famous
men of letters--currently including Jean Giono, Raymond Queneau,
Hervé Bazin, Alexandre Arnoux,
André Billy, Philippe Hériat,
Roland Dorgelès and Pierre Mac-
Orlan--was founded on December
21, 1903 to recognize "independent"
literature, in opposition to the
Académie Française, whose prizes
rewarded the conservative stylist
writing in the classic tradition.
The Goncourt brothers--Edmond
Goncourt (1822-1896) and Jules
Goncourt (1830-1870), French
critics and authors who collabor-
ated on a number of novels and
historical writings--founded the
Académie Goncourt with an endowment, and the amount of the
prize, currently 50 NF, is the
least significant aspect of the
award, which calls international
attention to the recipient and
insures increased sales of the
winning work.
The prize is awarded for a
prose work, preferably a novel,
published during the year, and
brings recognition to a younger
writer of imaginative literature,
as it emphasizes "youth, originality, and style." The jury
meets according to tradition in
the famous Drouant restaurant,
and the announcement of the award
winner is made to an eager crowd,
similar to that attending a Hollywood premier.
Laureates, who have received
the honor with the traditional
"vin d'honneur," are:
    1903 John-Antoine Nau. Force
    ennemie
    1904 Léon Frapié. La mater-
    nelle
    1905 Claude Farrère. Les
    civilisés
    1906 Jérôme et Jean Tharaud.
    Dingley, l'illustre écrivain
    1907 Emile Moselly. Terres

lorraines
1908 Francis de Miomandre.
Ecrit sur de l'eau
1909 Marius-Ary Leblond.
En France
1910 Louis Pergaud. De
Goupil à Margot
1911 Alphonse de Chateau-
briant. Monsieur des
Lourdines
1912 André Savignon. Filles
de la pluie
1913 Marc Elder. Le peuple
de la mer
1914 Not awarded until 1916
1915 René Benjamin. Gaspard
1916 Adrien Bertrand. L'appel
du sol; Henry Barbusse. Le
feu (1914 prize)
1917 Henri Malherbe. La
flamme au poing
1918 Georges Duhamel. Civil-
isation
1919 Marcel Proust. A l'ombre
des jeunes filles en fleurs
1920 Ernest Pérochon. Nène
1921 René Maran. Batouala
1922 Henri Béraud. Le
vitriol de lune; Le martyre
de l'obèse
1923 Lucien Fabre. Rabevel
1924 Thierry Sandre. Le
chèvrefeuille
1925 Maurice Genevoix.
Raboliot
1926 Henry Deberly. Le sup-
plice de Phèdre
1927 Maurice Bedel. Jérôme,
60° latitude nord
1928 Maurice Constantin-
Weyer. Un homme se
penche sur son passé
1929 Marcel Arland. L'ordre
1930 Henri Fauconnier.
Malaisie
1931 Jean Fayard. Mal
d'amour
1932 Guy Mazeline. Les
loups
1933 André Malraux. La
condition humaine
1934 Roger Vercel. Capitaine
Conan
1935 Joseph Peyre. Sang et

lumière
1936 Maxence Van der Meersch.
L'empreinte du Dieu
1937 Charles Plisnier. Faux
passeports
1938 Henri Troyat. L'araigne
1939 Philippe Hériat. Les enfants gâtés
1940 Not awarded until 1946
1941 Henri Pourrat. Vent de
Mars
1942 Marc Bernard. Pareils à
des enfants
1943 Marius Grout. Passage
de l'homme
1944 Elsa Triolet. Le premier
accroc coûte deux cents francs
1945 Jean-Louis Bory. Mon
village à l'heure allemande
1946 Jean-Jacques Gautier.
Histoire d'un fait divers
Francis Ambrière. Les
grandes vacances (1940 prize)
1947 Jean-Louis Curtis. Les
forêts de la nuit
1948 Maurice Druon. Les
grandes familles
1949 Robert Merle. Week-end
à Zuydcoote
1950 Paul Colin. Les jeux
sauvages
1951 Julien Gracq (pseud of
Louis Poirier). Le rivage des
Syrtes (award refused as
author opposed to literary
prizes)
1952 Béatrix Beck. Léon
Morin, prêtre
1953 Pierre Gascar. Le temps
des morts, et les Bêtes
1954 Simone de Beauvoir. Les
Mandarins
1955 Roger Ikor. Les eaux
mêlées
1956 Romain Gary. Les
racines du ciel
1957 Roger Vailland. La loi
1958 Francis Walder (pseud
of Francis Waldburger--
Belgium). Saint-Germain
ou la négociation
1959 André Schwarz-Bart. Le
dernier des justes
1960 Vintila Horia. Dieu est

né en exile (revealed as
former fascist by the Communist Daily, "L'Humanité;"
Horia then refused prize;
the Académie then withdrew
award)
1961 Jean Cau. La pitié de
Dieu
1962 Anna Langfus (Poland--
France). Les bagages de
sable   481.

GOSLAR CULTURAL PRIZE
(Germany)
A 5000 DM cultural award of
the city of Goslar, granted annually since 1956 to persons who
have made a significant contribution to the Arts or Sciences
through their entire work or a
single work, has included prizes
for Literature and for Drama.
Authors receiving the honor include:
1955 Ernst Jünger
1956 Heinz Hilpert
1958 Wilhelm Hochgrave
1960 Gerhard Cordes   482.

L. GOULANDRIS PRIZE (Greece)
One of five prizes granted each
year since 1950 by a group of
writers known as the "Group of
Twelve," and so also called "The
Group of Twelve Prize," the
Goulandris Prize is among the
"principal literary awards of
Greece." It offers a premium of
Drs 15,000 for the best work of
Literary Criticism, Travel
Impressions, or Essay, published
in Greece during the preceding
year, and deposited in the Greek
National Library. Among recent
winners are:
1957 Athanasiadis-Novas
1958 Manolis Kriaras
1959 Pantelis Prevelakis
1960 Emilios Hourmouzios
                            483.

GREEK NATIONAL PRIZE
This national literary honor
of the Greek government, awarded

by the Greek Ministry of Education and Religion (Department of
Letters and Fine Arts, 2 Evange-
listrias Street, Athens) is the
highest official recognition given
an author in Greece. The prize,
also known as the "Greek State
Awards," and the "Greek Ministry
of Education Awards," is conferred
each fall, with a premium ranging
from Drs 10,000 to 30,000, on
the "best work" in the categories
of writing: Poetry; Short Story;
Essay; Novel; Biography or
Biographical Novel; Published
Drama; Travel Impressions.
Awards are made on the basis
of recommendations of a committee of literary authorities
(professors, writers and critics),
and any Greek citizen may receive the honor, provided the
work considered for award is
deposited with the Greek National
Library. In addition to the
monetary premium, 100 copies of
each prize-winning book are purchased by the Greek Ministry of
Education and sent to libraries
throughout Greece. Another
"Greek National Prize" of Drs
30,000 is granted for the best unpublished and unproduced stage
play. This award was presented
for the first time to Pant.
Prevelakis for his play, "The
Volcano."
Recipients of First and Second
Prizes in these Greek "State A-
wards," for "works judged the best
of the year from the point of view
of content, quality and form of
presentation," include:
Biography and Biographical Novel
(20,000 Dr)
1956 Tasos Athanasiadis.
Dostoevsky: From the Galley
to Pathos
1957 Ioannis Theodorakopoulos.
Faust
1958 Michael Peranthis.
Souliotes; Vranousis. Rigas
Ferreos
1959 Stratis Tsirkas. Cavafy

and his times
Drama (30,000 Dr)
  1956 Nikos Kazantzakis.
    Theater
  1958 Theophilos Frangopoulos.
    Patience
  1959 P. Kagias. Theater
  1960 Alexander Matsas.
    Croesus
Essay (15,000 Dr)
  1956 Cleon Paraschos. Forms
    and ideas
    Yannis Hatzinis. Greek texts
  1957 G. Theotokas. Problems
    of our times
    Hrysos Evelpidis. Civilisa-
    tion Civilisations
  1958 Timos Malanos. Cavafy
    Apostolos Sahinis. Historical
    novel
  1959 Panos Karavias. March
    without stars
  1961 Petros Spandonidis.
    Kazantzakis
    Kitsos Makris. Folk art of
    Pilion
Novel (25,000 Dr; 10,000 Dr)
  1956 N. Kasdaglis. The
    teeth of the millstone
  1957 Aris Dikataeos. The
    state
    I.M. Panagiotopoulos. The
    seven sleeping children
    Costas Soukas. The criminal
    record of an era
  1958 Angelos Terzakis. Secret
    life
    Stelios Xefloudas. Odysseus
    without Ithaca
  1959 G. Manglis. Men, my
    brothers
    Rodis Provelengios. The
    other bank
  1960 Pantelis Prevelakis. The
    sun of death
    Galateia Saranti. Our old
    house
  1961 Stelios Xefloudas. You,
    Mr. X and a small Prince
    Yiannis Sfakianakis. The
    guilty
    William Abbot. Dimitrios
    Gabriel
Poetry (20,000 Dr; 10,000 Dr)

  1956 Nikiphoros Vrettakos.
    Poems 1929-51
    Yeorgios Themelis. Orchard
    Zoe Karelli. Cassandra and
    other poems
  1957 Yiannis Ritsos. Moonlight
    Sonata
    Minas Dimakis. Dark passage
  1958 Nikos Engonopoulos. In
    the flowering Greek word
    G. Geralis. Reception room
  1959 G. Kotsiras. Sisyphos
    Nano Valaoritis. Central
    Arcade
  1960 Odysseas Elytis. It is
    worthy
    Nik. Papas. 5 past 12
  1961 Minas Dimakis. The
    voyage
    Costas Steryiopoulos. The
    shadow and the light
Short Story (20,000 Dr; 10,000
Dr)
  1956 Michael Karagatsis. Grand
    procession
    Spiros Plaskovitis. The
    storm and the beacon
  1957 Thanasis Petsalis-
    Diomidis. Exaltation of the
    Sweet Land Cyprus
    Tatiana Milliex. We change
    Yiannis Maglis. Sinners don't
    exist
  1958 Angelos Vlahos. Hours of
    life
    K. Makistos. The upset
  1959 G. Grigoris. State un-
    covered
  1960 Kosmas Politis. Crab-
    apple tree
    Renos Apostolidis. Stories
    from the Southern States
  1961 Mona Mitropoulou. Holiday
    Dim. Zade. Gull nests in
    Phymaena
Travel Impressions (15,000 Dr)
  1956 Ioannis Marmaryadis (pen
    name: Petros Haris). Cities
    and seas
  1957 Pavlos Paleologos.
    Kerkyra, my love
  1958 D. Mostratou. Kargeze
  1959 Man. Gialourakis. Sina-
    Crete   484.

GREEK WOMEN'S LITERARY
GROUP AWARDS
Several prizes for children's
literature are offered by the
organization, "Women's Literary
Group," (Vasileiou Publishing
House, 40 Stadium Street,
Athens). For 1962 these awards
include:
Aglaia TAKOVIDOU PRIZE--
5,000 Dr premium for a
poetry collection for children
Simon SIKIARIDIS PRIZE--
5,000 Dr premium for short
stories for children
Vasileiou PUBLISHING HOUSE
PRIZE--illustration and publication of the winning book
for children   484a.

GREGORY MEDAL (Ireland)
Awarded triennially for "distinguished work in Irish Literature," this medal, administered
by the Irish Academy of Letters
(c/o Abbey Theatre, Pearse
Street, Dublin) is one of several
literary honors granted by the
Academy. Padraic Colum received the medal in 1953.
                                 485.

Leon de GREIFF PRIZE (Latin
America--Venezuela)
The Premio Interamericano
de Poesía Leon de Greiff is a
biennial poetry prize, established
by the Architect Carlos Celis
Apero on May 5, 1956 in Caracas
to honor the Colombian poet,
Leon de Greiff (1895-), and to
"encourage poets of the Spanish
language all over the world."
The prize, which is administered
under the auspices of Asociación
de Escritores Venezolanos (Centro Profesional del Este, oficina
104, Calle Vilaflor, Sabana
Grande, Caracas), consists of a
premium of Bs 4.000, a gold
medal, a diploma, and publication of the winning poems in a
book.
A jury of scholars and writers

has awarded the prize to:
1956 Juan Manuel González
(Venezuela). La Heredad
Junto al Viento
1958 Sebastian Salazar Bondy
(Peru). Conducta Sentimental
                                 486.

GRENFELL FESTIVAL AWARDS
(Australia)
Grenfell's annual prize, in
honor of its native son, Henry
Lawson, Australia's first great
writer of short stories and bush
ballads, is offered for the best
poem and the best prose work
submitted in competition at the
Henry Lawson Festival, held on
the Queen's Birthday holiday week-
end in June.
The "Lawson Prize"--a bronze
Ampol (statuette)--awarded each
year since 1958 includes among
honored writers:
Prose
1960 Cyril E. Goode
1961 R.N. Callender
1962 Griffith Watkins. Down at
the Twenty One Hundred
Poetry
1960 Eric Rolls
1961 J. Kennedy
1962 Len Fox. The conquest of
Australia   487.

GRILLPARZER PRIZE (Austria)
Since 1872, several prizes of
this name (commemorating the
Austrian poet and playwright,
Franz Grillparzer, 1791-1872)
have been granted in Austria.
Such a literary honor was won in
1908 by Artur Schnitzler.
Winners of the current Grillparzer Prize, since 1937 when a
triennial Grillparzer-Preis was
instituted by the Austrian Academy
of Science (Österreichischen
Akademie der Wissenschaften), include:
1947, 1950 Rudolf Holzer
1953 Rudolf Bayr
1956 Fritz Hochwälder
                                 488.

GRIMM BROTHERS PRIZE
(Germany)
This prize for children's literature was established in Berlin in 1961 to encourage the writing of modern fairy tales and plays for children. The award brings a premium of 10,000 DM to be granted each two years on December 16, date of the death of Wilhelm Grimm.   489.

GROVE PRESS INDIAN FICTION PRIZE (India---U.S.A.)
A publisher's award, granted a single time in 1956 by Grove Press (64 University Place, New York 3), was directed to furthering "cultural relations between the United States and India." The $1,000 premium offered for the best novel manuscript in English submitted by a citizen of India, rewarded the work of Khushwant Singh, who won the prize with "Mano Majra."   490.

GRUPPE 47 PRIZE (Germany)
A group of approximately 100 young authors and critics, seeking to recognize and encourage the work of younger writers of talent, established the prize in 1947. The prize premium has increased over the years from 3000 DM to 5000 DM, and the award--granted for the best unpublished work presented for consideration--is announced on the annual festival of the group--Herbsttagung, held in Munich each October.
Among writers honored are:
1950 Günter Eich
1951 Heinrich Böll
1952 Ilse Aichinger
1953 Ingeborg Bachman
1954 Adrian Morrien
1955 Martin Walser
1958 Günter Grass. Die
   Blechtrommel   491.

GUANABARA STATE PRIZE
(Brazil)
The Guanabara State Secretary of Education and Culture (Secretaria de Educação e Cultura) annually grants a number of literary awards for unpublished writings, submitted anonymously in three copies for the prize. Guanabara State is the administrative region in which Rio de Janeiro, former capital of Brazil is located, and the literary honors it grants include: Five prizes of Cr $ 50.000 each for Novel (Prêmio Manuel Antonio de Almeida); Short Story or Chronicle (Prêmio Machado de Assis); Poetry (Prêmio Olavo Bilac); Essay and Criticism (Prêmio Carlos de Laet); Biography and History (Prêmio Barão do Rio Branco). Four prizes for unpublished works of Children's Literature are also offered with premiums that include awards of Cr $ 50.000 and Cr $ 30.000 for authors (Authors--Prêmio José Bento Monteiro Lobato; Illustrators--Prêmio Alfredo Storni).
In 1960, recipients of literary prizes included:
Almeida Prize (Novel)--Emi Bulhoes Fonseca de Carvalho. Nós três (published as "Os Sete Silêncios")
de Laet Prize (Criticism--Osvaldino Ribeiro Marques. O Laboratório poético de Cassiano Ricardo
Olavo Bilac Prize (Poetry)--Rute Silvia de Miranda Sales. Canção para Ubutuba; Walmir Ayala. A rosa no pulso
Monteiro Lobato Prize (Children's Literature)--Walmir Ayala. O Canario eo Manaquim   492.

GUATEMALA CITY NATIONAL FAIR PRIZE (Guatemala)
The highest literary award of the "Concurso Literario" of the Guatemala City Feria Nacional, first held in 1938, brought a Flor

Natural and a gold medal to Augusto Meneses (pen name: Balamjuya) for "Mi Guatemala Criolla."   493.

John Simon GUGGENHEIM MEMORIAL FELLOWSHIPS (International --U.S.A.)

Established in 1925 by Mr. and Mrs. Simon Guggenheim, in memory of their son who died April 26, 1922, with a four million dollar grant, these annual awards are directed to improving cultural relations between the republics of the Americas, encouraging scientific investigation, and securing a community of scholarships between the countries in the Western Hemisphere.

The Becas de Intercambio entre Las Repúblicas de la América Latina y Los Estados Unidos de América are announced in April or May each year by the Foundation Trustees, who select Fellows to receive awards from nominees of a Committee of Selection. Men or women who have made distinguished contributions in the sciences and arts are eligible for consideration as Fellows (provided they are citizens or permanent residents of the United States of America, including Puerto Rico; the Latin American Republics; British Caribbean; Canada; or the Republic of the Philippines). Applications must be made in writing before December 31 of the year preceding award, and applications of Fellows for renewal of grants must be received by February 15 of the year of grant. Renewal and Application forms may be obtained from the John Simon Guggenheim Memorial Foundation (551 Fifth Avenue, New York 17), or from Latin American representatives of the Foundation: Mexico (Arq. Carlos Contreras, Edificio La Nacional, Despacho 1004, Avenida Juarez

4, Mexico, D.F.); Argentina (Dr. Luis Baudizzone, San Martin 345, Buenos Aires); Chile (Dr. Joaquin Luco, Universidad Catolica de Chile, Santiago).

In the areas of Creative Writing and Literary History and Criticism, fellowship winners include:
Argentina--
    Emilio Carilla (1958--Style of Spanish American Literature)
    Rosa Chacel (1959--Creative writing; fellowship renewed 1960)
    Julio Fingerit (1932--Contemporary literature of the United States)
    Raimundo Lida (1939--The aesthetics and poetics of George Santayana)
Caribbean Area--
    John Errol (Trinidad) (1958--Creative writing: Drama)
    George Lamming (Barbados) (1954--Creative writing)
    Pierre Marcelin (Haiti) (1951--Creative writing)
    Edgar Austin Mittelholzer (Barbados) (1952--Creative writing)
    Felix Andrew Alexander Salkey (Jamaica) (1960--Study of Afro-Caribbean folk and dialect story as material for creative writing)
    Victor Stafford Reid (Jamaica) (1959--Creative writing)
    Samuel Selvon (British West Indies) (1955--Creative writing)
    Philippe Thoby-Marcelin (Haiti). (1951--Creative writing)
Chile--
    R. Fernando Alegría (1946--Influence of the poetry of Walt Whitman on the poets of the Americas)
Cuba--José Antonio Portuondo Valdor (1948--Literary criticism in Spanish America)
Mexico--
    Antonio Alatorre V. Chavéz (1959--Study of influence of Ovid on Spanish American literature)

Agustí Bartra Lleonart (1948--
Creative writing; fellowship
renewed 1960)
Octavio Paz (1943--Poetic
expression of the concept of
America)
Antonio Sánchez Barbudo
(1947--Comparative study of
Ralph Waldo Emerson and
Miguel de Unamuno)
Ramón Sender (1941--Creative
writing)
Republic of the Philippines--
Emigio Alvarez Enriquez
(1959--Creative writing)
Bienvenido N. Santos (1960--
Creative writing)
Edilberto K. Tiempo (1955--
The Philippine Short Story;
and creative writing)
Puerto Rico--
René Marqués (1954--Creative
writing)   494.

Mario Colombi GUIDOTTI PRIZE
(Italy)
A biennial literary award of
L 500.000 offered in Parma
(Presso l'avv. Giancarlo Artoni,
via Petrarca 16) is granted
alternately to a published fiction
book and to a work of criticism.
Since the first award in 1955,
recipients of the honor are:
1955 Pier Paolo Pasolini.
Ragazzi di vita
1957 Leone Piccioni. Tradizi-
one letteraria e idee correnti
1959 Roman Bilenchi. Rac-
conti   495.

GUILDE DU LIVRE PRIZE
(Switzerland)
The Prix Littéraire de la
Guilde du Livre is a publisher's
novel award that is granted biennially in Lausanne (4 avenue de
la Gare). The 5,000 fr sw
premium (3,000 fr sw outright
grant; 2,000 fr sw royalty advance on the first edition of
10,000 copies), presented each
autumn since 1941, is awarded
for an unpublished manuscript

in French--a minimum of 200
typed pages, with the only subject
restriction: "non-political"--sub-
mitted for consideration before
May 1 of the year of award.
Novelists recognized by the
award include:
1941 Jane Loisy. La vie de
Catherine Baron
1943 Gilbert Cesbron. Les
innocents de Paris
C.-L. Paron. Et puis s'en
vont
E.-E. Landry. Le mas
Méjac
1945 Gaston Baissette.
L'étang d l'or
Raymond Dumay. Les raisins
de maïs
1948 Jacques Mercanton. Le
soleil ni la mort
1951 Paul Pilotaz. La part du
ciel
1952 Anna Pollier. Grand Quai
1955 Nadine Lefébure. Les
portes de Rome
1957 Alain Le Breton. Pour-
suites
1959 Arthur Nisin. Un journal
de Russie
1961 Reine-Marie Sorel. Les
petites filles   496.

GUINNESS POETRY AWARD
(Ireland)
An annual literary award of the
brewer, Arthur Guinness, Son &
Company (Park Royal N.W., 10,
London) grants L 700 in prizes
(300, 200, and 100 pounds) for
the three best poems appearing
in print in England or Ireland
during the previous 12 months'
period. The 1959 prize was
divided equally between: W.H.
Auden, "Goodbye to the Mezzo-
giorno;" Robert Lowell, "Skunk
Hour;" Edwin Muir, "Impersonal
Calamity;" Edith Sitwell, "La
Bella Bona Roba"--with a L 50
award to William Plomer for "A
Young Jackdaw."   497.

GUJARAT BOOK AWARDS (India)

One of the regional or state literary prizes of India, this award offers Rs 36,000 for books in Gujarati--one of the major languages of India--in eight categories of literature for adults; and in four categories of literature for children.   498.

Calouste GULBENKIAN PRIZES (International--Portugal)
Established in 1962 by the Fundação Calouste Gulbenkian and administered by the Portuguese National Academy of Fine Arts (Academia Nacional de Belas Artes, Lisbon, Portugal), the prizes are monetary premiums for literary works in the Fine Arts: Esthetics, Art History and Archaeology (30 contos); Art Criticism (15 contos). Portuguese writers and authors of other nationalities may compete for the annual awards,which will be granted by a jury for a book published during the year, or to an unpublished work. For the Art Criticism award, critical articles published during the year in magazines or newspapers of Portugal, or abroad, by authors of any nationality, will be considered for the prize, as well as unpublished critical essays.
499.

GUTENBERG BOOK GUILD PRIZE (Switzerland)
Offered at infrequent intervals by the Zurich organization Büchergilde Gutenberg since 1935, the prize was presented in 1951 to: Otto Steiger; Hans Walter; and Alfred Frankhauser.   500.

GUTENBERG PLAQUE (Germany)
The city of Mainz presents the prize for outstanding cultural contributions. Among the authors so honored are: Carl Zuckmayer (1948); Josef Glückert (1951); Ludwig Berger (1957); and Kurt Goetz (1958).   501.

GUTENBERG PRIZE OF LEIPZIG (Germany, East)
This prize, granted each year for service to "socialist book promotion," was presented in 1959 to the International Book Exhibit.   502.

Søren GYLDENDAL PRIZE (Denmark)
The currently awarded Gyldendal Prize of 10,000 D kr, established by the publisher Søren Gyldendal (3 Klareboderne, Copenhagen) in 1958, is presented each year on April 12, the birthday of the founder of the firm--Søren Gyldendal (1742-1802). The prize is given "to one or more Danish authors, from any field, whose work is considered worth stimulating by the board of Gyldendal."
Previous literary awards of this name have been offered from time to time for a number of years. In the 1920's the Gyldendal Prize, offered jointly by the publishers Gyldendal and Bonnier (Stockholm), granted 3,500 D kr for the "best novel." Winners of this novel prize included Herman Wildenvey, and--in 1924--J. Anker-Larsen, with "Philosopher's Stone."
The present Gyldendal Prize has honored:
1958 Willy August Linnemann. Bogen om detskjulte ansigt
1959 K. E. Løgstrup; Sven Møller Kristensen
1960 Thorkilk Bjørnvig
1961 Jørgen Haestrup   503.

Guy HACHETTE PRIZE (France)
The Syndicate des Journalistes et Écrivains prize for young people's literature designates the best book for children from 12 to 16 years of age published since January 1 of the year of award. In 1960 Simone Voskressensky won the prize with "Le coeur d'or, L'escapade des marionnettes;" and in 1961 the winners were

Rene Violaines with "Pieds d'or," and Ry de La Touche with "Péricaud détective."   504.

HAITI LEGISLATURE PRIZE

The Prix du Corps Légis- latif was granted to Stéphen Alexis (1956?) for his patriotic play, "Le faisceau."   505.

HAITI PRESIDENT'S PRIZE

The highest official honor in Haiti was awarded to Placide David and Dominique Hippolyte (1956?) for "Le torrent."   506.

Joost HALBERTSMA PRIZE (Netherlands)

Since 1948 this biennial prize offered by the Friesland Province (Provinciale Staten van Fries- land, Leeuwarden) has been an alternate annual award with the Gysbert Japicx Prize. The literary honor, granted for his- torical writing in the Frisian language, is named for the regional writer Joost Halbertsma (1789-1869), a Mennonite clergy- man in Bolsward, and rewards with a premium of 500 fl the best publication of the preceding four years on the general or local history of Friesland, with the prize given alternately to an amateur and to a professional writer. Winners, determined with the advice of the Friesland Academy, include:

1958 H. Halbertsma. His- torical and archaeological writings

1960 A. Algra. Contribution to the history of church and school in Friesland in the 19th and 20th centuries, collected in the volumes: De historie gaat door het eigen dorp (History passes through each village)   507.

HALLE ART PRIZE (Germany, East)

The cultural awards of the city of Halle, first granted in 1953, are offered in the fields of: Painting, Music, Literature. The prize for writers, a total of 5000 DM, is given in three classes for a single work or for the entire literary work of an author. Recipients of the medals and premium, presented on October 7, anniversary of the founding of the DDR, include:

1956 Werner Reinowski. Der kleine Kopf
Friedrich Döppe. Forster in Mainz (novel)
1961 Christa Wolf. Moskauer Novelle   508.

HALLMARK INTERNATIONAL TELEPLAY COMPETITION (Inter- national--U.S.A.)

Established in 1960, "to en- courage the writing of meaning- ful, and original drama for television," the biennial prize of the greeting card manufacturer, Hallmark Cards, Inc. (680 Fifth Avenue, New York) offers a monetary premium for the best original 90-minute television script submitted during the con- test period. An official entry blank must accompany each manu- script sent for consideration. Hallmark Fund for Television Drama (P. O. Box 2805, Grand Central Station, New York 17) administers the contest, with a $250,000 grant from Hallmark Cards. Plays entered in compe- tition must be in English and the authors must be at least 18 years of age. The contest is not held on a regular basis, and winner of the first competition, which closed September 1, 1960, was David Mark, with "The old ball game."   509.

HAMBURG ACADEMY OF ART PLAQUE (International--Germany)

The annual prize of the Akademie der Künste, a general honor established in 1955 for out-

standing service to Literature,
Music, and Painting, consists of
a bronze plaque. Recipients of
the award, honored for their
literary achievement, include:
>   1955 Thomas Mann (Germany
>   --U.S.A.)
>   1957 John Cowper-Powys
>   (United Kingdom)
>   1959 Peter Huchel (Germany,
>   East)   510.

HAN KUK CULTURAL PRIZE
FOR PUBLISHING (Korea)

The annual prize of the Han
Kuk Newspaper (Han Kuk Ilbo
Sa, Chunghak-dong, Chongno-ku,
Seoul) is awarded each November for outstanding books or
other writings, including Korean
books or foreign books written
in Korean. The prize was
established in 1960, and the
prize rules require that competing works be submitted by
October 15, to qualify for consideration for the awards--which
consist of a citation, prize cup,
purse, and certificate of merit.
511.

HANAZIV PRIZE (Israel)

One of the literary honors of
the municipality of Haifa was
established in 1954 to recognize
outstanding writings in Rabbinical
literature. A monetary prize,
named for Rabbi Naftali Zvi
Berlin (Hanaziv), the award is
designed to stimulate research
in rabbinical affairs or to encourage popular religious literature. Two juries determine
prize winners: Original Research Work Jury--appointed by
Chief Rabbinate of Israel,
Chief Rabbinate of Haifa, and
representatives of the Talmudic
Encyclopedia, Jerusalem; Popular Rabbinical Work Jury--ap-
pointed by Haifa municipality
or by an institution authorized
by Haifa, in consultation with
the Chief Rabbinate of Haifa, the

Institute of Jewish Learning at
the Hebrew University of Jerusalem, and the Rav Kuk Institute,
Jerusalem.

Prize winners, honored by
presentation of the prize in the
month of Shwat of the Jewish
calendar, include:
>   1957 Chayim Druck. Oroth
>   ha-chayim (On the hours of
>   the day and night in the
>   halakha)
>   Mair Uriyan. Hamoreh
>   ledoroth (On Maimonides)
>   1958 Meir Sirovitz. Sefer
>   hassadeh (Mishna tractates
>   Peah and Demai)   512.

HANSEATIC SHAKESPEARE
PRIZE (International--Germany)

A literary honor awarded by
Hamburg University was granted
in 1938 to John Masefield
(United Kingdom), but was not
presented until January 1952,
due to health and social problems
postponing the ceremony.   513.

HARMSWORTH LITERARY
AWARD (Ireland)

The Ł 100 prize of the Irish
Academy of Letters (c/o Abbey
Theatre, Pearse Street, Dublin)
is granted for "the best work of
imaginative literature by an
Irish author." Recipients include:
>   1933 Lord Dunsany. The
>   curse of the wise woman
>   1934 Joseph O'Neill. Wind
>   from the North   514.

HARPER PRIZE NOVEL (Inter-
national--U.S.A.)

A biennial publisher's award--
the "largest prize regularly presented for fiction by any American institution"--brings $10,000
($2,000 outright grant, and
$8,000 minimum royalty guaran-
tee to be paid within six months
after publication) to the winning
author. Writers of any nationality are eligible to compete for
the prize, and manuscripts of

novels unpublished in book form, written in English, and at least 30,000 words in length, must be presented during the contest period (most recently, June 1, 1961 to June 1, 1962) to the editorial board of Harper & Brothers (49 East 33rd Street, New York 16). This board selects the submitted manuscripts for final judging by a jury of three distinguished authors.

The prize, directed to bringing "the full weight of critical and public attention to an author of fiction and his work," has signified recognition of exceptional literary achievement for such recipients as:

1929 Julien Green (France).
The dark journey
1937 Frederic Prokosch.
The seven who fled
1948 Joseph George Hitrec.
Son of the Moon   515.

Wilhelm HARTEL PRIZE
(Austria)

An annual prize of S 30.000, offered by the Austrian Academy of Science (Österreichischen Akademie der Wissenschaften) for an outstanding work in the sciences, was awarded in 1959 to Albin Lasky for "Geschichte der griechischen Literatur."
516.

K. HATZIPATERA PRIZE
(Greece)

One of five prizes offered each year since 1950 by a group of writers known as the "Group of Twelve," and so also called "The Group of Twelve Prize," this award grants Drs 15,000 for the best collection of poetry published in Greece during the preceding year, and deposited in the Greek National Library. Poets honored include:

1958 Nikos Karydis
1960 Takis Varvitsiotis   517.

Gerhart HAUPTMANN PRIZE
(Germany)

Several German literary prizes have been named for Gerhart Hauptmann (1862-1946), the famous German writer who won the 1912 Nobel Prize for Literature "in special recognition of the distinction and wide range of his creative work in the realm of dramatic poetry." An early Hauptmann Prize was presented in 1928 to Heinrich Hauser for his novel "Brackwasser (translated as "Bitter Water"), and in 1930 the award was given to Hulson for "Der Schatz im Acker."

The currently awarded Gerhart Hauptmann Prize is an annual award for drama, which was established by the West Berlin theater group, "Freien Volksbünne," in 1953. Presented each November, the prizes (totalling 15.000 DM to 20.000 DM) are offered for the advancement of dramatic writing of the "rising generation," and have been given to such "unknown or not widely known playwrights" as:

1953 Claus Hubalek. Der Hauptmann und sein Held
1954 Herbert Asmodi; Gert Weymann. Generationen
1955 Leopold Ahlsen. Philomen und Baukis
1956 Hermann Gressieker; Peter Hirche
1957 Wolfgang Altendorf. Entire work; Theodor Schübel. Kürassier Sebastian und sein Sohn
1960 Matthias Braun; Richard Hey; Hermann Moers; and a stipend of 2500 DM to Tankred Dorst   518.

Johann Peter HEBEL MEMORIAL MEDAL (Germany)

In addition to the Baden-Württemberg State Prize--the Hebel Gedenkpreis--this Hebel Gedenkmedaille was established in 1959 and first awarded in 1960 on the

second centenary of Swiss-born
poet Hebel's birth. Appropri-
ately granted to encourage writing in the Alamannic dialect--
Johann Peter Hebel (1760-
1826) wrote his famous collection of poems "Allemannische
Gedichte" in 1803 in that dialect
--the prize was presented to
Ernst Niefenthaler in 1960 for
"Der Weg berguf."   519.

Johann Peter HEBEL MEMORIAL
PRIZE (Germany)
   Each year on May 10, the
birthday of the famous poet of
the Baden-Württemberg region,
Johann Peter Hebel (1760-
1826), a memorial prize is presented by the Minister of Culture
of the State of Baden-Württemberg (Kultusministerium Baden-
Württemberg, Schillerplatz 5B,
Stuttgart) to a writer or poet
of the Upper Rhine area. The
5000 DM award (prior to 1960
the premium has ranged from
2500 to 4000 DM), established
in 1935 to honor the best regional
literary work, is directed to distinguishing valuable accomplish-
ments in contemporary literature
--both as an encouragement to
aspiring young authors and as
public recognition of the literary
contribution of established
writers.
   Winners of this literary honor,
which is granted without application, include:
   1936 Hermann Burte
   1937 Alfred Huggenberger
      (Switzerland)
   1938 Emil Strauss
   1939 Herman Eris Busse
   1940 Benno Rüttenauer
   1941 Eduard Reinacher
   1942 Wilhelm Weigand
   1943 Wilhelm Schäfer
   1944 Jacob Schaffner
   1946 Anton Fendrich
   1947 Franz Schneller
   1948 Traugott Meyer

   1949 Wilhelm Hausenstein
   1950 Wilhelm Altwegg
   1951 Albert Schweitzer
   1952 Max Picard
   1953 Reinholf Zumtobel
   1954 Otto Flake
   1955 Wilhelm Zentner
   1956 Lina Kromer
   1957 Immanuel Stickelberger
      (Switzerland)
   1958 Friedrich Alfred Schmid-
      Noerr
   1959 Carl Jacob Burckhardt
      (Switzerland)
   1960 Martin Heidegger
   1961 Albin Fringeli (Switzer-
      land)   520.

Heinrich HEINE PRIZE (Germany,
East)
   An annual literary prize of
the East German Ministry for
Culture (Ministerium für Kultur)
is granted only for poetry and for
work publicizing writers, publishing, and literary organizations
(Kollektive). The premium of
12.500 DM, which is presented
each December 13, has been divided between:
Lyric
   1957 Karl Schnog
   1958 Max Zimmering
   1959 Walter Stranka
   1960 Gerd Semmer
Publizistik
   1957 Walther Victor
   1958 Bruno Kaiser
   1959 Weiland Herzfelde
   1960 Lothar Kusche   521.

HELDEN DER ARBEIT (Germany,
East)
   Fifty or more annual awards,
consisting of the honorary title
"Hero of Labor" and a monetary
prize of 10.000 DM, are granted
by the national government of
East Germany to honor workers in
all areas of labor, including
"workers with the pen."   522.

HELGAFELL PRIZE (Iceland)

The Bókmenntaverölaun Hel-
gafells, a prize of the publisher,
Hélgafell (Veghusastigur 7, Reykjavik) was awarded in 1960 to
Hannes Pétursson for his poetry.
523.

Ernest HEMINGWAY JOURNAL-ISM PRIZE (Spain)

For the second time in 1962
the newspaper, "Pueblo" (calle
de Narvaez 70, Madrid) is offering a prize for an article or
a collection of articles appearing in Spanish newspapers or
magazines between January 1,
1961 and April 30, 1962 on the
subject: 'Ernest Hemingway--
His Life, His Work, and His
Death." Competing works, entered for the 30,000 pts premium,
were submitted in six copies by
May 15, 1962.   524.

Ernest HEMINGWAY PRIZE (Italy)

The L 100.000 prize was
established as an annual award
from 1949 to 1953 for the best
unpublished novel submitted to
Hemingway's Italian publisher,
Arnoldo Mondadori Editore (via
Bianca di Savoia 20, Milan).
Winners of the award include:
Romualdo Romano (1949), with
the novel "Sirocco;" and in 1953
--Sergio Maldini with "I
sognatori;" and Mario Schettini
with "Il paese dei bastardi."
525.

Alexandre HERCULANO PRIZE (Portugal)

One of several literary prizes
of Secretariado Nacional da
Informação, this award for historical writing was established
in 1934. Recipients of the
premium, now a biennial award
of 15.000$, include:
    1941 João Ameal. História
      de Portugal
    1945 Amadeu Cunha. Sertões
      e Fronteiras do Brasil

    1951 Salvador Dias Arnaud.
      A Batalha de Trancoso
    1952 Miguel Paile. Santo
      Antoñio dos Portugueses em
      Roma
    1954 Joaquim Veríssimo Serrão.
      Portugueses no Estudo de
      Toulouse
    1959 M. de Almeida Trinidade.
      O Padre Luís Lopes de Melo
      e sua Época
    1961 Avelino de Jesus da
      Costa. O Bispo D. Pedro
      e a Organização de Diocese
      de Braga   526.

Edouard HERRIOT PRIZE (France)

The 25.000 fr novel prize of
the French government was established in 1951 by Assemblée
nationale (126 rue de l'Université,
Paris) under the patronage of
the French Secretary of State
and the Fonction publique et de
l'Union artistique interministérielle.
Granted each year on May 31, the
prize honors an unpublished novel
judged the best entered in competition (manuscript sent in four
typed copies to Assemblée nationale before the second Wednesday of February.
Novelists recognized by the
prize are:
    1952 Georges Belloni. Le
      miracle des innocents
    1953 Delauney. Toute honte
      bue
    1954 André Devaux. Le
      gerbe et le fagot
    1955 Jean- Louis Boncoeur.
      Le moulin de la veille morte
    1956 Henry Jacomy. Le
      journal d'une ombre
    1957 F. Duplouy. Un si
      profond silence
    1958 André Lamoureux. Le
      second souffle
    1959 Robert Escarpit. Les
      Dieux du Patamba
    1960 Jacques Carton. Croix
      au coeur
    1961 Louis Dario. La terre
      de Mathias   527.

HERTZOG PRIZE (South Africa)
The South African Academy of
Arts and Sciences (Suid-Afrikaanse Akademie vir Wetenskap
en Kuns, Engelenburg House,
Hamilton Street, Pretoria)
awards a number of literary
honors, including the Hertzog
Prize, instituted as an annual
prize in 1916 to "encourage
the expansion of the Afrikaans
language." A monetary premium
(about R 100) is granted to the
writer of the best literary work
or belles lettres in Afrikaans.
Literary forms eligible for
award include: Poetry, Drama,
Narrative Art (Essay, Novel,
Short Story), and Other Prose
(Criticism, Causerie, Journey
Writing).   528.

HERVORRAGENDER WISSEN-
SCHAFTLER DES VOLKES
(Germany, East)
A high honor of the national
government of the Deutsche
Demokratische Republik brings
the officially bestowed title,
"Hervorragender Wissenschaftler
des Volkes," and a monetary
premium of 40.000 DM for outstanding cultural contributions by
citizens of East Germany.
                                  529.

HESPERIDES INTERNATIONAL
ACADEMY PRIZE (International
--France)
Among a number of literary
prizes granted by the Académie
Internationale des Hespérides
(74 rue de l'Université, Paris)
is this prize, which was established in 1958 from the Academy headquarters in Morocco,
and continues since 1960, when
the Academy moved its offices
to Paris. The prize, pre-
sented each year for writing
expounding and illustrating
the fundamental values of Western Culture in literature and
the arts, consists of a box of

oranges (Pommes d'or des
Hespérides), and a work of art.
Laureates are:
1959 Nikos Kazantzakis (Greece)
1960 Denis-Bernard Drucker
1961 Pierre Grimal. A
  la recherche de l'Italie
  Jean Prasteau. Fenêtres
  sur Seine   530.

Herman HESSE PRIZE (Germany)
The Förderungsgemeinschaft
der deutschen Kunst in Karlsruhe
awards the Hesse Prize each
five years for an outstanding
work in the German language by
an author of any nationality. In
1957 the 10.000 DM premium
was presented, as an encouragement prize, to Martin Walser
for "Ehen in Philippsburg."
                                  531.

Edouard von HEYDT CULTURAL
PRIZE (Germany)
The entire life's work of
creative artists, especially those
associated with the area of
Bergisch Land, is honored by the
prize, presented each year by
the city and area of Wuppertal,
in the Ruhr Valley. The award,
designated "Kulterpreis der Stadt
Wuppertal" until 1958, consists
of 5000 DM and a plaque. Authors
whose work has been given recognition by the prize include:
1950 Gerhard Nebel
1953 Ernst Bertram
1956 Flora Klee-Palye. For
  translation of European
  poetry
1957 Max Burchartz
1958 Heinrich Böll
                                  532.

HILVERENBEEK PRIZES
(Netherlands)
Granted on the occasion of
the "Groot Kempische Cultuur-
dagen" to authors of Belgium or
the Netherlands writing in Dutch,
these literary awards have been
presented such authors as:

1955 Ward Ruyslinck. De
ontaarde slapers (novel)
Jan Carstens. Brabantse
Madonna (poetry)
F. Babylon. Goudvissen in
aquarium (poetry)
1959 R. Bellefroi (Belgium)
Het Huis on de St. Allegon-
diskaai   533.

HISPANIC CULTURAL INSTI-
TUTE PRIZE (Spain)

The Instituto de Cultura Hispanica (Avenida de los Reyes
Católicos, Madrid) has offered
a variety of prizes for literature. Awards with varying
eligibility requirements and
forms of literature given recognition include: AGRUPACION
DE ESCRITORES ESPANOLAS--
two prizes for Novel and Poetry;
PREMIOS BELLAS ARTES
CULTURA HISPANICA--awards
for Poetry and Novel; PREMIOS
MUNDO HISPANICA--three
awards; and PREMIOS LITERA-
TURA Y CULTURA HISPANO-
AMERICANAS.

Recipients of prizes include:
1951 Tomás Salvador.
Garimpo
1953 Ernesto Giménez Caballero. Para las juventudes
de America y España (libro
de texto)
1954 Juana de Ibarbourou.
Romances del Destino
(50,000 pts premium)
1955 José Luis Castillo
Puche. Con la Muerte al
Hombre (novel)   534.

HISTORIA PRIZE (France)

The publisher Éditions Tal-
landier (17 rue Remy-Dumoncel,
Paris 14e) created the prize as
an annual award in 1960, to
honor a writing in the area of
history--a book resurrecting the
past on a grand scale from
antiquity to our day. Books
considered for award included:
Biography; Archaeology; Study

of an epoch or of a society, of
economic or intellectual life, of
customs; or related subject.
Winner in 1961 was duc de
Castrie with "Mirabeau."
                             535.

Hugo von HOFMANNSTHAL
PRIZE (Austria)

A prize of S 10.000 for an
essay related to Austrian problems or people was established
by the Austrian Minister of
Education (Bundesminister für
Unterricht) in 1959 to commemorate the 30th anniversary
of the death of the Austrian poet
and playwright, Hugo von Hofmannsthal (1874-1929). In 1960 the
prize was presented to Ernst
Randak and Ignaz Zangerle.
                             536.

HOFMEYR PRIZE (South Africa)

This R400 literary award was
instituted in 1954 in memory of
the late Dr. W. A. Hofmeyr,
one of the founders of the Nasionale Pers, parent company
of Nasionale Boekhandel. It is
awarded only to authors of books
published by Nasionale Boekhandel
(P. O. Box 122, Parow, South
Africa) in the rotating categories:
Drama, Prose, Poetry.   537.

HOLBERG MEDAL (Denmark)

The Holbergmedaillen, consisting of a medal and 5.000 D
kr, is awarded to honor the
Danish writer, Ludvig Holberg
(1684-1754)--generally regarded
as the founder of Danish litera-
ture--each year on his birthday,
December 3.

The Award Committee, including professors of Danish Literature and representatives of the
Danish Authors' Association with
the Minister for Cultural Affairs
as Chairman, has selected as
authors to be honored:
1934 Vilh. Andersen
1935 Sven Clausen

1937 Vald. Roerdam
1938 Th. A. Muller
1939 Jacob Paludan
1940 Thit Jensen
1941 Henrik Pontoppidan
1942 Fr. Poulsen
1943 Otto Rung
1944 Johs. Joergensen
1945 Tom Kristensen
1946 Harry Soiberg
1947 Carl Erik Soya
1948 Paul La Cour
1949 Karen Blixen (pen name:
   Isak Dinesen)
1950 Hans Hartvig Seedorff
1951 Torben Krogh
1952 Martin A. Hansen
1953 Helge Topsoe-Jensen
1954 H. C. Branner
1955 Knuth Becker
1956 Palle Lauring
1957 Kjeld Abell
1958 F. J. Billeskov Jansen
1959 Knud Soenderby
1960 William Heinesen
1961 Robert Neiiendam   538.

Nils HOLGERSSON MEDAL (Sweden)

The prize of the Swedish Library Association (Tornavagen 9, Lund), awarded annually on November 20--Selma Lagerlöf's birthday--honors "the most outstanding book for children or young people written in Swedish and published during the preceding year." Suggestions for award must be submitted by March 20 of the year of award, and the final decision of the prizewinners is made at the beginning of April. A prize for the best illustrated children's book--the ELSA BESKOW MEDAL--has been awarded each year since 1958.

The jury, "consisting of two children's librarians, two school librarians, a member of the Board of Education, and a representative of the Board of the Swedish Library Association," has granted the Nils

Holgerssonplaketten to:
1950 Astrid Lindgren. Nils
   Karlsson Pyssling
1951 Lennart Hellsing. Summa
   Summarum
1952 Sten Bergman. Vildar och
   paradisfaglar
1953 Tove Jansson. Hur gick
   det sen?
1955 Harry Kullman. Hemlig
   resa
1956 Olle Mattson. Briggen
   Tre Liljor
1957 Edith Unnerstad. Farmor-
   sresan
1958 Hans Peterson. Magnus,
   Mattias och Mari
1959 Anna Lisa Wärnlöf. Pellas
   bok
1960 Kai Söderhjelm. Mikko i
   kungens tjänst
1961 Åke Holmberg. Ture
   Sventon, privatdetektiv
1962 Britt G. Hallqvist.
   Festen i Hulabo   539.

HOLON PRIZE FOR LITERARY AND SCIENTIFIC ACHIEVE-MENTS (Israel)

The Municipal Council of Holon grants the prize, in memory of the first Mayor of the town, the late Dr. H. Kugel, in February each year "to encourage literary and scientific talents in Israel." Two monetary premiums are granted of IL 500 each--one for Literary Works; one for Scientific Works. Application for consideration for award is made with four copies of the work to the municipality of Holon, and a prize-winning author cannot apply again until five years have elapsed since his award. Minimum length of works entered in competition is: Poetry--no less than one printed sheet; Prose, Science, and Jewish Science--no less than two printed sheets.

A separate jury picks the winners in the two subject sections (Literature and Science), and both juries are selected by

the Israel Literary Assembly.
Recipients of the prize include K. Zetnik (1954), 3rd
prize; Y. Tversky, "an encouragement prize" in 1956;
and
Literature
1953 Y. Ogen; Sh. Hyllel's
1954 J. Arihs
1955 Sh. Meltzer
1956 Y. Cohen
1957 A. Broides
1958 G. Mishkowsky
1960 Y. and A. Sand
1961 Lea Goldberg
1962 Z. Gylad
Jewish Science
1953 D. Ziv
1954 Z. Har-Zahav
1955 B. Kurtzvail
1956 Av. N. Polak
1957 D. Etinger
1958 D. Sedan
1960 Y. Klozner
1961 B. J. Myhaly
1962 D. Knaany   540.

Henriette Roland HOLST PRIZE
(Netherlands)
Winners of the annual prize
are such authors as:
1957 Louis-Paul Boon. De
kleine Eva uit de Kromme
Bijlstraat
1958 F. de Jong. Om de
plaats van der arbeid
1959 E. Verbeck. Arthur
Rimbaud   541.

P. C. HOOFT PRIZE (Nether-
lands)
An annual award established
in 1947 by the Netherlands
Ministry of Education, Arts and
Science (Ministrie van Onderwijs,
Kunsten en Wetenschappen), the
Hooft Prize is also known as the
NETHERLANDS GOVERNMENT
PRIZE FOR LITERATURE
(Staatsprijs voor letterkunde).
Named to commemorate the
Dutch historian, poet and play-
wright who was a leader in the
Dutch renaissance, Pieter

Corneliszoon Hooft (1581-1647),
the award honors "Dutch authors
of important literary works written in Dutch." Authors writing
in a variety of literary forms
are eligible for the prize: Fiction, Nonfiction, such as Studies
and Essays; Poetry. A work to
be considered for award must
have appeared in print during the
three-year period preceding July
1 of the award year. In addition
to honoring a single work of an
author, the prize may also be
awarded in recognition of a
writer's entire literary contribution.
The prize, which is presented
in May and now brings a premium
of 4.000 fl, has been granted:
1947 Fiction--
Arthur van Schendel. Hed Oude
Huis
Amoene van Haersholte.
Sophia in de Koestraat
1948 Nonfiction--
A. M. Hammacher. Eduard
Karsen en zijn vader Kaspar
1949 Poetry--
Gerrit Achterberg. En Jezus
Schreef in 't Zand
1950 Fiction--
S. Vestdijk. De Vurraanbid-
ders
1951 Nonfiction--
E. J. Dijksterhuis. De
Mechanisering van het Werel-
beeld
1952 Poetry--
J. C. Gloem. Avond
1953 F. Bordewijk. De Doop-
vont; and Studien in Volks-
structuur
1954 L. J. Rogier. Chapters
I, II and IV in "In Vrijheid
Herboren Katholiek Neder-
land 1853-1952"
1955 Poetry--
A. Roland Holst. Late Telgen
1956 Anna Blaman (Miss J.
P. Vrugt). Complete works
1957 P.C.A. Geyl. Complete
historical works
1958 Pierre Kemp. Complete

poetical works
1960 V. E. van Vriesland.
Complete works, especially
for "Onderzoek en vertoog"
542.

HÖRSPIELPREIS DER KRIEGS-
BLINDEN (Germany)
One of the most popular and
best-known literary honors in
Germany, the Radio Play Prize
of the War Blinded, most famous
radio prize, is offered annually
by the organization, Bund der
Kriegsblinden Deutschlands in
Bonn. Founded in 1951, the
prize distinguishes the best
original radio play that has been
presented on a West German or
West Berlin radio station during
the previous year. The prize--
a sculpture made by a person
blinded in the war--is determined
by a jury of nine radio critics
and 9 war-blinded persons.
Such distinguished German
authors have received the honor
as:
1951 Erich Wickert. Darfts du
die Stunde rufen?
1952 Günter Eich. Die andere
and ich
1953 Heinz Oskar Wuttig.
Nachtstreife
1954 Wolfgang Hildesheimer.
Prinzessin Turandot
1955 Leopold Ahlsen. Philomen und Baucis
1956 Friedrich Dürrenmatt
(Switzerland). Die Panne
1957 Benno Meyer-Wehlack.
Die Versuchung
1958 Ingeborg Bachmann. Der
gute Gott von Manhattan
1959 Franz Hiesel. Auf
einem Maulwurfshügel
1960 Dieter Wellershoff. Der
Minotaurus   543.

HÖRSPIELPREIS VON RADIO
BREMEN (Germany)
One of several prizes offered
by Radio Bremen for radio writing (a "Feature-Preis" of 10.000

DM was announced in 1961), this
prize for a radio play was won
in 1955 by Herbert Eisenreich.
544.

HOUGHTON MIFFLIN LITERARY
FELLOWSHIP (International--
U.S.A.)
"Designed to help authors
complete literary projects in fiction and nonfiction," this award
established in 1935 is the "oldest
publisher-sponsored award of its
kind." The fellowship brings
$5,000 ($2,000 outright grant and
$3,000 royalty advance) for a
finished work, as well as work
in progress, provided the writing
has not previously been published
in book form. Applications--
together with at least 50 pages
of the actual project, description
of its theme and intent; examples
of past published or unpublished
work; brief biography--may be
submitted at any time to Houghton
Mifflin (2 Park Street, Boston
7, Massachusetts).
Recipients of the grant include
David Cornel DeJong (Nether-
lands--U.S.A.), with the published work 'Old Haven" from his
1938 fellowship.   545.

Matica HRVATSKA PRIZE
(Yugoslavia)
In 1953, this literary honor
was awarded Josep Povicic for
his work, "Kniga o davnini"
(The book of olden times).
546.

Constantijn HUYGENS PRIZE
(Netherlands)
Awarded by the Jan Campert
Foundation (Jan Campert Stichting) each year in November or
December, the prize established
by the municipality of The Hague
is a "Master-Prize" honoring the
entire work of a recognized author. Since the initial award
in 1947, the premium (currently
2.500 fl--an increase over the

2.000 fl awarded prior to 1955/
56) has brought a respected
Dutch literary honor to:
- 1947 P. N. van Eyck. Poetry
- 1948 A. Roland Holst. Poetry
- 1949 J. C. Bloem. Poetry
- 1950 Geerten Gossaert (F.C. Gerretson). Poetry
- 1951 William Elsschot (Alfons de Ridder). Novels
- 1953 M. Nihoff. Posthumous award for poetry; money returned to the Foundation and used in 1956 to commission S. Vestdijk to write a book on poet Nihoff's life and work
- 1954 Jan Engelman. Poetry
- 1955 S. Vestdijk. Novels
- 1956 Pierre Kemp. Poetry
- 1957 F. Bordewijk. Novels; Short Stories
- 1958 Victor E. van Vriesland. Poetry; Essays
- 1959 Gerrit Achterberg. Poetry
- 1960 Anton van Duinkerken (W. Asselbergs). Poetry; Criticism; Essays
- 1961 Simon Carmiggelt
- 1962 Hendrik de Vries
547.

Ruedo IBERICO NOVEL PRIZE
(Spain)
   The Paris publisher, Ediciones Ruedo Iberico (27 boulevard Malesherbes) offers the prize of a million francs (approximately 120,000 pts) for an unpublished novel in Spanish. Works entered in competition for the award were submitted in two copies by December 31, 1961. The initial prize, presented in Cillioure, France, where the Spanish poet, Antonio Machado, is buried, was won by Armando Lopez Salinas with the novel, "Ano tras ano." The same publisher also offers the Antonio MACHADO POETRY PRIZE, and will award an additional honor in 1963: Juan de MAIRENA PRIZE--for an ideolog-ical, travel, or descriptive essay.
548.

Henrik IBSEN PRIZE (France)
   The critics' organization, Syndicat de la Critique Dramatique et Musicale (52 rue Richer, Paris 9e), has granted this prize since 1948 for a drama, written in the spirit of Ibsen. Among the playwrights honored are:
- 1948 Maurice Clavel. Les incendiaires
- 1950 Roger Vailland. Héloïse et Abelard
- 1955 Jean Vauthier. Le personnage combattant
- 1959 Soria. L'étrangère dans l'île
- 1961 Yves Jamiaque. Les cochons d'Inde
549.

ICELANDIC STATE BROADCAST SERVICE AUTHORS' FUND AWARD
   The Rithofundasjoour Rikisutvarpsins is an annual prize granted to two authors by the Icelandic State Broadcast Service (I.S.B.S., Skulagata 4, Reykjavik). The Award is not confined to a specific work, but honors an author's or a poet's entire literary output. Winners include: Loftur Guðmondsson; Snorri Hjartarson (poetry); Jónas Árnason; Guðmundur Frímann (poetry); Hannes Sigfússon (poetry); Matthías Johannessen (poetry); Stefán Júlíusson; Guðmundur Ingi Kristjánsson (poetry); Jón úr Vör (poetry); Ólafur Jóhann Sigurðsson.
550.

ICELANDIC STATE BROADCAST SERVICE BIRTHDAY FUND AWARD
   Grants under the Birthday Fund of the Iceland State Broadcast Service (I.S.B.S., Skulagata 4, Reykjavik) are awards to authors for the writing of literary works or for research. The "Afmaelissjoour Rikisutvarpsins" has been presented to one foreign

guest (Arnold Toynbee, for a lecture in history); and to Icelandic authors, including: Agnar Þórðarson, playwright; Guðmundur L. Fridfinnesson, author; Ludvík Kristjánsson, historian.   551.

ICELANDIC STATE GRANTS TO AUTHORS

An allowance made by the national government of Iceland to writers is the most significant acknowledgement of literary achievement or potential, as the major "form of public and official recognition to creative artists in Iceland, is as a rule, not in the form of literary or art prizes, but in the form of regular yearly grants or salaries specified in the State Budget as passed annually by the Icelandic Althing (Parliament)."

Such government grants are typical of awards made for creative workers in the arts, including writers, in the Scandinavian countries. In the 1960 budget of Iceland the grants for literature and art were distributed in four groups: 33.220 Icl Kr--14 grants; 20.000 Icl Kr--16 grants; 10.000 Icl Kr--48 grants; 5.000 Icl Kr--30 grants. Of these 108 allowances, 53 were to writers, including Halldór Kiljan Laxness (33.200 Icl Kr); Snorri Hjartarson (20.000 Icl Kr); and 10.000 Icl Kr allotments to: Agnar Þórðarson; Guðmundur Ingi Kristjánsson; Hannes Pétursson.   552.

Karl IMMERMANN PRIZE
(Germany)

One of the long-established cultural prizes of the city of Dusseldorf, (Landeshauptstadt), this award was initially granted in 1936 in memory of Karl Immermann, the famous German writer (1796-1840) whose works include "Munchhausen."

The literary honor, originally a 3000 DM and currently a 5000 DM premium, has been supplemented since 1954 by a 2000 DM encouragement prize. With the 1961 award, the prize will be granted each three years.

Among the authors whose talent is recognized by the prizes, which may be given on the occasion of the celebration of the Founding Day of Dusseldorf, August 14, are:

Immermann-Preis
  1936 Albert Bauer
  1937 Hermann Stahl
  1938 Karl Matthias Busch
  1939 Curt Langenbeck
  1941 Josef Wenter
  1942 Wilhelm Schäfer
  1948 Emil Barth
  1951 Wolf von Niebelschütz
  1952 Friedrich Georg Jünger
  1953 Georg Britting
  1954 Ernst Penzoldt
  1955 Ilse Aichinger
  1956 Heinz Risse
  1957 Marie Luise von
    Kaschnitz
  1958 Wolfdietrich Schnurre
  1959 Gerd Gaiser
  1960 Eckart Peterich
  1961 Sigismund von Radecki
Förder-Preis
  1954 Erhart Kaestner
  1955 Rolf Schroers
  1956 Otto Heinrich Kühner
  1957 Alfred Hellmuth Andersch
  1958 Hans Peter Keller
  1959 Christopher Merkel
  1960 Ingrid Schwarze Bachér
                                   553.

INDEPENDENT CULTURAL MOVEMENT PRIZE (Italy)

The Premio Movimento Indipendente di Cultura, a poetry award of the M.I.C. (via Lucullo 6, Rome) has been offered each year since 1959 for the best poetry.   554.

INDIA CHILDREN'S BOOK AWARDS

The Indian Ministry of Education annually offers approximately 25 prizes of Rs 500 for the best books for children written in the major languages of India.   555.

INDIA HINDI BOOK PRIZE

Every fourth or fifth year the Indian Ministry of Education offers a prize of Rs 500 for the best books written in Hindi (up to ten prizes are granted at a time), published since the previous year of award.   556.

INDRADEVI PRIZE (Cambodia)

This biennial award, established by the Association of Kmer Writers in 1961 "to encourage writers and develop Kmer literature," with the patronage of the Cambodian Ministry of Education and the financial aid of the Asia Foundation and private donors, offers literary awards in three areas of writing: Novel; Poetry; Drama.

Open to all Kmer writers, the competition grants three prizes in each section--Premiums of 15.000, 10.000, and 5.000 Cambodian Riels--and several "encouragement" awards. Unpublished works are submitted anonymously, with an accompanying identification sheet, during a specified five-month period, for consideration by a jury of writers and Kmer intellectuals.

Among the First Prize winners in 1961 are:
Novel--Suon Sorin. Un
   Nouveau Soleil se Lève sur
   l'Ancienne Terre
Poetry--Chap Pin. Commen-
   taire sur cinq Maximes
Drama (shared 2nd prize)
   Nuon Kan. Certaines feuilles
   tombent loin du pied de
   l'arbre
   Chheng Phon   557.

INNER SANCTUM MYSTERY CONTEST (International--U.S.A.)

The author of the best mystery, detective or suspense novel submitted in the publisher's competition (Simon and Schuster, 630 Fifth Avenue, New York 20) receives a prize of $3,500 ($1,000 outright grant, and $2,500 royalty advance), and a contract for the next three books written. Manuscripts entered in the contest must be in English and from 55,000 to 80,000 words in length. Most recent winner (1962) of the prize is Herbert Monteilhet (France) with "The Praying Mantises," a book which also won the 1960 French Grand Prize for Mysteries (Grand Prix de Littérature Policière) as "Les mantes religieuses."   558.

INNERSCHWEIZ PRIZES (Switzerland)

Cultural and literary awards of Innerschweizerische Kulturstiftung with headquarters in Lucerne (Ehrungsdirektion des Kantons Luzern, Herr. Dr. Hans Rogger, Sempacherstrasse 10, Luzern)--an organization of six Swiss cantons (Luzern, Uri, Schwyz, Obwalden, Nidwalden, and Zug)--have been offered since 1953, and include honors for various categories of writing.

Usually granted biennially and awarded in the month of December, the prizes are:
INNERSCHWEIZ LITERATURE
PRIZE--Biennial prize of 1000
   to 2000 fr for a writer native
   to or five years resident in
   the Innerschweiz cantons,
   who is author of a work of
   outstanding literary worth,
   with no limitation on theme.
   Awarded in 1957 to Walter
   Hauser (Sisikon) for "Feier
   des Lebens," and in 1962
   to Josef Vital Kopp.

KULTURPREIS DER INNER-
SCHWEIZ--Biennial prize of
   1000 to 2000 fr for a significant
   scientific publication on the
   Innerschweiz region, written
   by an author of any nationality or place of residence.
   Recipients of the highest
   prize (2000 fr) include:
   1957 Kuno Muller (Luzern).
   Scientific publications on the
   Innerschweiz district
   1959 Rudolf Henggeler (Einsie-
   deln). Scientific publications
   on the Innerschweiz district
   Robert Blaser (Luzern).
   Original historical studies on
   the subject of book printing
   and the press
   1961 Jakob Wyrsch (Stans).
   Essays and folk-psychology
   studies of Innerschweiz
   1962 Linus Birchler. Publications in art history

GROSSE LITERATURPREIS DER
INNERSCHWEIZ--A special award
   of at least 3000 fr granted for
   outstanding literary achievement by a writer native to the
   Innerschweiz cantons, or
   resident there for at least
   10 years. Winners of this
   prize:
   1953 Meinrad Inglin (Schwyz).
   Entire literary work
   1956 5000 fr prize--Hans Urs
   (Basel). Major work as
   writer, editor, translator
   and critic in the general
   area of Literature, and of
   Music History, Philosophy
   and Theology

GROSSER KULTURPREIS DER
INNERSCHWEIZ--A special award
   of at least 3000 fr for an
   author of significant scientific
   works concerning the Innerschweiz region   559.

INNSBRUCK PRIZE (Austria)
   The Preis der Landeshauptstadt Innsbruck zur Förderung
künstlerischen Schaffens is a
general cultural award of the

city of Innsbruck (Landeshauptstadt
Innsbruck, Stadtgemeinde Innsbruck, Rathaus) was established
in 1952 as an annual prize to
further artistic work in Literature; Music; and Painting. The
Literary prize rotates each award
for: Poetry, Drama, Fiction.
Since 1955 the literature award is
granted triennially.
   Authors honored include:
   1952 Ingeborg Mülhofer; Albert
   Köller
   1953 Gertrud Theiner-Haffner;
   Hermann Kuprian
   1954 Robert Skorpil; Ernst
   Meister
   1955 Helmut Schinagl; Gertrud
   Theiner-Haffner; Ingeborg
   Teuffenbach
   1958 Lyric 2nd and 3rd prize--
   Heinrich Klier; Walter Miess
                                560.

INSTITUT DES POÈTES PRIZES
(France)
   The Académie internationale
des Poètes (rue Rene-Boulanger
20, Paris) offers six prizes for
poetry in French: GRAND PRIX
DU LAURIER D'OR DE LA
POÉSIE--For best unpublished
poetry collection, to be published
in the "Laurier d'or Series;"
PRIX DE L'INSTITUT DES POÈTES
--For best published poetry collection issued during the preceding
five years; PRIX DU PARNASSE--
For poem of at least 300 verses;
PRIX JOSÉ-MARIA DE HEREDIA--
for a sonnet; PRIX VERLAINE--
For a sonnet on a set subject--
as in 1961: Mains de femme;
PRIX VILLON--for a poem of set
form.   561.

INSTITUT D'ESTUDIS CATALANS
PRIZES (Spain)
   Since 1915 this Catalan learned
society in Barcelona has granted
awards for literature, geography,
history, and cultural subjects pertaining to Catalonia, to such writers as: Francisco Cambó; Jaime

I. Rubió; Francisco Eiximenis;
Eduardo Brossa. 562.

INTERALLIÉ PRIZE (France)
One of the four or five most
important and respected French
literary honors is the novel
prize (Pierre Loiselet, 55 rue
Condorcet, Paris) established in
1930 and awarded annually in
December to an author, usually
a journalist, for "a novel of
good quality with international
interest." The significance of
the prize is reflected in the professional recognition of high
achievement and in the increased
public sale and translation of
winning works, rather than a
monetary premium.

The jury of twelve, including
the laureate of the previous
year, has granted the honor to:
1930 André Malraux. La voie
royale
1931 Pierre Bost. Le scandale
1932 Ratel. Maison des Bor-
ies
1933 Bourget-Pailleron.
L'homme du Brésil
1934 Marc Bernard. Annie
1935 Jacques Debû-Bridel.
Jeunes ménages
1936 René Laporte. Chasses
de novembre
1937 Romain Roussel. La
vallée sans printemps
1938 Pierre Nizan. La
conspiration
1939 Roger de Lafforest. Les
figurants de la mort
1945 Roger Vailland. Drôle
de jeu
1946 Jacques Nels. Pous-
sières du temps
1947 Pierre Daninos. Les
carnets du Bon Dieu
1948 Henri Castillou. Cortiz
s'est révolté
1949 Gilbert Sigaux. Les
chiens enragés
1950 Georges Auclair. Un
amour allemand
1951 Jacques Perret. Bande

à part
1952 Jean Dutourd. Au bon
beurre
1953 Louis Chauvet. Air sur
la quatrième corde
1954 Maurice Boissais. Le
goût du péché
1955 Félicien Marceau. Les
élans du coeur
1956 Armand Lanoux. Le
Commandant Watrin
1957 Paul Guimard. Rue du
Havre
1958 Bertrand Poirot-Delpech.
Le grand dadais
1959 Antoine Blondin. Un
singe en hiver
1960 Jean Portelle. Janitzia
ou la dernière qui aima
l'amour
Henry Muller. Clem
1961 Jean Ferniot. L'ombre
portée
1962 Henri-François Rey. Les
pianos mécaniques
563.

INTERAMERICAN CULTURAL
ASSOCIATION PRIZES (Latin
America--Venezuela)
A literary competition of
Asociacion Cultural Interameri-
cana (Salas a Altagracia 28,
Caracas) open to all writers in
Spanish with prizes for Novel
(TERESA DE LA PARRA PRIZE--
Bs 3.000); Poetry (ANDRES
ELOY BLANCO PRIZE--Bs
3.000); and Journalism (CON-
CEPCION DE THAYLHARDAR
PRIZE--Bs 1.000). Winner of
the journalism award in 1957 was
Aya Mercedes Perez du Duque
Arango. 564.

INTERNATIONAL ACADEMY OF
CULTURAL INFORMATION
PRIZE (Italy)
Since 1958 the Accademia Inter-
nazionale di Propaganda Culturale
under the direction of Francesco
Gligora (casella postale 6152,
Rome) has offered through its
review, "Rondine," competitions for

poetry: "Sagra del sonetto italiano"--an Academy Medal; and "Quindici anni di poesia." Books of published poetry are honored by award--a gold cup for the winning author, and an Academy Medal for the publisher of the winning work. Recent first prize winners (1959) were: Sagra del sonetto--Pasquale Cafaro; Quindici anni di poesia--Rodolfo Pucelli, with "Poesie vecchie e nuove."   565.

INTERNATIONAL ALLIANCE OF JOURNALISTS AND WRITERS PRIZE (Italy)
The A. I. G. S. L. (Alleanza Internazionale Giornalisti e Scrittori Latini, viale Medaglie d'oro 190, Rome) has offered the prize each year since 1959 for several categories of writing: Poetry--L 500 for an unpublished poem not exceeding 30 verses; Novella--L 1.000 for an unpublished story not over five typed pages long; Critical Essays--L 1.000 for published or unpublished writing on the subject of contemporary poetry in the Romance Languages; Stories for Children--L 800 for "racconti" not exceeding four typed pages in length. In addition to receiving the monetary premium, winning works are published in "Corriere Letterario Latino."
Prize winners include:
1958 Carlo Cuini. Luna
1959 Gina Donenti Mira D'Ercola. La Pioggia   566.

INTERNATIONAL BENJAMIN FRANKLIN SOCIETY MEDAL
A gold medal was awarded in 1957 to Peter Freuchen (Denmark), author-traveller, for "service to mankind in opening new frontiers."   567.

INTERNATIONAL FANTASY AWARD (International--England)
The Fantasy Book Center (10 Sicilian Avenue, London, W. C. 1) offers this prize each year to the authors of a fiction book and a nonfiction book, which are judged best from the standpoint of "artistic merit or creative fantasy." The award, consisting of a "desk ornament in the form of a silver spaceship mounted on an inscribed plinth of polished oak, which also supports a table lighter," has been granted to:
1951 George R. Stewart. Earth abides
1952 Clifford D. Simak. The city (nonfiction)
L. S. de Camp and Willy Ley. Lands beyond
1953 T. Sturgeon. More than human
1954 Edgar Pangborn. A mirror for observers
2nd prize--Hal Clement. A mission of gravity
3rd prize--J. T. McIntosh. One in three hundred
Isaac Asimov. The caves of steel
1957 J. R. R. Tolkien. Lord of the rings   568.

INTERNATIONAL FIRST NOVEL PRIZE (International--France)
Just established in 1961, the Prix International du Premier Roman is presented for an unpublished novel around December 15 each year (Jean-Louis Bory, Secretary, 34 rue de l'Université, Paris 7e). The eight best manuscripts entered in competition for the prize will be selected and published by Éditions Julliard-- usually these will be four or five manuscripts in French and three or four manuscripts translated into French that have not already won a literary prize. The initial prize winner in 1961 was Michel Servin with "Deo gratias;" and in 1962 Marie Cardinal with "Ecoutez la mer."   569.

INTERNATIONAL GRAND PRIZE

FOR POETRY (International--
Belgium)

One of the richest awards in
recognition of the poetic work
of a living writer is the Grand
Prix International de Poésie
with a premium of 100.000
francs belges, established in
1956 by Maison Internationale de
la Poésie.

The prize, awarded during
the biennial international poetry
competition "to a living poet
whose published works in any
language have universal value,"
has honored such distinguished
poets as:

1956 Giuseppe Ungaretti
(Italy)
1959 St. John Perse (pseud
of Aléxis Saint-Léger
Léger) (France)
1961 Gorge Guillén (Spain)
570.

INTERNATIONAL INSTITUTE
OF AFRICAN LANGUAGES AND
CULTURES PRIZE FOR BIOG-
RAPHY

Samuel Yosia Ntara (Nyasaland) won the prize in 1933 for
his "Man of Africa," an account
of the life of an African chief,
arranged and translated from
the original Nyanja by T. Cullen
Young.   571.

INTERNATIONAL LITERARY
COMPETITION FOR THE BLIND
(International--U.S.A.)

The competition sponsored
by the Jewish Braille Institute
of America (48 East 74th Street,
New York 21) offers cash prizes
of $1,000 for writings of authors
of any nationality. Also designated
the "Jewish Braille Review
Literary Competition," the International Literary Braille Competition for the Blind, sponsored
by the "Jewish Braille Review,"
has been held from time to
time--with nine competitions
in the last 30 years.

Initiated to "uncover literary
talent to express themselves
creatively among the blind of all
faiths, nations, and colors," the
next Literary Braille Competition is planned for 1964. In
1957-1958 prose and poetry
manuscripts from 39 nations in
27 different languages competed
for 28 prizes presented to representatives from many countries,
who accepted awards on behalf
of winners from India, Japan,
Poland, Italy, Greece, Turkey,
Canada, and other nations.
572.

INTERNATIONAL LITERARY
PEACE PRIZE (International--
Belgium)

The annual award of 50,000
francs for "a book about World
War II or underground fighters"
was presented in Chaudfontaine,
Belgium to Robert Jungk (Austria)
for his work, "I lived in Hiroshima."   573.

INTERNATIONAL NONFICTION
CONTEST (International)

The competition, also called
the "Econ Nonfiction Contest,"
is conducted by ten cooperating
publishers (Econ-Verlag, Dussel-
dorf-- organizer of the contest;
Gyldendal, Denmark; Hodder &
Stoughton, England; Kustannusosakeyhtio Otava, Finland; Hachette,
France; Uitgerverij W. Gaade,
Holland; Aldo Garzanti, Italy;
Gyldendal Norsk Forlag, Norway;
Bokforlaget Forum, Sweden;
Editorial Noguer, Spain; Mc
Graw-Hill, U.S.A.) Prizes
totalling $24,000 (First Prize--
$12,000; Second Prize--$7,200;
Third Prize--$4,800) were of-
fered "as an advance against
royalties and other earnings" for
the best unpublished work dealing
"with a scientific, technical,
economic, or cultural subject in
such a way that the basic facts
are presented in a lively fashion

to attract a large readership."

Authors from all countries of the world were encouraged to compete with manuscripts written in English, French, or German (manuscripts in Italian, Dutch, Danish, Finnish, or Swedish could be submitted to publishers in participating countries for possible translation into one of the three specified languages, if considered for the prize) that were from 250 to 500 typed pages in length.

An international jury of six members selected three prize winners from the three to five manuscripts selected in preliminary choice by the participating publishers in their own language areas. From the first contest--deadline for entries October 31, 1961--a prize winner, whose work was to be published simultaneously in 10 countries, was announced on January 10, 1962:

> F. L. Boschke (Germany),
> "Die Schöpfung ist noch
> nicht zu Ende" "Creation
> still goes on).   574.

INTERNATIONAL P.E.N.
SHORT STORY CONTEST

This INTERNATIONAL SHORT STORY COMPETITION of the International Writers' Fund open to P.E.N. members and administered by the world association of writers, International P.E.N. (62 Glebe Place, London, S. W. 3) was won by Carl Erik Martin Soya, Denmark's leading dramatist, novelist, and short story writer, with "On Order"--in the U.S.A. magazine "Story," November 1962 issue. Additional winners were: 2nd prize--Ersi Seferidades Haztimihali (Greece), "Apou;" 3rd prize divided equally --Wladimir Kostetsky (USSR-- USA), "Adam, I, and Kapitasha;"

Constance Young (South Africa), "And Ezolini smiled."   575.

INTERNATIONAL PUBLISHERS'
PRIZE (International)

The Prix Internationale des Éditeurs, one of two international literary awards (the other, the Prix Formentor) founded at an international meeting of publishers in Formentor on the Island of Mallorca in May 1960, is a "confirmation" prize "given to an author of any nationality whose existing body of work will...be of lasting influence on the developments of various national literatures."

Nominations for the award, honoring the "work of a mature author whose merits have not been fully recognized," are made only by the 13 participating publishers (see Formentor Prize for list of participating publishers), and entries are not solicited and no application is made for the prize. An international jury of authors and critics selects the winner of this prize in May, at the time the winner of the Formentor Prize is selected, during the award meeting at the Club des Poètes in Formentor.

The rich premium ($10,000) has honored:

> 1961 Jorge Luis Borges
> (Argentina). Entire literary
> work, as "Latin America's
> most distinguished man of
> letters," especially for his
> collection of short stories,
> "Ficciones"
> Samuel Beckett (Ireland-
> France). Entire literary
> work, especially his tetralogy:
> Malone, Malone Dies, Unnameable, Comment d'est. Premium
> shared equally by Borges and
> Beckett, with a special citation
> for Henry Miller (U.S.A.) as
> "one of the important literary
> figures of the twentieth century"
> 1962 Uwe Johnson (Germany).

Das dritte Buch über Achim, as the "best work of fiction by a living author"
1963 Carlo Emilio Gadda (Italy) La Cognizione del Dolore 576.

IRAN ROYAL PRIZES

To honor "the best writers and translators, who have offered valuable works to the nation," the prizes were established in 1953 by His Imperial Majesty the Shahanshah through the Pahlavi Foundation. Administered by a Selection Committee whose members are professors at Tehran University, the prizes are awarded each year to "the best writers, compilers, and translators" in four subjects: Literature, Science, History, and Geography, Ethics and Education. The premium, varying with the type of work, is: Writers---50,000Rls; Compilers ---30,000 Rls; Translators--- 20,000 Rls.

The Pahlavi Foundation through a published notice in newspapers "invites candidates to participate in the contest for best book of the year," by sending "three copies of their book to the Education and Social Section of the Foundation before October 20 each year."

Recent winners of the "Iran Imperial Prize" (also called the "Pahlavi Foundation Prize"), presented by the Shah on March 21 each year, include:
1953 Mohammad Hijazi (Motiod Doleh). Sereshko Parvaneh (Tear and butterfly)
Zeinalabedin Motaman. She'ro Adabe Farsi (Persian poems and literature)
Shoja'adin Shafa. Iran va Adabiyat Jahan (Iran and the world's literature)
Zabiholah Safa. Tarikh Adabiyat Iran (History of Persian literature)
Ali Akbar Norad. Sherkathai Ta'Avoni va Bank baraye

Keshavarzan (Cooperatives and Bank for Farmers)
1954 Ali Pasha Saleh. Tarikhe Adabi Iran (Literary history of Iran)
Ali Javaher Kalaam. Tarikhe Tamadon Slam (the history of Islamic civilization)
1955 Abdolreza Mahdavi. Dovomin Shans (The second chance)
Ahmad Matin Daftari. Ravabete Bein-o-Imellali az Ghadim-olay' yam Ta Sazamane Melale Motahed (International relations from olden times to the beginning of the United Nations organization)
1956 Abolghasem Payandeh. Nehj-olfosaha (Manners in eloquence);
Tarjomehe Korane Majid (Translation of Great Koran); Eshghe zanashoo'i (The marriage love)
Mohammad Ebrahim Aayati Birjandi. Afkare Javide Mohammad (The Eternal Islamic Percepts)
Reza Zadeh Shafaq. Iran az Nazare Khavar Shenasan (Iran as judged by Orientalists); Tarikhe Adabiyat Iran (History of Persian literature); Nader Shah (Nader the King of Persia); Eskandare Maghodooni (Alexander, the Great, King of Macedonia)
Aman-olah Jahanbani. Marzhaye Iran va Shoravi (Irano-Soviet boundaries)
1957 Abdor-rahim Homayoon Farokh. Dastoor Zabane Farsi (Persian grammar)
Ehsan Yar Shater. Dastanhaye Shahnameh (Stories of the "Shahnameh"--Book of Kings, the most celebrated epic poetry and legendary history of Persia, by Ferdowsi)
Ali Asghar Hedayati. Aayin Koshbakhti (Institution of happiness)
Mansoor Sharif Zandiyah. Translation of Maurice Maeterlinck's "Fourth dimension"--

Bo'd Chaharom (received award also in 1959)
1958 Sa'id Nafisi. Aarezoohaye Bar Badrafteh (Destroyed aspirations)
Hamid Enayat. Translation of Aristotle's "Politics"-- Seyasat
Nezam'e-din Mojir Sheybani. Tarikhe Tamaddon (History of civilization) (received award also in 1960)
1959 Hadi Hedayati. Translation of Herodotus' works
Abdor-rahim Homayoon far-rokh. Dastoor Jame Zabane Farsi (Comprehensive grammar of the Persian language)
Amir Jalal-e-din Qafari. Farhanghe Farsi-Faranseh (Persian-French dictionary)
Ehsan Yar Shater. Dastanhaye Iran Bastan (Stories of ancient Iran)
1960 Javad Mosleh. Falsafaye Ali (Supreme philosophy)
Hamid Enayat. Translation of Aristotle's "Politics"   577.

IRAQI ACADEMY PRIZES

The year after it was established in 1947, the Iraqi Academy offered literary awards for the scholastic year 1948-1949. "Three prizes of 200 Iraqi dinars each were offered in two categories: (1) The best work written by an Iraqi; and (2) The best translation by an Iraqi." The three prizes offered in 1954, 1958, and 1960 were withheld from award as "there were no works which met the Academy's standards."
Winners include:
1948-9 Jafar Khayatt. Friend of the village
Abdul Azz Al-Douri. History of the economy of Iraq during the fourth century of the Hejira
Abdul Razzak Al-Hassani. History of political life in Iraq

1950-51 Mohammed Ahmed Al-Omar. The application of jurisdiction
2nd prize for translation-- Hassan Ahmed Al-Salman. Doreen Doris, "Earth and poverty"
1951-52 Ameen Al-Mumayiz. America as I saw it
2nd prize--Abdul Hak Fadil. The revolution of Al-Kayyam
2nd prize for translation-- Baha Al-Din Nuri. A windy trip in Iraq   578.

IRISH ACADEMY OF LETTERS

The literary honors granted by the Academy include: AE Memorial Prize; Casement Award; Gregory Medal; Harmsworth Literary Award; O'Growney Award. Academy members include such famous dramatists, poets, historians, novelists and critics as: Elizabeth Bowen, Padraic Colum, Mary Lavin, Frank O'Connor. Sean O'-Faoláin became a charter member of the Academy in 1932 with his volume of short stories, "Midsummer Night Madness and Other Stories."   579.

IRISH CREATIVE LITERATURE PRIZE

"Occasional monetary awards to creative writers" are among the literary prizes of the Irish Arts Council (An Chomhairle Ealaion, 70 Merrion Square, Dublin). A prize of Ł250 was offered for "published poetry in the English language" in 1961 and conditions of the award have included such requirements as that the winner be Irish-born, but competition rules, which may vary, are specified as each prize is announced.   580.

IRISH PLAY PRIZE

The annual prize of the Irish Arts Council (An Chomhairle Ealaion, 70 Merrion Square,

Dublin) for "the best one-act play in Irish submitted for the Oireachtas Art Competitions" (See Gaelic League Prizes) was established in 1952 to encourage the writing of plays in Irish. Rules of competition for the Ł 50 prize, part of the All-Drama Festival (held since 1961 in May, to accommodate the large number of play entries previously judged at the regular Festival in October) are set by the Gaelic League (Connradh na Gaeilge, 14 Parnell Square, Dublin).   581.

IRISH POETRY PRIZE

These awards of the Irish Arts Council (An Chomhairle Ealaion, 70 Merrion Square, Dublin) are granted from time to time in the form of scholarships and monetary premiums. Differing from the Denis Devlin Memorial Foundation Prize for poetry, also administered by the Irish Arts Council, these Irish poetry prizes are for works in the Irish language, while the Devlin prize honors poetry in English. The purpose of these prizes is "to reward and encourage the practice of poetry in the Gaelic language."

Eligibility for the prize may vary with each competition, and conditions of award are established by the Arts Council, including the requirement that competitors be Irish citizens. Winner in 1961 was Thomas Kinsella with his book, "Poems and Translations."

Also awarded by the Irish Arts Council is a triennial prize of Ł 300 "for the best book of poetry in the Irish language published by an Irish citizen in the preceding three years." First award will be granted in 1965 for works published during the competition period 1962-1964, and brought to the attention of the Council. Eugene Watters won a 1959 verse-tragedy award.   582.

Washington IRVING PRIZES (Spain)

Casa Americana, Madrid, offered the Irving Prizes in 1959 to commemorate the centenary of the death of Washington Irving (1783-1859), American author whose travels and residence in Spain as an American diplomatic representative resulted in such writings as "The Alhambra;" "History of...Christopher Columbus;" and "A Chronicle of the Conquest of Granada." Open to "Spanish writers resident in Spain and under 30 years of age," the prize, which was granted for the best 25-page stories submitted for consideration, was won by: Aquilino Duque (First Prize--15,000 pts); Eduardo Tijeras (Second Prize--7,500 pts).
583.

ISRAEL STATE PRIZE

The Israel State Prize for Literature, one of the official cultural honors of the government of Israel, together with awards in Science and the Visual Arts, consists of a certificate signed by the Israeli Minister of Education and Culture, and IL 2,000 premium. Presented on May 14, Israel Independence Day, the award is available to every writer in Israel "on the merit of work done during the last five years." Applications may be submitted by candidates, or by publishers, institutions, organizations, and societies. A jury of three members considers candidates for each prize--from 1953, founding date of the prize, to 1959 there were ten awards of IL 1,000 each; since 1959 there are five prizes of IL 2,000.

"Humanities" prize winners include: S. G. Bergman (1954); Y. Levy (1957); M. Buber (1958); L. A. Mayer (1959); Y. Kutscher

(1961). Among the State Prize for Literature laureates are:
1953 Y. Cohen; H. Hazaz
1954 D. Shimoni; S. Y. Agnon
1955 Z. S. Shimoni; Y. Lamdan
1956 G. Shofman; Mrs. M. Shtekelis-Yalon (Children's and Young People's Literature)
1957 G. Fikhman; U. Z. Greenberg; A. Smoli (Children's and Young People's Literature)
1958 S. Y. Agnon; Y. D. Berkovitz; Y. Cohen
1959 S. Yizhar; Y. Goley
1961 Y. Bouria   584.

ITALIA PRIZE (International-- Italy)

Founded in 1948 at Capri by cooperative action of radio representatives from a number of countries, this award--the only international prize for radio and television writing--was initiated and is presently administered by Radiotelevision Italiana (Segretaria RAI, via del Babuino 9, Rome). The 22 participating countries are the founding nations (Italy, Austria, France, United Kingdom, Monaco, Holland, Portugal, Switzerland), and those joining the prize activity since 1948 (Belgium, Germany, United States of America, Luxembourg, Canada, Ireland, Japan, Poland, Sweden, Yugoslavia, Israel, Australia, Republic of South Africa, Greece).

The original prize offered premiums for "the best dramatic, literary, and musical works for radio"--alternating each year between (1) Literary and Dramatic Works; and (2) Musical Works.

In 1952, the rules and prizes were changed to include works for the media of television and to award several prizes each year in major categories: Opere musicali; Opere letterarie o

drammatiche. Present awards, offering premiums that reach a total of L 8.000.000 a year, include a number of separate prizes, each granted by a separate jury with representatives from various participating countries:

ITALIA PRIZE FOR LITERARY OR DRAMATIC WORKS (current premium--14,500 Swiss francs)
RADIOTELEVISIONE ITALIANA PRIZE (current premium-- 1,040,000 Lires).

Writers who have been honored by various awards, for plays, poetry, and documentary programs, include:
1951 René Clair and Jean Forest (France). Dramatic adaptation of Théophile Gautier, "Una lacrima del diavolo"
1953 Charles Bertin (Belgium). Cristoforo Colombo (radio-drama)
1954 Dylan Thomas (United Kingdom: Ireland). All'-ombra del bosco latteo (Under Milkwood)
Louise Macneice (United Kingdom: Ireland). Il viaggio del prigioniero
Paul Louyet (Belgium). Un mondo si sveglia in Africa
1955 Claude Aveline (France). È vero ma non bisogna crederci
Peter Hirche (Germany). Il ritorno
1956 Carlo Castelli (Switzerland). Ballata per Tim, pescatore di trote
1957 Herbert Eisenreich (Germany). Perche viviamo, perche moriamo (Wovon wir leben und woran wir sterben)
1958 Friedrich Dürrenmatt (Switzerland). Una sera d'Autunno (Abenstunde im Spatherbst)
Aleksandr Obrenovic (Yugoslavia). L'uccello

HUMAN RIGHTS PRIZE, offered by UNESCO for a literary, dramatic, or documentary production:

Ernst Schnabel (Germany). Anne Frank--Spur eines Kindes

1959 Samuel Beckett (Ireland-France). Ceneri

Ivan Smith (Australia). Death of a wombat

Riccardo Bacchelli. La notte di un Nevrastenico (musical libretto)

1960 Maurice Picard (Switzerland). La vita di un uomo

Jacques Armand and Claude Barma. (France). Dramatic adaptation of Honoré de Balzac, "La grande Bertesca"

Kenichi Koyama (Japan). Risveglio della montagna

1961 Michael O'haodha (Ireland). The weaver's grave

Nebojsa Nikolic (Yugoslavia). Monsieur Joseph

CITY OF PISA PRIZE for musical works: Kafka, Franz. The Trial, adapted by Boris Blacher and Heinz von Cramer (Austria)

1962 Spark, Muriel (United Kingdom). The ballad of Peckham Rye

Yukio Doi (Japan). I was not afraid of the mountain

Izuho Sudo (Japan). The volcano (after Yasushi Inoue's novel)

EAST WEST PRIZE, a special prize of $1,000 offered by UNESCO: Studs Terkel (U.S.A.). Born to live   585.

ITALIAN ACADEMY OF POETRY PRIZE

A national competition for poetry has been held since 1960 by Accademia Italiana dei Poeti (viale Mazzini 55, Rome). The prize consists of a gold cup and publication of the winning poem in an anthology of poetry. Roberto Berardi won the award in 1960.   586.

ITALIAN CRITICS OF ART PRIZE

The highly-regarded Premio per la Critica d'Arte for writings in art history is offered by Instituto Italiano di Storia dell'-Arte in Florence, through Ente Provinciale del Turismo, Florence.   587.

ITALIAN CRITICS PRIZE

The Premio della Critica, also called the "Premi Biennale Critica," has been awarded since 1959 by a jury of critics (Giacomo Debenedetti, via Governo Vecchio 78, Rome). Winners of the L 300.000 premium include:

1959 Guglielmo Petroni. Poesie

1961 Gastav R. Hocke; Elda Fezzi; Andre Kuenzi   588.

ITALIAN CULTURAL PRIZE

The Premio della Cultura is an official national award, announced from time to time by Presidenza del Consiglio dei Ministeri, which has honored such writers as: Mauro Musiacchio; Giuseppe M. Musso; Giuseppe Gerini, the Florentine poet; and---in 1962---Anna Lo Monaco Aprile, who received the prize for her general literary work, especially her book of poetry, "Dove la terra muore;" Arturo Fornato, resident of Zurich and distributor of Italian poetry and books throughout Western Europe; Giuseppe Porto dell'Aquila, for his general literary work, especially his most recent publication, "L'ocarina."   589.

ITALIAN DRAMA INSTITUTE PRIZE

Currently offering two drama prizes (also called "Premio Nazionale IDI--per il Commedia, and per il Dramma"), the Instituto del Dramma Italiano (I.D.I., via Salandra 6, Rome) honors dramatic works--drama and comedy--written by an Italian citizen for approximately a two-hour performance in Italian. Plays that have not been produced or published or received a previous literary prize, are eligible for consideration, and are submitted in six copies to the jury before June (1962). The prize in each of the two classes (Drama; Comedy) consists of a gold medal, a premium of L 1.000.000, an additional L 1.000.000 royalty advance when the play is produced in the theater or on the radio or television, and production of the prize-winning play. The Institute also offers the D'AMICO PRIZE (which see) for drama criticism.

Playwrights who have received the high honor, for plays which are staged during the theatre season (July 1 to June 30 of the following year), include:

1949 Ugo Betti. Corruzione a Palazzo di Giustizia
1950 Diego Fabbri. Inquisizione
1951 Eduardo Di Dilippo. La paura numero uno
1952 Cesare Giulio Viola. Salviamo la giovane
1953 Dino Buzzati. Caso clinico
1954 Silvio Giovaninetti. Sangue verde
1955 Diego Fabbri. Processo a Gesu
1956 Cesare Meano. Bella
1957 Riccardo Bacchelli. Amleto
1958 Giuseppi Patroni Griffi. D'amore si muore; Giuseppe Marotta and Belisario

Randone. Bello di papa
1959 Giuseppe Dessi. La giustizia
1960 Eduardo Di Filippo. Sabato, domenica, lunedi; Carlo Terron. Lavinia fra i dannati
1962 Diego Fabbri. Ritratto di ignote

The PREMIO I.D.I. - SAINT VINCENT, 1961-1962--two L 2.000.000 prizes for unpublished plays--was granted to Silvano Anbrogi for his comedy, "I burosauri;" and to Rossano Ferrini (pen name: Giulio Gatti for his drama, "Antigone Lo Cascio."   590.

ITALIAN MINISTER OF PUBLIC EDUCATION PRIZE

The Premio del Ministero della publica Instruzione, a scholarly literary honor, administered by Accademia Nazionale dei Lincei (via della Lungara 10, Rome), was established in 1947 and is granted each year in four of eight subjects: Philology, Literary Criticism, Art; Mathematics; Physics; Chemistry, Biological Sciences; Philosophy; Law, Economics, Social Sciences; History and auxiliary subjects.

A jury, composed of members of the Academy and authorities in the subject area of the award, considers works submitted in competition before February 16 each year. Prizes of L 250.000 are granted to original writings which are unpublished or issued during the five years preceding the year of award, with each of the eight subject areas considered for award biennially.

Recipients of prizes in Philology and Literary Criticism include:

1948 Filippo Donini. Vita e Poesia di Sergio Corazzini
1950 Giuseppe Corsi. Dittamondo, di Fazio Degli Uberti

1953 Franca Ageno Brambilla.
Critical edition of Jacopone
da Todi, "Laudi"
1955 Rosetta Faccini da Rios.
Editing of Aristosseno da
Taranto, "Elementa Harmon-
ica"
1957 Maria Corti. Definitive
linguistic study of Pietro
Jacopo de Gennaro, "Rime;"
"Lettere"
1959 Antonio Quaglio. Entire
philological works
1961 Gaetano Fichera (mathematics and mechanics);
Ferdinando Milone (social
and political science)
1962 Antonio Marussi (astron-
omy, geodesy and geophysics)
Antonino Pagliaro (philology
and linguistics)   591.

ITALIAN NATIONAL PRIZE

Italy's highest official recognition of scholarly and cultural
work is the Premio Nazionale
del Presidente della Republica,
administered by Accademia
Nazionale dei Lincei (via della
Lungara 10, Rome). The prize
which carries on the Royal Prizes
(Premi Reali) conferred by the
King of Italy from 1879 to
1943, offers a premium of L
5.000.000 each year for two
major classes of work: (1)
Physics, Mathematics, and
Natural Science; (2) Moral Science, History, and Philology.

The administering agency,
Accademia Nazionale dei Lincei,
Italy's national Academy, was
established by Italian President
Luigi Einaudi in 1939 to continue in the scholarly and cultural tradition of the Academia
d'Italia (which it replaced),
founded by King Umberto I in
1878. Among the literary
honors bestowed by the Academy
are such prizes as the Donegani,
Einaudi, Feltrinelli, Novaro,
Trenta.

Included in the laureates recently recognized by Premi Na-
zionali are:
1957 Vincenzo Caglioti
(chemistry)
Luigi Ronga (art and poetry
criticism)
1958 Piero Leonardi (geology,
paleontology, mineralogy)
Gian Piero Bognetti (history,
geography, anthropology)
1959 Giuseppe Montalenti
(botany, zoology)
Ugo Spirito (philosophy)
1960 Giulio Stella (physiology
and pathology)
Emilio Betti (jurisprudence)
1961 Carlo Miranda (physics,
mathematics and natural
science)
1962 Natalino Sapegno (moral
and historical science, and
philology)   592.

IVORY COAST REPUBLIC
LITERARY PRIZE

The Grand Prix Littéraire de
la Côte d'Ivoire, established in
1960 to give recognition to the
literary work of an author of the
Ivory Coast Republic, was founded by the S.F.A.D.E.C.O.
(B. P. 301, Abidjan), at the suggestion of the organization's
Director, M. Spoliansky. The
premium of 50.000 frs C.F.A.
is awarded by a jury which includes M. Clerici, Inspecteur d'A-
cadémie de la Côte d'Ivoire. In
1960 Sidiki Dembele was honored
with the prize for his novel,
"Les inutiles."   593.

IZVESTIA COMPETITION (USSR)

In a literary competition conducted by "Izvestia," one of the
Communist Party's official
Moscow Russian-language newspapers, a number of prize-winners were named in 1962, including:

Poetry--Sergei Ostrovci.
Ballad of love
Petrya Dariyenko. My spring
Short Story--A. Useinov.

Silence in the ether
Iv. Koshcheyev. How Yegora
grew in the field
A. Virigo. Pedagogical road
Z. Tumanova. The bag
Leonid Pestin. Flowers
S. Naumov. The watercolor
Anna Sidorova. The Troika
V. Bovkun. Night concert
Anatoly Ferenchuk. The
passerby   594.

JABUTI PRIZE (Brazil)
The annual award of the
Câmara Brasileira do Livro (Av.
Ipiranga 1267, Sao Paulo), con-
sisting of a statue of some
character from Brasilian folk
lore, is offered for many types
of writing: Novel; Short Story;
Poetry; 'Revelação de Autor;''
Literary Personality; Book of the
Year; Essay; Literary History;
Scientific Discovery; Children's
and Young People's Literature;
Biography; Technical Writing.
Writers honored with the
1959 award include: Sergio
Milliet, José Paulo Moreira da
Fonseca, Jorge Amado, Jorge
Medauar, Isa Silveira Leal,
Aldemir Martins.   595.

Max JACOB PRIZE (France)
A major French prize for
poetry, this award was established in 1951 with a premium
of 3.000 NF for a work of
poetry published during the preceding year, preferably by a little
known poet. A work is entered
in competition by depositing nine
copies, before January 30, with
Librairie Le Pont Traversé
(16 rue Saint-Séverin, Paris).
Laureates include:
1951 Louis Guillaume. Noir
comme la mer
1952 Armen Lubin. Sainte
patience
1953 Marcel Sauvage. Oeuvre
d'or
1954 Jean Grosjean. Fils de
l'homme

1955 Marie-Josèphe. Les
yeux cernés
1956 Edmond Humeau. Entire
work
1957 Marc Alyn. Les temps
des autres
1958 Charles Le Quintrec.
Les noces de la Terre
Pierre Oster. Solitude de la
lumière
1959 Gabriel Dheur. Monde
transparent
Henry Bauchau. Géologie
1960 Alain Bosquet. Deuxième
testament
1961 Lena Leclercq. Poèmes
insoumis   596.

Hugo JACOBI PRIZE (Germany)
In this award, which is
named for a Strassbourg poet,
the Jacobi-Stiftung offers 1000
DM to a young poet writing in
the German language--''Stil und
Existenz ringende Dichter.''
Among winners of the award are:
Rainer Brambach, Hans Magnus
Enzensberger, Cyrus Atabey,
Peter Ruehmkorf, Helmut Heis-
senbüttel.   597.

JACOBSON PRIZE (Netherlands)
One of several awards granted
under the Tollens Fund, the
Jacobson Prize, established in
1925, was presented in 1960
to Marie Schmitz for her entire
literary work.   598.

JĀIZAT AL-DAULAH (Egypt)
The annual prize, one of the
State awards for cultural achievement, brings official government
recognition for literary contribution.   599.

JALISCO STATE PRIZE (Mexico)
A literary award of the
second most populous of Mexico's
29 states, the prize has been
presented by a prize committee
consisting of ''three ranking
writers'' to such authors as:
1951 Olivia Zúñiga. Retrato

de una nina triste
1953 Juan José Arreola
600.

Kalevi JÄNTTI PRIZE (Finland)

The annual award of the
Jäntti Foundation, "established
to support young authors," has
been won by:
1951 Veikko Huovinen
1952 Eeva Joenpelto
1953 Marko Tapio
1954 Kirsi Kunnas
1955 Martti Palkispää
1956 Paavo Rintala
1958 Satu Waltari
1959 Pentti Saarikoski
1960 Martti Joenpolvi
1961 Harri Kaasalainen
601.

JAPAN ACADEMY OF ARTS PRIZES

As one of its activities in
advancing the arts in Japan, the
Japan Art Academy (prior to
1947 the "Japan Imperial
Academy of Arts") annually awards
prizes in the fields of Visual
Art, Literature, and Music "to
those who have contributed an
excellent artistic work or toward
the development of the arts."
Two of the cultural prizes--
IMPERIAL PRIZE (Onshi-sho)
and JAPAN ACADEMY OF ARTS
PRIZE (Nihon Geijitsuin-sho)--
established in 1941 to "honor
works and persons that specially
contributed to development of
art," consist of a Diploma of
Honor, a medal, and a monetary
premium. The jury for prizes
in literature is composed of
novelists, poets, and critics who
are members of the Literary
Department of the Academy.

Among writers receiving Japan
Academy of Arts recognition
are:
Imperial Prize--Novelists, poets,
critics, and literary scholars
who have won this distinguished
honor for their entire literary

contribution or for a single work
include:
1949 Ryohei Handa, poet.
Saiwaigi
1957 Shinobu Origuchi, writer
1959 Syohachi Kimura.
Flourishing annals of Tokyo
Japan Academy of Arts Prize--
Twenty-seven recipients of this
respected award (through 1961)
are:
Poetry--
1942 Kotaro Takamura. Dotei
(A course of life)
1943 Yonejiro Noguchi
1951 Tokujiru Oyama
1953 Tatsuji Miyoshi
Tampu Hattori
1958 Ryuko Kawaji. Wave
Novel--
1950 Jiro Osaragi. Kikyo
(Homecoming)
1952 Yasunari Kawabata.
Senbazuru (One thousand
cranes)
1956 Masuji Ibuse. Hyomin-
Usaburo
1957 Ata Koda. Nagareru
(To drift)
1959 Yasushi Inoue. Ice Cliff
1961 Ashihei Hino. Before
and after of revolution Jun
Ishikawa
Literary History and Research--
1948 Shinobu Origuchi
1953 Bummei Tsuchiya
1955 Shintaro Suzuki. Studies
of French literature
Criticism--
1951 Hideo Kobayashi
1952 Konosuke Hinatsu
1954 Toyotaka Komiya
1956 Syomu Nobori
1957 Yoshie Hoshida. Ichiyo
No Nikki (Diary of Ichiyo)
1958 Ryozo Niizeki. Dramatic
history of Greece and Rome
1959 Seiichi Yoshida. Study of
naturalism
1961 Tettaro Kawakami
Children's Literature--
1951 Mimei Ogawa
1955 Joji Tsubota
Translation--

1950 Yoshio Yamauchi. Translation into Japanese of
Roger Martin du Gard's
"Les Thibault"
1953 Kinichi Ishikawa   602.

JAPAN ACADEMY PRIZES

Outstanding contributions to
science and learning are honored
by the Japan Academy (Ueno Park,
Tokyo) by two annual prizes:
The **IMPERIAL PRIZE** (Onshi
Sho)--established in 1910;
The **JAPAN ACADEMY
PRIZE** (Gakushi-in Award)
--established in 1911.

These prizes, awarded "for
specified papers and books of
eminent merit, mainly concerned with literature and social
sciences and natural sciences and
their applications," consist of a
medal, a Certificate of Merit,
and a monetary premium.

Among the scholars and
writers awarded this high public
honor are:

Osamu Takata; Takuji Ito;
Kazuo Yamasaki; Aki Uyeno;
Taka Yanagisawa; Tsugio
Miya. Wall-paintings in the
Daigo-ji Pagoda
Shigetoshi Kawatake. A his-
tory of the Japanese theatre
Toshio Takeuchi. Aristotle's
theory of Art
Masami Ito. Freedom of
speech and press
Shigeo Kishibe. A historical
study of the music of the
T'ang Dynasty: The First
Installment--Music Organiza-
tions
Tomoichi Sasabuchi. A study
of Romanticism in modern
Japanese literature
Koya Nakamura. A study of
the documents of Tokugawa
Ieyasu
Yoichi Kodama. A study of
the development of the salt
fields in the Tokugawa
Period.   603.

JAPAN DETECTIVE STORY WRITERS CLUB PRIZES

The Nippon Tantei Sakka
Kurabu, awarded annually in
three categories (Novels, Short
Stories, and New Writers), is
granted by the Detective Story
Writers' Club. The prize was
established in 1947, and like the
Edogawa Rampo Prize (established in 1956) it is designed to improve the quality of Japanese
detective, mystery and crime
writing, and to encourage new
writers in the field. Members
of the jury include well-known
writers, such as Edogawa Rampo,
famous author of mystery stories.
Among the winners are:

1947 Masashi Yokomizo. Hon-
jin Satsujin Jiken (A murder
case at headquarters)
1948 Ango Sakaguchi. Furen-
zoku Satsujin Jiken (A murder case by an atmospheric
discontinuity)
1949 Akimitus Takagi. Noh-
men Satsujin Jiken. (Murder
by a man with the Noh mask)
1950 Udaru Oshito. Ishi no
Shita no Kiroku (Records
under the rock)
1951 Jun Mizutani. Aru Ketto
(A duel)
Rampo Edogawa. Gen-Ei-Jo
(The castle of illusion)
1953 Sango Nagase. Baikoku-
Do (A traitor to one's
country)
1955 Jokichi Hikage. Kitsune
to Niwatori (A fox and a
cock)   604.

JAPAN ESSAYISTS CLUB PRIZE

The Japan Essayists' Club
grants 50,000 yen each year for
"the best theses and essays,
including those in book form."
Winners of the award--granted
primarily for the writing of new
authors--include:

1953 Toru Uchida. Kitsutsuki
no Michi (Woodpeckers'
roads)

1954 Sakae Suda. Ichiya
(A thousand and one nights)
1957 Mori Maru. Chichi no
Boshi (Father's hat)   605.

JAPAN WOMAN WRITERS LITERARY PRIZES

Created as an annual award for the best novel published during the previous year, this prize, offered each spring by the Women Writers' Association, "was established in 1947 in order to encourage the literary work by women novelists of both veteran and young talents".

Members of the Association nominate and select works for consideration by a jury which determines the winner. Information about the prize-winner is published each year in "Fujin-Koren," a leading women's magazine in Japan.

Recipients of the Nippon Joryu Bungakusha Kyokai (17, Yanaka-Shimizucho, Daito-ku, Tokyo), which consists of a monetary premium and a medal, are:

1947 Taiko Hirabayashi.
Such a woman
1948 Kiku Amino. Golden
coffin
1949 Fumiko Hayashi. Late
chrysanthemums
1952 Nobuko Yoshiya. Fire of
Hell
Yohko Ohta. The ragged ones
1953 Fujiko Ohtani. Tsurube
no oto (Sound of Tsurube, a
Japanese well; or Sound of
a sweep-bucket)
1954 Fumiko Enchi. Homojii
Tsukihi (Hungry Years;
Hungry days)
1955 Sakae Tsuboi. Kaze
(Wind)
1957 Yasuko Harada. Banka
(Requiem)
Tomie Ohhara. Sutomai
Tsumbo (Streptomycin-deaf)
1958 Chiyo Uno. O-Han
1960 Masako Yana. Hiden-in

1961 Yoshiko Shibaki. Yuba
Yumiko Kurahashi. Die
Partei
1962 Kiku Amino.   The cherry
blossoms   606.

JAPANESE EDUCATIONAL MINISTER'S PRIZE FOR ARTIS-TIC ACHIEVEMENT

An official national prize created in 1950 by the Japanese Ministry of Education as an annual recognition of "meritorious services in the field of juvenile literature, fiction, and criticism." Recipients of the government award include:

1950 Michi Takeyama. Biruma
no Tategoto (The sound of a
harp echoing through the
jungles in Burma)
1952 Mimei Ogawa. General
work in Children's Literature
1954 Takashi Saita. Saita
Takashi Jidogeki Zenshu
(Collected children's dramas
of Takashi Saita)
1955 Rinzo Shiina. Utsukushii
Onna (A pretty woman)
Seiichi Yoshida. Gendai Bunga-
kuron Taikei (A representative selection from con-
temporary literary theories
and criticism)   607.

JAPANESE IMPERIAL POETRY CONTEST

Each year thousands of poems are submitted in this poetry contest (7,490 in 1956; 23,000 in 1960; 31,000 in 1962). The competition, which is more than a thousand years old, honors the 15 persons whose poems are selected as the "best of the year" by a reading at a Royal poetry party (televised for the first time in 1962) of the winning poems. Poems entered in the Emperor's New Year's Poetry Contest are on set subjects (announced each year) and in a set form--"tanka:" a 31-syllable

poetry form of unrhymed sen-
tences of seven syllables, except the first and third sen-
tences of five syllables, expressing a lyrical thought.

In the 1963 competition, the
subject is "Grassy Fields;" and
the deadline for entries was
October 15, 1962, which were
to be submitted to Kunaicho,
Marunouchi, Tokyo, Japan,
Eishinka. Included among winning poets, who have written
on such assigned themes, as
"Light," and "Youth," are
several from the United States:

  1957 Lucille Nixon--first
    foreign-born poet to be
    among winners
  1962 Mrs. Yuriko Takahashi
                            608.

JAPANESE ORDER OF CULTURAL MERIT

An official government award,
founded by the "Order of Cultural
Merits Ordinance," enacted on
February 11, 1937, to recognize
"those who have made the most
outstanding contributions to the
growth of culture," the honor is
assigned by a Selection Committee of 10 outstanding representatives of Japanese culture
appointed by the Japanese Ministry of Education.

The Order, which is worn
suspended on a ribbon, is con-
ferred by the Emperor at the
Imperial Palace on November 3,
Cultural Day. Among the au-
thors receiving this major public
recognition for distinguished
work in literature are: Roban
Koda; Setsurei Miyake; Shigeo
Iwanami; Kunio Yanagida;
Mokieni Saito; and Kafu Nagai.
Living laureates include: Naoya
Shiga; Nobutsuna Sasaki;
Junichiro Tanizaki; Hakucho
Masamune; Saneatsu Mushanokoji;
Mantaro Kubota; Ton Satomi;
Haruo Sato; Eiji Yoshikawa;
Yasunari Kawabata.   609.

JAPANESE PENSION FOR MEN OF CULTURAL MERIT

Writers, together with other
creative persons who have made
outstanding cultural contributions,
are recognized by a national law,
enacted April 13, 1951, designed
to honor "those who are specifically meritorious for furtherance and development of culture!"
The selection procedure and committee are the same, generally,
as those for the Japanese
Order of Cultural Merit. Recipients of the pension are announced once a year, usually in
November, and the maximum
number receiving the premium
is set at ten.

Usually conferees of the
Japanese Order of Cultural Merit
are the recipients of the Japanese
Pension, so that the existing
pension holders are the ten living laureates of the Japanese
Order of Cultural Merit, and, in
addition, Utsuho Kubota.
                            610.

Gysbert JAPICX PRIZE (Netherlands)

Since 1947, the Frisian Novel
and Poetry Prize for the best
prose and poetry (alternately) in
the Frisian language, published
during the preceding four years,
has been granted by Friesland
Province (Provinciale Staten van
Friesland, Leeuwarden, Friesland) each year. In 1953 the
prize became a biennial award,
granted alternately with the Joost
Halbertsma Prize for scientific
writing. The 750 fl (formerly
500 fl) premium is awarded on
the second Friday in October in
the town hall of Bolsward, the
Frisian town which was "the
dwelling-place of the 17th century poet, Gysbert Japicx"
(1603-1666), who "is considered
the founder of Frisian literature."

Winners of the prize, who
are determined with the assis-

tance of the Frisian Academy, are:

1947 O. Postman. It sil bistean (It will exist)
1948 N. Haisma. Simmer (Summer) (posthumous award)
1949 Fedde Schurer. Simson, and rhymed translation of the Psalms
1950 Y. Poortinga. Elbrich, 2nd volume
1951 Sjoers Spanninga (pseud of Jan Dijkstra). Spegel-skrift (Mirror writing); and Nunders (Seashells)
1952 Anne Wadman. Kritysk konfoai
1953 Rixt (Miss H. A. van Dorssen). De gouden rider (The Golden Rider)
1955 Ulbe van Houten. De hillige histoarje (The Holy history); De sunde fan Haitse Holwerda (Haitze Holwerda's sin)
1957 D. A. Tammingo. Bal-laden
1959 E. B. Folkertsma. Essays (prize refused)
1961 Marten Sikkema (pseud of G.G.G. Meerburg). Poetical works.   611.

JOCS FLORALS DE LA LLEN-GUA CATALANA (International)
These Floral Games of the Catalan Language, like the Floral Games of Toulouse, repre-sent the oldest traditional liter-ary competitions of the Western World that were first held in the Middle Ages as the trouba-dour "Court of Love and Beauty." Catalan games, which "flourished in Catalonia for three centuries," have been held annually since their revival in 1859. The competition was traditionally held in Barcelona on the first Sunday in May, but, since with-drawal of Catalan liberties in Spain, now takes place in exile in a different city each year,

including such locations as: Mexico City (1942); London (1947); Montevideo (1949); New York (1951); Paris (1959); Buenos Aires (1960); Santiago (1962). The Jocs Florals are open to all writers of poetry and prose in Catalan throughout the world.

The prizes consist of tradi-tional emblems of excellence-- flowers of gold or of silver, and often a monetary premium is given with three "Traditional Prizes" (Premis Ordinaris), corresponding to the three words of the Jocs Florals de Barce-lona: Patria, Fides, Amor--
Englantina d'Or--best patriotic poem
Viola d'Or and d'Argent--best religious or moral poem
Flor Natural--best love poem.
Approximately 30 other prizes (Premis Extraordinaris) may be given for five classes of writing: Poetry; Novel, Drama, Stories; Music; Philology, History, Current Events; Economics and Sociology. Prizes are supplied by cultural groups in Europe, Latin America and the United States--all organizations associ-ated with the Catalan language.
At the Catalan Floral Games of New York (Juegos Florales de Neuva York), organized by the Ibero-American Writers' and Poets' Circle of New York, which were held on October 16, 1955 at Columbia University, the first prize for reporting was won by Jesus de Galindez, for "A Basque Looks at Columbia," an article that appeared in the English edition of "Américas" in June 1954.   612.

Sir William JONES MEMORIAL MEDAL (India)
One of several awards of The Asiatic Society (1 Park Street, Calcutta 16) "for encouragement of studies in letters and humani-ties," this honor is granted trien-

nially "to a person who in the opinion of the Council (of the Asiatic Society) has made conspicuously important Asiatic Researches in one of the two divisions of Knowledge, namely (1) Science, including medicine; and (2) Philosophy, Literature, and History." Recipients of the medal include:
  1953 Jules Bloch
  1956 R. N. Chopra
  1959 L. D. Bernett   613.

JORNAL DE LETRAS PRIZE
(Brazil)

The literary periodical of Rio de Janeiro (Avda. Erasmo Barga 255) has conducted several contests for Brazilian writers: PREMIO JUSCE LINOKUBITS-CHEK; PREMIO ADOLFO CAMINHA, for a first novel; PREMIO MARTINS PENA, for drama.   614.

Dieciocho di JULIO PRIZE
(Spain)

The Julio Prize, offered by the Secretaría General del Movimiento (Alcalá 44, Madrid), grants 50,000 pts for a published work in the fields of political or social science.   615.

JUNGE GENERATION PRIZE
(Germany)

The annual "Younger Generation Prize," part of the Fontane Prize, is a general cultural award granted by the Senate of West Berlin (Der Senator für Volksbildung, Charlottenburg 9, Berlin) in: Painting, Architecture, Music, Literature, and Motion Pictures. Authors honored with the 2500 DM prize include:
  1956 Jens Rehn
  1957 Heinz Piontek
  1958 Wolfdietrich Schnurre
  1959 Heinz von Cramer
  1960 Cyrus Atabay
  1961 Rudolf Hogelstange;

Rudolf Hartung. Vor grünen Kulissen (collected poems) 1962 Annemarie Lorenzen-Weber. Korso (novel), and her entire literary work

A recent winner of the JUNGE GENERATION PRIZE OF "DIE WELT," organized by the journal "Die Welt," was Max Frisch, Swiss playwright and novelist, who received a 10,000 DM premium.
                               616.

JUNGMANN PRIZE (France)

A newly established 10.000 NF prize, first granted in 1960, the award was founded by the Président-directeur of the Société Louis Jungmann (52 rue Marquette, Nancy) to honor a published or unpublished imaginative writing, preferably a novel, set in an industrial milieu and demonstrating the great technical advances of the 20th century. Winners include: Philippe Diole with "L'eau profonde;" Henri Queffélec with "Les frères de la brume;" Roger Chateaneu with "Les harpes de fer."   617.

JUVENIL CADETE PRIZE
(Spain)

In 1960, the Barcelona publisher Editorial Mateu (San Gervasio 84) offered this 70,000 pts award for children's literature, which was won by Luis Carbonell, author of a novel about a teacher.   618.

JUVENTUD PRIZES (Spain)

A total of 11 prizes have been granted by the publisher Editorial Juventud of Madrid, who issues "Revista Juventud." The awards, which vary in monetary premium from 5,000 to 10,000 pts, have been granted for: Novel, Poetry, Short Story, Narration.

Recipients include:
GIBRALTAR PRIZE of 5,000 pts:
  1953 José María Sánchez-Silva;

1954 Rafael Morales;
1955 Luis López Anglada;
1956 Julián Andujar
José Luis HIDALGO PRIZE
5,000 pts prize for novel:
   Carlos Sahagún. Requiem
   ante un retrato de primera
   comunión
Antonio MACHADO PRIZE:
   1956 Prado Nogueira
Juan de MENA PRIZE for novel:
   José Luis Gomez Alfaro.
   Cordoba
Samuel ROS PRIZE for short
stories:
   1956 Daniel Sueiro. La
   Rebusca   619.

K. R. O. POETRY PRIZE
(Netherlands)
   Poets winning the prize in
1960 include: J. W. Schulte
Nordholt, and Hubert van
Herreweghen.   620.

KALINGA PRIZE (International)
   The Kalinga Prize is named
after an Indian empire conquered
more than 2,000 years ago by
Asoka (King of Magadha, 273-
232)--an extensive domain
corresponding to modern India--
at such cost that Asoka pledged
that he never again would wage
war. Granted on a world-wide
basis for the best popular science writing, the annual award,
founded by the Indian industrialist of the state of Orissa,
M. B. Patnaik, is administered
by UNESCO (Department of
Exact and Natural Sciences, 2
Place Fontenoy, Paris 7e).
Directed to offering recognition to
leading interpreters of science
and to strengthening scientific
relations between India and other
nations, the prize brings a
premium of L1000 and a trip
to India to the winner--a writer
or journalist, or a motion picture, radio, television director--
who through his work has made
"an important contribution to the

wider dissemination and better
understanding of science among
the general public."
   Laureates, who have been
honored for their entire work in
popularization of science by the
international jury appointed by
the Secretary-General of UNESCO,
are:
   1952 Luis de Brolie (France)
   1953 Julian Huxley (United
      Kingdom)
   1954 Waldemar Kaempffert (U.
      S.A.)
   1955 August Pi Suner (Venezue-
      la)
   1956 George Gamow (U.S.A.)
   1957 Bertrand Russell (United
      Kingdom)
   1958 Karl von Frisch (Ger-
      many--Austria)
   1960 Jean Rostand (France)
   1961 Ritchie Calder (United
      Kingdom)
   1962 Arthur C. Clarke (United
      Kingdom)
                              621.

KALOKAIRINEIOS DRAMA CON-
TEST (Greece)
   The annual drama contest,
with awards since 1919, was
initiated by art patron Andreas
L. Kalokairinos, who also found-
ed a contest for poetry in 1919.
The prize, administered by the
Parnassus Literary Society
(Square Aghiou Gheorghiou Kary-
tsi 8, Athens), is given for "the
best dramas and comedies, his-
toric or patriotic works in
Greek, which are performed on
the stage."
   Kalokairineios Theatrical
Competition: recent winners of
First Prize and Honorable Men-
tion, with a premium of 7,000
drachmae, are:
1953 Michael Anastasiou. The
   young ones (three-act drama)
   Honorable Mention--G.
   Biniaris. Velvet curtains
   Sot. Riganakos. The honest
   ones

P. Samartzis. In the Cave
of Polyphimus
1954 Mich. Anastasiou. Mr.
Stephanos Vrettos
Honorable Mention--Them. K.
Mitsotakis. How far back
Yiannis Economidis. Yiannis
Kaloyiannis
P. Tsakonas. Longer nails
1955 George D. Kaloyeropoulos.
The wounded partridge
Honorable Mention--Efstathios
Liakopoulos. Vasilios
Digenis Akritas
Theodoros Dervos. There
aren't many in the world
1956 Panos I. Kontellis. Sor-
rows of the valley
Maria Panayiotopoulou. The
terrible dilemma
Honorable Mention--Vas.
Georgoutsos. Jealousy
P. Tsakonas. The strangler
1957 Dora Moatsou-Varnali.
Under the Lion of Venice
Rodopi Vasileiadou. The
pauper's son
1958 Antonio Leonardos. Michael
Kourmoulis-Hussein bey
1959 Dimitrios Bourounis. Under
the palm of God
Hostas Maiandros (pen name:
Constantine Kourtis).
Lambros Katsonis
Honorable Mention--Constan-
tine Asymakopoulos. We
did not live today
Haris Sakellarious. Kleitos
Yiannis Skevakis. Factories
should have large ... wide
windows   622.

Halpérine KAMINISKY PRIZE
(France)
    The prize of the Société des
Gens de Lettres (38 rue du
Faubourg-Saint-Jacques, Paris
14e), one of some fifty literary
honors given by the organization,
was established in 1937 as an
annual award for the best translation into French by a French
author of a foreign literary work.
Winners of the 500 NF prize

with the book judged the best
translation published during the
year are:
1937 Claudine Decourcelle. Translation of Younghill Kang, Au
pays du matin calme
1940 Pierre-François Caille.
Translation of Margaret Mitchell, Autant en emporte le
vent
1945 Jean Talva. Translation of
Rosamund Lehmann, La bal-
lade et la source
Anne-Mathilde et Pierre Paraf.
Translation of V.-J. Jensen,
La rameau de myrte
1947 Max Morize. Translation
of Frédéric Prokosch, Les
asiatiques
1948 Marcelle Sibon. Translation
of Graham Greene, La puis-
sance et la gloire
1949 Michel Arnaud. Translation
of Dino Buzatti, Le désert
des Tartares
1950 Jacqueline Peltier. Translation of M. Liberaki, Trois
étés
1951 Blaise Briod. Translation
of Jacob Wassermann, l'Ulri-
que
1952 Pierre Javet. Translation
of Jan de Hartog, Thalassa
1953 Bernard Lesfargues. Translation of Rafael Sanchez Mazas,
Pédrito de Andia
1954 Maurice-Edgar Coindreau.
Translation of William Goyen,
La maison d'Haleine
1955 Charles-du-Bos (Mme).
Translation of Bernard Beren-
son, Esquisse pour un portrait
de moi-même
1956 Claude Sylvian and Jaakes
Ahokas. Translation of
Vaïno Linna, Soldats inconnus
1957 Imre Laszlo. Translation
of Tibor Dery, Niki ou l'histoire d'un chien
1958 Lou Bruder. Translation of
Jens Rehn, Rien en vue
1959 Jean Dutourd. Translation
of Truman Capote, Les muses
parlent

1961 Yvonne Davet. Translation
of Vladimir Nabokov. Autre
rivage
1962 Mme. Hofer-Bury. Translation of Ernst Wiechert. La
Commandante   623.

KARISTO COMPANY PRIZE
(Finland)

Among the winners of this
publisher's prize, which has
been awarded by the Finnish
Literature Union to "young
promising authors" annually since
1952, are:

1952 Pentti Holappa; Otto
Varhia
1953 Jarmo Ruoste
1954 Jarmo Ruoste
1955 Veijo Merki
1956 Esko Koivu
1957 Ester Erhomaa; Pentti
Kivistö
1958 Pentti Saarikoski
1959 Leo Kalervo
1960 Kekka Lounela
Tyyne Saastomoinen
1961 Kaarlo Isotalo   624.

KARLSRUHE CULTURAL
PRIZE (Germany)

Outstanding works in Literature, as well as those in Painting, Graphic Art, Sculpture, and
Music, are honored by the annual cultural awards of the city
of Karlsruhe, available to artists
who were born or who resided
in the area of Baden-Baden,
Bruchsal, Karlsruhe, Pforzheim,
or Rastatt. The literary prize,
with a premium of 2000 DM and
a Second Prize of 1000 DM, has
honored such writers of prose and
poetry as: Gustav Faber; Macha
Kropp; Ernst Feuerstein; Otto
Gillen; Erna Lotte Goosens-
Heller; Werner Walz; Walter
Helmut Fritz.   625.

Charles KAUFFMANN PRIZE
(France)

The Fédération Des Artistes
Prize brings a 5.000 NF pre-

mium from the Fondations Louis
Jungmann (52 rue Marquette,
Nancy) for writing directed to
increasing public interest in
travel (voyages). Michel Déon
won the prize in 1961 with "Le
balcon de Spetsai."   626.

Gottfried KELLER PRIZE (Swit-
zerland)

This 10.000 fr sw award of
the Martin-Bodmer-Stiftung (Le
Grand Cologny, Geneva) is one
of the major literary prizes in
German and Continental letters,
and the highest Swiss literary
award. The Gottfried-Keller-
Preis was established in 1922
and is awarded from time to
time--usually every two or three
years--"to honour an important
literary, philosophical, or historical performance...in accordance with the traditional Swiss
spirit (Helvetia mediatrix)." Winning works must be in one of the
Swiss languages, especially German or French, and no application is made for the award,
which is determined by a jury of
scholars and writers. The Martin-Bodmer-Stiftung, in addition
to awarding the Keller Prize,
has conferred "some 60 honorary
donations" to writers.
Recipients include:

1922 Jakob Bosshart, novelist
1927 C. F. Ramuz, novelist
in French
1929 Joseph Nadler, Austrian
historian of literature
1931 Hans Carossa, German
poet
1936 Hermann Hesse, novelist
and poet
1938 Ernest Gagliardy, historian
1942 Robert Faesi, novelist,
poet, historian of literature
1945 Eduard Korrodi, critic
1952 Gertrud von Le Fort,
German poet
1954 Werner Kaegi, historian
1956 Max Rychner, critic and

poet
1959 Maurice Zermatten,
    novelist and poet in French
1962 Emil Staiger, historian
    of literature and translator
                            627.

Josef KELLER VERLAG DRAMA
PRIZE (Germany)
    The Dramenpreis des Josef
Keller Verlages, a publisher's
prize of Josef Keller Verlag
(Posstenhofener Strasse 43,
Starnberg 13B) although not cur-
rently given has been awarded
such playwrights as: Roland
Ziersch, Fred Siebeck, Fried
Mass, Heimut Harun, Joachim
Wichman, Heinz Rieder, Otto
Mielke.   628.

Matthias KEMP PRIZE (Netherlands)
    Since 1953 the prize of the
Province of Limburg has been
awarded to authors of the Netherlands and Belgium writing in the
Dutch language, including:
    1958 Paul Haimon. Mense-
        wissers
        Jos Vanderloo (Belgium).
        De Muur
    1960 Bernard Kemp (pseud of
        B. F. van Vlierden)
        (Belgium). De Dioskuren
        Jo Nabben. Hagar   629.

KIEL CULTURAL PRIZE
(Germany)
    An annual award of the city
of Kiel, granted by the govern-
ing cultural council of the city
(Kultursenat), has been offered
since 1951 for artistic or
scientific achievement, especially to persons whose work concerns Kiel, or the Schleswig-
Holstein district in which the
city is located. The 5000 DM
premium, presented during the
city holiday in celebration of
Kiel Woche, honors writers
whose work contributes to the
mainstream of contemporary

literature. Among writers
honored are:
    1956 Hans-Egon Holthusen
    1960 Wolfgang Liepe
    1961 Hal Koch (Copenhagen)
    1962 Lilli Martius   630.

KIKUCHI PRIZE (Japan)
    Named for Hiroshi (Kan)
Kikuchi (1888-1948), Japanese
playwright and novelist who
founded the publishing company,
Bungei Shunjusha, this prize established in 1939 by the Japanese
literary magazine "Bungei Shunju,"
and the Japanese Society for the
Promotion of Literature (Bungaku
Shinkokai) was awarded to recognize the literary achievements
of established writers. Among
the authors honored until 1944,
when the prize was temporarily
suspended, were such "writers
over the age of 46 with long
literary careers" who had published a work of merit during the
preceding year, as Shusei Tokuda,
who received the prize for his
book "Kaso Jimbutsu" (Characters
in disguise); and for general
literary activities during a year:
Saneatus Mushanokoji, Ton Satomi
(1940); Saise Muro (1941); and
Haruo Sato (1943).
    Since its reestablishment in
1953 the prize is given each year
for distinguished achievement in
Japanese letters, designating individuals or groups "making the
newest and most creative contributions during the year in such
fields as literature, drama,
cinema, newspaper and magazine
publication." Award-winning authors are:
    1953 Eliji Yoshikawa. Shin
        Heike Monogatari (New tales
        of the Heike Family)
    1954 Momoko Ishii. General
        work in children's literature
    1955 Hideo Aragaki. Tensei
        Jingo (Heavenly voices and
        human words)
    1956 Hakucho Masamune.

General activity in literary
criticism
1962 Donald Keene (U.S.A.--
first non-Japanese honored)
631.

KISHIDA PRIZE FOR DRAMA
(Japan)
The Shinchosha Publishing
Company established this annual
prize in 1954 in commemoration
of the playwright, Kunio Kishida
(1890-1954). Granted "for
outstanding contributions to the
theatre," the prize has honored
such playwrights and translators
of plays as:
1954 Junji Konoshita. Furo
(Storms and swells)
Tadasu Iizawa. Nigo (A
mistress)
1955 Yukio Mishima. Shiro-
ari No Su (Termites' nests)
Tsuneari Fukuda. Transla-
tion into Japanese of William
Shakespeare's complete
works   632.

Aleksis **KIVI FOUNDATION
PRIZE** (Finland)
To commemorate Aleksis
Kivi, Finnish dramatist and
novelist (1834-1872) who wrote
the famous novel of peasant
life, "Seven Brothers," this a-
ward has been granted each year
since 1936 by the Finnish Liter-
ature Society. Recent winners
of the honor, which is presented
in October "for support of the
creative work of Finnish litera-
ture," are:
1950's
Ilmari Kianto
Heikki Toppila
Yrjö Jylhä
Lauri Viljanen
P. Mustapää
Aale Tynni
Lauri Viita
Lauri Pohjanpää
Helvi Hämäläinen
Viljo Kajava
1960's

Väinö Linna
Eeva-Liisa Manner   633.

Heinrich von **KLEIST PRIZE**
(Germany)
Founded in 1911 by a group of
eminent German writers, including F. Engel, to commemorate
the hundredth anniversary of the
death of Heinrich von Kleist
(1777-1811), German novelist
and poet, this prize, once a
major literary honor of Germany
and German language writing, was
granted annually for over 20 years,
1912 through 1933. The honor
was assigned by a single judge,
with the judge changing each
year. The famous writers
honored were:
1912 Hermann Burte.Wiltfeber
der Ewige Deutsche (novel)
Reinhard Johannes Sorge.
Der Bettler (drama)
1913 Oskar Loerke. Pastor
Ephraim Magnus
1914 Fritz von Unruh. Drama
1915 Arnold Zweig. Entire
work
1916 Agnes Niegel. Poetry
Heinrich Lersch. Herz!
Ausgluehe dein Blut
1918 Leonard Frank. Die
Räuberbande; Die Ursache
(novels)
1919 Dietsenschmid.
Koenig Tod
1920 Paul Gurk. Drama
1921 Otto Baumgard. Dichter
als Freiwilde
1922 Berthold Brecht. Trom-
meln in der Nacht (drama)
1923 Wilhelm Lehmann. Bil-
derstürmer (novel)
Robert Musil (Austria). Die
Schwärmer (drama)
1924 Ernst Barlach. Entire
work
1925 Karl Zuckmayer. Der
Fröliche Weinberg (drama)
1926 Alexander Lernet-Holenia
(Austria). Demetrius (drama)
Alfred Neumann. Der Teufel
(novel)

1927 Gerhard Menzel. Tobog-
gan
Hans Meisel. Tortstenson
1928 Anna Seghers. Der Aus-
stand der Fischer von St.
Barbara (novel)
1930 Reinhard Goering. Die
Suedpolexpedition des Kapitan
Scott
1932 Richard Billinger. Rauh-
nacht (drama)
Else Lasker-Schüler. En-
tire work   634.

Jochen KLEPPER PLAQUE
(Germany)
The Klepper Plaque, a
drama award offered since 1949
by the Vaganten-Bühne in Berlin
in memory of the evangelical
religious writer, Jochen Klepper,
is presented on December 11--
date of Klepper's death--for the
play of the current theater season judged the most outstanding
"by the public and by the press."
The award, an honorary
prize with no monetary premium, has been granted:
1949 Armand Payot
1950 Günter Rutenborn
1951 Walter Gutkelch
1952 Stefan Andres
1953 Christopher Fry. Ein
Schlaf Gefangener
1954 Ingeborg Drewitz
1955 Manfred Hausmann
1956 Kurt Ihlenfeld. Das
verlorene Haus
1957 Wolfgang Borchert.
Draussen vor der Tür
(posthumous award)
1959 Erwin Sylvanus. Korczak
und die Kinder   635.

KNIGHT OF THE ORDER OF
LEOPOLD (Belgium)
The high State honor of
Belgium, not frequently awarded,
was granted to George Alfred
Leon Sarton, the Belgian-Ameri-
can author of many works in the
history of science, especially
those in Ancient and Renais-

sance Science.   636.

Laura KOCH PRIZE (Italy)
The poetry award of Lyceum
di Genova (piazza De Ferrari 4,
Genoa) was established in 1957
as an annual prize to honor the
50th anniversary of the death of
Laura Koch, poet of Genoa. In
1961 two poets shared the L
200.000 prize: Carlo Galasso of
Florence, and Martino Vitali of
Bergamo.   637.

KOCO RACIN PRIZE (Yugoslavia)
The literary prize of the
publisher, Koco Racin of Skoplje,
chief town of the Federated
Republic of Macedonia, was established in 1957 to distinguish
the most outstanding work published by the firm during the
year. Dimitar Mitrev won the
prize with "Kriterium i dogma."
638.

KOGGE RING PRIZE (Germany)
The city of Minden grants a
5000 DM prize for poetry each
year to a member of the "Kogge,"
which includes German, Belgian
and Dutch authors. Recent winners are Manfred Hausmann
(1958), and Hans Franck (1959).
639.

KORDELIN PRIZE (Finland)
Grants by the Alfred Kordelin
Foundation have been made for a
number of years to Finnish authors.
A. Kallas received such an award
in 1929. The present literature
prize, one of the Foundation's
cultural awards, was established
in 1957, and is assigned by the
Finnish Literature Society to
"a prominent Finnish author."
Prize winners are:
1957 Artturi Leinonen
1958 Reino Kalliola
1961 Helvi Hämäläinen   640.

KOREAN REPUBLIC POETRY

PRIZE FOR ENGLISH LYRICS
The Literary award of the
Seoul newspaper, "Korean
Republic" (31 Taepyong-no 1,
Chong-ku) was granted in 1959
to Richard Hertz, the German
Ambassador to Korea.   641.

Theodor KÖRNER PRIZE
(Austria)
Established as an annual
award in 1954 by the Theodor-
Körner-Stiftungsfond zur Förder-
ung von Wissenschaft und Kunst
(Vienna), this prize has been
granted--as a Förderungspreis--
to:
    1954 Othmar Lang
    1956 Theodor Kramer;
        Hermann Lienhard
    1960 Karl Wawra
    1961 Lisolotte Buchta-Hruby,
        Bertrand Alfred Egger,
        Vera Ferra-Mikura, Arthur
        Fischer-Colbrie, Hans
        Lebert, Hermann Lienhard,
        Agnes Muthspiel, Georg
        Rauch, Felice Rotter, Oskar
        Jan Tauschinski, Herbert
        Zand.
Other authors honored with a
Körner Prize are:
    1955 George Saiko
    1956 Kurt Benesch; Gerhard
        Fritsch   642.

KOSSUTH PRIZE (Hungary)
The Kossuth Prize, highest
Hungarian cultural award, is an
official honor granted by the
Council of Ministers each year
on the 15th of March, the anniversary of the 1948 Hungarian
War of Independence. Its four
sections (Natural Sciences;
Humanities; Arts and Literature;
Social Reconstruction) were established in the Hungarian National Law in 1948 (Law 1948:
XVII) to reward creative work
in Hungary--"outstanding results
in all fields of life, including
literary works." Recipients of
the award are recommended

for the honor by the Kossuth
Prize Committee (Kossuth-dij
Bizottsag-Kossuth Lajos-Ter 1,
Budapest 5) to the Council of
Ministers. The prizes, which
are made public in the Official
Gazette ('Magyar Kozlony'), con-
sist of a diploma, a medal, a
monetary premium, and the
right to use the title, "Kossuth-
dijas" (Kossuth Prize-Winner).
From 1948 to 1961, 270 of the
972 prizes awarded were "for
contributions to literature and
art."
Awards are given in four
classes: Grand Prize--75,000
Forints; First Prize--50,000
Forints; Second Prize--35,000
Forints; Third Prize--20,000
Forints. Winners of the Grand
Prize and the First Prize in
Literature--highest state award
for outstanding contribution to
letters--are:
    1948 Jozsef Attila (posthumous
        award); Lajos Nagy; Tibor
        Déry; Gyula Illyés (Gyula
        Háy)
    1949 J. Jenö Tersánsky and
        Sándor Gergely; Oszkár Gel-
        lért and Zoltán Zelk; Sándor
        Nagy and Tamás Aczél
    1950 Peter Veres; Gyula
        Illyés
    1951 Pál Szabó
    1st Prize--Gyula Háy; Ferenc
        Juhász; György Hámos;
        György Parragi
    1952 1st Prize--
        László Benjamin; Peter
        Veres; Ernö Urbán
    1953 Guyla Illyés; Andor Gábor
    1st Prize--Kálmán Sándor;
        Lajos Konya; László Kardos;
        Tibor Méray
    1954 Pál Szabó
    1st Prize--Tibor Barabás;
        Sándor Rideg; Aron Tamási;
        Zoltán Zelk
    1955 György Bölöni
    1st Prize--Bela Illés
    1956 József Darvas
    1st Prize--Lajos Barta; Sándor

Gergely
1957 Jenő Heltai
1st Prize--László Németh
1962 Lajos Mesterhazi; Antal
Hidas; Istvan Vas   643.

Harry KOVNER MEMORIAL
AWARDS (International--U.S.A.)
Honors for Hebrew and
Yiddish poetry, as well as for
English-Jewish poetry, are part
of the Kovner Memorial Awards,
established in 1950 by the Jewish Book Council of America
(145 East 32nd Street, New York
16). An Awards Committee
determines the winners, and
the prize--a citation and a premium of $100--which is award-
ed each May brings recognition
for a book of poetry published
in New York or in Israel during
the preceding year, or honors
the entire literary contribution
of a poet writing in Hebrew or in
Yiddish. Among recent recipients are:
Hebrew Poetry
1960 Eisig Silberschlag.
Kimron Yamai
1961 Ephraim E. Lisitzky.
K'Mo Hayom Rad
1962 Gabriel Preil. Mapat
Erev
Yiddish Poetry
1960 Ephraim Auerbach.
Gildene Shekiah
1961 Joseph Rubinstein.
Megilath Russland
1962 Israel Emiot. In Nigun
Eingehert   643a.

KRAFT PRIZE (Argentina)
The Premio Kraft para la
Novela Argentina is a biennial
publisher's prize of Editorial
Guillermo Kraft, Ltda (Recon-
quista 319, Buenos Aires) a-
warded for unpublished novels.
The award was established in
1954 to further the writing of
novels in Argentina, and is directed particularly to encouraging
young and unknown authors. The

original premium of $30.000 has
increased to $50.000, and, in
addition to this outright grant,
the winner receives royalties for
his book, which is published by
Kraft in the series, "América en
la Novela." Kraft publishes not
only the "Premio Kraft para la
Novela Argentina" winner, but also
other novels "recommended" by
the prize jury. Recipients of the
award--with "recommended" books
following the prize-winner--are:
1954 Marco Denevi. Rosaura
a las Diez
Pilar de Lusarreta. Niño
Pedro
Alejandro Ruiz Guiñazú.
La Deuda
Juan Manuel Villarreal. Mi
Propia Horca
Arturo Cerretani. Maria
Donadei
1956 David Viñas. Un Dios
Cotidiano
Bernardo Verbitzky. Villa
Miseria también es América
1958 Federico Peltzer. Com-
partida
Arturo Cerretani. El
Pretexto
1960 Silvia Guerrico. Dulce
Raiz Dormida   644.

KRIEGSBESCHÄDIGTEN ART
PRIZE (Germany)
Literature, together with Painting, Music, and Sculpture, are
the arts honored by the award
of the organization, Verband der
Kriegsbeschädigten, Kriegshinter-
bliebenen, und Sozialrentner
Deutschlands, in Bad Godesberg.
A biennial prize, established in
1955, the Literature Award of a
gold medal and 1000 DM has been
presented to such writers as:
1955 Hermann Buddensieg.
Morbus Sacer
1958 Lother Franke. Das tapfere
Leben   645.

Leo J. KRIJN PRIZE (Belgium)
Described as the "Prix Gon-

court of Belgium," this award, established in 1946, is granted each four years for a Flemish novel. Winners include:
1950 Hugo Claus. The duck hunt
1958 Jan Walravens. Negatief 646.

KRZYWE KOLO PRIZE (Poland)
The Polish debating club, "Crooked Circle" (Krzywe Kolo), only discussion group and "forum of unlimited debate in Poland," created news in January of 1962 by granting their annual literary award to Loszela Kolakowski for "literary achievement," as the current writing of this author had been officially censored--his play, "Entrance and Exit." The dramatic work "satirizing bureaucracy" was closed in 1961 after four performances in Warsaw's Atheneum Theater. (New York Times, January 21, 1962, 21:1) 647.

"KULTURA" LITERARY PRIZE (Poland)
Established in 1954 as an annual award of the Polish literary journal "Kultura," which is published in Paris (91 Avenue de Poissy, Maisons Laffitte, S et O), this prize of 1000 fr is directed to "encouraging literary production of Polish writers in exile." Published or unpublished works are eligible for the prize, and award winners include:
1954 Marian Pankowski. Smagla Swoboda
1955 Leo Lipski. Noc i dzien; Andrzej Chciuk. Smutny usmiech--shared prize
1957 Czeslaw Milosz. Sraktat poetycki--also awarded this year to Polish writer living in Poland: Marek Hlasko. Cmentarze. Nastepny do raju
1958 Gustaw Herling Grudzinski. Wieza

1959 Hanna Guilley Chmielowska. Spotkania na galerii
1960 Witold Gombrowicz. Pornografia
1961 Jozef Lobodowski. General works 648.

KULTURBUCH NOVEL PRIZE (Germany)
The publisher's award of Kulturbuch-Verlag (4 Passauerstrasse, Berlin 30) was announced in 1954, and awarded the next year to Karla Höcker. Further awards of 2500 DM are planned. 649.

KUNSTENAARSVERZET YOUTH LITERATURE PRIZE (Netherlands)
Offered by Stichtun Kunstenaarsverzet voor zijn Kinderverzen, the prize has been granted such authors as:
1957 Hans G. Hoekstra
1958 W. F. Hermans. Novellas
1959 Belcampo (pseud of H.P. Schonfeld Wichers)
1960 Alfred Kossmann. Entire work 650.

LAMDAN PRIZE FOR CHILDREN'S LITERATURE (Israel)
One of four literary prizes distributed by the municipality of Ramat-Gan, this award of IL 500 is presented annually to two writers of "original children's literature." The award is named for the late poet, Isaac Lamdan, and writers apply directly to the Cultural Department of the city of Ramat-Gan, sending four copies of the work to be considered with their application.
The prize winners from 1954 to 1962 are:
Moshe Stavi. On the road to Happyland
Simoha Nachmani. The adventures of Sasson and Giora
Gurit Axelrod. Sing Song and I
Menchem Talmi. Daringly
B. Dagon-Fishko. A wing to

a wing
Jacob Churgin. The diamond of
    miracles
Zvi Zaviri. The adventures of Yval
Nachum Gutman. The great
    vacation
Abraham Weinberg. Few against
    many
Izhar Smilansky. Bare-footed
Nathan Yonathan. Between
    spring and the cloud   651.

LA MED PRIZE FOR YIDDISH FICTION (International)

The literary award for novels and
collections of short stories in
Yiddish has been granted to such
writers as:
  B. Demblin (pseud of Benjamin
    Teitelbaum). Erev nakht
  B. Demblin (pseud of Benja-
    min Teitelbaum). Tzanken-
    dike likht
  I. Metzker. Gots bashefenishn
    (short stories)   652.

LANGEN-MÜLLER LITERATURE PRIZE (Germany)

The publisher's novel award of
Verlag Langen-Müller (13 B
Krailling, Munich), the firm of
Albert Langen and Georg Müller,
brought a 5000 DM prize to Walter
Meckauer in 1952.   653.

LANGLOIS PRIZE (France)

This annual translation prize
of Académie Française is granted
to the work which is the best translation into French of a verse or
prose writing in Greek or Latin, or
other language. Among recent
recipients are:
  1952 Jean Minassian. Avedik
    Issanakian. Abou-Lala-Mahari
    (French-Armenian poem)
  1955 Guillot de Saix. Translation
    of writings of Oscar Wilde
  1956 André Mirambel. Transla-
    tion of "Tasso Tassoulo" and
    other novels of Thrasso
    Castonakis
  1957 Anne-Marie Paraf and
    Pierre Paraf. Hans-Christian
    Andersen. Les deux baronnes.
  1958 Antoine Gentian. Sudhin-

dra Natha Gose. Le berceau des
    nuages (Cradle of the clouds,
    English autobiography of the
    Indian writer)
  1959 Marcel Thomas. Life of
    J. K. Huysmans
    Berthe Lacombe. Translation of
    Don Juan de Naranon
  1961 René Herval. Florilege de
    Nina, infante Ferraguti
  1962 André Robinet. Edition cri-
    tique de Malebranche.
    Pierre and Yves Hebert. Trans-
    lation of Poèmes mystiques de
    Saint Jean de la Croix.
    Corbeau, Authier, and de Toni.
    Editing of manuscript B of
    Leonardo da Vinci.   654.

Miguel LANZ DURET PRIZE (Mexico)

One of the most famous literary awards in Mexico, this novel
prize was established in 1941
by Miguel Duret, Junior, in
honor of his father, Miguel Lanz
Duret, who founded the Mexico
City newspaper, "El Universal"
(Diario El Universal, Bucareli 8,
Mexico, D. F.). The prize was
initiated on the occasion of the
Silver (25th) Anniversary of the
paper, June 3, 1941. The award,
with an annual premium of 1,000
pesos and possible publication in
"El Universal" and in "El Universal Grafico" (book rights reserved
to the author), was established
"to stimulate young novelists into
action and to encourage and direct
their efforts with art and intelligence." (Yeats, p. 123).

The competition required that
book-length manuscripts (200-
250 typed pages) be submitted
anonymously during the contest
period of October 1 to January 1,
with the award being given to "the
best-written work... most in ac-
cord with Mexican reality, judged
from the standpoint of setting and
national idiosyncracy." (Yeats,
p. 12).

Winners of the nation-wide novel

contest include such well-known and popular Mexican writers as:

1941 José María Benítez. Ciudad

1942 Adriana García Roel. El Hombre de Barro

1943 Sara García Igelesias. El Jagüey de las Ruinas

1944 Jesús Goytortua Santos. Pensativa

1945 Gustavo Rueda Medina. Las Islas También son Nuestras

1946 Gilberto Chávez. Playa Paraíso

1947 Miguel N. Lira. La Escondida

1948 Rogelio Barriga Rivas. Río Humano

1951 Evelina Bobes Ortega. Otono esteril

1955 G. Chavez. Una sombra en los brazos

1956 Rafael Trujillo. La mujer dormida   655.

LA PAZ PRIZES (Bolivia)

Several literary honors have been granted from time to time by the municipality of La Paz, capital city and most populous area of Bolivia. These city awards include:

LA PAZ CITY PRIZE (Premio Municipal). Among winners is Humberto Guzman Arze, honored in 1948 for 'Esteban Arze, caudillo de los valles.''

LA PAZ MEDAL OF MERIT (Medallo al Mérito de la Ciudad de La Paz). Cultural honor, whose recipients include Abel Alarcón.

LA PAZ FLORAL GAMES (Juegos Florales de La Paz). The highest honor of these floral games--Flor Natural y Banda del Gay Saber--has been won by leading literary figures of Bolivia, such as Eduardo Diez de Medina, winner in 1919 with his poem, ''Mallcu-Kaphaj;'' Raul Otero Reiche; Claudio Penaranda.   656.

René LAPORTE PRIZE (France)

Established in 1956 in memory of poet René Laporte, this 500 NF award is granted each year on March 2 for the best work of poetry published during the preceding five years. The jury (Secretary, 40 bis, rue Boissiere, Paris 16e) has assigned the prize to:

1957 Claudine Chonez. Les portes bougent

1958 Michel Manoll. Entire work

1959 Léna Leclercq. Pomme endormie

1961 Mohamed Dib (Algeria). Ombres gardiennes

1962 Louis Foucher. Eponine et le puma   657.

LARRAGOITI PRIZE (Spain)

The Cervantes Society (Sociedad Cervantina, Correo 4, Madrid) founded this award in 1954--offering 25,000 pts for the best book of specified types of writing published in Spain during the previous year by a Spanish author. The prize, granted for such forms of writing as: Novel, Short Stories, Journalism and Biography, has honored Gerardo Diego for ''Amazone,'' and

1954 José de Zunzunegui. La Vida Como Es

1956 Antonio de Obregon. Articles in ''Madrid,'' ''Alerta,'' ''La Voz de España,'' ''Amanecer''

1958 Rafael Láinez Alcalá. Don Bernardo do Sandoval y Rojas, Protector de Cervantes Tomás Borrás. Yo, Tú, Ella (short stories)   658.

LATIN AMERICAN PRIZE NOVEL COMPETITION (Latin America--U.S.A.)

Designed by the publisher Farrar & Rinehart and 'Redbook Magazine'' to ''stimulate interest in the novel among Latin American writers and to present the best work of Latin American writers to readers in the United

States," this competition considered manuscripts from each
Latin American country (except
Uruguay whose entry arrived too
late).

"Organized in all Latin American countries with the assistance
of the Division of Intellectual
Cooperation of the Pan American Union," this 1941 contest
for the best unpublished novel
picked four international winners
from the 27 manuscripts sent to
New York by the National Committees in each country. Final
decision of winners was made by
a jury of three--consisting of
U.S.A. writers Blair Niles and
John Dos Passos, and the Chilean
journalist, Ernesto Montenegro.

Premiums totalling $7,500
were distributed, with the official presentation in New York,
April 14, 1941, as part of the
celebration of Pan American Day.
The four prize winning novels,
published in English translation
by Farrar & Rinehart (sections
from three of the books were
also published in "Redbook
Magazine"), were:
Winning Novel:
   Ciro Alegría (Peru). El
   Mundo es Ancho y Ajeno
   (Broad and alien is the
   world)
Honorable Mention Novels (re-
warded in view of "the excellence
of the manuscripts received"):
   Enrique Gil Gilbert (Ecuador).
   Nuestro pan (Our daily
   bread)
   Cecilio J. Carneiro (Brazil).
   A Fogueira (The bonfire)
   Miguel Angel Menéndez
   (Mexico). Nayar   659.

LATINITA PRIZE International--
Italy)
   The Premio della Latinita,
offered in Siena, was awarded in
1957 to Ribeiro Couto of Brazil.
                                660.

LATINITAS CONTEST (Interna-
tional--Italy)
   The prize of the quarterly
Vatican publication, "Latinitas,"
for Latin prose and poetry was
established to promote and encourage the study of Latin. The
annual international competition
for writing in Latin on fixed subjects is open to Latinists of the
world. Two prizes are awarded
in the contest, which is administered by the Editor of "Latinitas,"
who writes most of the Vatican's
documents in Latin: A First
Prize (gold medal and $160) and
a Second Prize (silver medal and
$80) in each of two classes--
(1) Latin teachers and scholars;
(2) Students of all schools,
including universities.   661.

LAUREL DEL LIBRO (Spain)
   Established by the publisher
Editorial Escelicer, Madrid, this
award was won in 1956 by Jose
Luis Castillo Puche with his novel
"Hicieron Parte." Other prizes
granted under the name "Laurel
del Libro" include: APRIL AND
MAY PRIZE, for writing of young
people; BIBLIOTECA DE LEC-
TURAS EJEMPLARES PRIZE,
which awarded 10,000 pts to
Emilio Teixico for "Patucho;"
and JUVENTUD FEMINA PRIZE.
                                662.

LAZARILLO PRIZE (Spain)
   Honoring good writing for children and young people, the
Lazarillo Prize has been offered
annually since 1958 by the
Comision de Literature Juvenile
e Infantil (Spanish Book Institute,
I.N.L.E.--Instituto Nacional del
Libro Español--Ferraz 13,
Madrid). The award, "patron-
ized by the Ministry of Education
and Information," is granted to
stimulate Spanish writers and illustrators to produce books for
children and young people "of
the highest literary quality,

published or unpublished."

Authors and illustrators of winning books receive a monetary premium (at present 40,000 pts), and publishers of prize-winning books are given a citation (mencion honorifica). Competing works are submitted during the months of December and January and the prizes are presented at the time of the Fiesta del Libro, celebrated throughout Spain on April 23, the anniversary of the death of Cervantes.

Winners of the prize from 1958 to 1962 are:
Authors--
Alfonso Iniesta Corredor. Dicen las Florecillas
Miguel Buñuel. El Niño, la Golondrina y el Gato
Montserrat del Amo. Rastro de Dios
Joaquín Aguirre Bellver. El Juglar del Cid
Concha Fernandez-Luna. Fiesta en Marylandia
Illustrators--
José Francisco Aguirre. El Libro del Desierto
Rafael Munoa. Exploradores de Africa
M. Jiménez Arnalot. Yo soy el Gato
José Narro Celorio. Robinson Crusoe
José Picó. Fantasía
Editors--Editorial Mateu, Barcelona
Dalmau y Jover, Editorial Molino
Ediciones Gamma
Doncel
Ediciones Gaisa, Jorge Juan 28, Valencia   663.

Francisco LAZO MARTI PRIZE FOR POETRY (Venezuela)

One of several official national literary honors offered by the Venezuelan Ministry of Education (Ministerio de Educacion, Direccion de Cultura y Bellas Artes, Caracas), this prize for poetry is given alternately with the official national prize for prose writing (see Venezuelan National Prize for Literature).   664.

LEBANESE ARAB AUTHORS PRIZE

The Beirut Municipal Council donated this prize of 2.000 LP to be awarded to the Arab author of the best book published in Lebanon in the Arabic language during 1961. The prize, determined and presented by the "Book Friend Society," was won by Abdul Jabbar Goumrad with "Yazid Ben Mazid Al-Chinani."   665.

LEBANESE DRAMATIC PRIZE

Like the Lebanese Arab Authors Prize, this drama award was determined and presented by the "Book Friend Society." The award, a premium of 2.000 LP donated by Mr. Majib Salha of Lebanon, was established in 1960, and was to be granted to the Lebanese author writing the best drama in Arabic during 1960-1961. The prize was not awarded for that year.   666.

LEBANESE PRIZE FOR MOST BOOKS IN ARABIC

This award, offered by His Excellency Fouad Chehab, President of the Lebanese Republic, is to give public and official recognition for outstanding literary production to the Lebanese author who has written the largest number of books in Arabic. The prize of 5.000 LP, determined by a jury of the "Book Friends Society," was presented to Dr. Michael Naimeh.   667.

LEBANESE RESEARCH PRIZE

The Lebanese Ministry of Orientation and Information offered a premium of 3.000 LP for the best research book pub-

lished in Lebanon in Arabic during 1960-1961. Areas of research considered eligible for
award by the "Book Friends
Society," who judged entries,
included: Literature; Society;
Education; Economy; Agriculture; Arts; Sciences. The premium was divided equally between two authors: Anwar El
Khatib, "Parliamentary principles
in Lebanon and the Arab world"
Adib Mrouwa, "Arab journalism."
                                    668.

LEBANESE SCIENCE PRIZE
    The "Best scientific book
written and published in the Arabic
language by a Lebanese author
during 1960-1961" was honored
by the prize of 2.000 LP, subscribed by Mr. Chukri Chammas
of Lebanon. The "Book Friends
Society" selected as winner Dr.
Fouad Sarruf for his writing,
"The man and the world."   669.

LEBANESE TRANSLATION
PRIZE
    One of a number of Lebanese
literary awards administered by
the "Book Friend Society," the
translation prize, offered by Mr.
Emil Bustani, member of the
Lebanese Parliament and head of
the C.A.T. Company, offers a
2.000 LP premium for the best
translator of a scientific book
(theoretical or applied) translated into Arabic in 1960-1961.
Two translators shared the prize
equally: Munir Baalbeki, with
"The pioneer in communist literature;" and Burhan Dajani, with
"Fabian Communism."   670.

Pierre LECOMTE DU NOUY
PRIZE (International--France)
    This 2.000 NF prize, given
each spring alternately in France
and in England or the United
States, honors a work published
during the two years preceding
the distribution of the award.

Established in 1953 by Mme Lecomte du Nouy in honor of Pierre
Lecomte du Nouy, philosopher
and scientist for many years associated with the Rockefeller
Institute, the prize is given for
a book of philosophy, science,
or biography written in or translated into the French language or
written in English.
    Winners of the prize, with
books distinguished by a particular interest in the spiritual life
of our time and for the defense
of human dignity, include:
    1954 Marcel Senrail. Le ser-
        pent et le miroir
    1955 C. A. Coulson (United
        Kingdom). Sciences and
        Christian belief
    1956 Maurice Vernet. L'homme,
        maître de sa destinée
    1957 William Ernest Hocking
        (U.S.A.). The coming
        world civilization
    1959 Michael Polanyi. Con-
        naissance personnelle; Étude
        de l'homme
    1960 Henry Breuil. Entire
        work
    1961 Loren Eisely (U.S.A.).
        Firmament of time
    1962 Marie Noël. Notes intimes
        Henri Gouhier. Bergson et
        le Christ des Evangiles
                                    671.

Eino LEINO PRIZE (Finland)
    Winners of the prize of the
Eino Leino Society, consisting of
a monetary primarily "to give
medal, granted primarly "to give
attention to authors whose work
has not received fair public attention" are such Finnish authors
as: Viljo Kajava, Helvi Juvonen,
Rabbe Enckell, Juha Mannerkorpi,
Simo Puupponen, Olavi Paavolai-
nen.   672.

Nikolaus LENAU PRIZE (Austria)
    The prize of the Austrian
Ministry of Education (Bundesministerium für Unterricht) was

offered in 1960 to authors who had returned to Austria within the last decade after residing outside the country. The S 5.000 premium was awarded to Georg Drozdowski for his collection of poems, "Der Steinmetzgarten."   673.

LENIN PEACE PRIZE (International--USSR)

This international honor, communism's counterpart of the Nobel Prize for Peace, is awarded annually to intellectuals and international figures by the Lenin Peace Prize Committee in Moscow. Presented each year on the eve of the Soviet Union's May Day Celebration, the prize brings recognition to public figures in many countries for their contribution to world peace. The Lenin Peace Prize replaced the Stalin Peace Prize in 1956, and on March 15, 1962 the USSR announced that foreign holders of the Stalin Peace Prize could exchange the award for the Lenin Peace Prize.

Recent winners of the award, one of the USSR's highest official honors, with a premium of 10,000 rubles which cannot be converted into currency of another country, include: Kostas Varnalis (Greece); Ivor Montagu (United Kingdom); Louis Aragon (France); Arnold Zweig (Germany, East) and:
1959 Achmed Sukarno
   (Indonesia)
   Cyrus Eaton (U.S.A.)
   Laurent Casanova (France)
   Asis Scharif (Iraq)
1960 Fidel Castro (Cuba)
   Rameshwari Nehru (India)
   Sekou Touré (Guinea)
   Mikhail Sadoveanu (Rumania)
1961 Kwame Nkrumah
   (Ghana)
   Pablo Picasso (Spain-France)
   Istvan Dobi (Hungary)
   Olga Poblete de Espinosa

(Chile)
Faiz Ahmad Faiz (Pakistan)
                                                 674.

LENIN PRIZE (USSR)

The highest official cultural award of the USSR for "outstanding works in science, technology, literature, and art," includes prizes for the best works of literature and literary research, journalism and publicity. Granted each year by the Soviet Academy of Sciences (Akademiia Nauk SSSR, Moscow), the prize consists of a diploma, a gold medal, and a monetary premium (in 1957 literary awards ranged up to 75,000 rubles).

The Lenin Prize was offered from 1925 to 1935, when it was replaced by the Stalin Prize as Russia's major official cultural honor until 1953. Reestablished by decree of the Central Committee of the Communist Party in 1956, the Lenin Prize was again awarded in 1957, and--subsequent to the year 1958, when no writer appeared on the annual list of Lenin Prize Winners--approximately 8 of the 50 Lenin Prizes presented each year honor writers and artists. The prize competition is announced annually in "Pravda," official party newspaper, as are candidates for the award ("Lenin Prize Nominations") who are suggested for award by a large number of cultural, political and professional groups, and the previous Lenin Prize Winners. Names of winners, who receive the award on April 22, the birthday of I.V. Lenin, "founder of the Soviet State," also appear in "Izvestia," official daily paper, Moscow, and in the Bulletin of the Academy of Sciences, USSR (Vestnik Akademii Nauk, SSSR).

Laureates of the Lenin Award are such writers as: P. Brovka, E. Mezhelaitis, M. Pylskii,

Kornei Chukovskii; and the
journalists N. M. Gribachev, V.
Exhov, G. A. Zhukov, R.
Karmen, V.I. Orlov. Recipients of literary prizes of
various years include such
"workers in culture" as:
1957 Leonid Leonov. The Russian forest (novel)
  Musa Dzjalil. Moabit's Book
  (translation from the Tatar
  poet, executed by the Nazis
  in 1944 in Berlin Moabit
  Prison)
1959 Mikolas F. Pogodin. Che-
  lovek s ruzhyom (The man
  with the gun); Kremlevskie
  Kuranty (Kremlin chimes);
  Thirt Pathetique--three
  parts of a trilogy about
  Lenin
  A.P. Dovzhenko. Poem about
  the sea, dramatic film-
  poem in his "Selected works"
  Mukhtar O. Avezoz. Abai
  (2 volume novel translated
  from Kazakh)
1960 Litsom K Litsu c Amerikoi
  (Face to face with America--
  joint award for the report
  of the group of 12 journalists
  and writers who accompanied
  N.S. Khrushchev on his
  State visit to the U.S.A.,
  September 15-27, 1959)
  Maksym F. Rylsky. Rozy i
  vinograd (Roses and grapes
  --collected verse); Daleki
  Nebosklony (The distant
  horizons--poem)
  Mirza Tursun-Zade. Golos
  Azii (The voice of Asia);
  Hasan Arbakesh (verses and
  poems translated from
  Tadzhik)
  Mikhail Sholokhov. Podnyataya
  tselina (Virgin soil upturned
  --novel)
1961
  Alexander Prokofiev. V Puti
  (Invitation to a journey--
  song and folklore verse)
  Mikhail A. Stelmakh. Bread
  and salt (3rd volume of a

novel trilogy translated from
Ukranian; other volumes:
Blood is thicker than water,
or Human blood isn't water;
The great family, or Many
kinsfolk)
Alexander Tvardovsky, editor
of "Novy Mir" (New World--
leading literary periodical).
Za dalyu dal... (lyrical
philosophical poem, title
variously translated: Space
beyond Space; Further...
Further...; Beyond this
horizon another; Distance
beyond distance)
Johan U. Smuul. The ice
chronicle (The ice book,
Antarctic travel diary,
translated from Estonian)
Valentin Ivanovitch Yezhov.
Ballad of a soldier (film
scenario)
1962 Kornei Ivanovich Chukovsky
(Lithuania). Nekrasov's
mastery
A.V. Ivanov. The Pogonophora
V. Vorobskii. Best achievement in journalism
Pyotr (Petrus) Ustinovich
Brovka. And the days pass
(poems--also awarded by the
State of Belorussia the honorary title, "Belorussian Republic People's Poet")
Nikolai A. Nevsky. For
linguistic work, published in
1959, deciphering the language and script of "the
obscure Tangut People, who
flourished in Central Asia
from the 9th to the 13th
century"   675.

Fray Luis de LEÓN PRIZE
(Spain)
  The Spanish Association of
Translators (Asociacion Española
de Traductores) offers the prize
for technical and scientific trans-
lation, with a second sponsor, the
National Ministry of Education
(Ministerio de Educacion Nacional,
Alcala 34, Madrid). Winners of

the 25,000 pts premium, since
it was first granted in 1956,
are:
  1956 Consuelo Berge´s. His-
    toria de la España Cristiana
    (Jean Descola's work)
  1957 José López Toro.
    Epistolario de Pedro Mártir
    de Anglería
  1958 Eduardo Prado and Julio
    López Morales. A history
    of the firm of Siemens (from
    the German)
  1960 J. M. Valverde. Fifty
    poems of Rainer Maria Rilke
    (Agora, 1958)
  1961 Julio Gómez de la Serna.
    General de Gaulle, "Mem-
    orias de la Guerra"
                                676.

LERICI-PEA PRIZE (Italy)
  The publisher's prize,
organized by Marco Carpena of
Sarzana, brings a premium of
L 300.000 each year for the best
unpublished poetry entered in
competition. Poets honored
include:
  1954 Giovanni Titta Rosa.
    I giovani morti del mare
  1955 Giorgio Caproni. La
    piccola porto
  1956 Biagia Marniti. I rami
    della vita
  1960 Ugo Reale. Finestra
    felice
  1961 Massimo Grillandi
  1962 Corrado Govoni   677.

LERMA PRIZES (Spain)
  Two prizes offered by the publisher, Faro de Vigo, for literary and scientific works were
won in 1961 by:
  Mercedes de Lerma Prize
    (30,000 pts)--J.M. Castro-
    viejo and A. Cunqueiro.
    Teatro Venatorio y con-
    quinorio gallego
  Josefina de Lerma Prize
    (20,000 pts)--J.M. Alvarez
    Blázquez and F. Fernández
    del Riego. Excolma de

Poesía gallega (4 vols)
                                678.

Gotthold LESSING PRIZE
(Germany, East)
  Like the Heine Prize, this
annual literary award, named
for the famous German dramatist
and critic, Gotthold Ephraim
Lessing (1729-1781), is granted
by the East German Ministry for
Culture (Ministerium für Kultur).
The Lessing Prize, honoring
playwrights and theatre critics,
with a 10.000 DM premium since
1954, has been presented to such
dramatists and critics as:
  1955 Herbert Ihring. Life's
    work as a drama critic
  1956 Peter Hacks. Die Eröff-
    nung des indischen Zeitalters;
    Die Schlacht von Lebositz
    Fritz Erpenbeck. Drama
    criticism
  1957 Max Schroeder. Drama
    criticism
  1958 Hans Lucke. Kaution;
    Der Keller
  1959 Harald Hauser. Im
    himmlischen Garten
    Johanna Rudolph
  1960 Hedda Zinner. Was
    wäre wenn...
    Hans Koch. Literary theory
  1961 Erwin Strittmatter. Die
    Holländerbraut
    Elisabeth Hauptmann. Many
    years' collaboration with
    Bertolt Brecht   679.

LESSING PRIZE (Germany)
  To commemorate the 200th
birth date of the German dramatist and critic, Gotthold Ephraim
Lessing (1729-1781), this triennial prize consisting of a certificate and a premium of 10,000
DM was established in 1929 by
the legislative body of Hamburg
(Senat, Rathaus, Hamburg 1).
The prize is presented each year
on January 22, Lessing's birthday, to poets and writers for
outstanding literary accomplish-

ment and to scholars contributing to the knowledge of Lessing and his writings.

Winners of this major German honor, presented in a ceremony by the Senat of Hamburg, following the recommendation of a seven-member jury, and a 5.000 DM stipend for independent literary work--awarded since 1956--include:

1930 Friedrich Gundolf
1934 Friedrich Griese; Konrad Beste
1938 Andreas Heusler
1942 Hermann Claudius
1944 Fritz Schumacher
1947 Rudolf Alexander Schröder
1951 Ernst Robert Curtius
1953 Wilhelm Lehmann; Albrecht Goes
1956 Hans Henny Jahnn. Thomas Chatterton (play) Stipend--Monika George; Grund; Helmut Heissenbüttel; Gerd Oelschlägel
1959 Hannah Ahrendt Stipend--Heinz Albers; Mattrias Braun
1962 Werner Haftmann   680.

IL LETTERATO PRIZE (Italy)

The prize of the Culture Organization of the Review 'Il Letterato" (O.C.R.I.L. -- Organizzazione Culturale Revista 'Il letterato," via Roma 74, Cleto, Cosenza) has been offered annually in four literary forms: Collection of Poetry--150 to 500 verses; Collection of Novella-- at least two unpublished stories, each not exceeding 100 typed pages; Novel--unpublished manuscript less than 200 typed pages; Drama--unpublished comedy or drama, or radio play. In 1962, the ninth "Concurso Poetico" was won by Carmelina Grimaldi with "Preghiere e lacrime."   681.

Grace LEVEN PRIZE FOR POETRY (Australia)

One of the most important continuing literary awards in Australia is granted each year "for the best volume of poetry published in each calendar year, by a writer either Australian-born, and writing as an Australian, or naturalized in Australia and residing in Australia for not less than ten years." Established by the will of Australian poet William Baylebridge, who died in 1942, the prize is named for Grace Leven, the woman to whom Baylebridge's sonnet-sequence ('Love Redeemed") was addressed.

To be considered for the Ŀ 100 premium (originally Ŀ 50), printed volumes of poetry written by authors eligible for the award should be sent to The Perpetual Trustee Company, Ltd (33 Hunter Street, Sydney). Winners from the first award in 1947 are:

1947 Nan McDonald. Pacific sea
1948 Francis Webb. A drum for Ben Boyd
1949 Judith Wright. Woman to man
1951 Rex Ingamells. The Great South Land
1952 Robert D. Fitzgerald. Between two tides)
1954 John Thompson. Thirty poems
1955 A. D. Hope.The Wandering Islands
1956 James McAuley. A vision of ceremony
1957 Leonard Mann. Elegiac and other poems
1958 Geoffrey Dutton. Antipodes in shoes
1959 Robert D. Fitzgerald. The wind at your door
1960 Colin Thiele. Man in a landscape   682.

LEVSTIKOV PRIZE (Yugoslavia)

The publishing firm, Mladinska kniga (Youth Book) of Ljubljana, capital city of the Federated

Republic of Slovenia offers this literary award to Slovene writers. Among recipients of the prize, which is granted for writing in a number of literary forms, including journalism, are:

1949 Prezihov Voranc. Solne (The sun--children's stories)
France Bevk. Ostroska leta (Ostroska's summer)
Tone Seliskar. Mule (Mules)
Josip Ribicic. Tince in Bince (Tince of Bince--drama)
Katja Spurova. Plugi orjejo (Plowed furrows--journalism)
1957 Lojze Zupanc
Miroslav Adlesic
Miroslav Zej   683.

LIBERA STAMPA PRIZE
(Switzerland)

The Premio "Libera Stampa" is a literary prize awarded writers in the Italian language, without restrictions as to nationality, by the socialist newspaper "Libera Stampa" (via Canonica 3, Lugano) in the "Italian" region of Switzerland. The award is granted for various forms of writing--including Poetry, Fiction, Scholarly Works --and is assigned by a jury of nine Italian and Swiss scholars, writers and critics.

The amount of the monetary premium varies from year to year (recently 3.500 fr sw), and the prize is presented each Spring (since 1955 when the award was reestablished after a period of inactivity from 1948 to 1955) to a distinguished author--participants in the ceremony have included Vasco Pratolini and Leonardo Sciascia. The "Vincitori del Premio," with "Special Prize" winners shown, are:

1946 Vasco Pratolini. Cronache di poveri amanti (novel)
1947 Antonio Manfredi. Poesie
1948 Loredana Minelli. Un

mantello alla citta (stories)
1955 Mario Colombi-Guidotti. Il grammofono (novel)
"Premi Speciali"--Alberto Bevilacqua. A collection of poetry
Nino Palumbo. L'intoppo e altre cose (collected stories)
1956 Vittorio Sereni. Poesie
1957 Leonardo Sciascia. Gli zii di Sicilia (stories)
1958 Giancarlo Artoni. Los stesso dolore (poetry)
1959 Antonio Delfini. Misa Bovetti e altre cronache (stories)
1960 Giorgio Orelli. Un giorno della vita (stories)
"Riconoscimento Speciale"-- Mario Agliati. L'erba voglio
1961 Nelo Risi. Pensieri elementari (poetry)
"Premio Speciale" (offered by the Revista 'Questo e altro" of Milan--Editor Arrigo Lampugnani Nigri--for the best work in French or Italian on the Algerian question appearing during the two years, 1960-1961)--Francis Jeanson. La Révolution algérienne

The 1962 Premio Letterario "Libera Stampa" is offered for fiction works which must be entered in competition (in five copies) by January 15, 1963-- both unpublished writings and works published during 1962 are eligible. A fr sw 2.000 prize is also offered for the work of a Spanish writer. Both awards are to be announced before April 1963.   684.

LIBERTY PRIZE (France)

The Prix de la Liberté is an annual award of the newspaper, "Le Populaire" (61 rue La Fayette, Paris) to honor a work in the French language that is written in defense of Liberty and of Democracy. The prize, initiated in 1957 by the newspaper, 'Franc-Tireur," has brought a premium of 1000 NF, presented on May 1, to such writers as:

1957 Suzanne Labin. Entre-
tiens de Saint-Germain
1958 Milovan Djilas. La
nouvelle classe dirigeante
1959 Paul Tillard. L'outrage
1960 Léon Leneman. Tragédie
des juifs en U.R.S.S.
1961 Georges Paloczi Horvath.
La délivrance   685.

LIBRAIRES DE FRANCE
LITERARY PRIZE (France)
An award for imaginative
literature--Novel, Novella, Fictionalized travel or biography--
is offered each year in January
by Selection des libraires de
France (Cercle de la Librairie,
117 boulevard Saint-Germain,
Paris 6e). The honor carries
no monetary premium as such but
consists of the designation
"Prize-Winner," with resulting
publicity and increased sales of
the winning work. Laureates
designated by Fédération Française des Syndicats de Libraires
include:

1955 Michel de Saint-Pierre.
Les aristocrates
1956 Albert Vidalie. Le grande
Ferté
1957 Françoise Mallet-Joris
(Belgium). Les mensonges
1958 Jean Bassan. Nul ne
s'évade
1959 Georges Bordonove.
Deux cents chevaux dorés
1960 Georges Conchon. La
corrida de la victoire
1961 Andrée Martinerie. Les
autres jours
1962 Jean Anglade. La foi et
montagne   686.

LIFE EN ESPAÑOL PRIZE
(Latin America--U.S.A.)
Announced in 1959, this Gran
Concurso Literario de Life en
Español offered prizes totalling
$10,000 for the best unpublished
short story or novella (not ex-

ceeding 20,000 words) by any
Latin American author, submitted
in competition before March 15,
1960. Designed "to give recognition to deserving Spanish A-
merican authors and to encourage
them to continue trying to improve the quality of their work,"
the contest was open to permanent
residents or citizens of any of
twenty Latin American countries
and Puerto Rico.

From nearly 3,000 manuscripts
received, a panel of distinguished
literary judges--including Federico
de Onis (Puerto Rico), Arturo
Uslar Pietri (Venezuela), Octavio
Paz (Mexico), Hernán Díaz Arrieta (Chile), Emir Rodríguez
Monegal (Uruguay)--selected three
prize winners and eight honorable
mentions:

$5,000 Prize--
('Premio Life en Español')--
Marco Denevi (Argentina).
Ceremonia secreta (novel)
$2,000 Prize--
Carlos Martínez Moreno (Uru-
guay). Los aborígenes (story)
$1,000 Prize--
Alfonso Echevarría Yáñez
(Chile). Nausicaa (novel)
Honorable Mentions (8 prizes
of $250 each)
Juan Carlos Onetti (Uruguay).
Jacab y el otro
Carlos Rozas Larrain (Chile).
Barco negre
Laura del Castillo (Argentina).
Una ciruela para Coco
Augusto Jose Antonio Roa
Bastos (Paraguay). La sed
Tomas Mojarro (Mexico). El
arpa
Dalmiro Antonio Sáens (Argen-
tina). No es
Ramón Ferreira López (Cuba).
Sueño sin nombre
Faustino González Aller (Cuba).
El yugo   687.

LIMA SHORT STORY CONTEST
(Peru)
The competition for the "best

short story," sponsored by the television station in the city of Lima, was won in 1962 by Cata Podestá with the story, "The seashell."   688.

José LINS DO RÉGO PRIZE (Brazil)

Named for the powerful Brazilian novelist, José Lins do Régo (1901-1957), who wrote of the rural life in Brazil's northeast sugar plantations, the publisher's prize of Livraria José Olimpio (Av Nilo Pecanha 12-6º Andar, Rio de Janeiro; rua dos Gusmoes 100/104, Sao Paulo) was established in 1961 by Manuel de Sousa Pinto. The prize of Cr $500.000, founded in celebration of the publisher's 30th anniversary and granted alternately with the Tarquinio de Souza Prize, was first presented to Fernando Namora for the second part of his work, 'Retalhos de vida de um Medico."   689.

José LINS DO RÉGO PRIZE (Portugal)

Like the Brazilian prize of the same name, this literary award of 40.000$ for an unpublished novel in Portuguese was established in memory of the Brazilian writer and man of letters, Lins Do Régo (1901-1957). The annual award is directed 'to encouraging literary works of the highest quality and contributing to the prestige and growth of modern Portuguese literature--especially outside of Portugal." The sponsoring agency--the publisher Editorial "Livros do Brasil"--requires that manuscripts entered in competition be submitted in five copies to "Livros do Brasil" (Rua dos Caetanos 22, Lisbon 2), or to the firm's agents in any Portuguese-speaking country (as, Editora Globo, Rua dos Andradas 1, 416, Porto Alegre, Brazil).   690.

LITHUANIAN WRITERS' ASSOC. AWARD (U.S.A.)

Since 1950, a $500 prize has been offered by the Association (address, 1962-1963: Bernard Brazdzionis, Lithuanian Days Magazine, 4364 W. Sunset Boulevard, Hollywood, California, U.S.A.) for the best Lithuanian writing submitted in competition. Winners include: Vernardas Brazdzionis, "The great crossroads;" Jurgis Jankus, "The house on a good street."   691.

LITTLE THEATRE GUILD PLAY CONTEST (Australia)

Prizes of ₤1000 are offered by the Little Theatre Guild and J. C. Williamson (240 Exhibition Street, Melbourne) for the manuscript of the best radio or stage play submitted in competition.   692.

LJUS PRIZE (Sweden)

A jointly sponsored award (Ljus Publishing Company, Stockholm; Thomas Y. Cromwell Company, New York; Metro-Goldwyn-Mayer Motion Picture Company, Hollywood; and George G. Harrap & Company, London) offered $25,000 for "a novel in a Scandinavian language." Winners of the 1946 prize--the next richest Scandinavian literary reward after the Nobel Prize for Literature--with novels to be printed simultaneously in Sweden, Norway, France and Netherlands, were: Thore Ericson with "Im Letzten Augenblick;" with Nanna Lindefjeld, winner of a special award with "Echo eine Stimme!" 693.

Manuel LLORENTE PRIZE (Spain)

The prize granted by the Real Academia Española, established in 1925 by Manuel Llorente Vazquez with an endowment of 100,000 pts, is offered every five years to a work of prose or verse on a patriotic theme that will enrich the knowledge of children concerning Spanish history and traditions. Writings about memorable historic locations in Spain are eligible for award. Winner the 12,000 pts premium in 1957 was Francisco Ferrari Billoch for his book 'Ramon y Cajal-- Un gran Sabio Español." 694.

LODZ POETRY PRIZE (Poland)
The Lodzka Wiosna Poetow (Lodz Poetical Spring) award is granted each year in June to a young poet by the Lodz section of the organization, Association PAX (Lodzki Oddzial Stowartzyszenia PAX, Piotr-kowska 49, Lodz). Poets honored since the first presentation in 1959 are:
    1959 Marian Grzesczak
    1960 Stanislaw Chacinski;
        Czeslaw Kuriata
    1961 Czeslaw Kuriata; Maciej
        Bordowicz; Janusz Onopa
                                695.

LODZ PRIZE (Poland)
A prize granted by the Lodz Publishing House in an "All-Poland Literary Competition" was won in 1960 by Wojciech Kaider with his work "Smierc Jest Swiatelm" (Death is the light).   696.

LONGFELLOW-GLOCKE (Germany)
Founded in 1949 by the group, "Longfellow Gemeinschaft der Steuben-Schurz-Gesellschaft" in Frankfurt am Main, this cultural award, in the form of a Longfellow-Glocke, is offered each four years to two outstanding public figures distinguished "for an original contribution to the mutual understanding between peoples." Among the winners are:
    1950 Rudolf Alexander
        Schröder; Reinhold Schneider
    1954 John J. McCloy; Theodor
        Heuss
    1958 J. William Fulbright;
        Robert Schuman   697.

LOPE DE VEGA PRIZE (Spain)
The most coveted of Spain's drama prizes (according to the authority on Spanish literary honors, José Sanchez), this award was established by the Ayuntamiento de Madrid in March 1932 as an annual prize. Named in honor of the Spanish dramatic poet and founder of the Spanish national drama, Lope Félix de Vega Carpio (1562-1635), the award offers 25,000 pts and presentation of the winning play at the Teatro Español, the "Official Spanish Theater," on Calle del Principe in Madrid.
Dramatists honored with this respected award include:
    1932 Alejandro Casona. La
        Sirena Varada
    1949 Buero Vallejo. Historia
        de una escalera
    1950 Faustino Gonzalez Aller
    1952 José Antonio Giménez-
        Arnau. Murió hace quince
        años
    1954 Julio Trenas. El Hogar
        invalido
    1955 Luis Delgade Benavente.
        Media hora antes
    1956 Jaime de Armiñán Oliver.
        Nuestro fantasma
    1957 Emilio Hernández Pino.
        La galera
    1958 José Martiñ Recuerda.
        El Teatrito de Don Ramón
                                698.

Julia LOPES DE ALMEIDA PRIZE (Brazil)
The Academie Brasileira de Letras (Avenida Presidente Wilson 203, Rio de Janeiro) offers this Cr $7,200 prize for the best work by a woman writer. Recipients include:
    1956 Zilah Corrêa de Araújo
        Maria José Morais Pupo
        Nogueira. Natal solitário
        (novel)
    1958 Consuelo dos Reis Melo.
        A Amazonia
    1959 Rosita Fleury. Elos de

Mesma Corrente
1960 Stella Leonardos. Estátua
de sal
Maria Eugênia Pôrto Oliveira
Ribeiro. A sensitiva
1961 Berenice Grieco de Barros Moreira. Caliban
Stela M. da Câmara Leol
Tostes. Paixão de Mulata
1962 Maria Cibeira Perpétuo.
E continuamos a viver
                              699.

LOSADA CONCURSO INTER-
NACIONAL DE NARRATIVA
(International--Argentina)

The publisher's fiction con-
test, conducted by Editorial
Losada (Alsina 1131, Buenos
Aires) in 1959 for the best
novels and short stories in Span-
ish submitted as unpublished
manuscripts, brought prizes to:
First Prize--
Augusto Roa Bastos (Para-
guay). Hijo de hombre
Second Prize--
Ofelia Machado (Uruguay).
Un Ángel de bolsillo
Third Prize--
Victor Sáiz (Spain). El
banquete
Honorable Mention--
Jorge Masciangoli (Argentina).
El último piso
Marcos Victoria (Argentina).
Un verde paraíso
The winning works were novels,
with the exception of the Third
Prize winner and the second
honorable mention--which were
short stories.

In 1958 a CONCURSO INTER-
NATIONAL DE NOVELAS EDI-
TORIAL LOSADA awarded a
prize to Cecilio Benítez de Cas-
tro for the novel,"La illuminada!"
Another literary prize award-
ed by Editorial Losada--The
Ricardo GÜIRALDES PRIZE,
named for the Argentine novelist
Güiraldes (1886-1927)--was
granted in 1940 to Bernardo
Verbitsky for his book, 'Es

dificil empezar a vivir."   700.

LOUBAT PRIZES (International--
U.S.A.)

Offered quinquennially since
1893 by Columbia University
(Loubat Prize Competition, Secretary of Columbia University,
New York 27), the Loubat Prizes
are open to writers who are
citizens of any country. Books
eligible for competition "must be
publications in English" that have
appeared prior to January of the
year of award. Two premiums--
a First Prize of $1,200 and a
Second Prize of $600--are granted
"in recognition of the best works
printed and published in the
English language on the history,
geography, archaeology, ethnology,
philology, or numismatics of
North America." The current
award will be granted in 1963,
and works entered for the prize
should be submitted in four
copies by January 1, 1963.

Most recent winners (1958)
are Douglas Southall Freeman,
with 'George Washington, a
biography;" and Henry A. Poch-
mann, with 'German culture in
America, 1600-1900."   701.

Torcuato LUCA DE TENA
PRIZE (Spain)

A journalism award of the
ABC, Madrid newspaper (Calle
de Serrano 61), the prize with
a current premium of 25,000
pts has been granted such writers
as: Manuel Sánchez del Arco,
Victor de la Serna, José Luis
Vázquez Dodero, Pedro de
Lorenzo, Victoriano Fernández
Asis, Luis María Anson, Gonzalo
F. de la Mora.   702.

LUGANO PRIZE (International--
Switzerland)

A literary award consisting
of a novel prize (Grand Prix
International de la Nouvelle d'Anticipation) and a prize for the

best science fiction novel dealing with the future, has been won by such authors as:

1947 Vasco Pratolini.
Cronache de poveri amanti
1960 Van den Esch (France).
Janvier de l'an 2000
Pierre Versins (Switzerland).
Die entfernte Gegenwart
(technical book)   703.

LUPO DA GUBBIO PRIZE
(Italy)

To qualify for this annual poetry award, established in 1961 by L'Associazione internazionale per la Protezione e la Conoscenze degli Animali (Linda Samaritani, via Bitinia 19, Rome) competing works (unpublished poems or poems published within three years of the contest period) must be submitted in five copies by August 31. The prize consists of a special cup, "Lupa da Gubbio," and of gold, silver and bronze medals, and is announced each December. The initial "Lupa da Gubbio" winner was Sonio Serpieri; and Michele Carta was awarded the gold medal in the same contest.
704.

LUXEMBOURG ASSOCIATION OF WRITERS IN FRENCH PRIZE

First awarded in 1954, this triennial prize of SELF (Société des Écrivains Luxembourgeois de Langue Française) offers 30,000 fr for the best literary works in the French language written by a native-born citizen of Luxembourg. Designed to encourage creative writing and literature in Luxembourg, the prize is offered for works in a number of literary forms. Published works, issued during a specified period preceding each contest, and unpublished works (Novels, Collections of Poetry, Drama, Collections of Short Stories or Novellas, Travel Impressions, Memoirs, Essays) are submitted in competition by sending five copies of the work to the Secretary of SELF. Recent recipients include:

1954 Paul Palgen. General works
1957 Albert Borschette.
Continuez à mourir (novel)
1960 Pierre Frieden. General works   705.

LUXEMBOURG LITERATURE PRIZE

The highest cultural award of Luxembourg, including prizes in Literature, Science and the Arts, was created in 1938 and awarded for the first time the following year. Granted by the Minister of Arts and Sciences (Ministère des Arts et des Sciences, 19 Côte d'Eich, Luxembourg), the prize has increased in value from an initial premium of 5,000 fr to 15,000 fr in 1957, and 25,000 fr in 1961. This amount is awarded to each of three winning works, written in the three official languages of the country-- Luxembourgese, French, German. A jury of six members determines prize winners. In 1957, the award, generally presented every three years, was granted to:

French--M. Edmond Dune.
Les Taupes
German (shared equally)--
Felix Mersch. Die Bruche
Leon Nilles. Leningrad
Alex Jacoby. Der Fremde
706.

LUZAN PRIZE (Spain)

The city of Zaragoza (Ayuntamiento de Zaragoza) offers this 10,000 pts prize for the best dramatic work in competition.
707.

William J. B. MACAULAY FOUNDATION FELLOWSHIPS
(Ireland)

Established in 1958, these

general cultural scholarships of approximately Ŀ 1,000 are a-warded annually for Painting, Sculpture, Music, Literature, and Drama by the Irish Arts Council (An Chomhairle Ealaion, 70 Merrion Street, Dublin). Eligible for consideration as a grant awardee are Irish-born creative workers in the arts, who are under 30 years of age--or, in exceptional cases, under 35 years of age.

The fellowship, announced in the early summer, generally is granted in literature and in drama once during a five-year period. Formal application forms are submitted to the Arts Council, and a committee of two judges from outside Ireland determines the recipients from among applicants.   708.

Jean MACÉ PRIZE (France)

A prize honoring a book for young people, granted by the organization, Ligue Française de l'Enseignement (3 rue Recamier, Paris 7e)/, brings 2000 NF to the winning author. Writers enter the competition by submitting a 200 to 300 page manuscript by October 1. There is no subject restriction on writings entered in the contest, except they must not be of a political or a religious nature. Laureates include:

1958 A. Laredo and J. Franceschi. Sidi-Safi
1959 P. Counillon. L'extra-ordinaire voyage de M. Ricou
1961 Étienne Cattin. L'express du soir   709.

MACEDONIAN WRITER'S SOCIETY PRIZES (Yugoslavia)

Among the winners of the Drustvo knjizevnika Makedonije, awarded in the Federated Republic of Macedonia, are such writers of novels, poetry, and other forms of literature, as:

Dimitar Mitev. Vapcarov (Vapcarov--collected essays, 1954)
Dimitar Solev. Pod usijanoscu (Under intense heat--prose work, 1957)
Jordan Leov. Collected children's stories, 1957
Novel--
Stoleta Popov. Krpen zivot (The patched life, 1953)
Slavko Janevski. Dve Marije (Two Mary's, 1956)
Poetry--
Blaza Konesko. Pesni (Poems, 1953)
Srba Ivanovski. Sredbi i razdelbi (Those in the middle and on the edge, 1953)
Gogo Ivanovski. Senki na dalecnoto (Shadows afar, 1954)
Mateja Matevski. Dozdovi (The rains, 1956)
Aco Sopov. Vetar nosi lepo vreme (The wind blows nice weather, 1957)
Drama--
Vasil Ijoski. Kuzman Kapidan (Captain Kuzman, 1954)
                                                710.

MACHADO DE ASSIS PRIZE (Brazil)

One of Brazil's highest literary prizes, and a major literary honor granted by the Academia Brasileira de Letras (Avenida Presidente Wilson 203, Rio de Janeiro), this annual prize of Cr $200.000 is granted for the entire literary work of a Brazilian writer--including that published during the three years preceding the year of award.

Named for Brazil's famous author, Joaquim Maria Machado de Assis (1839-1908), whose novels and short stories have been designated "most Brazilian" of the country's writing, and whose poetry was a forerunner of the Brazilian Parnassian School, this prize, one of the

best-known and most-respected
in all Latin America, has
honored such authors as:
  1955 Onestaldo Penaforte
  1956 Luís de Câmara Cascudo
  1957 Tasso da Silveira. Col-
    lected Canzoniere
  1958 Raquel de Queiroz
  1959 José Maria Belo
  1960 Eduardo Freiro
  1961 João Guimarães Rosa
  1962 Antenor Nascentes
  In 1961 William L. Gross-
man (U.S.A.) received an award
called the MACHADO DE ASSIS
MEDAL for his translation of
the 1881 novel by Machado de
Assis into English: Memórias
Pósthumas de Braz-Cubas (Epi-
taph of a small winner).   711.

Antonio MACHADO POETRY
PRIZE (Spain)
  A 25,000 pts prize offered
by the Paris publisher, Ediciones
Ruedo Iberico (27 Boulevard
Malesherbes) for poetry--a
minimum of 700 verses--required
two copies of manuscripts competing for the award be entered
in competition by December 31,
1961. The initial award was
presented in Cillioure, France--
where the Spanish poet, Antonio
Machado, is buried--to Angel
Gonzalez for his book of poems,
"Grado elemental." The publisher also offers the Ruedo
IBERICO NOVEL PRIZE, and
will award an essay prize--
MAIRENA PRIZE--in 1963.
                                712.

Jessie MACKAY POETRY
AWARD (New Zealand)
  An annual award of the P.E.
N. New Zealand Centre (P.O.
Box 9016, Wellington), this
prize of L 50 established
in 1940 honors the best poetry
written or published during a
calendar year by a New Zealand
writer (a native New Zealander,
or any other person who has

resided continuously in New
Zealand during the previous five
years).
  Winners of the award, which
is granted without application,
are:
  1940 Douglas Stewart. Elegy for
    an airman
  1941 Paula Hanger. Three
    fronts of war
  1942 R.I.F. Pattison. Youth
    passes
  1943 Mary Greig. Year's wane
  1945 Mary Stanley. The new
    philosopher
  1947 Ruth Gilbert.   Lazarus
  1948 Ruth Gilbert. Sanitorium;
    Behold it was Leah
  1950 James K. Baxter. Seven
    poems in "Landfall," March
    1950
  1951 Charles Spear. Twopence
    coloured and other poems
  1952 Mary Stanley. Starveling
    year
  1953-4 Patrick Wilson.
    Staying at Ballisodare in
    "Landfall"
  2nd Prize--Charles Doyle. A
    splinter of glass in "Landfall"
  1955 Paul Henderson (pseud
    of Ruth France). Unwilling
    pilgrim
  2nd Prize--Gloria Rawlinson.
    Islands where I was born
  1956 W. H. Oliver. Group of
    poems in "New Zealand
    Poetry Yearbook, 1956"
  1957 Allen Curnow. Poems
    1949-57
  1958 James K. Baxter.   In
    fires of no return
  1959 M. K. Joseph. The living
    countries
  1960 Basil Dowling.   A letter
    to D'Arcy Cresswell   713.

MACMILLAN FICTION AWARD
(International--U.S.A.)
  The publisher's prize of $7,500
($2,500 outright award, and
$5,000 royalty advance) for fic-
tion was first announced January
1, 1959 by The Macmillan Com-

pany (60 Fifth Avenue, New York 11). Any work of fiction (except mystery stories, westerns and juvenile stories) in the English language, between 50,000 and 200,000 words, is eligible for the competition. There is no restriction as to the nationality or citizenship of the author. Manuscripts must be submitted during the contest period (1962 contest period: December 1, 1961 to February 28, 1962), must be unpublished, and may be translations into English, "but preference will be given to novels of particular significance to American readers." No contest forms are required, and the editorial staff of The Macmillan Company choses the prize winner. Winners of the Macmillan Fiction Award are:

    1959 John Berry. Krishna fluting
    1960 David Storey. The sporting life
    1961 Ann Hebson. The Lattimer legend   714.

MADRID PRIZE (Spain)

One of a number of cultural honors granted by the city of Madrid, this award for books or articles about Madrid grants 10,000 pts to the winning author. Among recipients of the prize of the "Concurso de Libros sobre Madrid" are:

    1954 Víctor Ruiz Albéniz
    1957 Augusto Martinez Olmedilla. Anecdotario del Siglo XIX
    1958 Tomás Borrás. Madrid gentil, torres mil
    1959 Jaime Oliver Asín. Historia del nombre Madrid
    1960 Miguel Molina Campuzano· Planos de Madrid de los siglos XVII y XVIII   715.

Ramon MAGSAYSAY AWARDS FOR JOURNALISM AND LITERATURE (Philippines, Republic of)

Established in 1958 in honor of the late President of the Republic of the Philippines, Ramon Magsaysay, who was killed in an airplane crash in 1957, these Pan-Asian awards annually grant-- in "recognition of Magsaysay's ideals and service to the people" --a rich prize of 10,000 pesos and an inscribed certificate of award.

Citizens of the Philippines or of any country of Asia are eligible for the awards, which are administered by the Ramon Magsaysay Award Foundation (P.O. Box 3350, Manila). Initial financing of the prizes was sponsored by the Rockefeller Brothers Fund of New York City, with a grant of 500,000 pesos. As many as five ₱10,000 prizes--one in each of five categories: Government Service; Public Service by a private citizen; International Understanding; Community Service; Journalism and Literature-- may be awarded each year.

A formal presentation ceremony in Manila on August 31, the birthday of Ramon Magsaysay, designates the recipients of this high honor, representing a continuation of the humanitarian and democratic ideals of President Magsaysay. Publishers and authors receiving the award for "effective writing and publishing as a power for the public good" are:

    1958 Robert McCulloch Dick. Publisher of the "Philippines Free Press"
    1959 U Law Yone (Burma). Editor and founder of "The Nation," Rangoon
    Tarzie Vittachi (Ceylon). Editor of the Ceylon "Observer," for his book, "Emergency '58," and his crusading editorials
    1960 Amitabha Chowdury (India). Courageous reporting for the Calcutta newspaper "Jogantar"

216   International Literary Awards

1962 Chang Chun-ha (Korea).
Journalism and literature
work   716.

MAINICHI PRIZES (Japan)
  The Mainichi Newspaper Publishing Company awards the
prize to "the authors and publishers of works contributing to
human culture." Another literary award, offered by the publisher is the SUNDAY MAINICHI
CHIBA PRIZE, granted since
1949 in memory of the literary
critic, Kameo Chiba (1878-1935),
by the Sunday Mainichi, a weekly magazine of the Company,
to the best popular story submitted for consideration.
  Winners of the Mainichi
Prizes, since the initial award
in 1947, are:
    1947 Yuriko Miyamoto.
    Banshu Heiya (The Banshu
    Plain); Fuchiso (A cool-
    ness-bringing bush)
    Jun-ichiro Tanizaki. Sasame-
    yuki (Light snow)
    1948 Minoru Kida. Kichigai
    Buraku Shuyu-ki (Records of
    wandering about a madman's
    community)
    Michio Takeyama. Biruma
    no Tategoto (The sound of
    a harp echoing through the
    jungles in Burma)
    1949 Atsushi Nakajima.
    Nakajima Atsushi Zenshu
    (Complete works)
    1950 Tatsuo Hori. Hori
    Tatsuo Sakuhin-shu (Works)
    Yutaka Tatsuno. Figaro no
    Kekkon (Japanese translation
    of the "Mariage de Figaro")
    1951 Konosuke Hinatsu,
    Tatsuji Miyoshi, Shigeharu
    Nakano, Makoto Sangu,
    Hojin Yano. Nippon Gendai
    shi Taikei (A representative
    selection from Contempo-
    rary Japanese Poems)
    Torahiko Tamiya. Ehon (A
    picture book)
    1952 Hiroshi Noma. Shinku

Chitai (Zone of emptiness)
1953 Temma Shibata. Ryosai
Oshii (To wish the common,
to attempt the uncommon--
a Japanese translation from
the Chinese text)
1954 Fumi Kuroyanagi. Shimai
(Sisters)
Sue Sumii. Yoake Asayake
(The early and late hours of
the morning)
1955 Shigeharu Nakano.
Muragimo (The soul)
Suekichi Aono, and others.
Gendai Bungaku-ron Taikei
(A representative selection
from contemporary literary
theories and criticisms)
1956 Tatsukichi Nishino.
Chichibu Konmin-to (The
Chichibu Poor Workers'
Party)
1958 Endo Shusaku. Umito
Dokuyaku (The sea and poison)
                    717.

MAINZ ACADEMY PRIZE (Ger-
many)
  The Grösser Akademiepreis
für Literatur of the Mainz
Academy for Science and Literature (Mainzer Akademie der
Wissenschaften und der Literatur,
Geschwinter-Scholl Strasse 2,
Mainz), with a premium of
10.000 DM, has been awarded
twice. Winners of the two
prizes (future awards are not
planned at this time) are:
    1950 Divided equally:
    Werner Helwig; Hans Hennecke;
    Oda Schaefer; Arno Schmidt;
    Heinrich Schirmbeck
    1954 Alfred Döblin   718.

MALAGA PRIZE (Spain)
  The Malaga-Costa del Sol
Prize, offered by Diputacion
Provincial, Malaga, since 1960,
grants a monetary premium for
various forms of writing, as
specified in the rules at each
award. In 1957, 25,000 pts was
presented Salvador Rueda as

the "MALAGA PRIZE." The first award offered under the name "Malaga-Costa del Sol Prize" was a 100,000 pts premium in 1960, which was won by D. Torcuato Luca de Tena for "Edad Prohibida," as the best published novel during the period December 1, 1957 to December 31, 1959, which obtained a literary prize of at least 5,000 pts. The 1961 prize, granted for newspaper articles in Spanish published in newspapers in Spain, America, or the Philippines, excluding Malaga, with the theme "Costa del Sol," was won by D. José Antonio Torreblanca with "La costa que hace famosa al Sol," which appeared in "Informaciones," Madrid,on February 1, 1961. The 1962 prize, also offered for journalism, was granted for the best articles entered in competition that were written in any officially recognized language and published outside of Malaga in any newspaper or magazine, with "Malaga and the Costa del Sol" as theme. Award winner was Jesús Vasallo with "Carta a mister Thant sobre una rosa," appearing in "Arriba" of Madrid, January 14, 1962.
719.

Ricardo MALHEIROS PRIZE (Portugal)
The Lisbon Academy of Sciences (Academia des Ciencias de Lisboa) grants a prize of 5.000$ for a work of imaginative literature, prose or poetry. Winners of the prize in recent years--usually novelists--include:
1958 José Campos de Figueiredo. Obed (lyric-dramatic poem, 1956)
1960 Mario Braga. O livro das sombras   720.

MALINCA DETECTIVE NOVEL COMPETITION (Argentina)
The publisher's contest for the best "Novelas Erotico Policiales" with a first prize of 20,000 pesos and a second prize of 15,000 pesos was won in 1960 by Ansolmo Leoz with "Los muchachos del lápiz;" and Victor Sáiz (Spain) with "El Crimon Metafísico."   721.

Lucien MALPERTUIS PRIZE (Belgium)
A 10,000 fr biennial award for Belgians writing in French has been granted since 1940 by the Belgian Royal Academy of French Language and Literature. The prize rotates each year, honoring in succession: Drama, Poetry, Short Story, Essay. Recent winners are:
1953 Mme Louis Dubrau. Double jeu
1955 Denis Marion. Les masques du destin
1957 Noël Ruet. La Boucle de Temp (poetry)
1959 Gérard Prévot. Le nouvelle Eurydice
1961 Pierre Demeuse. Entire work   722.

MANDAT DES POÈTES (France)
A major French prize for poetry and one of France's richest premiums for French poetry is granted each year (Pierre Bearn, 60 rue Monsieur-le-Prince, Paris 6e) to allow a French poet --young or old--to realize his talent. The honored writer may be called a "Poet's Poet," as the prize, usually about 4.500 NF, is determined by secret vote of some 250 poets who sponsor the award. The assembled poets usually designate the prize-winner in November, and their members include such distinguished men of letters as Jean Cocteau, Daniel-Rops, Georges Duhamel, François Mauriac, André Maurois, and Jules Romains of the Académie Française; and Hervé Bazin, Mac Orlan, and Raymond Queneau

of the Académie Goncourt.

Official and professional groups participate in the award (such as Direction des Lettres, of the French National Ministry of Education; Société des Gens de Lettres; Société des Poètes Français), as do literary publications (among these are: "Figaro littéraire;" "Nouvelles littéraires;" "Journal des poètes," of Brussels).

Laureates of this high honor, with premiums ranging up to 440.000 francs, are:

1950 René-Guy Cadou
1951 François-Paul Alibert; Armen Lubin
1952 Jean de Boschère; Albert Flad
1953 Louis de Bonzague Frick; Roger Lannes; Jean Germon
1954 Pierre-Albert Birot; Colette Benoite
1955 Angèle Vannier; Vincent Monteiro; Charles Le Quintrec
1956 André Mary; Philéas Lebesgue; Adrien Maitlev
1957 Renée Rivet; Robert Lorho
1958 Paul Fort; Jean Laugier
1959 Blaise Cendrars
1960 Claire Goll; André Druelle
1961 Ginette Bonvalet; Louis Depierris
1962 Michel Manoll; Marie-Madeleine Machet   723.

Heinrich MANN PRIZE (Germany, East)

The literary honor of the German Academy of Arts of East Berlin (Deutsche Akademie der Künste; also called "Ostberliner Akademie der Künste") is awarded each year on the birthday of Heinrich Mann, March 27. Winners of the award, which may be granted in First, Second, and Third Prizes in one year, include:

1954 Theo Harysch. Hinter den schwarzen Wäldern;

Im Geiseltal (novels)
1956 Franz Fühmann. Die Fahrt nach Stalingrad
Wolfgang Schreyer. Unternahmen Thunderstorm (novel)
Rudolf Fischer. Martin Hoop IV (novel)
1957 Margarete Neumann. Der Weg über den Acker (novel)
Hanns Maassen. Die Messe des Barcello
Herbert Nachbar. Der Mond had einen Hof (novel)
1958 Herbert Jobst. Der Findling (novel)
Rosemarie Schuder. Der Sohn der Hexe (novel)
Hans Grundig. Zwischen Karneval und Aschermittwoch (reminiscences)
1959 Hans Lorbeer. Entire work, including his novel about Luther, "Das Fegefeuer"
Inge and Heinrich Müller. Lohndrücker; Korrektur (plays)
1960 Annemarie Reinhard Helmut Hauptmann
1961 Dieter Noll. Die Abenteuer des Werne Holg (novel)
1962 Ludwig Renn. Lyrical work concerning Günter Kuhnert   724.

Katherine MANSFIELD MEMORIAL AWARD (New Zealand)

A biennial award administered by the New Zealand Women Writers' Society was founded in 1959 "to commemorate the genius of New Zealand's most famous writer, and to help New Zealand writers to gain prestige and recognition in their own country." Funds for the award are provided by the Bank of New Zealand--of which Sir Harold Beauchamp, Katherine Mansfield's father, was Board of Directors member for 38 years, and Chairman of the Board for 15 years. Dual prizes of Ł 50 are granted in each award--one for the best published short story,

the other for another form of
writing, specified at each award
period. New Zealand writers
(those born in the country or
having resided there for five
years or more) are eligible for
the prize, which is presented
(Katherine Mansfield Memorial
Award Committee, Box 8016,
Wellington) on a convenient day
near October 14, Katherine
Mansfield's birthday.

Winners are:
1959 Published short story--
Maurice Duggan. The de-
parture (in "Image," April
5, 1959)
Published essay or article--
Elsie Locke. Looking for
answers (in "Landfall,"
December 1958)
1961 Published short story--
C. K. Stead. A race apart
(in "Landfall," June 1960)
Published or unpublished
essay not less than 5,000
words of a critical or biographical nature--C.K. Stead.
'Hulk of the world's between'
(to be published in a series
"dealing with the effects of
remoteness on New Zealand")
725.

Katherine MANSFIELD PRIZE
(International--France)
A triennial, bilingual prize
for a short story is offered by
the village of Menton (Marie
de Menton, Alpes-Maritimes,
France) to commemorate
Katherine Mansfield, who spent
the last years of her life in her
villa "Isola Bella," in Menton.
The prize, which was established
in 1959 and is administered by
the French and the Great Britain
P.E.N. Clubs (P.E.N. Club de
France, 66 rue Pierre-Charron,
Paris 8e; P.E.N. Club of Great
Britain, 62/63 Glebe Place,
Chelsea, London, S. W. 3),
divides the prize premium
equally between the winning au-

thor of a short story in French
(1.500 NF) and in English
(L100), which has already been
published in a book or in a
periodical during the three years
preceding year of award. Stories
considered for award must not exceed 10,000 words in length.

The prize, presented on
October 14, the birthday of
Katherine Mansfield, has honored
such English writers (from United
Kingdom, Ireland, and the
Commonwealth and South Africa)
and such French authors as:
1959 Frank Tuphy. The
admiral and the nuns
Luce Amy. La grand-mère
1962 Mary Lavin (Ireland).
The great wave
Nicol Briacq. La Lande
726.

Alessandro MANZONI PRIZE
(Italy)
The Catholic Publishers of
Italy (Unione Editori Cattolic
Italiani-U.E.C.I., Via di Porta
Angelica 63, Rome) offers the
prize for "narritiva" which must
be submitted in competition in
four copies before December 31
each year. Premiums for the
winning works--unpublished novels
concerned with the conception of
Christian ethics and values--
are a First Prize of L 1.000.000
and a Second Prize of L 500.
000.

Recipients of the award's First
Prize, granted since 1954, include:
1954 Adriana Zarri. Giorni
feriali; Bruno Russello.
Trent'anni
1957 Andrea Pagano. La lunghi
notti
1959 Silvestro Volta. Scozia
senze Natale   727.

Eugene MARAIS PRIZE (South
Africa)
An award for poetry and
drama, granted by the South Afri-

can Academy of Arts and Science
(Suid-Afrikaanse Akademie vir
Wetenskap en Kuns, Engelenburg
House, Hamilton Street Pretoria),
the prize is one of several literary rewards directed to promote
Afrikaans literature. First
recipient of the honor in 1961
was Audrey Blignaut.   728.

Gregorio MARAÑON PRIZE
(Spain)
  The 50.000 pts premium of-
fered by the periodical "Gran
Via," Barcelona, was won in
1961 by E. Barco Tervel with
'Elogio y Nostalgia de Marañon."
                              729.

MARCH FOUNDATION PRIZES
(Spain)
  Since 1956 La Fundacion Juan
March (Nuñez de Balboa 68,
Madrid), as established by Juan
March Ordinas, continues as one
of the great endowed foundations
of Europe, offering various
grants and prizes "to help the
scholar." Grants are awarded
in recognition of high professional and scholarly achievement
--as "Ayuda de Investigación"
of half a million pesetas--to
distinguished scholars for research or for past contributions
in their fields. In addition,
100 annual scholarships of 50,000
pts are given as encouragement
of creative work--including
writing--to young scholars for
study in Spain. Some of the
Foundation's grants and prizes
are administered by Real Academia Española, others by professional and learned societies.
  Among writers receiving
awards of 50,000 pts are:
    1959 Ana María Matute; José
    María Espinás; Antonio
    Vilanova
    1962 Manuel Alcántara; Car-
    men Bravo Villasante; Juan
    Antonio Cabezas; Carmen
    Conde; J. Fernández de la

    Reguerra; Vicente Gaos;
    Rafael Garcia Serrano;
    César González Ruano;
    Manuel Iribarren; Leopoldo
    de Luis; Enrique Moreno
    Baéz; Domingo Paniagua;
    Domaso Santos; José Luis
    Vázquez Dodero
  The March Foundation Literary Prizes (one aspect of the
Foundation awards in the Sciences, Letters, and Arts) are
of the highest prestige in Spain
as in the "mundo hispanico,"
and--with the exception of the
Nobel Prize for Literature--are
the richest monetary premiums
for literature in Europe. The
Literature Prize (Premio Literatura) and the Letters Prize
(Premio de Letras) are honors
recognizing general contributions
to literature with a lifetime of
work and achievement. Other
literary honors granted are those
for creative literature, regional
prizes, and --since 1959--
specific contributions to literature
of designated form.
  Award winners include:
Literature Prize (Premio Litera-
tura--500,000 pts)
    1956 (jury of Real Academia
    de la Lengua) Ramón
    Menéndez Pidal
    1957 (jury of Mesa del In-
    stituto de España) José María
    Pemán
Letters Prize (Premio de Letras--
500,000 pts)
    1958 (jury of President of In-
    stituto de España and of
    Presidents of the 8 component
    Reales Academias)
    José Martínez Ruíz (pen name:
    Azorín)
    1959 (jury same as in 1958)
    José María Millás Vallicrosa
    1961 (jury of Director, Real
    Academia Española, and
    member academicians) Gerardo
    Diego Cendoya
Imaginative Literature Prize
(Premio de Literatura de

Creación--500, 000 pts)
1960 (jury of six academicians)
Ramon Pérez de Ayala
Regional Literary Prizes:
Madrid, Cataluna, Galicia
1962 Awarded to writer who
has made the greatest contribution to the literature of
three specified regions of
Spain, granted by juries composed of members of educational organizations, professional and learned societies.
Madrid: Ramón Gómez de
la Serna
Cataluña (Catalonia):Miguel
del Riquer Morera
Galicia: Ramón Otero
Pedrayo
Prizes for Specified Literary
Form (300, 000 pts in each
category)
1959 Premio de Novela, Teatro y Poesia (jury of 4
representatives of Real
Academia Española, 10 newspaper critics, and 3 representatives of Spanish literary reviews)
Novel: Gonzalo Torrento Bal-
lester.   El Señor Llega
Drama: Antonio Buero Val-
lejo.   Hoy es Fiesta
Poetry: José Hierro. Cuanto
Sé de Mí
1960 Premio de Ensayo de
Creación, Periodismo Lit-
erario y Critica en General
(jury of representatives from
Real Academia Española and
Academia de la Historia, and
literary critics)
Essay: Dámaso Alonso
Journalism: José Plá
Criticism: Melchor Fernández
Almagro   730.

Marcial MARTINEZ CUADROS
PRIZE (Chile)
The triennial award of the
Facultad de Ciencias Juridicas
y Sociales of the University of
Chile was established in 1950.
The prize, with a small mone-

tary premium but high national
prestige, is granted for a literary work published during the
three years preceding the year of
award.   731.

Joanot MARTORELL PRIZE
(Spain)
Awarded each year for the
best novel written in Catalan, the
publisher's prize of Editorial
Selecta (Ronda Sant Pere 3,
Barcelona) has recently been
jointly sponsored by Ayamá,
Sociedad Anonima Editora (Tra-
vesera de Gracia 64, Barcelona).
Since the prize was first awarded in 1947, the premium--cur-
rently 40, 000 pts--has been won
by such writers as:
1947 Celio Suñol. Priemera
parte
1951 Josep Plá.   El Carrer
Estret
1953 Josep María Espinas.
Con Ganivets O Flames
1955 Joan Slaes. Incerta
gloria
1956 Ramón Folch y Camarasa.
La Maroma
1957 Blas Bonet.   El mar
1960 Ricardo Salvat. Animals
destructors de lleis   732.

MARVA PRIZE (Spain)
Since 1930 the National Planning
Institute (Institut Nacional de Previsión, Alcala 56, Madrid) has granted
over 20 awards for the best work
during the year on a specified theme
in economics or social science.
Winners of the prize--presently a
20, 000 pts premium--include:
1930 Gregorio Blanco Santamaría.
El emigrante y los Seguros
Sociales
José María and Ignacio López
Valencia. El emigrante y los
Seguros Sociales
1931 Leandro Silván. Estudio
Médico-social del Convenio
sobre reparación de enfermedades
profesionales
Vincente de Andrés Bueno. Estudio Médico-social del Convenio
sobre reparación de enfermedades

profesionales.
1932 Subject; Los Seguros
Sociales en el medio rural: Ex-
tensión de los Seguros sociales
a los trabajadores del campo.
Procedimiento de hacer más
eficaz esa extensión--José
López Valencia; Enrique
Luño Peña
1933 María Palamcar and
Eugenio Pérez Botija. La
prevención de los accidentes
del trabajo por los modernos
medios psicológicos, gráficos
y mecánicos: Eficacia com-
parativa de unos y otros
desde el punto de vista hu-
manitario y económico
1934 Enrique Luño Peña. El
problema de la unificacion de
los Seguros sociales fuera de
España
1935 Jose Pérez Serrano. Or-
ganizacion y funcionamiento
de los Tribunales de Trabajo
en la Legislacion comparada
y su posible aplicacion a
España
1940 Pedro Arnaldos Jimeno.
Los Seguros Sociales en los
Estados totalitarios
1941 José Lledó Martín. La
Pesca Nacional
1942 Antonio Rumeu de Armas.
Historia de la Previsión
Social en España--Cofradía;
Gremios; Hermandades;
Montepíos
1945 Eugenio Pérez Botija.
El Derecho del Trabajo. Con-
cepto, substantividad y
relaciones con las restantes
disciplinas jurídicas
1947 José Lledó Martín. La
participación de los trabajadores en los beneficios de
las Empresas
1948 Pedro Arnaldos Jimeno.
Estudio comparado del Seguro
de Invalidez y Muerte y de
su posible implantación en
España
1950 Pablo and Hilario Salvador Bullón. La Teoría del

"Full-Employment"
1952 Pablo and Hilario Salvador Bullón. El Seguro contra
el Paro forzoso
1953 Antonio Agúndez Fernández.
El Patrimonio familiar
1956 Manuel Alonso Olea and
Enrique Serrano Guirado.
La Seguridad Social de los
funcionarios públicos en
España en el extranjero
1957-8 Jesús María Vázquez.
El Servicio Doméstico en
España   733.

Karl MARX ART PRIZE (Ger-
many, East)
The cultural award, established
by the council of the city of
Karl Marx (Rat des Bezirkes
Karl Marx), distributes a total
of 50,000 DM in prize premiums
each year. In 1960 the literature
prize was won by Hermann Heinz
Wille.   734.

MARZOTTO PRIZE (Italy)
Among the best-known and most
significant prizes in Italy, are
these richly-endowed cultural
awards--with premiums that may
reach a total of L 30.000.000
each year. Rewarding outstanding
work in a number of scientific and
art areas (Prose and Poetry; Art
History; Journalism; Drama;
Medicine and Surgery; Painting;
Music), the prizes (Segretaria
Premio Marzotto, via Barberini
3, Rome) were established in
1950 by Count Paolo Marzotto.
Significant for their prestige,
diversity and generous premium,
the literary awards are granted
to Italian and to foreign writers
for as many as 18 forms of
imaginative and factual works,
including: MARZOTTO PRIZE--
for works of Philosophy and History, Criticism and Literary
History; ZIGNAGO PRIZE--for
works in Economics, Agricultural
Economics and Food; CASTEL-
VECCHIO PRIZE--journalism.

Current awards in Literature and Philosophy--biennial since 1960--are:
Marzotto Prose or Poetry Prize (Marzotto Narrative o Poesia) --L 3.000.000
Marzotta Philosophy Prize (Marzotto Filosofia) --L2.000.000, for work in philosophy or history of philosophy published in the six years preceding the year of competition
Marzotto "Choice" Prize (Marzotto Selezione) --L 500.000 to L 3.000.000 each for Prose, Poetry, Children's Book published in the two years preceding the competition, and for Philosophy published in the six years preceding the competition
Marzotto Laureat Prize (Premio di laurea Marzotto) --L 250.000 to L 500.000 for a dissertation in Literature or Philosophy
Among the recipients of major awards are the novelists Giuseppo Berto (1951) for 'Il brigante;" Carlo Cassola (1952) for "Fausto e Anna;" and Anna Banti (1955) for "Alarme sul lago." Other writers honored by chief awards for imaginative and factual works are:
Prose and Poetry Prize-- L 2.000.000, increased in 1954 to L 3.000.000
1951 VALDAGNO PRIZE -- Amedeo Maiuri. Passeggiate compane
1952 Giovanni Papini. Libro nero
1953 Aldo Palazzeschi. Roma
1954 Alberto Moravia. Racconti romani
1955 Ardengo Soffici. Thirty years of literary work, and for "Autoritratto d'artista italiano nel quadro del suo tempo"
1956 Bruno Cicognani. Le novelle

1957 Umberto Saba. Riccordi e racconti
1959 Riccardo Bacchelli. I tre schiavi di Giulio Cesare
Carlo Cassola. Il taglio del bosco
1961 Gianna Manzini. Un'altra cosa
Economics
1958 Pasquale Jannaccone. Moneta e lavoro; El costo di produzione
1960 Costantino Bresciani Turroni. Corso di economic politica
1962 Giorgio Mortara. Economia della popolazione
History
1957 Carlo Guido Mor. L'Eta feudale (2 vol)
Criticism--L 2.000.000
1952 Giuseppe Antonio Borgese. Entire critical work
1954 Mario Praz. La crisi dell'eroe del Romanzo Vittoriano
Drama
1957 Luigi Squarzina. Romagnola
1959 Giorgio Prosperi. La congiura
1961 Diego Fabbri. Ritratto d'ignoto
Poetry
1956 Eugenio Montale. La bufera e altro
1957 Mario Luzi. Onore del vero
1959 Giorgio Vigolo. Canto del destino   735.

Gabriel MAURA PRIZE (Spain)
The award of the Ayuntamiento de Palma de Mallorca, with a premium varying from 20,000 to 50,000 pts, is granted for a novel or prose narrative with a Balearic setting, if any. In 1961 Manuel Pico won a prize of 25,000 pts for his novel 'El Llanto de la Cigarra."   736.

MAY PRIZE (France)
The Prix de Mai, representa-

tive of "non-literature," "non-novel" contemporary French writing, is designed to honor not the "best novel of the year" in the conventional sense of the novel form, but rather the work of a writer who evidences concern for rediscovering--through a renewal of the form of the novel--the significance which the traditional novel form has allowed to escape. Laureates, named by a jury (Bernard Pinguad, Secretary, 9 rue du Val-de-Grâce, Paris 6e) which includes among its members Nathalie Sarraute and Alain Robbe-Grillet, are:
   1957 Jean Lagrolet. Les vainqueurs du jaloux
   1958 Marguerite Duras. Moderato cantabile
   1959 Jean Douassot. La Gana
   1960 Yves Velan. Je...
   1961 Pierre Klossowski. Le Souffleur   738.

MÉDICIS PRIZE (France)
   Established by the Italian, Maecenas, with a grant of 333, 333 francs, this prize for an avant-garde book (Novel, Story, or Collection of Novella) is granted to an author whose fame does not equal his talent. The jury of ten (c/o Mme Gala Barbisan, 20 rue Cortot, Paris 18e) discusses books entered in competition by the deadline November 1, at the Alexandre Restaurant and awards the prize for writing representing new trends on the Sunday preceding the Monday announcement of the Prix Fémina.
   Prize winners since 1958, date of the first award, are:
   1958 Claude Ollier. Le mise en scène
   1959 Claude Mauriac. Le Diner en ville
   1960 Henri Thomas. John Perkins
   1961 Philippe Sollers. Le Parc

1962 Colette Audry. Derrière la baignoire   739.

Juan MEJÍA BACA FICTION PRIZE (Peru)
   The publisher's award of Libreria Juan Mejía Baca (Jiron Azangaro 722, Lima) was offered during the three years 1957-1959 for the best unpublished novel submitted in competition by Peruvian writers (citizens by birth, or by naturalization with at least five years' residence in the country). Novel manuscripts were submitted by December 30, and winner was announced the following April. Winners of prizes, which ranged in premium from 5,000 to 20,000 ejemplares, include: Francisco Vegas Seminario with "Taita Yoverague;" and Luis Felioe Angell with "La Tierra prometida."   740.

MELANTRICH PRIZE (Czechoslovakia)
   A major literary award in Czechoslovakia during the 1930-1940's--but not given since World War II--was offered by the publishing house, Malentrich, which has since been absorbed in the currently active publisher, Svobedne slovo. Winners include:
   1933 Benesora. Bozena (Works)
   1934 Durych. Pisen oruzi Hrubin. Zpivano z dalky
   1944 J. Toman. Don Juan: The life and death of Dan Miguel de Manara   741.

Ferñao MENDES PINTO PRIZE (Portugal)
   An annual 10.000$ award for a novel, one of several literary prizes offered by the Portuguese government department, Agencia Geral do Ultramar, is directed to encouraging new writing by Protuguese citizens on subjects dealing with overseas topics. Winner in 1957 was Manuel Fer-

reira, with his collection of
tales, "Morabeza."   742.

Ramon MENENDEZ PIDAL PRIZE (Spain)

A scholarly award for works
in the fields of philology and
historical or literary criticism,
the 30,000 pts premium granted
by the Real Academia Española
was presented in 1961 to
Eulalia Rodón Binué for the
work, "El Lenguaje Técnico del
Feudalism en el Siglo XI en
Cataluña," as the "best writing
published since 1957." Works
entered for the award must be
written on a set subject announced
at each competition. In 1962
the subject is: "A philological
study on one or more peninsular
romance texts of the Middle
Ages;" and the study must be
unpublished, must not previously
have won a prize, and must be
submitted by December 31,
1962.   743.

MENENDEZ Y PELAYO NATIONAL PRIZE (Spain)

Offered as one of several
prizes in 1956 in celebration of
the centenary of the birth of
Marcelino Menendez y Pelayo
(1856-1912), "Spain's great
historian and critic of literature," the national government
award was established in 1952
by the Ministry of Information
and Tourism. The prize,
honoring the best essay--historical, literary, or cultural--
in competition, has recently
been granted:
  1956 José Camón Aznar.
  Picasso y el cubismo
  1957 Santiago Galindo Herrero.
  Donoso Cortés
  1958 José Gomá Orduña.
  La Guerra en el Aire
  1959 José Luis Alborg. La
  Hora Actual de la Novel
  Española
  1960 Raimundo Paniker. La

India--gente, cultura, y
  creencias
  1961 Gonzalo Fernández de la
  Mora. Ortega y el 98
                               744.

MENORCA PRIZE (Spain)

The works of Spanish and Hispano-American writers were to be
honored by the award, established
in 1955 with a premium of 200,
000 pts, to be granted annually,
in successive years, for: Novel;
Biography; Criticism and Research. The author first receiving the prize was Carmen
Laforêt, with "La mujer neuva."
                               745.

MERGENTHALER PRIZE (Latin America--U.S.A.)

The journalism prize, offered
each year by Sociedad Interamericana de Prensa (Inter-
American Press Association, 667
Madison Avenue, New York 21),
was initiated in 1952 upon a
grant from the Mergenthaler
Linotype Company, New York.
Included in the five prizes of
$500 given each year are awards
for journalists who have contributed most in public service
with the best reporting or regular
columns, and for journalists
whose information and reporting
are judged the best
  Latin American writers
honored by the prize include:
  1955 Jorge Luis Martí, "El
  Mundo," Havana, Cuba
  Juan Ramón Ardón, "El Dia,"
  Tegucigalpa, Honduras
  1956 René Silva, "El Mercurio,"
  Santiago, Chile
  Etienne Dupuch, "The Nassau
  Tribune," Bahamas
  1958 Alejandro Miró Quesada,
  "El Comercio," Lima, Peru
  Víctor Gutiérrez Salamador,
  "El Dia," Montevideo,
  Uruguay
  1959 Andrés Borrasé, "La
  Prensa Libre," San Jose,

Costa Rica
Horacio de Dios, "La
Razon," Buenos Aires,
Argentina
1960 Marco Tulio Rodríguez
Martínez, "El Espectador,"
Bogota, Colombia
1961 Luis Loli Roca and
Victor Orzero Villegas,
"Ultima Hora," Lima, Peru
746.

Aruther MERGHE LYNCK PRIZE
(Belgium)
The Flemish literature award
of the Belgian Royal Academy of
Flemish Science, Letters and
the Arts has been won (1958) by
Johan Daisne with "Lago Mag-
giore;" and Jan Veulemans with
"Onbestendig."   747.

MEXICAN DRAMA CENTER PRIZE
The Premio del Centro
Mexicano de Teatro is an annual 10,000 pesos prize offered
by Centro Mexicano de Teatro
(Antonio Magana Esquivel,
Secretary, Av. 3 num 67,
Colonia Independencia, Mexico
13, D.F.) for a play not previously performed, by a playwright who is Mexican by birth
or by naturalization. Plays
submitted in the first contest,
which closed January 15, 1961,
had an optional theme, but
preferably one "applicable to
present-day problems." The
initial first prize winner, whose
play became eligible for competition in the international play
contest of the International
Institute of Drama and of
UNESCO in Paris, was Emilio
Carballido, author of the
drama "Medusa."   748.

MEXICAN NATIONAL DRAMA COMPETITION
The national prize of the
Concurso Nacional de Teatro,
granted by the Mexican govern-

ment agency, Instituto Nacional
de Bellas Artes (Direccion General, Palacio de Bellas Artes,
Mexico, D.F.), is also known as
the "PREMIO I.N.B.A.," after
the awarding agency. The National Competition in 1954 was
the result of a series of local
theater contests inaugurated "to
stimulate the amateur stage."
Mexican playwrights winning
national awards include:
1955 Carlos Ancira. Despues
nada
Juan José Arreola. La hora
de todos
Maria Luisa Algarra. Los
Anos de prueba
Emilio Carballido. Felicidad
1957 Hugo Argüelles. Veloria
en turno
1958 Pablo Salinas. Los
hombrecillos di gris   749.

MEXICAN NATIONAL PRIZE FOR ARTS AND SCIENCES
The Premio Nacional de
Artes y Ciencias, highest national cultural award of the
Mexican government, is administered by the Secretaria de
Educacion Publica. The prize
was established by federal law
on December 30, 1946 and is
granted in successive years to an
outstanding artist, author, and
scientist. The award, consisting
of a diploma and a premium of
20,000 pesos, may be granted in
literature for significant contributions in the field of the novel,
poetry, essay, biography, drama,
or motion picture script. The
Instituto Nacional de Bellas
Artes acts as the advisory jury in
selecting prize winners in the
arts and literature. Only two authors have received the major official recognition of the Mexican
government--presented to a
Mexican writer of at least 40
years of age--
1946 Alfonso Reyes. "For
work in classical criticism"

1949 Mariano Azuela. Entire
literary work, including
"Los de abajo" (The under-
dogs)
Other literary awards of the
Mexican Government or of non-
official national groups have
been called: "National Prizes."
In 1935, a "Mexican National
Prize," or "Mexican National
Prize in Literature," was
granted Gregorio López y
Fuentes for "El Indio;" and the
same year a "Mexican National
Prize in Journalism" was pre-
sented to Gustavo Ortiz Hernan.
    In 1940 the Secretaria de
Educacion Publica (by official
Mexican government decree of
November 15, 1940) was named
administrator of the "Mexican
National Literary Award," which
was to be granted each year in
November--following a national
competition--for the best novel,
story, biography or poetry written during the year.   750.

MEXICAN WRITERS' CENTER
FELLOWSHIPS
    Centro Méxicano de Escritores
(Rio Volga 3, Col Cuauhtemoc,
Mexico 5, D.F.) annually offers
a fellowship to writers in Mexico
and the U.S.A. "for completion
of works of creative literature."
The grants--ranging in amount
from 16,500 to 25,000 pesos--
are generally given to younger
writers and critics.
    The fellowships, directed "to
encouraging greater literary
exchange between Mexico and
the United States of America," a
are sponsored by such organizations as Banco de Mexico,
Rockefeller Foundation, Instituto
Nacional de Bellas Artes, "The
News," and Universidad Nacional
Autonoma de Mexico. Among
Mexican recipients of the grant
are: Juan José Arreola (twice a
fellow); Antonio Montes de Oca
(1956); Elena Poniatowska (1959);

Carlos Fuentes (1956-1957).
                              751.

MEXICO CITY PRIZE
    The literary honor of Ciudad
de Mexico has been granted such
popular Mexican novelists as:
    1951 Antonio Magaña Esquivel.
    La tierra enrojecida
    Luis Spota. Wounds of hunger
    1956 Juan Garcia Ponce. El
    canto de los grillos   752.

Auguste MICHOT PRIZE (Belgium)
    A biennial award of 10,000
fr granted by the Belgian Royal
Academy of French Language and
Literature since 1924 to a Belgian author writing in French
(prose or poetry). Works competing for the Michot Prize must
be on the set subject: The
Beauty of Flanders. Both unpublished and published (during the
two years preceding close of
competition) works are eligible,
and must be submitted by January
1, following the two years of
competition.
    Recent winners are:
    1951 Simone Bergmans.
    Faligan (novel)
    1953 Joseph Van der Elst.
    L'Age d'Or de la Peinture
    flamande
    1955 Jean Kestergat. Petit-
    biquet (novel)
    1957 Etienne Schoonhoven.
    Anvers, son fleuve et son
    port
    1961 Liliane Wouters. Les
    belles heures de Flandre
                              753.

MILAN PRIZE (Italy)
    Premio Milano, offered for
unpublished poetry by the University of Milan (Segretaria,
presso l'Universita degli Studi
di Milano), consists of a gold
medal and a premium of 1500.000.
In 1962 the jury, whose chairman
was Salvatore Quasimodo, awarded a number of prizes including

one to Mario Cicognani for his work, "Controluce."   754.

MINAS GERAIS CULTURAL PRIZES (Brazil)

The cultural honors of the State of Minas Gerais are offered by the Secretário da Educação for achievement in Literature and the Arts (Music, Painting, Sculpture and Architecture), and bring a premium of Cr$1.000.000 each year to the winners of the various competitions (Concursos de Letras e Artes). The literary contests and their winners in 1961, honoring the best book published during the year with the diploma and premium presented on December 31, were:

Cláudio Manoel da COSTA PRIZE--poetry: Pièrre Santos. Invenção da Rosa
João Alphonsus GUIMARÃES PRIZE--fiction (Novel, Short Stories, Novela): Maria Soledade (pseud of Zilah Correa de Araújo). Bezerro de Ouro
Pandiá CALÓGERAS PRIZE-- scholarly writing: Oiliam José A propaganda Republicana em Minas Gerais

In 1962 three prizes (Cr$300.000, Cr$200.000, Cr$100.000) will be awarded for published works on the history of Minas Gerais.

Two Cr$75.000 prizes are also offered each year for unpublished children's and young people's literature, entered in competition in three copies. These Premio de Literatura Infanto-Juvenil are presented on October 30, in connection with the celebration of "Dio do Professor."   755.

Gabriel MIRO PRIZE (Spain)

Named for Gabriel Miro (1879-1930), Spain's novelist and short story writer, this annual prize of the Ayuntamiento de Alicante (Caja de Ahorros, San Fernando 38) offers 50,000 pts to a Spanish or a Spanish-American novelist for a novel manuscript (minimum length: 200 pages) to be submitted in competition in April, each year.

Novelists winning the prize include:

1956 Jesús Fernández Santos. En la Hoguera
1958 José Albí. La Espera
1959 José Albí. El Silencio de Dios
1960 Juan Antonio Cabezas. La Montaña Rebelde
1961 Rodrigo Rubio. Un Munda a Cuestas   756.

MR. H'S PRIZE (Japan)

The award of the Japan Contemporary Poets' Society (Genai Shijin Kai), which is named for the anonymous donor who established the prize in 1950, is presented each year to the author of the best verse. Among recent winners is Yoshioka Minoru (1959).   757.

Gabriela MISTRAL PRIZE (Chile)

The city of Santiago established the literary honor upon the death of Gabriela Mistral (1889-1957), the distinguished Chilean-born Latin American poet and educator (real name: Lucila Godoy de Alcayaga) who was presented with both the Nobel Prize (1945) and the Chilean National Prize for Literature (1951). The prize, initiated in 1958 "as an expression of the highest homage to the great poet," is composed of three awards (Tres Sueldos Vitales-- $210; Dos Sueldos Vitales-- $140; Un Sueldo Vital--$70) which designate outstanding unpublished writing in each of five categories: Novel; Poetry; Drama; Essay; Collections of Stories.

Recent recipients of the prize, directed to assisting young authors with the distribution of new literary works, include:
Poetry--Jorge Teillier; Luis

Vulliamu; Emmio Moltedo
Novel--Enrique Lafourcade;
Jaime Talciani; Jorge Rubén
Morales
Stories--Edesio Alvarado;
Francisco Brzovíc; Manuel
Miranda
Drama--Enrique Molleto;
Fernando Lamberg; Egon
Wolf
Essay--Yerko Moretíc; Raul
Francisco Jiménez; Miguel
Saidel   758.

MLADA FRONTA AWARD
(Czechoslovakia)
A monetary award is granted
each year in March by the publishing house, "Mlada fronta"
(Young Front) for imaginative
and factual writing (including
such forms as Fiction, Poetry,
Journalism, and Popular Science),
and translation. Works eligible
for award are those published
by Mlada fronta during the preceding year.
Winners include:
Fiction--
1957 Cestmir Vejdelek. Duha pro
muy den (The soul of my day)
1958 Bohumir Polach. Navrat
Jiriho Skaly (The return of
George Skaly)
1959 Arnost Lustig. Demanty
noci (Diamonds of the night)
1960 Josef Nesvadba. Einsteinuv
mozek (Einstein's brain)
Journalism--
1959 Jaroslav Mrnka. Zazrak
bez nadeje (Miracle without
hope)
Jaroslav Putnik. Svedomi (Conscience)
1960 Ludwig Svoboda. Z
Buzuluku do Prahy (From
Buzuluku to Prague)
Poetry--
1957 Jiri Sotola. Svet nas
vesdejsi (Blessed is our
World)
Miroslav Florian. Zavrat
(Dizziness)
1958 Ivan Skala. Ranni

vlak nadeje (Hopes of the
morning train)
1959 Josef Kainar. Cloveka
horce mam rad (People I
love with passion)
1960 Miroslav Holub. Achiles
a zelva (Achilles and the
giraffe)
Karel Siktanc. Heinovske
noci (The nights of Hajnovsky)
Popular Science--
1957 Bares. Zrozeni atomoveho
veku (The birth of the atom
age)
1958 Josef Maran. Jak
zvirata zabydlila zemi (How
the animals covered the earth)
1960 Augusta. Ztraceny svet
(Lost world)
Translation--
1957 Jarmila Fastrova.
Charlotte Bronte's "Jane
Eyre"
1958 Lumir Civrny. Nicollas
Guillen's "Pisne a elegie"
(Song and elegies)
1960 Frantisek Vrba. John
Braine's "Misto nahore"
(Room at the top)
Jiri Valja. William Faulkner's
"Divoke palmy" (wild palms)
                                759.

Albert MOCKEL GRAND PRIZE
FOR POETRY (Belgium)
A major award for poets of
Belgium writing in the French
language, this 50,000 fr prize
is granted every five years by the
Belgian Royal Academy of French
Language and Literature. The
two poets honored since the award
was initiated in 1953 are:
Armand Bermier; and Marcel
Thiry.   760.

MODERN LANGUAGE ASSOCIA-
TION HONORARY FELLOWS
(International--U.S.A.)
The Modern Language Associa-
tion of America (6 Washington
Square North, New York 3),
a professional organization of
scholars in language study and

teaching, established the category of organization affiliation "Honorary Fellow" in 1959 "in order to bring into the Association distinguished men and women of letters of any nationality." The number of Honorary Fellows is limited (maximum of 40, by constitutional provision), and the names of such members are recommended by a committee of the Association to the Executive Council of the group, who proposes the names it chooses for election, for action by the members at the annual meeting of the Association.

Creative writers in the field of poetry, prose, drama, or criticism elected Honorary Fellow include:

1959 T. S. Eliot (U.S.A. -- United Kingdom)
Jorge Guillén (Spain)
Alexis Legér (St.-John Perse) (France)
Jean-Paul Sartre (France)
1960 André Malraux (France)
Ignazio Silone (Italy)
Giuseppe Ungaretti (Italy)
1961 Jorge Luis Borges (Argentina)
René Char (France)
Friedrich Dürrenmatt (Switzerland)
Rómulo Gallegos (Venezuela)
Aldous Huxley (United Kingdom--U.S.A.)
François Mauriac (France)
Pablo Neruda (pseud of Neftali Ricardo Reyes) (Chile)   761.

MOINHO SANTISTA PRIZE (Brazil)
One of the richest cultural rewards in Latin America, this honor has distributed a total of Cr $2. 000. 000 in premiums each year since its establishment in 1955. The prize was founded by the Moinho Santista Corporation, with the organization of the Moinho Santista Foundation (308

Rua São Sento, São Paulo), in celebration of the 50th anniversary of the corporation (S. A. Moinho Santista--Industries Gerais) in Brazil. The sponsor, "among the largest industrial groups of Latin America," annually offers two prizes in Science, Letters or Arts--according to the following yearly schedule: (1) Biology and Physiology, Medicine and Hygiene; (2) Physics, Chemistry; (3) Mathematics, Economics; (4) Philosophy, Science of Education; (5) Social Sciences in General, Legal Science; (6) Arts in General, Music; (7) Literature, Linguistics.

A gold medal, a diploma describing distinguished services to Science, Arts and Letters, and a premium of Cr $1. 000. 000 are presented in each category of award. A jury of scholars and leaders in the professions selects the winners of the prize, which is not applied for, from candidates suggested by Special Committees of award, nominated by the heads of major Academies and Universities of Brazil.

The prize, awarded each year on September 30, signifies outstanding cultural achievement based on the entire life and works of the laureate, and has honored such distinguished Brazilians as writer Alceu Amoroso Lima, who won the award for "Artes e Letras" in 1959. The next regularly scheduled prize for literary achievement will be granted in 1966.   762.

MONACO LITERARY COUNCIL PRIZE (International--Monaco)
The Prix du Conseil Littéraire de Monaco, also designated the "Rainier III Prize," is a rich literary honor (premium 10, 000 NFO which was founded in 1950 by Prince Rainier III of Monaco. Assigned by the Conseil Litté-

raire de Monaco (2 boulevard des Moulins, Monte Carlo), the annual prize distinguishes "an author of considered merit writing in the French language" who has made an unusual literary contribution through his entire work.

A jury of famous writers (Georges Duhamel, André Maurois, Maurice Pagnol, Henri Troyat, Marcel Achard, André Billy) and representatives of French literature from Switzerland, Belgium and Canada has named as laureates (first honored in April 1951 during the national celebration in Monaco):

1951 Julien Green, Works, including "Moira"
1952 Henri Troyat. Works, including "The mountain"
1953 Jean Giono
1954 Jules Roy
1955 Louise de Vilmorin, Works, including "Le violin"
1956 Marcel Brion
1957 Hervé Bazin, Works, including "A tribe of women"
1958 Jacques Perret
1959 Joseph Kessel, Works, including "The lion"
1960 Alexis Curvers (Belgium), Works, including "Tempo i Roma"
1961 Jean Dutourd (Switzerland), Works, including "Au bon beurre"
1962 Gilbert Cesbron   763.

Elisenda de MONCADA PRIZE (Spain)

The award of the review, "Garbo," is granted by a jury composed of women novelists. Since its establishment in 1953, the 25,000 pts premium has been won by such writers as:

1953 Carmen Conde. Las oscuras raíces
1956 Mercedes Rubio de Juan. Las siete muchachas del

Liceo
1957 José Poblador. Pensión
1959 María Jesús Echevarría. Las medias pala bras
                                764.

MONDADORI PRIZE (Italy)

The publisher's prize, no longer awarded, but a significant literary honor in the 1920-1930's, paid L 5.000 each year to a winning novelist, including such recipients as:

1928 F. Perri. Enough of dreams
1929 Vincenzo Cardarelli. Sinatzenith
1930 D. Cinelli. The trap
1933-4 Segre. Agenzia Abram Lewis   765.

MONTEFELTRO PRIZE (Italy)

A joint award of the Libera Universita degli Studi di Urbino and the Amministrazione Provinciale di Pesaro-Urbino (Segreteria del Premio Montefeltro, via Saffi 2, Urbino), the prize offers L 2.000.000 to a living writer, who by his entire literary work, has contributed in an eminent manner to "affirming the Italian creativity in contemporary culture." A second prize of L 500.000 is granted for a scholarly work in Literature, History or Morals. The work should represent an original treatment of a theme vital to the present, and may be published (since January of the year preceding the award) or unpublished.

The prize, which is announced in September each year, has honored:

1960 Giuseppe Ungaretti. Entire poetical work
Arturo Massolo. Prime ricerche di Hegel
1961 Carlo Betocchi. Entire work, including his most recent collection of poems, "L'estate di S. Martino"
Piero Bigongiari. Poesia

italiana del novecento   766.

MONTEIRO LOBATO PRIZE
(Brazil)
The publisher's award, named
for the Brazilian writer, Jose
Bento Monteiro Lobato, was established in 1956 by Companhia
Editora Nacional (rua Sete de
Setembro 97, Rio de Janeiro)
to celebrate the 30th anniversary of the founding of the firm.
The prize is awarded for new fiction, and consists of a Cr
$50.000 premium and publication
of the winning work. Recipients
of the prize, which is administered by Sociedade Paulista de
Escritores, include Osman
Lins, with his collection of
tales, "Os Gestos;" and Geraldo
Santos.   767.

MONTENEGRO PEOPLE'S
REPUBLIC PRIZES (Yugoslavia)
The writers prizes offered
by the People's Republic of
Montenegro (Crna Gora), since
1945 a Federated Republic of
Yugoslavia, have honored such
authors as:
1950 Mihajlo Lalic. Izabrane
pripovijetke (Selected
stories)
Aleksandar Ivanovic. Stihove
(Rhymes)
1954 Radoslav Rotkovic. Lada
tone (The ship is sinking--
novel)   768.

MONTEVIDEO HISTORY PRIZE
(Uruguay)
In a recent Concurso Lit-
terario Municipal, conducted
under the auspices of the
Concejo Departamental de
Montevideo, for the best book of
history published during the
years 1960-1961, the PREMIO
DE HISTORIA winner was Serafín
Cordero, with "Los Charruas,"
which received special commenda-
tion for the research in prehistory.   768A.

Tomás MORALES PRIZE (Spain)
The Casa de Colon de Las
Palmas de Gran Canaria offers
this prize for unpublished poetry
"written in any of the peninsular
vernaculars--Portuguese, Catalan,
Gallego." To compete for the
three prizes offered (12,000;
9,000; and 4,000 pts) poems
must be entered in the contest
by June 1, 1962. Poets winning
the prize include: Rafael Morales, José García Nieto, Pina
Ojeda, María Paz de la Puebla
Franco.   769.

Thomas MORE ASSOCIATION
MEDAL (International--U.S.A.)
The medal, bestowed by the
directors of the Thomas More
Association (210 West Madison
Street, Chicago 6), is given
annually to the publisher "making
the most distinguished contribution to Catholic publishing."
Publishers submit entries for the
bronze medal and plaque, which
have distinguished such works as:
1956 Knopf--José María
Gironella (Spain). The
cypresses believe in God
1959 Hawthorn Books--Henri
Daniel-Rops (France). The
twentieth century encyclopedia
of Catholicism   770.

Fernando MORENO POETRY
COMPETITION (Argentina)
One of several literary honors
awarded by La Sociedad Argentina
de Escritores (Calle Mexico 564,
Buenos Aires), the prize for the
Competition winner in 1961 was
presented to Saúl Yurkiovich for
"Pablo Pájarol" (Paul, the bird).
771.

Justus MÖSER MEDAL (Germany)
Named for Osnabrück's distinguished citizen, Justus Möser
(1720-1794), the historian, statesman and writer who influenced the
thought of his famous contempo-
raries--Goethe and Herder--this

award, consisting of a medal and a certificate, has been granted by the Osnabrück city council (Rat der Stadt Osnabrück, Postfach 1308) since 1944, when it was first presented on January 8, the 150th commemoration of the death of Bürger Möser.

The medal is a general cultural honor, distinguishing outstanding work in Art and Science concerning the work and achievements of Justus Möser, or advancing the cultural life of the city of Osnabrück or the Osnabrück region. Winners of the medal include:

1944 Ludwig Bäte
1952 Christian Dolfen. Work on the "Codex Giole"
1955 Wilhelm Fredemann
1956 Theodor Heuss   772.

Samuel Eduard MQHAGI PRIZE (South Africa)

A literary honor granted for a novel in Zulu, the prize is awarded by the South African Academy of Science and Arts (Suid-Afrikaanse Akademie vir Wetenskap en Kuns, Engelenburg House, Hamilton Street, Pretoria) in its program for the promotion of Bantu literature. The initial prize, granted in 1962, was won by Mosis J. Ngeobo for his novel, "Inkunga Mazulu" (Beware of ignorance, Zulu).   773.

MUNICH LITERATURE PRIZES (Germany)

Since 1927 the city council of Munich (Stadtrat der Landeshauptstadt München) has awarded a prize for literature ("Literaturpreis der Stadt München;" Kulturpreis für Literatur der Stadt München") as one of its general cultural honors Kunstpreise), and since 1957 these cultural prizes have been continued as encouragement prizes (Förderungspreise). Two additional prizes are also offered currently by the city of Munich, and writers as well as other creative artists may be given the awards: CULTURAL AWARD OF HONOR (Kulturellen Ehrenpreis); and SWABIAN ART PRIZES (Schwabinger Kunstpreise). The DM 1.000 premium for each of the Swabian Art Prizes is given by "the three important Munich newspapers: Süddeutsche Zeitung, Münchner Merkur, Abendzeitung." Administered by the Kulturreferat of Munich, with the assistance of prominent scholars and professional persons who form the Committees selecting prize winners, the three prizes that are presently awarded by the city of Munich each year are:

KULTURELLEN EHRENPREIS-- a premium of 15,000 DM to a person who has made eminent contributions in the Arts or Sciences, and who has achieved international recognition in his field. Award winners include: Werner Heisenberg (1958); Bruno Walter (1959); Martin Buber (1960); and Karl Schmidt-Rottluf (1961); and Fritz Kortner (1962).

FÖRDERUNGSPREISE--five awards of 3000 DM each for Painting, Sculpture, Architecture, Music, and Literature (with a sixth prize added in 1961 for "Interpretive Art"). These prizes are granted to young artists working or living in Munich, or the Munich area, and are awarded not so much for completed work or accomplishment, as for the promise of future achievement.

Literary winners of the Kunst- and Förderunfspreise are:
1927 Hans Carossa
1928 Willy Seidel
1929 Josef Magnus Wehner
1930 Hans Brandenburg
1931 Ruth Schaumann

1933 Hans Zoberlein
1934 Ziska Luise Dresler-
    Schember
1935 Georg Britting
1936 Erwin Guido Kolbenheyer
1937 Josef Ponten
1941 Ludwig Friedrich Barthel
1942 Richard Billinger
1943 Wilhelm Weigand
1945 Peter Dörfler
1947 Gertrud von Le Fort
1948 Ernst Penzoldt
1949 Georg Schwarz
1950 Annette Kolb
1951 Gottfried Kölwel
1952 Eugen Roth
1953 Mechtilde Lichnowsky
1954 Wilhelm Hausenstein
1955 Erich Kästner
1956 Wilhelm Herzog
1957 Lion Feuchtwanger.
    Jefta und sein tochter
1958 Georg von der Vring
1959 Oda Schaefer
1960 Walther Kiaulehn
1961 Wolfgang Koeppen
1962 Herbert Schneider

SCHWABINGER KUNSTPREISE-
established in 1961 under the
direction of a Kuratorium of
four members, with an additional member from each of
the five areas of art in which
the 1000 DM prize is awarded,
this annual recognition for art
"in the tradition of the Grand
Swabian Era" was presented
in 1961 to author Peter Paul
Althaus, and in 1962 to Ernst
Hoferichter.   774.

MUSGRAVE MEDALS (Jamaica)
The Gold and Silver Musgrave
Medals of The Institute of
Jamaica (Kingston, Jamaica, W.
I.), established in 1889 as
prizes in national contests and
bestowed since 1906 in the present form, are named for Sir
Anthony Musgrave, Governor
of Jamaica from 1877 to 1883
and founder of The Institute and
other Jamaican cultural and
educational organizations, such

as Jamaica College.
The Medals, general cultural
honors giving recognition to outstanding work in the sciences
and arts--including literature--
have been given historians,
creative writers, and philologists.
The Gold Musgrave Medal,
awarded for "distinguished emi-
nence in literature, science or
art, or for public services in
their promotion in connection
with the West Indies, especially
Jamaica," has been granted
twice in Literature:
    1954 W. Adolphe Roberts.
    History and Literature
    1958 J. E. Clare McFarlane
    (Poet Laureate of Jamaica).
    Poetry
The Silver Musgrave Medal,
not more than two of which may
be granted each year--one during
the month of December--is
awarded for "outstanding merit
in the promotion of literature,
science and art in connection
with the West Indies, especially
Jamaica."
Silver Medalists in Literature
are:
    1924 C. A. Bicknell
    1950 Victor Reid
    1962 Lucille Iremonger
    Poetry--
    1912 Claude McKay
    1930 Una Marson
    1931 L. King
    1935 J. E. Clare McFarlane
    1941 Adolphe Roberts
    1950 Albinia C. Hutton-Davis
    1960 Vivian L. Virtue
    Philology--1961 Frederic G.
       Cassidy   775.

Joaquim NABUCO PRIZE (Brazil)
The Cr $50.000 prize of
Academie Brasileira de Letras
(Avenida Presidente Wilson 203,
Rio de Janeiro) is offered for
writing in social history, political
science, or memoirs--either
unpublished or published during
the two years preceding award.

Winners include:
1956 Brígido Tinoco
1958 Joâo Camilo de Oliveira
Torres. A Democracia
Coroada
1960 Djacir Menezes. Hegel
e a Filosofia Soviética
1962 Nelson Omegna. A
Cidade Colonial
Leandro Tocantins. Forma-
ção Histórica do Acre
776.

EL NACIONAL SHORT STORY
CONTEST (Venezuela)
The publisher's prize of "El
Nacional" (Puerto Escondido a
Puente Nuevo, Caracas) for the
best short story submitted for
consideration has been presented
each year since 1945. Recent
first prize winners include:
Martín de Ugalde, with "Un
real de sueño;" and Hector
Malave Mata, with "La metamor-
iósis."   777.

Eugenio NADAL PRIZE (Spain)
Spain's oldest and most famous
popular novel prize, awarded annually since 1944 by the publisher
Ediciones Destino, S. L. (calle de
Balmes 4, Barcelona), was established in honor of the editorial secretary of the weekly,
'Revista Destino'--Eugenio Nadal,
the Catalan intellectual who died
in 1944. Judges traditionally
meet at the Hotel Oreinte in
Barcelona during the Christmas
holidays to designate from the
unpublished manuscripts entered
for the prize (minimum length 200
typed pages) "the best young
novelist of the year."
The prize, presented each
Spring--with public announcement
of the winner in January--is
considered by some students of
Spanish literature "the most important event in Spanish literary
life." The value of the premium
has increased from the first
award of 5,000 pts to 150,000

pts in 1962. The publisher
acquires all rights for a first
edition of 20,000 copies of the
winning manuscript.
The Nadal Prize, similar to
the Goncourt Prize in the public
interest and prestige of the award
reflected in sales of the winning
fiction work, has been granted:
1944 Carmen Laforêt. Nada
1945 José Félix Tapia. La
luna ha entrado en caso
(entered under the pseud
Eduardo Ayala)
1946 José M. Gironella. Un
hombre
1947 Miguel Delibes. La
sombra del cipres es
alargada
1948 Sebastián Juan Arbó.
Sobre las piedras grises
1949 José Suárez Carreño.
Las ultimas horas
1950 Elena Quiroga. Viento
del norte
1951 Luis Romero. La noria
1952 Dolores Medio. Nosotros.
Los rivero
1953 Luisa Forrellad. Siempre
en capilla
1954 Francisco José Alcántara.
La muerte le sienta bien a
Villalobos
1955 Rafael Sánchez Ferlosio.
El jarama
1956 J. L. Martín Descalzo.
La frontera de Dios
1957 Carmen Martín Gaite.
Entre visillos
1958 José Vidal Cadellans. No
era de los nuestros
1959 Ana María Matute.
Primera memoria (1st part of
a trilogy: "Los Mercaderes")
1960 Ramiro Pinilla. Las
ciegas hormigas
1961 Juan Antonio Payno. El
curso   778.

NAE SUNG LITERARY PRIZE (Korea)
The annual novel award of
the Kyung Hyand Newspaper
(Kyung Hyand Shinmun, Sogong-
dong, Chung-ku, Seoul)

was established in 1958, and
offers a citation, a prize cup,
and a monetary premium of
300,000 hwan to the winner,
who must enter the competition
by the last day of March to be
considered for the award--
granted in January following the
year of application. Recipients
include: Han Suk Chung, with
"The season of the dark;" Ho
Yoo, with "The Moon Season;"
and Hyung Hee Park, with
"Drifting island."   779.

NAMI JAFET PRIZE (Brazil)
    The general cultural award
of the Nami Jafet Institute for
the Advancement of Science and
Culture (Instituto Nami Jafet
para o Progresso da Ciência
e Cultura, 1455 Rua Agostinho
Gomes, São Paulo), established
June 24, 1961, offers annual
premiums of Cr$2.000.000 for
achievement in science and
culture. The prize--consisting
of the premium of two million
cruzeiros in cash, a gold medal,
a diploma; and scholarships--
was founded in memory of the
late industrialist and scholar,
Nami Jafet. The award rotates
as: Scholarships (to be granted
1962, 1964); and Prizes--in the
fields of Science (to be granted
1961, 1966), Technology (to be
granted 1963, 1968), Culture
(including Music, Visual Arts,
Cinema, Architecture--to be
granted 1965, 1970. An advisory
council composed of scholars
(University of São Paulo; Mackenzie University) assists in
administering the honor.
    In 1961, the initial Nami
Jafet Prize was granted to
Academia Brasileira de Ciencias
(Brazilian Academy of Science).
                              780.

NAOKI PRIZE (Japan)
    This prize, like the Akutagawa
Prize, was established in 1935

by Hiroshi (Kan) Kikuchi (1888-
1948), founder of the publishing
company (Bungei Shunjusha) in
which the awarding group--
Japanese Society for the Promotion of Literature (Bungaku
Shinkokai) is located. Awarded
semiannually in memory of the
popular novelist Sanjugo Naoki
(1891-1934), this honor is given
to writers of light fiction--when
the award was first established
it distinguished promising new
writers, more recently it has
been presented to established
authors.
    Recipients of the prize include:
1935 Matsutaro Kawaguchi.
    Tsuruhachi Tsurujiro
    (Tsuruhachi Tsurujiro)
1936 Chogoro Kaionji. Jinsei
    no Ago (Fools of life)
1937 Matsuki Ibuse. Jon
    Manjiro Hyoryuki (John Man-
    jiro, the man who discovered
    America)
1942 Norio Taoka. Gojo
    Ichigo (Obstinate strawberries)
1950 Hidemi Kon. Tenno No
    Boshi (The Emperor's hat)
    Itoko Koyama. Shikko Yuyo
    (Probation)
    Kazuo Dan. Chokonka (Songs
    of deep regret); Shinsetsu
    Ishikawa. Goemon (A true
    story of Goemon Ishikawa, a
    famous chivalrous burglar)
1951 Keita Genji. Eigoya San
    (Mr. Professional English
    User)
    Juran Hisao. Suzuki Mondo
    (Mondo Suzuki, a Samurai)
    Renzaburo Shibata. Iesu No
    Sue (Offspring of Jesus)
1952 Shinji Fujiwara. Tsumina
    onna (A sinful woman)
    Nobuyuki Tateno. Hanran
    (Revolts)
1954 Yoriyoshi Arima. Shushin
    Miketsu Shu (Lifelong un-
    convicted prisoners)
    Haruo Umezaki. Koanken
    Monagatari (Tales of dogs of
    Koan)

1955 Jiro Nitta. Goriki Den
(Lives of guides of Mt.
Fuji)
Kyu Ei-Kan. Honkon (Hong-
kong)
1956 Norio Nanjo. Todai Ki
(A demon in a lighthouse)
Kan-ichi Kon. Kabe no
Hana (Flowers near the wall)
Toko Kon. O-Gin Sama
(O-Gin)
1957 Masanori Ezaki. Ruson
No Tanima (Valley of
Luzon)
1958 Toyoko Yamazaki. Hana
Noren (Proprietress)
Eiji Shimba. Akai Yuki
Saburo Shiroyama. Sokaiya
Kinjo
Kyo Takigawa. Ochiru
1959 Kieko Watanabe.
Mabuchigawa
Yumie Hiraiwa. Haganeshi
Shiro Shiba. Fukuro no Shiro
Koji Toita. Danjuro Seppuku-
jiken
1960 Shotaro Ikenami. Sakuran
Daikichi Terauchi. Hagure
Nenbutsu
Juro Kuroiwa. Haitoku no
Mesu
1961 Tsutomu Minakami. Kari
no Tera
Keiichi Ito. Hotaru no Kawa
781.

NAPLES PRIZE (Italy)
Naples literary prizes, one of
several cultural honors of the
city granted each year with other
awards for achievement in the
arts and sciences, are given
for several forms of writing
(Narritiva, Scholarly Works,
Literary Criticism, Radiotelevision Writing, History) by
the Naples Prize Foundation
(Fondazione Premio "Napoli,"
Palazzo Reale, Naples). Currently premiums are offered
(1962) for: Narratives;
Radiotelevision Documentaries;
Drama; and Poetry. In addition, an international prize of

L 3.000.000 is announced for a
book of poetry published between
January 1, 1960 and December 1,
1962 (works entered in competition to be submitted in seven
copies to the Foundation before
December 31, 1962).
Prize recipients include:
Novel--
1954 Dino Buzzati. Il crollo
della Baliverna
1956 Enrico Pea. Peccati in
piazza
1959 Mario Pomilio. In nuovo
corso
1960 Giuseppe Marotta. Gli
alunni del tempo
History--
1954 Gaetano de Santis. Storia
dei Romani; Storia dei
Greci
1958 Domenico Demarco. Il
Banco delle due Sicilie
Edmondo Cione. Napoli
romantica
Romeo De Maio. Le origini
del Seminario di Napoli
1961 Edmondo Cione. Fran-
cesco De Sanctis
Domenico Demarco. Il crollo
del Regno delle due Sicilie
Ruggero Moscatti. La fine
del Regno di Napoli
Antonio Saladino. L'estrema
difesa del Regno delle due
Sicile
Rosario Villari. Mezzo-
giorno e contadini nell'eta
monderna
Scholarly Works--
1958 Raffaello Franchini.
Metafisica e storia
1960 Vittorio Lugli. Bovary
italiane
Art History--
1957 Giovanni Oscar Onorato.
Iscrizioni pompeiane
1958 Raffaello Causa. Pittura
napoletana dal XV al XIX
secolo
1960 Mario Napoli. La pittura
antica in italia
Radiotelevision Documentary--
1961 Samy Fayad. Caccia agli

adorni (radio)
Ennio Mastrostefano. I fucili
sono amici (television)
Journalism--1961 Aldo
Gianfreda; Biagio Pavesio;
Egidio Sterpa; Marino
Turchi
Drama--
1954 Rosso di San Secondo.
Il ratto di Proserpina
Enrico Bassano. Il Pellicano
ribelle
1955 Cesare Giulio Viola.
Venerdi Santo
1957 Ezio D'Errico. Le
forze
1959 Giuseppe Luongo. Adonai
Poetry--
1954 Giulio Caprin. Un ospite
della vita
Mario Luisa d'Aquino. Rose
d'autunno
1955 Adriano Grande. Avventure
e preghiere   782.

NARCISO PRIZE FOR POETRY
(Italy)
Winners of the poetry prize
offered by the review "Il
Narciso" (via Foligno 44,
Torino) include: Nino Ferrari,
Mauro Donini.   783.

NARRATIVA PRIZE (Italy)
The rich literary honor with
a L 1.000.000 premium for
published prose and criticism
was founded in 1957 by the review "Narritiva" (via Villa Pam-
phili 199, Rome). The prize--
including publication of the winning work--has been granted to
such novels and scholarly works
as:
1957 Roberto Morilia. La
figlia di Zhara (novel)
1958 Francesco Foti. Storia
del saggio (criticism)
784.

NASCIMENTO PRIZE (Chile)
The literary award administered by the Sociedad de Escritores de Chile is a publisher's prize

(Editorial Nascimento, San
Antonio 390, Santiago). Ciro
Alegría (Peru) received the prize
in 1935 for "La serpiente de
oro;" and more recently--in 1953
--Carlos Droguett won the award
with "Sesanta muertos en la
escalera."   785.

NASE VOJSKO PRIZES
(Czechoslovakia)
On "Army Day," September 6,
the publishing house, Nase Vojsko
('Our Army") awards three prizes
each year: For a political book;
For a book of military theory;
For a book of fiction. The
premium of 20,000 Kcs is divided
among the three winners (not
necessarily into three equal sums).
Winners of the fiction prize are:
1960 Kysely. Deset ostrych
(Ten live bullets)
1961 Jan Kalcik. Kral Sumavy
(King of Sumava)   786.

NAUTILUS PRIZE (France)
A science fiction prize--for
popularization or anticipation of
science--was established in 1958
with a 1.000 NF premium (Mme
Andrée Petivon, 5 rue Rousselet
Paris 7e). The award, granted
each year in June, is presented
for the best work of published
science fiction, submitted for
consideration in six copies by
February 15.
Laureates include:
1959 Charles-Noël Martin.
Les 20 sens de l'homme
1960 Pierre Rousseau. Science
de l'avenir
1961 Philippe Tailliez. Plongées
sans cable
1962 Jean E. Chavors. Con-
naissance de l'Univers
787.

Vladimir NAZOR PRIZE
(Yugoslavia)
The award of the publication
"Mladost" (Youth) of Zagreb was
given in 1951 to two writers of

books for young people: Mato
Lovrak, and Josp Pavicic.
788.

Antonio de NEBRIJA PRIZE
(Spain)
The Higher Council for
Scientific Research honored
A. Hermenegildo Fernandez with
its prize for his work, "La
Tragedia en España en el
Siglo XVI." 789.

"NEVEN" PRIZE (Yugoslavia)
The award, granted for out-
standing literature for children,
is offered by the organization,
"Society of Children's Friends."
The "Neven" Drustiva prijatelja
dece, in 1954, was given Branko
Copic for his story, "Dozivljaji
macka Tose" (Adventures of
Tom, the cat). 790.

NEW YORK DRAMA CRITICS
AWARDS FOR THE BEST
FOREIGN PLAY OF THE SEA-
SON (International--U.S.A.)
One of several prizes for
drama granted by the New
York Drama Critics Circle, an
organization established in 1935
by the play reviewers who met
at the famous literary rendezvous
--The Algonquin Hotel--this a-
ward designates the best foreign
play of the New York theater
season, in the judgment of the
drama critics.
Winners include:
1944 Franz Werfel (Austria
--U.S.A.), and S. N.
Behrman. Jacobowsky and
the Colonel
1947 Jean-Paul Sartre (France).
No exit
1949 Maurice Valency.
Adaptation of Jean Giraudoux
(France). Madwoman of
Chaillot
1954 Maurice Valency. Adaptation of Jean Giraudoux
(France). Ondine
1956 Christopher Fry (United

Kingdom). Translation of Jean
Giraudoux (France). Tiger
at the gates
1957 Jean Anouilh (France).
Waltz of the toreadors
1959 Friedrich Dürrenmatt
(Switzerland). The visit
1962 Robert Bolt. A man for
all seasons 791.

NEW YORK HERALD TRIBUNE
CHILDREN'S SPRING BOOK
FESTIVAL PRIZE (International--
U.S.A.)
First awarded in 1937 to
stimulate the publication and sale
of children's books in the Spring
this annual prize is offered for
the best children's book published during the first half of
each year (January through May).
The book of any author may be
submitted in competition. Winners are determined by a panel
of six judges--two in each of
the age group categories: 4-8
years, Picture Books; 9-12
years, Middle-Age Books; 12
years and over, Older Books.
Prizes--$200 for the best book
in each category--are presented
in May at the New York Herald
Tribune offices (230 West 41st
Street, New York 36), and--in
addition--the winning book, and
four "Honor Books" in each age
group, are given special reviews
and mention in the issue of the
"Herald Tribune Book Review"
devoted to Spring children's books.
Among the winners are:
Picture Books--
1944 M. Ilin (pseud of Il'ia
Marshak), and E. Segal
(USSR). A ring and a riddle
1951 Françoise (pseud of
Françoise Seignobosc).
Jeanne-Marie counts her
sheep
1958 Tomi Ungerer (Germany
--U.S.A.). Crictor
Middle-Age Books--1958
Francis Kalnay. Chucaro,
wild pony of the Pampa

Older Books--
1953 Marto Benary-Isbert
(Germany). The Ark
1958 Hans Baumann (Ger-
many). Sons of the Steppe
1962 Paul-Jacques Bonzon
(France). The orphans of
Simitra   792.

NEW YORK HERALD TRIBUNE
WORLD SHORT STORY CON-
TEST (International--France)
A World Short Story Contest,
conducted in 1950-1951 by the
European Edition of the New York
Herald Tribune (21 rue de
Berri, Paris 8e), resulted in a
number of prize-winners, includ-
ing: Bienvenido N. Santos,
who won first prize in the
Philippine Division; K. T.
Mohamed of India, who received
first prize in the Malayalam-
language competition, organized
by the "Hindustani Times" in
India, for his story, "Eyes;" and
Sot Patatzes of Greece, second
prize winner with "Neraida tou
Bythou" (The Nereid of the deep).
                              793.

NEW ZEALAND AWARD FOR
ACHIEVEMENT
Available annually since 1958
to a New Zealand writer, this
Ŀ 100 award is granted by the
New Zealand Minister of Internal
Affairs, on the recommendation
of the Literary Fund Advisory
Committee. Applications are
not made for the award, which
is one of the best-known New
Zealand literary honors (Secretary of Internal Affairs, P.O.
Box 8007, Wellington). Winning
authors include:
1958 J. Frame. Owls do
cry (novel)
1959 R. France. The race
(novel)
1960 O. E. Middleton.
The stone (short stories)
1961 Frances Keinzly.
Tangahano

1962 Errol Brathwaite. An
affair of men   794.

NEW ZEALAND LITERARY FUND
An official government allowance for creative writing has
been made each year since 1947
--in the form of grants and other
aid--by the New Zealand Department of Internal Affairs, advised
by the Literary Fund Advisory
Committee. Approved categories
of assistance awarded by the
Minister of Internal Affairs from
the Fund (in recent years Ŀ2,000)
are:
(1)"Grants towards the publishing
costs (or by other appropriate
means) to enable the publication of writing of literary
merit in such fields as contemporary, creative literature,
historical writing, reprints of
New Zealand classics and
Maori literature;"
(2)"Grants to New Zealand authors
undertaking creative work on
approved projects;"
(3)"Grants towards the cost of
publication (or other appropriate means) of critical books
and studies, to encourage the
reading and study of New
Zealand literature;"
(4)"Such other assistance as the
committee, with better knowledge gained by its experience,
may deem desirable."
Applications for Fund awards
are made to: Secretary for Internal Affairs, P.O. Box 8007,
Wellington.   795.

NEW ZEALAND SCHOLARSHIP
IN LETTERS
An award of the New Zealand
government, "the scholarship is
intended to enable the recipient
to give all or most of his time
to the project or projects nominated
by him, either in New Zealand, or
abroad, during the year of
tenure." New Zealand writers

are eligible for the grant of
Ł 500, made by the New Zealand
Minister of Internal Affairs,
with the advice of the Literary
Fund Advisory Committee.
Candidates wishing to be considered for the Scholarship
should apply before August 31
of the year preceding the grant-
year to: Secretary for Internal
Affairs, P.O. Box 8007, Wellington. Writers who have received
the government grant include:
1957 E. McCormick
1958 P. Wilson
1959 S. Ashton-Warner
1960 M. Shadbolt
1961 M. Duckworth
1962 Maurice Gee
1963 Redmond Wallis; Noel
Hilliard   796.

Martin Andersen NEXÖ ART
PRIZE (Germany, East)
The Kunstpreis der Stadt
Dresden, a general cultural
award of the city of Dresden,
was established in 1958 in
honor of Martin Nexö (1869-
1954), Danish author of German
descent famous for his novels
and novellas of the peasant and
laboring classes, who lived for
several years before his death
in Dresden. The prize, which
is granted for Painting and
Music as well as for Literature,
has honored such authors as:
1959 Auguste Weighardt-
Lazar
1960 Lothar Kempe. Entire
literary work, especially
"Schlösser und Garten in
Dresden;" "Zwischen
Fichtelberg und Hiddensee"
1961 Karl Zuchardt   797.

NIEDERÖSTERREICH CULTURAL
PRIZE (Austria)
The cultural award of Nieder-
österreichischen Landesregierung
was granted in 1961 to: Wilhelm
Szabo, and Hans Hörler.   798.

NIEDERSÄCHSEN KUNSTPREIS
(Germany)
The tradition of literary honors
awarded in this region of Ger-
many is continued in the current
literary prizes included in the
two general cultural awards for
Visual Art, Literature, and Music
which were established in 1961
as annual honors of the Lower
Saxony area:
GROSSER NIEDERSÄCHSISCHER
KUNSTPREIS--25,000 DM prizes
to give recognition to distinguished works of young
German artists;
NIEDERSÄCHSISCHER FÖRDER-
UNGSPREIS FÜR JUNGE KUNST-
LER--10,000 DM prizes awarded
to three young artists.
These official prizes of the
Lower Saxony area (Niedersäch-
sische Landesregierung Hannover)
are administered by the Nieder-
sächsische Kultusminister (Am
Schiffgraben 7-9, Hannover).
A previous literary award of
5000 DM--LITERATURPREIS
DER LANDES NIEDERSÄCHSEN--
established in 1950 to bring recognition for outstanding literary con-
tributions--was presented to such
writers as: Albrecht Schaeffer
(1950); and Hans Henry Jahnn
and Georg von der Vring (1954).
799.

NIGERIAN FESTIVAL OF THE
ARTS PRIZE (Nigeria)
In 1953, the Poetry Award
presented in connection with the
Nigerian National Festival was
won by Gabriel Okara.   800.

NIGERIAN NATIONAL TROPHY
(Nigeria)
This official government prize
of Nigeria, awarded by the Niger-
ian Council of Art and Culture
(Permanent Secretary, Federal
Ministry of Information, Lagos,
Nigeria), honors an "outstanding
contribution in art and culture"

by a national of Nigeria with a
trophy (an open book of gold)
donated by the Nigerian Federal
government. Presented each
year on October 1, the anniversary of Nigerian Independence,
the prize was first won in 1961
by Albert Chinua Achebe for his
novels, "Things fall apart;" "No
longer at ease."   801.

NIGERIAN NOVEL COMPETI-
TION (Nigeria)
    The contest sponsored by the
Nigerian Ministry of Education
offered 25 gns for "novels in
Nigerian languages," with the
deadline for the first competition, September 1, 1960.
    "Specially organized in 1960
to mark the attainment of
Independence," the competition
was directed "to foster the
growth of realistic novels in the
various Nigerian languages," and
"any realistic novel in the
Nigerian language was eligible
for the prize." The jury--whose
members were skilled in one or
more of the languages of the
competing manuscripts; Yoruba,
Hausa, Ibo, Itsekiri (Midwest)--
selected the writings of three
Nigerians for award:
    First Prize--J. O. Jeboda.
    Olowolaiyemo
    Second Prize--A. Ogunranti.
    Puru kan ko yato si Puru
    Third Prize--H. Ogundepo.
    Ekuro 'Lalabaku Ewa
                                802.

Martinus NIJHOFF PRIZE
(Netherlands)
    Created in 1953, and first
awarded in 1954, this annual
prize is a grant of the Prince
Bernhard Fund (Prins Bernhard
Fonds, The Hague, Netherlands).
The award is named to commemorate the poet Martinus
Nijhoff, and the premium of
2.000 fl is presented on January
26, date of the poet's death,

"for translation of literary work
into or from Dutch--alternately,
if possible."
    Winners include:
    1954 Aleida G. Schot. Trans-
        lation of 19th century Russian
        authors
        Bertus van Lier. Translation
        of Sophocles. Antigone
    1955 James S. Holmes.
        Translation of Dutch poetry
    1956 H.W.J.M. Keuls. Trans-
        lation of Dante. La Vita Nuova
    1957 Dolf Verspoor. Transla-
        tion of Dutch poetry into
        French
    1958 Max Schuchart. Transla-
        tion of Tolkien. Lord of the
        Rings
        Bert Voeten. Translation of
        dramatic works--mainly
        English
    1959 Francisco Carrasquer.
        Translation of contemporary
        Dutch poetry into Spanish:
        Antologia de poetas holan-
        deses contemporaneos
        (Madrid, 1958)
    1960 Gerda van Woudenberg.
        Translation of contemporary
        Dutch poetry: Poesia Olan-
        dese contemporanea
        Evert Straat. General trans-
        lation work, especially of
        Shakespeare. Love's Labour
        Lost; Euripides. Heracles;
        and Iphigeneia in Aulis   803.

THE NINE PRIZE (Sweden)
    De Nios Pris, "Prize of the
Nine," awarded by the Society of
the Nine (Samfundet de nio,
Villagatan 17, Stockholm O) consists of annual awards granted
each September in the form of
monetary premiums (currently
two 10,000 kroner prizes, and
smaller awards totalling 8,000
kroner), or--in rare instances--
a gold medal. The prizes and
the Academy of Nine were founded by the Swedish author, Lotten
von Kraemer, at her death in
1913. One of the initial mem-

bers of the Academy of Nine (all of whom are distinguished Swedish literary figures) was Selma Lagerlöf. The major premiums of the "Prize of the Nine" are granted to an author of established reputation and outstanding literary achievement, while the smaller prizes are awarded 'to encourage young talented writers."

Among Swedish authors honored with the award are: Pär Lagerkvist, Vilhelm Moberg, Frans G. Bengtsson, Elin Wägner, Stig Dagerman, Erik Lindegren, Anders Österling, Evert Taube, Olle Hedberg, Karin Boye, Eyvind Johnson.

804.

NINOVA CRITICS' PRIZE
(Yugoslavia)

The annual literary award, established by the paper, "Nedeljne Informativne Novine" (Weekly Informative News), to bring public attention to an "Outstanding Yugoslav Novel," has been presented to:

1954 Dobric Cosic. Koreni (Roots)
1955 Mirko Bozic. Neisplakani (The unshed tears)
1956 Oskar Davico. Beton i svici (Cement and scrolls)
1957 Aleksandar Vuco. Mrtve javke (Dead hallucinations)
1958 Branko Copic. Ne tuguj bronzana strazo (Do not grieve, Bronze Sentinel)

805.

NOBEL PRIZE FOR LITERATURE (International--Sweden)

The world's most famous literary honor, the Nobel Prize for Literature, was established in 1901 by the will of Alfred Bernhard Nobel (1833-1896), Swedish chemical engineer and industrialist, usually identified as the "inventor of dynamite."

One of five Nobel Prizes--international awards financed by the Nobel Foundation (Physics; Chemistry; Physiology or Medicine; Literature; Peace)--the Nobel Prize in Literature is determined by the Swedish Academy (Nobel Committee of the Swedish Academy, Borshuset, Stockholm 2), which--patterned on the "40 immortals" of the Académie Française--is composed of "18 immortals."

Granted for the entire literary work of an internationally distinguished author, rather than for a single writing, the prize is not applied for, as candidates for the award are nominated before February 1 each year by members of the Swedish Academy, and of similar Academies in other countries, professors of languages or history of literature in universities or colleges, previous winners of the Nobel Prize for Literature, presidents of authors' organizations, and 'representatives of the literary activities of their respective countries."

Works of nominees are read and considered by the Nobel Committee of the Academy, and final determination of the prize winner is made about November 10, with public announcement of the award followed by presentation of the honor on December 10, the anniversary of the death of Alfred Nobel. The formal presentation ceremony in Stockholm's Concert Hall is an impressive spectable, when Sweden's King Gustav VI gives each winner a diploma, a gold medal, and a check. By tradition, the laureate in literature receives his award last.

Winners of the Nobel Prize for Literature--increased from an initial premium of $29,110 in 1901 to $48,300 in 1962--are:

1901 Sully Prudhomme (pseud of René François Armand Prudhomme) (France)

1902 Theodor Mommsen
(Germany)
1903 Bjørnstjerne Bjørnson
(Norway)
1904 Frédéri Mistral (France)
José Echegaray (Spain)
1905 Henryk Sienkiewicz
(Poland)
1906 Giosuè Carducci (Italy)
1907 Rudyard Kipling (United
Kingdom)
1908 Rudolf Eucken (Germany)
1909 Selma Lagerlöf (Sweden)
1910 Paul Heyse (Germany)
1911 Maurice Maeterlinck
(Belgium)
1912 Gerhart Hauptmann
(Germany)
1913 Rabindranath Tagore
(India)
1915 Romain Rolland (France)
1916 Verner von Heidenstam
(Sweden)
1917 Karl Gjellerup (Den-
mark)
Henrik Pontoppidan
(Denmark)
1919 Carl Spitteler (Switzerland). In special appreciation of his epic, "Olympian
Spring"
1920 Knut Hamsun (Norway).
For his monumental work,
"Growth of the Soil"
1921 Anatole France (pseud of
Jacques Anatole Thibault)
(France)
1922 Jacinto Benaventa
(Spain)
1923 W. B. Yeats (Ireland)
1924 Wladyslaw Reymont
(Poland). For his great
national epic, "The Peasants'
1925 G. B. Shaw (United
Kingdom)
1926 Grazia Deledda (Italy)
1927 Henri Bergson (France)
1928 Sigrid Undset (Norway)
1929 Thomas Mann (Germany)
Principally for his great
novel, "Buddenbrooks"
1930 Sinclair Lewis (U.S.A.)
1931 Erik Axel Karlfeldt
(Sweden)

1932 John Galsworthy (United
Kingdom). With mention of
"The Forsyte Saga"
1933 Ivan Bunin (Stateless)
1934 Luigi Pirandello (Italy)
1936 Eugene O'Neill (U.S.A.)
1937 Roger Martin du Gard
(France). With special
mention of the novel-cycle,
"Les Thibaults"
1938 Pearl Buck (U.S.A.
1939 F.E. Sillanpää (Finland)
1944 Johannes V. Jensen (Denmark)
1945 Gabriela Mistral (pseud
of Lucila Godoy y Alcayaga)
(Chile)
1946 Hermann Hesse (Switzerland)
1947 André Gide (France)
1948 T.S. Eliot (U.S.A. –
United Kingdom)
1949 William Faulkner (U.S.A.)
1950 Bertrand Russell (United
Kingdom)
1951 Pär Lagerkvist (Sweden)
1952 François Mauriac (France)
1953 Winston Churchill
(United Kingdom)
1954 Ernest Hemingway (U.S.A.)
With mention of "The Old
Man and The Sea"
1955 Halldór Laxness (Iceland)
1956 J.R. Jiménez (Spain)
1957 Albert Camus (France)
1958 Boris Pasternak
(U.S.S.R.). Declined prize
1959 Salvatore Quasimodo
(Italy)
1960 Saint-John Perse (pseud
of Alexis Saint-Léger Léger)
(France)
1961 Ivo Andric (Yugoslavia).
With mention of "The Bridge
on the Drink"
1962 John Steinbeck (U.S.A.)
The Prize was not awarded in:
1914, 1918, 1935, 1940 through
1943.   806.

NOBEL PRIZE FOR PEACE
(International--Norway)
The Nobel Prize for Peace,
granted for contributions toward

world peace, is awarded by the
Norwegian Storting (Parliament).
For the 14th year since the
Nobel Prizes were established
in 1901 from the $9 million
trust fund of Albert Bernhard
Nobel, the peace award was
omitted in 1962. While recipients of the other 1962 Nobel
Prizes--in Physics; Chemistry;
Physiology or Medicine; and
Literature--were selected by
Swedish agencies in Stockholm,
the Norwegian committee for the
peace prize made only a brief
announcement of its decision
not to make the award.

Previous abstentions of the
award occurred in periods of world
crisis-- such as the three years
of World War I and the five
years of World War II. While
the present world situation is
considered too "unsettled" for the
award, the prize may be given
belatedly, as it was in 1961--
when the 1960 prize, which had
been skipped, was granted to
Albert John Luthuli, a Negro
resistance leader of South Africa.
Luthuli was named 1960 Nobel
Prize for Peace winner at the
same time as the 1961 prize
was awarded posthumously to
Dag Hammarskjold (Sweden), the
United Nations Secretary-General
who died in an African plane
crash.

Candidates are nominated for
the award by previous Nobel
Peace Prize laureates and members of all national assemblies
in the world. Annual deadline for
nominations is February 1, and
the names of candidates are kept
secret until the winner is announced in November. This
prize, with the other Nobel
Prizes, is presented in traditional ceremonies on December
10, anniversary of Alfred
Nobel's death.

Winners of the Nobel Prize
for Peace since World War II

are:
1945 Cordell Hull (U.S.A.)
1946 E.G. Balch (U.S.A.)
     J.R. Mott (U.S.A.)
1947 The Friends Service
     Council (United Kingdom)
     The American Friends
     Service Committee (U.S.A.)
1949 J. Boyd Orr (United
     Kingdom)
1950 R. Bunche (U.S.A.)
1951 L. Jouhaux (France)
1952 Albert Schweitzer (France)
1953 G.C. Marshall (U.S.A.)
1954 Office of the United
     Nations' High Commissioner
     for Refugees, Geneva
1957 L.B. Pearson (Canada)
1958 G. Pire (Belgium)
1959 P. Noel-Baker (United
     Kingdom)
1960 Albert John Luthuli
     (South Africa)--granted in
     1961
1961 Dag Hammarskjold
     (Sweden). Posthumous award
                              807.

NOI DONNE PRIZE (Italy)
The prize for a novel was won
in 1955 by S.M. Bonfanti with
"La speranza."   808.

NOMA LITERARY PRIZE (Japan)
An annual award, established
in 1941 by the will of Seiji
Noma, founder of the Dainippon
Yubenkai Kodansha Publishing
Company, granted for "the one
best work" in a wide variety of
writing (Novel; Drama; Literary
Criticism; Essay; Juvenile
Literature; Nonfiction) published
during the previous year in
newspapers, magazines or in
book form.

Recipients of the prize, which
was discontinued for the years
1947-1953, include:
1941 Seika Mayama. Mayama
     Seika Zenshu (Complete
     Works of Seika Mayama)
1943 Roban Koda. Gen Dan
     (Tales of Phantoms)

1946 Mimei Ogawa. Ogawa
Mimei Dowa Zenshu (Col-
lected Nursery Stories of
Mimei Ogawa)
1953 Fumio Niwa. Hebi to
Hato (Snakes and Doves)
1954 Yasunari Kawabata. Yama
no Oto (The Sound of Mountains)
1956 Shigeru Tonomura. Ikada
(Rifts)
1957 Fumiko Enchi. Onnasaka
Chiyo Uno. Ohan
1958 Hideo Kobayashi. Kindai
Kaiga (Modern painting--
essay)
1959 Saisei Murou. Kagero
no Nikki ibun
1960 Shotaro Yasuoka. Umibe
no Kokei
Tomie Ohara. En to iu
Onna
1961 Yasuchi Inoue. Yodo dono
no Nikki   809.

NOMA PRIZE FOR FOSTERING
LITERARY ARTS (Japan)
In 1941 this prize was
established by the will of
Seiji Noma, the founder and first
president of the Kodansha Publishing Company. Administering
agency of the award is the
"Noma Memorial Foundation,"
and the prize is directed to the
encouragement of new talent
among writers. In 1946, the
prize honored:
    Kaoru Funayama. Fue (The
    flute)
    Makoto Hojo. Kangiku
    (Chrysanthemums in mid-
    winter)
    Katsuhiko Otaguro. Kobuna
    Monagatari (Tales of little
    Crucians)   810.

NORDISK RADS LITERATURE
PRIZE (Denmark)
The tenth anniversary of the
Nordisk Rads, February 1962,
was celebrated by the establishment of this 50.000 D kr prize
for the best literary work writ-

ten in the Scandinavian countries.
Initial winner of the prize was
Eyvind Johnson, with "Hans
nades tid."   811.

NORDRHEIN-WESTFALEN GRAND
ART PRIZES (Germany)
The annual cultural award of
the North Rhine-Westphalia
Region (Landesregierung Nordrhein-Westfalen), which is
administered by the minister for
cultural affairs of the area (Der
Kulturminister des Landes Nordrhein-Westfalen, Cecilienallee 2,
Düsseldorf), includes prizes
for the arts (Painting, Sculpture,
Architecture, and Music) as
well as for literature. The
literature prize, determined by
a committee and presented each
July 11 by the State President,
carries a premium of 10.000
DM. In addition to the major
literature prize, an encouragement prize has recently been
granted, and in 1961 the writer
Kay Hoff received the award.
Writers who have won the award
with a single outstanding literary
work or their entire contribution
to letters are:
1953 Emil Barth
1954 Stefan Andres
1955 Gertrud von le Fort
1956 Gottfried Benn
1957 Richard Benz
1958 Ina Seidel
1959 Heinrich Böll
1960 Friedrich Georg Jünger
1961 George Britting   812.

NORWEGIAN CHILDREN- AND
YOUTH-BOOK AWARD
An annual prize of 6.000 N
kr, established and first awarded
in 1951, distinguishes the best
books of Norwegian authors suitable for school libraries.
Granted by the government
agency--Norwegian Ministry of
Church and Education--to "stimulate an interest in good books
for children," the prize is

awarded as: First Prize, N kr 3.000; Second Prize, 2 prizes of N kr 1.000; Third Prize, 2 prizes of N kr 500.

A Committee of selection is annually appointed by the Ministry to "decide which books shall be included in the 'Catalogue of Books for School Libraries,'" and to award the prizes. Among the prize winners (1953) are: Bjorn Rongen, with "Berteken i Risehola" (Spirited off into the mountains); and Thorbjorn Egner, with "Klatremus og de Andre Dyrene i Hakkebakkeskogen" (Klatremus and other animals in Hakkebakkeskogen); and 1957: Nils Slettermark, for "Rull, rull, kjerre;" Ingvald Svinsaas, for "Gaupe i fjellet."   813.

NORWEGIAN LITERARY CRITICS' PRIZE

The Norwegian Federation of Literary Critics established the prize on June 3, 1957, as an honor to be granted to "a Norwegian writer of fiction for a book considered to be of particular artistic value," preferably the book of a young writer. The winning work is determined by vote of the members of the Federation, from nominations for the award made by the Board of the Federation. The prize consists of an etching. Recent winners of the prize (also called, "Norwegian Critics' League Prize") include:

1957 Emil Boyson. Poetry
1958 Gunnar Bull Gundersen. Martin (novel)   814.

NORWEGIAN STATE GRANTS FOR WRITERS

In Norway, as in other Scandinavian countries, the government makes encouragement grants to young writers, and an annual stipend to established authors who have made significant contributions to the national litera-ture. Public literary awards are included in the budget for the Norwegian Ministry of Church and Education (Chapter 233A). At present, these grants which "can be used abroad and are then tax-free," are (1961):

Government Grants, for Writers-
Four three-year grants for N kr 2.000 each;

Government Grants for Artists-
Among the grants for creative artists are those for writers: Five one-year grants for N kr 4.000 each; ten one-year grants for N kr 2.000 each.

In addition, "the following established, meritorious authors receive from the Government a tax-free Artist's Salary Grant for life of N kr 9.000 per year:"

Johan Borgen
Emil Boyson
Johan Falkberget
Mikkjel Fønhus
Magnhild Haalke
Ingeborg Refling Hagen
Hans Henrik Holm
Helge Krog
Inge Krokann
Alf Larsen
Arthur Omre
Tore Ørjasøter
Arnulf Øverland
Gunnar Reiss-Andersen
Nils Johan Ruud
Cora Sandel
Aksel Sandemose
Kristofer Uppdal
Tarjei Vesaas   815.

Angielo Silvio and Jacopo NOVARO PRIZE (Italy)

These awards of the Italian National Academy (Accademia Nazionale de Lincei, via della Lungara 10, Rome) include prizes for literature in various forms. Since it was established in 1944, the literature prize has been presented each five years to an Italian author for--in succession--Poetry; Prose; Criticism; and Philology.

Recipients of the prize, including the JACOPO NOVARO PRIZE--a student award for historical-political or political-economics writing, granted by special juries of the Academy, are:

1948 Criticism and Philology--
  Benedotto Riposati. Studi
  dei Topica di Cicerone
1951 Poetry--Umberto Saba.
  Entire work
  Jacopo Novaro Prize--
  Pietro Rossi. Writings in
  "Giornale degli Economisti,"
  and his journal, "Il Risorgimento" (1847-1850)
1957 Literature--Viola Paszkowsky Papini. La bambina
  guardava
  Jacopo Novaro Prize--
  Nicola Picardi. La vicenda
  dei preti operaie; and
  Orientamenti de tolicesimo
  del II dopoguerra   816.

NOVEMBER 13 PRIZE
(Yugoslavia)
The national honor of the 13 novemri nagrada has been granted to such collections of poems and stories as:
Stories--1953 Simon Drakul.
  Planinata i dalecinite
  (Mountains and distances)
  1954 Jovan Boskovski. Ljudi
  i ptice (Men and birds)
  Blazo Koneski. Lojze
  (Louis).
Poetry--1953 Gane Todorovski.
  Trevozni zvuci (Trevozni
  sounds)
  1954 Slavko Janevski.
  Klovnovi i ljudje (Klovnovi
  and men)   817.

"NOWA KULTURA" PRIZE
(Poland)
Since 1957 the Nagroda tygodnika "Nowa Kultura" has been awarded annually in December by the weekly "Nowa Kultura" (Wiejska 12, Warszawa). The jury, consisting of members of the editorial staff of the publication, selects the winner of the monetary premium from books in the fields of belles lettres and literary criticism recently published in Poland.
Winners are:
1957 Aleksander Wat. Wiersze
  (Poems)
1958 Kazimierz Brandys. Listy
  do pani Z.; and Czerwona
  czapeozka
  Andrzej Stawar. Tadesz Boy-
  Zelenski
1959 Tadesz Konwicki.
  Dziura w niebie
  Kazimierz Kumaniecki.
  Cyceron i jego czasy
1960 Stanislaw Wygodzki.
  Koncert zyczen (short stories)
  Maciej Putkowski. Poludnie
  (received a citation)
  Marek Jaroslaw Ryszkiewicz.
  Czlowiek z glowa jastrzebia
  (poems) (received a citation)
                        818.

"NEUVA ESPAÑA" NOVEL
PRIZE (Mexico)
The publisher's prize for a Mexican novel, offered by Compania General de Ediciones (Schiller 227 D, Mexico, D.F.), was won in 1958 by Victoriano Cremer with "Libro de Caín."
                        819.

OBERÖSTERREICH DRAMA
PRIZE (Austria)
The award, one of several offered by the province Oberösterreich (Landhaus, Klosterstrasse 7, Linz), was granted on June 26, 1954 in celebration of the 150th anniversary of the theater, Landestheaters Linz. Playwrights honored were:
Franz Pühringer (S 10.000 award); Helmut Schwarz (S 5.000 award); Herta Staub (S 3.000 award).   820.

OBERÖSTERREICH FÖRDERUNGS-
PREIS (Austria)

Offered each year by the
province Oberösterreich to encourage young authors, and most
recently carrying a premium of
S 10.000, The Upper Austria
Encouragement Prize is granted
to a number of writers at each
time of award. Among the winners are: Karl Kleinschmidt;
Kurt Klinger; Hanns Gottschalk;
Gerhart Baron; Karl Wiesinger;
Helmut Degner; Rudolf List.
821.

OCTOBER PRIZE OF BELGRADE
(Yugoslavia)
The Oktobarska Nagrada
Beograda, a literary honor of
Belgrade, the capital of Yugoslavia and of the Federated
Republic of Serbia, has been
awarded for such literary works
as:
1956 Branko Copic.
Dozivljaji Nikoletine (Adventures of Nicoletin Bursac)
1957 Milan Dedinac.Od nemila
do nedraga (From one who
doesn't care for me to one
who doesn't like me)
1958 Oskar Davico
Stevan Raickovic 822.

Adam Gottlob OEHLENSCHLÄGER
SCHOLARSHIP (Denmark)
The Scholarship is offered
in memory of Adam Oehlenschläger (1779-1850), Danish epic
and lyric poet and dramatist
who was a pioneer in the Romantic Movement in European letters.
An annual award of 2.000 D kr
established in 1954, the grant is
distributed by a "committee consisting of a representative from
the Danish Ministry for Cultural
Affairs, who acts as Chairman,
and from the board of the
Danish Authors' Association."
Among Danish writers
honored with the award are:
1954 Marin A. Hansen
1955 H. C. Branner
1956 Jacob Paludan

1957 Sigurd Elkjaer
1958 Hans Hartvig Seedorff
1959 Karl Bjarnhof
1960 Mogens Jermiin Nissen
1961 Carl Erik Soya 823.

O'GROWNEY AWARD (Ireland)
The award, administered by
the Irish Academy of Letters
(c/o Abbey Theatre, Pearse
Street, Dublin), is one of several
literary honors granted by the
Academy. The prize is presented for the "best imaginative
work published in Gaelic."
824.

OLAVO BILAC PRIZE (Brazil)
Named for Olavo Braz Martins
dos Guimarães Bilac (1865-1918),
Portuguese poet who is considered
the founder of Brazil's Parnassian School of poets, this Cr
$50.000 prize of Academie
Brasileira de Letras (Avenida
Presidente Wilson 203, Rio de
Janeiro) is granted for the best
book of poetry--unpublished or
published during the two years
preceding the year of award--
entered in competition.
Recipients of the honor, one of
Brazil's most important in the
public recognition of outstanding
work of a poet, include:
1956 João Cabral de Melo Neto
1957 Stella Leonardos. Poesia
em tres tempos
1959 Thiago de Melo. Vento
Geral
1961 Péricles Eugênio da
Silva Ramos. Lua de Ontem
825.

OLDENBURG DRAMA PRIZE
(Germany)
The award offered by the city
of Oldenburg and the Oldenburg
State Theater honors "an outstanding contribution to theatrical
literature." In 1957, the prize--
which is presented by the Olden-
burg-Staatstheater--was won by
Stefan Andres, with "Sperr-

zonen."   826.

OLYMPIC GAMES LITERATURE
COMPETITION (International)
Patterned on the contests of
the Olympic Games of Greece,
the present Olympic Games included a Literature Competition
as part of the Art Competition
held in connection with the
Games from 1912 to 1948. Prizes
were awarded for Literature (as
well as for Art, Music, Painting,
Sculpture), but beginning in 1952
with the Games in Helsinki, the
official rules of the contests
state: "Art and literary exhibitions which may be organized
during the Games and in connection with them are not fixed."
While art and literary exhibitions
may be held in connection with
the current Games, no prizes
are awarded and no competitions
are held.
    Laureates of literature, dur-
ing the years a Literature
Competition was an official part
of the Olympic Games, are:
    1912 Stockholm--George
      Horrod and M. Eschbach
      (Germany). Ode to Sport
    1920 Antwerp--Raniero
      Nicolai (Italy). Canzoni
      Olympioniche
    1924 Paris--G. Charles
      (France). The Olympic
      Games
    1928 Amsterdam--Kazimierz
      Wierzynski (Poland). Laur
      Olimpijski (Lyric and
      Speculative Works)
    F. Mezo (Hungary). L'His-
      toire des jeux Olympiques
      (Epic Works)
    1932 Los Angeles--Paul Bauer
      (Germany). Am Kangehen-
      zonga
    1936 Berlin--Felix Dhunen-
      Sondinger (Germany). Der
      Laufer (Lyrics)
    Uhro Karhumaki (Finland).
      Avoveteen--Ins Freie Wasser
      (Epic Works)

1948 London--Aale Tynni
  (Finland). Laurel of Hellas
  (Lyrics)
Giani Stuparich (Italy). La
  Grotta (Epic Works)   827.

OMEGNA PRIZE (Italy)
    A cooperative literary award
of thirty Italian cities--including
Milan, Torino, Bologna, Modena,
Reggio Emilia--with an endowment of L 1.000.000, the prize
is administered by the Comune of
Omegna in Novara Province. The
award, which is granted in
September each year, honors
works of poetry, fiction, and
scholarly writing "affirming moral
values in social questions." Among
the authors given recognition by
the award are:
    1959 Henri Alleg (France). La
      question (La tortura)
    1960 Jean-Paul Sartre (France).
      Entire work   828.

OMNIA PRIZE (Italy)
    The review "Omnia" (via
Bitinia 19; Casella postale 4120,
Rome) offers the prize annually
for writing in various categories
that have included: Poetry,
Drama, Prose (Novelle, Fiabe,
Racconti), Short Stories, Scholar-
ly Writing, Children's Literature.
The winners, whose work is
published by "Omnia," receive a
monetary premium (first to sixth
prize), or other award, such as
"Penna d'oro;" "Grande lauro
Omnia."
    Among the many writers re-
ceiving prizes each year are:
Poetry--
    1957 Franco Buttaglieri;
      Valentine Melecrinis (equally
      divided)
    1959 Dario Galli
Scholarly Writing--
    1957 Gastone Imbrighi (econom-
      ics); Gina Catanzaro
      (philosophy); Licia Garziano
      (literature)
    1958 Luigi Vita. Appunti

sulla poesia e sui poeti del
Dopoguerra
Drama--
1957 Maria Flori. Per te
uomo; Pio Macrelli.
Nuvole (equally divided)
829.

ONDAS PRIZE (Spain)
The organization Sociedad
Española de Radiodifusión (Caspe
6, Barcelona), which owns 42
radio stations in Spain, awards
this prize through the Revista
"Ondas" to an outstanding novel
in Spanish for "radiodifusion."
The premium, ranging from
30,000 to 75,000 pts and recently (1960) 50,000 pts, has been
awarded to such writers as
Alberto Oliveras, and:
1954 Enrique Nácher. Sobre
la Tierra Ardiente
1959 Ramón Nieto. La Fiebre
1960 A. Fraguas Saavedra.
Don Generoso y Los
Fantasmas
1961 Antonio Prieto. Elegia
por una Esperanza   830.

ORDER OF THE NETHERLANDS
LION (Netherlands)
This national honor of the
Netherlands, "can be awarded
by her Majesty the Queen
to those who have shown
patriotism, special zeal, and
loyalty in the performance of
their civic duties, or extra-
ordinary proficiency in science
and art." The decoration has
been presented to such distinguished men of Dutch letters
as:
1942 Hendrik Willem van Loon
1958 Adriaan Roland Holst
831.

Ramalho ORTIGÃO PRIZE
(Portugal)
The Portuguese government
biennial award of 8.000$,
offered by Secretariado Nacional
da Informacão, for the best

writing in essay form has been
granted essayists including:
1952 M. Simões Dias.
Aspectos da Canção popular
Portuguesa
1956 Francisco Dias Agudo.
Introdução à Vida Docente
1958 Carlos Eduardo Soveral.
A Nostalgia de Hesíodo
832.

Laura ORVIETO PRIZE (Italy)
The major Italian award for
children's literature, honoring
prose and poetry by Italian
authors which has not been published in book form, requires
that competing works be submitted
to Segretaria del Premio (via
Enrico Potti 1, Florence) by
October 31 each year. Recipients
of the prize--a monetary premium
(L 500.000 for novel or novella;
L 200.000 for poetry), and publication by Casa Editrice "Bem-
porad Marzocco," Florence--
are:
1958 Ada Bellandi Taddei. Il
meraviglioso mare
Poetry--Idilio Dell'Era. Il
canzoniere del fanciullo
1962 Lucia Tumiati. Salta-
frontiera
Dea Duranti. Il Melo (The
appletree, children's poems)
833.

OSLO PEACE LIBRARY AWARD
(International--Norway)
The Norwegian "Book of the
Library of Peace," was granted
in 1961 to Hans Helmut Kirst
(Germany) for, "Fabrik der Of-
fiziere."   834.

OSTDEUTSCH KULTURRAT
PLAQUE (Germany)
The annual award, established
in 1956 by the East German
Cultural Council (Ostdeutsch Kulturrat) in Bonn, consists of a
medal presented to two persons
who have made the most outstanding contributions to the

cultural life of the area. The prize is usually given in the autumn on Ostdeutschen Kulturtag. In 1957, the prize for literature honored Agnes Miegel.   835.

Lars K. and Ingeborg OSTERHOLT PRIZE (Norway)
Distributed annually on January 2, this prize of N kr 3.800 is awarded "by two representatives from the Literary Council and one person named by the Ministry of Church and Education."
                                   836.

OTAVA PRIZES (Finland)
These publisher's prizes, granted each year for prose and poetry ('Lyric Prize"), include among recent winners:
Prose--
    1959 Veijo Meri
    1960 Iiris Kähäri
    1961 Matti Hälli
Poetry--
    1959 Paavo Haavikko
    1960 Maila Pylkkönen
    1961 Tuomas Anhava   837.

OTHON LYNCH PRIZE (Brazil)
The Premio Othon Lynch Bezerra de Melo, offered by one of Brazil's most populous states, Minas Gerais (Secretaria da Educacão), grants Cr$20.000 to a resident author.   838.

Kosta OURANIS PRIZE (Greece)
One of a number of prizes offered each year since 1950 by a group of writers known as "The Group of Twelve," (and so also called "The Group of Twelve Prize"), the Ouranis Prize is named for Kosta Ouranis, Greek poet and chronicler. The award offers a premium of Drs 15,000 for the best prose narrative published in Greece during the preceding year and deposited in the Greek National Library. In 1961, Spyros Plaskovitis won the prize with his novel, "The

barrier." Other winners are:
    1951 Asteris Kovatris.
         Peasants (won majority vote
         but not the prize)
    1952 Eva Vlami
    1953 Markos Lazaridis
    1954 Galateia Saranti
    1955 Angelos Vlahos
    1956 Rodis Provelengios
    1957 Takis Hatzianagnostou
    1958 Nikos Athanasiadis
    1959 Julia Iatridi
    1960 Julia Davara   839.

PAESTUM PRIZE (Italy)
The Salerno prize of Accademia di Paestum (Eremo Italico--Sant'Angelo Mercato Sanseverino) is granted in alternate years for poetry and painting. The first prize for poetry--"La Rosa d'Oro"--has been won by:
    1958 Giorgio Croce
    1960 Aldo Ravina
    1961 Vicenzo D'Ambrosio
                                   840.

PAKISTAN PRESIDENT'S MEDAL FOR PRIDE OF PERFORMANCE
An award for literature is included in the Rs 100,000 granted each year by the President of Pakistan "in recognition of notable achievement" in a variety of Cultural and Professional Activities, that include the Arts, Science, Literature, Sports, Nursing, Farming. The Meritorious Awards, administered by the Pakistan Ministry of Education and Scientific Research, are granted on the national holiday, Pakistan Day, March 23.
Election to the award is made by the President of Pakistan on the recommendation of a Committee appointed by the Pakistan government. Various sub-committees in each area of award consider nominations made by subject groups and authorities. In the field of Literature, such nominating organizations are

the Pakistan Writers' Guild,
the Bengali Academy, the Board
for the Advancement of Literature.
 Recipients of the medal and
the monetary premium (Rs
10,000, except as indicated)
are announced in the "Gazette of
Pakistan" on the day of award,
and have included:
 Urdu Language
1958 Hafiz Jalandhari
1959 Moulvi Abdul Haq
1960 S.M. Abdullah (Rs 5,000)
 Bengali Language
1958 M. Shahidullah
 Hasimuddin (Rs 5,000)
1959 Maulana Akram Khan
1960 Ghulam Mustafa (Rs
 5,000)
1961 Farrukh Ahmad (Rs
 5,000)   841.

PAKISTAN WRITERS' GUILD
PRIZES
 In addition to administering
Pakistan's richest literary
award--the Adamjee Prize--
the Pakistan Writers' Guild
offers three other literary prizes
for outstanding writing by
Pakistan citizens:
1. PAKISTAN WRITERS' GUILD
AWARDS--Annual awards of Rs
 1,000 each, announced on the
 Guild anniversary of January
 31, for outstanding writing in
 Urdu and in Bengali in each
 of five forms of literature:
 Poetry; Novelette, Short
 Story, Reportage; Drama and
 One-Act Play; Literary Criticism; Humour--prose or
 poetry.
2. "HAM QALAM" AWARDS--
 Annual prizes of Rs 500,
 granted by the monthly Urdu-
 language publication of the
 Pakistan Writers' Guild "for
 the various contributions published in Urdu magazines during the year." First award
 period for July 1960 to June
 1961 included the following

prize winners:
 N.M. Rashad. Sahra
 Nawarde Peer Dil (poem)
 Hajra Masroor. Teesri
 Manzil (short story)
 Ghulam Mustafa. Saqafati Urdu
 (literary criticism)
 Shaikh Ayaz. Translation of
 Sindhi Kafees--regional
 languages
3. PAKISTAN WRITERS' GUILD
REGIONAL LANGUAGE AWARDS
 Annual honors, announced on
 the Guild anniversary of
 January 31, for various forms
 of creative writing (Prose--Rs
 1,000; Poetry--Rs 1,000;
 Publications in journals and
 periodicals--Rs 250 each for
 Essays, Essays in Research
 and Criticism, Short Story,
 Poetry) in four regions:
 Pushto, Punjabi, Sindhi,
 Gujrati.   842.

Carlos PALANCA MEMORIAL
AWARDS FOR LITERATURE
(Philippines)
 These annual literary honors,
established in 1950 by La Tondena,
Inc. (453 Echague, Manila),
in memory of the founder, Don
Carlos Palanca, Sr., offer prizes
for published short stories (3
awards--P 1,000; P 500; P 250),
and for one-act plays (3 awards--
P 500; P 300; P 200). Each of
the series of awards is granted
for works in English and in
Tagalog, the two officially recognized languages of the Republic
of the Philippines.
 Winning works are selected
from the short stories submitted
by any periodical in the Philippines
(five outstanding stories published
during the year may be entered in
competition by July 1 of the following year); and from the plays
--unpublished and unproduced--
submitted by any playwright.
Results of the competition are
announced by September 1 each
year.

First Prize winners have included:
English Language--Short Story
1951 Juan T. Gatbonton. Clay
1952 Patricia S. Torres
(pseud of Kerima P. Tuvera).
The virgin
1953 Andreo Cristobal Cruz.
The quarrel
1954 Romy V. Diaz. Death in
a sawmill
1955 J.C. Tuvera. Ceremony
1956 Kerima Polotan. The
trap
1957 J.C. Tuvera. High into
morning
1958 Nick Joaquin. La Vidal
1959 F. Sionil Jose. The God
stealers
1960 Kerima P. Tuvera. The
tourists
1961 Kerima P. Tuvera. The
sounds of Sunday
English Language--One-Act Play
1954 Alberto S. Florentine.
The world is an apple
1955 Magtanggul Asa. The
long dark night
1957 Jesus T. Peralta. Play
the Judas
1958 Azudena Grajo Uranza.
Versions of the dawn
1959 Epifanio San Juan.
In the tangled snare
1961 Jesus T. Peralta.
Longer than mourning
Tagalog Language--Short Story
1952 Pablo N. Bautista.
Kahiwagaan
1953 Buenaventura S. Medina.
Kapangyarihan
1954 Teodoro A. Agoncillo.
Sa Kamatayan Lamang
1955 Genoveva Edroza-Matute.
Paglalayag sa Puso ng Isang
Bata
1957 Pedro S. Sandan. Sugt
1958 P.B. Peralta-Pineda.
Ang Mangingisda
1959 Buenaventura Medina.
Dayuhan
1960 Eduardo Bautista Reyes.
Luntiang Bukid
1961 Genoveva Edroza-

Matute. Paruza
Tagalog Language--One Act Play
1954 Dionisio Santiago Salazar.
Ang Kuwatro de Hulyo
1955 Julita and Fidel Sicam.
Pitong Taon
1956 Ruben Vega. Karalitaan
1958 Amado V. Hernandez.
Muntinlupa
1960 Rolando P. Bartolome.
Kamatayan ng Mga Simulain
1961 Amado V. Hernandez.
Magkabilang Mukha ng Isang
Bangol   843.

PALMA DE MALLORCA PRIZES
(Spain)

The Premio Ciudad de Palma,
established by the city of Palma
(Ayuntamiento de Palma de
Mallorca) in 1956 is offered for
various forms of writing: History, Science, Statutory Law, Novel.
Three of these prizes are listed
separately (which see): Gabriel
Maura Prize--an award for a
novel of 20,000 to 50,000 pts;
Miguel de los Santos Oliver
Prize--an award for Journalism
of 2,500 pts; Juan Alcover Prize
--granted for poetry. Jose M.
Quadro Prize for works on the
prehistory of Mallorca and the
Bartolomé Ferrer Prize of
5,000 pts for drama are additional awards of the city of Palma.
Among the winning authors
are:
1956 Juan Bonet. Un poco
locos francamente
1957 Lorenzo Villalonga
(novel)
Rafael Jaume (poetry)
Rafael Guinar (folklore)
Rafael Rámiz (journalism)
1958 Gabriel Cortes. L'altre
Cami (novel)
Baltasar Porcel. Els con-
demnats (drama)
Guillermo Rosello-Bordoy
(history)
Valentin Arteaga (Castilian
poetry)
Baltasar Coll (Majorcan

poetry)
Joaquin Caldentey (journalism)
1959 Bartolome Goya. Los
Sonetos (poetry)
Alejandro Cuello. El Bosque
de la Abuela (drama)
Arturo Ponce. Ensayo de
Entomologia (science)
1960 Baltasar Porcell. Sol
Negro (novel)
Juan Nonet. Cuasi una dona
moderna (drama)
1961 Jaime Vidal. A dos
viatges per mar (poetry)
Manuel Pico. El llanto de la
cigarra (novel)
Jose Salas Guiror (journalism)
844.

Juan **PALOMO PRIZE** (Spain)
The award of the "Revista
Semana" (Paseo de Onésimo
Redondo 26, Madrid) is a "prize
that is not a prize," as it is a
literary honor "without monetary
prize, without competition, and
without jury." In 1961 Luis
Rosales was the recipient of the
award in recognition of his essay,
"Cervantes y la Libertad."
845.

PAMPLONA PRIZE (Spain)
The 25,000 pts prize of
Diputación Provincial of Pamplona
was awarded in 1955 to Luis
García Royo for his biography of
San Francisco Javier. 846.

**PAN AMERICAN CONGRESS OF
THE THEATER COMPETITION**
(Latin America--Mexico)
The Concurso of the Teatro de
Ensayo, conducted in Mexico
City in October 1957, granted
a prize to James Ernhard
(pseudonym of Camilo Perez de
Arce) for his play, "Comedia
para asesinos." 847.

**PAN AMERICAN ROUND
TABLE CONTESTS** (Mexico)
The Pan American Round
Table, an organization active in

Mexico City "in the promotion of
the writing of good children's
books in Spanish with a Mexican
background" (Sullivan, p. 12),
has sponsored several book contests for the best manuscript
suitable for children. In April
1954 the First Prize of the con-
test--the third held--was presented Sr. Antonio Roblés for
"Ocho Estrellas y Ocho Cenzontles!"
848.

**PAN SCANDINAVIAN FICTION
PRIZE** (Europe)
This award for the best novel
by a Scandinavian writer--
previously offered, but not granted
at present--was won in 1959 by
Bo Grandien with "Hem till
stallet," according to the publisher offering the honor--Wahl-
strom & Widstrand, AB (Reger-
ingsgatan 83, Stockholm). 849.

PARAGGI PRIZE (Italy)
The novel award was won in
1950 by Giuseppe Marotta, known
also for his short stories,
journalism and scenarios, with
"L'oro di Napoli" (The gold of
Naples). 850.

PARIS CITY PRIZE (France)
The Prix de la Ville de Paris,
for which the City Council of
Paris (Conseil d'Administration)
acts as the jury, is an annual
award of 10 NF for a prose
work--novel, essay, study, three-
act play. Under the sponsorship
of the Syndicat des journalistes
et Écrivains (1 rue Jules-Parent,
Rueil-Malmaison, Seine-et-Oise),
the award has been granted since
1953 to such writers as:
1957 Jacques Hillairet. Con-
naissance du vieux Paris
1958 Jacques Hillairet. Gibets,
piloris
1959 Mme L. Delapalme.
Consultez-moi 851.

PARIS GRAND PRIZE FOR
LITERATURE (France)
Granted each year for a different form of writing--in the order: Novel, Poetry, Criticism, Essay, History, Philosophy--the Grand Prix Littéraire de la Ville de Paris is a 4.000 NF prize of the Paris Municipal Council (Conseil Municipal de Paris, 4e Commission, Hôtel de Ville de Paris). Under the supervision of the Direction des Beaux-Arts de la Ville de Paris (14 rue François-Miron), the honor is awarded each January for a work of the previous year, and is determined by a jury composed of eight municipal council members and eight writers selected by the Société des Gens de Lettres.

Among the laureates, who are honored for their entire literary work, are:

1937 Roger Martin du Gard (novelist)
1938 André Dumas (poet)
1946 Léon-Paul Fargue (essayist)
1947 André Suarès (philosopher)
1948 Paul Vialar (novelist)
1949 Philippe Chabaniex (poet)
1950 Jean Paulhan (essayist)
1951 Jean Rostand (philosopher)
1952 Yves Gandon (novelist)
1953 Paul Fort (poet)
1954 Jean Guehenno (critic)
1955 Louis Madelin (historian)
1956 PRIX SPECIAL: Pierre Mac Orlan
     Francis Carco (essayist)
1957 Maurice Fombeure (poet)
1958 Gérard Bauer (essayist)
1959 Daniel Halévy (historian)
1960 Blaise Cendrars
1961 Eugène Pascal-Bonetti (poet)

Most recent prizes (3,000NF)of the Conseil Général de la Seine have honored:
1960 André Billy; 1961 Paul-

Marie Duval; 1962 Armand Lanoux.   852.

PARIS PRIZE (France)
The Prix de Paris of the Académie des Lettres et des Arts (13 rue des Archives, Paris 4e) is granted each year for a novel or other literary work published during the preceding 12 months. The 50 NF premium, granted during June since 1947, has been presented recently to:

1955 Michele Brunet. A l'ombre du troisième jour
1956 Pierre-Valentin Berthier. Cheri-Bonhomme
1957 Robert Sabatier. Boulevard
1958 Georges Montforez. Les enfants du marais   853.

Giovanni PASCOLI PRIZE (Italy)
Honoring the 50th anniversary of the death of the Bolognese poet, Giovanni Pascoli (1855-1912), various prizes are offered: For poetry in Italian--a prize of L 1.000.000 by Palazzo della Provincia, Lucca--closing date September 13, 1962; For an article published in an Italian journal or review from October 1, 1961 to July 31, 1962-- L 1.000.000; and a PREMIO PASCOLI, the First Prize of which was presented in July 1962 in Naples (via della Vergini 68) to the poet Pasquale Autiello.   854.

Banjo PATERSON FESTIVAL LITERARY PRIZES (Australia)
The Banjo Paterson Festival Committee (38 Allenby Road, Orange, New South Wales) awards these prizes each year in November "to foster Australian literature and to commemorate Andrew Barton Paterson, one of Australia's best-known poets, who was born near Orange on March 17, 1864." Various categories of writing (Poetry, Short Story, One-Act Play,

Literary Criticism) are awarded
monetary premiums ranging from
L50 to L100, and any Australian
citizen may compete for the
prizes by submitting manuscripts
--with an application form--
before October 1.

Winners of the awards, which
have been granted since 1960,
include:

G.J. COLES' PRIZE FOR SHORT
STORY (L100)--1960 Frank
Cusack. The last day of
summer
MACQUARIE WORSTEDS' PRIZE
FOR POETRY (L50)--1960 Eric
C. Rolls. The hare
SILVER JUBILEE PRIZE FOR
ONE-ACT PLAY (L50)--1960
John McKinney. Neighbors
ANGUS AND ROBERTSON PRIZE
FOR POETRY (L50)--1961
J.F. Kennedy. The stout
hearted poet
ORANGE CITY COUNCIL PRIZE
FOR SHORT STORY (L50)--
1961 B.W. Jackson. The
first bridge   855.

Jean PAUL MEDAL (Germany)
First awarded in 1925 and
reestablished after a lapse of
some years in 1950, this prize
of the Jean Paul Gesellschaft in
Bayreuth is named for Jean Paul
Friedrich Richter (1763-1825),
one of Germany's greatest
romantic novelists, who used the
pseudonym "Jean Paul" for many
of his romances. The medal is
granted to persons who through
their work on Jean Paul or on
the Gesellschaft have made a
special literary contribution in
the spirit of "Jean Paul."

Poets and prose writers who
have been honored with a Silver
Medal--a Bronze Medal is also
awarded--include: Willy Arndt,
Hermann Burte, Robert Linden-
baum, Otto Michel, Rudolf Pannwitz, Rudolf Paulsen, Armin
Renker, Rudolf Alexander
Schröder.   856.

Samuli PAULAHARJU PRIZE
(Finland)
To commemorate the writer
Samuli Paulaharju, this prize is
given every five years to an
author who has "skillfully portrayed
the Finnish popular culture."
Most recent prize-winner (1959)
was Pertti Virtaranta.   857.

PAULÉE DE MEURSAULT
PRIZE (France)
This award, which has been
granted to some of the most
famous of contemporary French
authors, brings 100 bottles of
Meursault wine (Grand vin blanc
de Meursault) to the honored
writer from Syndicate d'initiative
et de tourisme, Hôtel de Ville,
Meursault, Côte d'Or.

Works eligible for the award
are published books concerning
the French countryside--with
preference given writing concerning the area of Burgundy
(Bourgogne) or of its wines and
vineyards. The prize is granted
each year after the third Sunday
in November, and competing
works must be submitted for consideration in six copies by July
31. Among the prize winners
are:
1934 Paul Cazin. La tapisserie
des jours
1936 Pierre Rouget. Rimes
sans raisons
1951 Colette. En pays connu
1959 Francis Ambriere
1960 Maurice Druon
1961 Jacques de Lacretelle
1962 Michel de Saint-Pierre
858.

PAULIST ACADEMY OF LETTERS
PRIZES (Brazil)
Three Prêmios Academia Paulista de Letras (Largo do Arouche
312, Sao Paulo) of Cr$100.000
each are granted to works entered in competition by March
31: PRÊMIO ALVERES DE
AZEVEDO--for poetry; won in

1959 by Jamil Almansur Haddad;
PRÊMIO JULIO RIBEIRO--for
novel; and PRÊMIO AFONSO
D'E. TAUNAY--for essay.
                          859.

Cesare PAVESE PRIZE (Italy)
The fiction prize of Ente
Provincial per il Turismo of
Cuneo (Corso Nizza 17) was
awarded in 1957 to Lalla Romano
for the novel, "Tetto Murato."
                          860.

"PEOPLE'S EDUCATION"
PRIZE (Yugoslavia)
The prize of Narodne Prosvjeta
is an award of the Sarajevo publisher Narodne Prosvjeta (People's Education'), and was established in 1955 as a regular annual
prize for the "best contemporary
Yugoslav novel." Granted on the
basis of a competition held each
year, the prize is given to some
entries in the contest and other
entries are purchased for publication. Both works winning a
prize and those purchased for
publication are announced in the
publisher's series: "The Contemporary Yugoslav Novel."
Winners include:
1955 Camil Sijaric; Mihailo
Renovcevic; Dragoslav Grbic
1956 Berislav Kesier; Vuk
Filipovic
1957 Nane Marinovic;
Dragoslav Popovic; Gordana
Olujic   861.

Paul PELLIOT PRIZE (France)
Created in 1946 to honor the
memory of the famous French
scholar, Paul Pelliot, this prize
is granted annually in February
for scholarly works--published
by Presses Universitaires de
France--which are distinguished
by the importance of their content and the quality of their
literary style. Two awards of
1.000 NF are given--one for
the work of a mature scholar

or a professor with published
work; the other for the writing of
a beginning author (Secrétariat du
Prix Paul Pelliot, 108 boulevard
Saint-Germain, Paris 6e).
Among major award winners
are:
1955 Louis Reau. Iconographie
de l'art chrétien
1959 Jean Charbonneaux. Les
Bronzes grec
1960 Pierre George. Entire
work   862.

PELMAN DRAMA PRIZE (France)
The Prix Pelman du Théâtre
is an annual award generally
granted in May, and is one of
five prizes established in 1955 by
L'Institut Pelman de Psychologie
Appliquée (176 boulevard Haussmann, Paris 8e) to honor a
theatrical work of the highest
ideals; affirming the vital being,
drive and courage which are
basic to Pelman percepts; and
characteristic of the best of the
eternal drama of man in his
struggle for the ideal ('un idéal
supérieur à ses passions').
Winners of the 3.000 NF prize,
awarded in the Spring each year,
include such well-known French
authors as:
1955 Felicien Marceau.
Caterina
1956 Colette Audry. Soledad
1957 Robert Mallet. L'équipage
est au complet
1958 Jules Roy. Le fleuve
rouge
Serge Pitoeff. Mise en scène de
Luigi Pirandello, "Ce soir on
improvise"
1959 André Obey. Les Trois
coups de minuit   863.

PEREZ GALDOS PRIZE (Spain)
A triennial prize, awarded
under the auspices of "Casa de
Colón" of Las Palmas (Casa
Museo, calle de Colón), with
premiums of up to 50,000 pts for
novels--there are also awards

for short stories and drama--
about the Canary Islands region,
this honor has been granted:
1954 Rafael Narbona.
Ausencia sin Retorno
1955 José María Álvarez
Blázquez. Las Estatuas no
Hablan
1956 Enrique Nácher. Guanche
The 1962 prize offers 70,000
pts for a novel; and 30,000 pts
for short story and drama.
864.

Willibald PIRKHEIMER MEDAL
(Germany)
Named for the German human-
ist, Willibald Pirkheimer (1470-
1530), author of many books on
science and politics and translator of Greek classics into the
common tongue (Latin), this
Nuremberg award--also granted
from time to time as the WILLI-
BALD PIRKHEIMER PRIZE, with
a premium of 1000 DM--is presented by the Pirkheimer Kuratorium, Nürnberg.
Recipients, honored for their
contribution to Modern Human-
ism, include: Carl J. Burckhardt,
Heimito von Doderer, Albrecht
Goes, Reinhold Schneider, Leo
Weismantel, and--in 1960--Max
Rychner, Sigismund von Radecki.
865.

PERUVIAN NATIONAL PRIZE
The Prêmios Nacionales de
Fomenta a la Cultura, the official
cultural awards of the Peruvian
government, offer prizes in Literature, the Arts and Sciences.
This national literary prize,
which is granted in recognition
of winning the "Concurso
Nacional," was established by law
in 1942 and has been awarded
by the Ministerio de Educación
Pública del Peru since 1944.
Honoring published or unpublished
works in many fields of writing,
the awards--consisting of a
diploma and a premium of

7,500 soles--are determined by
a jury of scholars and subject
experts, and are presented by
the President and Rector of the
National University of San Marcos
in a national ceremony on July 28.
The 16 "Peruvian National
Culture Prizes" offered in 1961
include:
ALEJANDRO DRUSTUA PRIZE--
best philosophical study
ANTONIO MIRO QUESADA PRIZE--
best chronicle, editorial or
magazine article on a national
theme
ANTONIO RAYMONDI PRIZE--
best work on geography of Peru
INCA GARCILASO PRIZE--
best work on the history of
Peru
JOSÉ SANTOS CHOCANO PRIZE--
best poetical composition on a
Peruvian theme
MANUEL GONZALEZ PRADA
PRIZE--best literary study
RICARDO PALMA PRIZE--
best novel, short story or
drama
Among recipients--whose work,
if unpublished, is issued in an
edition financed by the Peruvian
government--are:
1952 Alberto Escobar. Car-
tones de cielo y tierra
(Santos Chocano Prize--
poetry)
Eudocio Carrera Vergara. La
docena del fraile o trece
cuentos demi abuela (Palma
Prize)
1954 Max Henriquez Urena.
Poesia peruana de sigle
viente
Luis Jaime Cisneros. Estudio
del discurso en loor de la
poesia
1955 Arturo D. Hernandez.
Selva trágica (Gonzalez
Prada Prize--literary study)
José Paroja Paz Soldán. Las
constituciones del Peru
1961 Francisco Bendezú. Los
Anos   866.

Camilo PESSANHA PRIZE
(Portugal)
This 10.000$ prize for
poetry is one of several awards
offered by the Portuguese government department, Agencia Geral
do Ultramar, in an annual
promotion of new writing by
Portuguese citizens on subjects
dealing with overseas topics. In
1955 the prize was won by Jorge
Barbosa (Cape Verde) with
"Caderno de um ilheu;" and in
1957 the award was presented
to Geraldo Bessa Vitor for
"Cubata abondanada."   867.

PEUSER AWARD (Argentina)
The publisher's prize offered
by Casa Jacobo Peuser
(Patricios 599, Buenos Aires)
has been given for different forms
of literature. In 1952-1953, the
prizes for unpublished prose
works--CONCURSO LITERARIO
DE EDICIONES PEUSER--were
won by Martin Alberto Noel with
the novel "La Balsa," and Enrique
Popolizio with the biography
"Vida de Lucio V. Mansilla."
A more recent contest in 1957
offered the prize for unpublished
stories for children and young
people. The 13 stories and
illustrations winning prizes for
writing for children (7 to 13
years of age) were collected in
the book, "Donde nacio el arco
iris y otros cuentos;" and the
10 stories and illustrations winning prizes for writing for young
people (14 to 18 years of age)
were published as "Los anteojos
azules y otros cuentos."   868.

PHILADELPHEA POETRY
COMPETITION (Greece)
Perhaps the longest-established
continuous literary award in
Greece, this Competition was
founded in 1888 by Christos
Philadelphea, in memory of his
grandson of the same name, who
was an honorary president of the

Society of Greek Writers. Contests are announced from time to
time, "whenever the interest of
the endowed principle accrues to
the amount of the designated
prize."
Some years ago, the Philadelphea family, represented by
Alexander Philadelphea, gave the
administration of the Competition
to the Society of Greek Writers,
and until recently the contest was
biennial, with a premium of Drs
2,000--an award which was accompanied in the early years of
the competition with an olive
branch and was presented following the public reading of the
prize allocations. At present,
in accordance with the request of
the Philadelphea family, the
amount of the premium and the
scope of the prize are being increased by spacing the competition at less frequent intervals
than two years, with a premium
of 20,000 Drachmas.
Winners of the Competition,
one of the "Parnassus" Literary
Society Awards, who have gen-
erally been honored for collec-
tions of lyric poetry, include:
Ar. Anthiotis
G. Athanas
N. Damianos
Stephanos Daphnis
G. Drosinis
K. Karyotakis
I. Krinaios
Sp. Livadas
Myrtiotissa
Kostis Palamas (two awards)
Pan. G. Papadopoulos
Ioannis Polemis
Bianca Romaiou
Stel. Sperantsas (two awards)
G. Stratigis
D. Zades   869.

PHILIPPINES FREE PRESS
ANNUAL SHORT STORY AWARDS
The "oldest English literary
contest in the Republic of the
Philippines" is that conducted

each year by the Philippines Free Press, Inc. (Free Press Building, 708 Rizal Avenue, Manila). Three prizes are offered (P 1,000; P 500; P 250) for the three best short stories published in the magazine during a 12-month period (November through October of the following year), and the results of the contest are announced in the magazine's "Christmas Number," issued in the second week of December.

Established, in part, "to raise the standard of short story writing in the Philippines," the contest requires that competing entries submitted for the prize and publication must be original and not previously published stories--preferably between 1,500 and 3,000 words in length.

First Prize has been awarded since 1949 to:

Nick Joaquin. Guardia de Honor
Gonzalo Villa. A voice in Rama
Juan T. Gatbonton. Clay
Kerima Polotan Tuvera. The virgin
Gregorio C. Brilliantes. The living and the dead
Gregorio C. Brilliantes. A wing over the earth
Edith L. Tiempo. The chambers of the sea
Gregorio C. Brilliantes. The distance to Andromeda
Bienvenido N. Santos. Brother, My Brother
Lilia Pablo Amansec. The lilies of yesterday
Edith L. Tiempo. The dimensions of fear
Bienvenido N. Santos. The day the dancers came
Wilfrido Nolledo. Rice wine
870.

PHILIPPINES LITERARY CONTESTS
The contests conducted dur-

ing the years 1940 and 1941 were sponsored by the Philippine Writers' League and administered by the Office of the President, Commonwealth of the Philippines. This first official literary contest of the Philippine government offered a first prize of P 1,000-- with an honorable mention of P 500--in several forms of writing.

Recipients of the high official recognition of literary achievement were:

1940 Novel--Juan Cabreros Laya. His native soil
N.V.M. Gonzalez. The winds of April (Honorable Mention)
Short Story--Manuel R. Arguilla. How my Brother Leon brought home a wife
Poetry--R. Zulueta da Costa. Molave
Doveglion (pseud of Jose Garcia Villa). Poems (Honorable Mention)
Essay--Salvador P. Lopez. Literature and society
Autobiography--P.C. Morantte. A biography (Honorable Mention)
1941 Fiction--Consorcio Borje. The automobile comes to town, and other stories.
871.

PHILIPPINES REPUBLIC CULTURAL HERITAGE AWARDS
These official government prizes, awarded for cultural achievement as part of the yearly Independence Day celebration of the Republic of the Philippines, were established in 1960 by the National Commission on Independence Day and are administered by the Committee on Republic Cultural Heritage Awards. Designed to "encourage cultural advancement to complement the country's program of economic development," the prize consists of a premium of P 1,000-- together with a medal, diploma,

or plaque--awarded in public recognition of achievement "to the most outstanding men in arts and sciences."

In addition to prizes for Musical Composition, Sculpture, and Painting, awards for writing are granted for published works in Literature; History; Science and Technology. Competing writings must have been completed during the preceding year (May 1 to April 30), and must be submitted in seven copies by April 30. Works in Literature and in History must have been published in book form and be in the English, Spanish, or Filipino language. Works in Science or Technology must have been published in book form, or in "reputable journals or magazines," and if not in English, Spanish, or Filipino language, must have with the original work a translation into English.

Writers honored by the formal presentation of these prizes-- also designated PHILIPPINE AWARD OF MERIT--on July 2 at Malacanang Social Hall, include:
Literature
  1960 N. V. M. Gonzalez. The bamboo dancers
  1961 Nick Joaquin. The woman who had two navels
History
  1960 Eliseo Quirino. A day to remember
  1961 Cesar Adib Majul. Mabini and the Philippine Revolution
Science and Technology
  1960 T. F. Pesigen, et al. Studies on Schistosoma Japonicum infection in the Philippines
  1961 Gertrude Aguilar-Santos. The constitution of Pychamine
                                    872.

PHILIPPINES REPUBLIC PRO-PATRIA AWARD
These awards were pre-sented by the Philippine government "at the inauguration of the National Library building on the occasion of the Rizal Centennial Celebration"on June 19, 1961. Named for the Filipino national hero, Jose Rizal (1861-1893), the award brought official public recognition to 32 individuals (Filipino and non-Filipino) and organizations, through citation by the President of the Republic of the Philippines "in recognition of their distinguished contributions to the promotion and advancement of national progress and stimulation and encouragement of love of country and civic citizenship responsibility to the general community and to the Republic."

Literary men so honored included: Antonio K. Abad; N. V. M. Gonzalez; Wilfredo Ma. Guerrero; Teodoro M. Locsin; Lope K. Santos; Jose Garcia Villa; Agustin C. Fabian; and Carmen Guerrero-Nakpil.

Additional prizes were given for essays (in Spanish, English and Tagalog); Tagalog poetry; and biography concerning Jose Rizal. Biography award winners (P 10, 000; P 5, 000; P 2, 500) were: Leon Ma. Guerrero, "The first Filipino;" Gregoria Borlaza, "Si Rizal, ang Ulirang Pilipino;" Camilo Osias, "Rizal, the Nationalist."   873.

Marianne PHILIPS PRIZE (Netherlands)
Winners of this commemorative award, established in 1951, have included:
  1958 Nico Rost. Goethe in Dachau; Nog draaft Beyaard; and De vrienden van mijn vader
  1960 C. J. Kelk.   Entire work
                                    874.

Wlodzimierz PIETRZAK AWARDS (Poland)

Annually in May, the Association PAX (Stowarzyszenie PAX, Mokotowska 43, Warszawa) has awarded the Nagroda im Wlodzimierza Pietrzaka--a monetary prize "for a work expressing religious convictions according to Roman Catholic faith." Separate prizes for Young Writers and for Foreign Authors are also awarded.

Recent winners of the Pietrzak Award, which was established in 1948, are such authors in the field of Belles Lettres as:

1956 Zofia Kossak. Entire work
1957 Wladyslaw Jan Grabski. Rapsodia Swidnicka (novel)
Stanislaw Cat-Mackiewicz. Dostojewski
1958 Roman Brandstaetter. Entire work
Zygmunt Lichniak. Literary criticism
1959 Artur Gorski
1960 Alexsander Rymkiewicz. Poems
1961 Ewa Szelburg-Zarembina

Recent winners of the Pietrzak Award for Young Writers are:
1957 Andrzej Piotrowski
1958 Zdzislaw Laczkowski
1959 Szczepan Balicki
Anka Kowalska
1960 Andrzej Palosz
Danuta Slon
Jan Wagner
1961 Zligniew Dalecki
Kazimierz Kania
Mieczyslaw Dalecki

Prize winning Foreign Authors since 1954 include: Jean Marie Domenach; Paul Cazin; Gilbert Cesbron; Bruce Marshall; Graham Greene (1960).   875.

PIQUER PRIZE (Spain)

Offered annually for dramatic works written for Spaniards and first played in Spain during the year, this 1,600 pts prize is granted by Real Academia Española.   876.

Luigi PIRANDELLO PRIZE
(International--Italy)

In recognition of the 25th anniversary of the death of the Italian dramatist and novelist, Luigi Pirandello (1867-1936), this award of L 1.000.000 was offered in 1961 to authors of any nationality. The premium was divided equally between two prize-winners: Arcangelo Leone (Italy); and Franz Rauhut (Wurzburg, Germany).

A PIRANDELLO PRIZE granted by Sicily (Regione Siciliana) for scholarly work about Pirandello was won by Leonardo Sciarscia in 1953 with "Pirandello e il pirandellismo."   877.

PISA PRIZES (Italy)

Since 1957 these literary awards for poetry and short stories, under the sponsorship of the Ente Provinciale per il Turismo, Pisa, have been granted by the cultural organization, "Soffita" (casella postale 19, piazzi San Giorgio, 3 bis).

Recent winners are:
1956 Gennaro Morra
1958 Martino Vitali (poetry); Andrea Rossi (fiction)
1959 Maria Clara Cataldi. Collina di Gela (poetry)
Antonio Candio. Colloqui sul crepuscolo
1960 Massimo Grillanti.   A un uomo del futuro (poetry)
Giovanni Curmi. Autoconfessione de un delinquente (fiction)
1961 Renzo Rocca. La volpe ed altri racconti
Garibaldo Alessandrini. Innamorata Memoria (poetry)
1962--Gold Bull Pendant (Torre pendente d'oro) and L 300.000: Carlo Martini.   Poesie
        878.

PLANETA PRIZE (Spain)
Established in 1952 by José
Manuel Lara Hernández, director
of the Barcelona publisher,
Editorial Planeta (Fernando
Agullo 12), this prize is awarded annually on October 15 for
the best unpublished novel submitted for consideration. One
of the highest literary awards
granted in Spain, the 10th
prize (1961) carried a premium
of 200,000 pts.
Conditions of each year's
award are announced in January
of the year, and according to
recent competition rules, authors
of any nationality may enter the
contest by submitting novels in
Spanish--minimum length 200
typed pages--by the closing date
of June 30.
Recipients of this major
Spanish literary honor are:
1952 Juan José Mira. En la
noche no hay caminos
1953 Santiago Loren. Una
casa con Goteras
1954 Ana María Matute.
Pequeno teatro
1955 Antonio Prieto. Tres
pisadas de hombre
1956 Carmen Kurtz. El
desconocido
1957 Emilio Romero. La paz
empieza nunca
1958 Fernando Bermúdez de
Castro. Pasos sin huellas
1959 Andrés Bosch. La
noche
1960 Tomás Salvador. El
atentado
1961 Torcuato Luca de Tena.
La mujer de otro
1962 Angel Vazquez. Se
enciende y se apage una luz
879.

Germán PLAZA PRIZE (Spain)
Established in 1957 by the
Barcelona bookseller, Germán
Plaza, this 75,000 pts premium
for an unpublished novel was
won by Pedro Espinosa with

"Todos somos accionistas." 880.

PLAZA Y JANÉS PRIZE (Spain)
A newly established (1962)
publisher's award, offered by
Editorial Plaza y Janés (calle de
Enrique Granados 88, Barcelona
8) will grant 600,000 pts an-
nually for the best writing in
Spanish from Spain or Latin
America. Monthly awards of
50,000 pts are given as advance
royalties for works to be in-
cluded in the publisher's series:
"Selecciones Lengua Española."
Winner in April 1962 is
Iñigo de Aranzadi with the novel,
"Historias del Bosque Fang;" and
in May 1962 Carmen Mieza re-
ceived the award for the novel,
"La imposible."   881.

Edgar POE PRIZE (International--
France)
One of a number of poetry
prizes offered by Maison de
Poésie (11 bis, rue Ballu, Paris
9e), this annual award is given
to foreign poets writing in the
French language. The 100 NF
premium, granted in June to
published works submitted for consideration by March 31, has
honored the poetry of:
1950 Albert Caraco. Livre des
combats de l'âme
1952 Robert Simon
1953 Armand Bernier. Migra-
tion des âmes
1954 Hilaire Theurillat.
Corymbe
1955 Joseph Ascar-Nahas.
Djénène
1956 Robert Choquette
1957 Mme Gentille Arditty-
Puller. Plaisir d'Istanbul
1958 Gaston Figuera (Uruguay).
Pour ton clavecin
1959 Armand Godoy
1960 Lionel Fiumi. Entire
work
1961 Sadi de Gorter   882.

Emile POLAK PRIZE (Belgium)
A biennial award of 10,000
fr was established in 1927 by
the Belgian Royal Academy of
French Language and Literature
to distinguish the work of a
Belgian writing in French--
preferably a poet at least 35
years of age.
Poets recently honored by the
award are:
 1951 Gérard Prévot. Récital
 1953 Frederic Kiesel. Ce jour
   qui m'est donné
 1955 Liliane Wouters. La
   Marche forcée
 1957 Philippe Jones. Amours
   et autres visages
 1959 Jacques-Gérard Linze.
   Confidentiel   883.

POLISH MINISTER OF NATIONAL
DEFENSE PRIZE
The Nagroda Ministra Obrony
Narodowej, established as an
annual award in 1958, is presented on October 12, "Polish
Army Day." The prize, consisting of a monetary premium,
is given "to writers dealing with
the history of Polish armed
forces, the contemporary life of
the Polish army, and the
problem of the defense of the
country."
 Winners of the prize are:
 1958 Leon Pasternak
   Wladyslaw Machejek
 1959 Waldemar Kotowicz.
   Frontowe drogi (novel)
 1960 Jan Gerhard. Luny w
   Bieszczadach
 1961 Wojceich Zukrowski.
   Skapani w ogniu   884.

POLISH P.E.N. CLUB PRIZES
The Nagrody Polskiego Kluba
Literackiego PEN are two
translation prizes offered by the
Polish P.E.N. Club (Palac
Kultury i Nauki, Warszawa)--
one for translations of Polish
literary works into foreign
languages; the other for translation of foreign literature into
Polish. The prizes were initiated
in 1928 and are awarded with no
specified frequency.
Winners include:
Translations of Polish Literary Works into Foreign Languages
Paul Cazin. Translation of A.
Mickiewicz "Pan Tadeusz"
into French, and other translations
Jan Tomcsanyi. Translation
of Wl. St. Reymont "Chlopi"
into Hungarian
Serge Repall Noyes. Translation of A. Mickiewicz "Pan
Tadeusz" and other works
into English
1948 Franisek Halas. Translation of works of A. Mickiewicz
and J. Slowacki into Czech
1957 Julije Benesic. Translation of Polish literary works
into Chorvatian
1960 Istvan Meszaros. Translation of Polish literary
works into Hungarian
Jean Bourilly. Translation of
works of J. Slowacki into
French
Translations of Foreign Literature into Polish
1928 Aniela Zagorska. Translation of Joseph Conrad,
"Victory;" and entire work of
translation
1932 Tadeusz Boy-Zelenski.
Translations of French
literary works
1935 Jozef Wittlin. Translation of the "Odyssey"
1937 Edward Boye. Entire
work, especially translation
of Cervantes, "Don Kichot"
1938 Gabriel Karski. Translations of French literature
1939 Maria Godlewska. Translation of English literary
works: J. Galsworthy; A.
Huxley; K. Mansfield
1948 Leopold Staff. Entire
work, particularly translation of Leonardo da Vinci
and Michelangelo, and the

poetical paraphrase of Goethe
"Reinecke Fuchs"
1949 Stefan Srebrny. Translation of classical Greek
literary works, particularly
Aeschylus,"Oresteia"
1950 Adam Wazyk. Entire
work, particularly translation of Pushkin, "Eugene
Onegin," and works of Rimbaud, Apollinaire, and V.
Maiakovskij
1951 Weclaw Rogowica.Trans-
lations of French literary
works
1952 Ludwik Hieronim Morstin.
Entire work, particularly
works of Calderon and Lope
de Vega
1954 Kazimiera Illakowiczowna.
Entire work, particularly
works of Tolstoi, Schiller,
and Hungarian writers
1956 Julian Rogozinski. Translation of French literary
works
1959 Zofia Jackimecka.
Translation of Italian works
Roman Koloniecki. Entire
translation work
1960 Branislaw Zielinski. Entire translation work
1961 Wladyslaw Broniewski.
Translation of Russian works.
885.

POLISH PRIME MINISTER'S
AWARD FOR WRITING FOR
CHILDREN AND YOUTH
Awarded annually on June 1
since 1958, the Polish Prime
Minister's award (Prezes Rady
Ministrow, Al. Ujazdowskie
1/3, Warszawa) recognizes
outstanding contributions in the
area of literature for children
and young people.
Winners of the monetary pre-
mium--receiving the Nagroda
Prezesa Rady Ministrow za
tworezosc dla dzieci i mlodziezy
for their "Entire Work" except
as otherwise noted--include:
1958 Irena Jurgielewiczowa

1959 Hanna Ozogowska
Stafania Szuchowa
1960 Halina Rudnicka
Czeslaw Janczarski
1961 Gustaw Morcinek. Works
for youth
Janina Dziarnowska. Gdy inna
dziecmi sa (novel)   886.

POLISH UNION OF SOCIALIST
YOUTH PROSE AWARD
The Literacka Nagroda
Mlodych w Dziedzinie Prozy, a
recently instituted prize, was
established in 1961 to honor a
young author--under 30 years of
age--for a book published during
the award period. To be granted
each year on May 1 by the Central Committee of the Union of
Socialist Youth (Komitet Centralny
Zwiazku Mlodziezy Socjalistycznej)
and the editorial staff of the
periodical, "Sztandar Mlodych"
(Wspolna 61, Warszawa), the
initial award was presented in
1961 to Janusz Krasinski for his
work, "Przerwany rejs 'Bialej
Marianny.' "   887.

Henrik PONTOPPIDAN MEMOR-
IAL FUND (Denmark)
The prize of the Danish
Authors' Association (Dansk
Forfatterforening, Ved Stranden
20, Copenhagen K) is granted to
honor Henrik Pontoppidan (1814-
1943), Danish novelist who shared
the Nobel Prize for Literature
in 1917.
Granted since 1946, the prize
currently brings a premium of
5. 000 D kr (previous premiums
were 3. 000 D kr from 1946 to
1953; and 4. 000 D kr from 1954
to 1956), and has honored such
authors from 1936 to 1962 as:
Johs. Joergensen
Karin Michaelis
Agnes Henningsen
C. E. Soya
Poul la Cour
Knud Soenderby
Thit Jensen

Kjeld Abell
Hans Hartvig Seedorff
Leck Fischer
Knuth Becker
Jacob Paludan
Cai M. Woel
Karen Blixen (Isak Dinesen)
Tom Kristensen
Per Lange
William Heinesen   888.

PORTUGUESE NATIONAL
LITERARY PRIZES
Official government recognition
of writers in Portugal is granted
by S. N. I. (Secretariado Nacional
da Informação) as Prémios
Literários Nacionais--eight cur-
rently granted prizes listed
under name (which see):
Andrede; Bragança; Herculano;
Ortigão, Quental; Queiroz;
Vaz de Carvalho; Vicente.
                                889.

PORTUGUESE WRITERS
SOCIETY PRIZES
   Two 50.000$ prizes estab-
lished in 1962 by Sociedade Portu-
guesa de Escritores (Rua da
Escola Politecnica 20-1o E,
Lisbon 2), with the Fundation
Calouste Gulbenkian as patron,
are the: Grand Prize for Poetry;
and the Grand Prize for Drama.
The prize winners for poetry
published during the years 1960
and 1961, and for drama pub-
lished or presented during this
period, were determined by a
jury meeting early in 1962:
GRANDE PRÉMIO DE POESIA
JOSÉ GOMES FERREIRA.
POESIA III.
   César Praţas. Post Scriptum
GRANDE PRÉMIO DE TEATRO.
   Luís de Sttau Monteiro.
   Felizmente há Luar
   Another group of prizes
offered by the Portuguese
Writers Society are the
"PRÉMIOS DE REVELAÇÃO"--
annual prizes since 1960 for
original writing: Novel or

Novella, Collection of Short Stories;
Poetry; Essay; Drama. Among
recipients of the prize, consisting
of a diploma and publication of
the winning work, are:
   1960 Fiama Hasse Pais Brandão.
   Os Guarda-Chuvas
   Marta de Lima. Album (fiction)
   1961 Almeida Faria. Rumor
   Branco (fiction)
   Maria Amália Ortiz de Fonseca.
   Introdução oa Estudo de João
   Penha (essay)   890.

POURFINA AWARDS (Greece)
   One of several prizes offered
each year since 1950 by a group
of writers known as the "Group
of Twelve," and so also called
"The Group of Twelve Prize,"
this award of Drs 25, 000 is
granted for the best literary writing extolling Greek Civilization,
published in Greece during the
preceding year and deposited in
the Greek National Library.
   Authors honored with the
prize--designating the "Purfina
Prize Book"--presented each
December, include:
   1958 Dionisios Romas
   1959 Angeliki Hatcimichali
   1960 Andreas Karantonis
                                891.

POZNAN POETICAL NOVEMBER
PRIZE (Poland)
   Annually awarded since November 1958, this monetary premium of the Poznan Municipal
Council (Rada Narodowa miasta
Poznania, Stalingradzka 18,
Poznan) brings public recognition
"to a young poet for the best
debut book of the year."
   Winners include:
   1958 Jerzy Sita. Wioze swoj
   czas na osle
   1959 Andrzej Bursa. Wiersze
   1960 Marian Grzeszczak.
   Lumpenizje
   1961 Czeslaw Kuriata. Niebo
   Zrownane z ziemia   892.

POZZALE PRIZE (Italy)
This award, offered since
1948 for a first work--Narrative
or Scholarly Writing--is offered
by the city of Empoli (Adminis-
trazione comunale di Empoli,
presso il Palazzo comunale,
Empoli). Recipients of the
L 500.000 premium include:
1959 Giuliano Palladino. Pace
e El Alamein
1960 Furio Monicelli. Il
Gesuitta perfetto (The perfect
Jesuit)
1961 Anonimo Trietino (pen
name of Giorgio Voghero
Fano, deceased). Il
Segreto   893.

PRATO PRIZE (Italy)
Since 1948 the city of Prato
(Segreteria del Comune di Prato,
Ufficio del Premio letterario
"Prato"), near Florence in
Tuscany, has offered a literary
award of L 1.000.000 for various
forms of writing--Poetry inspired
by the Resistance, and--more
recently (1962)--for Prose (Novel,
Memoirs, Diary). Currently
works published July 1, 1961 to
July 31, 1962 and submitted in
competition by July 31, 1962
are considered by a jury and
prizes are presented in a formal
ceremony on September 8.
Recipients include:
1949 Armando Meoni. L'ombra
dei vivi
1955 Marina Sereni. I giorni
della nostra vita
Fausto Nitti. Il maggiore e
un rosso
Carlo Cassola. I vecchi
compagni
1957 Maria L. Guaita. La
guerra finisce, la guerra
continua
1958 Pietro Secchia. Il monte
rosa
Cima Moscatelli. Sceso a
Milano
1959 Enrico Valle. Il cristallo
magico

1960 Leone Sbrana. Giorno che
sembrano ano (Days that
seem years)
Beppe Fenoglio. Primavera di
belle (Beautiful springtime)
Leonardo Scaiscia. Gli zii di
Sicilia (The uncles from
Sicily--short stories)   894.

PRESERNOV AWARD (Yugoslavia)
This prize, one of a number
of cultural and literary honors
granted by the component Republics of Yugoslavia, is awarded
by the People's Republic of
Slovenia to Slovene writers.
Established in 1949, the centennial of Presernov's death, the
award has brought official public
recognition to such authors as:
1949 Ciril Kosmac. Na svojoj
zemlji (On your own land--
film scenario)
Anton Ingolic. Put po nasipu
(Highway over filled land)
France Bevic. Toncek (Toncek
--youth book)
Vladimir Levstik. Translation
of Gogol, "Taras Bulba;"
of the German classic, "Till
Eulenspiegel"
1953 Ivan Potrc. Na kmetih
(The village mayors--novel)
1956 Cene Vipotnik. Drevo na
samem (Lonesome tree--
collected poems)
1957 Lojze Krajger. Entire
literary work
Beno Zupancic. Sedmina (The
seven--novel)
Boris Ziberl. Knjizevnost i
drustvo (Literature and
society)
Edvard Kardelj. Razvoj
slovenackog nacionalnog pitanja
(Development of the Slovene
National Question)   895.

José Antonio PRIMO DE RIVERA
NATIONAL PRIZE (Spain)
The 25,000 pts award of the
Spanish government (Ministry of
Information and Tourism) has
been granted since 1938 for var-

ious forms of writing--Novel,
Essay. Currently (1962) the
award is offered for journalism
published in papers or magazines
in Spain or a Spanish-language
country between February 1 and
October 31. Articles entered
in competition were to be sub-
mitted to the Subdireccion General
de Prensa before November 10,
1962.
Recent prizes have honored:
Rafael Laffon. La Rama
Ingrata
Fernando Canellas Rodriguez.
Journalism
J.L. Prados Nogueira.
Miserere en la tumba de
R.N. (poetry)
Rafael Montesinos. El Tiempo
en Nuestros Brazos
Luis López Anglada. Con-
templación de España   896.

**S. H. PRIOR MEMORIAL
PRIZE (Australia)**
This annual award, established
in memory of Samuel Henry
Prior, editor of the "Sydney
Bulletin," who died in 1933, by
his son, was awarded for ten
years (1935-1945), and then was
discontinued in 1946. The prize
was offered for a published
Australian novel that had not
previously won a literary award,
and the amount of the premium
increased during the years of
award from Ł100 to Ł500.
Among winners of the prize
are: Douglas Stewart; Brian
James; and
1935 Kylie Tennant. Tiburon
1936 Miles Franklin. All that
swagger   897.

PROCELLARIA PRIZE (Italy)
The review, "La Procellaria,"
(via da Nava 21 C, Reggio
Calabria), offers this prize for
unpublished poetry--maximum
500 verses--submitted in competition by July 31 each year.
Recent winners are:

1958 Salvatore Di Marco
1959 Mario Vernola. Colloqui
con il Padre
1960 Antenore Perilli. Le
colline aspettano il vento
1961 Raffaele Mangano.
Approdi d'anima   898.

PROSA LATINA PRIZE (Italy)
In a competition ('Certamen
Capitolinum") for Latin composi-
tion, sponsored by the Italian
Minister of Public Instruction
(Ministero della Pubblica Istruzione,
Rome) and administered by
Istituto di Studi Romani (Piazza
Cavalieri di Malta 2, Rome),
winners receive as prize a Silver
Wolf (Lupa d'Argento).   899.

**"PRZEGLAD KULTURALNY"
PRIZE (Poland)**
Since 1957 the weekly cultural
review, "Przeglad Kulturalny"
(Krakowskie Przedmiescie 21/23,
Warszawa) has awarded a monetary prize each December.
Writers of such literary forms as
poetry, prose, and drama are
eligible for the award, and winners are selected by a jury
composed of members of the
editorial staff of the publication.
Authors honored with the
Nagrody Artystyczne tygodnika
"Przeglad Kulturalny" include:
1957 Slawomir Mrozek. Slon
(short stories)
1958 Stanislaw Dygat. Podroz
(novel)
1959 Adolf Rudnicki. Stories
published in "Przeglad
Kulturalny"
1960 Tadeusz Breza. Urzad
(novel)   900.

**PUCCINI-SENIGALLIA PRIZE
(Italy)**
The literary prize, established
by the city of Senigallia (presso
Azienda Autonoma di Soggiorno di
Senigallia) to commemorate the
author, Mario Puccini, associated
with the city, offers L 1.000.000

--an annual premium since 1958
for a published writing of fiction
(Raccolta; Racconti; Novelle).
In 1962 a prize of L 2.000.000
was also offered for a published
or an unpublished scholarly work
about Mario Puccini.

Competing works must be
submitted by June 30 to the jury,
which has presented the honor
to:

1959 Giovanni Testori. La
Gilda del MacMahon (short
stories)
1960 Renzo Rosso. L'Adesca-
mento (The enticement)
1961 Libero Bigiaretti. I
racconti
1962 Mario Rigoni-Stern. Il
bosco degli Urogalli   901.

PUERTO RICAN THEATER FESTIVAL

The Festival of Puerto Rican
Drama, planned as a periodic
event, was first held in July
1958 in San Juan at Teatro
Tapia. Sponsored by the Puerto
Rican government and administered by Instituto de Cultura
Puertorriqueña (Apado 4184, San
Juan), the drama contest honored
four plays with performance during
the Festival de Teatro Puertorriqueña: Manuael Méndez
Ballester, "Encrucijada;" Francisco Arriví, "Vegigantes;" Emilio
S. Beleval, "La hacienda de los
cuatros vientos;" René Marqués;
"Los soles truncos."   902.

PUERTO RICO POET LAUREATE

This title of honor was bestowed upon Diana Ramirez de
Arellano in 1958 by Instituto de
Literatura Puertorriqueña de la
Universidad de Puerto Rico, for
her book, "Ángeles de Ceniza."
903.

PUERTO RICO PRIZE

The Premio Puertorriqueño,
granted for the best Puerto
Rican novel by Instituto de
Literatura Puertorriqueña de al
Universidad de Puerto Rico, was
presented in 1957 to Cesar Andrew
Iglesias for his book, "Los
derrotados."   904.

Agustín PUJOL PRIZE (Spain)
Awards totalling 400,000 pts
are distributed among three plays
and one novel. Recipients of the
honor, also known as "PREMIO
FUENTEOVEJUNA," include
Ignacio Luca de Tena, with "El
Cóndor sin alas."

Another prize of the same
name--JOSÉ M. PUJOL PRIZE--
grants 25,000 pts through Sociedad
Arqueological Tarraconense for a
writing about the city of Tarragona.
905.

PUSHKIN PRIZES (USSR)

These prizes are awarded
Soviet playwrights and other
authors of the U.S.S.R.   906.

PUTNAM AWARDS (International-- U.S.A.)

Publisher's awards "for
superior manuscripts in both the
fields of fiction and nonfiction"
are offered by G.P. Putnam's
Sons (200 Madison Avenue, New
York 16), but are not considered
the reward of a prize contest by
the publisher. "Although they
will pay an author a considerable
advance against royalties (a
minimum of $5,000), they are
intended primarily to establish a
standard of quality which will
become a guarantee of excellence
in the minds of the reading
public."

Manuscripts entered for the
awards must be unpublished, in
the English language, of a
minimum length of 65,000 words,
and must be a novel or nonfiction
work which "can be successfully
published to reach the widest
possible audience," written by an
author not previously published
by G.P. Putnam's Sons.

Recent winners are:
1960 William Mulvihill. The
sands of Kalahari
1961 Ian Brook. Jimmy Riddle
907.

QUADRANT LITERARY AWARD
(Australia)

Endowed by the Australian
philanthropist, Adolph Basser,
this annual prize of Ł100 "to
encourage Australian writing,"
is offered by the Australian
Association of Cultural Freedom
through the quarterly review it
sponsors--"Quadrant." The
prize--awarded each year for
five years beginning in 1959--is
granted for the best contribution
to "Quadrant," and winners are
chosen by the editors of the
magazine, "Encounter," published
in London.

Recipients include:
1959 Peter Hastings. Portrait
of Krishna Menon (article)
1960 Geoffrey Dutton. South
Australian almanac (poem)
1961 Desmond O'Grady. Old
Buffers (short story)
1962 Hugh Atkinson, Sydney
novelist
Stanly Tick (U.S.A.), teacher
in Department of English,
University of New South
Wales   908.

QUAI DES ORFÈVRES PRIZE
(France)

Jacques Catineau of the publishing firm, Société d'éditions,
established the annual award of
1.000 NF in 1946 to give recognition to the best unpublished
mystery (roman policier) submitted for consideration. The
prize, one of the significant
awards offered for detective novels
in France, has been continued
since 1951 by Éditions Hachette
(Secrétariat, 125 rue Montmartre,
Paris).

The award, granted on the
second Tuesday of each November,

honors the competing manuscripts
not only for a demonstration of
exact descriptive details and
procedures of French law en-
forcement and justice, but also
for the literary qualities of the
writing.

The jury, among whose members is the Chief of Police of
Paris, has awarded the prize to:
1946 Jacques Levert. Le singe
rouge
1947 Jean Le Hallier. Un
certain Monsieur
1948 Yves Fougères. Nuit et
brouillard
1949 Francis Didelot. L'assassin au clair de lune
1951 Dekobra. Opération
Magali
1952 Saint-Gilles. Ne tirez
pas sur l'inspecteur
1953 Cécil Saint-Laurent.
Sophie et le crime
1954 Alain Serdac, and Jean
Maurinay. Sans effusion de
sang
1956 Noël Calef. Echec au
porteur
1957 Louis Thomas. Poisson
d'avril
1958 André Gillois. 125, rue
Montmartre
1959 Jean Marcillac. On ne tue
pas pour le plaisir
1960 Coronel Rémy (pseud of
Gilbert Renault). Monocle
noir
1961 Robert Thomas. Huit
femmes
1962 Micheline Sandrel. Dix
millions de témoins   909.

Eça de QUEIROZ PRIZE
(Portugal)

The biennial prize of the
Secretariado Nacional da Informação grants 15.000$ to the
best novel published in Portugal
during the preceding two years.
Winners include:
1954 Agustina Bessa Luís.
A Sibila
1956 Alberto Lopes. A

Ultima Estação
1958 Maria da Graça Freire.
A terra foi-lhe negada
1960 Ester de Lemos. Com-
panheiros   910.

Antero de QUENTAL PRIZE
(Portugal)
The annual poetry prize of
the Secretariado Nacional da
Informação, established in
1934, offers 6.000$ premium
which has been won recently by:
1956 Carlos Lobo de Oliveira.
Alegre Melancolia
1957 Maria Madalena
Monteiro Ferin. Poemas
1958 Ruy Cinatti. Olivro do
Nómada meu amigo
1959 António Manuel Couto
Viana. Mancha Solar
1960 Fernando Guedes.
Viagem de Icaro   911.

QUITO CENTENNIAL ECUADOR
PRIZE
A literary prize, awarded on
December 6 as the anniversary
of the founding of the city of
Quito, was presented to Isaac
J. Barrera for his work,
"Historia de la Literatura
Ecuatoriana."   912.

Wilhelm RAABE PRIZE
(Germany)
This memorial prize, named
for the German writer, Wilhelm
Raabe (1831-1910), considered
one of the 19th century's greatest
novelists, is awarded by the
city of Brunswick (Stadt Braunschweig), where Dichter Raabe
lived from 1870 to 1910. Established in 1944 to honor a
single contemporary work of a
living author writing in the
German language considered
worthy of a prize named for
Raabe, or the entire work of
such an author, the 5000 DM
premium was granted annually
until 1954, when the frequency
of award was changed to three

years.
Winners, honored for their
entire literary work unless otherwise noted, include:
1944 Ricarda Huch
1946 Fritz von Unruh
1947 Werner Bergengruen.
Lyric and prose work
1948 Ina Seidel. Lyric and
prose work
1950 Hermann Hesse
1954 Max Frisch (Switzerland).
Stiller
1957 Friedrich Georg Jünger.
Entire work, especially the
book, "Zwei Schwestern"
1960 Gerd Gaiser. Schlussball
The RAABE MEDAL, awarded
for the first time in 1960 by the
city of Brunswick for service in
the dissemination of Raabe's work,
was presented to August Dresbach.
An earlier RAABE PRIZE
(Volkspreis) of the Wilhelm Raabe
Foundation was granted in 1934
to Gustav Frenssen for the work,
"Meino der Prahler."   913.

RAMAT-GAN LITERARY PRIZE
FOR HEBREW FICTION (Israel)
Established in 1955 "to
encourage original Hebrew fiction,"
this award of the municipality of
Ramat-Gan "is given for a book
published within the two years
immediately preceding the date
set for the distribution of the
prize." The literary judges,
appointed by the Authors' Association of Israel, may award the
prize for a specific book or for
the general literary contribution
of an author. To compete for
the IL 500 annual premium,
candidates send four copies of
the qualifying work with an application to the Cultural Department of Ramat-Gan.
Novelists, poets, and critics
honored with prizes (1955-1962)
are:
Jacob Fichman. Honorary
Prize
Jacob Horowitz. For man does

not lie
Abraham Kariv. Redeemed
crown
Avigdor Hameiri. Honorary
Prize
Joshua Bar-Joseph. A
Tabernacle of Peace
Abraham Broides. To the
hidden dawn
Israel Eldad. Reflections of
the Bible   914.

RAMAT-GAN PRIZE FOR
STUDIES IN JUDAISM (Israel)
"To encourage original re-
search and studies in Judaism,"
this municipal prize of IL 500
has been awarded since 1955.
Competing writers submit four
copies of their book to Cultural
Department, Ramat-Gan, for con-
sideration.
Among the winners of this
scholarly prize are:
Nachum Slusch. Honorary
Prize
Chaim Hillel Ben-Sasson.
Chapters in Medieval Jewish
history; and Meditation and
leadership
Chaim Bar-Droma. And this
is the boundary of the land
Avigdor Cherikover. The Jews
in the Hellenic and Roman
Worlds   915.

RAMOS PAZ PRIZE (Brazil)
The Academia Brasileira de
Letras (Avenida Presidente Wilson 203, Rio de Janeiro) offers
this Cr$3,625 premium for a
young Brazilian author who has
written an original unpublished
work in Portuguese on some
aspect of literature--especially
Brazilian Literature.
Winners with works of literary
criticism and history include;
1956 Ivolino Vasconcelos
1960 Abdon Vaz Tôrres.
Espera; Primeira Missão;
Ylanda e o Menino
1962 Henriques Losinkas
Alves. Antônio Bento.

Fantasma da Abolição   916.

REAL ACADEMIA ESPAÑOLA
(Spain)
Founded in 1714 and approved
by Royal Decree one year later,
the Spanish Academy (Felipe IV
4, Madrid) instituted literary contests and awards in 1778. Current prizes in literature include
the: Alba; Alvarez Quintero;
Cartagena; Castillo de Chirel;
Cerralbo; Espinosa y Cortina;
Llorente; Piquer; Rivadeneira;
San Gaspar (which see).
In addition to granting many
honors for literary and scholarly
writing (such as the prizes to
Ramón Solís for "El Cadiz de las
Cortes;" to Eduardo Marquina
for "historical plays;" 1912--to
Serafín and Joaquín Álvarez
Quintero for the drama,"Malvaloca;"
1923--to Carlos Maria Ocantos
for "La Cola de Paja;" 1945--
to Dámaso Alonso for "La Poesía
de San Juan de la Cruz;" 1955--
to J. Calvo Sotelo for his play,
"La Muralla") the Academy includes among its members many
of the national literary figures.
Election to the Academy, "most
respected recognition a writer may
receive in Spain," has been
achieved recently (1957) by Camillo
José Cela and Juan Antonio Zunzunegui, and previously by other
famous authors:
1861 Juan Valera
1874 Gaspar Núñez de Arce
1875 Pedro Antonio de Alarcón
1897 Benito Pérez Galdós
José María de Pereda
1902 Ramón Menéndez Pidal,
who became Academy Director
in 1925
1906 Armando Palacio Valdés
1913 Jacinto Benavente
1927 Antonio Machado y Ruiz
1928 Ramón Pérez de Ayala
1934 Ramiro de Maeztu
1935 Tomás Navarro Tomás
1936 Pío Baroja
1938 Manuel Machado y Ruiz

917.

RENCONTRE PRIZE (France
The publisher's prize of
Éditions "Rencontre" (51 rue de La
Harpe, Paris 5e) seeks to re-
vive interest in good novels pub-
lished earlier in the century
through granting the Recontre
Prize to those novels which were
issued in the early 1900's, and
are today most unjustly forgotten.
Laureates are:
1961
René Boylesve. L'enfant à
la balustrade (1903)
Emile Guillaumin. La vie d'un
simple (1904)
C. F. Ramuz. Aline (1905)
Abel Hermant. Les grands
bourgeois (1906)
Colette. La retraite senti-
mentale (1907)
Louis Codet. La petite
Chiquette (1908)
O. V. de L. Milosz. L'a-
moureuse initiative (1909)
Jean Giraudoux. Provinciales
(1910)   918.

RED BADGE PRIZE COMPETI-
TION (International--U. S. A.)
Dodd, Mead & Company (432
Park Avenue South, New York
16) offers this publisher's award
of $2, 500 (royalty advance) for
the best unpublished mystery-
detective-suspense novel submitted during the contest period--
closing dates April 15 and
October 15. Authors of any
nationality are eligible to compete, provided they have not
previously issued a book under
the "Red Badge" imprint. The
manuscript sent for consideration
must be in the English language
and at least 60, 000 words, and
preferably not over 80, 000 words,
in length.   919.

RÉFLEXION PRIZE (France)
The literary critics of Paris
constitute the jury of award for

the prize, offered by the journal,
"Arts" (140 Faubourg Saint-
Honoré, Paris) in the first week
of Spring. The prize, which
brings public attention to the best
work appearing during the preceding ten years which did not
obtain a wide reading public, was
initially presented, in 1960, to
Raymond Abellio, for "Les yeux
d'Ézechiel sont ouverts."   920.

REFUGEE BOOK AWARD
(International--U. S. A.)
Sponsored by the publisher,
Doubleday & Company (575
Madison Avenue, New York 22),
and the United States Committee
for Refugees (11 West 42nd
Street, New York 36), the prize
offered $500 for a "book-length
work of fiction or nonfiction
describing the experiences of a
refugee," written in English.
The award, which was granted
only once--in 1959, World Refugee
Year--was presented to Claire
Hedervary for "Broken bridges."
                          921.

Julius REICH PRIZE (Austria)
The Julius Reich Stiftung of
Vienna has presented the prize
to such authors as: August
Scholtis; Oskar Maurus Fontana.
                          922.

REINAERT PRIZES (Belgium)
Flemish language awards are
granted in several categories of
writing. Among recent winners
(1957) are: Felix Dalle for his
novel, "Beiten;" Gaston van der
Gucht for his book for young
people, "Boesjes uit mijn straat;"
and J. La Mote for his travel
book, "De kermis der profeten."
                          923.

Théophraste RENAUDOT PRIZE
(France)
This "Substitute Prix Goncourt"
award--named for the acknowledged
founder of the French press,

Théophraste Renaudot (1586-1653) with his "Gazette" (1631), the first regular journal in France--was established in 1926 by a group of writers and newspaper editors who were dissatisfied with the assignment of the Prix Goncourt, and determined to honor the novel "which should have received the prize."

Awarded annually on the same day as the Prix Goncourt--the first Sunday in December--and with the same rules of competition as that prize, the Renaudot Prize has brought professional and public prestige and book sales--not a monetary premium--to:

1926 Armand Lunel. Nicolo Peccavi
1927 Bernard Nabonne. Maitena
1928 André Obey. La joueur de triangle
1929 Marcel Aymé. La table-aux-crevés
1930 Germaine Beaumont. Piège
1931 Philippe Hériat. L'innocent
1932 Louis-Ferdinand Céline. Voyage au bout de la nuit
1933 Charles Braibant. Le roi dort
1934 Louis Francis. Blanc
1935 François de Roux. Jours sans gloire
1936 Louis Aragon. Les beaux quartiers
1937 Jean Rogissart. Mervale
1938 Pierre-Jean Launay. Léonie la bienheureuse
1939 Jean Malaquais. Les Javanais
1941 Paul Mousset. Quand le temps travaillait pour nous
1942 Robert Gaillard. Les liens de chaine
1943 André Soubiran. J'étais médecin avec les chars
1944 Roger Peyrefitte. Les amitiés particulières
1945 Henri Bosco. La mas Théotime
1946 David Rousset. L'univers concentrationnaire
Jules Roy. La vallée heureuse
1947 Jean Cayrol. Je vivrai l'amour des autres
1948 Pierre Fisson. Voyages aux horizons
1949 Louis Guilloux. Le jeu de patience
1950 Pierre Molaine. Les orgues de l'enfer
1951 Robert Margerit. Le Dieu nu
1952 Jacques Perry. L'amour de rien
1953 Célia Bertin. Dernière innocence
1954 Jean Reverzy. Le passage
1955 Georges Govy. Le Moissonneur d'épines
1956 André Perrin. Le père
1957 Michel Butor. La modification
1958 Edouard Glissant. La lézarde
1959 Albert Palle. L'expérience
1960 Alfred Kern. Le bonheur fragile
1961 René Bordier. Les blés
1962 Simonne Jacquemard. Le Veilleur de nuit   924.

RÉSISTANCE LITERARY PRIZE (France)

The jury for this prize is composed of the members of the Comité d'Action de la Résistance (10 rue de Charenton, Paris 12e), and the 2500 NF premium for the best writing contributing to the history of the Resistance and its spirit was granted in 1961 to Fernand Rodriguez--the initial award--for "L'escalier de fer."   925.

REUCHLIN PRIZE (Germany)

The cultural prize of the city of Pforzheim, not a literature prize in the strict sense, is granted for an eminent contribution to the German language, as determined by the Heidelberg

Academy of Science. The 5000
DM biennial premium has been
awarded:
1955 Werner Näf
1957 Rudolf Bultmann
1959 Hans Jantzen
1961 Richard Benz   926.

Fritz REUTER ART PRIZE
(Germany, East)
The council of Schwerin (Rat
des Bezirkes Schwerin) established this general cultural award
in 1956, in memory of the
Mecklenburg writer, Fritz
Reuter (1810-1874). The prize
grants a 3.500 DM premium in
each of three categories: Painting, Music, Literature.
Recipients include:
1955 Heinrich Behnken
1956 Benno Voelkner. Leute
von Karvenbruch (novel)
1957 Erich Kohler. Das
Pferd und sein Herr (story)
The Low German Fiction Prize
offered by the foundation,
Freiherr vom Stein, in Hamburg
is also named after Reuter--
FRITZ REUTER PRIZE.   927.

Ernst REUTER PRIZE (Ger-
many)
This 10.000 DM official prize
or the German government, first
offered in 1960 by the office,
Bundesministerium für Gesamt-
deutsche Fragen, honors the
best German language radio
station broadcast--either a play
or factual reporting--charac-
terized by a German theme.
The initial prize was presented
to Dieter Meichsner for "Rikchen
von Preetz."   928.

Alejandro REVERON PRIZE
(Venezuela)
The "best book on the life
and works of Venezuelan artists"
is designated by this award,
which was established by Edoardo
Crema in 1956.   929.

THE REVOLUTIONARY CIVIL
SERVANTS LEAGUE LITERARY
PRIZES (Viet-Nam)
Annual awards of the League
(17, Thong-Nhut Street, Saigon)
offer monetary premiums "to
encourage civil servants in the
art of writing, compilation, and
translation." First and Second
Prizes, and occasional "Encouragement Prizes," are offered for
literary works written by civil
servants in Vietnamese in three
categories:
Factual Writing--in specific
subject fields, as Administration, Law, Politics, Criticism,
Economics
Imaginative Writing--Novel, Short
Story, Essay and Criticism,
Poetry, Drama
Translations--including all styles
of imaginative and factual
literature   930.

RHEIN-RUHR LITERATURE
PRIZE (Germany)
The 3000 DM annual award of
the writers' group, Bund West-
deutscher Schriftsteller, in
Bochum, an industrial city in the
Ruhr valley, was presented in
1958 to Georg Breuker.   931.

RHEINLAND-PFALZ ART PRIZE
(Germany)
The entire work of an artist
or a single outstanding contribution associated with the cultural
life of the Rheinland-Pfalz region
is honored by this 5.000 DM
cultural prize, which was
established in 1956 by the Bundes-
land-Rheinland-Pfalz (Ministerium
für Unterricht und Kultus
Rheinland-Pfalz). The prize for
Literary Work was presented
in 1957 to Carl Zuckmayer.
A PFALZ LITERATURPREIS--
also Honor and Encouragement
Grants (Ehren-und Förderungsgaben)
to further literary work--was
established in 1959 by the literary

group, Literarischen Vereins der Pfalz, in cooperation with the Landesverband Rheinland-Pfalz des Schutzverbandes Deutscher Schriftsteller. The 2000 DM premium was awarded as an Ehrengab (Honorary Grant for the author's entire work) to Martha Saalfeld in 1959; and as a Föderungsgabe (Encouragement Grant for a native son or an author identified with the area through many years of work) to Wolfgang Schwarz in 1960.

932.

John Llewellyn RHYS MEMORIAL PRIZE (International--England)

Since 1942 this Ł50 prize has been awarded each year through the National Book League (7 Albermarle Street, London, W 1) for a book published during the preceding year by a citizen of the British Commonwealth under 30 years of age at date of the book's publication," which is considered "the most memorable and promising of any literary work" in the submitted entries.

Poems, Short Stories, Novels, Plays and other forms of imaginative literature are eligible, and books are submitted by publishers--not by authors--for consideration. Winners include:

1946 Oriel Malet (United Kingdom). My bird sings
1958 V.S. Naipaul (Jamaica). The mystic masseur
1959 Dan Jacobson (South Africa--England). A long way from London
1962 Edward Lucie Smith (Jamaica). A tropical childhood, and other poems

933.

Carlos RIBA PRIZE (Spain)

An annual prize for Catalan poetry was established in 1962 by the "Omnium Cultural"

(Montcada 20, Barcelona) with a premium of 25,000 pts, and publication of the winning work by Biblioteca Ossa Menor, as one of the publisher's series of Catalan poetry: "Poesia catalana." First winners of the award, established to encourage expression in Catalan, a language "being attacked by the present Spanish authorities," will be announced in 1962 on December 13, Santa Llúcia Day, in a traditional "fiesta de las letras catalanas."

934.

João RIBEIRO PRIZE (Brazil)

One of the many literary honors conferred by Academia Brasileira de Letras (Avenida Presidente Wilson 203, Rio de Janeiro), this Cr$50.000 prize is offered for the best book of philosophy, ethnography, or folklore--unpublished or published during the two years preceding the year of award.

Writers winning this scholarly literary award include:

1956 Marciel Pinheiro, Linguajar nordestino
Jesus Belo Galvão. Subconsciência e acceptividade na língua portuguesa
1958 Darcy Ribeiro and Berta G. Ribeiro. Arte Plumária dos índios Kaapor
1960 Armando Levy Cardoso. Toponímia Brasílica
1962 Angel Vaz Leão. O Período Hipocético Inicidado per se
Júlio Romão da Silva. Geonomásticos Cariocas de Procedência Indígena 935.

RICCIONE PRIZE (Italy)

Financed by contributions from such drama organizations as Societe Autori Drammatici Italiani, Istituto del Dramma Italiana, and Ente Italiana Scambi Teatrali, this prize, one of Italy's major drama awards,

offers L 500.000 annually for
plays which may have been produced but which must not be
published. Also offered is a
prize for plays which have been
neither produced nor published--
the EMILIA ROMAGNA PRIZE,
of L 100.000. Three copies of
competing plays must be sent
by June 20 to Segretaria del
Premio Riccione (via Luigi Serra
1³, Bologna).
Winners, announced by the
jury in September, include:
1947 Midi Manocci. Emmelina
1948 Gino Pugnetti. Paese
Ugo Betti. I morti parlano
1949 Carlo Terron. Giuditta
1950 Gennaro Pistilli.
Notturno
1951 Tullio Pinelli. Gorgonio
1952 Franco Monicelli.
Leonida non e qui
1953 E. Biagi. Giulia viene
da lontano
1954 Angelo Rognoni. La
flamma di Namu
1955 Renato Lelli. Sulle
strade di notte
1956 Massimo Binazzi. Gli
estranei
1957 Aldo Nicolaj. Le
formiche (television play)
1958 Paolo Levi. Lastrico
d'inferno
1959 Anton Gaetano Parodi.
L'ex maggiore Hermann
Grotz
1960 Ezio D'Errico. L'assedio
1961 Aldo Paladini. Svolta a
sinistra
1962 Dario Martini. Qualcosa
comunque   936.

RICHELIEU PRIZE (France)
The annual award offered by
the insurance company, Compagnie d'assurances générales
incendie (87 rue de Richelieu,
Paris 11e) brings 10.000 NF
each May to the author of a
prose work (Novel, Essay,
History) published during the
preceding year, that is judged

outstanding with regard to style
and in the best tradition of
French literature.
Winners are:
1957 Pierre Cosson. Et qui
laissent tomber leurs armes
1958 François Ponthier.
L'homme de guerre
1959 Andre Castelot. L'Aiglon
1960 Guy Ponce de Léon.
Le sang acide
1961 Robert Bourget-Pailleron.
La colombe du Luxembourg
1962 George Blond. Verdun
937.

Mary Roberts RINEHART FOUNDA-
TION AWARDS (International--
U.S.A.)
Grants-in-aid to help writers
to complete works in progress are
awarded each year by the Rinehart Foundation, which was established in 1959 by the three
sons of Mary Roberts Rinehart,
American novelist who died
September 22, 1958. The
$1,000 grants--as many as ten
each year--carry on the tradition
followed by Mrs. Rinehart in her
lifetime--that of "helping people
of creative ability who lacked the
means to complete their work."
Writers of any country or
nationality are eligible for the
grants, provided their work (a
definite project of biography,
autobiography, fiction, history,
poetry, drama, or science) is in
the English language. Application forms, which must accompany
an outline of work in progress
and "other supporting evidence for
consideration by the Administration Committee," may be obtained
from the Foundation (383 Madison
Avenue, New York 17).
Awards, which are determined
by a Committee of literary
critics and scholars, have been
granted such writers as Richard
Eunkook Kim (Korea--U.S.A.),
who received an award in 1961.
938.

RIO DE JANEIRO INDEPENDENT
CIRCLE OF THEATER CRITICS
AWARDS (Brazil)
Each year the drama critics'
group in Rio de Janeiro presents
an award--a bronze statue of
Father Ventura, "First Cariocan
Theatre Impresario"--for the best
work in the theatre.   In 1961 the
prize for "Best Playwright" was
given Nelson Rodrigues.   939.

RIO DE JANEIRO PRIZE
(International--Brazil)
A biennial 200,000 cruzeiros
Prêmio Cidade do Rio de Janeiro
is offered by the Municipal Government of the city of Rio de
Janeiro to honor the "best work
on the Brazilian capital published
in a foreign country and written
by a foreign author." Works in
any literary form and dealing with
any aspect of Rio de Janeiro are
eligible provided they meet the
specifications of minimum length:
Prose--150 pages; Poetry--1000
lines; Journalism--1000-word
articles.
Entries, which must have been
published during the two-year
contest period (1955 to January
1957; 1957 to January 1959),
may be submitted to any P.E.N.
center, or may be sent directly
to the Brazil P.E.N. Club
(Avenida Pechanha 26, Rio de
Janeiro 13).   940.

RIVADENEIRA PRIZE (Spain)
Offered by the Real Academia
Español for a "study on any
subject of linguistics or Spanish
literature," two premiums
(30,000 pts and 20,000 pts,
respectively) are granted. Next
contest period ends September
30, 1964.   941.

RIZZOLI PRIZE (Italy)
In 1959 a special prize of
500.000 lire was granted by the
Milan publisher, Rizzoli Editore
(Piazzi Carlo Derba 6) to Fiora

Vencenti.   942.

ROCKEFELLER FELLOWSHIPS
IN CREATIVE WRITING (Inter-
national--U.S.A.)
The Rockefeller Foundation (49
West 49th Street, New York) in-
cludes among its scholarships and
awards fellowships in creative
writing, which have been granted
since 1933.   Foreign writers from
Brazil, China, Denmark, Finland,
India, Italy, Mexico, Ghana,
Netherlands, Philippines, Sweden,
were given fellowships in the
period 1933-1950--including the
Filipino writers Edilberto K.
Tiempo (1948), and Nestor V.M.
Gonzalez (1949); and J.W.
Kwabena Nketia, the author from
Ghana who writes in Twi and in
English.
In the period 1951-1955, 14 of
899 awards were granted to foreign
authors including those from
Germany (Helmut Vierbrock);
India (Shripad Pendse); Italy
(Antonio Russi); Japan (Hiroyuki
Agawa, Ishi Momoko, Shohei
Ooka); Mexico (Ramon Xirau);
Philippines (Nick Joaquin y
Marques; Ricaredo D. Demetillo;
Virginia Moreno); and South
Africa.   943.

Pablo ROJAS PAZ PRIZE
(Argentina)
The prize of Sociedad Argentina
de Escritores (calle Mexico 564,
Buenos Aires) was established in
1958 for the best unpublished
biography presented in competition.   A recent winner of the
award (1961), which consists of a
monetary premium and publication
by Editorial Losada, was Jorge
Calvetti, with the "El Miedo
Immortal" (Immortal Fear).
      944.

Ricardo ROJAS PRIZE
(Argentina)
Named for Ricardo Rojas, the
Argentine writer and critic who

was the first professor of
Argentine Literature at the University of Buenos Aires, this
biennial competition of the city
of Buenos Aires offers prizes
($50.000; $30.000; $20.000)
for works in prose--imaginative
writing, criticism, and essays.
Recipients of the initial awards
in 1959 were:
  Angel J. Battistessa. Estaban
  Echeverria. La Cautiva
  Martin Fierro--critical and
  annotated editions
  Jose Hernandez. Bio-
  bibliographic study
  Boleslao Lewin. La Rebelion
  de Tupac Amaru
  Ismael Moya. El Arte
  de Los Payadores   945.

Aristides ROJAS PRIZE FOR
LITERATURE (Venezuela)
  The annual novel prize,
offered by Mrs. Ana Boulton de
Phelps, brings a citation and
5,000 bolivares to the winning
author. Recent recipients include:
  1955 Miguel Otero Silva.
  Casas muertas
  1957 Gloria Stolck. Fondos
  amargos
  1960 Arturo Croce. Los
  diablos danzantes   946.

ROME PRIZES (Italy)
  Among the best-known and
longest established city prizes
in Italy are the cultural awards,
Premi Roma, which are offered
each year for achievement in
various fields of contemporary
Italian art--including Literature;
Poetry; Drama; Cinema; Painting; and Music.
  The L 1.000.000 premium
offered in each section of creative
endeavor has been granted such
authors as: Giuseppe Ungaretti
(poetry); Giorgio Bassani; and
Ugo Betti, for his first play,
"La Padrona," in 1926.
  Other cultural and literary

awards have been granted under
the name, PREMIO ROMA, as the
Gold Medal--recently awarded the
Nagel Travel Guide Series--and a
CITTA' DI ROMA PRIZE for
published or unpublished poetry is
announced in 1962 by a publishing
firm, presso Paolo Diffidenti (via
G. Pitacco 35, Rome), with six
prizes consisting of medals and
cups.   947.

Silvio ROMERO PRIZE (Brazil)
  Directed to the "preservation
of Brazilian folklore," this Cr
$100.000 literary prize of the
Brazilian Minister of Education
and Culture (Ministério da
Educacão e Cultura de Letras) is
granted by the Brazilian Academy
of Letters (Academia Brasileira
de Letras, Avenida Presidente
Wilson 203, Rio de Janeiro) for
unpublished and original writings
in literary history and criticism
on a theme announced by the
donor--as, "Romances Tradicionais
do Brasil;" "Dimensões i Interpretação da Literatura Brasileira."
  Recipients of this official honor
include:
  1957 Brito Broca. A vida
  literária no Brasil
  1959 Eduardo Portella. Dimensões I"
  1961 Valdemar Cavalcanti.
  Jornal Literário   948.

RONSARD PRIZE (France)
  A 2.000 NF poetry prize was
created in 1961 by the insurance
company, Compagnie "La Nationale;"
and is awarded by a distinguished
jury including Jules Romains,
Maurice Rat, Paul Gilson, and
Alfred Rosset. Works are
entered in competition from
December 1 to February 15
(Secrétariat du "Prix Ronsard,"
c/o Compagnie d'assurances
contre l'incendie, 17 rue Laffitte,
Paris 9e).
                              949.

Ramon ROSA PRIZE (Honduras)
One of three National Prizes
of Honduras, established by the
National Congress of Honduras
on February 18, 1949, this annual award, consisting of a
diploma and 2.000 lempiras, has
been granted since 1954. Prize
winners are determined by the
Universidad Nacional Autonoma
de Honduras, and the honor is presented each September 19. 950.

Max ROSE PRIZE (Belgium)
This French-language award
was granted in 1960 to J. L.
Vanham for his work, "Les
Aubes exaucées."   951.

Peter ROSEGGER PRIZE
(Austria)
The province of Styria
(Landesregierung Steiermark,
Graz, Styria) established an
annual award in 1951 in memory
of the famous Styrian writer,
Peter Rosegger. The S 20.000
premium is offered to an author
whose usual place of residence
is Austria and who is associated
with Styria through birth, long
residence, or special work.
The prize, which honors the
entire literary output of a
writer or a single outstanding
work, has been won or shared
by:
1951 Rudolf Hans Bartsch;
Max Mell
1952 Paula Grogger;
Margarete Weinhandl
1953 Franz Nabl; Rudolf
Stilbill--Förderungspreis
1954 Julius Franz Schüttz;
Karl Adolf Mayer
1955 Eduard Hoffer; Paul
Anton Keller; Alois Hergouth
1956 Julius Zerzer; Kurt
Hildebrand Matzak; Anna
Lukesch
1957 Hild Knobloch; Rudolf
List; Herbert Zand
1959 Franz Taucher; Helene
Haluschka; Martha Wölger

1961 Bruno Brehm; Wolfgang
Arnold and Erwin Walter
Stein--Förderungspreis
952.

Victor ROSSEL PRIZE (Belgium)
The Rossel Prize is one of
the famous novel prizes awarded
in Belgium. It was founded in
1938 and is awarded each year
by "Le Soir," Brussels newspaper
(21, place de Louvain). The
published or unpublished novels
of Belgian authors writing in
French are eligible for the honor,
provided the works have been
written or published in the year
of competition.
Novelists whose work has been
brought to public attention by the
prize include:
1947 Maurice Carême. Contes
pour Caprine; Orladour
1952 Albert Ayguesparse.
Notre ombre nous précède
1955 Lucien Marchal. La chute
du Grand Chimu
1956 Stanislas D'Otremont.
L'amour déraissonable
1957 Edmond Kinds. Les
ornières de l'été
1958 Stéphane Jourat. Entends,
ma chère, entends...
1959 Jacqueline Harpman.
Brève Arcadie
1960 Victor Misrahi. Les
routes du Nord
1961 David Scheinert. Le
Homard aux longues oreilles
953.

Léopold ROSY PRIZE (Belgium)
The triennial award of the
Belgian Royal Academy of
French Language and Literature
for essays written in French by
Belgian authors was first awarded in 1942. Recent winners of
the 5,000 fr premium are:
1955 Jeanine Moulin. Textes
inédits de Guillaume
Apollinaire
1958 Claude Pichois. L'image
de la Belgique dans les

lettres françaises de 1930
à 1870
1961 Jacqueline Van-Praag
Chantraine. Gabriel Miro ou
le visage du Levant   954.

"ROTTERDAMSE NUTS" PRIZE
(Netherlands)
Granted by the Rotterdam
Society for Public Utility (Department Rotterdam der Maat-
schapij Tot Nut, van 't Algemeen)
since 1949, this 500 fl prize is
granted for "a novel of social-
ethical tendency," set in Rotterdam. Among the authors honored are:
B. Stroman. Kleine diefjes
worden groot (Little thieves
grow up)
P.A. Begeer. Wespen en
Horzels (Wasps and hornets)
J.M. van Krimpen. In de
oude stadswijk (In the Old
City District--the gospel
in a port town)   955.

Juan RUIZ DE ALARCÓN
PRIZE (Mexico)
The annual drama prize--
MEXICAN THEATRE CRITICS
BEST PLAY; MEXICAN DRAMA
CRITICS AWARD--is granted by
the critics' organization,
Agrupacion de Criticos de
Teatro de Mexico (Republic del
Salvador 31, deps 11 y 12,
Mexico 1, D.F.), for the best
dramatic work presented during
the preceding year's theatre
season.   Named for the Mexican-
born playwright, Juan Ruiz de
Alarcón (1581-1639), who was
the first American dramatist to
win critical acclaim in Spain,
the prize is an honorary award--
consisting of a diploma.
   Playwrights honored with this
significant Mexican prize include:
1950 Rodolfo Usigli. Comedies
   Xavier Villaurrutia. Drama
   (posthumous award)
1951 Rodolfo Usigli. El niño
   y la niebla

1952 Celestino Gorostiza. El
   color de nuestra piel
1953 Héctor Mendoza. Las
   cosas simples
1954 María Luisa Algarra.
   Los años de pureba
1955 Federico S. Inclán. Hoy
   invita la Güera
1956 Luis G. Basurto.
   Miércoles de Ceniza
1957 Emilio Cargallido.
   Felicidad
1958 Luis Moreno. Los sueños
   encendidos
1959 Federico S. Inclán.
   Detrás de esa puerta
1960 Fernando Sánchez
   Mayans. Las alas del pez
1961 Hugo Argüelles. Los
   Prodigiosos   956.

RUMANIAN ACADEMY PRIZES
   These cultural prizes of the
Academy of the Rumanian People's
Republic (Calea Victoriei, no.
125, Bucharest), which were
established in 1949, "to encourage
scientific, literary, and artistic
activity," consist of a monetary
premium and a diploma. Granted
with no specific frequency, "with
priority to the younger talents,"
the presentation of the prizes is
a solemn occasion when the win-
ners--proposed by a special committee of nine and approved by
the General Assembly of the
Academy and the Rumanian People's
Republic Council of Ministers--
receive the honor "in the presence
of the Presidium of the Grand
National Assembly, of the members of the Government and of
the Secretariate of the Central
Committee of the Rumanian
Workers' Party."
   Honored by prizes which are
granted in five fields (prose,
poetry, drama, criticism,
journalism)   are writers, poets,
and critics "in the early stages
of their literary career, but who
already show literary maturity."
Among the authors receiving this

State recognition for their professional achievement are:

I. L. CARAGIALE PRIZE FOR DRAMA
1956 A. Kiritescu. Theatre
1962 A. Mirodan. The Famous 702

ION CREANGA PRIZE FOR PROSE
1956 Ion Pas. Days of your life; Chains
1961 Alecu Ivan Ghilia. Cuscrii (The Kinsfolk; or Relatives) Teodor Mazilu. Bariera (The turnpike; or The barrier)
1962 Nicolae Velea. The gate

GH. COSBUC PRIZE FOR POETRY
1949 Radu Boureanu and Maria Banus
1956 Virgil Teodorescu. I write in black and white
1957 Miron Radu Paraschivescu. Translation of the poem "Pan Tadeusz," by A. Mickiewicz
1961 Aurel Rau. Sacred fires Ion Brad. Cu timpul meu (With my times)

CONST. DOBROGEANU-GHEREA PRIZE FOR CRITICISM
1949 Ion Vitner
1961 Alexendru Dima. Alecu Russo (monograph) Dumitru Micu. Romanul romilhesc contemporan (The contemporary-Rumanian novel--critique)

AL. SAHIA PRIZE FOR JOURNALISM
1949 The Review, "Contemporanul"
1956 Traian Cosovei. The giant prelude
1961 Simion Pop. Paralela 45 (45th parallel) Nicolae Tic. Profiluri (Profiles)
1962 Ervine Mike. The drive for reeds   957.

RUMANIAN GRAND PRIZE
This official award of the Rumanian government was presented to Robul Theodorescu, whose works became known in English with Oscar Leonard's English adaptation of his book, "One house contains us," in 1939.
958.

RUMANIAN MINISTRY OF CULTURE AND EDUCATION PRIZES
Among the writers distinguished with this contemporary literary honor of the Rumanian government--with a premium of 15.000 lei granted in 1956 for works published in 1958--are:
Titus Popovici. The stranger (novel)
Veronica Porumbacu. My generation (poetry)
Theodor Mazilu. Pocket book of insects
A. Mirodan. The journalists (play)
Radu Tudoran. The last story (prose)   959.

RUMANIAN STATE PRIZE
"The highest distinction that can be awarded to exponents of the arts and letters in the Rumanian People's Republic" is the Rumanian State Prize, which "is awarded to all writers and artists who have contributed and contribute by their works to enlighten the people, to enrich their country's artistic treasury, to safeguard the peace and understanding among peoples." Both older writers who have achieved a permanent place in Rumanian--or in world--literature, and younger writers whose literary efforts have brought them favorable public and critical attention have received the official state prize--"which crowns outstandingly fruitful literary activity" of "creators who have given to the national cultural patrimony works profoundly original by virtue of realism and authenticity, as well as high artistic merit."

The honor, established as an
award of the Rumanian Council of
Ministers in 1949 "for works of
an uncommon value, for the up-
building of socialism in the
Rumanian People's Republic,"
consists of an honorary title--
"State Prize Laureate" --a monetary premium, a badge, a diploma,
and an identity card. The prize,
currently granted biennially, is
determined by the Council of
Ministers with the recommendations of the State Prize Committee
and recognizes writers with
awards--First, Second, and Third
Class, which range from 20.000
to 50.000 lei premium--in four
areas: Prose (Novel, Short
Stories, and other forms);
Poetry; Drama; Criticism.

Among Rumanian writers
honored with their country's most
important cultural award are:
Mihail Sadoveanu (1880-1961);
the poet Tudor Arghezi; Mihai
Beniuc; Zaharia Stancu; and the
younger authors V. E. Galan, and
Marin Preda. Some of the
laureates have received the prize
more than once. Recent winners
include:
Novel and Other Prose
1949 Mihail Sadoveanu.
Mitrea Cocor
2nd class--Istvan Asztalos.
Vintul nu se stirneste din
senin (The wind doesn't
blow without cause)
1950-51
2nd class--Gyorgy Kovacs.
Cu ghiarele si cu dintii
(With one's claws and
teeth)
Eusebiu Camilar. Zorii
robilor (The dawn of slaves)
Ion Calugaru. Ovel si piine
(Steel and bread)
Valerien Em Galan. The
Foundation
3rd class--Istvan Horvath.
Brazda peste haturi
(Furrows without boundary
paths; or Blot out the

boundaries)
Nicolae Jianu. Cumpana
luminilor (Rise of lights; or
Well of light)
1952 Zaharia Stancu. Barefoot
(1952 edition)
3rd prize--Dumitru Mircea.
White bread
1953 Geo. Bogza. Anti
impotrivirii (Years of darkness; or Years of resistance);
and Meridiane sovietice
(Soviet meridians)
Camil Petruscu. Un om intre
oameni (A man amongst men)
2nd class--Istvan Asztalos.
Inima tinara (Young heart)
I. Ludo.   Domnul general
guverneaza (The general
governs)
3rd class--Vladimir Colin.
Basme (Fairy tales; or
Legends)
Dragos Vicol. Valea fierului
(Iron vale; or Valley of Iron)
Andras Suto. Pornesc oamenii
(People move; or People
work)
1954 Valerian Em. Galan.
Baragan, vol 1
2nd class--Dumitru Almas.
Spatarul Neculai Milescu (The
Sword-bearer Neculai Milescu)
3rd class--Franciscan Munteanu.
In orasul de pe Mures (In
the city upon Mures)
1955 Marin Preda. Moremetii
(Morometes)
Istvan Nagy.   La cea mai
inalta tensiune (At the
highest tension), second
issue
Poetry
1949 Alexandru Toma. Cintul
vietii (Song of life)
2nd class--Dan Desliu. Lazar
de la Rusca
1950-51 Dan Desliu. In numele
vietii (In the name of life);
and Minerii din Maramures
(Miners of Maramures)
Mihai Beniuc. Poems pub-
lished during 1950 and 1951
2nd class--Eugen Jebeleanu.

In satul lui Sahia (In Sahia's
village)
Veronica Porumbacu. Mar-
turii (Confessions; or
Testimonies)
Eugen Frunza. Zile slavite
(Glorious days)
Imre Horvath. Versuri (Verses)
3rd class--Miron Radu Para-
schivescu. Translation into
Rumanian of the poem
"Ruslan and Ludmila" by
A.S. Pushkin
Alex. Philippide. Translation
into Rumanian of Lermontov,
"Selected poems"
Nina Cassian. Nica fara
frica (Fearless Nica--fairy
tale in poetry)
1952 2nd class--Lajos Letay.
A new world is being built
3rd class--Mihu Dragomir.
Stars of peace
1953 Cicerone Theodorescu.
Un cintec din ulita noastra
(A song of our street); and
his translation of A. Tvardov-
ski, "Vasily Tiorkin"
2nd class--Demostone Botez.
Floarea soarelui (The sunflower)
Miron Radu Paraschivescu.
Laude (Praises)
Ferenc Szemler. A lupta cu
devotament (Fight with heart
and soul; Hungarian title--
Haroolni hiven)
3rd class--Alex Andritoiu. In
tara Motilor se face ziua
(Day dawns in the country
of Moti)
Stefan Iures. Cuvint despre
tinerete (A word about youth)
Eric Majtenyi. De straja (On
guard; Hungarian title--
Orsegen)
1954 Mihai Beniuc. Marul de
linga drum (The apple tree
by the road)
2nd class--George Lesnea.
Translation of A.S. Pushkin,
"Evgueni Oneguin," novel in
poetry
Mihu Dragomir. Razboiul

(The war)
Alfred Margul Sperber. Translation into German of his
work, Poezii populare
rominesti (Rumanian folk
poems)
3rd class--A. E. Baconsky.
Cintece de zi si noapte
(Songs of day and night)
Jeno Kiss. Wayfarer's
rhapsody
1957 Tudor Arghezi. 1907;
and Cintare omului (Song of
man)
Drama 1949 Camil Petrescu.
Balcescu
Maria Banus. Ziua cea mare
(The great day)
1950-51 Mihail Davidoglu.
Cetatea de foc (The fiery
fortress or The stronghold of
fire)
Nicolae Moraru, and Aurel
Baranga. Pentru fericirea
poporului (For the happiness
of the people)
2nd class--Mircea Stefanescu.
Matei Millo
Laurentiu Fulga. Ultimul mesaj
(The last message)
3rd class--Lucia Demetrius.
Vadul nou (The new crossing)
Andras Suto, and Zoltan Hajdu.
Mireasa desculta (Barefoot
bride)
1952 2nd class--Lucia Demetrius.
Men of today
3rd class--C. Constantin, and
Adrian Rogoz. Martin Rogers
discovers America
Ladislau Kiss, and Dezideriu
Kovacs. Storm in the
mountains
1953 2nd class--Aurel Baranga.
Mielul turbat (The furious
lamb)
Horia Lovinescu. Lumina de la
Ulmi (Light from the Ulmi)
3rd class--Mihail Davidoglu.
Schimbul de onoare (The
high shift; or Honour work-
shift)
Tudor Soimaru. Afaceristii
(The racketeers)

1955 2nd class--Horia Lovin-
escu. Citadela sfarimata
(The broken citadel)
3rd class--Ana Novac. Preludiu
(Prelude); and Familia
Kovacs (Kovacs Family)
Criticism 1953 2nd class--Ovid
S. Crohmalniceanu. Articole
si cronici (Articles and
book reviews)
D. Panaitescu-Perpessicius.
Mihail Eminescu's works--
critical edition of the poet
3rd class--Silvian Iosifescu.
Caragiale (monograph)
1954 2nd class--Ion Vitner,
and Ovid S. Crohmalniceanu.
Contribution to the 2nd
volume of "The History of
Rumanian Literature" 960.

RUMANIAN-UNITED STATES OF
AMERICA CULTURAL EXCHANGE
OF BOOKS
While not a literary prize, as
such, a high national honor is
given in the public recognition
afforded the books of contemporary Rumanian authors which are
selected by the Rumanian government as representative of the
best Rumanian writing, and
translated into English in accordance with the Rumanian-United
States cultural exchange agreement, entered into force December 9, 1960. Among authors
so honored is Mihail Sadoveanu--
Rumania's "greatest 20th-century
writer," who died in 1961 at
the age of 81--whose books
published recently in the U.S.A.
include: Evening Tales; Tales
of War; The Mudhut Dwellers
(Twayne Publishers, Inc., 31
Union Square West, New York 3).
961.

RUPPIN PRIZE (Israel)
This monetary cultural award
of the municipality of Haifa has
been granted once a year since
1945 for the best book published
in Hebrew, within the last three

years, or for an unpublished
manuscript in the fields of:
Literature, Sociology, or Science.
A jury composed of representatives of the city of Haifa, the
Haifa College, and the Technion
(Israel Institute of Technology)
determines the winning work.
The prize has been awarded
to such writers as:
1945 Devora Baron. L'eth 'ata
(For the time being)
1946 Yitzhak Shenberg. Yamin
Yedaberu (Time will tell)
1947 Nathan Altherman.
Kochavim bachuz, Simchat
'anyim, Shirei makkoth
Mitzrayim (poems)
Zvi Woislavsky. Chavlei tar-
buth (Conflicts of culture)
1948 S. Yishar. Hachursha
asher bagiv'ah (fiction)
Martin Buber. N'tivoth ba-
utopia (Ways in Utopia)
S. Raikoitz. Hakarkoath
hamelechim be'emek hayarden
1949 Lea Goldberg. 'Al
haprichah (poems)
1950 M. Tabib. Kéessewbassadeh
(Like the grass in the field--
fiction)
1951 Meir Mohr. 'Ayin be'ayin
(From eye to eye--poems)
1953 G. Shofman. Selected
works
1954 Anda Pinkerfeld-Amir.
Achath (poems)
1955 Yitzchak Shalev. Koloth
enosh chamim (poems)
1957 Naomi Frankel. Shaul and
Yohanna (fiction)
Shin Shalom. Bametach
hagavohah (fiction)
1958 Eliezer Steinmann. Selected works
1960 S. Melzer. Or sarua
(poems, ballads)   962.

RUSTICHELLO DA PISA PRIZES
(Italy)
Journalism awards, sponsored
by Ente provinciale per il Turismo of Pisa, and the "Spettacolo,"
since 1955, offer each year four

gold books--two for Italian, and two for foreign journalists--for the best article published during the year on any aspect of the history, art, or tourist attractions of Pisa. Previous winners include:
1958 Luigi M. Persone
1961 Gianna Manzini. Una strada come una donna, in "Giornale di Sicilia" Joseph Coolsaet. Pisa, in "Auto Touring," of Brussels
1962 Andres Travesi. Pisa y su Gioco del Ponte (Spain)
963.

SAARLAND ART PRIZE (Germany)
The general cultural prize of the Minister für Kultus, Unterricht und Volksbildung, was granted in 1960 for the first time in the subject of Literature. The award was presented to Gustav Regler, resident of Mexico, for his entire literary work, including "Das Ohr des Malchus." 964.

SAHARA GRAND PRIZE FOR LITERATURE (France)
Awarded by the writers' group, Association Nationale des Écrivains de la Mer et de l'Outre Mer (41 rue de la Bienfaisance, Paris 8e), the Grand Prix Littéraire du Sahara was established in 1959 with a 2000 NF premium. Winners of the prize, which is granted each November for a work expanding the present knowledge about the Sahara and its inhabitants, or concerning the French administration of the Sahara, or for the entire writings of an authority on the Sahara, are:
1959 Henri Lhote
1960 Paul Mousset. Ce Sahara qui voit le jour
1961 Guy Le Rumeur. Le Sahara avant le pétrole
965.

SAHITYA AKADEMI AWARDS (India)
The Sahitya Akademi--India's National Academy of Letters--was established by the government of India in 1954, as a "national organization to work actively for the development of Indian letters and to set high literary standards, to foster and coordinate literary activities in all the Indian languages and to promote through them all the cultural unity of the country." Annual awards of Rs 5,000 are granted to the authors of the most outstanding books of literary interest published during the contest period, in each of the 16 major languages of India recognized by the Sahitya Akademi--the 14 major languages enumerated in the Constitution of India, plus English and Sindhi.
The first award, granted in 1955, considered books published during the preceding seven years, and each year since that date books published during the three preceding years are considered for the award. The Executive Board of the Akademi determines the prizes on the basis of recommendations from "distinguished scholars and critics in the language concerned," and awards are presented each Spring by the President of India--who is also President of the Akademi--Sri Jawaharlal Nehru.
The Awards honor writing of fiction, nonfiction, and other literary forms, such as poetry, biography, essay, criticism. The Akademi also grants two additional prizes for Sanskrit--one for creative writing in Sanskrit, the other for original writing on or about Sanskrit literature written in any Indian language or in English. Winners of the Akademi Award, usually presented in January or February and also designated the "Presi-

dent's Award," include:
Novels and Short Stories
1955 Gopinath Mohanty.
Amrutara Santan (Oriya)
1956 Tarasankar Bandyopadhyaya.
Arogya-Niketan (Bengali)
Krashnamurti 'Kalki.' Alai
Osai (Tamil)
1957 Thakazhi Sivasankara
Pillai. Chemmeen (Malaya-
lam)
1958 Rajasekhara Bose.
Anandibai Ityadi Galpa
(Bengali--short stories)
Akhtar Mohiuddin. Sat Sangar
(Kashmiri--short stories)
Kanchucharan Mohanty. Ka
(Oriya)
1959 Gajednra Kumar Mitra.
Kalkatar Kachhei (Bengali)
1960 R. K. Narayan. The guide
(English)
'Uroob' (pseud of P. C. Kut-
tikrishnan). Sundarikalum
Sundaranmarum (Malayalam)
V. S. Khandekar. Yayati
(Marathi)
1961 Birendrakumar Bhat-
tacharya. Iyaruingam
(Assamese)
Bhagwaticharan Verma. Bhoole
Bisre Chitri (Hindi)
Nanak Singh: Ik Mian Do
Talwaran (Punjabi)
M. Varadarajan. Agal Vilakku
(Tamil)
Poetry 1961 Rehman Rahi.
Nauroz-i-Saba (Kashmiri)
Imtiaz Ali 'Arshi'. Diwan-i-
Ghalib (Urdu)
Nonfiction
1955 Suravaram Pratap Reddy.
Andrula Sanghika Charitramu
(Social history of the Andhras
as revealed through litera-
ture) (Telegu)
Tarakateertha Laxman Shastri
Joshi. Vaidik Samskriticha
Vikas (Cultural history of
Vedic India) (Marathi)
1958 C. Rajagopalachari.
Chakravarti Tirumagan
(Ramayana--retold in prose)
(Tamil)

K. P. Kesava Menon. Kazhinja
Kalam (Autobiography)
(Malayalam)
Rahul Sankrityayana. Nadhya
Asia Ka Itihas (History of
Central Asia) (Hindi)
1961 A. R. Krishna Sastri.
Bangali Kadambarikara
Bankimchandra (Kannada)
Godavaris Misra. Arhasatabdir
Odisa O Tanhire Mo Sthan
(Oriya)
Balanthrapu Rajanikantha Rao.
Andhra Vaggeyakar Charitramu
(Telugu)   966.

Josef SAILER PRIZE (Germany)
The drama award, offered
by the Josef Sailer Stiftung in
the city of Oetigheim, was granted as a 2000 DM premium in
1959 to Franz and Bernward
Kollmel for their play, "Josef und
Seine Bruder."   967.

SAINT VINCENT PRIZE (Italy)
The Saint Vincent Prize has
been awarded for poetry, and
most recently (1961) for journalism (Segretaria del Premio,
Corso Reggio Parco 2, Torino).
Recipients of the L 5.000.000
prizes include:
1948 Sergio Solmi; Afonso
Gatto
1949 Enrico Pea. Vita in
Egitto (prose)
Camillo Sbarbaro. Trucioli
(poetry)
1959 Paolo Monelli   968.

SAINTE-BEUVE PRIZE (France)
This highly-regarded literary
honor brings as a prize not a
monetary premium, but the
critical acclaim of a jury which
includes the laureates of the preceding year of four of France's
best-known annual literary awards:
Goncourt; Fémina; Interallié;
and Renaudot. Established in
1946 and awarded each year
shortly after Easter, the prize
consists of two awards for books

by Frenchmen and published in France: Novel Prize; and Prize for Poetry or Essays on general cultural subjects such as literary or art criticism.

Publishers may submit as many as six books which they have issued during the year for consideration. The prizes are granted to direct the attention of readers to literary works of quality, whose authors are not sufficiently known to the general public and which have not received a literary honor or award. Laureates include:

1946 Pär Lagerkvist (Sweden). Les nains
1947 Victor A. Kravchenko. J'ai choisi la liberté
1948 Armand Hoog. L'accident Gilbert Cesbron. Notre prison est un royaume
1949 André Dhôtel. David Claude Mauriac. André Breton (essay)
1950 Georges Poulet. Etude sur le temps humain (essay)
1952 Pierre Boulle. Le pont de la rivière kwai
1956 Henri Thomas. La cible
1957 Alex Curvers (Belgium). Tempo di Roma
Alain Bosquet. Premier testament (poetry)
1958 Henri D'Amfreville. Naufrage des sexes
Mongo Beti. Mission terminée (essay)
1959 Jean Cathelin. Marcel Aymé ou le paysan de Paris (essay)
1960 Nicole Védrès. Suite parisienne (essay)
Gilbert Prouteau. La peur des femmes
1961 Robert Abiracheb Casanova ou la dissipation Patrick Walberg. Le promenoir de Paris (essay)
969.

SAINTOUR PRIZE (France)
The annual prize of the Académie des Inscriptions et Belles-Lettres is granted successively to the best French work regarding the Orient; Classical Antiquity; and the Middle Ages and the Renaissance.

Recipients since 1950, date of the initial award, include:
1951 Henri Musset. Histoire du Christianisme, surtout en Orient (3 vol)
1957 Philippe Marcais. Le parler arabe de Djidjelli et les textes arabes de Djidjelli
1960 Jean Vercoutter. L'Egypt et le monde égéen préhéllenique
1961 Pierre Grenade. Essai sur les origines du Principat
1962 Le Hir and Hatzfeld. Essai de bibliographie critique de stylistique francaise et romane
Henri Morriér. Dictionnaire de Poétique et de Rhétorique
970.

SALA DE IMPRENSA PRIZE (Portugal)
The 3.000$ prize of the Portuguese government (Secretariado Nacional da Informação) was established in 1959 and is awarded four times a year to the author or the journalist having the best reporting published in a Portuguese newspaper. Competing articles must be presented in duplicate on the fifth of January, February, March, and September --the month following the three month's period of competition.
971.

SALENTO PRIZE (Italy)
The prose prize for novels and short stories (L 1.000.000) is the best-known of the many prizes (presso l' Amministrazione Provinciale di Lecce) including awards for Economics (L 2.000. 000 for unpublished works on the industrialization of the prov-

ince of Lecce offered in 1962);
Scholarly Works (Universita
Salenta Prize of L 500.000);
Journalism (L 200.000).
Recipients include:
    1953 Livia de Stefani (Livia
    Signorina). La vigna di
    Uve nere (first work)
    1956 Aldo Capitini. Canto
    corale (lyrics)
    1957 Ignazio Silone. Il
    Segreto di Luca
    1958 Carlo Cassola. Il Soldato
    Giuseppe Cassieri. I delfini
    sulle tombe
    1959 Dante Troisi. La strada
    della perfezione
    1960 Italo Calvino. I nostri
    antenati
    Giuseppe Bufalori. La
    masseria (first work)
    1962 Mario Fratti. La
    Menzogna   972.

SAMIL LITERARY PRIZE
(Korea)
    Since 1959, the Pacific Cement
Company (1st-ka, Ulchi-ro,
Chung-ku, Seoul) has offered
this annual prize of 2,000,000
hwan and a citation for the best
work of imaginative writing or
scholarly research. Works
must be submitted for consideration by November 15 of the year
preceding the year of award,
and the prizes are presented
on the first of March of the
following year.   973.

"SAN GASPAR" PRIZE (Spain)
    The prize and allowances of
"San Gaspar" are distributed
each year by Real Academia
Española.   974.

SANT JORDI PRIZE (Spain)
    One of the "Santa Lucia
Prizes," this award was instituted by Biblioteca Selecta
(Ronda de Sant Pere 3, Barcelona 10) for an unpublished
novel in Catalan--minimum
length 250 typed pages--and the

150,000 pts prize is now awarded
each year by "Omnium Cultural"
(Montcada 20, Barcelona). The
prize was established in 1960
as "stimulation to Catalan Liter-
ates who write this language
spoken by six million inhabitants
in Catalonia, Valencia, and the
Balearic Islands (Spain), and
Roussillon (France), and forbidden
for the public use by the present
Spanish authorities."
    The prize, "Premio San Jorge,"
which includes publication by
Biblioteca Selecta, is granted on
December 13, Santa Lucia Day,
in a traditional "fiesta de las
letras Catalanas," and has
honored such writers as:
    1960 Enrico Massó. Viure no
    és fàcil
    1961 Josep María Espinas.
    L'ultim replà   975.

SANTA LUCIA PRIZES (Spain)
    Literary awards for writing
in Catalan are presented in
Barcelona on Saint Lucia's Day,
December 13, and include such
prizes as: Catala; Yxart;
Sant Jordi; Aedos (which see).
Works entered in competition
must be submitted by October
31, and information about each
year's prizes is available from
Casa del Libro, Ronda de San
Pedro 3, Barcelona.   976.

SANTIAGO LITERARY PRIZES
(Chile)
    The Premios Literarios de la
Municipalidad de Santiago were
instituted in 1934 as an annual
literary competition under the
auspices of the city of Santiago.
Awards, formalized with the
Prize Rules in 1940, total E01-
200 and distinguish the best book
published during the preceding
year in one of five categories:
Novel; Poetry; Drama; Essay
(including biography, and social,
political, historical, and moral
studies); and--since 1954--

Short Stories.
The prizes, ranging in premium from four to one-half sueldos vitales, have been presented to:
1935 Julio Barrenchea.
Espejo del ensueno (poem)
1935 and 1941 Luis Durand
1936 Juan Marín. Paralelo 53 sur
1952 Antonio Campaña. La cima ardiendo (poem)
1956 José Donoso. Veraneo y otros cuentos (short stories)
Among more recent winners are:
Novel--
1958 José Manuel Vergara.
Daniel y los leones corados
Luis Enrique Délano. Puerto de Fuego
1960 Enrique Lafourcade.
Fiesta del Rey Acab
Leonardo Espinoza. Puerto Engaño
1961 Armando Cassigoli.
Angeles bajo la lluvia
Hernan Jaramillo. Crónica del Hombre
Poetry--
1958 Efraín Barquero. La Compañera
1960 Braulio Arenas. Poemas
1961 Juvencio Valle. Del monte en la ladera
Drama--
1958 Fernando Josseau. El prestamista
1960 Alejandro Sieveking.
Paracido a la felicidad
1961 Sergio Vodanovic. Deja quo los perros ladren
Essay--
1958 Hernan Ramierez Necochea.
Historia del morimiento obrero en Chile
Mario Naudón. Apreciación tetral
1960 Alberto Baltra. Crecimiento economico de America Latina
1961 Jorge Millas. Ensayos sobre la Historia Espiritual del Occidente

Stories--
1958 Francisco Coloane.
Tierra del Fuego
1960 Enrique Bunster. Aroma de Polinesia
1961 Maite Allamand. El Funeral del Diablo; Polí Delano. Fuente Solitaria
977.

Miguel de los SANTOS OLIVER JOURNALISM PRIZE (Spain)
One of a number of literary awards of Ciudad de Palma (See Palma de Mallorca Prizes), this prize was won in 1961 by José Salas Guiror.
977A.

João dos SANTOS PRIZE (Portugal)
The 10.000$ prize for essays is one of several literary awards offered by the Portuguese government (Agencia Geral do Ultramar) in an annual promotion of new writing by Portuguese citizens on subjects dealing with overseas topics. The award was granted in 1957 to Luis Silveira for "Ensaio de Iconografia das Cidades Portuguesas do Ultramar!"
978.

SAO PAULO P.E.N. CLUB PRIZE (Brazil)
The currently awarded prizes of the P.E.N. Club of Sao Paulo (Secretary, Caixa Postal 1.574) were granted for the first time in 1960 to books published in 1959. Among the forms of writing distinguished by the honor are: Poetry, Essays, Criticism. Winners of the prizes, each bearing a premium of Cr$50.000, are:
1960 Ofelia and Narbal Fontes.
Precisa-se de um Rei
Judas Isgorogota. A arvore sempre verde
Vicente Catalano. Sexy
Gilberto Freire. Ordem e Progresso
1961 Maria de Lourdes

Teixeira. Raiz Amarga
Pedro Xisto Pereira de Carvalho.
Haikais+Concreto
Georges Raeders. Bibliographie
Franco-Brésilienne
Olimpio de Sousa Andrade.
Historia e Interpretação de
"Os Sertões"
Péricles Eugênio da Silva
Ramos. Lua de Ontem
                                979.

SAO PAULO PRIZES (Brazil)
In 1954 the city of Sao Paulo
(Prefeitura de São Paulo, Departmento de Cultura, Parque
Iberapuera) established two annual prizes--Prêmios Municipais
de São Paulo--to recognize outstanding writing published during
the preceding year, from January
1 to November 10. A First
Prize (Cr$30.000) and a Second
Prize (Cr$20.000) recognize
major contributions of Brazilian
writers, who are nominated for
the award by publishers, and by
professional associations and
organizations of writers and
journalists. The two prizes are:
PRÊMIO CÂMARA MUNICIPAL
DE SÃO PAULO--A rotating
award distinguishing outstanding books in the literary
forms: Novel, Children's
Literature, Story, Essay,
Drama, Poetry. In 1960 no
entries qualified for the drama
prize; and in 1962 the award
will be presented for the best
novel in competition. Among
recent winners are:
1955 Novel--Mario Donato.
    Madrugada sem Deus
1957 Story--Ricardo Ramos.
    Terno de Reis
2nd prize--Osman Lins. Os
    Gestos
Honorable Mention--Luiz Lopes
    Coelho. A morte no
    envelope
1959 Essay--Divided Prize
    Alceu Maynard Araújo. A
    congada nasceu em Ron-

cesvales
José Goncalves Salvador. Os
    Transportes em São Paulo
    no periodo colonial
2nd prize divided--Antonio
    Rangel Bandeira. Jorge de
    Lima
Octacilio de Carvalho Lopez.
    A cor do gosto
PRÊMIO PREFEITURA MUNICI-
PAL DE SÃO PAULO--A journalism award for the best work
appearing in newspapers or
magazines. Among First
Prize winners are:
1957 Maria de Lourdes
    Teixeira
1959 Miguel Angelo Barros
    Ferreira. O Brasil já leu
    mais em outros tempos; é
    priciso estimular o hábito da
    leitura
1960 Leonardo Arryo. Vida
    Literaria   980.

Sir Jadunath SARKAR GOLD
MEDAL (India)
    One of several medals award-
ed by the Asiatic Society (1 Park
Street, Calcutta 16) "for encouragement of studies in letters
and humanities," this honor is
granted biennially to "a person
who is considered to have made
conspicuously important contributions to any of the following
subjects: History, Religion, Art,
Archaeology, and Literature,
with special reference to India
from 1300 A.D. to 1802, the year
of the treaty of Bassein."
    The medal has been awarded
for the scholarly writings of:
    1951 Kalikaranjan Quanungo
    1953 Ashirbadilal Srivastava
    1955 O.C. Gangoly
    1957 G.S. Sardesai
    1959 C.C. Davies   981.

SARMIENTO PRIZE (Argentina)
    Granted by the Sociedad
Argentina de Escritores to distinguish the "best book of prose
of the year," this literary honor,

named for Domingo Faustino
Sarmiento (1811-1888), Argentine
political leader and educator famous throughout the Americas,
was presented in 1951 to Vicente
Barbieri for his book, "Desenlace
de Endimión."   982.

SARPAY BEIKMAN PRIZE
(Burma)
   The Burma Translation
Institute, government-subsidized
cultural organization which was
formerly called the Burma Translation Society (361 Prome Road,
Rangoon), annually awards prizes
for the best Burmese novel, the
best translation of a Great Book,
the best work of Belles Lettres,
the best work on any subject of
general knowledge, and the best
collected short stories.
   These prizes, described by U
Nu as "an attempt to stimulate
the production of 'New Life
Literature,' that should go hand
in hand with 'New Life Culture'
that Burma is building as an
independent and sovereign
country," offer 1,000 Burmese
Kyats for each category of
award, except Translation, where
the premium is 750 Burmese
Kyats.
   Winners include:
Novel
   1948 Min Aung. Moe-Auk-
   Myai-Byin (The earth under
   the sky)
   1950 Tet Toe (pseud of U On
   Pe). Min-HmuHtan (The
   civil servant)
   1951 Tha Du. Tat Hte Ga
   Myat ko ko. Story of the
   Burmese army
   1954 Sagaing U Po Thin. Nga
   Mai Kyun. A tale of ancient
   Burma
   1955 Journalgyaw Ma Ma Lay.
   Mone Ywe Ma Hu (Not
   because of hatred)
   1956 U Ba Thaw. Ko Twe
   Sone Htauk Hmu (True
   detectives)

1957 Du Wun. Gun Pon
1958 U Thein Pe Myint. Ashay
   Ka Nai Win Htwet Thi Pama
   (As if the sun rises in the
   East)
1959 Mg Thin. Saya Zat Lan
   Sone. (A doctor's experiences)
1960 Bhamo Tin Aung. Ma Ma
   Gyi
   Aung Lin. A Yine Sapai (Wild
   jasmine)
Belles Lettres
1951 Shwegaing Tha, and U
   Thaw Bi Ta. Sin Yin Htone
   Pwae Hmu (A book of Bur-
   mese costumes)
1952 Journalgyaw Tint Swe.
   Thadinsar Achaykhan Pyinnya
   (Fundamentals of journalism)
1955 Zawgyi. Thakin Kodaw
   Hmaing Dika (Critical study of
   Thakin Kodaw
1956 Man Tin. Moscow Hma
   Yangon Tho (From Moscow to
   Rangoon)
1957 Ludu U Hla. Htaun Hnyint
   Luthar (Man and prison)
1959 Natmauk Phone Kyaw.
   Min Hla Khan Tat (Minhla
   Ford)
Translation
1945-1952 Shwe U Daung.
   Htway Ta Lint Lint (Charles
   Dickens, "Great Expectations")
1954 Min Yu Wai, and Nywe
   Tar Yee. Aesop Pon Pyin
   Myar (Aesop's "Fables")
1955 Shwe U Daung. Thway
   Sote Myai (Upton Sinclair,
   "The jungle")
1956 Theikpan Soe Hla. Bawa
   A Htway Htway (Pearl Buck,
   "My several worlds")
1957 Bo Aye Maung. Lu Lor
   Nana Barwa Lor
1958 Tint Te. Pyo do Achittaw
   (Guy de Maupassant, "Bel
   Ami")
1959 Dagon Shwe Hmyar.
   (Daniel Defoe, "Robinson
   Crusoe")
General Knowledge
1953 U Myo Sin. Local govern-
   ment

294   International Literary Awards

1955 Dagon Nat Shin.
  Biographies of authors
1957 Thuriya Kan Ti. A
  technique of writing novels
Short Stories
1960 Khin Hnin Yu. Kyay
  Mon Yeik Thwin   983.

SARZANA PRIZE (Italy)
  The prize offered by Sarzana
(La Spezia) for a scholarly work
on the subject of "The Resistance
and the New Generation," grants
L 250.000 as First Prize, with
a Special Prize of L 50.000, in
a second contest ending in 1962.
                              984.

Eugene F. SAXTON MEMORIAL
TRUST AWARD (International--
U.S.A.)
  The publisher's award, established by Harper & Brothers (49
East 23rd Street, New York 16)
in 1923 in memory of Eugene
F. Saxton, Harper's chief literary
editor for many years, offers
"fellowships, with substantial outright grants of money, to creative
writers, especially those who
have never had books published and
who lack established publishing
connections or other means of
financial assistance."
  Designed to "encourage distinguished writing in the fields of
fiction, poetry, biography, history, criticism, and the essay,
as well as outstanding jobs of
reporting, needed popularizations
of knowledge, and original inter-
pretations of cultural trends,"
the fellowships may be applied
for at any time. Writers of all
nationalities may apply on an
official entry blank, obtained
from Harper & Brothers, accompanied by about 10,000 words
of an unfinished fiction or nonfiction manuscript, which must
be in English.
  Recipients of the award, which
may reach $2,500, include:
1945 Celia Chao--novel

1947 Sara de Ford--poetry
1948 Frank Mlakar. He, the
  Father l
1951 Sebastien De Matto--novel
1952 Katherine Baccaro--novel
1956 Nick Joaquin y Marquez--
  novel
1960 Gerhart Reichlin--novel
                              985.

SCARRON PRIZE (France)
  Named in honor of Paul
Scarron (1610-1660), the French
comic poet, novelist, and dramatist, this prize has been awarded
each November since 1949 for the
best humorous writing published
in book form during the year.
Authors or publishers submit two
copies of the competing works
(René Virard, 4 rue Fabre-
d'Eglantine, Paris 12e) before
November 10, and--after announcement of the winner--all books
entered in the contest are sent to
Bibliothèque de l'Association des
Paralysés de France.
  Recipients of the 5.000 fr
award--given in a purse with
Scarron's arms and in 500 ten-
franc crowns duplicating the allowance that Scarron received from
the Queen of France--include:
1950 Ernestine and Frank
  Gilbreth (U.S.A.). Treize
  à la douzaine
1951 Alexandre Breffort. Mon
  taxi et moi
1953 Francis Didelot. Adam
  est Eve
1955 Marc Benoni. Arthur et
  la planète
1956 Jacques Chabannes.
  Prince Carolus
1959 Serge. Paris mon
  coeur
1960 Claude Pasteur. Éternel
  Adam
1961 Jean Grandmoujin.
  Noenoeil, homme d'État
                              986.

SCHEEPERS PRIZE FOR YOUTH
LITERATURE (South Africa)

This annual literary honor, granted by the South African Academy of Arts and Science, (Suid-Afrikaanse Akademie vir Wetensekap en Kuns, Engelburg House, Hamilton Street, Pretoria) as part of its program of promoting Afrikaans Literature, was established in 1956 as a monetary prize for the "best Afrikaans literary work for the more advanced youth."   987.

Rene SCHICKELE PRIZE (International--Germany)
Considered at the time of its award as the "most significant international literary prize for German language authors," this honor, established in 1952 and awarded in Munich, was granted by a jury of such distinguished authors as Thomas Mann, Alfred Neumann, Hermann Kesten. Winners of the prize include:
Hans Werner Richter. They fell from God's hands
Luise Rinser
Ilse Aichinger
Heinrich Böll
Franziska Becker
Heinz Risse
Siegfried Lenz   988.

SCHILLER FOUNDATION PRIZE (Europe--Switzerland)
Of the several literary honors offered by the Schweizerischen Schillerstiftung (Stadthausquai 5, Zurich), the most important is the SCHILLER GRAND PRIZE (Grösser Schillerpreis), an annual award for outstanding service to literature, granted for a distinguished work in German, French, or Italian. Winners of the premiums (5.000, 2.000, and 1.000 swiss francs) include:
1932 Auer. Bonvouloir
1951 Josef Kopp (also prize-winner in 1947)
1954 Marguerite Janson (also prize-winner in 1949)

Martin Strubs
1955 Max Frisch
1956 Hans Moser (also prize-winner in 1954)
1959 Olga Mayer; Pierre Courthion; Piero Bianco
1960 Friedrich Dürrenmatt
989.

SCHILLER MEMORIAL PRIZE (Germany)
Established in 1955 to commemorate the 150th anniversary of the death of Freidrich von Schiller (1759-1805), Germany's most famous dramatist, triennial (prior to 1960 biennial) literary prizes are granted by the area of Friedrich von Schiller's birthplace--Landesregierung Baden-Württemberg:
HONOR AWARD (Ehrenpreis)--a premium (increased from 10,000 to 15,000 DM) for outstanding literary work, either a single writing or the entire literary output of an author-- a poet or a prose writer worthy of being honored in Schiller's memory--with dramatic work, including radio and television plays, given preference;
ENCOURAGEMENT PRIZE (Fördergabe)--two 7,500 (formerly 5,000) DM stipends for young playwrights to enable them to study staging and directing of plays. Playwrights qualify for the monthly grant of the stipend by having a play produced within three years of the year of award, by being engaged currently in presenting their play, by having had a play published, or if not otherwise qualified, by being recommended by a drama editor or a play publisher for the award.
The prizes are administered by the Minister of Culture of the State of Baden-Württemberg (Kulturministerium Baden-Württemberg, Schillerplatz 5B, Stuttgart), and are bestowed on

November 10, Schiller's birth
date. Recipients include:
Ehrenpreis
1955 Rudolf Kassner
(Switzerland)
1957 Rudolf Pannwitz
1959 Wilhelm Lehmann
1962 Werner Bergengruen
Fördergabe
1955 Stefan Barcava
Richard Hey
1957 Karl Wittlinger
Leopold Ahlsen
1959 Dieter Meichsner
Bruno Meyer-Wehlack
1962 Heinar Kipphardt
Dieter Waldmann   990.

SCHILLER PRIZE OF MANNHEIM
(Germany)
The cultural award, as was
the Schiller Memorial Prize, was
founded to commemorate the
150th anniversary of the death of
Friedrich von Schiller (1759-
1805). The 10,000 DM biennial prize is offered by the city
of Mannheim (Rathaus E 5) to
an artist who--in the spirit of
Schiller--through his entire work,
or a single work, has served
to advance the cultural life in
the field of German language in
a significant way. In 1958,
Friedrich Dürrenmatt, the Swiss
dramatist, won the prize as
the "most important living playwright in German."
The city of Mannheim also
awards an annual SCHILLER
PLAQUE for outstanding service
to the cultural life of Mannheim.
In 1960 this Schiller-Plakette was
granted publisher Fritz Knapp.
991.

SCHILLER RELIEF (Germany,
East)
An honorary award in the
form of a relief sculpture of the
German poet and playwright,
Friedrich von Schiller (1759-
1805), is granted by the Ger-
man Schiller Foundation

(Deutsche Schillerstiftung) for
writing of unusual merit. In
1960 Ludwig Bäte won the award.
992.

SCHLESWIG-HOLSTEIN ART
PRIZE (Germany)
Awarded for the first time in
1950 through the Ministerprasident
of the region of Schleswig-Holstein,
this cultural prize is offered for
an outstanding work of an artist
born in the area, or especially
associated with Schleswig-Holstein
through his work. The biennial
premium, which has increased
from an initial 2000 DM to the
current 5000 DM, was granted in
Literature in 1952 to Wilhelm
Lehmann.   993.

SCHLEUSSNER-SCHÜLLER PRIZE
(Germany)
The Hessian Broadcasting
System (Hessischen Rundfunk),
Frankfurt, founded the prize in
1954 and granted it annually
through 1959, when it was
terminated. The "Hessian Broadcasting System Prize" brought a
premium of 3000 DM to the
author of the "best radio play."
Playwrights honored by the
award are:
1954 Max Frisch (Switzerland)
1955 Walter Jens
1956 Walter Oberer. Der
Fiend des Prasidenten
1957 Kurt Heynicke. Das
Lächeln der Apostel
1958 Alfred Andersch. Aktion
ohne Fahnen
1959 Gunter Eich. Die Mädchen
aus Viterbo   994.

Eugene SCHMITS PRIZE
(Belgium)
First granted in 1924, this
triennial prize of the Belgian
Royal Academy of French Language and Literature is presented
for moral treatises by Belgian
authors writing in French.
Published or unpublished

works submitted or published
during the three years of
competition are considered for
the award. Recent winners are:
1951 Maurice Beerblock. De
Paris et d'ailleurs
1954 Jacques Biebuyck. N'em-
pechez pas la musique
1960 Jean-Louis Van Ham.
Apotheóse et Chants
Prisonniers 995.

Olive SCHREINER PRIZE
(South Africa)
Named for the famous South
African writer, Olive Schreiner
(1855-1920), author of the
widely-read "The Story of an
African farm" (1883), the prize
is awarded by the South African
Academy of Arts and Sciences
(Suid-Afrikaanse Akademie vir
Wetenskap en Kuns, Engelen-
burg House, Hamilton Street,
Pretoria) in furtherance of
English Literature. 996.

Henrich SCHUCK AWARD
(Sweden)
This prize of the Swedish
Academy (Svenska akademien,
Borshuset, Stockholm C) was
presented to Alrik Gustafson
for his book, "A History of
Swedish Literature" (University
of Minnesota Press). 997.

Albert SCHWEITZER BOOK
PRIZE (Germany)
The children's book publisher,
Kindler Verlag, Munich, established the prize in 1955 with a
10,000 DM premium, which has
since increased to 20,000 DM.
Recipients of the honor, which
is presented on January 14,
Schweitzer's birthdate, include:
1956 Walter Bauer. Die
langen Reisen
1957 Roger Ikor. Die Söhne
Abrahams
1959 Charlie May Simon
Kagawa. Gischichte eines
Lebens (translation of "A

seed shall serve," the life of
Tojohiko Kagawa, Japanese
Protestant theologian)
1961 Philipp Noel-Baker.
Wettlauf der Waffen--Konkrete
Vorschläge für die Abrüstung
998.

Albert SCHWEITZER PRIZE
(France)
The 5.000 NF prize, awarded
for the first time in November
1959, is presented for a published book on the problems of
the handicapped and the social
responsibility for their adjust-
ment (c/o Confédération des
aveugles, sourds-muets et grands
infirmes, 19 rue Germain-Pilon,
Paris). Recipients are:
1959 Jean Adnet. D'un autre
monde
1960 Denise Legrix. Née
comme ça
1961 Edita Morris. Fleurs
d'Hiroshima 999.

SELSKABET PRIZE (Denmark)
This 1.500 D kr award
(Selskabet Til de Skionne og
nyttige videnskabers forfremmelse)
has been presented to:
1947/48 F.J. Billeskov Jansen
1950 Sigurd Strangen
1952 Johannes Wulff
1955 Clara Pontoppidan
1959 H.C. Branner 1000.

SEOUL CITY SPECIAL LITERARY
PRIZE (Korea)
The general cultural award of
the city of Seoul (The Seoul City
Hall, Seoul), granted annually
in November since 1952, offers
200,000 hwan, a gold medal and
a citation to the person who has
performed the most outstanding
service in each of a number of
scholarly and cultural fields
(currently 12)--Literature, Press,
Publishing, Art, Motion Pictures,
Drama, Music, Architecture,
Natural Science, Political Science,
Technology, and Physical Culture.

SEPASS BADGE (Iran)
The Ministry of Education of
the Imperial Iranian Government
awards this badge for scientific
and educational books that have
been written, translated, or
published with private funds, and
which render "a valuable service
to the country's education." The
jury determining the award meets
twice a year--in March and in
August--to recommend works to
receive the Badge for final
decision by the Ministry of
Education. Three classes of
prizes are granted: Gold Badge,
Silver Badge, Bronze Badge.
1002.

SERBIAN PEOPLE'S REPUBLIC
PRIZES (Yugoslavia)
As part of the celebration of
July 7, in observance of The
Insurrection, the following
writers were honored with a
literary award (Vlade NR Srbije)
in 1950:
Isidora Sekulic. Zapisi o
mome narodu (Chronologies
about my people)
Tanasija Mladenovic. Collec-
tion of poems
Desanka Masimovic. Reka
Pomocnica (The river as a
helper)
Mladen Leskovac. Clanci i
eseji (Articles and essays)
Prizes were also presented
to "Literary Work on the Lan-
guages of Minorities:" Mihajlo
Majtenija, Rade Flora, Esad
Mokulia.
Translators were honored:
Jelisaveta Markovic; Natalija
Lukic and Konstantin Stepanovic
for "Posechon Antiquities;"
Saltikov Scedrina.   1003.

SERBIAN WRITERS' ASSOCIA-
TION PRIZE (Yugoslavia)
Novels, poetry, and essays
given recognition by this award

1001. (Udruzenja Knijizevnika Srbije)
include:
Novel
1954 Radomir Konstantinovic.
Daj nam danas (Give us today)
1955 Mihajlo Lalic. Raskid
(The break-up)
Poetry
1952 Miodrag Pavlovic. 87
Pesama (Eighty-seven poems)
1954 Dusan Kostic. Zov lisca.
(The call of leaves)
1955 Stevan Raickovic. Balada
o predvecerju (Ballad about
twilight)
Essay
1952 Dusan Matic. Jedan vid
francuske knjizevnosti (One
aspect of French Literature)
1004.

SÉSAMO PRIZE (Spain)
Perhaps the best-known and
most-coveted short story and
novella prize in Spain, this award
was founded by Tomás Cruz,
proprietor of the cafe, "Cuevas
de Sésamos" (Principe 7), popular
meeting place of young writers
in Madrid. Winners of the
5,000 pts premium (currently
granted quarterly) include:
1955 Medardo Fraile. Presencia
de Berta
1956 Luis de Goytisolo. Niño
Mal
1957 Ramón Nieto. La Cala
(novella)
Pascual Martín Criado. Calor
1959 Manuel Alonso Alcalde.
Ha Caido una Piedra en
Estangue
1960 Victor Mora. La Cometa
Azul
Pablo Antoñana. No estamos
solos
1961--1st quarter Marua Muñiz
La paga
2nd quarter Andrés Castellanos.
Uno
3rd quarter Francisco Regueiro.
Las muchachas
4th quarter Jaime Borell. Urge
un camarero hablando

inglés 1005.

T. P. SVENSMA PRIZE
(International)

The prize of the International Library Committee, Library of the League of Nations (Fédération internationale des Associations de Bibliothécaires, Geneva), was established by subscription of members of affiliate Library Associations to honor Dr. T. P. Svensma, the first and only secretary of the International Federation of Library Associations. Founded as an annual award for the best essay on a specified subject, the competitions were limited to members of the affiliate Library Associations, and further restricted to members who were at least 40 years of age. 1006.

SEVILLE PRIZE (Spain)

Many distinguished literary honors are conferred by the City of Seville. Prizes vary in amount of premium, and have included: Biennial Novel Prize--for a published or an unpublished work, with a premium of 50,000 pts; Annual Award for Journalism--15,000 pts premium; Book of Poetry--a premium of 50,000 pts for an unpublished work relating to Seville.

Recipients of the prizes are announced on November 22, the eve of the city holiday--Anniversary of the Reconquest of Seville. Winners of the honor include Rafael Montesinos, who won the Seville Prize in 1957. 1007.

Miles SHEROVER and Juan de CASTELLANOS PRIZES (Venezuela)

Recent winners of these literary awards--Sherover with a premium of 10,000 bolivares; Castellanos, with a premium of 5,000 bolivares--include:
1956 Isaac J. Pardo. Esta

tierra de gracia (history) Guillermo Morón. Libro de la Fe
1958 Caracciolo parra Perez. La monarquía en la gran Colombia
Lowell Dunham. Romulo Gállegos 1008.

SHINCHO PRIZES (Japan)

These awards of the Shinchosha Publishing Company, established in 1936 with a yearly prize (500,000 yen in 1962) for the "Best work published during the preceding year," are also known as the SHINCHOSHA PRIZES. A jury of authors and critics and editorial staff of the monthly, "Shincho" (New Trends) selects the most commendable literary work, including stories for children and dramatic works, for the honor.
Recipients of the prize are:
1951 Kiyoshi Madono. Kido (The way of spirits)
1953 Reiko Sakaguchi. Banchi (A savage land)
1954 Yukio Mishima (pseud of Kimitake Hiraoka). Shiosai (The sound of waves)
1955 Haruo Umezaki. Suna-Dokei (A sand-glass)
Kenkichi Yamamoto. Basho (A study of Basho Matsuo, the Greatest Haikist)
1956 Aya Koda. Nagareru (To drift)
1957 Kenichi Yoshida. On Japan (essay)
1958 Shusaku Endo. Umito Dokuyaku (novel)
1959 Tetsutaro Kawakami. Japan's outsiders (essay)
1960 Junzo Shono. Seibutsu (novel)
1961 Shohei Ooka. Kaei (novel) 1009.

SHOGAKKAN CHILDREN'S CULTURE PRIZE (Japan)

The Shogakkan Company, publisher of children's magazines,

created this annual award in
1954.   1010.

SHOSETSU SHINCHO PRIZE
(Japan)
Established in 1954 by the
magazine, "Shosetsu Shincho"
(New Fiction Trends), a publication of the Shinchosha Publication
Company, this award is granted
yearly to a new writer "in the
field of the novel."   1011.

SHUMAWA PRIZE (Burma)
The prize of the magazine
publisher, Shumawa Company
(146/147 West Wing, Bogyoke
Market, Rangoon) offers 1,000
Burmese Kyats for the best
Burmese novel written during the
year. Established as an annual
award, but granted irregularly
over a period of years, the
honor includes among its winners:
Ngwe Lin. Ei Ya Mon (At
    the river side)
Sein Sein. Thar Lein Mar
    (An obedient son)
Mg Thain Kha. Thi Kyar
    Sai (Let it be known)
Mg Shwe Kyi. Kyar so Thor
    Kyar (Tiger! Tiger!)
Tin Mying Aung. Ye Nant
    Thar U (Among the oil
    fields)   1012.

SICILY PRIZE (Italy)
Offered by the review, "Eco"
(via 24 Maggio, isol. 250, no.
39, Messina), the Sicily Prize
is granted for unpublished poetry,
and also for fiction and drama.
Recipients of the award--a premium of L 50,000 with Second
and Third Prizes--include:
1958 Giorgio Croce. Sicilia
1959 Anna Lo Monaco Aprile.
    Giobbe
    Antonio Tagliacarne. L'arte
    e missione
    Attilio Agar Pace. Le cose
    (fiction)
1960 Antonio Barletta. Incubo
    Carmelo Sandro. Colloquio

con la Morte (novela)
Vanda Verratti. Un abito
bianco per Lili (story)
                               1013.

Renato SIMONI PRIZE (Italy)
The drama prize, established
in 1957 by the city of Verona and
Milan in commemoration of the
death of Renato Simoni, Italian
theatrical figure who devoted his
life to prose drama, is conferred
each year "per la fedelta al teatro
di prosa." The award, granted by
a jury of six judges--three from
each of the two cities participating
in the prize--has brought the premium of L 1.000.000 to the following playwrights, whose careers
have been devoted in entirety or
major part to prose drama:
1958 Lucio Ridenti
1959 Emma Gramatica
1960 Renzo Ricci   1014.

SINERGIA PRIZE (Spain)
"Sinergia," a Spanish magazine
(Apartado 919, Barcelona), offers
this cultural award of 25,000 pts
for an unpublished novel by a
member of the medical profession.
"Sinergia" is a general cultural
review of the professional association of pharmacists, Sociedad
General de Farmacia, and works
submitted for the prize must be
sent by June 30 to the Madrid
office (Calle Sagasta, 13, 3º
Ctro.). Dr. Enrique Nácher won
the honor in 1960 with "Cerco de
Arena."   1015.

SKIARIDEIOS COMPETITION FOR
CHILDREN'S THEATRE (Greece)
First Prize for children's
drama in the 1960 Skiarideios
Competition was awarded in 1960
to Melissanthe, for the play,
"The little brothers."   1016.

SLOVENE WRITERS' ASSOCIA-
TION PRIZE (Yugoslavia)
One of a number of prizes
offered by the Writers' Associa-

tions of the Republics of Yugo-
slavia, the Drustva Slovenackih
Knjizevnika was presented in
1954 to:
   Lojze Kovacic. Ljubljanske
   razglednice (Views of
   Ljubljana)
   Peter Levic. Zeleni val (The
   green wave--collected poems)
   Beno Zupancic. Veter in cesta
   (Veter in cesta--novela col-
   lection)   1017.

**W. H. SMITH & SON LITERARY
AWARD (International--England)**
   The publisher's award of
Ł 1, 000 is offered each year by
the London Company, W. H. Smith
& Son, Ltd. (Strand House,
Portugal Street, London, W. C.
2) for the book by a Commonwealth author that makes "the
most outstanding contribution to
English Literature." Competing
works must be written originally
in English and published in the
United Kingdom--either as a first
publication or within six months
of the first publication elsewhere
--within the two calendar years
preceding the year of award.
   Established in 1959 and
granted in the Autumn--usually
in October--the prize requires
no application or submission of
published books for consideration.
Among recipients are:
   1959 Patrick White (Australia).
   Voss
   1960 Nadine Gordimer (South
   Africa). Friday's footprint
   1962 J. R. Ackerley. We
   think the world of you
                   1018.

**SONNING FOUNDATION PRIZE
(Europe--Denmark)**
   The highest privately endowed
premium of any literary prize in
Denmark is carried by this
general cultural award, which
offers 100. 000 kr each year to a
person who has made a major
contribution to European culture.

The award, financed by the Sonning Foundation of Copenhagen, and
administered by the University of
Copenhagen, has honored such
distinguished Europeans as:
   1959 Winston Churchill
        Albert Schweitzer
   1960 Bertrand Russell
   1961 Nils Bohr   1019.

**SOTAN PREY CHEA EN PRIZE
(Cambodia)**
   The literary prize of the
Cambodia Ministry of Education
was established in 1959 to honor
outstanding Kmer writing and to
encourage new writers.   1020.

**SOUTH AFRICAN ACADEMY FOR
SCIENCE AND ART PRIZES
(South Africa)**
   The Suid-Afrikaanse Akademie
vir Wetenskap en Kuns (Engelen-
burg House, Hamilton Street,
Pretoria, Transvaal) offers a
number of annual literary prizes
and honors for writing of South
African authors. Six such
awards (which see) are:
   Honors for Writing in Akfriaans:
   HERTZOG PRIZE; SCHEEPERS
   PRIZE FOR YOUTH LITERA-
   TURE; MARAIS PRIZE;
   Honors for Writing in English:
   OLIVE SCHREINER PRIZE;
   Honors for Writing in Afrikaans
     and in English: SOUTH
   AFRICAN BROADCASTING
   CORPORATION PRIZE FOR
   RADIO PLAYS;
   Honors for Writing in Zulu
     (Bantu Literature):
   MQHAGI PRIZE.
Other prizes granted by the
Academy, which may include
awards for literature, are:
**SOUTH AFRICAN ACADEMY FOR
SCIENCE AND ART PRIZE FOR
TRANSLATED WORK--A R 50**
premium, granted from time to
time, for the best translations
from any foreign literature into
Afrikaans--Drama, Prose,
Poetry;

STALS PRIZE--An annual general cultural award for the promotion of the Humanities, which brings recognition of outstanding contributions in Language and Literary Science, as well as in Fine Arts and Music; SOUTH AFRICAN ACADEMY FOR SCIENCE AND ART MEDALS OF HONOR--one of the most important recognitions of the Academy for achievements in the Arts, Humanities, and Natural Sciences, including an annual Medal of Honor for Afrikaans Language and Literature; HAVENGA PRIZE--Medals and prizes for achievement in Science, Technology, and Medicine.   1021.

SOUTH AFRICAN BROADCASTING CORPORATION PRIZE FOR RADIO PLAYS

The prize, sponsored by the S.A.B.C., is one of a number of literary and cultural honors administered by the South African Academy for Science and Art (Suid-Afrikaanse Akademie vir Wetenskap en Kuns, Engelenburg House, Hamilton Street, Pretoria). The award honors outstanding radio plays in Afrikaans and in English.   1022.

SOUTH AFRICAN C.N.A. LITERARY PRIZE

Among the richest literary honors in South Africa are the two annual prizes of R 1,000 each offered since 1961 by the Central News Agency, Ltd. (P. O. Box 1033, Johannesburg) "for the best book published during the calendar year, in English and in Afrikaans, respectively, by a South African author (citizen of South Africa, but not necessarily a resident), in the following categories: Novel (and Short Stories); Poetry; Biography; Drama; History; Travel."

Books entered in the competition must be published by British or South African publishers; must not be anthologies, translations, or reprints; and must be submitted in three copies by December 31. A panel of six judges--three English, and three Afrikaans--announces the prize in January of the year following the contest. Winners of the first year's prize--which was announced in January 1962--received the monetary premium and an inscribed plaque in March:

Afrikaans--Chris Barnard.
Die Bekende Onrus
English--Siegfried Stander.
This deserted place   1023.

SOUTH AFRICAN NATIONAL ADVISORY COUNCIL FOR ADULT EDUCATION PRIZES

The awards of the South African government agency, N.A.C.A.E. (Secretary for Education, Arts, and Sciences, Pretorius Street, Van der Stel Buildings, Pretoria, Transvaal), are presented each March for winning works in the national literary competition held annually since 1957 for writing in a specified genre (1959--poetry; 1961--drama). First and Second Prizes, varying in amount of premium from R 400 to R 600, are granted for the best writing in English and in Afrikaans. Recipients include:

English Language
  1957--Drama: 2nd prize
    James Ambrose Brown.
    Seven against the sun
  1959--Poetry: R.N. Currey;
    A. Delius;
    2nd prize, S.D. Clouts
Afrikaans Language
  1959 Poetry: 2nd prize
    P.J. Philander. Vuurklip
  1961 Drama: 2nd prize
    Joan Retief. 'n Vroumens
    is 'n Snaakse ding; and

Die Hoe Drif   1024.

SOUTH AFRICAN SHORT STORY CONTEST

In a national competition organized jointly by the P.E.N. Centres in Johannesburg and Cape Town in 1962, six winning stories--selected from 700 entries--were each rewarded with a premium of Rand 40:

Bonnie Morne. Shoes for Mdala

Peggy Butler. The mail train to Johannesburg

Berry Colsen. The unwanted Kwela. Four I had to him

Richard Rive. Strike

-- (Anonymous). Pardon Ma'am, Pardon Sir
                              1024A.

SOUTH AMERICAN PRIZE (Brazil)

The Prêmio Sul-América, a government award for the "best study on the Brazilian theatre" offered by Instituto Brasileiro de Educação, Ciencia e Cultura, Ministérie das Relações Exteriores, brought a premium of Cr$100.000 in 1958 to J. Galante de Sousá for "O teatro no Brasil."
                              1025.

SOUTH AMERICAN PRIZE FOR POETRY (Latin America)

The First Prize of the PREMIO SUDAMERICANA DE POESÍA CÉSAR VALLEJO was presented to the Bolivian poet, Javier del Granado.   1026.

SPANISH CRITICS' PRIZE

Granted for various forms of the writing of Spanish authors --Novel, Poetry, Essay, Biography, and Short Story--the Premio de la Critica has been termed the "most authoritative, and least authoritarian" literary award in Spain (Kerrigan, p. 7; p. 13). An annual honor under the patronage of the publisher,

Editorial A.H.R. (24 Leon XIII, Barcelona) and Radio Zaragoza, the prize is determined by a jury composed of seven literary critics from Madrid and an equal number from Barcelona, and critics from Saragossa papers. Saragossa (Zaragoza) is the meeting place of the jury and the scene of presentation of the prize.

Among recent recipients are: Rafael Montesinos, who won a premium of 50,000 pts in 1958, and--

Novel--
1956 Camillo-José Cela. La Catira
1957 Rafael Sánchez Ferlosio. El Jarama
1958 Ignacio Aldecoa. Gran sol
1959 Ana María Matute. Los hijos muertos
1960 Elena Quiroga Tristina. Tristura
1962 Ramiro Pinilla. Las ciegas hormigas
Catalan Language--Lorenzo Villalonga. Blarr

Biography--
1960 Juan Ramon Jiménez. Españoles de Tres Mundos

Poetry--
1957 Victoriano Crémer. Furia y paloma
Vicente Gaos. Profecía del Recuerdo
1958 José Hierro. Cuanto sé de Mí
1959 Blas Otero. Ancia
1960 J.A. Valente. Poemas de Lázaro
1962 José María Valverde
Catalan Language--Blai Bonet

Short Story--
1959 Jesús Fernández Santos. Cabeza Rapada

Essay--
1958 Pedro Laín. La espera y la esperanza
1959 Eugenio G. de Nora. La novela española contemporánea   1027.

SPANISH NATIONAL PRIZES

The designation, "Premio
Nacional," has been applied to
many literary awards and honors
in Spain, but currently "Spanish
National Prizes" generally refers
to four awards (which see):
FRANCO PRIZE--for political
and social essays, journalism,
and--more recently--novels
CERVANTES NATIONAL PRIZE--
for novel
MENÉNDEZ Y PELAYO PRIZE--
for historical essay
PRIMO DE RIVERA PRIZE--for
poetry, and occasionally for
essay and journalism
Highest official formal recognition of an authors' work in
Spain, the prizes are granted by
Dirección General de Bellas
Artes, and entries for the awards
"must support the Catholic conception of the world and man,
as well as the ideology of the
National Movement" (Spanish
Cultural Index, July 1959, p.
769; August 1960, p. 819), must
be submitted in two copies, and
must have been published originally between December 1 of the
previous year and November 30
of the year of award (November
30 is also the deadline for
entries) in a Spanish-speaking
country.

Authors whose works have
been entered in the CONCURSO
NACIONAL DE LITERATURA,
and who have been honored with
the PREMIO NACIONAL DE
LITERATURA, include:
History
1959 Claudio Miralles.
Empresas Africanas en el
Reinade de Carlos V
Poetry
1925 Rafael Alberti. Marinero
en Tierra
Gerardo Diego. Versos
Humanos
1927 Concha Espina de Serna.
Altar Mayor
1932 Casona. Flor de Layendas
1950 Dionisio Ridruejo. En

once anos
Novel
1927 Pérez de Ayala. Tiger
Juan (5,000 pts)
Florez. Las siete columnas
(2,000 pts)
1933 R. Vicente Aleixandre.
La Destrucción e el Amor
1934 Adriano del Valle. Mundo
sin travesía
1936 Ramon J. Sender. Pro
patria
1942 Luis Diaz del Corral. El
Archipiélago
Ernesto Giménez Caballero.
Amar a Catalina
1945 Ignacio Agustí. Mariano
Rebull
1946 Ignacio Agustí. El Viudo
Reus
1947 Eulalia Galvarriato. Cinco
sombras
1948 Juan Antonio Zunzunegui.
La úlcera
1949 Pedro Rocamora
1952 Pedro Álvarez. La espera
1954 Ramón Menéndez Pidal
1955 J. Mancisidor. El alba
en las simas
1956 José María Sánchez-
Silva. Tres novelas y pico
(4 short stories)
Miguel Delibes. Diario de un
Cazador
1957 García Nieto. Geografía
es Amor
1959 Daniel Sueiro. Los
Conspiradores
Essay
1935 Damaso Alonso. La
Langua Poetica de Gongora
1959 José Luis Alborg. La
hora actual de la novela
española
1961 José María Azcárate.
Alonso Berruguete   1028.

SPANISH NATIONAL THEATER
PRIZE
These annual awards of the
Ministry of Information and
Tourism have been presented for
three forms of dramatic writing
--Best Drama of the Year

(produced play); Best Comedy of
the Year (produced play, also
called "Benavente Prize"); and
Best Drama Article of the Year.
Among the playwrights and
critics honored are: Ruiz
Castillo; Joaquín Calvo Sotelo
for "El Criminal de Guerra," and
1950 Claudio de la Torre.
El Río que Nace en Junio
1953 Miguel Mihura. Tres
sombreros de Copa (comedy)
1954 José López Rubio. La
Venda en los Ojos
1955 Torcuato Luca de Tena
Miguel Mihura. Mi Adorado
Juan (comedy)
1958 Alfonso Paso. El Cielo
Dentro de Casa
1959 A. Buero Vallejo. Un
Soñadar para un Pueblo
1960 Miguel Mihura.
Miribel y la Extraña Familia
1029.

STALIN PEACE PRIZE (Inter-
national--People's Republic of
China)
This award of the Chinese
People's Committee for World
Peace, Peking, was created in
1962 so that "the struggle for
peace should continue to be
linked with the glorious name of
Comrade J.V. Stalin." The ac-
tion was taken to continue the
Stalin Peace Prize, formerly
awarded by the U.S.S.R. but
replaced in 1956 with the Lenin
Peace Prize (New Republic,
April 9, 1962).   1030.

STALIN PEACE PRIZE (Inter-
national-USSR)
The "International Stalin Peace
Prize" was established December
20, 1949 in honor of Josef
Stalin's 70th birthday, and was
awarded by a Special International
Stalin Prize Committee "for the
promotion of peace among
nations," "for outstanding service
in the struggle against war-
mongers, and for the promo-

tion of peace."
The honor--a diploma, a gold
medal with Stalin's portrait
embossed, and a premium of
100,000 rubles--was presented to
five or ten laureates each year--
from the time of the initial award
in 1950--on December 2, the date
of national celebration of Stalin's
birthday.
The international award, an
official honor of the Soviet Union,
replaced in 1956 with the Lenin
Peace Prize, was granted a
number of intellectuals and public
figures outside Russia. Writers
receiving the prize include:
Berthold Brecht, Germany, in
1955; Pablo Neruda, Chile; and
Howard Fast, U.S.A.
The USSR, in a public announcement released on March 15, 1962
(New York Times, March 16,
1962, 3:4) indicated that
foreign holders of the Stalin
Peace Prize could exchange the
award for the Lenin Peace Prize.
1031.

STALIN PRIZE (USSR)
This annual prize replaced the
Lenin Prize as the highest national cultural honor officially
awarded by the USSR from 1939,
when it was established on December 20 in celebration of
Stalin's 60th birthday, until 1953,
the year of Stalin's death.
Granted for specific actions and
achievements in a wide range of
cultural fields, including "writing
of a specific book," the original
92 prizes of 1941--with premiums ranging from 25,000 to
100,000 rubles--were increased
in number through the years to
more than 160 awards--with First
Prizes in various categories
(Literature, Art, Dance, Theatre,
Science, Music, Medicine,
Film) carrying a premium of
200.000 rubles (Guillebraud, p.
499;503). In 1952, 102 Stalin
Prizes awarded had a total pre-

mium of 4 million rubles.
The Stalin Prize, initially
given only to writers of Russia,
was awarded to other than Soviet
citizens for the first time in
1952, when it was granted to
André Stil (France), and to
several Hungarian and Chinese
writers. Halldór Kiljan Laxness,
Nobel Prize-winning Icelandic
novelist, received a Stalin Prize
in 1953. In more recent years,
some of the Stalin Prize works
of novelists, dramatists, and
poets have been criticized in
the USSR as "harmful and not
conforming to 'social idealism.' "

Information on the prize winners was contained each year in
"Pravda" and "Izvestia," and--
from 1949 until 1953--in "Current Digest of the Soviet Press,"
which indexes Stalin Prize
notices and articles. These
sources were used by Seymour
M. Rosen in preparing a "Complete List of Stalin Prizes in
Prose and Drama, 1941-1952,"
as an Appendix to a Columbia
University Master's Essay in
the Slavic Languages.

Among authors of books of
fiction, drama, poetry, and
literary criticism receiving the
Stalin Prize are: Leonid Leonov,
with two awards for "Crown of
Thorns" and "Road to the
Ocean;" Monica Felton; George
Amadu; Stepan Shchipachev,
for "Pavlik Morozov," a tale;
Anna Seghers for "The seventh
cross;" George Markov for "The
Strogovs;" and
Poetry
   1941 Alexander Trifonovich
      Tvardovsky. Strana
      Muraviya (The Land of
      Muravia--long poem)
   1942 Margarita Aligher. Zoya
      (poem)
   1944 Alexander A. Prokofiev.
      Russia (poem)
      Mikolay Tiakhonov. Kirov
      s nami (Kirov is with us--

long poem)
Vera Inber. Pulkovsky
   meridian (The Pulkovo Meri-
   dian--long poem)
1948 Nikolay Gribachov. Vesna
   v "Pobede" (Spring in "Victory"
   --poem)
1949 Alexander Yashin (pseud
   of Alexander Yakovlevich
   Popov). Alyona Fomina
   (narrative poem)
1950 Aleksei Surkov. Peace for
   the World (collected poems)
   Semen Kirsanov. Makar
   Mazai (narrative poem)
1951 Samual Marshak. Col-
   lected poems for children
   V. Zamiatin. Green Shelter
   Belt (long poem)
Prose
1935 to 1940 (Years preceding
   official establishment of the
   honor)
A.N. Tolstoi. Pyotr pervy
   (Peter, the First)
S.N. Sergeyev-Tsenski.
   Sevastopolskaya strada (The
   ordeal of Sevastopol)
Mikhail A. Sholokhor. Tikhi
   Don (The silent Don; or
   Quiet flows the Don, 1934;
   also The Don flows home to
   the sea, 1940)
1941 Ilya Ehrenburg. Padenie
   Parizhe (The fall of Paris)
V.G. Yancheveschki. Ghingis-
   Khan (Ghenghis Khan)
Alexey Tolstoy. Khozhdenie po
   mukam. Road to Calvary,
   (trilogy--alternate titles:
   Ordeal; The path of suffering;
   A way through Hell)
2nd prize Serghei Borodon
   (pseud of Amir Sargidzhian).
   Dimitry Donskoy
   Nicolas Virta (pseud of
   Svertzev). Odinochestvo
   (Loneliness, or Solitude)
1942 Wanda L. Wasilevska.
   Raduga (The rainbow)
2nd prize P.P. Bazhov. Mala-
   khitovaya shkatulkn (The
   Malachite Casket--short
   stories)

Leonid S. Sobolov. Morskaya dumn (Soul of the sea-- short stories) 1943 and 1944

Viacheslav Y. Ghishkov. Emelyan Pugachyov (Emelyan Pugachov)

A.N. Stepanov. Port-Artur (Port Arthur)

2nd prize Boris L. Gorbator. Nepokorennia (The Unvanquished, or The Taras Family)

Benjamin Kaverin (pseud of Benjamin Zilberg). Dva Kapitana (The two captains)

Wanda L. Wasilevska. Prosto lyubov (Simple love)

Konstantin M. Simonov. Dai i nochi (Days and nights)

1945 Alexander A. Fadeyev. Molodaya gvardiya (The young guard)

Aibek. Navoi

1946 Elmar Green. Veter s yuga (The wind from the South)

Vera F. Panova. Sputniki (Fellow travelers, or--English translation title: The train)

2nd prize Boris N. Polevoi. Pvest o nastoyashchem chelovoka (Story of a real man)

1947 Mikhail Bubennov. Belaya berega (The silver birch, vol 1)

Peter A. Pavlenko. Schastye (Happiness)

Ilya Ehrenburg. Burya (The storm)

1948 Vassily N. Azhayev. Daleko ot Moskvy (Far from Moscow)

M.O. Auezov. Abai

Konstantin A. Fedin. Servye radosti (First joys); and Neobyknovennoe leto (No ordinary summer)

Semion P. Babayevski. Kavaler solotoi zvezdy (Cavalier of the golden star, or Knight of the golden star)

2nd prize T.Z. Semushkin. Alitet ukhodit v gory (Alitet leaves for the mountains, or Alitet goes to the hills)

Boris Polevoi. Mya sovetskie lyudi (We are the Soviet people--short stories)

A.T. Gonchar. Zlata Praga (Golden Prague--sequel to "The Standard Bearers")

1949 Semion P. Babayevski. Svet nad semloi (Light over the land-- vol 1 of 2 vol sequel to "Knight of the golden star")

E. Mal'tsev. Heart and soul

2nd prize Fyodor V. Gladkov. Povest o destve (A story of childhood--autobiography)

Emanuel G. Kazakovich. Vesna na Odore (Spring on the Oder)

Alexander N. Voloshin. Zemlya kuznotskaya (Kuznetsk Land)

3rd prize Vasily P. Ilyenkov. Bolshaya doroga (The highway)

Alexander B. Chakovski. U nas uzhe utro (It is morning here)

Grigory Medynaki (Medynsky-- pseud of N.M. Pokrovsky) Marya

Antonin Kopyayeva. Ivan Ivanovich

Vera F. Panova. Yasny bereg (Bright shore, or Gleaming shore)

1950 Fyodor V. Gladkov. Volnitsa (Free men)

Galina P. Nikolayeva. Zhatva (The harvest)

Gaider Guseinov. From the history of Public and Private Thought of Azerbaijan in the 19th century (Prize committee requested withdrawal of award the same year)

2nd prize Semion P. Babayevski. Svet nad semloi (Light over the land--vol 2 of 2 vol sequel to "Knight of the golden star")

Alexei V. Kozhevnikov.
Zhivaya voda (Life giving
water)
Nicolai N. Nikitin. Severnaya
avrora (Northern Aurora)
3rd prize Sergei F. Antonov.
Do dorogam idut mashiny
(Machines drive along the
roads, or Lorries on the
road--short stories)
Vitalii A. Zakrutkin. Plo-
vuchaya stanitsa (Floating
Stanitsa)
Anna A. Karavayeva. Rodnoi
dom (Native home--last vol
of trilogy: Rodina (Home)--
Ogin (The lights), Razberg
(A running start))
Yuri V. Trifonov. Studenty
(Students)
1951-1952 Stepan P. Zlobin.
Stepan Razin
Vilis T. Latsis. K novomu
beregu (To the new shore)
2nd prize Tin Lin (also Din
Lin, Ting Ling) (China).
Solntse nad rekoi Sangan
(Sun shines over the Sangan
River)
Nicolai Zadornov. Kokeanu
(Toward the ocean--last vol
of a trilogy--vol 1 and 2:
Amur-batyushka (Amur),
Daleki krai (Distant land))
André Stil (France). Pervy
udar (The first blow)
3rd prize Tamas(h) Atsel
(Hungary). Pod senyu
svobody (Beneath the canopy
of freedom)
Sandor Nagy (Hungary).
Primirenie (Reconciliation)
Lev V. Nikulin. Rossee
vernye cyny (Russia's loyal
sons)
Chou Lee-Bo (also, Chou Li-
Po) (China). Uragan
(Hurricane)
Children's Literature
1947 3rd prize I. I. Likstanov.
Malyshok (Little tot)
1948 2nd prize V. A. Lyubimova.
Snezhok (Snow--drama)
1949 3rd prize I. D. Vasilenko.

Zvezdochka (The little star)
A. I. Musatov. Stozhary
1951 3rd prize V. P. Belyayaev.
Staraya Kropost (The old
fortress)
N. N. Nosov. Vitya Naleyev v
Shkole i doma (Vitya Maleyev
at school and at home)
V. A. Oseyeva. Vasek Tru-
bachev i evo tovarishchi
(Vasek Trubachev and his
comrades)
Drama
1935 to 1940 K. A. Trenev.
Lyubov Yarovaya
A. E. Korneichuk. Platon
Krechet; Bogdan Khmelnitski
N. F. Pogodin. Chalovek s
ruzhyem (The man with the
gun)
1941 K. M. Simonov. Paren iz
nashevo goroda (A fellow
from our town)
A. E. Korneichuk. V Stepyakh
Ukrainy (In the steppes of
the Ukraine)
1942 A. E. Korneichuk. Front
(The front)
Leonid M. Leonov. Nashestvie
(Invasion)
2nd prize K. M. Simonov.
Russkie lyudi (The Russian
people)
1943 A. N. Tolstoi. Ivan grozny
(Ivan the Terrible)
Leonid Leonov. Lyonushka
2nd prize Samuel Y. Marshak.
Desyat mesyatsev (Twelve
months)
1945 B. A. Lavrenev. Zd tokh,
kto v moro! (For those out at
sea)
2nd prize V. A. Solovyov.
Veliki gosudar (The great
sovereign)
1946 K. M. Simonov. Russki
vopros (The Russian question)
Anatoli Surov. Daleko ot Stalin-
grada (Far from Stalingrad)
B. Chirskov. Podediteli (Vic-
tors)
1947 B. S. Romashov. Velikaya
sila (The great force)
A. M. Yakobson. Borba bez

linii fronta (The struggle
without a battle line)
2nd prize P. E. Virta. Khleb
nach nasushchny (Our daily
bread)
1948 A. V. Sofronov. Moskov-
ski Kharakter (Moscow
character)
N. E. Virta. Zagovor obrechen-
nykh (Conspiracy of the
doomed); V odnom strane
(In a certain country)
2nd prize A. E. Korneichuk.
Makar Dubrava
Anatoli A. Surov. Zolysnaya
ulitsa (Green Street)
1949 Vsevolod Vishnevski.
Nezabyvasmy 1919-i (Un-
forgettable 1919)
2nd prize Sergey V. Mikhailkov.
Ya khochu domoi (I want to
go home); Ily Golovin (Ilya
Golovin)
K. M. Simonov. Ghuzhaya ten
(Someone else's shadow)
Boris A. Lavrenyov. Golos
Ameriki (The voice of
America)
1950 2nd prize Anatoli A.
Surov. Rassuet nad Moskvoi
(Dawn over Moscow)
1951-1952 2nd prize
Hei Chin-Chi (also, Hi Tzin
Schzhi) (China). Sodaya
devuahka (White haired girl)
1032.

STANVAC JOURNALISM AWARDS
(Philippines)
Annual prizes have been offered
since 1954 for a variety of
journalistic activities, including:
Distinguished Reporting; Feature
Articles; Editorials; Provincial,
Tagalog, and Chinese Language
Reporting. Recent winners of
the Grand Prize and the title,
"Journalist of the Year," are:
1957 Carmen Guerrero-Nakpil
Teodoro M. Locsin
1958 Napoleon G. Rama
1959 Teodoro M. Locsin
1033.

STELLA MARIS PRIZE (Italy)
The L 100.000 poetry prize of
the Stella Maris Committee (Comitato "Stella Maris," via Edoardo
Scarfoglio 22, Pescara), granted
for an unpublished poem on the
life and works of St. Francis,
was presented to Vincenzo D'Am-
brosio in 1961 for, "Fate
quanto Egli vi dira." 1034.

STELZHAMER-PLAKETTE
(Austria)
The literary honor of the Province of Upper Austria (Landes
Oberösterreich) is named for the
famous writer of that region,
Franz Stelzhamer, whose birthday
on November 29 the prize honors.
In addition to administrative
officials and cultural leaders of
Upper Austria who have been
presented with the plaque, the
award has given public recognition
to authors, such as Otto Jungmair,
who gained the honor in 1953.
1035.

Rolf STENERSEN AWARD
(Norway)
The drama prize of N kr
7.000 is distributed usually as
one award to a young author.
The award is given for each of
two successive years, and then
withheld from presentation for one
year. Selection of playwrights
to be honored is "made by the
Norwegian Association of Writers
on the nomination by two representatives from the Literary
Council and the chairman of the
Norwegian Dramatist's Federation." 1036.

Adalbert STIFTER MEDAL
(Austria)
This official honor, one of the
many prizes of the Bundesministerium für Unterricht (Minoritenplatz 5, Vienna 1), was
founded in 1955 in commemoration
of the 150th birthday of Adalbert
Stifter. It offers a silver medal,

a diploma, and a premium of S
20.000--granted without applica-
tion--to distinguish the entire
literary work of an author.
Among recipients are:
 1955 Felix Braun
 1957 Max Mell; Karl Heinrich
   Waggerl
 1960 Josef Nadler   1037.

Adalbert STIFTER PRIZE OF
OBERÖSTERREICH (Austria)
 Established first in 1951 with
a memorial premium of S
10.000, the cultural honor of the
Province of Oberösterreich (Linz,
Upper Austria) included among
winners honored: Linus Kefer,
August Karl Stöger.
 Also granted were a Förde-
rungspreis of S 5.000 to Johann
Pauk, and Franz Pühringer; a
Förderungspreis for writers in
exile of S 5.000 to Gertrud
Fussenegger and Robert Hohlbaum.
The award was reestablished in
1961 with a premium of S 30.000.
                            1038.

STONEHILL LITERARY AWARDS
(Philippines)
 This literary prize, administered by the Philippine P.E.N.,
was established in 1959 and
offers a six-month grant to a
Filipino writer, of at least 25
years of age, for completion of
a book in progress. Books
finished with the aid of the grant
(P 1,000 a month for five months,
and P 2,500 on the sixth month
when the completed manuscript
is submitted) are published by
Alberto Benipayo, and royalties
of the first edition belong to the
Philippine P.E.N. Club, with
royalties from subsequent
editions reverting to the author.
 Authors assisted by the grants
include:
 1960 Nick Joaquin. The
   woman who had two navels
 1961 Kerima Polotan. Hand
   of the enemy   1039.

STRADANOVA PRIZE (Italy)
 The annual publisher's prize
of L 300.000 for fiction, offered
by presso La Bancarella di Libri
Gigetto "Bonometto" (SS Apostoli
4392, Venice) for "un racconto
lungo inedito," is presented in the
setting appropriate to the award
--before the book carts of Venice
in Strada Nova. The award has
been granted such writers as:
 1958 Nullo Cantaroni. L'afoso
   autunno
 1959 Mauro Senesi. Quattro
   regali per i negri
 1960 Luigi Grande. I piedi
   di carta
 1961 Silvestro Amore. Essere
   uomo tra gli uomini
 1962 Gian Luigi Zucchini. La
   processione di Verges
                            1040.

STREGA PRIZE (Italy)
 This "Roman" prize, the most
famous Italian literary award, is
offered for the best Italian novel
published during the contest year
(from April 30 of the previous
year to May 1 of the year of
award). In addition to selecting
the "best novel of the year," the
honor stimulates interest in
literature through publicity given
the prize.
 Established in 1947 with a
grant from Guido Alberti and
named for the Strega liqueur
manufactured by fratelli Alberti
di Benevento, the award is also
popularly referred to as the
"Bellonci Prize," from Salotto
Bellonci, the literary salon in
which the idea of such a literary
prize developed. The salon was
composed of writers, artists,
musicians, and intellectuals--"Gli
Amici della dominica," The Sunday
Friends (via Fratelli Ruspoli 2,
Rome)--who first met at the
home of Maria Bellonci (literary
biographer and critic) and Gofredo
Bellonci during World War II,
as a secret gathering to discuss

aid to intellectuals and literati
who suffered in the political,
social, and economic strictures
of the time.

At present the "Amici," a
group of approximately 370 members, determines annually the
recipient of the L 1.000.000
Strega Prize premium. Novels
published during the contest
year, that have "not already won
a literary award," are entered
in competition for the prize by
the sponsorship in writing of at
least two members of the "Amici."
The winner is selected by two
sealed ballots of the group--an
initial vote in June to reduce
the hundreds of competing books
to five finalists; and a final vote
in July. The results of the
deciding ballot are publicly tabu-
lated each year at a reception
in the gardens of Villa Giulia--
one of the show-places of Rome,
now an Etruscan museum.

Recipients of Italy's major
novel award are:

1947 Ennio Flaiano. Tempo
di uccidere
1948 Vincenzo Cardarelli.
Villa Tarantola
1949 G.B. Angioletti. La
memoria
1950 Cesare Pavese. La
bella estate
1951 Corrado Alvaro. Quasi
una vita
1952 Alberto Moravia. I
racconti
1953 Massimo Bontempelli.
L'amante fedele
1954 Mario Soldati. Lettere
da Capri
1955 Giovanni Comisso. Un
gatto attraversa la strada
1956 Giorgio Bassani. Cinque
storie ferraresi
1957 Elsa Morante. L'isola
di Arturo
1958 Dino Buzzati. Sessanta
racconti
1959 Giuseppe Tomasi. Il
Gattopardo
1960 Carlo Cassola. La
ragazza di Bube
1961 Raffaele La Capria.
Ferito a morte
1962 Mario Tobino. Il
clandestino   1041.

SUNNMØRE PRIZE (Norway)
The Norwegian prize of N Kr
1.000 is distributed by the Sunnmøre Patriotic Youth League.
1042.

SVENSKA AKADAMIEN PRIZES
(Sweden)
The Swedish Academy Prizes
are awarded by the Academy, an
exclusive body, founded in 1786
by Gustav III with the motto,
"Snille Och Smak" (Genius and
Taste), of eighteen nationally
recognized Swedish authors and
cultural leaders such as Pär
Lagerkvist and Harry Martinsson,
and the two "leading prose
writers" recently elected (1957) to
the group: Ollo Hedberg, Eyvind
Johnson.

"The total sum at the disposal
of the Academy for awards to
authors is about 100,000 kroner
a year." During the period
1864-1939, the Swedish national
government gave the Academy a
"special grant to be distributed
among authors." At present, the
group's literary awards are
derived from the yield of a "number of legacies and donations,"
and profit accruing "from the
official periodical of the Swedish
government, 'Post och Inrikes
Tidningar,' the oldest existing
periodical in the world, founded
in 1645."

In addition to administering the
world's most famous literary
honor, the Nobel Prize for Literature, the Swedish Academy
(Borshuset, Stockholm C) presents prizes to Swedish writers
for outstanding work, and to
authors of other Scandinavian
countries for their literary con-

tributions. These awards include
the Bellmann Prize (which see),
and a SWEDISH TRANSLATOR'S
PRIZE (Oversattarpriset), a
SWEDISH GOOD USAGE PRIZE
(Sparkvardspriset), and the
highest official honor of the national government for a Swedish
writer--KUNGLIGA PRISET
(Swedish Royal Prize), also
known as the SWEDISH NATIONAL
LITERARY PRIZE, awarded in
1961 to Arthur Lundkvist.

The Academy also grants a
prize to Norwegian writers--the
DOUBLAUG PRIZE, with a
premium of 15,000 kroner each
year.   1043.

SVENSKA DAGBLADET
LITERARY PRIZE (Sweden)
The 5.000 Swedish Crowns
literary prize of the Stockholm
newspaper, "Svenska Dagbladet"
(Karduansmakargatan 11, Box
594, Stockholm 1) is one of the
best-known awards for authors
in Sweden. Granted annually
"just before Christmas," the
prize was established in 1944 in
connection with the celebration
of the 60th anniversary of the
"Svenska Dagbladet," "to lend
support to one or several new,
or so far as age goes, young,
Swedish authors having during
the past year made a remarkable
debut or having showed in his
or her production a remarkable
development."

Among authors receiving the
initial prizes in 1944 are Lars
Ahlin, now "one of Sweden's
most outstanding literary talents,"
and Harry Martinsson, now an
internationally-known member of
the Swedish Academy. The jury
--composed of staff members of
"Svenska Dagbladet" Literary
Section, and public figures and
professional writers, such as
Prince Wilhelm, President of
the Swedish P.E.N. Club,
President of the Swedish Writers

Association--has granted the
award in the last five years to:
1957 Birgitta Trotzig. De
     utsatta (The exposed)
     Erland Josephson. En berat-
     telse om herr Silberstein
     (A tale about Mr. Silberstein)
1958 Lars Gyllensten. Senatorn
     (The senator)
     Ake Wassing. Dodgravarens
     pojke (The gravedigger's boy)
1959 Bengt Söderbergh. Vid
     flodens strand (At the river
     side)
     Kurt Salomonson. Sveket (The
     deceit)
1960 Lars Gustafsson. Broderna
     (The brothers)
1961 Bo Carpelan (Finland).
     Den svala dagen (The cool
     day)
1962 Gunnar E. Sandgren.
     Fursten (The prince)   1044.

SVJETLOST PRIZES (Yugoslavia)
These publisher's prizes, offered by the firm, Svetlost (The
Light) of Sarajevo, capital city
of the Republic of Bosnia and
Herzegovinia, have honored such
writers as:
1954 Ivo Andric. Travnicka
     hronika (Chronicle of travel--
     novel)
     Branko Copic. Odabrane ratne
     pripovijetke (Selected war
     stories)
     Bodoljub Colakovic. Zapisi iz
     N.O. rata (Chronicles from
     the People's Liberation War)
1955 Vojo Caric. Beli vuk (The
     white wolf--collected stories)
                               1045.

SWEDISH AUTHORS' FUND
"Since 1954 this fund has granted
(a) compensation from State
means to authors whose works are
lent or used in public and school
libraries according to the number
of times the works of respective
authors are lent out, and (b)
awards--400,000 kroner--and
pensions--200,000 kroner. The

individual awards range from 2000 to 5000 kroner a year, and the pensions--which may be granted to both authors and deceased authors' survivors-- from 4000 to 10,000 kroner; the most usual sum at present is 7000 kroner" (Letter, Swedish Authors' Fund) 1046.

SWEDISH BOOK LOTTERY
The Book Lottery, "an exclusively Swedish phenomenon," has awarded financial assistance to Swedish authors since 1947. Funds are derived from lottery tickets "sold to the public through popular political, economic and cultural movements." Winners of the lottery receive prizes of "parcels of books." The 240,000 kroner annual profit from the lottery is distributed in awards to authors as the BOKLOTTERIETS STORA PRIZE, with premiums varying from 2000 to 25,000 kroner. 1047.

SWISS TEACHERS' ASSOCIATIONS YOUTH BOOK PRIZE
The Jugendbuchpreis des schweizerischen Lehrer- und Lehrerinnenvereins is offered each year by the Swiss Teachers' Associations "for the best children's book or the best work done in the field of children's literature by a Swiss author and published in Switzerland."
Children's authors honored include:
1945 Olga Meyer
1946 Elisabeth Müller
1947 Adolf Haller
1948 Hans Fischer
Alois Carigiet
Selina Chonz
1949 Traugott Vogel
1953 Max Voegeli
1954 Gertrud Hausermann.
Heimat am Fluss (Home on the River)
1955 Ernst Kreidolf
1956 Olga Meyer

1957 Felix Hoffmann 1048.

SYDNEY MORNING HERALD LITERARY COMPETITION (Australia)
This major literary competition of Australia, the richest held in amount of premiums awarded-- with a first prize of Ŀ2000 for a novel (Second and Third Prizes of Ŀ1000 and Ŀ500), and smaller premiums for short stories (Ŀ 100, Ŀ50) and poems (Ŀ50, Ŀ25)-- was established in 1947 as an annual event. The contest was temporarily discontinued in 1952-1955, reestablished in 1955, and finally terminated in 1957.
The contest was open to all Australian citizens, and among the authors honored by the prize were:
Novel Prize (Ŀ2000)
1947 Ruth Park. Harp of the South
1948 George Johnston and Charmain Clift. High Valley
Smaller or Shared Novel Prize--
Esther Roland, D'Arcy Niland, Mabel W. Smith, C.V. Crockett, Nancy Phelan, and
1947 Jon Cleary. You can't see around corners
1949 T.A.G. Hungerford. Sowers of the wind
1950 T.A.G. Hungerford. The ridge and the river
Barbara Jeffris. Return via Canterbury
1954 Barbara Jeffris. Contango Day
1957 A.M. Harris. A tall man
War Story Prize (Ŀ1000)--- one-time award to John Hetherington
Poetry Prize--Rosemary Dobson, Raemonde Alain, T. Inglis Moore, Muir Holburn 1049.

SZOT LITERARY PRIZE (Hungary)
Established in 1956 by the Hungarian Trade Unions Council for "outstanding literary composi-

tions," this award carries a premium of 12,000 Forints for the First Prize and 8,000, 6,000 and 4,000 Forints for Second, Third, and Fourth Prize. Among the First Prize winners are:

1959 Mate Timar
1960 Geza Molnar   1050.

Maila TALVIO PRIZE (Finland)
Named to commemorate the Finnish writer, Maila Talvio, the prize, which is awarded by the Tàlvio Literature Prize Committee, has honored such authors as:

1951 Martti Merenmaa
1956 Väinö Linna
1958 Veikko Huovinen   1051.

TAMPERE PRIZE (Finland)
The regional literary award for local authors is granted by Tampere, the second largest city in Finland, each year. Winners include:

1954 Esti Heiniö
     Laura Virkki
1955 Väinö Linna
     Eila Pennanen
1956 Hannu Lehtinen
     Veikko Pihlajamäki
     Jaakko Syrjä
     Rauha Virtanen
1957 Aili Somersalo
1958 Kirsi Kunnas
     Mirkka Rekola
1959 Helvi Erjakka
     Esti Heiniö
     Matti Hyvonen
     Alex Matson
     Kalle Päätalo
     K. H. Seppälä
1961 Matti Saariaho
     Rauha Virtanen   1052.

TARQUINIA-CARDARELLI PRIZE (Italy)
Ente Provinciale del Turismo di Viterbo (Pro Tarquinia, Piazza Cavour 21, Viterbo, Tarquinia) sponsors this annual L 1.000.000 award, which is named for the poet Vincenzo Cardarelli. The premium is divided among three forms of writing: Poetry (L 500.000); Critical Essays (L 300.000); and Journalistic Articles published in reviews (L 200.000). Winners in 1962 shared prizes in each category:

Poetry Dianella Selvatico Estense
     Annarosa Panaccione
Essay Gaetano Salveti. Article in
     "La Fiera Letteraria"
     Giuseppe Tedeschi. Article in
     "Il Popolo"
Journalism Elio Filippo Accrocca.
     Articles in "La Giustizia"
     R. M. De Angelis. Articles
     in "Il Tempo"   1053.

Otavio TARQUINIO DE SOUZA PRIZE (Brazil)
A prize alternating in year of award with the novel prize, José Lins do Rêgo Prize, is the Tarquinio de Souza Prize, offered by the publisher, Livraria José Olimpio (Rua Gusmoës 100, São Paulo) in celebration of the firm's 30th anniversary. In 1963 a premium of Cr$500.000 will be presented for the best manuscripts of biographies or Brazilian studies submitted in competition for the award.   1054.

Saul TCHERNICHOFSKY PRIZE (Israel)
This translation prize has been awarded Simon Halkin for his work in translating Walt Whitman's "Leaves of Grass" into Hebrew.   1055.

TERAMO PRIZE (Italy)
The L 400,000 premium awarded for an unpublished short story --with several additional prizes for poetry and journalism--is conferred by the city of Teramo (Ente Provinciale per il Turismo, c.s.o. S. Giorgio 62). Winners of the "Racconto Inedito" prize include:

1959 Maruo Senesi. Il leone

di Antula
1960 Michle Lalli. Costruivamo
una diga
Giose Rimanelli. Il vestito
rosso
1961 Giovanni Pirelli. L'otto
settembre della vedova
Bianchi
1962 Fulvio Longobardi. Ciao
1056.

THAILAND ROYAL INSTITUTE
OF ARTS AND SCIENCES ESSAY
CONTEST
This prize, the only continuing
literary honor in Thailand at
present, is awarded in an annual
contest "for essays on a Buddhist
theme to be used for the instruction of youngsters." While entries
"are judged mainly according to
originality of approach, clarity
of exposition, and soundness of
doctrinal interpretation," "in-
trinsic literary merit is also
taken into account."   1057.

THREE CROWNS LITERARY
PRIZE (France)
The Prix Littéraire des Trois
Couronnes for an unpublished
work in verse or prose--a novel
or a history concerning the
Basque country in France or
Spain--was first granted in 1958.
Books may be entered in the
annual competition by sending
three copies of the manuscript
before May 1 to the Secretary
(Pierre Espil, Hasparren,
Basses-Pyrénées). The 500 NF
premium, announced each year
toward the end of August in a
different village in the Basque
country, has been presented to:
1958 Marie Cossa. Fileuse de
verre
Luce Laurand-Dupin. L'oiseau
sur la lande
1959 Madeleine Mayi. Itinéraire
du passé
1960 Bernard Candeul. Il avait
l'accent de chez nous
1961 Michel Lauret. La lande

brûlante
1962 Claude Rivière. Terres
d'ombre pensive
Claudie Planet. Campagne
landaise   1058.

Nestor de TIERE PRIZE (Belgium)
The Flemish language award,
offered by the Belgian Royal
Academy of Flemish Science,
Letters and the Arts, was won by
Robert van Passen with "De
matroos," 1958.   1059.

TIERRA DEL FUEGO BEST BOOK
OF THE YEAR (Chile)
This prize of the Sociedad de
Escritores de Chile brought the
title of honor, "Mejor Libro del
Año a Tierra del Fuego" in 1957
to Francisco Coloane's collection
of eight short stories.   1060.

TIRSO DE MOLINA PRIZE (Spain)
The Spanish government awards
a 40,000 pts drama prize--De-
partmento Audio visual, Instituto
de Cultura Hispanica, Avda de los
Reyes Catolicos 16, Madrid--
which is named for the 17th
century Spanish dramatist, Gabriel
Tellez, who wrote under the pen
name of Tirso de Molina. The
prize is offered for the best work
of a playwright of any nationality
writing in Spanish. Winner of the
award in 1961, with an "original
unpublished drama of the length of
an ordinary play," was Martin
Iniesta with "Final del Horizonte."
1061.

TOBAR PRIZE (Ecuador)
Included among the literary
winners of this cultural honor of
the city of Quito is Jorge Carrera
Andrade.   1062.

TOLLENS PRIZE (Netherlands)
Among the winners of this prize,
which has been awarded since
1903 by the Tollens Fund, is
Maria Dermout, who received
the honor in 1958 for her entire

literary work.   1063.

Leo TOLSTOY MEMORIAL
MEDAL (USSR)
This prize of the Maxim Gorky
Institute of World Literature (Ul.
Vorovskogo 25a, Moscow)--the
Soviet Writers Union "school for
the training of writers"--was
awarded in 1960 to the German
author, Hermann Kasack. 1064.

TOPELIUS-PALKINTO (Finland)
A publisher's prize, donated
by Werner Söderstöm, has been
granted each year since 1947 for
the best children's book. The
prize, which is administered by
"Nuorten Kirja" (The Book of the
Youth), has brought a premium
of 75.000 Fmk to such authors
as:
    1951 Aili Somersalo. Metsolan
    Iapset
    1952 Leena Härmä. Tuittupää
    ja Rantakylän Sisu
    1953 Marjatta Kurenniemi. Oli
    ennen Onnimanni
    1954 Juuso Tamminen.
    Varjagien aarre
    1955 Martti Haavio. Kultaomena;
    and Tuhkimus
    1956 Aale Tynni. Heikin
    salaisuudet
    1957 Aira Kokki. Avattu ovi
    1958 Hellin Tynell. Rohkeu-
    skeinu Haakana, and O. Veikko.
    Luolamiehen pojat   1064A.

TOR MARGANA PRIZE (Italy)
The Premio Tor Margana,
an award in the form of a
replica of the Renaissance doors
of Piazza Margana--a reproduction in silver following the design
of Roberto Ruta--is granted by the
restaurant, Angelino (Armando
Biasciucci, Director, Piazza
Margana 37, Rome). The prize
honors outstanding writers, publishers, and publications, as
well as other artists--architects,
painters, sculptors, actors.
The Tor Margana is awarded

each two or three months by a
jury of young writers, most of
whom are in their 30's, at
"Hosteria Angelino," a gathering-
place for artists, located in Piazza
Margana in the old quarter of
Rome.
Among the winners of the award
--symbol of 15th century Italian
art--are such authors and publishers as:
Recent Awards--
     P. Monelli, G. Bigorelli,
     Maria and G. Bellonci, C.
     Bernari, G. Debendetti. S.
     Quasimodo, G. Villaroel,
     Paolo Lechloano, Gracinto
     Spagnoletti
1958 G. B. Angioletti
     Nezi Pozza
     Vincenzo Cardarelli
     Alfredo Montelli
     Mario Praz
1959 Cesare Zavattini and Valen-
     tino Bompiani. New edition
     of "Almanacco Letterario"
     Giuseppe Ungaretti
     Antonio Baldini
1960 Giovanni Scheiwiller
     Libero Bigiaretti   1065.

TÖREHAN PRIZE (Turkey)
This translation prize was recently awarded A. Kadir for his
work in translating Homer's
"Iliad" in free verse.   1066.

TOULOUSE FLORAL GAMES
(France)
The Concours des Fleurs
Traditionnelles, one of numerous
floral games held in Latin countries each year, are conducted
by the Académie des Jeux Floraux
(Hôtel d'Assézat et Clémence
Isaure, Toulouse) and are considered the original literary
competitions of this type in
Europe. Said to be founded in
1323 by seven troubadours who
invited all troubadours to compete
the following year for the award
of one golden violet--indicating
the best poem about the Virgin

(Oxford Companion to French Literature, p. 371), the competitions are held currently for writing in set form and subject.

Carrying on the long tradition of the Floral Games of Toulouse, winning poems--and writing in other literary forms--read at the annual festival are rewarded with flowers of gold and silver in such forms as Amarante, Violette, Souci, Eglantine, Primevère, Lys, and Jasmin. 1067.

Georg TRAKL PRIZE FOR POETRY (Austria)

Established in 1954 by the Salzburg City officials to commemorate the 40th anniversary of the death of the famous Salzburg poet, Georg Trakl, this award is a cooperative literary honor granted jointly by the Salzburger Landesregierung and the Bundesministerium für Unterricht. Recipients of the prize--carrying a premium of S 15.000 in 1962--include: Christine Busta, Christine Lavant, Michael Gottenbrunner, Wilhelm Szabo, and Juliane Windhager. 1068.

TREBBO POETRY PRIZE (Italy)

The poetry award of L 500.000, instituted by the organization, "Amici della Cultura," includes among its recent winners S. Angeli. 1069.

TRENTA PRIZE (Italy)

Italy's National Academy of Letters (Accademia Nazionale dei Lincei, via della Lungara 10, Rome) grants this literary prize for such writing as:
1931 Fabio Tombari. La vita
1940 Dino Buzzati. Il deserto
    dei Tartari 1070.

TRICOLOR PRIZE (Italy)

A joint award of the Comune di Reggio Emilia and the Societa Italiana Autori Drammatici is offered as a special prize in commemoration of the Risorgimento Italiano. The honor will be presented an Italian playwright for an unpublished dramatic work about the Risorgimento. The premium for the winning work, which must be entered in competition before February 28, 1962 with Segreteria del Concorso presso, Municipio di Reggio Emilia, is L 1.000.000. In addition to the monetary award, the winning play will be brought to public attention by presentation at Teatro Municipale di Reggio Emilia. 1071.

TRYSIL AWARD (Norway)

Winners of this N Kr 2.000 prize are nominated by the Literary Council and distribution is made by the city, Trysil Municipality. 1072.

TUNISIAN ACADEMY OF FLORAL GAMES GRAND PRIZE

Offered for all forms of literature, since the first year of award in 1937, the Grand Prix de L'Académie des Jeux Floraux de Tunisie is given each year, as a monetary award and a plaque. The prize is granted for work submitted during the period of competition--January 1 to June 30--to Felix de La Croix (Secrétaire Général, 23 avenue de Carthage, Tunis). Recent laureates include:
1953 Mme Vona Palaa
    Ludovic Bernero--diploma and
    medal
1954 Mme Lavier
1955 Mme Hallex
1956 Mlle Roi
1957-1958 Mme Vona Palaa
1959 Mme A. Pujol
1960 Col. Moreau
1961 Jean Chavigny
    Wilfred Lucas 1073.

TURKISH LANGUAGE FOUNDATION SCIENCE AND ART PRIZE

The Turk Dil Kurumu San'at

318   International Literary Awards

ve Bilem Armaganlari is an annual   grocer's store)
prize of the Turkish Language   Cahit Sitki Taranci. Otuzbes
Foundation, which was initiated   Yas
in 1955 and is awarded each   Ahmet Muhip Dranos. Golgeler
year for various forms of imagin-   Yahya Kemal Beyatli. Golgeler
ative writing, criticism, and   1075.
factual writing. Among the win-
ners of the premium--decreased   TWELVE PRIZES (Greece)
from 3.500 TL presented in the   These literary honors, awarded
first two years to the present   by the "Group of Twelve" (10
2.000 TL--are: Othonos, Athens), an informal and
   1955 Cahit Kulebi. Yeseren   unofficial organization of literary
      Otlar   men--poets, critics and novelists--
   Ali Gunduz Akinci. Abdulhak   were established in 1950 and are
      Hamit   five annual prizes. The "Group
   1956 Orhan Hancerlioglu. Ali   of Twelve" has been described as
   1957 Sabahattin Kudret Aksal.   "the acknowledged though unofficial
      Yarali Hayvan   Greek Academy," and includes
   Cahit Orhan Tutengil. Montes-   such famous contemporary Greek
      quieu'nun siyasi ve iktisadi   authors as Pandelis Prevelakis,
      Fikirleri   and the literary honors it bestows
   1958 Fazil Husnu Daglarca.   are collectively designated "The
      Delice Bocek   Group of Twelve Awards," or
   Oktay Akbal. Sucumuz Insan   "Awards of the Twelve." Current
      Olmak   prizes (which see) are:
   1959 Tahsin Yucel. Duslerin   G. FEXIS PRIZE--for new writer
      Olumu   with promising literary talent
   S. Eyuboglu-N. Ali Cimcoz.   L. GOULANDRIS PRIZE--for
      Devlet   literary criticism, essay, or
   Nermin Uygur. Edmund   travel impressions
      Husserl'de Baskasinin Ben'i   K. HATZIPATERAS PRIZE--for
      Problemi   collected poetry
   1960 Onat Kutlar. Ishak   OURANIS PRIZE--for prose nar-
   Orhan Asena. Tanrilar ve   rative
      Insanlar   POURFINA (PURFINA) PRIZE--
   Teoman Akturel. Sarlo   for literary writing extolling
   Huseyin Batuhan. Batida   Greek civilization   1076.
      Tolerans Fikrinin Gelismesi
   1961 Tarik Dursun K. Guzel   "U" PRIZE (France)
      Avrat Otu   A drama prize of 1.000 NF,
   E. Erhat-A. Kadir. Ilyada   awarded since 1955 for the best
   Mehmet Fuat. Dusunceye   play of the current theatre season
      Saygi   1074.   in Paris, has honored such play-
                                      wrights as:
TURKISH REPUBLICAN PARTY   1955 Yves Jamiaque
LITERARY PRIZE   1956 Colette Audry. Soledad
   The Cumhuriyet Halk Partisi   1957 Robert Mallet. L'Equipage
Edebiyar Armagani, a prize of   au complet
Inonu (C.H.P.), has been award-   1958 Georges Soria. L'Étrangère
ed since 1940 for a variety of   dans l'île
literary work including novels and   1959 François Billetdoux.
poetry. Winners include: Tchin-Tchin
   Halide Edip Adivar. Sinekli   1960 René de Obaldia.
   Bakkal (The fly-blown   Genousie

1961 Roland Dubillard.
Naïves hirondelles   1077.

UL YOO LITERARY PRIZE FOR
TRANSLATION INTO KOREAN
(Korea)
Presented for the superior
translation of literary works
into Korean, this annual prize
of 200,000 hwan, a citation, and
a medal is offered by the Ul Yoo
Publishing Company (Kwanchul-
dong, Chongno-ku, Seoul) each
November since 1957. Works
entered in competition must be
submitted by the last day of
March of the year of award.
                          1078.

UNANIMOUS PRIZE (France)
The Prix de L'Unanimité of
Comité national des écrivains
(2 rue de l'Elysée, Paris 8e)
requires unanimous vote of the
jury to award the 2.000 NF
premium to a distinguished
writer, or the two 2.000 NF
purses to assist the work of two
young writers.
Laureates since 1955, initial
year of award, are:
1955 Julien Benda
1956 Gustave Cohen
1957 Marie Noel
1958 Francis Carco. Entire
   literary work
1959 Pierre Mac Orlan
Bourses--Grants to young writers
1955 Claude Lipardi
   Gérard Prévost
1956 J.J. Robert
   Cowlet
1958 Roger Rudigoz. Le
   dragon Solassier
   Michel del Castillo. Tanguy
   et la guitare
   Henri Alleg. La question
1959 Henri Crespi. La
   cigarette
   André Liberati. Vieux
   capitaine
   Ferdinand Oyono (Cameroon).
   Une vie de Boy; Le vieux
   nègre et la médaille

1960, 1961, 1962 No prize
granted   1079.

UNESCO INDIAN PRIZE FOR THE
NEW READING PUBLIC (India)
Some thirty prizes of Rs 500
each are offered by the Indian
Ministry of Education for books
in all the major languages of
India, which are suitable for the
new reading public. Seven prizes
of Rs 1,900 each were awarded
by the Ministry of Education in
1961, the year of the second
annual competition, for works in
Hindi (winning authors: Ramesh
Chandra Varma, Umesh Varma,
Vikas Ki Kahani); and Tamil
(winning authors: Devendra
Kumar, Shiv Chandra Dutta and
Bimla Dutta, Kishor Garg).
                          1080.

UNITA D'ITALIA PRIZE (Inter-
national--Italy)
In celebration of the Centenary
of the Unity of Italy (Centenario
dell'Unita d'Italia) this award is
offered by the Italian Minister
of Foreign Affairs for an unpublished monograph on the Italian
Risorgimento. Open to both
Italian and foreign scholars, the
contest carries a prize premium
of L 2.000.000, a gold medal,
and the right to publish the winning work in Italian.
Unpublished monographs are
accepted in various languages
provided they treat a single
period, aspect or individual of the
Risorgimento, and present a
critical review of the domestic
and foreign events that enabled
the Italians to unify their country.
Competing writings must be submitted in five typed copies by
June 30, 1962 to Ministero degli
Affari Esteri, Direzione Generale
delle Relazione Culturali (Ufficio
II, Rome).   1081.

UNITED KINGDOM ROYAL
SOCIETY OF LITERATURE

AWARD (International--England)
This prize is granted under
the W.H. Heinemann Bequest and
was formerly known as "The
W.H. Heinemann Award for Literature." One of several literary
honors granted by the Royal
Society of Literature of the
United Kingdom (1 Hyde Park
Gardens, London, W 2), the
award was established in 1944
with a bequest of the publisher
W.H. Heinemann for "the encouragement of genuine contributions to literature," preferably
those forms of writing less
likely to command large public
sale--poetry, biography, criticism, philosophy, history--al-
though novels of distinction are
also considered for the prize.

Publishers submit books published during the year to the
Committee for consideration.
Books must be written in English
--translations are not eligible--
and "works of younger authors
who are not yet widely recognized"
are given preference in determining the winner.

Among the winners of the a-
ward, which is usually presented each year in July at the
annual meeting of the Society,
are:

1960 Morris West. The
devil's advocate
C.A. Trypanis. The cocks
of Hades
1961 James Morris. Venice
Vernon Scannell. The masks
of love   1082.

UNITED KINGDOM ROYAL
SOCIETY OF LITERATURE
PRIZES (International)
The Royal Society of Literature (1 Hyde Park Gardens,
London, W 2), founded in 1825
by King George IV, includes
among its Fellows and Members
distinguished authors, as well
as critics, teachers, and
scholars whose work in the field

of literature is internationally
known. Among the Fellows are
English authors famous as novel-
ists, poets, dramatists, and
masters of factual writing: H. E.
Bates, Phyllis Bentley, John
Betjeman, Catherine Bowen,
Agatha Christie, Noel Coward,
Cecil Day-Lewis, Daphne Du
Maurier, Lawrence Durrell,
William Golding, Elizabeth Goudge,
Graham Greene, Elizabeth Jennings,
Bruce Marshall, John Masefield,
Somerset Maugham, Bertrand
Russell, V. Sackville-West, Edith
Sitwell, Osbert Sitwell, Charles
Snow, G. B. Stern, Rebecca West,
T. H. White.

Fellows and Members identified
with countries outside the British
Isles include:

Fellows

Australia	Morris L. West
Austria	Arthur Koestler
India	
Ghana	Sarvepalli Radhakrishnan
Pakistan	Itrat Husain
South	Alan Paton
Africa	Mary Renault (pseud
	of Mary Challans)
U.S.A.	Van Wyck Brooks
	Rachel Carson
	Hardin Craig
	Robert Frost
	Gilbert Highet
	Louise Booker Wright

Members

Australia	P. Brian Cox
Burma	Maung Maung Pye
Ceylon	S. Kumaravelu
Ghana	J.W. Harvey Ewusi
India	M. N. Gupta
	Brahma Swarup
Italy	Pietro Festa
Mauritius	Moonasur Kooraram
New Zealand	Peter Hickson
	Keith J. Wyness-
	Mitchell
Nigeria	G. N. Ukabiala
Pakistan	Abdullah Hasham
	Mohammad Owais
South Africa	Sesham Jivaratnam
	John

South Africa   T. H. Lawrence
Uganda   Raymond Tong
  Among literary honors awarded by the Society is the newly
instituted dignity, Companion of
Literature (C. Lit.), established
in 1961 "to honor English writers
who have given exceptional distinction to English Literature."
Companions of Literature--
limited to a maximum number of
10 at one time--must be elected
by unanimous vote of the Council
of the Royal Society, and were
first designated on May 10,
1961: Winston Churchill, E. M.
Forster, John Masefield, W.
Somerset Maugham, G. M.
Trevelyan. T. S. Eliot, also invited, preferred not to accept the
award. In 1962, two additional
authors honored were: Aldous
Huxley and Edmund Blunden.
Two other prizes of the Society
are the Benson Medal, and the
United Kingdom Royal Society
of Literature Award (which see).
                            1083.

UNITED NATIONS ESSAY
PRIZE (International)
  One of several literary awards
offered from time to time by the
United Nations, this prize for
an essay on a "United Nations
Topic," was established in 1948
in memory of the late François
Steffani, Director of the Bureau
of Technical Services of the
United Nations. The subject of
the competition was, "The Role
of the Individual in the United
Nations," and the prize for
winners--selected from the
competing writings of members
of non-governmental organizations between 20 and 30 years
of age--was a fellowship to
work at the United Nations Headquarters (then Lake Success) for
30 days. During the period of
fellowship, winning essayists
served as interns--studying the
administration of the United Na-

tions. Transportation was paid
to the Headquarters and a main-
tenance allowance of $10 a day
granted each winner.   1084.

UNITED NATIONS ONE-ACT
PLAYWRIGHTING CONTEST
(International)
  In 1959 the United Nations
awarded three prizes for the
winning one-act plays submitted
in the competition:
1st prize--$1,000 Ronald
  Dunlavey. Border incident
2nd prize--$500 Willard Weiner.
  Leave it to the little people
3rd prize--$250 Ruth Purkey.
  God's alarm clock
  Other literary prizes offered
by the United Nations include
the UNESCO SPECIAL PRIZE,
granted Ernest Schnabel (Germany)
for "Anne Frank--Spur Eines
Kindes."   1085.

UNITED STATES NATIONAL
INSTITUTE OF ARTS AND
LETTERS GRANTS IN LITERA-
TURE (International--U.S.A.)
  The National Institute of Arts
and Letters (633 West 155th
Street, New York 32), a private
organization "for the furtherance
of literature and the fine arts in
the United States," was founded
in 1898 and is composed of 250
members who are "qualified by
notable achievements in art,
literature, or music."
  Six grants in literature have
been awarded each year by the
Institute since 1941 to honor
"published work showing creative
achievement." The $1,000 pre-
miums, which are not applied for
and which are presented in a
formal joint ceremony each April
in a session of the Institute and
the American Academy of Arts
and Letters, have been won by
such writers as:
  1941 Mary M. Colum (Ireland
    --U.S.A.)
  1943 Jose Garcia Villa

(Philippines--U.S.A.)
1944 Hugo Ignotus (pseud of
Hugo Veigelsberg) (Hungary)
1948 Bertolt Brecht (Germany,
East)
1951 Vladimir Nabokov (USSR-
U.S.A.)   1086.

UNIVERSALITY OF THE FRENCH LANGUAGE PRIZE (International --France)

The Prix de L'Universalité de la Langue Française, a biennial publisher's prize offered by Librairie Bonaparte (31 rue Bonaparte, Paris 6e)--formerly called the "Prix Rivarol," or "Antoine de Rivarol Literary Prize"--is granted for the best work written in French by a foreign author in one of five literary forms: Novel, Drama, Criticism, Essay, Poetry. The 1.000 NF prize for other than French authors is presented to those writers from countries where French is not the official language or one of the official languages. Both published works (those issued during the four years preceding the year of award), and unpublished books in manuscript may be entered in competition.

A distinguished jury, including François Mauriac, Emile Henriot, Gabriel Marcel, Jules Romains, Daniel-Rops, Henry Troyat, has awarded the honor to:
1949 Wladimir Weidle
En marge de l'Occident (Russie d'hire et d'aujourd'hui)
Farjallah Haïk (Lebanon).
Abou Nassif
1950 Elie Cioran (Rumania).
Précis de décomposition
1951 Emineh Pakravan (Iran).
Le prince sans histoire
1952 Gloria Alcosta (Argentina). Visages (poems)
Gardner Davies (Australia).
Le tombeau de Mallarmé
1953 Costa du Rels (Bolivia).

Les Croisés de la Haute-Mer
1954 Georges Spiridaki (Greece)
La Grèce et la poésie moderne; Mort lucide
1955 Armen Lubin. Transfert nocturne
Constantin Amariu (Rumania).
Le paresseux
1957 Vahé Katcha. Oeil pour oeil
1959 José Luis de Villalonga.
L'homme de sang
1961 Bruce Lowery. La cicatrice
1087.

UNIVERSITY OF THE PHILIPPINES GOLDEN JUBILEE SHORT STORY CONTEST

In celebration of the Golden Jubilee of the University in 1958, a contest was held for Philippine short stories. The First Prize was presented Bienvenido N. Santos.   1088.

URUGUAY NATIONAL LITERARY PRIZE

In 1954 this official national literary award was presented to the poet, Carlos Sabát Ercasty.
1089.

USSR ORDER OF THE HERO OF SOCIALIST LABOR

This official State award of the USSR, established in the latter part of 1938 as the "supreme grade of distinction in the sphere of economic and cultural construction" (Guillebaud, p. 497), carried rank and privilege equal to those of the State award, Hero of the Soviet Union, which was established in 1936.

The initial honor was presented on December 20, 1939 to Josef Stalin on the occasion of his 60th birthday, but since World War II the Order of the Hero of Socialist Labor has been identified as an official public reward for agricultural workers through the presentation of nearly 6500 such

Orders for contributions in Agriculture.   1090.

USSR ORDER OF LENIN
According to an authority on Russian literature (Slonim, Russian Soviet Literature, p. 2), this "Highest Soviet Decoration," is an "eagerly coveted" honor. The Order of Lenin was established, along with the USSR ORDER OF THE RED STAR (primarily a military decoration), by government decree of April 30, 1950 (General Regulations About Order of the USSR).

Offered for "artistic activities," not specified by subject area, the Order carries certain privileges, exemptions and rights-- such as, pension rights, monthly payments, transportation privileges, income tax exemption (Guillebaud, p. 493). Writers receiving this high public recognition include: Maxim Gorky, Nikolay Ostovsky (1935), Fyodor Gladkov (1953), Aleeksandr Korneichuk (1955--on the occasion of his 50th birthday), Ilya Ehrenburg (1961--for "services to the development of Soviet Literature"), Vesevolod A. Kochetov (1962--on the occasion of his 50th birthday)--two published novels: "The Yershov Brothers 1956; "The Regional Party Secretary," 1961), Konstantin Fedin (1962--on the occasion of his 70th birthday, for "outstanding contribution to the advancement of Soviet Literature").   1091.

USSR ORDER OF THE RED BANNER OF LABOR
Recipients of this USSR official honor include writers--"workers with the pen"--as well as outstanding members of other professions. Mikhail Zoshchenko received a Red Labor Banner Medal in 1939. More recent winners of the honor are such authors as Ilya Ehrenburg (1961

--on the occasion of his 60th birthday for "outstanding achievements in the sphere of Belles Lettres"), and in 1962: K. G. Paustovsky (on his 70th birthday); N. N. Gusev; Mikhailo A. Stelmakh (on his 50th birthday), V. N. Sobko (on his 50th birthday).
                                          1092.

USSISHKIN PRIZE (Israel)
The Jewish National Fund (Karen Kayemet) grants the literary award, which has been won by such writers as:
1948 Moshe Shamir. He who went into the fields
1954 I. Mossinshohn. The way of man
Aharon Megged. Hedva and I
                                          1093.

UZIEL PRIZE FOR RELIGIOUS LITERATURE (Israel)
Named for the late Rabbi Ben-Zion Uziel, this prize is applied for by sending with an application four copies of the work entered in competition to the Cultural Department of the municipality of Ramat-Gan. Rabbi Isaac Izik Halevi Prague won a First Prize with his book, "The Shrub of the Field."   1094.

Severo VACCARO PRIZE (Argentina)
The journalist, writer, or scientist who in his professional work has made an outstanding contribution, which honors Argentina and is beneficial to all mankind, is given public recognition for his achievement by the Vaccaro Prize. The award is granted biennially by the Severo Vaccaro Foundation (Avenida de Mayo 628, Buenos Aires) as endowed by Vicente Vaccaro, and consists of a gold medal, a diploma and a premium of 10.000 pesos.

The prize, presented on June 7, anniversary of the first number of "La Gazeta de Buenos Aires," first newspaper after the Argen-

tine Revolution of May 1910,
has been won by such intellectual
leaders as: Enrique Banchs,
poet; Eduardo Mallea, novelist;
the journalists: Alberto Cainza
Paz ('La Prensa"), David Michel
Torina ('El Intransigente"),
Américo Ghioldi ('La Vanguardia');
Enrique Nelson, educator;
Francisco Romero, philosopher;
and the scientists: Oscar Orías,
physiologist; and Luis F. Leloir,
biochemist.   1095.

VALENCIA PRIZES (Spain)
   In 1950 Diputacion Provincial
of Valencia established the prize
which offers premiums of 10, 000
pts in each of several classes of
literature--Biography, Novel,
Drama, Poetry.   Native-born
authors, or those with a specified
length of residence in the region,
who are honored with the prize
include:
Novel
   1958 Tomás Casillas García.
   El Camarada Darío
   1959 M. Beneyto Cuñat. El
   Río Veine Creciendo
   1960 Vicente Beltrán. Los
   don Nadie
Biography
   1961 S. Rodríguez Garcia.
   Life of the painter, Muñoz
   Degrain
Drama
   1958 Santiago Iborra. Ni a
   la Farsi ni a la Vida
   1959 M. Rodríguez Cuevillas.
   La Luna esta sobre el
   Camino
Poetry
   1958 Vicente Andrés Estellés.
   La Llave que abre Todas
   las Cerraduras
   1959 J.M. Pérez Martín.
   Música Olvidada
   1960 Carlos Senti. Dos
   Rompeintes
   1961 V. García del Real.
   En Contra del Viento y la
   Marea
Valencian Dialect--

1959 J. Brú Vidal. Retrova-
   ment
1960 Matilde de Lloria.
   Altissim Regne
1961 Jean Valls. Versos y Sara
      1096.

VALLOMBROSA PRIZE (Italy)
   Since 1953 this annual prize
has been awarded for various
forms of published writing:
Poetry, Short Stories, Journalism.
Culturale Artistico di Vallombrosa
(via Targioni Tozzetti 28, Florence) has distributed the L 1. 000.
000 premium to such authors as:
Poetry
   1958 L 300. 000 Guglilmo Lo
   Curzio. Il nemico; and
   Favola
   3 "Lupa d'Oro"--Renato
   Colombo, Nunzio Cossu,
   Leonardo R. Patane
   1961 L 1. 000. 000 Alessandro
   Paranchi. Coraggio di vivere
   1962 Divided: Luigi Fallacara.
   Il fruto del tempo
   Piero Jahier. Oualche Poesia
Short Stories
   1958 Ercole Mazzaccara. La
   foresta viv
   1960 Luigi Seomma. Laura,
   lotte e il professore
Journalism
   1958 2nd award Andrea M.
   Rossi   1097.

Joost VAN DEN VONDEL PRIZE
(Netherlands)
   Winners of this award, presented for the entire literary
output of a Dutch writer of
Netherlands or Belgium, include:
   1959 Antoon Coolen (Netherlands)
   1960 Max Lamberty (Belgium)
      1098.

Lucie B. and C. W. VAN DER
HOOGT PRIZE (Netherlands)
   A long-established award of
the Society of Netherlands Literature (Maatschappij der Nederlandse

Letterkunde, Rapenburg 12, Leiden) has been presented each year in the summer since 1925 for encouragement of authors. Writers honored with the prize are:

1925 R. van Genderen Stort. Kleine Inez (novel)
1926 Dirk Coster. Collected prose works
1927 Herman de Man. Het wassende water (novel)
1928 Aart van der Leeuw. Het aardsche paradijs
1929 Anthonie Donker (A.N. Donkersloot). Grenzen
1930 Antoon Coolen. Het donkere licht
1931 Arthur van Schendel. Het fregatschip Johanna Maria (novel)
1932 Johan Fabricius. Komedianten trokken voorbij
1933 Anton van Duinkerken (W.J.M.A. Asselbergs). Dichters der Contra-Reformatie
1934 J. Slauerhoff. Soleares (poetry)
1936 H. Marsman. Porta Nigra (poetry)
1937 Henriëtte van Eyk. Gabriël
1938 S. Vestdijk. Het vijfde zegel (novel)
1939 Ed. Hoornik. Mattheus (poetry)
1940 Clara Eggink. Het schiereiland
1941 M. Vasalis (M. Droggleever Fortuyn-Leenmans). Parken en woestijnen (poetry)
194- Bep Vuyk (E. de Willigen-Vuyk). Het laatste huis van de wereld (novel)
194- Ida Gerhardt. Het veerhuis (poetry)
194- Muus Jacobse (K. Heeroma). Vuur en wind (poetry)
1946 Bert Voeten. Doortocht (prose)
1947 J.J. Klant. De geboorte van Jan Klaassen

1948 Hendrik de Vries. Toorvertuin (poetry)
1949 Anna Blaman. Eenzaam avontuur (novel)--prize refused
1950 Leo Vroman. Gedichten, vroegere en latere (poetry)
1951 Alfred Kossmann. De nederlaag
1952 J.W. Schulte Nordholt. Verwilderd landschap
1953 Adriaan van der Veen. Het wilde feest
1954 Guillaume van der Graft. Vogels en vissen (poetry)
1955 Willem G. van Maanen. De onrustzaaier
1956 W.J. van der Molen. De onderkant van het licht
1957 Jacob Presser. De nacht der Girondijnen (novel)
1958 Hans Warren. Said
1959 A. Koolhaas. Er zit geen spek in de val
1960 Christine d'Haen. Gedichten 1946-1958 (poetry)
1961 Bert Schierbeek. Het boek Ik   1099.

H. G. VAN DER VIES PRIZE (Netherlands)
Since 1939 the award for stage plays has been presented by the Association of Men of Letters, Department of Theatre. Winners include:
1958 Jan Staal. De laatste verlofganger
1960 G.K. van het Reve. Moerlandshuis   1100.

VARLIK NOVEL PRIZE (Turkey)
Established by Varlik Yayinevi in 1954, this prize with a premium of 1.000 TL was presented the following year to Yasar Kemal for his book, "Ince Mehmed."   1101.

Georges **VAXELAIRE PRIZE** (Belgium)
Awarded on April 23--St. George's Day--by the Belgian Royal Academy of French Lan-

guage and Literature, this 10.000
fr annual prize is granted to a
Belgian playwright for a play
set in Belgium. Radio and
television plays, as well as stage
productions, are considered
for the prize. Recent winners
include such dramatists as:
1954 Claude Spaak. La
   Rose des Vents
1955 Charles Bertin.
   Christophe Colomb (television play)
1956 Paul Willems. Off et la
   Lune
1958 André Frère. La
   Répétition générale
1959 Myriam Lempereur. La
   Moisson de Pilar
1960 Jean Sigrid. Les
   Cavaliers
1961 Edmond Kinds. Les
   Moineaux de Baltimore
   (radio play)   1102.

Maria Amalia VAZ DE CAR-
VALHO PRIZE (Portugal)
   A prize for children's literature with a premium of 6.000$
has been offered annually since
1937 by the Portuguese Secretariado Nacional de Informação.
Among recent recipients of the
government award for Literatura Infantil are:
1952 Aurora Constança.
   Estrelinha de Oiro, Grinalda
   de Prata
1953 Maria Cecília Correia.
   Histórias de Minha Rua
1954 Maria Elisa Nery de
   Oliveira. A Quinta das
   Amendoeiras
1957 Maurício Queiroz.
   História Linda de Portugal
1958 Ricardo Alberty.
   Galinha Verde
1961 Isabel Maria Vas
   Raposo. O menino gordo;
   A formiga; O Sábio ea
   Borboleta   1103.

VAZ FERREIRA PRIZES
(Uruguay)

Literary awards of 10,000
pesos are offered by La Facultad
de Humanidades y Ciencias of the
Universidad de la Republica for
unpublished works in Spanish on
set themes. Writings entered
in the first competition were submitted by March 31, 1960 to
Secretaria de la Facultad, Universidad de la Republica (Cer-
rito 73, Montevideo).   1104.

VEA Y LEA DETECTIVE SHORT
STORY CONTEST (Argentina)
   The competition conducted
by "Vea y Lea," the Buenos
Aires magazine, for stories in
the "genero policial," was first
held in 1950, and more recently
in 1961. Both the First and
the Second Prize in the recent
contest "for original short fiction
in Spanish," were won by one
writer--Adolfo Pérez Zelaschi,
with "Las Señales," and "El
Banquero, la muerte y la luna."
                          1105.

Charles VEILLON PRIZE (Inter-
national--Switzerland)
   Since 1947 this triple international prize of 5,000 Swiss
francs has been granted each
year for three novels--one each
in French, in Italian, and in
German. Winners of the award,
which was established by the Swiss
industrialist, Charles Veillon, are
determined by three international
juries: Italian Language Jury--
judges from Italy and Switzerland;
German Language Jury--judges
from Germany, Austria, and
Switzerland; French Language
Jury--judges from France, Belgium, and Switzerland.
   The three prizes are presented each Spring--usually in May--
in a ceremony conducted in successive years in one of the three
major cities of Switzerland bor-
dering three neighboring countries
--France, Italy, and Germany--
Lausanne, Lugano, and Zurich,

respectively. The award, honoring the best published or unpublished novel or collection of novelas of the contest year submitted for consideration, has brought public recognition to: French Language (French authors, unless otherwise indicated)

1947 Pierre Gamarra. La maison de feu
1948 Bert Huyber (Belgium). Jozefa des Flamands
1949 Alexandre Vialatte. Les fruits du Congo
1950 C.-F. Landry (Switzerland). La devinaize
1951 Pierre Moinot. Armes et bagages
1952 Marie Mauron. Le Royaume errant
1953 Camara Laye (Guinea). L'enfant noir
1954 Jacques Audiberti. Les jardins et les fleuves
1955 Pernette Chaponnière (Switzerland). Toi que nous aimons
1956 Jean-Pierre Monnier (Switzerland). La clarte de la nuit
1957 Alfred Kern. Le clown
1958 Elizabeth Petit. Mademoiselle Simon
1959 Maud Frère (Belgium). La Grenouille
1960 Anna Langfus. Le sel et le soufre
1961 Jean-Pierre Chabrol. Les fous de Dieu
Italian Language (Italian authors, unless otherwise indicated)
1948 Adolfo Jenni (Switzerland). Il tempo che passa
1949 Societa degli scrittori della Svizzera Italiana
1950 Carlo Coccioli. Il Giuoco
1952 Natalia Ginzburg. Tutti i nostri ieri
1953 Lalla Romano. Maria Giovanni Bonalumi (Switzerland). Gli ostaggi
1954 Giuseppe Cassieri. Dove abita il prossimo

1955 Giorgio Bassani. Gli ultimi anni di Clelia Trotti
1956 Mario Tobino. La brace dei Biassoli
1957 Anna Banti. La Monaca di Sciangai
1958 Nino Palumbo. Il Giornale
1959 Saverio Strati. Tibi e Tascia
1960 Vasco Pratolini. Lo Scialo
1961 Enrico Emanuelli. Settimana Nera
German Language (German authors, unless otherwise indicated)
1953 Hertha Trappe. Was ich wandre Dort und hier
1954 Carola Lepping. Bela Reist am Abend ab
1955 Franz Tumler (Austria). Der Schritt hinueber
1956 Johannes Urzidil (Austria--U.S.A.). Die verlorene Geliebte
1957 Max Frisch (Switzerland). Homo Faber
1958 Otto Friedrich Walter (Switzerland). Der Stumme
1959 Heinrich Böll. Billard um Halbzehn
1960 Karl Eska (Austria--U.S.A.). Der Kreidestrich
1961 Edzaard Schaper (Finland). Der vierte Konig
                                    1106.

VENEZUELAN NATIONAL PRIZE FOR JOURNALISM
    One of several official national literary honors granted annually by the Venezuelan government-- Ministerio de Educacion, Direccion de Cultura y Bellas Artes, Caracas--the Premio Nacional de Periodismo consists of a gold medal for a newspaper, and a diploma and a premium of Bs 3.000 for journalists in three different areas of newspaper and magazine writing. Recent awards have brought recognition to:
    1958 Omar Pérez
        Ciro Urdaneta Bravo

1959 Eleazar Diáz Rangel
Alejandro Borges
Alberto Ravell
1960 Pedro Nolasco Hernández
Miguel Otero Silva
D. F. Maza Zavala
1961 Arístides Bastidas
José Moradell
Eduardo Feo Calcaño
1962 Miguel de los Santos
José Antonio Ugas Morán
Guillermo José Schael
1107.

eternidad y poemas
italicos
57 Rómulo Gallegos.
Dona Barbara
58 Juan Manuel González.
La herdad junto al viento
59 José Fabiani Ruiz. A
Orillas del sueno
1959-60 José Ramón Medina.
Memorias y Elegias
61 José Antonio de Armas
Chitty. Poet and his-
torian   1108.

VENEZUELAN NATIONAL PRIZE FOR LITERATURE

Venezuela's highest official literary honor, the Premio Nacional de Literatura is awarded annually--alternating between poetry (the Premio Anual de Poesia Francisco Lazo Marti) and prose--by the Ministerio de Educacion (Direccion de Cultura y Bellas Artes, Caracas). A premium of Bs 10.000 is granted for the prize-winning work, with a prize of Bs 5.000 for the runner-up.

Recipients of Venezuela's major literary honor are nominated by the countries leading writers for award--even years for poetry, odd years for prose. Among distinguished Venezuelan authors presented with the Premio Nacional, in a ceremony held each March, are:
1947-48 Carlos Augusto León
49 Santiago Key Ayala
1949-50 Juan Liscano
51 Ramón Díaz Sánchez
52 Félix Armando Núñez
53 Arturo Uslar Pietri.
Las Nubes
Mariano Picón Salas. Los dias de cipriano castro
54 Manuel F. Rugeles.
Cantos de sur y norte
55 Miguel Otero Silva.
Casas muertes
Augusto Mijares. La luz y le espejo
56 Juan Beroes. Materiade

VENEZUELAN WRITERS' ASSOCIATION PRIZE

The Premio de la Asociacion de Escritores (Centro Profesional del Este, oficina 104, Calle Vilaflor, Sabana Grande, Caracas), offered by the same group of writers who grant the international poetry prize--Leon de Greiff Prize--is an annual honor recognizing the best writing--including such literary forms as Novel, Poetry, Essay, and Biography. Recent winners include:
1957 Pascual Pla y Beltran.
Habra en algun lugar mas claridad
1958 José Antonio Escalana-Escalona. Jose Antonio Maitin (biographical study)
Arristides Parra. Notalgia de la Egogla (poetry)   1109.

VENICE PRIZE (Italy)

The Premio Venezia (also called the Premio Letterario Venezia, and from 1953 the Premio delle Nove Nazioni) is an annual prize awarded to such writers as:
1949 Dante Arfulli. I superflui
1951 Elda Bossi. I poveri (short stories)
1952 Livia de Stefani
1953 Ugo Facco de Lagarda--2nd prize
1110.

Orio VERGANI PRIZE (Italy)
The award, sponsored by the
publication, "Corriere della
Sera" (via Solferino 28, Milan),
was a single prize offered in
1961 for a book of fiction published in 1960. Alberto Denti
di Pirajno won the L 2.000.000
premium with "Ippolita.
1111.

José VERÍSSIMO PRIZE (Brazil)
One of the many literary honors presented by the Academia
Brasileira de Letras (Avenida
Presidente Wilson 203, Rio de
Janeiro), this Cr$50.000 prize
is granted for an essay or a
scholarly writing--unpublished
or published during the two
years preceding the year of
award. Recipients include:
1955 Antonio Rangel Bandeira
1957 Celso Cunha. O can-
cioneirio de Martim Codax
1959 Raymundo Aoro. Os
Donos do Poder
1961 Paulo Cavalcanti. Eça
de Queiroz Agitador no
Brasil   1112.

VÉRITÉ GRAND PRIZE (France)
The Grand Prix Vérité,
an annual journalism award of
the newspaper, "Le Parisien
libéré" (124 rue Réaumur,
Paris 11e) offers 2.000 NF for
the best writing of the year concerning current events, observation or document directly
recreating a period in contemporary history of France or another
country--reporting characterized
by exactness and feeling for the
human condition.
Works are entered in competition by sending two copies of
the topical works (not over 50
typed pages in length and unpublished)to the newspaper by
September 15. Winners of the
December award, which "honors
the truth" and considers the
significance of the events re-

ported and the literary quality of
the writing, are such journalists
as:
1947 Pierre Nord. Mes
camarades sont morts
1948 Jacques Le Bourgeois. A
Saigon, prisonnier des
Japonais
1951 Renée Bidault. La petite
Madame Gateau
1953 Étienne Cattin. Trains
en détresse
1956 Christian Berntsen and
Robert Soulat. Un viking chez
les Bédouins
1959 Alain Manevy. L'Algérie
a vingt ans
1960 Anne Michel. J'ai adopté
un enfant
1961 Jean Coubeyre. Faire
face
1962 Victoire Cosnelle.
Dame et sa fille cherchent
emploi   1113.

Paul VERLAINE PRIZE (France)
Among several poetry prizes
offered by Maison de Poésie
(11 bis, rue Ballu, Paris 9e)
is the annual award of 100 NF
presented each June for published
works submitted in competition
by March 31. The award is
granted for the best book of any
type of poetry, without any
special conditions regarding form
of writing or author. Laureates
include:
1952 Marguerite Henry-Rosier
1953 Elisabeth Borione.
Couleurs des jours
1954 Georges Belloni. Sous
le signe du bélier
1957 Alexandre Guinle. Pour
Béatrice
1959 Mary Cressac. Les
ombres s'allongent
1960 Claude Fourcade. Au-delà
du sommeil
1961 André Lo Celso   1114.

Jules VERNE PRIZE (France)
This publisher's prize offered
by Librairie Hachette (79 boule-

vard Saint-Germain, Paris) for
the best unpublished science fiction manuscript, brings a token
premium of 10 NF, and publication in Hachette's "Le roman
fantastique" series. Winners,
who have been presented the
honor on May 25, include:
1958 Serge Martel. L'adieu
   aux astres
1959 Daniel Drode. Surface
   de la planète
1960 Albert Higon. La
   machine du pouvoir
1961 Jérôme Seriel. Le sub-
   espace
1962 Philippe Curvel. Le
   ressac de l'espace   1115.

VERSILIA PRIZE (Italy)
   Winners of this poetry and
novel award, offered by Ente
Provinciale del Turismo,
Viareggio (see also, Viareggio
Prize) include:
1948 Sibilia Aleramo. Selva
   d'amore
1949 Ugo Moretti. Vento caldo
   Biagio Zagarrio. Sereno;
   Libero de Libero; Banchetto
   (poetry)
1951 Attilio Bertolucci. La
   capanna indiana (poetry)
1953 Raffaele Carrieri. Il
   trovatore (poetry)
1954 Vieri Nannetti. Poesie
1955 Carlo Betocchi
1956 Giacomo Noventa. Versi
   e poesie
1958 Salvatore Quasimodo.
   La terra impareggiabile
                          1116.

Antonio de VIANNA PRIZE
(Spain)
   The "Little Nadal Prize," a
50,000 pts novel award, is
granted by the town of Santa Cruz
de Tenerife. Winner of the
"Pequeño Nadal" in 1962 was Juan
Antonio Cabezas, with "La casa
sin cimientos."   1117.

VIAREGGIO PRIZE (Italy)
   Longest-established Italian
literary honor next to the Bagutta
Prize, and "second in importance
after the Strega Prize," the
Viareggio Prize includes eight
different awards in several categories of writing. According to
an authority on Italian literary
honors, the prize is "undoubtedly
the best known to the general
public and the most lucrative for
the writers chosen" (Golino, p 47).
   Established in 1929 by a group
of writers and journalists who
spent their summers in Viareggio,
a Tuscany seaside resort on the
Ligurian Sea, the prize has been
financed by the city of Viareggio
with the exception of several
post-World War II years when industrialist Adriano Olivetti provided the funds for the contest.
Each year's prize offers a major
premium of L 2.000.000, and
additional premiums of L 1.000.
000 each for: Novel, Poetry,
Drama, First Work, Journalism
and three categories of "Saggistica"--essays.
   Publishers submit books in
competition to the jury (Comitato
del Premio e Comune di Viareggio,
l'Azienda Autonoma della Versilia, via Giacomo Puccini 164,
Viareggio) for consideration, and
the contest is open to "novels,
books of poetry, and essays" and
other specified literary works
published between August 1 of the
previous year and July 31 of the
award year.
   Among authors distinguished by
this respected literary honor are:
Viareggio Major Prose Award
1930 Divided prize--Anselmo
   Bucci. Il pittore volante
   Lorenzo Viani. Ritorna alla
   Patria
1931 Carrado Tumiati. Tetti rossi
1932 Antonio Foschini. Avven-
   tura di Villon
1933 Achile Campanile.
   Cantilena all'angolo della

strada
1934 Raffaele Calzini. Segan-
tini, romanzo della montagna
1935 Divided prize--Mario
Massa. Un uomo solo
Stafano Landi. Il muro di
cass
1936 Riccardo Bacchelli. Il
rabdomante
1937 Guelfo Civinini. Trat-
toria di paese
1938 Divided prize--Vittorio
G. Rossi. Oceano
Enrico Pea. La Maremma
1939 Divided prize--Maria
Bellonci. Lucrezia Borgi
Arnaldo Fratelli. Clara fra
i lupi
Orio Vergani. Basso profundo
1946 Divided prize--Umberto
Saba. Canzoniere
Silvio Micheli. Pane duro
1947 Antonio Gramsci. Lettere
dal carcere
1948 Divided prize--Aldo
Palazzeschi (pseud of Aldo
Giurlani).
Fratelli Cuccoli
Elsa Morante. Magia e
sortilegio
1949 Carlo Arturo Jemolo.
Stato e Chiesa in Italia
negli ultimi cento anni
1950 Divided prize--Carlo
Bernari. Speranzella
Francesco Jovine. Terre del
Sacramento
1951 Domenico Rea. Gesu fate
luce
1952 Tommaso Fiore. Un
popolo di formiche
1953 Carlo Emilio Gadda.
Novelle del Ducato in fiamme
1954 Rocco Scotellaro.
E'fatto giorno
1955 Vasco Pratolini. Metello
1956 Divided prize--Carlo
Levi. Le parole son pietre
Gianna Manzini. La
Sparviera
1957 Umberto Saba (Prize of
Honor)
Divided for Narrativa--Italo
Calvino. Il barone rampante

Arturo Tofanelli. L'uomo
d'oro
Natalia Ginzburg. Valentino
1958 Ernesto De Martino.
Morte e pianto rituale del
mondo antico
1959 Marino Moretti. Tutte le
novelle
1960 G. B. Angioletti. I grandi
ospiti (Great guests--essays
on famous Europeans)
Narrativa--Laudomia Bonanni.
L'imputata
1961 Alberto Moravia. La Noia
1962 Giorgio Bassani. Il
Giardino dei Finzi-Contini
Additional awards under the
Viareggio Prize include:
Viareggio Poetry Prize (See also
"Versilia Prize," the name given
to some poetry awards under the
Viareggio Prize)
1957 Divided prize--Sandro
Penna. Poesie
Alberto Mondadori. Quasi una
leggenda
Pier Paolo Pasolini. Le
ceneri di Gramsci
1959 Giorgio Caproni. Il seme
del piangere
1960 Paolo Volpini. Le porte
dell'Appennino
Viareggio Critics Prize
1950 Massimo Mila
1952 Mario Praz
1953 Roberto Battaglia
1954 Divided prize--Giuseppe
Ravegnani. Uomini visti
Eugenio Garin. Cronache di
filosofia italiana
1956 Divided prize--Nino Valeri.
Da Giolitti a Mussalini
Giancarlo Vigorelli. Gronchi,
battaglie di ieri e di oggi
1958 Tomasso Landolfi.
Ottavio di Saint Vincent
Viareggio First Work Prize
("Opera Prima")
1950 Giorgio Piovano
1951 Pietro Sissa
1952 Marcello Venturi. Dalla
Sirte a casa mia
1953 Mario Rigoni Stern. Il
sergente nella neve

1955 Giovanni Russo. Baroni
e contadini
1956 Nicco Tucci. Il segreto
1957 Felice Del Vecchio. La
chiesa di Canneto
1958 Anita Fazzini. Ritorno in
pianura
1959 Michel Lacalamite. La
civilta contadina
1960 Sergio Saviane. Festa
di laurea
Viareggio Journalism Prize
("Inchiesta Giornalistica")
1959 Giuseppa Boffa. La
grande svolta
1960 Divided prize--Ugo
Moretti. Nuda ogni giorno
Silvio Micheli. L'Artiglio ha
confessate
Viareggio Drama Prize
1960 Eduardo De Filippo.
Contata dei giorni pari
Viareggio International Prize
1959 Narrativa--Marek Hlasko
L'ottavo giorno della
settimana
Franco Lucentini. Translation
Critica--Will Grohmann.
Kandinsky
                        Kandinsky
Viareggio Thirtieth Anniversary
Prize ("Trent'anni del Viareggio")
1959 Giuseppe Villaroel. La
bellezza intravista
Viareggio Scholarly Works Prize
("Saggistica")
1960 Divided prize--Ettore Lo
Gatto. La vita di Pushkin
Bruno Migliorini. Storia
della lingua italiana
Saggistica cinematografia--
Umberto Barbaro. Il film e
il risarcimento marxista
nelle arti
1962 C. L. Ragghianti.
Mondrian e l'arte del XXe
secole   1118.

"VIATA ROMINEASCA" AWARDS
(Rumania)
One of several prizes offered
to young writers by the literary
review, "Viata Romineasca," these
awards are presented for works

of fiction winning the competitions
held from time to time. The
monthly publication of the Rumanian People's Republic Writers'
Union has honored a number of
writers with monetary prizes,
ranging from 2.000 to 8.000 lei.
Among Rumanian authors distinguished by the awards are:
1958 V. E. Galan; Luca Stefan;
Simion Pop; Niculae Tic
1959 Nicolae Jianu; Vasile
Nicorevici; Niculae Tic
1961 Dumitru Micu; Ion
Gheorghe; Niculae Velea
                               1119.

Gil VICENTE PRIZE (Portugal)
The Portuguese government--
Secretariado Nacional da Infor-
mação--has offered this drama
prize of 6.000$ each year since
1935. Among the 12 playwrights
honored since the award was
initiated are:
1954 Almeida Amaral, Fernando
Santos, and Leitão de Barros.
Prémio Nobel
1958 Costa Ferreira. Um dia
de Vida
1959 José H. Saraiva.
Caminhos da Esperanza
1961 Francisco Ventura. Auto
de Justiça   1120.

VIENNA ART FUND PRIZE
(Austria)
Among recent recipients of the
yearly stipend and grant awarded
by Wiener Kunstfond der Zentral-
sparkasse der Gemeinde Wien
are: Fritz Hochwälder, Hubert
Werner Beyer (pseud of Ludo
Gerwald), Walter Buchebner,
Humbert Fink, Ernst Kein,
Franziska Klinger, Heinrich
Leopold Marresch, Anny Tichy,
Dorothea Zeemann-Holzinger.
                               1121.

VIENNA CHILDREN'S AND YOUTH
BOOK PRIZE (Austria)
Youth book prizes offered since
1954 and Children's book prizes

granted since 1960 are the literary recognition of Amt für Kultur, Volksbildung und Schulverwaltung of the city of Vienna. The Kinder- und Jugendbuchpreise der Stadt Wien are given for the best children's or young people's book by a living Austrian author, published in Vienna during the contest year--August 1 through July 31 of the following year. A diploma and a premium of S 8.000 designate the best such book for Children (ages 6-14), and Young People (ages 14-18). In addition, a prize of S 3.000 is granted for the best illustrated book, and an award of S 15.000 is presented for the best textbook.

The authors honored with the award are:

1954 Karl Bruckner. Giovanna und der Sumpf
1955 Franz Lang. Die Männer von Kaprun; Georg Schreiber. Der Weg des Bruders
1956 Vera Ferra-Mikura; Der Teppisch der Schönen Träume; Lilli König. Gringolo
1957 Karl Bruckner. Der goldene Pharoa
1958 Karl Bruckner; Emmy Feiks-Waldhäusl; Helga Pohl
1959 Christine Busta. Die Sternenmühle
1960 Fritz Habeck. Der Kampf um die Barbacane Kinderbuchpreis--Helmut Leiter. Martin gegen Martin
1961 Karl Bruckner; Fritz Habeck Kinderbuchpreis--Mira Lobe
1122.

VIENNA FÖRDERUNGSPREIS (Austria)

Next to the Vienna Prizes (Preisen der Stadt Wien), the Vienna Förderungspreisen are the highest literary awards for Austrian writers who live in Vienna or have gained their fame as authors there. The grants are general cultural awards that may be given to painters, composers, and scientists, as well as to writers.

Among the authors honored by the grants are Wieland Schmeid, and

1951 Johann Gunert; Vera Ferra
1952 Fritz Habeck; Rudolf Bayr
1953 Johann Lebert; Elfriede Ziering
1954 Gerhard Fritsch; Franz Kiessling
1955 Karl Anton Maly; Georg Rauchinger
1956 Helmut Schwarz; Herta Staub
1957 Oskar Jan Tauschinski; Herbert Zand
1958 Wieland Schmied; Ida Thomas
1959 Kurt Benesch; Wolfgang Fischer
1960 Hans Bausenwein; Erich Pogats
1961 Jeanni Ebner; Doris Mühringer
1123.

VIENNA PRIZES FOR LITERATURE (Austria)

The Preise für Kunst, Wissenschaft und Volksbildung, general cultural honors of the city of Vienna, that recognize achievement in various fields--Letters, Publicity, Musical Composition, Architecture, Painting and Graphic Art; Applied Art; Folk Art; Cultural Sciences; Natural Sciences; Technology--carry premiums ranging from S 15.000 to S 150.000. Awarded annually since 1947, the prizes honor a life's work or a single outstanding achievement by the presentation of 15 awards. Authors distinguished by the Würdigungspreise für Literatur are:

1947 Felix Braun
1948 Erika Mitterer

334

1949 Alma Holgersen
1950 Rudolf Brunngraber
1951 Alexander Lernet-Holenia
1952 Franz Nabl
1953 Franz Theodor Csokor
1954 Franz Karl Ginzkey
1955 Fritz Hochwälder
1956 Rudolf Henz
1957 Ferdinand Bruckner
1958 Theodor Kramer
1959 Georg Saiko
1960 Ernst Waldinger
1961 Heimito Doderer   1124.

VIERA Y CLAVIJO PRIZE
(Spain)
Awarded under the patronage
of the Casa de Colón (Cabildo
Insular de Gran Canaria), this
25,000 pts prize for an unpublished work in Spanish with a
theme concerning the Canary
Islands was won in 1960 by S.
de la Nunez Caballero with,
"Unamuno, en Canarias."
1125.

VIET-NAM LITERARY PRIZE
Since 1954, this official annual
literary prize of Viet-Nam
(Office of Cultural Affairs, Department of Information, 165 Tu-
Do Street, Saigon) offers a
monetary premium for the best
published works, "in accordance
with the people's interest and the
national spirit," written in
Vietnamese in four literary
forms: Novel, Essay or Criticism, Poetry, Drama.   1126.

VIJVERBERG PRIZE (Nether-
lands)
A novel award granted by the
Jan Campert Foundation (Jan
Campert Stichting), instituted
by the municipality of The
Hague, has brought a premium of
1.500 fl to the winner each
year since 1948. Among authors
presented with the award--usually
given in November/December--
are:
1948 Jo Boer. Kruis of munt
1950 Josepha Mendels. Als

International Literary Awards
wind en rook
1951 Theun de Vries. Anna
Casparii of het heimwee
1952 Albert Helman. De
laaiende stilte
1953 Max Croiset. Amphitryon
1956 Albert van der Hoogte.
Het laatste uur
1957 Marga Minco. Het bittere
kruid
1958 Jos. Panhuysen. Wandel
niet in het water   1127.

VIKINGS PRIZE (Europe--France)
Granted in May since 1928 as
a biennial prize of 1.000 NF,
this award was established by a
Norwegian friend of France to
honor a prose work written in
French by a French or Scandinavian author who was not over 45
years of age during World War
II and who has not previously
received a literary award equal to
or greater than the Prix des
Vikings.
The forms of writing considered for award are reports of
lengthy voyages or explorations
demonstrating the qualities of
character of the Vikings--courage,
endurance, and energy. Works
entered in competition may be
in a wide range of literary
forms--provided the book en-
hances Franco-Norwegian friendship: Novel, Essay, Criticism,
Factual Report, or Fictionalized
Biography.
Among laureates are:
1930 Édouard Peisson. Courrier
de la mer Blanche; Hans le marin
1952 Alain Gheerbrant. Orénoque-
Amazone
1956 Jacques Legray. D'amour et
de gloire, and for his entire
work
1958 Jean-Pascal Benoist.
Kirdi au bord du monde
1128.

Benedict Wallet VILAKAZI
MEMORIAL AWARD (Africa--South
Africa)
Any African writer may com-
pete for this annual prize, estab-

lished in 1951 in memory of Dr. Vilakazi (1906-1947), Zulu language poet, novelist, and linguist, who was a member of the University of Witwatersrand Department of Bantu Studies. The award-- consisting of a premium of R 20, and a Certificate--is granted by the University of Witwatersrand (Milner Park, Johannesburg) "for the most meritorious contribution by an African to Nguni literature."

Recipients of the literary honor, which is presented by the Vice-Chancellor of the University on the advice of a Selection Committee, include:

1951 R.R.R. Dhlomo
1952 J.J.R. Jolobe
1953 E.H.A. Made   1129.

VILLA SAN GIOVANNI PRIZE
(Italy)

This award, instituted by Circolo di Cultura Calabrian (Southern Italian) writers, "Cenide" (via di Villa Patrizi 4, Rome), has been granted each year since 1956 in two categories:

(1) L 1.000.000 for a novel in Italian published during the year;

(2) L 500.000 (1962: L 200. 000) for journalistic writing on aspects or problems of Calabria (1962: essay on contemporary Calabrian Literature) published in newspapers or periodicals (reviste) during the contest period.

Among winners of the novel prize are:

1956 Saverio Strati. La Marchesina
1958 Leonida Repaci
1959 Francesco Perri. L'amante di zia Amalietta
1960 Virgiliao Lilli. Una donna s'allontana   1130.

Xavier VILLAURRUTIA PRIZE
(Mexico)

Named for the Mexican man of letters, Xavier Villaurrutia (1903-1950), known for his writings (poetry, stories, plays) as well as for his translations (Gide, William Blake), this prize has been granted each year since 1957 by Sociedad de Amigos de Xavier Villaurrutia (Paseo de la Reforma 18, Galeria Excelsior, Mexico 1, D.F.). Offering a premium of 5.000 pesos for the best work of a new author published during the preceding year, the prize may be given for creative writing in several forms--Poetry, Prose (novel or story), Drama, Essay.

Recipients, designated by a jury of three--composed of such distinguished writers as Carlos Pellicer, Rodolfo Usigli, and Francisco Zendejas--include:

1957 Juan Rulfo. Pedro Páramo (novel)
1958 Octavio Paz. El arco y la lira (essay)
1959 Josefina Vicens. El Libro Vacío (novel)
1960 Marco Antonio Montes de Oca. Delante de la luz cantan los pajaros (poetry)
1961 Rosario Castellanos. Ciudad Real (stories)

A XAVIER VILLAURRUTIA PRIZE was also offered by Agrupacion de Criticos de Teatro de Mexico for the best experimental play of the year. In 1961, this prize was won by Hector Azar for his adaptation of Fernandez de Lizardi, "El Periquillo Sarniento."   1131.

VINCULA POETRY COMPETITION
(International--Monaco)

The Concours de Poésie Vincula of the Union Mondiale des Intellectuels (villa "Emma," 40 boulevard d'Italie, Monte Carlo) was established in 1958 to recognize the outstanding work of poets writing in French, Italian, or English--whether members of the Union or not. Poems entered in competition should not exceed 60 lines in length, and must be submitted in three copies. The prize winner, announced in January, receives 20 NF a month during the year and a premium of 500 NF at the end of the year. In 1958, the two winners were: Princesse Marguerite de Broglie, and Gisèle Perlot.   1132.

VIRGEN DEL CARMEN PRIZE (Spain)
    An annual book or journalism award for writing on a sea theme --published or unpublished--is sponsored by Presidencia del Gobierno (calle de Alcalá Galiano 10, Madrid). The book prize of 50,000 pts was won in 1961 by Ciriquiáin Gaiztarro with "Los Vascos en la Pesca de Ballena." In 1962, prizes of a citation, a diploma, and a premium of 300,000 pts were offered for works on a set theme in six classes, to be submitted in competition during the month of March, with award winners to be announced in July.   1133.

VISSER-NEERLANDIA PRIZE (Netherlands)
    Award winners have include: C. Nooteboom; J. Staal; Abel Herzberg; and--for their stage plays: Lo van Hensbergen, with "Het twinfest;" Harry Mulisch, with "Tanchelijn."
                                1134.

VLIEBERG PRIZE (Belgium)
    One of the awards of the Davids Fund, this prize was won in 1958 by Cor Ria Leeman with, "De grote Heer."   1135.

Emmanuel VOSSART PRIZE (Belgium)

Recognizing an outstanding Belgian writer's work in prose or poetry--especially a literary essay, this 10,000 fr biennial award is granted by the Belgian Royal Academy of French Language and Literature. Since the first award in 1952, the winners have been:
    1952 Nelly Cormeau. L'Art de
        François Mauriac
    1954 Charles Moeller. Littérature de XXe siècle et Christianisme
    1956 Marcel Doisy. Jacques Cocteau ou l'absolu dans l'art
    1960 Daniel Gilles de Pelichy. Tolstoï (essay)
    1962 Arsène Soreil   1136.

William Gaston WALKLEY NATIONAL AWARDS FOR AUSTRALIAN JOURNALISM (Australia)
    These awards, endowed by the Australian industrialist and businessman, William Gaston Walkley, were founded in 1955 with annual premiums of Ł1,000 a year, since increased to Ł1,300, and a statuette, or "Oscar." Nine prizes for different aspects of journalism--newspaper reporting, feature story, magazine story, provincial newspaper story, as well as headings, pictures, cartoons, illustrations, and press artwork--are offered.
    Any resident of Australia may compete provided his entry was published in Australia during the year, and is "accompanied by a statement of not more than 200 words explaining the circumstances in which the story was prepared." The best three entries in each class are selected by each Australian Journalists' Association District and forwarded to the Federal Judges for final selection.
    Winners in Reporting and Story categories include:

Best Newspaper Reporting
1957 Eva M. Sommer--"The Sun," Sydney
1958 Lionel Hogg--"Melbourne Herald"
1959 Douglas Lockwood-- Melbourne
1960 John E. Coulter--"The News"
1961 E.W. Tipping--"Melbourne Herald"
Best Feature Story
1957 Allan Nicholls. "The Age," tied with Athol Thomas. "Week End Mail"
1958 Selwyn Speight. "Sydney Morning Herald"
1959 J.G. Patin. "A.B.C. Weekly, and T.V. News Times," Sydney
1960 Graham Perkins. "The Age," Melbourne
1961 Gavin Souter. "Sydney Morning Herald"
Dan O'Sullivan. "Daily News," Perth
Best Magazine Feature Story
1957 Keith Finlay. "Woman's Day"
1958 H. H. Cox. "Associated News," Melbourne
1959 H. Cox. "People," Melbourne
1960 Graham Perkin. "The Age," Melbourne
1961 John Hetherington. The boy from the bush, in "Southerly"
Best Provincial Newspaper Story
1957 Albert E. Stephens. "South Pacific Post"
1958 Ron Burnett. "Daily Bulletin," Townsville
1959 J.G. Coleman. "The Bulletin," Townsville
1960 James Bowditch. "The News," Darwin
1961 R.J. Manning. "Daily Mercury," Mackay   1137.

WAR AGAINST FASCISM MEDAL (Germany, East)
A government honor of the DDR--Medaille für Kämpfer gegen der Faschismus--has been awarded such writers as Ludwig Renn.   1138.

WARSAW CITY PRIZE (Poland)
In the 1930's a prize of this name with a premium of 10,000 zloty was awarded to Poland's leading writers, including Berent (1933), Askenozy (1934), and M. Kuncewiczawa (1937), who won the honor for "The Strangers."
Since World War II, the Warsaw City Prize--Nagroda miasta Warszawy--has been granted annually to commemorate the liberation of the city of Warsaw in 1945. The awarding agency, the Warsaw Municipal Council (Department of Culture, Stoleczna Rada Narodowa, Wydzial Kultury, Pl. Dzierzynskiego 3/5, Warszawa), has presented the honor on January 16, anniversary of the Liberation of Warsaw, for writing for children and young people. Among writers given public recognition are:
1948 Ewa Szelburg-Zarembina
1949 Janina Broniewska
1950 Lucyna Krzemieniecka
1951 Maria Kownacka
1954 Jan Brzechwa
1956 Hanna Januszewska
1957 Janina Poraziuska
1958 Czeslaw Janczarski
1959 Irena Jurgielewicz
1960 Jan Zabinski   1139.

WARSAW CITY PRIZE FOR YOUNG POETS (Poland)
The Doroczna Nagroda Poetycka Mlodych miasta Warszawy is an annual monetary prize granted in November since 1961 by the Warsaw Municipal Council (Stoleczna Rada Narodowa, Pl. Dzierzynskiego 3/5, Warszawa). Active in financing and administering the award are the Students' Club Hybrydy (Klub Studentow "Hybrydy"), the Warsaw Creative Youth Club (Warszawski Klub Tworczy Mlodych), and the editorial staff

of the periodical, "Nowa Kultura" (Mokotowska 48, Warszawa). Winners for 1961 are Maciej Bordowicz, with "Testament zanium przyjde;" and Edward Stachura, who received the honor for his lyrical poems.   1140

WARSAW STUDENT AND YOUTH AWARD FOR YOUNG POETS (Poland)

Each April since 1960 an annual premium has been presented by the Central Youth Club of Warsaw Students (Centralny Klub Studentow Warszawy), and the Warsaw Creative Youth Club (Warszawski Klub Tworczy Mlodych, Mokotowska 48, Warszawa). Poems by young poets--under 30 years of age--are eligible for award, either published or unpublished. Winners include:
1960 Zbigniew Jerzyna. Lokacje
Krzysztof Gasiorowski. Apostrofa
1961 Roman Sliwonik. Poszukiwanie domu
Jaroslaw Markiewicz. Do robotnika   1141.

G.J. WATTUMULL AWARDS (India)

Presentation of literary awards is one of the functions of the Wattumull Foundation, established in 1942. The organization is also active in making grants for the exchange of scholars and teachers in India and the United States, and in "encouraging literary, scientific, cultural and technical work of a high order in India."

One of 11 grants awarded in New Delhi in 1961 was given to Mrs. Welthy Honsinger Fisher, founder of Literary House, in Lucknor.

The WATTUMULL PRIZE, awarded "in even numbered years for the best work on the

history of India originally published in the United States," was presented in 1962 to Stanley A. Wolpert, Professor at the University of California at Los Angeles, for his book, "Tilak and Gokhale."   1142.

Edmond WEIL PRIZE (France)

This rich literary honor (10.000 NF), founded in 1960 by the F.S.J.U. (Fonds social juif unitié, 19 rue de Teheran, Paris) and the Association des amis d'Edmond Weil, is granted each year to encourage an original contribution to Jewish culture or Jewish social work, with the purpose of stimulating or recognizing service to Judaism. The award--which may be assigned to an individual or to an institution entering as a candidate for the prize before February 1--was presented to Léon Poliakov in 1961 for "Histoire de l'antisemitisme."   1143.

WEIMAR LITERATURE AND ART PRIZE (Germany, East)

The city of Weimar first established this cultural honor in 1948, and--after an interval of some years--reestablished the prize in 1958. Currently, the prize brings a medal and a premium of 10.000 DM to an artist who was born in or who worked in Weimar, provided his work has special significance for Weimar. Also eligible for award is an author who carries on the humanistic tradition of Weimar, and at the same time advances the development of the culture of East Germany. Winners include:
1948 Georg Maurer. Gesänge der Zeit
1959 Louis Fürnberg
1960 Armin Müller. Entire literary work   1144.

Erich WEINERT ART PRIZE

(Germany, East)
The cultural award of the
East German Youth Organization
(F.D.J.--Freie Deutsche
Jugend) was established in 1957
as an annual prize for Literature, Painting, Drama, and
Motion Pictures. The honor--
consisting of a medal--is presented by the central council
of FDJ (Zentralrat), and has
been awarded such writers as:
  1957 Erwin Burkhart; Kuba
    (pseud of Kurt Bartel);
    Max Zimmering; Wolfgang
    Kohlhaase
  1958 Peter Kast; Helmut
    Hauptmann; Walter Stranka
  1960 Gustav von Wangenheim;
    Rainer Kerndl; Armin
    Müller   1145.

F.C. WEISKOPF PRIZE (Ger-
many, East)
  This award is granted by the
same agency that gives the
Heinrich Mann Prize--the German Academy of Arts (Deutsche
Akademie der Kunste) of East
Berlin. Established in 1957
with a grant of 5.000 DM by
Margarete Weiskopf, the widow
of F.C. Weiskopf, the prize has
been presented to:
  1957 Ernst Stein
  1958 Stephen Hermlin
  1960 Viktor Klemperer
                           1146.

WELTI-STIFTUNG FÜR DAS
DRAMA PRIZE (Switzerland)
  The award of the Swiss
Schiller Foundation (Schweizeris-
chen Schiller-Stiftung) brought a
4.000 sw fr premium in 1961 to
Louis Gaulis, author of
"Capitaine Karogheuz."   1147.

WEMMEL POETRY FESTIVAL
PRIZE (Belgium)
  This Flemish-language prize
has recently been won by: Jan
Veulemans (1958), and Hubert
von Herreweghen (1959).   1148.

WEST FLANDERS PRIZE
(Belgium)
  The Flemish literary honor,
granted for writing in various
genres, includes among latest
winners:
  1957 Essay--J.W. Walgrave.
    Ortega y Gasset
  1958 Novel--Andre Demedts.
    De levenden en de doden
                           1149.

Carton de WIART PRIZE
(Belgium)
  Founded in 1912 by the Belgian
Ministry of Public Education
(Ministère de L'Instruction
Publique), this 10,000 fr award
is granted every five years--
alternately to a work in French
and in Flemish--for a book in the
field of literary history, or in
any literary form, provided the
subject concerns episodes or
aspects of Belgian life--past or
present.
  The jury of three are alternately members of the Royal
Academy of French Language
and Literature, and the Royal
Academy of Flemish Language and
Literature. Among recent French
language winners are:
  1926 Lucien Christophe
  1936 Pierre Nothomb
  1946 Carlo Bronne
  1956 Luc Hommel   1150.

WIHURI FOUNDATION AWARD
(Finland)
  Among the many cultural
grants of this major Scandinavian
foundation (Kärkikallionkuja 3,
Kulosaari, Helsinki)--richly endowed by the Finnish manufacturer and shipping magnate, Antti
Wihuri--are scholarships and
awards to authors. In 1958,
the writer Lauri Viljanen received
a Wihuri award.   1151.

C.J. WIJNANDTS FRANCKEN
PRIZE (Netherlands)
  Winners of the award, granted

since 1935 by the Society of
Netherlands Literature (Maatschappij der Nederlandse Letterkunde, Rapenburg 12, Leiden),
include: C. Bittremieux, who
received the prize in 1957, for
his essay, "De dichter Jan van
Nijlen." 1152.

Margaret WRONG MEMORIAL
PRIZE (Africa--United Kingdom)
   The Wrong Memorial Prize--
consisting of a medal (silver and
later bronze) and a monetary
premium (increasing from L5 in
1950 to L50 in later awards)
is directed to "advance literature
in Africa," and has been granted
annually since 1950 "for an outstanding contribution to literature in Africa by a person of the
African race."
   Friends of Margaret Wrong--
who spent the last twenty years
of her life "largely in the service of Africa and inspiring the
production of Christian literature
to meet the social, cultural and
educational needs of that conti-
nent," established the Memorial
Fund to commemorate Miss
Wrong, Secretary of the International Committee on Christian
Literature for Africa, who
"died suddenly in Uganda in
1948 when she was carrying out
a visit."
   Each year the Administrative
Committee of the Prize (Margaret Wrong Memorial Fund, University of London Institute of
Education, Malet Street, London
W.C. 1) announces required
area of residence of competitors:
   in 1960--Somaliland and
      Somalia, Kenya, Uganda,
      Tanganyika, Congo Belge
      and Zanzibar;
   in 1961--Republic of South
      Africa, trusteeship territory
      of South-West Africa, High
      Commission Territories of
      Basutoland, Bechuanaland,
      and Swaziland, the Rhodesias

and Nyasaland, Angola, and
Mozambique;
   in 1962--West Africa.
The procedure of award,
followed in the last few years
is to invite recommendations
from a large number of individuals
and organizations, for Africans in
the geographic areas considered
for award that year "who had
rendered outstanding services to
literature in recent years."
Deadline for recommendations is
November 30, and, from writers
nominated for the prize in the
recommendations, the Medal- and
Prize-Winners are selected and
announced in June of the following year.
   Recipients of the honor--grant-
ed for the entire work of a writer
or for a single work of imaginative or factual writing in English,
French, Portuguese, Afrikaans,
or an African language--include:
   1950 G.A. Ngbongo. Belgian
      Congo
   Q. Ayom. Anglo-Egyptian
      Sudan
   1951 D. Nicol. Nigeria
   1952 Oscar Ribas. Angola--A
      Praga (The plague--short
      story)
   1954 M.A. Naimbi. Uganda
      Issa Kaita. French Sudan
      (Mali)
   1955 D.O. Fabunwa (F.O.
      Fagunwa.) Nigeria
      S. Layare. French Cameroons
      (Cameroon)
   1956 M.C. Mainza. Northern
      Rhodesia (Federation of
      Rhodesia and Nyasaland)
      A. W. Kayper Mensah. Ghana
      W. Soyinka. Nigeria
      A. Wandira. Uganda
   1957 Y.Y.R. Yolobe. South
      Africa
   1958 Alexis Kagame. Ruanda
   1959 Chinuah Achebe. Nigeria--
      Things fall apart
   1960 Shaaban Robert. Tanganyika
   1961 S.A. Mpashi. Northern
      Rhodesia (Federation of

Rhodesia and Nyasaland)--
for "considerable and beneficial influence on the growth
of a real interest in reading
and writing...particularly...
in the Northern, Luapala,
and Western Provinces (of
Northern Rhodesia) where
Bamba, his own language, is
current" 1153.

XANATHOUDIDEIOS FOLKLORE COMPETITION (Greece)

The contest of the Society of
Historical Studies Concerning
Crete was won in 1960 by G.
Karatarakis with his monograph,
"Burial in Crete." 1154.

Leib YAFFE PRIZE (Israel)

United Israel Appeal (Keren
Hayesod, P.O.B. 583, Jerusalem)
has awarded their literary prize
to:

Gershon Shalom. Shabtai Zwi
N.M. Gelber. Zionist move-
ment in Galicia
I.I. Rivlin. Shirat Yehudai
Hatargum
Yaakov Katz. Masoret U'
Mashber
Zeev Rabinowitz. Litvisch
Hassidut since the beginning
to our time
Alex Bein. Theodore Herzl
1155.

YEDITEPE POETRY PRIZE (Turkey)

Yeditepe Siir Armagani, established in 1954, is awarded
in several classes--300 TL
and 500 TL. Among the honored
authors are: Oktay Rifat, Fazil
Husnu Daglarca, Behcet Necatigil,
Edip Cansever, Arif Damar,
Cemal Sureyya for the work
"Uvercinka." 1156.

Riichi YOKOMITSU PRIZE (Japan)

Riichi Yokomitsu (1898-1947),
"one of the greatest novelists of
The Taisho and Showa periods,"

is commemorated by the prize
bearing his name. The award has
been given twice:
1948 Shohei Ooka. Furyoki
(Records of a prisoner's life)
1949 Tatsuo Nagai. Asagiri
(Morning mists) 1157.

YOMIURI LITERARY PRIZE (Japan)

Each year since 1950 the
Yomiuri Newspaper Company has
awarded literary prizes for the
best work in five fields: Novel,
Drama, Literary Criticism,
Literary Study and Translation,
Poetry and Haiku. Among the
winners of the well-known
Japanese award for writers are:

Novel
1950 Masuji Ibuse. Honjitsu
Kyushin (Closed for today)
1951 Koji Uno. Omoi Gawa
(The river of reflections)
1952 Shohei Ooka. Novi (Fires
on the plains, or A field of
fire)
1953 Hiroyuki Agawa. Haru No
Shiro (A castle in Spring)
1955 Hauro Sato. Akiko Mandara (Akiko Yosano, the
great lady-poet, in Buddhist
Paradise)
1956 Ton Satomi. Koigokoro
(A tender feeling)
1957 Yukio Mishima. Kinkakuji
(The Golden Pavilion in
Kyoto)
Saisei Muroo. Anzukko
Yaeko Nogami. Meiro
1959 Hakucho Masamune.
Kotoshi no Aki
Shigeharu Nakano. Nashi no
Hana
1960 Shigeru Tonomura.
Miotsukushi

Drama
1952 Juro Miyoshi. Honoo no
Hito (Men in flames)
1953 Tsuneari Fukuda. Ryu o
Nadeta Otoko (Men who
stroked a dragon)
1961 Yukio Mishima. Toka no
Kiku

Literary Criticism and Literary
Study and Translation
1951 Katsuichiro Kamei. Literary criticisms during 1950
1953 Masao Yonekawa.
Dosutoefusukii Zenshu (Trans-
lation of F.M. Dostoevsky's
Complete Works)
1955 Motohiro Fukase. Eriotto
(A critical study of T. S.
Eliot's Works)
1956 Kenkichi Yamamoto.
Koten to Gendai Bungaku
(The Classics and Con-
temporary Literature)
1957 Yoshishige Abe.
IWANAMII Shigeo (biography)
Kenji Takahashi. For his
studies of Hesse and his
work as a translator
Toyoji Hongo. Ryokan
1958 Mitsuo Nakamura.
FUTABATEI Shimei (biog-
raphy)
Michio Chidani. Hidejuro Yawa
Moichi Kure. Homer's "Iliad"
1959 Yoshio Nagayo. Waga
Kokoro no Henreki (biography)
Kazuo Watanabe, Masaaki
Sato, and Masataka Okabe.
Senichiya Monogatari
1960 Tsuneari Fukuda. Wat-
akushi no kokugo kyoshitsu to
Sakunendo no shosakuhin
Mizuho Aoyagi. Sasayakana
Nihon Hakkutsu
Rintaro Fukuhara. Studies of
Thomas Gray
1961 Michio Takeyama. For his
journals of his travels abroad
Yoshizo Kawamori. A history
of the French literary world
Poetry and Haiku
1950 Mokichi Saito. Tomoshibi
(Lights)
1954 Takashi Matsumoto.
Ishidama (Spirit of the
stones)
1957 Miyoko Goto. Haha no
Kashu
Tatsue Ubukata. Shiroi Kaze
no nakade
1958 Hideo Chidani. Yoshino
Hideo Kashu

Daigaku Horiguchi. Yube no
Niji
1959 Shiro Murano. Boyoki
1960 Hekido Ozawa. Hekido
kushu
1961 Shuji Miya.   Ohku no Io
no Uta   1158.

YUGOSLAV CENTRAL COMMITTEE
OF THE FEDERATION OF SYN-
DICATES PRIZE
    The literary honor awarded by
Centralnog veca Saveza sindikata
Jugoslavije was won in 1952 by
Branko Copic with his novel,
"Prolom" (Breakthrough).
                            1159.

YUGOSLAV CENTRAL COUNCIL
FOR THE PEOPLE'S YOUTH
PRIZE
    Literary prizes for young
writers were established by the
Centralnog veca narodne omladine
Jugoslavije to give recognition to
new writers in several literary
fields: Poetry, Prose, Children's Literature, Literary
Criticism, and Journalism. A
recent winner (1957) was
Vjekoslav Kaleb, who received
the prize for his novel, "Divota
prasine" (Wonders of dust), which
also won the Yugoslav Writers'
Association Prize in 1954.
                            1160.

YUGOSLAV FEDERATION OF
HUNTING SOCIETIES PRIZE
    The literary award of Saveza
lovackih drustava was granted
to Danko Andelinovic in 1954 for
his novel, "Proslednja zelja" (The
last wish).   1161.

YUGOSLAV LITERARY PRIZES
    The Yugoslav National Prize,
awarded by the Committee for
Culture and Art (Komitetaza
Kulturu i Umetnost), is the
highest official cultural honor in
Yugoslavia, and includes prizes
for writing in various literary
forms, such as Children's

Books, Journalism, and Transla-
tion. Among Yugoslav writers
whose work has been distinguished
by one of the "Prizes of the
Government of the Federate
People's Republics of Yugoslavia"
--The "Vlade FNRJ"--are:
Novel
  1947 Misko Kranjec. Fara
    svetega Ivana (Parish of St.
    John)
  Oto Bibalji-Merin. Dovidenja
    u oktobru (Till we meet in
    October)
  1949 Ande Slodnjak. Pogine naj
    pes (Death on Pes)
Short Stories
  1947 Vjekoslav Kaleb. Brigada
    (Brigade--six short stories)
  Isak Samokovlija. Nosac; Samuel
    (Samuel, the porter)
  1949 Ivo Andric. Nove pripovetke
    (New stories)
  Veljko Petrovic. Prepelica u
    ruci (Quail in the hand)
  Branco Copic. Surova skola
    (The brutal school)
  Mihajlo Lalic. Izvidnica (The
    outpost)
Prose (Prose pieces) Ranko Marin-
  kovic.
Collected Poems and Poetry
  1947 Radovan Zogovic. Prkosne
    strofe (Rhymes of spite)
  Branco Copic. Ratnikovo
    proljece (The warrior's
    springtime)
  Janko Donevic. Gorski Tokovi
    (Mountain streams)
  1949 Oskar Davico. Zrenjanin
    (The Zrenjanin)
  Skender Kulenovic. Zbor
    dervisa (Meeting of the
    dervishes)
  Slavko Janevski. Pesni
    (Poems)
Drama
  1947 Skender Kulenovic.
    Vecera (The supper)
  Joza Horvat. Prst pred
    nosom (Finger before your
    nose)
  1949 Mirko Bozic. Povlacenje
    (The retreat, or The with-
    drawal)

Children's Literature
  1947 Franc Slokan. Povest o
    belem kruhu (Story about
    white bread)
  Slavko Janevski. Respejani
    bukvi (Flowering trees)
  1949 Prezihov Voranc. Solnce
    (The sun)
  France Bevk. Ostroska leta
    (Ostroska's summer)
  Josip Pavicic. Radost mladog
    pok olenja (Happiness of the
    younger generation)
Journalism
  1947 Oskar Davico. Medu
    Markosovim partizanima
    (Among the Markosov partisans)
Translation
  1949 Mihovil Kombol. Danteovog,
    "Pakla" (Dante's "Inferno")
                                1162.

YUGOSLAV SOCIETY FOR
EDUCATION AND CARE OF
CHILDREN PRIZE
  The award for books for children, offered by Drustava za
Vaspitanje i brigu o djeci, was
given to Aleksa Mikic in 1954 for
her book, "Suncana obala" (Sunny
shore).   1163.

YUGOSLAV WRITERS' ASSOCIA-
TION PRIZE
  The national association of
Yugoslav writers (Saveza knjizevnika
Jugoslavije) at a meeting of its
Council on January 16 and 17,
1953 inaugurated several prizes
to honor established writers and
outstanding currently published
works. These awards recognize
the entire literary contribution of
leading Yugoslav authors, and
bring public notice to literary
works in several forms that are
currently issued in Yugoslavia.
Among authors honored by the
prize are:
Entire Literary Work
  1949-1952 Miroslav Krleza
  1953 Veljko Petrovic
  1954 Viktor Emin
  1955 Ivo Andric

1956 Jus Kozak
1957 Milan Bogdanovic--a
joint award granted with
the Yugoslav Publishers'
Association (Udruzenja
izdavackih preduzeca
Jugoslavije)
Novel
1949-1952 Oskar Davico.
Pesma (The poem)
1953 Mahajlo Lalic. Zlo prolece
(The bad springtime)
1954 Aleksandar Vuco. Raspust
(The vacation)
Vjekoslav Kaleb. Divota
prasine (Wonder of the dust)
1955 Novak Simic. Braca i
Kumiri (Brothers and
relatives)
1956 Ivan Doncevic. Mirotvorci
(The peacemakers)
Collected Stories and Short Story
1949-1952 Vladan Desnica.
Olupine na sunca (Junk on
the sun)
1953 Ranko Marinkovic. Ruke
(Hands)
1954 Ivo Andric. Prokleta
avlija (The cursed yard)
1956 Erih Kos. Veliki mak
(The big poppy)
Collected Poems
1953 Dobrisa Cesaric.
Osvijetljeni put (The lighted
way)
Mladen Leskovac. Antologiju
staije srpske lirike
(Anthology of older Serbian
lyrics)
1955 Blaze Koneski. Veziljke
(Embroideries)
1956 Cene Vipotnik. Drevo
na samem (The lonesome
tree)
Essays
1949-1952 Milan Bogdanovic.
Stari i novi, IV (The old
and the new, part 4--literary
criticism)
1953 Peter Segedien. Na putu
(On the road--travelogue)
1954 Mate Balota (pseud of
Mijo Mirkovic). Puna je
Pula (Pula is full--mono-

graph)
Josip Vidmar. Meditacije
(Meditations)
1955 Marko Ristic. Tri mrvta
pesnika (Three dead poets)
1956 Isidora Sekulic. Govor i
jezik kulturna smotra
(Speech and language, a
cultural examination of People)
                                        1164.

Josep YXART PRIZE (Spain)
One of the Santa Lucia Prizes,
this award, named for the
Spanish journalist, poet and liter-
ary critic of Tarragona (1852-
1895), is offered by the publisher
Editorial Selecta (Fonda de San
Pedro 3, Barcelona) for an essay
in Catalan "of a philosophico-
critico-biographical character."
Winners of the honor--which
currently bears a premium of
15,000 pts--include:
   Juan Fúster. Figuras del
   tiempo
   Capmany, et al. Cita de
   Narradores
   Juan Triadu. He Calgut
   Escullir
   Oswaldo Cardona. Verdaguer i
   Lamartine
   Jose Maria Corredor. La
   societat industrial i
   nosaltres   1165.

ZAGREB PEOPLE'S PRIZE
(Yugoslavia)
   One of the most important
literary awards granted by cities
in Yugoslavia, this prize presented by Zagreb, capital city of
the Republic of Croatia, was
awarded in 1954 to Slobodan
Novak for his story, "Izgubljeni
zavicaj" (Lost homeland);
Dusanka Popovic for his novel,
"Nocne ptice" (Night birds); and
Peter Segedin for his collection
of novella, "Mrtvo more" (The
Dead Sea).   1166.

ZARAGOZA PRIZE (Spain)
   A prize of 10,000 pts is

awarded by the Ayuntamiento de Zargoza for a work on Aragon history. In 1954 the Premio de la Diputación Provincial was won by Luis López Anglada with "Canto a la Virgen." 1167.

Mariusz ZARUSKI LITERARY PRIZE (Poland)
In 1958 the Marine Club of the League of the Friends of Soldiers (Klub Morski Ligi Przyjaciol Zolnierza, Chocimska 14, Warszawa) established the Nagroda Literacka im Mariusza Zauskiego--a literary honor to be awarded each year on June 24, the day consecrated to the sea. Among the winners are:
1958 Jerzy Boydan Rychlinski. Entire work
1959 Stanislaw Maria Szlinski. Entire work
1960 Lech Badkowski. Polo nadziei (novel)
Bronislaw Miazgowski. Entire work
1961 Karol Borhardt. Znaczy kapitan (novel) 1168.

ZIG-ZAG PRIZE (Chile)
The publisher's prizes of Editora Zig-Zag (Santa Maria 076, Porto Fernandez, C. 936, Santiago) have been offered from time to time over a period of years. Although no prize is currently given by Zig-Zag, previous awards were granted such writers as:
1939 Ciro Alegría (Peru). Los perros hambrientos (The hungry dogs)
1956 Luis Merino Reyes. Regazo amargo (Bitter refuge) 1169.

ZMAJ PRIZE (Yugoslavia)
Named for the famous Serbian journalist and author, Jovan Jovanovic (1833-1904), who used the pen name "Smaj," or "Zmaj," this award is offered by Matica Srpska (Society for Belles

Lettres). Award winners include:
1954 Antonije Isakovic. Velika deca (The big children--story)
1955 Velibon Gligoric. Srpski realisti (Serbian realists)
1956 Vasko Popa. Nepocinpolje (The Field of Nepocin-- collected poems)
Bosko Petrovic. Lagano promicu oblaci (The clouds pass slowly--collected stories)
1957 Vladan Desnica. Projjece Ivana Galeba (The spring of Ivan Galeb--novel)
1958 Desanka Maksimovic. Miris zemlje (The smell of earth) 1170.

Enrique ZOBEL DE AYALA PRIZES (Philippines)
An annual "Concurso Literario Enrique Zobel de Ayala" is conducted by Casino Español (663 San Luis, Manila), offering a premium of P 1,000 "for the best writing in Spanish, regardless of genre, submitted or published during the year." 1171.

ZURICH LITERATURE PRIZE (Switzerland)
The cultural honor of the city of Zurich has been granted since 1932. Originally the premium of fr 8.000--more recently fr 5.000--was offered for literary works only, but since 1942 the Literature Award has been presented triennially--rotating with the award for Visual Arts and for Music. Authors distinguished by the prize include: C.G. Jung; Felix Moeschilin; Maria Waser; Hermann Hiltbrunner; Friedrich Dürrenmatt, honored in 1947 for his first play; and--more recently--
1945 Robert Faesi
1948 Traugott Vogel
1951 Fritz Ernst
1955 Kurt Guggenheim
1959 Max Frisch 1172.

346 International Literary Awards

"ZYCIE LITERACKIE" PRIZE
(Poland)

In 1958 this award for literary
criticism, journalism, and
essays was established by the
weekly, "Zycie Literackie"
(Wislna 2, Krakow). The yearly
premium, assigned by the editorial board of the publication, has
been given each December to
such authors as:

1958 Kazimierz Wyka.
Literary criticism published
over the past two years
Ludwik Flaszen. Literary
criticism and articles
Jerzy Lovell. Journalism,
particularly the book
"Raport w sprawie aniolow"
1959 Zbigniew Kwiatkowski.
Journalism
Andrzej Kijowski. Literary
criticism
1960 Mieczyslaw Jastrun.
Essays and literary criticism
Jan Blonski. Literary criticism
Konstanty Grzybowski.
Journalism
Wilhelm Szewczyk. Journalism
1173.

Sources of Information About Literary Awards--
Selected Bibliography

Academia de la Lengua Española.
In Almanaque Mundial, 1962,
Eduardo Cárdenas, editor.
Editors Press Service, 551 Fifth
Avenue, New York 17
   Lists learned academies in 20
Latin American countries with
lists of members. Includes some
information about Latin American
prizes and their winners, as
Alberdi-Sarmiento, Cabot Prizes.
                                 B-1.
Académie Royale des Sciences, des
Lettres, et des Beaux-Arts
de Belgique. Concours
Annuels et Fondations Academi-
ques. Brussels. 1961. 58p.
   Gives the set questions of
annual literary competitions for
the years 1962, 1963, and 1964.
Also describes prizes and awards
of learned societies and foundations for factual and literary
writing in Belgium.   B-2
Académie Royale de Langue
et de Littérature Françaises.
Annuaire, 1961. Brussels.
66p.
   The lists of prizes awarded
by the Academy may include
names of prize winners and
titles of winning works as well
as description of the prize.
                             B-3.
Accademia Nazionale dei Lincei.
Annuario. Rome, 1960, 316p.

   Includes rules for prizes and
honors awarded: Feltrinelli,
Nazionale, Novaro, Saintour,
Donegani. Gives prize winners
for some awards, as Feltrinelli,
and "Premi Reali"--shows winners from 1879-1943.   B-4.
All-India Library Conference.

Souvenir of Baroda. Baroda
Central Library, 1946. 41p. Supplement, 1946. 23p.   B-5.
Almanacco Letterario Bompiani
Milan, V. Bompiani.
   The 1960 edition listed (p. 267-
270) 85 Italian literary awards
by month of award, showing
literary form for which awarded;
may give amount of premium
and names of winning authors.
Period covered: September
1958-September 1959.   B-6.
Americana Annual. New York,
Americana Corporation.
   This yearbook of the Ency-
clopedia Americana lists prizes
in literature each year under
the article, "Prizes and Awards
--Literature;" and under the index entry: "Prizes and Awards."
Winners of such foreign awards
as Prix Fémina; Prix Goncourt;
Prix Médicis; Prix Théophraste
Renaudot; Prix Interallié; Grand
Prix de la Critique Littéraire,
and other prizes are shown under
"Prizes and Awards," or under
the articles about national
literatures: French, German,
Italian, Latin American, Soviet
Spanish. New York Drama
Critics Circle Awards, including
"Best Foreign Play," are given
under "Theater and Motion Pic-
tures." There is a separate
article on the Nobel Prize.
                             B-7.
Américas. Washington, Pan
American Union
   A monthly illustrated magazine
--English, Spanish, and Portu-
guese editions-- "about folklore,
art, music, history, geography,
agriculture, industry, economics,

347

and culture of countries in the
Western hemispheres!' Includes
incidental listing of prizes as
news notes, in special announce-
ments, and in articles.   B-8.
Annual Register of World Events:
A review of the year, 1958.
Longmans, 1959. Previous titles:
Annual Register, 1954-1957
    Chapter on "Literature" gives
major French prize winners.
                             B-9.
Asian Recorder, weekly digest
of Asian events. January 1955-
New Delhi.
    Issued in 3 separate quarterly
issues, and a cumulative annual
issue with index. Includes major
cultural awards, such as the
Indian prizes of the Sahitya
Akademi.   B-10.
Association des Écrivains
Belges de Langue Française.
Annuaire. Brussels.
    Lists foreign literary awards
and Belgian literary prizes
available to Belgians. Does not
list prize winners.   B-11.
The Author's Annual, 1929.
New York, Payson & Clarke Ltd.
    Includes an article by Bessie
Graham, "Famous Literary
Prizes," a reprint from "Pub-
lishers' Weekly;" describes (p.
26-34) 16 prizes, including the
Nobel Prize for Literature,
Goncourt Prize, French Academy
Prize, Fémina Prize, and gives
"Miscellaneous prize notes,"
with descriptive annotations of
winning works.
    The 1930 edition article by
Bessie Graham, "1929 Literary
Prizes and Their Winners," de-
scribes 16 literary awards--
mostly American and British, but
some French--as Goncourt Prize,
Brentano Prize.   B-12.
Benet, William Rose. The
Reader's Encyclopedia. New York,
Crowell, 1955
    Includes some literary honors:
Nobel Prize--lists winners, giv-
ing nationality birth and death

dates, area of work; Goncourt
Prize--incidental mention; under
"Academy"--briefly describes
eight learned societies.   B-13.
Der Bibliothekar; Zeitschrift für
das Bibliothekswesen. Zentralin-
stitut für Bibliothekswesen,
Berlin C 2 (Georgenkirchstrasse
24)
    Incidental and occasional sum-
mary listing of East German
Literary awards.   B-14.
Book Review Digest. New York,
H.W. Wilson.
    Indexes "Fiction--Translated
Stories;" with incidental mention
of prize awards in reviews.
                             B-15.
Booklist and Subscription Books
Bulletin. Chicago, American
Library Association.
    From September 1954 lists
bibliographies of foreign-language
books from time to time, as
"French Books;" "Lithuanian
Books;" with prize information
in descriptive annotations.
                             B-16.
Books Abroad; a quarterly publication devoted to comments on
foreign books, v 1, 1927- University of Oklahoma.
    Prize information about books
published outside the United States
appears incidentally in reviews of
foreign books, and in articles on
foreign literatures.   B-17.
Books for Africa. Q. Christian Literature Council, Edinburgh House, 2
Eaton Gate, London, SW1.
    Announces literary competitions
and awards for writing in Africa.
                             B-18.
Braun, Sidney Z., editor.
Dictionary of French Literature.
Philosophical Library, 1958
    Lists Académie Française and
Académie Goncourt.   B-19.
Britannica Book of the Year
    Lists, as do other encyclopedia
yearbooks, information about
literary awards in articles on
"Literary Prizes," and on specific
prizes, as the Nobel Prize.

Highlights of publication and writing in national literatures are carried under national literature articles, as for: France (Académie Française Grand Prix, and Prix du Roman, Renaudot Prize, Grand Prix Littéraire de la Ville de Paris, Prix Fémina, Prix Goncourt); Germany; Italy; Jewish Literature; Latin America; Soviet Literature; Spain.

B-20.

Brockhaus' Konversations-Lexikon. Der grosse Brockhaus. 1955 edition Wiesbaden, F.A. Brockhaus

Brief world review of literary awards under "Literaturpreis," vol 7, p. 275.

B-21.

Brook, Herbert. Blue Book of Awards. Chicago, Marquis-Who's Who, 1956

Includes some literary and some journalism awards--Condor of the Andes; Merganthaler Awards. Describes and may give recent winners.

B-22.

Bulgarska akademiia na naukite. Laureates of the Dimitrov prize in scientific areas, 1950-1953. Sofia, 1959

One of several publications of the Bulgarian Academy of Science giving bio-bibliographic information on winners of the Dimitrov prizes, with incidental mention of awards in letters. Joint Publications Research Service: 1513-N English language-text.   B-23.

Bulgarska akademiia na naukite. Laureati na Dimitrovski nagradi. Sofia, 1955

Bulgarian edition of the information in B-23.

B-24.

Bulgarska akademiia na naukite. Laureati na Dimitrovski nagradi za literatura. Sofia, 1953

In this publication devoted to the literary winners of the Di-

mitrov Prize, information given about each prize-winner includes: Portrait, works for which specially cited, biography, and bibliography of writings.

B-25.

Bungei nenkan. Japanese yearbook of literature, drama, and the arts. Edited by Nihon Bungei-ka Kyokai (Text in Japanese)

Lists current literary awards granted in Japan (not seen).

B-26.

Carlos Palanca Memorial Awards for Literature. Prize stories, 1950-1955, edited by Kerima Polotan. Manila?, 1957

A collection of 1st, 2nd, and 3rd prize winning writings in the Philippines short story contest; with text in English or Tagalog.

B-27.

Cendán Pazos, Fernando. Premios literarios en España. Madrid, 1960. 5 p.

In this publication of Instituto Nacional del Libro Español Ferraz 13, Madrid , 8 the 90 most important literary honors periodically awarded in Spain are listed alphabetically. Information given for each award is form of literature for which granted, nature of award, awarding or sponsoring agency.

B-28.

Cassell's Directory of Publishing in Great Britain, The Commonwealth, and Ireland, 1961 edition. London, Cassell

"Literary Prizes," p. 295-305, described are generally those of Great Britain and the Commonwealth, including international awards such as Macmillan Fiction, Putnam, Mansfield Short Story (Menton). Incidental prize information in sections concerning "Government Agencies Concerned in the Selling and/or Promotion of Books," "Literary Foundations." Lists Afrikaans, and describes in detail English-

language prizes in South Africa.
B-29.
Cassell's Encyclopedia of
Literature, 2 v. London,Cassell,
1953; New York, Funk &
Wagnalls, 1954
In the most comprehensive
description of world-wide literary
honors in English, lists ("Prizes,
Literary," v 1, p. 460-463)
awards by country with coded
information to show: Official
name of prize; year in which
first offered or awarded; type
of work for which given; value;
name of awarding body.
B-30.
Chamber's Encyclopaedia World
Survey. London, George
Newnes Ltd.
Annual publication, including
a paragraph on "British Honours
and Awards;" a table of Nobel
Prize Winners (through the
current year); and in a major
Division of the encyclopaedia,
"Literature and the Arts," contains sections discussing prize-
winning authors and their works:
"Literature in English," "Literature in Western Europe,"
"Slavonic Literature," "Arabic
Literature," and--in the 1960
edition--"Japanese Literature."
B-31.
Chapsal, Madeleine. Goncourt
prize winner: How people
become French, Reporter 14:38-
40, January 26, 1956
In a brief description of the
Prix Goncourt, reports the award
given every fall since 1903,
from funds left in 1896,"to the
best work of fiction written within
the year." Current value of
premium in 1957: $28.57.
Colette presided over the Academy of 10 writers until her
death in 1954. The Goncourt
Prize award sells 200,000 copies
of the winning title.
B-32.
The Children's Book Council.
Children's Books: Awards and

Prizes, 1960/1961. Prepared by
Westchester Library System,
Mount Vernon, New York.
Available from Council, 175
Fifth Avenue, New York
In a listing (alphabetical by
name) of literary awards for
writing for children, lists prizes--
mainly U.S.A.--with description
of history and purpose of award,
and winners for 1960 and 1961.
A 1961/1962 Supplement lists
1961 and 1962 prize winners.
B-33.
China Yearbook, 1960-1961
Includes incidental information
about literary awards in China,
such as: Central Daily News
Prize, China Association of
Literature and Art Prize, and
China Ministry of Education and
Literature Award.
B-34.
Ciardi, John. Poets and prizes,
English Journal, 39:545-52,
December 1950
Critical review of prize award
procedure in several literary
honors granted in the U.S.A.--
Bollingen Prize administration
changed from Fellows in Ameri-
can Letters of the Library of
Congress, to Yale Library,
after "public furor" upon award
of the prize to Ezra Pound (p.
545); "Pulitzer judges will
prefer an easy clarity, even the
clarity of mediocrity, in preference to a potentially rewarding
difficulty" (p. 547).
B-35.
Conditions of Lenin Prizes and
other decisions. In"Questions
of Ideological Work," Glossary
of most important decisions of
the Communist Party of the
USSR, 1954-1961. Moscow,
State Printing House, 1961, p.
218-223.
B-36.
The cultural scene in Pakistan,
1960-1961, Literature. Karachi,
Pakistan Publications,1962?
68 p.
English-text excerpts from

four prize-winning works of the
Adamjee Prize, initially awarded
in 1960.
                              B-37.
Current Digest of the Soviet
Press. Joint Committee on
Slavic Studies, American Council of Learned Societies and
Social Science Research Council
   Weekly translations and index
of selections from various newspapers and magazines in the
USSR, and index of contents of
"Pravda," and "Izvestia." Includes cultural honors of the
USSR: Lenin Prize, Order of
the Red Banner of Labor, and
others.
                              B-38.
"Dangerous thoughts," Nation,
171: 13, July 1, 1950
   A brief satirical editorial
suggesting an "Ignobel Prize," to
honor the "smallest mouse
brought forth by the biggest
elephant," and to mark "greatest
editorial credulity and contempt
for reader's intelligence," in
literary works.
                              B-39.
Diccionario de la Litteratura
Latino Americana, Argentina.
Primera Parte. Autores Argentinos de la Colonia al Presente,
1960, 218p;   Segunda Parte.
Autores Argentinos Vivos,
1961, p. 219-392. Pan American
Union
   Incidental mention of literary
honors in the brief biographies
and bibliographies of outstanding
writers of Argentina.
                              B-40.
Diccionario de la Literatura
Latino Americana, Bolivia. Pan
American Union, 1960, 121 p'
   Incidental mention of literary
honors in the brief biographies
and bibliographies of outstanding
writers of Bolivia.   B-41.
Delta, Netherlands Government
   A review in English of the
arts, life and thought in the
Netherlands; contains some

literary prize information.
                              B-42.
Los Doce mejores artículos del
premio Cabotín 1957. Lima,
Garcilaso, 1958, 102 p.
   Collection of Peruvian essays
honored with the Cabotín Prize
(not seen).
                              B-43.
Estaciones, Revista Literaria de
Mexico. Mexico. No 1, Spring
1956-
   Quarterly review of Mexican
literature; mentions contests,
prizes, and prize winners.
                              B-44.
Europa Year Book, 1961, 2nd ed.
v. 1. Europe; v. 2. Africa, The
Americas, Asia, Australasia.
London, Europa Publications
   Section "European Prize
Foundations" gives address,
organization officers, recent prize
winners for Nobel Prize Founda-
tion, Lenin Prize Committee.
                              B-45.
Facts on File Yearbook. New
York, Facts on File
   The Five Year Index, 1956-
1960, lists the Nobel Prize,
Goncourt Prize, Lenin Prize
(under "USSR-Arts and Sciences").
"News Year, 1960" lists under
"Names that made news" winners
of major awards, as Erasmus
Prize of Copenhagen, Guggenheim
International Award. Also gives
Nobel and Pulitzer Prize winners
for current year (1960).
                              B-46.
Ferro, Antonio. Prémios
literários, 1934-1947. Lisboa,
Edições S. N. I., 1950. 217p.
   Discusses Portuguese litera-
ture competitions (not seen).
                              B-47.
Fiction Catalog, 1950, and
cumulative supplements of 5 and
3 years. New York, H.W. Wilson.
   Fiction translations from a
variety of languages (as, Chinese,
Czech, Danish, Dutch, Finnish,
Flemish, French, etc.) are
listed and descriptive notes may

mention prize received.
B-48.
Fischer Weltalmanach. Annual-
Frankfort am Main, S. Fischer-
Verlages, Zeil 65/69
  Presents the most complete
information on major art and
literary prizes throughout the
world of any publication examined.
Prepared under the direction of
Dr. Gustav Fochler-Hauke. The
1961 edition gives prize infor-
mation (description of awards,
name and address of awarding
agency, winners) for the years
1945-1960. The 1962 edition
continues prize information,
citing current winners.
B-49.
Florilege de Jeux floraux du
Languedoc. Lamalou-les-Bains,
Eds de La Rev du Languedoc,
1953, 32p.
  Describes floral games of
the region (not seen).
B-50.
Forfattern. Denmark
  Information from this Danish
periodical was used in preparing
a list of Danish literary prizes
compiled by Det Kongelige
Bibliotek.
B-51.
French News. Cultural Services
of the French Embassy, 972
Fifth Avenue, New York 21.
  Descriptions and lists of
French literary awards and their
winners appear from time to
time: "French literary awards
for 1960," No. 11, p. 4, January
1961--lists 22 awards giving
authors and titles; "Literary
prize giving," No. 15, p. 5-6,
January 1962--describes prize
procedure, with pictures of
some winners; April 1962, p.
10--lists winners of 1961 literary prizes: Goncourt, Fémina,
Renaudot, Médicis, Interallié.
B-52.
Fitch, Morrison. "The French
literary prizes," Publishers'
Weekly, p. 2311-2, December

22, 1951
  List of major French prizes
in order of importance, with
brief evaluative comments.
B-53.
Frank, Joseph. "Notes on the
literary situation," Partisan Review, 18:450-8, July 1951
  Quotes André Rousseaux from
a weekly column in "Figaro littéraire:" "Literary prize week in
France is a phenomenon in the
history of modern manners
related to the sweepstakes or the
Tour de France (annual bicycle
race)."
B-54.
G. H.'S-Gravesande, Letterkundige prijzen in Nederland,
1952
  Vereeniging ter Bevordering
van de Belangen des Boekhandels
indicates this publication gives
particulars of Dutch literary
awards (out of print; not seen).
B-55.
Genet. "Letter from Paris,"
New Yorker, 37:104, December
16, 1961
  Each mid-December major
French literary award winners
are given.
B-56.
"Académie Française ceremony
makes a rebel immortal," Life,
39:158-60, November 7, 1955
  Illustrations of Jean Cocteau
in the uniform of the Academy
(color) and quotations from his
comments on his election; "You
have given an expatriate identity
papers, a resting place to a
vagabond, a body to a ghost."
After this "official" statement,
Cocteau commented: "Since
it is now fashionable to laugh at
the Academy, I have remained a
rebel by joining it."
B-57.
Golino, Carlo L. "Italian literary
prizes, 1960 edition," Italian
Quarterly, 4:16, p. 43-55, Fall
1961, No. 19, v. 5
  Description of major awards
and award procedure by an

authority who secured the information during fellowship-residence
in Italy.   B-58.
Gorchakov, Nikolai A. The
theater in Soviet Russia. Columbia
University Press, 1957
    Several references to Stalin
Prize plays.
                                 B-59.
"Green fever," Time, 66:20,
October 31, 1955
    Reporting the election of Jean
Cocteau to the Académie
Française, describes the mythi-
cal "41st chair" occupied by those
who never made the grade. Annual stipend of Academy member: 60,000 francs ($171).
Cocteau predicted in his acceptance speech that the time was
coming when few will read or
write: "I would like to think
that our door would be open for
the singular persecuted by the
plural."   B-60.
Guatemala (City) Feria nacional.
Concurso literario, organizado
por el Comité central de la
Feria nacional. 1st- Guatemala,
C.C. Tipografía nacional,
1938-
    Collection of prize-winning
literature, including the first
prize-winner: Flor Nacional y
Medalla de Oro.
                                 B-61.
Guggenheim Memorial Foundation.
Reports of the Secretary General
and the Treasurer, 1959-1960.
New York, Author, 1961, 485p.
    Includes list of grantees.
                                 B-62.
Guggenheim Memorial Foundation.
Becas de Intercambio entre las
Republicas de la America Latina
y Los Estados Unidos de America.
New York, Author, 1962, folder
    Description of grants available
to Latin American writers.
                                 B-63.
Guide des prix littéraires;
lauréats primés, jurys, règle-
ments. 1st ed. Paris, Cercle
de la librairie, 1952-

Most recent edition (1959, 656
p; with two supplements--"Additif"
for 1960 and 1961) of prize information in this publication of
the French syndicate of the book
trade--principal associations of
publishers, book-sellers and
printers--is the most complete
listing of literary awards issued
in any country. Prizes alphabetical by name or awarding
agency (as Académie Française)
giving address, genre, history,
rules, jury members, laureates.
Indexes by name of award;
jurors; laureates; subject or
genre. Includes international
and European French-language
prizes; Algerian; Belgian; and
Swiss prizes; and some others.
                                 B-64.
Guillebraud, Philomena. "Role of
honorary awards in the Soviet
economic system," American
Slavic Review, 12:486-505,
December 1953
    Honorary awards--titles,
orders, and medals--conferred by
the central government of the
USSR are a widely used social
incentive. "One of the first acts
of the Soviet government after the
Revolution was the abolition of all
Tsarist orders and medals"
(p 489).
                                 B-65.
Handbook of Latin American
Studies. Gainesville, University
of Florida
    Standard annotated bibliography
of books and articles prepared
by authorities; includes some
prize information in annotations.
                                 B-66.
Hespelt, E. Herman. An outline
history of Spanish American literature 2nd ed Appleton 1942
    Mentions some literary awards
in biographical notes of contemporary period writers.
                                 B-67.
"Hatpins and the Fémina," Time,
71:94, January 13, 1958
    Brief note on the Fémina

Prize, labels jury "12 eccentric
old ladies." Politics influence
award of the premium (cash
value: 5,000 francs or $12)
which through prestige of the
prize guarantees a sale of
100,000 copies of the winning
work.   B-68.
Hispania: A Teachers' Journal
Devoted to the Interests of the
Teaching of Spanish and Portuguese. American Association
of Teachers of Portuguese and
Spanish, 19-
  Notes and reviews in this
quarterly--as well as some
articles--give descriptions and
winners of Spanish-language and
Portuguese awards.
                                 B-69.
Holst, Eva. "Forfatterprisen
for Borne-og ungsdomsboger"
(Author awards for children's
and youth's books). Bibliotekaren,
16, No. 4-5: 111-12, 1954
  Among Danish awards for
children's and young people's
books are those of the Football
Pools and the Danish Ministry
of Education.
                                 B-70.
"Forfatterprisen for borne-og
ungdomsboger" (Author awards for
children's and youth books).
Bogens Verden, 36:337-8,
October; 557-8, December 1954
  Articles concerning Danish
literary awards appear in various
issues of this periodical, issued
eight times a year by Danmarks
Biblioteksforening (Odensegade
14, Copenhagen).
                                 B-71.
Husain, Yusuf Jamal. World
literary awards and the Adamjee
Prize for literature. Karachi,
Writers' Guild, 1960, 15p.
  Brief descriptions of famous
literary honors awarded through-
out the world--France, United
Kingdom, Germany, U.S.A.,
U.S.S.R., and the Adamjee
Prize of Pakistan.
                                 B-72.

Hughes, Langston, ed. An
African treasury; 30 stories,
articles, and other writings by
contemporary African authors.
New York, Crown, 1960
  Incidental mention of literary
awards won by African writers.
                                 B-73.
India. Ministry of Information
and Broadcasting. India, A
Reference Annual. Delhi,
Publications Division, Govern-
ment of India, 1953
  The 1961 edition lists winners
of the Sahitya Akademi Awards.
                                 B-74.
Indian Council for Cultural
Relations. Cultural news from
India. New Delhi, Author
  Bi-monthly, mentions news of
Indian literary prizes.
                                 B-75.
Information Please Almanac. New
York, McGraw, 1947-
  Lists some international and
American prizes: Nobel and
Pulitzer Prizes (complete lists
of winners, showing nationality
of laureates); New York Drama
Critics' Circle Prizes, and
Overseas Press Club of America
Awards--winners and winning
works.
                                 B-76.
Instituto de Cultura Puertorriqueña.
Teatro puertorriqueño. San Juan,
P.R, 1959, 461 p.
  Describes and lists winners in
First Festival of Puerto Rican
Drama held in San Juan, July
1958, at Teatro Tapia.
                                 B-77.
Instituto de Literatura Chilena.
Boletin. v 1, no 1- Sept 1961-
Santiago
  Several sections give infor-
mation on literary awards granted
in Chile: "Premio Nacional de
Literature" (p 3-9) chronological
list of annual winners with brief
biography, list of works, and
major bio-critical information
sources; "Premios Literarios
Vigentes en Chile" (p 31) gives

winners of four additional awards through 1961: Alerce Prize, Atenea Prize, Mistral Prize, Santiago City Prizes.

B-78.
Instituto Internacional de Literature Iberoamericana. An outline history of Spanish Literature. 2nd ed. New York, F.S. Crofts, 1942
Incidental prize information by authors receiving awards.

B-79.
International Literary Annual, no 1, 1959- . London, John Calder
Information about major literary prizes: Nobel Prize; English Awards; French Awards. Lists winning author, title of winning work, publisher.

B-80.
Introduction to Contemporary Japanese Literature. Edited and published by Kokusai Bunka Shinkokai (Society for International Cultural Relations). Tokyo. 1959,296 p.
"A list of literary prizes" (Part II--1935-1955, p. 279-82)--photostat from National Diet Library, Tokyo--lists 22 prizes of Japan by name of award, giving date of establishment, purpose, form of prize, names of some recipients.

B-81.
Italian Books and Periodicals (English edition of Libri e reviste d'Italia, Rassegna bibliografica mensile). Presidenza del Consiglio dei Ministri, Rome
This standard source for information about Italian publications includes incidental prize information. B-82
"Jackpots," Time, 56:32, December 18, 1950
Account of some famous French literary awards--including the Goncourt Prize. Académie Goncourt meetings are distinguished by the customary costume of the academy members: Cocktail

dresses for women (noon meeting), mufflers and overcoats for men (regardless of weather).

B-83.
Handbook of Jamaica. Gillespie & Company, 96 Wall Street, New York 5
Includes information about the Musgrave Medal (1960 ed, p 592)

B-84.
The Japan Annual
Mentions major Japanese literary honors (1958 ed, p.346): Akutagawa, Yomiuri, Naoki, Women Writers'. B-85.
Japan, National Commission for UNESCO. Japan.
"Encouragement for Good Publications" (p. 473-4) lists public and publishers' awards, literary awards of writers' societies and foundations (14), and science awards of public and private groups (5).

B-86.
Jones, Willis Knapp. "Recent Novels of Spain: 1936-1956," Hispania, 40:303-11, 1957
Discusses literary awards in Spain: "Prize contests are largely responsible for the discovery of the present-day crop of Spanish novelists..." p.305.

B-87.
Jong, E.S. de., ed. Oer de skied fan't hjoed. Tinkboekje utjown ta gelegenheit fan de utrikking fan de Gysbert Japiczen Dr. Joast Halbertsma-priis, respectivelik oan de hearen Dr. Y. Poortinga en Mr. D.J. Cuipers. Boalsert, A. J. Osinga, 1950
30 p
Discussion of two prize-winners of the Japicx Prize and the Halbertsma Prize (not seen).

B-88.
Der Journalist, Handbuch der Publizistic, v 2-4. Bremen, Heye, 1956-1958
Amerika-Gedenkbibliothek, Berlin, indicates as source of German literary prize information (not seen). B-89.

Kerrigan, Anthony. "A literary letter from Spain," New York Times Book Review, 62:7, 13, July 7, 1957
Spanish literary awards for 1957 are reviewed, including the Nadal Prize.
B-90.
Koninklijke Vlaamse Academie voor Wetenschappen, Letteren, en Schone Kunsten van Belgie. Jaarboek, 1960
Describes and lists winners of Belgian Flemish-language literary honors in the sciences, social sciences, and some forms of literature.
B-91.
Kurschners Deutscher Literatur-Kalender. Berlin, de Gruyter
"Literarische Preise und Auszeichnungen" (v 53, 1958, p 911-919) lists alphabetically by name 119 literary awards, including Austrian and Swiss prizes, as well as West and East German awards. Gives date established, awarding and sponsoring agencies, names of prize winners--usually a selective rather than a complete listing.
B-92.
Kurtz, Maurice. "Immortals all," New York Times Magazine, p. 45-6, December 6, 1959
Description of Académie Française--"one of world's most exclusive clubs," with a limit of 40 members: 600 in 324 years. Mentions famous authors not members: Gide, du Gard, Romain Rolland; and other famous absentees: Camus, Aymé, Anouilh, Sartre, Balzac, Stendhal, Zola, and Descartes-- who was excluded as a founding member of the Academy as "too independent a thinker."
B-93.
Library Journal. New York, R. R. Bowker
American Library Association awards, citations and scholar-

ships announced each year.
B-94.
Library Literature. New York, Wilson, 1934-
Indexes literary honors under "Awards, Citations, and Prizes," in issues from 1952 to present.
B-95.
El Libro Español. Revista mensual del Instituto Nacional del Libro Español. Madrid
The section "Concursos y Premios" describes Spanish and Spanish-language and other literary awards, mentioning winners.
B-96.
"Life en Español," December 12 and 26, 1960
These issues show winners of the "Life en Español" Latin American literary contest, with portraits.
B-97.
Lincoln Library of Essential Information. Buffalo, New York, Frontier Press
Discusses Nobel and Pulitzer Prizes; lists Nobel Prize winners.
B-98.
Literary and Library Prizes. New York, Bowker, 1963
The best single source of information about literary honors awarded in the United States, Canada, United Kingdom. Also lists some International, prizes.
B-99.
Literary Market Place. New York, Bowker
Annual handbook lists literary honors: "Literary Awards;" Prize Contests;" "Literary Grants and Fellowships." All awards of United States and Canada, with few exceptions: Kalinga Prize, Hans Christian Andersen Prize, Centro Mexico de Escritores.
B-100.
McLeod, A. L. The Commonwealth Pen; An introduction to the literature of the British Commonwealth. Cornell Univer-

sity Press, 1961
   Chapters by authorities on the literature of the Commonwealth (including Australia and New Zealand) mention literary honors incidentally.
                              B-101.
McNab, Roy, ed.   Poets in South Africa.   Capetown, Maskew Miller Ltd., 1958
   Incidental mention of selec- tions winning awards: Vilakazi; Van Riebeock.
                              B-102.
Magill, Frank.   Cyclopedia of world authors.   New York, Harper, 1958
   Some prize awards mentioned under authors.
                              B-103.
Maurois, André.   "The forty immortals," Holiday, 21: 74-5, April 1957
   Sketch of the Académie Française created in 1635 by Cardinal Richelieu.   Portrait (in color) of Georges Duhamel in the uniform of the Academy in the Academy's private study.
                              B-104.
"Medals for Germans," Economist, 185:1135-6, December 28, 1957
   Civilian decorations awarded by Hitler, as well as military decorations won in either of two World Wars, were proscribed "soon after surrender of Ger- many" in World War II.   In 1957 a new law made legitimate the Federal Republic's Order of Merit (1914-1918), and some awards of 1939-1945--provided they were de-Nazified by removal of swastika.   Shops selling medals and ribbons are licensed by the government, and customers must produce evidence to show decoration may be worn.   Penalty for fraudulent wearing of a decoration may be 12 months' imprisonment.
                              B-105.
Il Merito.   Sarzana, Italy,

Editoriale Costruire.   Annual, 1962-
   This 929 page volume--"An- nuario dei Premi e dei Premiati d'Italia"--consists of an alpha- betical list of cultural awards (Italian, Swiss, some International) for literature and other arts and services.   Shows for each: address of awarding agency; cultural area for which awarded; history; description of award; prize winners through 1960--with a supplement (p. 871-894) of prizes and laureates through 1961.   A Biographical Dictionary of prize winners for 1959-1960 (p. 401-868) gives brief bio-bibliographic in- formation about writers, artists, architects, and public figures honored by awards.   Index of prizes by area of award, as "Lit- erature"--general; "Poetry;" "Teatro."
                              B-106.
"A multitude of awards; literary prizes and their uses," London Times Literary Supplement, 3111: 733, October 13, 1961
   Varying European awards are alike only in their great number. The international Formentor Prize may be a direct means of assessing the worth of literary works--as prize winners are now widely translated.
                              B-107.
Murray, Charlotte Ellen.   Famous literary prizes, Jamaica.   N. Y., Queensborough Public Library, 1934, 31p.
   Description of 12 literary prizes --including several no longer awarded: Prix fémina vie heureuse; Prix fémina vie heureuse améri- cain; Prix fémina vie heureuse anglais; French-American award; Kleist-preis.   List of prize win- ners through 1933.
                              B-108.
New International Year Book. Funk, v 1- , 1932-
   Brief summaries of the year's events may include major literary happenings by national literature,

including evaluative reviews of major works, mentioning prize awards. Wide subject coverage of national literatures: French, German, Italian, Latin American, Spanish, Russian; and also Netherlands and Flemish, Portuguese, Swiss, Norwegian, Swedish, and Japanese.

B-109.
"News note," New Republic, April 9, 1962
   Description of notice of Stalin Peace Prize, People's Republic of China.

B-110.
"New York Times."
   "Recent Mexican awards noted," New York Times, VII, 26:1, April 30, 1950--with information about winners of Mexican National Prize of Arts and Sciences and Lanz Duret Prize. Also, notice of other prizes and literary prize winners.

B-111.
New Zealand. Department of Statistics. New Zealand Official Yearbook, 1961, 66th issue. Wellington, Government Printer
   "Cultural Awards" (p. 1100-1101) describes eight scholarships and achievement awards--most of them for literature.

B-112.
Newmark, Maxim. Dictionary of Spanish Literature. New York, Philosophical Library, 1956
   Describes some literary awards under "Spanish and Spanish American Literature," as Fastenrath Prize. Mentions awards under authors receiving honors.

B-113.
Nobel Foundation. Nobelstiftelsen Kalender, 1961-1962. Stockholm, P. A. Norstedt, 1961, 120 p.
   This Nobel Foundation Calendar, issued biennially, lists laureates, giving reason for award in Swedish and in English.   B-114.
Nobel Prize Lectures. New York, American Elsevier Pub-

lishing Company, 1963-1964
   Collected Nobel Prize lectures will be issued in a series for each area of the Nobel Prize. Beginning in 1962 the Nobel Prize in Physics lectures will be available. The collected lectures of the winners of the Nobel Prize in Literature, published for the Nobel Foundation for the first time in English, will be available in 1964. Each lecture is preceded by the presentation address for the prize winner.

B-115.
Nobel Prize Yearbook. New York, American Elsevier Publishing Company, 1962- , v 1-
   Beginning in 1962 English editions of the Nobel Prize Yearbook will be issued.   B-116.
Norway. Public and School Libraries Law. Chapter 3. Compensation to Authors, May 13, 1955 (English Translation). Oslo, Royal Norwegian Ministry of Church and Education
   Legal basis of the Norwegian national government regular salaries for authors.

B-117.
Oxford Companion to French Literature. Harvey, Paul, and Janet E. Heseltine, eds. New York, Oxford University Press, 1959
   "Prix littéraires" (p. 576) gives some general information about French literary awards. There is also information under names of awards, as: Académie Goncourt; Goncourt; Fémina; Renaudot; Nobel; Institut de France; Société des Gens de Lettres; Grand Prix des Meilleurs Romans du Demi-Siècle.

B-118.
Ozersky, Mikhail, and Yuri Grafsky. Choosing the Lenin Prize Laureates. USSR, July 1961, p. 8-14
   Lenin Prizes in Literature and the Arts, as well as Lenin Prizes in Science and Technology, and Lenin Peace Prize, discussed and

some winners named.   B-119.
Pacifici, Sergio. A guide to
contemporary Italian literature.
New York, Meridian, 1962,
352 p.
  Incidental mention of famous
Italian literary prizes, such as
Viareggio, Strega, Chianciano.
                         B-120.
"Poetry." Chicago, monthly
  Each November issue, under
"Poetry Awards," contains an
announcement of prizes and
awards for the year, with a
brief statement of the prize his-
tory, and a chronological list of
winners since establishment.
Prizes are those given in the
U.S.A.
                         B-121.
Polish Library Association.
Librarian's and Bookseller's
Guide. Annual.
  Polish literary prizes are
listed each year, with a list of
current prize winners (not seen).
                         B-122.
Porter, Dorothy B. "Fiction by
African authors: A preliminary
checklist," African Studies
Bulletin, 5:54-66, May 1962
  The brief descriptive annota-
tions on some listings of the
novels, novelettes, and short
stories (arranged by country of
the writer) contain some infor-
mation about awards won by
writer.
                         B-123.
Porter, Dorothy B. "Notes on
some African writers." In U.S.
National Commission for
UNESCO. Africa and the United
States Background Books, 8th
National Conference, Boston,
October 22-26, 1961. U.S.
State Department Publication
7332 (p. 167-173)
  Incidental mention of literary
awards to African writers.
                         B-124.
Portteus, Elnora M., ed. Awards
in the field of children's books.
Kent State University, Kent,

Ohio. Department of Library
Science, 1959, 43 p. (Aspects of
Librarianship, Fall 1959, No 1)
  Awards in U.S.A. (also one
including Canada and U.S.A.) for
books for children. National,
regional, and state prizes giving
awarding agency, description of
prize, qualifications for award,
chronological list of winning
authors and titles.
                         B-125.
Los Premios de novela Ciudad
de Barcelona, 1949-1953.
Barcelona, Pareja, 1959.
  Collection of Spanish fiction
winning the city of Barcelona
Prizes (not seen).
                         B-126.
"Présence Africaine." Paris
  Incidental mention of literary
awards and prize winners in this
magazine. The publisher Présence Africaine has also issued:
John A. Davis, ed. "Présence
Africaine; Africa as seen by
American Negroes;" 1958, 418 p.
--with chapters by authorities
including those on the arts and
literature.
                         B-127.
Presidenza del Consiglio dei
Ministri. Ufficio della Proprieta'
Letteraria Artisticae Scientifica.
"Elenco Premi Letterari Assegnati
a Roma," 23-page typescript, 1962
  This catalogue of literary
prizes awarded in Rome gives
description and winners of 25
literary awards--by public and
private agencies and groups--show-
ing awarding agency with name
and address; type of writing
honored; history, rules and nature
of prize; jury; winners.
                         B-128.
"Publishers' Weekly, the American book trade journal." New
York, Publishers' Weekly
  The annual summary number
in January (January 21, 1963,
p. 76-80) includes a section:
"Literary Prizes and Awards."
Additional news notes and

articles throughout the year list
literary award information,
especially for French, Canadian,
English and Latin American
prizes.
                              B-129.
Ramos, Maximo. Philippine
Cross-Section; an anthology of
outstanding Filipino Short Stories
in English. 1950
   Brief biographical statement
introducing each story includes
some information about literary
honors won by the writer.
                              B-130.
Real Academia Española. Boletin.
   This official publication of
the Spanish Academy includes a
section "Información Académica,"
which may contain a paragraph:
"Premios y Concursos."
                              B-131.
Reitz, M. Prystoekennings aan
jeugboeke (Awards to youth
books), Cape Librarian, 1:2-4,
September 1958
   Mentions Republic of South
Africa awards for children's
and young people's books.
                              B-132.
Revista Interamericana de
Bibliografia (Inter-American Re-
view of Bibliography). Washington, D.C., Pan American Union,
Department of Cultural Affairs,
Division of Philosophy and
Letters. 1951-
   This quarterly publication may
contain articles, book reviews,
bibliographic annotations mentioning literary awards in Latin A-
merica. Under "News and Notes"
by country, literary awards may
be announced or winners given.
                              B-133.
Righetti, Renato, ed. Gran
Premio. La Spezia, via Don
Minzoni 41R
   Monthly publication devoted to
prize information in Italy and
some international and Europe.
Covers awards in the visual
arts, and sciences as well as
literature; gives announcements

of prize competitions and contests;
names winners as prizes are
awarded with description of winning work and information about
winner. Ceased publication 1963.
   A summary publication, "L'Almanacco dei Premi Artistici e
Letterari," for Italian cultural
awards is planned for 1963.
                              B-134.
Rockefeller Foundation. Directory
of Fellowship Awards, 1917-
1950; 1951-1955; and Annual
Reports
   Lists grants showing award
winners and purpose of award.
                              B-135.
"Room for 'Immortals', "Newsweek,
50:78, December 23, 1957
   Brief report of the Académie
Française prize awards. Men
under sixty years of age have
been "rarely elected" to the
Academy.   B-136.
Rosen, Seymour N. The Soviet
Communist Party literary policy
as reflected in the Stalin Prizes
in Prose and Drama. Master's
essay, Slavic Languages, 1952,
Columbia University, 1952, 100p.
   The "Complete List of
Stalin Prizes in Prose and Drama,
1941-1952" ('Appendix," p. 76-83)
contains the transliterated author's
name and title, and the English-
language title for each winning
work (as listed in "Izvestia,"
"Pravda," and other Russian-
language sources).
                              B-137.
Rutherfoord, Peggy. Darkness
and light: An anthology of
African writing. London, Fath,
1958
   Includes some prize awards.
                              B-138.
Sahitya Akademi. National
Academy of Letters. Annual Report. New Delhi.
   Each year the Akademi report
contains information about literary honors of India awarded by
the Akademi; including an Appendix:
"Books which have Won the

Akademi Award." B-139.
Sanchez, Jose."'Adonais': A poetic landmark,'' Hispania, 41: 236-7, 1958
In his description of Spanish literary honors, states: "Perhaps the most coveted prizes in Spain are the Nadal for novel, Sésamo for short story, Lope de Vega for drama, and in poetry definitely the Adonais, with the Boscán perhaps trailing" (p 236).

B-140.
Sanchez, Jose. "Literary awards in present-day Spain," Books Abroad, 31:365-7, Fall 1957
Evaluative review of current Spanish literary honors, mentioning as best-known and most-coveted of some 146 major awards the Nadal Prize and Planeta Prize for novel; the Adonais Prize for poetry--"most distinguished honor a poet can receive today in Spain" (p.366).

B-141.
Sanchez, Jose. Los premios literarios españoles (Supplement to the "Kentucky Foreign Language Quarterly"). Scripta humanistica Kentuckiensia, IV, Lexington, 1958, 20p.
Lists 160 Spanish literary prizes, giving description and winners, name and address of awarding agencies, current jury (as of 1957, Omits floral games.

B-142.
Santini, Aldo. Breve curiosa avventurosa Storia del Premio Viareggio. Il Cavallucio Marino, Editore Viareggio, 1961, 187 p.
Illustrated history of the Viareggio Prize, with brief biographies of winners through 1960.

B-143.
Scherf, Walter, ed. Children Prize Books. Munich, International Youth Library, 1959, 48 p.
The editor of this catalogue prepared for an exhibition of books for children and young people is Director of the International Youth Library (11 A Kaulbach Strasse, Munich 22). Describes prizes by country (14 European nations, Canada, U.S.A., and the International Andersen Medal) giving winners through 1957 or 1958.

B-144.
"Schrijversalmanak," 1957 (last issue)
This Dutch annual (now out of print) included a list of prize winning Dutch books, according to the Vereeniging ter Bevordering van de Belangen des Boekhandels (not seen). B-145.
"Sex and salvation; French literary prizes," Time, 73:88, March 9, 1959
Mentions six famous literary honors in a brief news note. B-146.
Simmons, Ernest J. "Soviet literature, 1950-1955." In Annals of the American Academy of Political and Social Science, January 1956, p. 89-103
An outstanding American authority on Russian writing reviews literature in the USSR during a six year period, mentioning literary honors incidental to discussion of major works.

B-147.
Sitwell, Osbert. "Some laments of literary corruption." In Penny Foolish; a book of tirades and panegyrics. New York, Macmillan, 1935
A critical assessment of literary honors, concluding that prizes "have seldom picked a real winner of whom little had previously been known" (p. 320).

B-148.
Slonim, Marc. Modern Russian literature from Chekhov to the present. New York, Oxford University Press, 1953
Incidental mention of Stalin Prize winners. B-149.
Slonim, Marc. "Russian Soviet

literature. In Perspectives: Recent literature of Russia, China, Italy, and Spain. Lectures presented under the auspices of the Gertrude Clarke Whittal Poetry and Literature Fund, Library of Congress, Reference Department, 1961

"Education of the masses... supreme goal of fiction" in the USSR, where aims and style of Communist writers have been directed by Central Committee of the Communist Party resolutions.
B-150.

Smith, Horatio E., ed. Columbia dictionary of modern European literature. New York, Columbia University Press, 1947

Prize information incidental, as mention of Goncourt Prize under "Goncourt, Edmond de and Jules de."
B-151.

Sociedad Amantes de la luz, Santiago de los Caballeros, Dominican Republic. Certamen de La Trinitaria. Santiago..., Editorial El Diario, 1938, 4 v

Collection of poetry and prose winning awards of La Trinitaria (Political Society of the Dominican Republic), sponsored by President Trujillo.
B-152.

Spanish Cultural Index. Spain, Cultural Relations Department. Madrid.

English edition of the publication of Dirección General de Relaciones Culturales of the Spanish Ministry of Cultural Affairs--a monthly issue including descriptive lists of writing classified by form or type: "Literature"--including information under "Prizes," "Awards;" and such subject fields as History, Science and Technology. Also includes regularly a section: 'News from Hispano-America and other countries," which may announce prizes and list award winners.
B-153.

"Spanish writers' prizes and privations," Economist, 198:666, February 18, 1961

Analyzes the cause and effect of the system of Spanish literary prizes, most of which have been established within the last 15 years.
B-154.

"Spoofing the Académie," Newsweek, 39:42, May 26, 1952

Reports the one anonymous vote, given in an Academy canvas for honors, for "Absinthe."
B-155.

Stahle, Nilsk. Alfred Nobel and the Nobel Prizes. Stockholm, Nobel Foundation and The Swedish Institute, 1960, 15 p·

An illustrated pamphlet by the Executive Director of the Nobel Foundation describing the determination and presentation of the Nobel Prizes; biographical statement about Alfred Nobel.
B-156.

Struve, Gleb. Soviet Russian literature, 1917-1950. University of Oklahoma Press, 1950

Descriptions of Stalin Prize, and mention of winners.
B-157.

Sullivan, Frances A. "Children's book awards in other countries," Top of the News, 11:11-13, December 1954

Mentions children's book prizes in Canada, Mexico, England, France, Norway, Sweden, and Switzerland. Discusses awards and gives recent winners with titles of winning works.
B-158.

Tauro del Pino, Alberto. Bibliografia Peruana de Literatura.

Instituto Cultural Peruano indicates this publication contains notice of Peruvian literary prize winners prior to 1958 (not seen).
B-159.

Times, Manila.

Each September, at time of award, carries notice of the

Palanca and the Magsaysay
Awards.   B-160.
Times of India. Directory and
Yearbook, including Who's Who.
    Indian literary prizes, with
winners, are listed (1961-2
edition, p.1200-1).
                            B-161.
Trumpf, Peter. Preise, Praemien, Privilegien. Heidelberg,
Keysersche Verlagsbuchhandlung.
1959, 204 p·
    Includes information about
European, English, and American
and Canadian prizes and honors
for the arts, sciences and
general humanitarian and intellectual endeavor. Chapters
give a short history of the granting of awards and honors; discuss
world-famous prizes (as, Nobel
Prize, Prix Goncourt); prizes of
specific countries (as, American
prizes, German prizes, Swiss
prizes). | This information is
followed by an alphabetical "List
of Prizes" (p.125-204), which
may show date of founding of
award, frequency and nature of
award, purpose, and prize
winners of recent years (1958-
1959). Majority of prizes listed
are German, including awards
granted in East Germany--
which appear not readily available in other printed sources.
                            B-162.
U On Pe. "Modern Burmese
literature," Atlantic, 201:152-
6, February 1958
    Includes some description of
the literary activities of the
Burmese Translation Society.
                            B-163.
USSR Academy of Sciences.
Annual Meeting, February 2-4,
1961 (U.S. Joint Publications
Research Service--JPRS 8558,
August 3, 1961); OTS 61-31,
517
    Mentions literary awards
among others granted by the
Academy.   B-164.
Vukovic, Milan T. Mali

knjizarski leksikon; bibliografsko-
bibliofilsko-bibliotekarski
prirucnik. Belgrade. 1959
    This handbook of Yugoslav
literature includes "Yugoslav
Literary Prizes" (p.705-715),
arranged by year of award--
1947-1958, lists prize winners
and titles of winning works; may
include a brief description of the
prize, as, awarding agency, date
established. Also lists major
literary awards in other countries
(as, British, Austrian, Italian,
German, Spanish, French) with
descriptions and winners of some
(Nobel Prize, Prix Goncourt,
Pulitzer Prize).
                            B-165.
West, Rebecca. "Prizes and
handicaps." In Enduring in earnest;
a literary log (p 81-90). New
York, Doubleday. 1931.
    Mentions Fémina-Vie Heureuse;
and British prizes.
                            B-166.
Whitaker, Joseph. Almanack.
London
    Annual including mention of
the Nobel Prizes--with winners;
and description and winners of
major British Awards: "Prizes
for Literature," of the current
year.
                            B-167.
Wilson Library Bulletin. New
York, H.W. Wilson
    "Awards" may be described or
announced, or winners shown.
Prize information also given in
news notes; and some special
articles.
                            B-168.
Winkler Prins Boek van het
Jaar. Amsterdam, Elsevier
    Encyclopedia yearbook under
"Letterkunde" briefs outstanding
literary events of the year in
Netherlands and Belgium, including prizes and honors, in Dutch,
Flemish and French language.
Also, literary awards in other
national literatures.
                            B-169.

World Almanac, a book of facts. New York, World Telegram

"Awards--Medals--Prizes" includes table of Nobel Prize winners, and list of Pulitzer Prize winners. "Book Awards" under "Special Awards, Grants, Fellowships" shows U.S.A. awards of some 35 donors.

B-171.

World biography, 1940- . New York, Institute for Research in Biography

This dictionary of biography includes "all living Nobel Prize winners," with comprehensive resumés of their significant achievements.

B-172.

Writer. Boston

Includes a regular section, "Prize Offers and Awards," in each monthly issue.

B-173.

Writers' and Artists' Year Book. New York, Macmillan

List of major British literary awards--"Literary Prizes and Awards"--referring to such journals as "The Author," "John O' London" for details of prizes and literary competitions for novels, short story, poetry, nonfiction.

B-174.

Writers' Digest. Cincinnati, F. & W. Publishing Company

"Prizes and Awards" is a regular department (or "Contests and Awards"--in 1959). Also, special articles on awards.

B-175.

Yarmolinsky, Avrahm. Literature under Communism. The literary policy of the Communist Party of the Soviet Union from the end of World War II to the death of Stalin. Indiana University Press, 1960, 165p.

Primary sources of information used in this study include: Rulings of the Central Committee of the Communist Party," "pronouncements of top political and

literary figures," proceedings of literary conferences. References to the Stalin Prize winners.

B-176.

Yeats, Elen F. A study of the Lanz Duret Prize Novels. Mexico?, 1950?, 125 p.

Description of Prize and discussion of Prize winners from 1941-1948.

B-177.

Literary Awards By Country

C-1	International	C-42	Congo
C-2	Europe	C-43	Ghana
C-3	Austria	C-44	Guinea
C-4	Belgium	C-45	Ivory Coast
C-5	Bulgaria	C-46	Nigeria
C-6	Czechoslovakia	C-47	Rhodesia-Nyasaland
C-7	Denmark	C-48	South Africa, Republic of
C-8	Finland	C-49	Australia
C-9	France	C-50	Burma
C-10	Germany	C-51	Cambodia
C-11	Germany, East	C-52	China, Republic of
C-12	Hungary	C-53	China, People's Republic
C-13	Iceland		of
C-14	Ireland	C-54	India
C-15	Italy	C-55	Japan
C-16	Lithuania	C-56	Korea
C-17	Luxembourg	C-57	Malaya, Federation of
C-18	Netherlands	C-58	Mongolian People's Repub.
C-19	Norway	C-59	New Zealand
C-20	Poland	C-60	Pakistan
C-21	Portugal	C-61	Philippines, Republic of
C-22	Rumania	C-62	Thailand
C-23	Spain	C-63	Viet-Nam, South
C-24	Sweden	C-64	Latin America
C-25	Switzerland	C-65	Argentina
C-26	Union of Soviet Socialist	C-66	Bolivia
	Republics	C-67	Brazil
C-27	Wales	C-68	Chile
C-28	Yugoslavia	C-69	Colombia
C-29	Algeria	C-70	Cuba
C-30	Egypt	C-71	Dominican Republic
C-31	Greece	C-72	Ecuador
C-32	Iran	C-73	El Salvador
C-33	Iraq	C-74	Guatemala
C-34	Israel	C-75	Haiti
C-35	Lebanon	C-76	Honduras
C-36	Tunis	C-77	Mexico
C-37	Turkey	C-78	Nicaragua
C-38	Africa	C-79	Paraguay
C-39	Burundi-Rwanda	C-80	Peru
C-40	Cameroon	C-81	Puerto Rico
C-41	Central African	C-82	Uruguay
	Republic	C-83	Venezuela
		C-84	West Indies

INTERNATIONAL

Most of the major international literary awards and honors are offered by publishers for unpublished manuscripts, either as cooperative undertakings of publishers in a number of countries (the All Nations Prize Novel Competition; the Corning Science Prize; the Formentor Prize; International Nonfiction Contest; International Publisher's Prize), or as the award offered by a single publishing company (Abingdon Award; Encyclopaedia Britannica Press Prize; Dutton Animal-Book Award; Losada Concurso Internacional de Narrativa; Smith and Son Literary Award).

Best known of all literary honors is the Nobel Prize for Literature of the Swedish Academy. The Stalin Prize and the Lenin Prize, counterpart of the Nobel Prize, awarded to citizens of the USSR have also been granted to other than Russian authors.

International literary honors may be cultural or other groups,' recognition for the best book by a foreign writer (as Académie Française Prize for the Best Book in French by a Foreigner; Camões Prize; "Frances Extérieures" Literary Prize; French Prize for the Best Foreign Book; New York Drama Critics' Circle Award for the Best Foreign Play of the Season), may bring recognition for an author's entire contribution to letters (American Academy of Arts and Letters Award of Merit Medal; Goethe Medal) or for a particular area of writing (Andersen International Award, granted for literature for children and young people; Italia Prize, for radio and television writing), or may mark a specific occasion (Dante Medal; Pirandello Prize; Unita d'Italia Prize; Nigerian Novel Competition).

Additional international liter-ary awards are CERCLE DU LIVRE DE FRANCE PRIZE, Ottawa (won in 1961 by Diane Giguere with "Le temps de jeux"); the Hans Christian ANDERSEN MEDAL (Kelvin Lindemann is the youngest author to receive this honor); "TRIBUNE DE PARIS" LITERATURE PRIZE, offered for the best work of any author (granted in 1953 to Heinrich Böll of Germany); Jose JANES INTERNATIONAL PRIZE, offered by a Barcelona publisher for the "best first novel published in Spanish (granted in 1947 to Rodolfo L. Fonseca of Uruguay for "Turris eburnea," Tower of Ivory; Francisco Gonzalez Ledesma, "Sombras viejas;" 1951 to Manuel Gil for "La moneda en el suelo," and Antonio Rabinat Muniesa for "La noche de Juan Doriac"); the PORTUGAL PRIZE, offered by the National Secretary of information of Portugal for the best poems entered in competition written in Italian, French, or Spanish; ATLANTIC PRIZES of the Netherlands, awarded in 1958 in literature to Hella S. Haasse, for "De ingewijden," and to A. Rutgers van der Loeff Basenau, for "Je bent te goed Giocomo."

Additional international awards for specific forms of writing include the American prizes in journalism (OVERSEAS PRESS CLUB AWARDS, given "to a foreign national for his faithful adherence to the highest journalistic code under unusual harassment and political pressure," and the NIEMAN FELLOWSHIPS, offered to foreign newsmen for study at Harvard University); prizes for mystery stories (ELLERY QUEEN'S MYSTERY MAGAZINE SHORT STORY CONTEST, won by such writers as Alfredo Segre (1948) with "Justice has no number," and Georges Simenon (1949) with "Blessed are the

meek") and prizes in such specialized areas of Science as the Ocean
Floor (BODENSEELITERATUR-
PREIS, offered each year by the
city of Überlingen); History of
Pharmacy (URDANG MEDAL of
the American Institute of the
History of Pharmacy to "honor
unusually distinguished historical
publication on pharmacy appearing
anywhere in the world," granted
in 1960 to Otto K. Zekert of
Vienna for his biographical essays
on Carl Wilhelm Schelle,
"Berühmte Apotheker"). Among
international prizes no longer
awarded are: INTERNATIONAL
L.I.P. LITERARY AWARD,
granted by the London International
Press "to encourage original work
of an exceptionally high standard,"
which was discontinued "in view of
the lack of outstanding material
coming forward;" PARTISAN RE-
VIEW AWARD, which granted
$1,000 in 1949 to George Orwell
for "significant contribution to
literature."

Sources of Information--The
best single survey of world literary prizes in the English language
is the article in "Cassell's Encyclopedia of Literature," v 1,
p.460-463. Prizes for children's
and young people's literature have
been listed and described in
"Children's book prizes," Walter
Scherf, editor, International Youth
Library, Munich; E.M. Portteus,
editor, "Awards in the field of
children's books;" Frances A.
Sullivan, "Children's book awards
in other countries," in Top of the
News, 11:11-13, 1954; and in the
Children's Book Council publication, which is supplemented or
revised each year, "Children's
books: Awards and prizes."

Literary Prizes, Awards, and
Honors are listed in periodical
indexes ("Library Literature;"
"Awards, Citations, Prizes;"
"Readers Guide;" "International
Index;" "New York Times Index;")

and in a number of periodicals:
"Library Journal," annual list
each January of American Library Association awards, citations, and scholarships; "Wilson
Library Bulletin," under "Awards"
section and also as general news
information; "Publishers' Weekly," annual summary number in
January lists "winners of most
publishers' contests," with notes
on French Literary Prizes, and
other literary awards appearing
throughout the year; "Booklist
and Subscription Books Bulletin,"
including foreign literary awards
in descriptions of books included
in bibliographies of foreign books,
appearing since September 1954;
"Book Review Digest," listing in
cumulated indexes--"Fiction-
Translated Stories;" "Fiction
Catalog," including books translated from a variety of European
and other languages, such as
Danish, Dutch, Finnish, Flemish,
French, German, Greek,
Hungarian, Japanese, Provençal,
many of which have won literary honors; "Books Abroad,"
showing incidental literary awards
in reviews of books published outside the United States; "International Literary Annual," with
special sections on American
Awards, Nobel Prize, English
Awards, French Awards; and the
professional writers' magazines:
"Writer," listing "Prize Offers
and Awards;" "Writers Digest,"
with "Prizes and Awards," as a
regular department, and additional
special articles on contests and
awards; "Poetry," with "Poetry
Awards," in each November issue,
and additional award information
throughout the year.

The most complete periodically
revised description of American
Literary Prizes is in "Literary
and Library Prizes," (most recent
issue 1963) which also lists
English, Canadian, and a few
major French, German, and Inter-

national Prizes. Older books listing literary awards are "The
Author's Annual," with "Famous
literary prizes," p. 26-84; Charlotte Ellen Murray, "Famous
Literary Prizes," describing
awards from various countries,
and listing prize-winners through
1933; Herbert Brook, "Blue Book
of Awards," a listing of prizes,
medals, honors, and distinctions,
which include prizes for journalism, general cultural achievement,
and some for literature.

The major continuing sources
of general literary prize information are yearbooks: "Americana Annual," giving information
about French, German, Italian,
Latin American, Soviet, and
Spanish awards under the "Literature" entries for these countries
and areas, and regularly listing
under the article, "Prizes and
Awards," winners of the Prix
Fémina , Prix Goncourt, and
Prix, Médicis; "Britannica Book
of the Year," with comparable
sections, listing literary prize
winners under the articles on
national literature--as French
Literature: Académie Française
Grand Prix, Prix du Roman,
Prix de la Ville de Paris, Prix
Théophraste Renaudot; "New International Yearbook," with reports
on various national literary
awards, including oriental countries such as Japan.

Annuals such as the "World
Almanac," "Information Please
Almanac," and "News Year" include
description and lists of winners
for the Nobel, Pulitzer and other
literary prizes. "Facts on File
Yearbook" gives Lenin Prizes as
well as the Nobel and Goncourt
Prizes; "Literary Market Place,"
summarizes each years' honors
under "Literary Awards;" "Prize
Contests;" and "Literary Grants
and Fellowships"--these literary
awards are those of the United
States and Canada, including such

international prizes as the Jane
Addams Award, Andersen Inter-
national Award, Centro Mexicano
de Escritores; Benet's "Reader's
Encyclopedia" mentions the Prix
Goncourt and gives winners of
the Nobel Prize for Literature;
"Lincoln Library of Information"
discusses Nobel and Pulitzer
Prizes; "Magill's Cyclopedia of
World Authors" mentions prizes
incidentally under authors who
have been honored; "World
Biography" lists "all living Nobel
Prize Winners, with comprehensive
resumés of their significant
achievements." Details of English,
United Kingdom, and Commonwealth literary awards are sum-
marized in "Writers' and Artists'
Yearbook," under "Literary Prizes
and Awards;" "Whitaker's Almanack," listing major British literary honors under "Prizes for
Literature;" "Cassell's Directory
of Publishing in Great Britain,
the Commonwealth and Ireland;"
and in the survey of literature
of the British Commonwealth:
A. L. McLeod, "The Commonwealth Pen."

Of foreign language annuals
listing literary prizes on a world
basis, "Fischer Welt-Almanach"
appeared to give the widest and
most up-to-date coverage; general
literary award information is also
included in Trumpf, "Preise,
praemien, privilegien;" and in the
monthly review of the Instituto
Nacional del Libro Español,
Madrid: "El Libro Español."

Periodic reports of foundations,
learned societies, and professional
groups give reports of honors
and grants (as Guggenheim Foundation, Rockefeller Foundation).
The Nobel Prize for Literature
is the most frequently represented
prize in books of reference, and
in addition to two publications of
the Nobel Foundation (Stahle,

"Alfred Nobel and the Nobel Prize;"
"Nobelstiftelsen Kalendar"--issued
every second year with a list of
laureates, giving reason for award,
Swedish and English texts) will
be further represented in two new
publications: "Nobel Prize in
Literature Lectures," and "Nobel
Prize Yearbooks," to be issued in
1962-1963 by American Elsevier
Publishing Company.
INTERNATIONAL LITERARY
  PRIZES
  ABINGDON AWARD
  ACADÉMIE FRANÇAISE PRIZE
    FOR A BOOK WRITTEN IN
    FRENCH BY A FOREIGNER
  ACADÉMIE INTERNATIONALE
    DE TOURISME PRIZE
  ADDAMS CHILDREN'S BOOK
    AWARD
  ALL NATIONS PRIZE NOVEL
    COMPETITION
  AMERICAN ACADEMY OF ARTS
    AND LETTERS AWARD OF
    MERIT MEDAL
  AMITIÉS FRANÇAISES PRIZE
  AMITIÉS LATINES PRIZE
  ANDERSEN INTERNATIONAL
    AWARD
  ANDORRA INTERNATIONAL
    CULTURAL CONTEST
  ANISFIELD-WOLF SATURDAY
    REVIEW AWARDS
  ATENEO ARENYS PRIZE
  ATHENS POETRY PRIZE
  ATLANTIC FICTION AND NON-
    FICTION CONTESTS
  BALZAN FOUNDATION PRIZES
  BARBOSA PRIZE
  BENSON MEDAL
  BOLIVAR PRIZE
  BRASILIA PRIZE
  BRENTANO PRIZE
  BROSS PRIZE
  CAMÕES PRIZE
  CHATRIAN PRIZES
  CHRISTIAN FICTION CONTEST
  CHRISTOPHER AWARD
  "CLUB ESPAÑA" NOVEL PRIZE
  COLUMBIA-CATHERWOOD
    AWARDS
  CORNING SCIENCE PRIZE
  CRAWSHAY PRIZE FOR

  ENGLISH LITERATURE
  CREOLE FOUNDATION PRIZE
  DALMIA PEACE PRIZE
  DANTE MEDAL
  DELTA PRIZE NOVEL AWARD
  DOUBLEDAY CATHOLIC
    PRIZE CONTEST
  DUTTON ANIMAL-BOOK
    AWARD
  ENCYCLOPAEDIA BRITANNICA
    PRESS PRIZE
  ENFANCE DU MONDE PRIZE
  ETNA-TAORMINA INTER-
    NATIONAL POETRY PRIZE
  FERRO PRIZE
  LA FONTAINE PRIZE
  FORMENTOR PRIZE
  "FRANCES EXTÉRIEURES"
    LITERARY PRIZE
  FREIDENSPREIS DES
    DEUTSCHEN BUCHHANDELS
  FRENCH PRIZE FOR THE
    BEST FOREIGN BOOK
  GENEVA PRIZE
  GOETHE MEDAL
  GOETHE PRIZE OF HAMBURG
  GUGGENHEIM MEMORIAL
    FELLOWSHIPS
  GULBENKIAN PRIZES
  HALLMARK INTERNATIONAL
    TELEPLAY COMPETITION
  HAMBURG ACADEMY OF ART
    PLAQUE
  HANSEATIC SHAKESPEARE
    PRIZE
  HARPER PRIZE NOVEL
  HESPERIDES INTERNATIONAL
    ACADEMY PRIZE
  HOUGHTON MIFFLIN LITER-
    ARY FELLOWSHIP
  INNER SANCTUM MYSTERY
    CONTEST
  INTERNATIONAL BENJAMIN
    FRANKLIN SOCIETY MEDAL
  INTERNATIONAL FANTASY
    AWARD
  INTERNATIONAL FIRST NOVEL
    PRIZE
  INTERNATIONAL GRAND PRIZE
    FOR POETRY
  INTERNATIONAL LITERARY
    COMPETITION FOR THE
    BLIND
  INTERNATIONAL LITERARY

PEACE PRIZE
INTERNATIONAL NONFICTION
   CONTEST
INTERNATIONAL P. E. N.
   SHORT STORY CONTEST
INTERNATIONAL PUBLISHERS'
   PRIZE
ITALIA PRIZE
JOCS FLORALS DE LA
   LENGUA CATALANA
KALINGA PRIZE
KOVNER MEMORIAL AWARDS
LA MED PRIZE FOR YIDDISH
   FICTION
LATINITA PRIZE
LATINITAS CONTEST
LECOMTE DU NOUY PRIZE
LENIN PEACE PRIZE
LOSADA CONCURSO INTER-
   NATIONAL DE NARRATIVA
LOUBAT PRIZES
LUGANO PRIZE
MACMILLAN FICTION AWARD
MANSFIELD PRIZE
MODERN LANGUAGE ASSOCIA-
   TION HONORARY FELLOWS
MONACO LITERARY COUNCIL
   PRIZE
MORE ASSOCIATION MEDAL
NEW YORK DRAMA CRITICS
   CIRCLE AWARD FOR THE
   BEST FOREIGN PLAY OF
   THE SEASON
NEW YORK HERALD TRIBUNE
   CHILDREN'S SPRING BOOK
   FESTIVAL PRIZE
NEW YORK HERALD TRIBUNE
   WORLD SHORT STORY CON-
   TEST
NOBEL PRIZE FOR LITERATURE
NOBEL PRIZE FOR PEACE
OLYMPIC GAMES LITERA-
   TURE COMPETITION
OSLO PEACE LIBRARY
   AWARD
PIRANDELLO PRIZE
POE PRIZE
PUTNAM AWARDS
RED BADGE PRIZE COMPE-
   TITION
REFUGEE BOOK AWARD
RHYS MEMORIAL PRIZE
RINEHART FOUNDATION
   AWARDS

RIO DE JANEIRO PRIZE
ROCKEFELLER FELLOW-
   SHIPS IN CREATIVE WRIT-
   ING
SAXTON MEMORIAL TRUST
   AWARD
SCHICKELE PRIZE
SEVENSMA PRIZE
SMITH & SON LITERARY
   AWARD
STALIN PEACE PRIZE
   (People's Republic of China)
STALIN PEACE PRIZE (USSR)
UNITA D'ITALIA PRIZE
UNITED KINGDOM ROYAL
   SOCIETY OF LITERATURE
   AWARD
UNITED KINGDOM ROYAL
   SOCIETY OF LITERATURE
   PRIZES
UNITED NATIONS ESSAY PRIZE
UNITED NATIONS ONE-ACT
   PLAYWRIGHTING CONTEST
UNITED STATES NATIONAL
   INSTITUTE OF ARTS AND
   LETTERS GRANTS IN LITERA-
   TURE
UNIVERSALITY OF THE
   FRENCH LANGUAGE PRIZE
VEILLON PRIZE
VINCULA POETRY COMPE-
   TITION   C-1.
EUROPE
   Among the major continuing
European awards for writing are
the Cortina-Ulisse Prize; Schiller
Foundation Prize, and--for
specific forms of writing or
single language works--Mansfield
Prize for Short Story; Atlantic
Council Prize for a research
thesis; various French-Belgian
literary awards; the French
Scandinavian Vikings Prize; and
the general cultural honors which
include awards to literary figures:
Erasmus Award; Sonning Founda-
tion Prize. Additional awards are
the regional prize for Mediteran-
nean Countries, offered for poetry
(Prix de la MEDITERRANÉE);
the Scandinavian prize INTER-
SCANDINAVIAN LITERARY CON-
TEST, with a 10.000 kr premium

won in 1931 by authors from Nor-
way, Sweden and Denmark; ALL-
SCANDINAVIAN LITERARY
PRIZE, granted A. Skoven in 1947
for "Stoker's mess;" the SCANDI-
NAVIAN NOVEL PRIZE, awarded
Hakon Morne of Sweden for "Slaves
of the sea;" and a pre-World
War II EUROPEAN CULTURAL
AWARD (the HERDER PRIZE),
presented in 1942 to F.C. Weiskopf
for his work, "Dawn breaks."

Sources of Information--Rules
and information from some awarding agencies; "The Europa Yearbook;" incidental information in
Horatio Smith, "Columbia Dictionary of Modern European Literature;" "Guide des Prix Littéraire,"
listing European as well as
French awards; "Cassell's Encyclopedia of World Literature,"
with an over-all review of the
world's major literary prizes;
various encyclopedias, as Brockhaus, Winkler; annuals, as "Fischer Welt-Almanach;" and articles,
as the "London Times Literary
Supplement," "A multitude of
awards; literary prizes and their
uses," of October 13, 1961.
EUROPEAN LITERARY PRIZES
   ATLANTIC COUNCIL PRIZE
   CORTINA-ULISSE PRIZE
   COUNCIL OF EUROPE PRIZE
   EIFEL-ARDENNEN LITERA-
     TURE PRIZE
   ERASMUS AWARD
   EUROPEAN LITERARY PRIZE
   FIUME-LEROUX PRIZE
   FRENCH-BELGIAN GRAND
     PRIZE FOR LITERATURE
   FRENCH-BELGIAN LIBERTY
     PRIZE
   PAN-SCANDINAVIAN FICTION
     PRIZE
   SCHILLER FOUNDATION
     PRIZE
   SONNING FOUNDATION PRIZE
   VIKINGS PRIZE   C-2.
AUSTRIA
Major literary prizes and
honors of Austria are the Aus-
trian government honors--Förde-

rungspreise and Würdigungspreise
--offered, respectively, to young
authors and to established writers
by the Bundesministerium für
Unterricht; Province and City
prizes offered by such areas as
the Innsbruck Prize; Niederösterreich and Oberösterreich prizes;
Trakl Prize of Salzburg; Vienna
Prizes; and the awards of learned
and scholarly groups, such as the
Grillparzer Prize of Österreichischer Akademie der Wissenschaften; and of foundations, such
as the Körner Stiftungsfond; Reich-
Stiftung, Vienna; Wiener Kunstfond
der Zentralparkaase der Gemeinde
Wein.

Additional Austrian literary a-
wards are granted by the city of Vienna, including DRAMATIKER-WETT-
BEWERB DES THEATERS IN
DER JOSEFSTADT IN WIEN,
bringing grants to six playwrights;
EHRENPREIS FÜR DICHTKUNST,
an annual prize since 1957 honoring such authors as Maurus
Fontana, and more recently (1961)
Heimito von Doderer; WURDIGUNS-
PREIS FÜR PUBLIZISTIK, an
annual award since 1951 recently
(1960) presented to Jacques
Hannak.

Sources of Information--Letters
from some prize-awarding agencies, such as Magistrat der
Stadt Wien; and Amt der Oberös-
terreichischer Landesregierung.
Letters from Austrian Consulate
General, Cultural Affairs Section,
527 Lexington Avenue, New York
17, describing Austrian State
Prizes; from Austrian Ministry
for Education, giving information
about ten awards of the Austrian
government; from Austrian National Library (Österreichische
National Bibliothek, Josefsplatz
1, Vienna 1) listing 22 major
Austrian prizes, giving awarding
agency, premium, and recent
winners. Also, printed sources
of information as for German
prizes, especially "Fischer Welt-

Almanach," and Trumpf.
AUSTRIAN LITERARY AWARDS
AUSTRIAN LEAGUE FOR THE
UNITED NATIONS DRAMA
PRIZE
AUSTRIAN STATE FÖRDERUNGS
PRIZE
AUSTRIAN STATE GRAND
PRIZE
AUSTRIAN STATE PRIZE FOR
CHILDREN'S BOOK
AUSTRIAN STATE PRIZE FOR
YOUNG PEOPLE'S LITERA-
TURE
AUSTRIAN STATE SPECIAL
PRIZE
GRILLPARZER PRIZE
HARTEL PRIZE
HOFMANNSTHAL PRIZE
INNSBRUCK PRIZE
KÖRNER PRIZE
LENAU PRIZE
NIEDERÖSTERREICH CULTUR-
AL PRIZE
OBERÖSTERREICH DRAMA
PRIZE
OBERÖSTERREICH FÖDE-
RUNGSPREIS
REICH PRIZE
ROSEGGER PRIZE
STELZHAMER-PLAKETTE
STIFTER MEDAL
STIFTER PRIZE OF OBERÖS-
TERREICH
TRAKL PRIZE FOR POETRY
VIENNA ART FUND PRIZE
VIENNA CHILDREN'S AND
YOUTH BOOK PRIZE
VIENNA FÖRDERUNGSPREIS
VIENNA PRIZES FOR LITERA-
TURE   C-3.
BELGIUM
    As in many multi-language
countries, Belgian literary prizes
are offered in the two languages
of the country: Flemish and
French. The Belgian government
grants awards for writings in both
languages, and there is a close
relationship with Dutch literature
on the one hand (Belgian writing
in Flemish has received or is
eligible for such awards as:
Dutch Literature Prize, Dutch

Mastership of Letters Prize,
Hilvarenbeek Prizes, Kemp Prize,
Van den Vondel Prize); and
French literature on the other
hand (Belgian authors have won
the Fémina Prize, Goncourt
Prize, Saint-Beuve Prize, and
literary honors of the Académie
Française--Maurice Maeterlinck, Belgian Nobel prize-winner,
declined membership in the
Académie as he was not willing
to renounce his Belgian citizenship to become a French citizen).
    Belgian academies' prizes are
granted for literature in Flemish
and in French. Publications'
prizes (as the Ark Prizes of the
"Vrije Woord," "Audace" Prize,
"Le Soir" Rossel Prize) are
offered for works in both languages.
There are a number of literary
awards for Flemish writing from
cities and areas in the "Flemish
Area" of north Belgium: Antwerp
Prizes, Brabant Prize, East
Flanders Prize, Flemish Provinces Prize, Ghent Prize, Wemmel
Poetry Festival Prize. Additional
prizes for Belgian writing in
French are the E. BERNHEIM
PRIZE (awarded Luc Hommel in
1959 for "Marguerite d'York");
VERHAEREN PRIZE (a significant
honor in the 1930's: Dubois,
"La tentation" (1929); Jose Gers,
"Jeanne" (1930); Bolsee, "Ligne
de Songe" (1933); Cammen,
"Sommeil du Laboureur" (1933)).
Additional Flemish literature
awards are: BORMAN PRIZE
(given in 1950 to A. Smeets and
H. Casteur for "Inleiding tot de
hedendaagse schilderkunst");
OPENBARE BIBLIOTHEN PRIZE
(won by Jozef Droogmans for
"Verzamelde opstellen," and Leo
de Wachter for "Repertorium der
Vlaamse gouwen en gemeenten");
PASTOR DE CRAENE PRIZE
(granted in 1958 to Odette Huys
and Zulma Denis); SABAM
PRIZE (won in 1958 by Mark
Tralbaut, "In de schaduw van de

raven''); AD. MAX PRIZE (granted
in 1958 to Jan Walravens for "Hier
is Brussel"); Alice NAHON
PRIZE (whose winners include
Blanka Gijselen, 1958); Jaak
BALLING PRIZE (presented in
1957 to Albert Swerts for "Als je
niet wordt als deve kleinen").

A literary form important in
German prizes is also recognized
by Belgian awards--the radio play:
FLEMISH NETHERLANDS RADIO
PLAY PRIZE (Vlaams-Nederland-
stalig Luisterspel, won in 1957
by Jozef Cohen with "Het staat op
de muren"), and YOUNG PEO-
PLE'S RADIO PLAY PRIZE
(granted in 1948 to René Strulens).

A children's literature award,
the PRIX "LE LIGUER-ROITELET,"
is a joint award of "La Liguer,"
the publication of the organization
Ligue des Familles Nombreuses
de Belgique, and the collection
"Roitelet" of the Brussels publisher
Durandel. Directed to recognizing
adventure books in French by
authors of any nationality which
are written for children 10 to 14
years of age, the initial prize in
1951--to be granted each four
years--was given, on the basis of
literary quality, originality, and
educational value of the writing,
to Robinson, "Les troubadours du
Far-West;" and G.V. Leclercq,
"Chameau blanc."

Sources of Information--Letters
and rules of some awarding agen-
cies. Three publications of
Belgian academies: Académie
Royal des Sciences, des Lettres,
et des Beaux-Arts de Belgique,
"Concours Annuels et Fondations
Académiques, 1961;" Académie
Royale de Langue et de Littéra-
ture Françaises," Annuaire, 1961;"
Koninklijke Vlaamse Akademie voor
Wetenschappen, Letteren en Schone
Kunst, "Jaarboek, 1960."

Additional important annually
published records of Belgian prize-
winners writing in the French language are "Guide des Prix Littér-

aires," which includes Belgian
awards such as the Engelmann
and Rossel Prizes. "Winkler
Prins Encyclopedie. Boek van
het Jaar," under the article,
"Letterkunde-België," discussing
outstanding literary events of the
year, lists major prize-winners
and their works, emphasizing
Flemish-language literature.

BELGIAN LITERARY AWARDS
  ANTWERP PRIZES
  ARK PRIZE OF THE "VRIJE
    WOORD"
  "AUDACE" PRIZE
  BAEKELMANS PRIZE
  BEERNHAERT PRIZE
  BELGIAN CATHOLIC WRITERS
    PRIZE
  BELGIAN GOVERNMENT
    PRIZES FOR LITERATURE
  BELGIAN GRAND PRIZE
  BELGIAN GRAND PRIZE FOR
    COLONIAL LITERATURE
  BELGIAN TRANSLATION
    PRIZE
  BOON PRIZE
  BOUVIER-PARVILLEZ PRIZE
  BRABANT PRIZE
  COOPAL PRIZE FOR TRANS-
    LATIONS
  COUNSON PRIZE
  DAVIDS FUND PRIZE FOR
    COLONIAL LITERATURE
  DENAYER PRIZE
  EAST FLANDERS PRIZE
  EEKHOUT PRIZE
  ENGELMANN PRIZE
  FLEMISH PROVINCES LITER-
    ATURE PRIZES
  GARNIER PRIZE
  GEZELLE PRIZE
  GHENT PRIZE
  KNIGHT OF THE ORDER OF
    LEOPOLD
  KRIJN PRIZE
  MALPERTUIS PRIZE
  MERGHELYNCK PRIZE
  MICHOT PRIZE
  MOCKEL GRAND PRIZE FOR
    POETRY
  POLAK PRIZE
  REINAERT PRIZES
  ROSE PRIZE

ROSSEL PRIZE
ROSY PRIZE
SCHMITS PRIZE
TIERE PRIZE
VAXELAIRE PRIZE
VLIEBERG PRIZE
VOSSART PRIZE
WEMMEL POETRY FESTIVAL
   PRIZE
WEST FLANDERS PRIZE
WIART PRIZE   C-4.

BULGARIA
   While a number of Bulgarian literary awards are granted by societies, institutions, and publications, the major literary honors are the state prizes: Dimitrov Prizes; and the Union of Bulgarian Writers Prizes.
   Sources of Information--Letter from V. Iltchev, Head of Department, Committee for Friendship and Cultural Relations with Foreign Countries, People's Republic of Bulgaria (5 Ruski Boulevard, Sofia); Letter from National Library of Bulgaria. Dimitrov prize-winners are discussed in publications of the Bulgarian Academy of Science (Bulgarska akademiia na naukite), two of which were examined: "Laureati na Dimitrovski Nagradi za Literatoura za 1949ᵣ1950, i 1950;" and "Laureati na Dimitrovski Nagradi v Oblasta na Naukata, 1950-1953." Dimitrov Prize awards are announced in the Bulgarian "Izvestia" at time of presentation.
BULGARIAN LITERARY AWARDS
   BULGARIAN WRITERS' UNION
      PRIZES
   DIMITROV PRIZES   C-5.

CZECHOSLOVAKIA
   The most important literary awards in Czechoslovakia are the Czechoslovak State Prize of Klement Gottwald, which continues a CZECHOSLOVAK NATIONAL AWARD, granted since 1920, and the title "National Artist." Publishers' prizes are directed to recognizing the best book issued by each firm during the year,

such as the Mlada Fronta, Nase Vojsko, and the Melantrich Prize (not awarded since World War II).
   Additional literary awards are various city prizes: PRAGUE PRIZE, an award presented on the Anniversary of the February Revolution, for "the best creative work, which has enriched human knowledge, contributed to the solution of tasks imposed by socialist construction, and furthered the development of culture in the capital of Prague;" BRNO PRIZE, awarded on the anniversary of the liberation of the town of Brno by the Soviet army on April 26; BRATISLAVA PRIZE for the best work in a five year period pertaining to the town of Bratislava, and awarded on the anniversary of its liberation.
   Prizes are also awarded in honor of Czech and Slovak writers: Julius FUCIK PRIZE for prose; Petr BEZRUC PRIZE; Jiri MAHEN PRIZE; Frano KRAL PRIZE for the "best literary work for youth;" Jaroslav HASEK PRIZE; I KRASKO PRIZE for "best first work of poetry."
   Literary competitions held regularly or to mark special occasions include: Czechoslovak ANTIFASCIST FIGHTERS' FEDERATION ANNUAL LITERARY COMPETITION; and the CZECHOSLOVAK TWENTIETH ANNIVERSARY LITERARY CONTEST, which will end on May 9, 1965.
CZECHOSLOVAK LITERARY AWARDS
   CZECHOSLOVAK NATIONAL
      ARTIST
   CZECHOSLOVAK STATE
      PRIZE OF KLEMENT
      GOTTWALD
   CZECHOSLOVAK WRITER
      PRIZE
   MELANTRICH PRIZE
   MLADA FRONTA AWARD
   NASE VOJSKO PRIZE
                        C-6.

Finland										375

DENMARK
The most extensive public recognition of Danish writers is in
the form of Danish government
Grants to Authors. In addition to
these stipends, the Danish Ministry for Cultural Affairs participates
with the Danish Authors' Association in the granting of other literary prizes: Andersen Prize,
Danish Authors' Colleagues' Prize
of Honor, Danish Authors' Lyric
Prize, the Ewald and Oehlenschläger
Scholarships, and Holberg Medal.
  Publishers' awards include:
Årets Kritikerpris of the Danish
Publishers' Association, and the
Gyldendal Prize.
    Among the literary honors
presented to Danish novelist Martin
Andersen Nexö (1869-1954) was
the celebration of his eightieth
birthday in 1949 as a national
holiday.
    Sources of Information--Letter
from Det Kongelige Bibliotek (The
Royal Library, Christiansgade 8,
Copenhagen) giving prizes and
prize-winners, mostly from the
publication, "Forfatteren." Letter
from Danish Information Office
(588 Fifth Avenue, New York
36) describing and giving winners
of eight major literary awards.
Articles from "Bogens Verden,"
and "Bibliotekaren," such as that
by Eva Holst on Danish Prizes for
Children's and Youth's Books.
DANISH LITERARY AWARDS
    AARESTRUP PRIZE
    ANCKER PRIZE
    ANDERSEN PRIZE
    ÅRETS KRITIKERPRIS
    BLICHER PRIZE
    DANISH ACADEMY'S PRIZE
    DANISH AUTHORS' COLLEAGUES'
        PRIZE OF HONOR
    DANISH AUTHORS LYRIC
        PRIZE
    DANISH PRIZE FOR CHIL-
        DREN'S AND YOUTH'S BOOKS
    DANISH STATE GRANTS TO
        AUTHORS
    DRACHMAN PRIZE

    EWALD SCHOLARSHIP
    GYLDENDAL PRIZE
    HOLBERG MEDAL
    NORDISK RADS LITERATURE
        PRIZE
    OEHLENSCHLÄGER SCHOLAR-
        SHIP
    PONTOPPIDAN PRIZE
    SELSKABET PRIZE   C-7.
FINLAND
    Government salaries for crea-
tive work, and Finnish State
prizes are among the most important literary honors in Finland,
including the FELLOWSHIP OF
THE STATE ACADEMY (VAL-
TION AKATEMIO-APURAHA);
and the FELLOWSHIP OF THE
FINNISH CULTURAL FUND
(SUOMEN KULTTUURIRAHASTON
APURAHA).
    Publishers' prizes (Karisto
Company, Otava), and Founda-
tion grants and awards (Kivi
Foundation, Kordelin Foundation,
Leino Foundation, Wihuri Founda-
tion) also offer significant en-
couragement to writers, as do
the city prizes of Tampere,
and the writers' groups prizes
(Finnish Literature Society Award,
Finnish Literary Union Award)
    Sources of Information--
Letter from Embassy of Finland.
(1900 24th Street, N.W., Washing-
ton 8, D.C.) listing 17 major
Finnish literary honors and prize-
winners.
FINNISH LITERARY AWARDS
    FINNISH CULTURAL FOUNDA-
        TION AWARD
    FINNISH GOVERNMENT
        SALARIES FOR CREATIVE
        WORK
    FINNISH LITERATURE
        SOCIETY AWARD
    FINNISH LITERATURE UNION
        PRIZE
    FINNISH STATE PRIZE FOR
        LITERATURE
    JANTTI PRIZE
    KARISTO COMPANY PRIZE
    KIVI FOUNDATION PRIZE
    KORDELIN PRIZE

LEINO PRIZE
OTAVA PRIZE
PAULAHARJU PRIZE
TALVIO PRIZE
TAMPERE PRIZE
TOPELIUS-PALKINTO
WIHURI   FOUNDATION
AWARD   C-8.

FRANCE

The best-known French literary prizes are the four end-of-
the-year awards: Goncourt,
Fémina, Interallié, and Renaudot,
and the literary honors (including
membership) of Académie Française, such as the Grand Prix
de Littérature, and the Grand
Prix du Roman.

The many annual literary
awards are generally given by
cultural groups, publishers, writers' professional organizations,
and memorial foundations rather
than by the government of France,
or of Provinces or Cities--al-
though several literary prizes are
granted with the title "Prix de
Paris." The number of annual
prizes exceeds 500 (Brockhaus
7:275), including awards for "best
works," manuscripts. The entire
literary achievement of a writer
may be recognized by membership
in a number of Academies (Georges
Duhamel and Henri Mondor belong
to 5 major academies), or by
official government recognition in
the form of a state decoration
(Romain Gary is a Chevalier of
the Légion d'Honneur).

A number of French prizes are
given on a European or an International basis to non-French writers for books in French, or for
works translated into French.
Additional significant awards are
the newly established HERMES
NOVEL PRIZE, whose jury--
laureates of the five major French
literary prizes--awarded the 1962
prize to Philippe Jaccottet for
L'obscurité;" the James JOYCE
PRIZE (given in 1960 to Maurice
Clavel for "Le temps de

Chartres"); the JULES PRIZE,
an award by a jury of men for
the best book by a woman,
granted initially in 1960 to
Annabel, wife of the painter
Bernard Buffet for her book, "L'a-
mour quotidien;" and the Sylvio
PELLICO PRIZE of 1.000 fr for
a work dealing with the fundamentals of politics, ethnology or
ideology and granted in 1956
to Hungarian writers in exile, as
a group.

Among the many French literary
honors once significant prizes
but now no longer awarded are:
awards for American and English
writing reciprocating the Fémina
Prize, such as the PRIX FÉMINA-
VIE HEUREUSE ANGLAIS (known
after 1938 as the STOCK PRIZE),
granted for 20 years (1920-1939)
for "the best English work suitable for translation into French;"
and the AMERICA-FRANCE
AWARD, reciprocal of the
FÉMINA-AMÉRICAIN, for a French
book to be translated and published in the United States by
Harcourt Brace; HEINEMANN
PRIZE (formerly NORTHCLIFFE
AND BOOKMAN'S PRIZE),
English prize for French letters
(1934-1936); PRIX FÉMINA-
AMÉRICAIN, established in 1932
and continued for some years,
honoring a book of imaginative
writing in prose or poetry "most
worthy of expressing to France
the spirit and character of America."

Other former prizes are:
PRIX BALZAC, founded by Sir
Basile Zaharoff, and bringing a
20.000 fr prize to an unknown
writer, the first of whom in
1922/23 was Jean Giraudoux with
"My friend from Limousin;"
PRIX BEAUJOUR, offered by
Académie de Marseille for novels
of the sea (granted in 1933 to
Edouard Peisson for his entire
work);   PRIX BINOUX

OF THE ACADÉMIE DES SCI-
ENCES OF PARIS, given two times
to George Alfred Sarton, Belgian
science historian; PRIX BREN-
TANO, an annual 25.000 fr prize
offered for several years to "encourage Franco-American cultural
relations by bringing to the American public in translation each
year a book which will illustrate
eminently the French cultural
ideal" (won by Jean Giono in 1929
with "Hill of Destiny," the translated title of "Colline," and Jeanne
Galzy in 1930 with "Burnt offer-
ings"); PRIX CARVEN, offered for
a book with a "good" woman
character, won in 1957 by F.
Hebrard for "Month of September;" PRIX PAUL FLAT, annual
award of 1.000 fr (whose winners
include: 1924--Joseph Kessel,
"Pilot and observer," in "Pure
in heart;" 1928--Julien Green,
"Closed garden;" 1931--Daniel-Rops;"
"Notre inquiétude"); the GRAND
PRIX FLAUBERT of the 1920's
bringing a 30.000 fr premium
to Pierre Mille, and Jean Violles;
PRIX GRINGOIRE, whose 10.000
fr premium for "best reporting
which appears in book form after
its appearance in a journal" was
won by Chadourne, with a report
on China; and Daniel-Rops, with
"Two men and me;" OSIRIS
PRIZE, 100.000 fr "awarded
for the whole of a literary career"
triennially by five academies of
the Institut de France for "the
most remarkable work on any
subject," given in 1924 to Tiarko
Richepin, for "The Academician."
    Significant awards no longer
offered include: PRIX DE LA
PLÉIADE, of Éditions Gallimard
(won in 1944 by Marcel Mouloudji
for "Enrico"); PRIX DE LA
PRESSE LATINE, a 200.000 fr
prize for a writer less than 35
years of age of Latin origin;
PRIX DE LA RENAISSANCE, an
annual award given 1922-1935
(won in 1923 by P. Morand with

"Closed all night"); PRIX
STENDHAL, for a prose work by
a young author, won by Robert
Lafforet.
    Sources of Information: The
most complete record of any
literary prizes is the serial,
"Guide des Prix Littéraires,"
supplemented with Additif between
periodic revisions (latest edition
1959, with two supplements for
1960 and 1961). This work
describes literary prizes (French,
French language, Belgian and
Swiss, European, and some International), and lists prize-winners
and titles of winning books. Information about current French
prize winners is also found in
English language annuals of encyclopedias (Americana, Britannica, International) and
almanacs (World Almanac, Information Please Almanac); Genêt,
Letter from Paris," appearing
each December in the "New
Yorker;" and the "French News,"
quarterly news bulletin of the
Cultural Services of the French
Embassy, Washington, D.C.
French literary prizes are most
frequently reported and described
of all foreign literary awards
mentioned in English reference
and periodical publications. Other
English language descriptions are
in "Oxford Companion to French
Literature;" Sydney Braun,
"Dictionary of French Literature;"
and special articles in "Publishers'
Weekly," as Morrison Fitch, "The
French literary prizes," December
22, 1951; "Partisan Review,"
Joseph Frank, "Notes on the literary situation, July 1951; "Time,"
("Sex and salvation; French literary prizes," "Jackpots"). Articles
on specific awards include the
Goncourt (Chapsal, "Goncourt
prize winner"); Fémina ("Hatpins
and the Fémina," in "Time"); and
the Académie Française membership and awards: André Maurois,
"The forty immortals," with

illustrations showing Georges
Duhamel in uniform of the Acadé-
mie; the "LIFE" report of Jean
Cocteau's Académie installation,
"Académie Française makes a
rebel immortal," with colored
portraits of Cocteau in Académie
robes; "Room for immortals," and
"Spoofing the Academy" in "News-
week;" the "New York Times
Magazine" article, "Immortals all"
by Maurice Kurtz; and the article
in "Time"--"Green fever."
FRENCH LITERARY AWARDS
  ACADÉMIE DES INSCRIP-
    TIONS ET BELLES-LETTRES
    PRIZES
  ACADÉMIE FRANÇAISE GRAND
    PRIX DE LITTÉRATURE
  ACADÉMIE FRANÇAISE GRAND
    PRIX DU ROMAN
  ACADÉMIE FRANÇAISE PRIZE
  ACADEMY OF 13 PRIZE
  ALLAIS PRIZE
  AMBASSADORS PRIZE
  ANTIRACISM PRIZE
  APOLLINAIRE PRIZE
  BROQUETTE-GONIN GRAND
    PRIZE
  CAZES PRIZE
  CLAIROUIN PRIZE
  COMBAT PRIZE
  COURTELINE PRIZE
  DELACROIX PRIZE
  DELARUE PRIZE
  DEUX MAGOTS PRIZE
  DUCA FOUNDATION PRIZE
  DUMONCEL PRIZE
  DURCHON-LOUVET PRIZE
  ENFANTS TERRIBLES PRIZE
  ENGHIEN-LES-BAINS GRAND
    LITERARY PRIZE FOR
    DRAMA
  "L'EXPRESS" PRIZE
  FANTASIA PRIZE
  FÉDÉRATION DES ARTISTES
    PRIZE
  FÉMINA PRIZE
  FÉMINA-VACARESCO PRIZE
  FÉNÉON PRIZE
  THE FIVE PRIZE
  FOUR JURIES PRIZE
  FRATERNITÉ PRIZE
  FRENCH CATHOLIC GRAND

  PRIZE FOR LITERATURE
  FRENCH CRITICS PRIZE
  FRENCH DRAMATIC AUTHORS
    AND COMPOSERS SOCIETY
    GRAND PRIZE
  FRENCH GRAND LITERARY
    PRIZE FOR NOVELLAS
  FRENCH GRAND NATIONAL
    PRIZE FOR LETTERS
  FRENCH GRAND NOVEL
    PRIZE
  FRENCH GRAND PRIZE FOR
    ADVENTURE NOVELS
  FRENCH GRAND PRIZE FOR
    CHILDREN'S LITERATURE
  FRENCH GRAND PRIZE FOR
    ESPIONAGE NOVELS
  FRENCH GRAND PRIZE FOR
    HUMOR
  FRENCH GRAND PRIZE FOR
    MYSTERY STORIES
  FRENCH GRAND PRIZE FOR
    YOUTH LITERATURE
  FRENCH LITERARY CRITICS
    GRAND PRIZE
  FRENCH POETS GRAND PRIZE
  FRENCH POPULAR NOVEL PRIZE
  FRENCH YOUTH PRIZE
  FRIEDENSPREIS DES DEUTSCHEN
    BUCHHANDELS
  GENS DE LETTRES SOCIETY
    PRIZES
  GILES PRIZE
  GOBERT PRIZE
  GONCOURT PRIZE
  HACHETTE PRIZE
  HERRIOT PRIZE
  HISTORIA PRIZE
  IBSEN PRIZE
  INSTITUT DE POÈTES PRIZES
  INTERALLIÉ PRIZE
  JACOB PRIZE
  JUNGMANN PRIZE
  KAMINSKY PRIZE
  KAUFFMANN PRIZE
  LANGLOIS PRIZE
  LAPORTE PRIZE
  LIBERTY PRIZE
  LIBRAIRES DE FRANCE
    LITERARY PRIZE
  MACÉ PRIZE
  MANDAT DES POÈTES
  MAY PRIZE
  MÉDICIS PRIZE

NAUTILUS PRIZE
PARIS CITY PRIZE
PARIS GRAND PRIZE FOR
   LITERATURE
PARIS PRIZE
PAULÉE DE MEURSAULT
   PRIZE
PELLIOT PRIZE
PELMAN DRAMA PRIZE
POE PRIZE
QUAI DES ORFEVRES PRIZE
RÉFLEXION PRIZE
RENAUDOT PRIZE
RENCONTRE PRIZE
RÉSISTANCE LITERARY
   PRIZE
RICHELIEU PRIZE
RONSARD PRIZE
SAHARA GRAND PRIZE FOR
   LITERATURE
SAINTE-BEUVE PRIZE
SAINTOUR PRIZE
SCARRON PRIZE
SCHWEITZER PRIZE
THREE CROWNS LITERARY
   PRIZE
TOULOUSE FLORAL GAMES
"U" PRIZE
UNANIMOUS PRIZE
VÉRITÉ GRAND PRIZE
VERLAINE PRIZE
VERNE PRIZE
WEIL PRIZE   C-9.
GERMANY
   The many literary prizes and
awards in Germany (a recent
estimate set the total of annual
literary premiums as "in excess
of three million marks") are
granted by national public agencies
(German Youth Book Prize of the
Bundesministerium für Familien-
und Jugendfragen), national learned
societies, and professional groups,
but the large majority of literary
awards are the continuing prizes
offered by regional and city
governments and cultural groups.
Some of Germany's most famous
literary honors are no longer
awarded. These include--in addition to the Kleist Prize, which
was not reestablished after World
War II--the KLOPSTOCK PRIZE of

1953; the LITERATURPREIS DER
STADT LEIPSIG; LYRIKPREIS
DER KOLONNE, given Horst
Lange in 1932; LYRIK-PREIS
DER "DAME," awarded Rudolf
Hagelstange in 1942; the Carl
SCHÜNEMANN-PREIS of the
Bremen publisher, which was
awarded for the "best" novel to
Ernst Wiechert in 1932 for "Jeder-
mann;" the PREIS DER DEUTS-
CHEN BUCHGEMEINSCHAFT; the
SÜDOSTDEUTSCH KULTURWERKE
LITERATURE PRIZE OF 1953;
the George KAISER-PREIS of
Munich; "DIE NEUE LINIE",
15.000 mark novel prize of 1932
and 1933; the Theodor WOLFF
PRIZE of "Stiftung Die Welt," an
annual journalism award of 30.000
DM; the FRIEDER LITERARY
AWARD, given to David Weiss for
"Guild Makers;" the Heinrich
HEINE PRIZE OF GERMAN
EXILES, won in 1938 by H.W.
Katz, with "The Fishmans."
   Also, such "specific occasion
awards" as the Carl SCHURZ
CENTENNIAL GRANT for a West
German Newsman, of 1952; the
HARPER & HEINEMANN PRIZE
of $2,500, offered for the trans-
lation rights of a new German
novel or biography in 1930, and
won by Bernhard Guttman with
"Ambition."
   Additional current awards are
the German government honor,
POUR LE MÉRITE, for distin-
guished cultural achievement,
recently conferred on Gerhard
Ritter; the DEUTSCHE HOCH-
SEEFISCHEREI-PREIS, won in
1957 by Felix Berner and by
Hans Lipinsky-Gottersdorf with
"Finsternis über den Wasser;" and
the publishers' prizes: "TEXTE
UND ZEICHEN" novel prize
established in 1956; WELT IM
BUCH (Verlag Kurt Desch), won
by Rudiger Syberberg in 1955,
and Hebert Frank in 1956;
FRANZ SCHNEIDERVERLAG
JUGENDBUCHPREIS for "Das

beste Mädchenbuch" in 1954.
Also, many prizes of private
foundations and organizations:
Rudolf Alexander SCHRÖDER
STIFTUNG LITERATURE PRIZE,
to be awarded in Bremen for the
first time in 1962; the Heinrich
STAHL PRIZE of the Judischen
Gemeinde, Berlin, given in 1959
to Ernst Schnabel for his television writing--"Anne Frank--Spur
eines Kinde," and to Hans Scholz
for his radio program--"Am
grünen Strand der Spree;"
MEERSBURGERDROSTE-PREIS,
a 2000 DM biennial award, given
in 1960 to Nelly Sachs; BLAUER-
RING DER DEUTSCHEN
DICHTUNG, presented initially
in 1953 to Hermann Burte;
GANGHOFER PRIZE, offering
5000 DM each year "to a distinguished German writer;" Adelbert
STIFTER LITERATURE PRIZE of
the Schutzgemeinschaft Deutscher
Wald, Koblenz, awarded for
nature writing of Heino Landrock
(1955), Friedrich Schnack (1956),
and Erich Hornsmann (1958); and
the FREUDENTHAL PRIZE, given
in 1957 to Adolf Woderich; and
two drama awards: DRAMA-
TIKERPREIS DES DEUTSCHEN
BUHNENVEREINS, and MANN-
HEIMER NATIONAL THEATERS
WETTBEWERBE.
Additional city and regional
prizes are those of;
AALEN--SCHUBERT LITERA-
    TURE PRIZE, 2000 DM
    awarded biennially on March
    26 since 1956
AMBERG--NORDGAUEHREN-
    PREIS and NORDGAUEHREN-
    PLAKETTE, cultural prizes
    established in 1952
BREGENZ--Hugo von MONTFORT
    PRIZE, an encouragement
    grant first awarded in 1957
FREIBURG--Reinhold SCHNEI-
    DER PRIZE, biennial prize
    established in 1960 with
    5000 DM premium
HAGEN--Karl Ernst OSTHAUS

PRIZE, biennial cultural honor
    given since 1946
NURNBERG--NURNBERG
    KULTURPREIS, for Art and
    Science, established in 1952
PADERBORN--PADERBORN
    KULTURPREIS, given in
    1961 initially to Therese
    Pöhler
PRÜM/EIFEL--LOTHER
    PRIZE, annual award since
    1959 for a novel
REGENSBURG--ALBERTUS
    MAGNUS MEDAL, granted
    since 1949 in recognition of
    achievement or as an en-
    couragement award to Georg
    Britting (1961), Florian
    Seidl (1953), Heinz Schau-
    wecker (1954)
SCHWEINFURT-SCHWEINFURT
    BUCHPREIS, established in
    1961 by the city, certain
    industrial groups, and the
    publisher, "Neues Forum,"
    offering 6000 DM for a novel
    (with 2nd and 3rd prizes of
    3000 and 2000 DM), and
    4000 DM for a book about
    politics
STEIERMARK--Peter ROSEGGER
    PRIZE, several awards
    granted each year since 1951
SUDETENDEUTSCH LANDS-
    MANNSCHAFT--CULTURAL
    PRIZE of 5000 DM, pre-
    sented each year in Pfingsten
    --awarded in 1958 to Erwin
    Guido Kolbenheyer for his
    entire literary work
    Sources of Information--Letter
from "Internationes," non-profit
informational organization, with
typed information from "Fischer
Weltalmanach;" letters from libraries and cultural and educational groups, such as Kulturamt,
Stadt Braunschweig (Postfach
507); and rules and letters from
many prize-awarding agencies
and groups.
    In addition to English language
sources ("Britannica Book of the
Year," "Americana Annual,"

"New International Yearbook"),
German language sources include:
"Der Grosse Brockhaus" article,
"Literaturpreis;" Trumpf, "Preise,
Praemien, Privilegien," which lists
German and other awards in many
areas of achievement; and three
serial publications: "Fischer
Weltalmanach;" "Kurschners
Deutsche Literatur-Kalendar,"
with an alphabetical list of Ger-
man language prizes; and--reported
as a significant source of prize
information, but not seen--"Der
Journalist. Handbuch der Pub-
lizistic."
GERMAN LITERARY AWARDS
  BAECK PRIZE
  BALZAC PRIZE
  BAYERISCHE AKADEMIE DER
    SCHÖNEN KÜNSTE LITERA-
    TURE PRIZE AND AWARD
    OF HONOR
  BERLIN DRAMA PRIZE
  BERLIN PRESS GOLDEN
    PLAQUE
  BERTELSMANN PRIZES
  BIELEFELD CULTURAL
    PRIZE
  BODENSEE LITERATURE
    PRIZE
  BREMEN LITERATURE PRIZE
  BÜCHNER PRIZE
  BUNDESVERBAND DER
    DEUTSCHEN INDUSTRIE
    PRIZE
  CAMPE PRIZE
  COLOGNE LITERATURE
    PRIZE
  DARMSTADT "BOOK OF MAY"
  DEUTSCHE AKADEMIE FÜR
    SPRACHE UND DICHTUNG
    TRANSLATION PRIZE
  DROSTE-HÜLSHOFF PRIZE
  DROSTE LITERATURE PRIZE
  DUDEN PRIZE
  EYTH PRIZE
  FISCHER DRAMA PRIZE
  FISCHER PRIZE
  FONTANE PRIZE
  FÖRDERUNG DES SCHRIFT-
    TUMS PRIZE
  FRIEDENSPREIS DES VER-
    BANDES DER KRIEGSBE-

    SCHÄDIGTEN
  FRIEDLANDPREIS DER
    HEIMKEHRER
  FREIHERR VOM STEIN
    PRIZES
  GERMAN CRITICS' PRIZE
  GERMAN STAGE ORGANIZA-
    TIONS DRAMA PRIZE
  GERMAN YOUTH BOOK PRIZE
  GERMAN YOUTH BOOK PRIZE
    OF FRANZ SCHNEIDER PUB-
    LISHING COMPANY
  GERSTÄCKER PRIZE
  GOETHE PLAQUE
  GOETHE PRIZE (Frankfurt)
  GOSLAR CULTURAL PRIZE
  GRIMM BROTHERS PRIZE
  GRUPPE 47 PRIZE
  GUTENBERG PLAQUE
  HAUPTMANN PRIZE
  HEBEL MEMORIAL MEDAL
  HEBEL MEMORIAL PRIZE
  HESSE PRIZE
  HEYDT CULTURAL PRIZE
  HÖRSPIELPREIS DER
    KRIEGSBLINDEN
  HÖRSPIELPREIS VON RADIO
    BREMEN
  IMMERMANN PRIZE
  JACOBI PRIZE
  JUNGE GENERATION PRIZE
  KARLSRUHE CULTURAL
    PRIZE
  KELLER VERLAG DRAMA
    PRIZE
  KIEL CULTURAL PRIZE
  KLEIST PRIZE
  KLEPPER PLAQUE
  KOGGE RING PRIZE
  KRIEGSBESCHÄDIGTEN ART
    PRIZE
  KULTURBUCH NOVEL PRIZE
  LANGEN-MÜLLER LITERATURE
    PRIZE
  LESSING PRIZE
  LONGFELLOW-GLOCKE
  LOTHAR PRIZE
  MAINZ ACADEMY PRIZE
  MÖSER MEDAL
  MUNICH LITERATURE PRIZES
  NIEDERSÄCHSEN KUNSTPREIS
  NORDRHEIN-WESTFALEN
    GRAND ART PRIZES
  OLDENBURG DRAMA PRIZE

OSTDEUTSCH KULTURRAT
PLAQUE
PAUL MEDAL
PIRKHEIMER MEDAL
RAABE PRIZE
REUCHLIN PRIZE FOR ART
AND CULTURE
REUTER PRIZE
RHEIN-RUHR LITERATURE
PRIZE
RHEINLAND-PFALZ ART PRIZE
SAARLAND ART PRIZE
SAILER PRIZE
SCHILLER MEMORIAL PRIZE
SCHILLER PRIZE OF
MANNHEIM
SCHLESWIG-HOLSTEIN ART
PRIZE
SCHLEUSSNER-SCHÜLLER
PRIZE
SCHWEITZER BOOK PRIZE
                        C-10.
GERMANY, EAST (DEUTSCHE
DEMOKRATISCHE REPUBLIK)
Many East German literary and
cultural prizes are awarded and
financed by the national govern-
ment (as the East German National
Prize for Literature), and by the
East German Ministry for culture,
and by cities and other adminis-
trative units of local government.
These literary honors are often
granted each year on the Founding
Day of the DDR (October 7), or
on the DDR Independence Day
(October 31).

Second to the national government in number of literature
awards is the state labor union
of the DDR--FDGB: Freie
Deutsche Gewerkschaftsbunde. An
additional literary honor is membership in the Institut für Schriftsteller, whose members have
included such well-known East
German authors as Anna Seghers,
Berthold Brecht, Arnold Zweig,
and Ludwig Renn.

Sources of Information--Letter
from Dr. Heinrich Roloff, Ab-
teilungsdirektor, Deutsche Staats-
bibliothek (East Berlin 8), listing
and describing 20 literary prizes

of East Germany, with prize-
winners through 1960/1961. German language sources: same as
for West Germany, and in addition: "Der Bibliothekar,"
Zeitschrift für das Bibliothekwesen,
issued by the Zentralinstitut für
Bibliothekwesen (Georgenkirchstrasse 24, Berlin C-2, East
Germany).

EAST GERMAN LITERARY
AWARDS
BAIMLER MEDAL
BART-CISINSKI PRIZE
BECHER PRIZE
BLECHEN PRIZE
BRINCKMANN PRIZE
DOMOWINA LITERATURE
PRIZE
DRESDEN LITERATURE
PRIZE
EAST GERMAN MINISTRY
FOR CULTURE PRIZES
EAST GERMAN NATIONAL
PRIZE FOR LITERATURE
EAST GERMAN ORDER FOR
SERVICE TO THE FATHER-
LAND
EAST GERMAN PEACE
MEDAL
EAST GERMAN WRITERS
ASSOCIATION PRIZE
FONTANE PRIZE
FRANKFORT-ODER ART
PRIZE
FREIE DEUTSCHE GEWERK-
SCHAFTSBUNDE LITERA-
TURE PRIZE
GOETHE PRIZE OF EAST
BERLIN
GOETHE PRIZE OF EAST
GERMANY
GUTENBERG PRIZE OF
LEIPZIG
HALLE ART PRIZE
HEINE PRIZE
HELDEN DER ARBEIT
HERVORRAGENDER WISSEN-
SCHAFTLER DES VOLKES
LESSING PRIZE
MANN PRIZE
MARX ART PRIZE
NEXÖ ART PRIZE
REUTER ART PRIZE

SCHILLER RELIEF
WAR AGAINST FASCISM
    MEDAL
WEIMAR LITERATURE AND
    ART PRIZE
WEINERT ART PRIZE
WEISKOPF PRIZE   C-11.

HUNGARY

Major literary prizes currently
granted on a continuing basis in
Hungary are four awards pre-
sented on specified dates by
official state organizations (Presi-
dential Council, Ministry of Cul-
ture, Hungarian Trade Unions
Council): Attila Prize, Gabor
Prize, Kossuth Prize, and Szot
Literary Prize. Pre-World War
II prizes that received international
notice include the JOKAI PRIZE
FOR HUNGARIAN NOVEL. In
1934 the HUNGARIAN LITERARY
PETOFI SOCIETY'S HONORARY
DIPLOMA was presented as
"highest literary honor" to Selma
Lagerlöf.

Sources of Information--Letters
from: Legation of the Hungarian
People's Republic (2437 15th
Street, N.W., Washington, D.C.);
and Dr. Magda Jóbord, Head, National Széchenyi Library (Muzeum
Korut 14-16, Budapest 7).

HUNGARIAN LITERARY AWARDS
    ATTILA PRIZE
    GABOR PRIZE
    KOSSUTH PRIZE
    SZOT LITERARY PRIZE
                        C-12.

ICELAND

In Iceland major "public or
official" recognition of authors
takes the form of a regular yearly
grant or salary from the Icelandic
government, which is included
each year in the budget of the
Icelandic government. Less
regular prizes are awarded by
private publishers, such as
Almenna and Helgafell.

Iceland's best-known writer--
Halldor Kiljan Laxness (1902-   )--
received both the Stalin Prize
(1953) and the Nobel Prize for

Literature (1955).
Sources of Information--Letters
from Landsbokasafn Islands
(Icelandic National Library,
Reykjavik); from Icelandic Minis-
try of Foreign Affairs (Reykjavik).

ICELANDIC LITERARY AWARDS
    ALMENNA BOKAFELAGSO
        PRIZE
    HELGAFEL PRIZE
    ICELANDIC STATE BROAD-
        CAST SERVICE AUTHORS'
        FUND AWARD
    ICELANDIC STATE BROAD-
        CAST SERVICE BIRTHDAY
        FUND AWARD
    ICELANDIC STATE GRANTS
        TO AUTHORS
                        C-13.

IRELAND

Contemporary literary prizes
in Ireland are generally granted
by three organizations: Irish
Arts Council; Gaelic League;
and Irish Academy of Letters.

Additional awards made during
the 1930's and no longer granted
include: IRISH WOMAN WRIT-
ERS' CLUB PRIZE, a nonfiction
award granted in 1939 to Mary
Colum for "From these roots;"
IRISH NOVEL PRIZE, a £150
premium offered for "the best
novel in Irish," by the National
Department of Education, divided
in 1931 between Barra O'Caoch-
laigh, and Sean O'Ruadhain.

Sources of Information--Letters
from R.J. Hayes, Director,
National Library of Ireland
(Kildare Street, Dublin); Irish
Arts Council (70 Merrion Square,
Dublin); Gaelic League, including
press releases about awards pre-
sented at the annual festival.

IRISH LITERARY AWARDS
    A E MEMORIAL PRIZE
    CASEMENT AWARD
    DEVLIN MEMORIAL FOUNDA-
        TION PRIZE
    GAELIC LEAGUE PRIZES
    GREGORY MEDAL
    GUINNESS POETRY AWARD
    HARMSWORTH LITERARY

AWARD
IRISH ACADEMY OF LETTERS
IRISH CREATIVE LITERATURE
PRIZE
IRISH PLAY PRIZE
IRISH POETRY PRIZES
MACAULAY FOUNDATION
FELLOWSHIPS
O'GROWNEY AWARD   C-14.

ITALY

Several hundred prizes for literature are offered each year in Italy by the Italian government, by municipalities, societies, academies, and publishers of books and reviews. Literary awards may be included among the general cultural recognition of a prize (as the Feltrinelli Prize, Italian National Prizes, Marzotto Prize, Rome Prize); they may be offered for various forms of writing (as the Gastoldi Prize, Novaro Prize, Naples Prize, Omnia Prize, Viareggio Prize), or for a single form of writing--as the Strega Prize, for novel; the Orvieto Prize, for children's literature; and the many prizes for poetry (35 of the approximately 100 Italian prizes listed in International Dictionary of Literary Awards, offer a prize for poetry, and 20 of these are granted for poetry only), such as the Cittadella Prize, Cervia Prize, Florence Prize (Premio Firenze), and the Chianciano Prize--which honors poetry as well as novels and journalism.

Two of the most significant Italian literary awards are granted for the "Best Book of the Year" (Bagutta Prize), and the "Best Seller of the Year" (Bancarella Prize).

Additional literary awards are the MARCHE PRIZE of Amici della Cultura (via Loggia 1, Ancona); BRACCO PRIZE, awarded in 1959 to G.C. Monti (poetry) and G. Tesini (Narrativa); CALABRIA LETTERARIA PRIZE offered for poetry, journalism, novel;

CASSINO PRIZE, granted in 1959 to N. Modica for "Il cuore di pietra;" COLLI EUGANEI PRIZE, including among winners Andrea Zanzotto; GELA PRIZE, awarded for poetry and journalism; LA GRANDE CERNITA PRIZE, presented such writers as Penelope Larcan Lanza; JUGLAR PRIZE FOR NOVEL AND POETRY; MASSAROSA PRIZE for novella, including other awards--AZIENDA DELLA VERSILIA PRIZE for monograph, and YORK PRIZE for poetry; O.C.R.I.L. PRIZE for novel, poetry and other forms of writing; PONTE PRIZE, awarded C. Francovich in 1955 for "Un anno di lotta a Firenze; PREMIO GRIFONE D'ORO, of Assoziane Pro Loco, Presso Enal Provinciale (via Cavour 15, Grosseto), offered since 1959, and granted in 1960 to Carlo Cassola; MEDALE D'ORO AL MERITO PROFESSIONALE of Confederaz. Gen. Ital. Professionalistie Artisti (20 via Romagnosi, Rome), honoring (1959) Aldo Palazzeschi, and (1960) Dino Buzzati Traverso, and Renato Angiolillio.

Older awards, offered before or immediately after World War II, which are not presently granted include: CORRIERE LOMBARDO PRIZE, given in 1946 to Carlo Levi for "Cristo si a fermata a Eboli;" FUSINATO FOUNDATION PRIZE, won by Rossi in 1933 with "Non erano Castelli in aria;" GRAND PRIX DIX, awarded in 1932 to Natalie Terni-Gialente; LA STAMPA PRIZE, offered by Turin's daily paper, and presented in 1931 to Corrado Alvaro for his entire literary work; BOLOGNA PRIZE, granted for several classes of literature, and won by Maria Puccini in 1933 with "La Prigione;" CERVINIA PRIZE, presented Giuseppe Marotta for "San Gennaro non dice mai no;" FRACCHIA PRIZE, given Arturo Loria in

1933 for "Il flauto magico;"
ITALIA LETTERARIA PRIZE, given
Carlo Emilio Gadda in 1929 for
"Deckhand."
Additional novel prizes are:
CASTELNUOVO GARFAGNANA
PRIZE, bringing a premium of L
100.000 in 1958 to S. Somigli;
BARI PRIZE, given in 1958 to
V. Di Mattia, and in 1959 to G.
Battaglia; Mario MOLES PRIZE,
awarded L. Saputi and C. M.
Setteneri in 1959.

The drama prize I RABDOMAN-
TI PRIZE of Centro di cicerche
teatrali (via Albani 27, Milan)
was won in 1961 by Galeazzo
Galeazzi with "La rupe delle
vergini."

Additional awards for children's
literature are the CASTELLO
PRIZE, sponsored by the Italian
National Commission for UNESCO,
divided equally in 1958 between
A. G. Dossena and B. Paltrinieri;
in 1959 by Dino Beretta and Roberto
Costa; and also won by Luigi
Ugolini (1957); the PREMIO
COLLODI of Milan, sponsored in
later years (1948-1956) by Comitato Nazionale per il Monumento
a Pinocchio, brought a premium
of 300.000 lire in 1956 to Fabio
Tombari for "Il libro di Tonino."

In the area of journalism,
additional prizes are the PREMIO
BRUNO REZZARA(via Borgogna 2,
Milan) presented in 1959 to Guido
Piovene; and the PREMIO NASTRO
D'ARGENTO of the Sindicate Naz.
Giornalistica Cinematografica
Ital. (via Basento 52, Rome),
honoring Pier Paolo Pasolini in
1960 for "soggetto" of the motion
picture, "La Notte Brava."

Among the numerous poetry
prizes are the ARTI PRIZE,
granted A. Parini in 1958;
BOCCADASSE PRIZE (via Fausto
Berretta 3-28, Genoa), presented
in 1958 to G. Gerini; CASTEL-
LAMMARE PRIZE given in 1959
to M. Grillandi; Ceccardo R.
CECCARDI PRIZE won by R.

Del Grata in 1958; CHIABERA
PRIZE, awarded S. Lo Piano
(1959); CHIETI PRIZE, granted
Gigino Morgione (1959) for "Una
vita;" CINZA-IRRADIO PRIZE,
awarded in 1959 to M. Gori;
COLUMBIAN PRIZE--a joint award
of the Columbian Academy, St.
Louis, U. S. A., and the "Pungolo
Verde" of Campobasso--including
among winners F. Boneschi
(1959) and Ersilia Nicodemi
(1961); COREGLIA PRIZE,
divided equally in 1961 between
Maruo Musciacchio and Emilia
Villoresi; FLORA PRIZE (via
Plinio 45, Milan), divided in 1959
between M. G. Ferraroni and E.
Villoresi; GHIANCIANO PRIZE of
L 1.000.000, won in 1959 by R.
Carrieri; LA SITUAZIONE PRIZE,
awarded G. Gramigna in 1958;
Giacomo LEOPARDI PRIZE
(Linda Samaritani, via Bitinia
19, Rome); A. MANCINI PRIZE,
granted F. L. Imbasciati in 1958);
DE MARIA PRIZE, won by M.
Musciacchio in 1959; MASTRO-
LONARDO PRIZE, awarded G.
Schiavi 1959); NICASTRO CITY
PRIZE, given in 1959 to A. Lo
Monaco; PARTENOPE PRIZE,
divided equally in 1959 between A.
Di Vadi and G. Costantini; LIVIO
RIZZI PRIZE, offered by Rovigo
and presented in 1960 to Mario
Bottari for "La Sagra di Villa-
marzana;" SELVA PRIZE, whose
1959 winner was G. M. Siercovich;
RENATO SERRA PRIZE, granted
in 1947 to Antonio Rinaldi for
"La notte;" VADO LIGURE PRIZE,
awarded R. Pascutto (1958).

Sources of Information--
Letters from some awarding
agencies, and from such official
and cultural groups and agencies
as: Presidenza del Consiglio
dei Ministri, Ufficio della Proprieta' Letteraria, Artistica,
Scientifica (via Boncompagni 15,
Rome) "Catalogue of Literary
Prizes Awarded in Rome"--23-
page typescript describing 51

Italian literary awards; Associazione Italiana Editora (via delle Muratte 25, Rome)--list of five prizes and information about Deledda prize; Italian Information Center (686 Park Avenue, New York 21)--letter from Dr. A. Zamparutti, Cultural Division, listing 16 major literary awards granted in Italy.

English sources, including Yearbooks of encyclopedias. Italian language serials, issued each year or more frequently, giving information about literary prizes in Italy include: Accademia Nazionale dei Lincei, "Annuario," which gives rules, prizes and lists some winners of honors granted by the Accademia, such as the Feltrinelli Prize, Italian National Prizes, and Novaro Prize; "Il Merito," issued annually either as a cumulated list of prizes and prize-winners or as a supplement to the basic volume; "Almanacco Letterario Bompiani," listing literary awards and prize winners by month--1960 edition lists prizes from September 1958 to September 1959; "Gran Premio," a monthly publication edited by Renato Righetti (via Don Minzoni 41 R, Spezia), carrying news of cultural awards and winners (the German annual "Fischer Welt-Almanach" includes a section on recent Italian literary prizes quoted, according to note, from "Gran Premio"). Two other notable sources of information on Italian literary awards are: Carlo L. Golino, "Italian Literary Prizes--1960 Edition," in Italian Quarterly, 4:16, p.43-55, a descriptive review of major awards prepared from information obtained during a year's fellowship residence in Italy; and Sergio Pacifici, "A guide to contemporary Italian literature," with incidental mention of authors winning such prizes as Viareggio, Strega, Chianciano.

ITALIAN LITERARY AWARDS
ALPI APUANE-PEA PRIZE
ALVARO PRIZE
AMICI DEL LIBRO PRIZE
AMICI DI VENEZIA PRIZE
AUDITORIUM PRIZES
BAGUTTA PRIZE
BALZAN PRIZE
BANCARELLA PRIZE
BERGAMO E PROVINCIA
  PRIZE
BORGIA PRIZE
BORLETTI PRIZE
BORSELLI PRIZE
BRAIBANTI PRIZE
BUAZZELLI PRIZE
CAPITOLINE WOLF PRIZE
CAPRI PRIZE
CARDUCCI PRIZE
CASALECCHIO PRIZE
CEPPO PRIZE
CERVIA PRIZE
CHIANCIANO PRIZES
CITTADELLA PRIZE
CIVITATE CHRISTIANA PRIZE
COSENZA PRIZE
CROTONE PRIZE
D'AMICO PRIZE
D'ANNUNZIO PRIZE
DAVID PRIZE
DELEDDA PRIZE
DE SARIO PRIZE
EINAUDI PRIZES
ENTE NAZIONALE PER LE
  BIBLIOTECHE POPULARI
  E SCOLASTICHE PRIZE
FALCO PRIZE
FELTRINELLI PRIZE
FIERA LETTERARIO PRIZE
FILA INES ED ADOLFO
  PRIZE
FLORENCE PRIZE
FONTE CIAPAZZI PRIZE
GASTALDI PRIZE
GIRAFFE PRIZE
GOLDEN BOOK PRIZE
GOLDEN MADONNA PRIZE
GOLDEN QUILL PRIZE
GUIDOTTI PRIZE
HEMINGWAY PRIZE
INDEPENDENT CULTURAL
  MOVEMENT PRIZE
INTERNATIONAL ACADEMY
  OF CULTURAL INFORMA-

TION PRIZE
INTERNATIONAL ALLIANCE
OF JOURNALISTS AND
WRITERS PRIZE
ITALIAN ACADEMY OF
POETRY PRIZE
ITALIAN CRITICS OF ART
PRIZE
ITALIAN CRITICS PRIZE
ITALIAN CULTURAL PRIZES
ITALIAN DRAMA INSTITUTE
PRIZE
ITALIAN MINISTER OF PUBLIC
EDUCATION PRIZE
ITALIAN NATIONAL PRIZE
KOCH PRIZE
LERICI-PEA PRIZE
IL LETTERATO PRIZE
LUPA DA GUBBIO PRIZE
MANZONI PRIZE
MARZOTTO PRIZE
MILAN PRIZE
MONDADORI PRIZE
MONTEFELTRO PRIZE
NAPLES PRIZE
NARCISO PRIZE FOR
POETRY
NARRATIVA PRIZE
NOI DONNE PRIZE
NOVARO PRIZE
OMEGNA PRIZE
OMNIA PRIZE
ORVIETO PRIZE
PAESTUM PRIZE
PARAGGI PRIZE
PASCOLI PRIZE
PAVESE PRIZE
PISA PRIZES
POZZALE PRIZE
PRATO PRIZE
PROCELLARIA PRIZE
PROSA LATINA PRIZE
PUCCINI-SENIGALLIA PRIZE
RICCIONE PRIZE
RIZZOLI PRIZE
ROME PRIZES
RUSTICHELLO DA PISA
PRIZES
SAINT VINCENT PRIZE
SALENTO PRIZE
SARZANA PRIZE
SICILY PRIZE
SIMONI PRIZE
STELLA MARIS PRIZE

STRADANOVA PRIZE
STREGA PRIZE
TARQUINIA-CARDARELLI
PRIZE
TERAMO PRIZE
TOR MARGANA PRIZE
TREBBO POETRY PRIZE
TRENTA PRIZE
TRICOLOR PRIZE
VALLOMBROSA PRIZE
VENICE PRIZE
VERGANI PRIZE
VERSILIA PRIZE
VIAREGGIO PRIZE
VILLA SAN GIOVANNI PRIZE
                    C-15.
LITHUANIA
   Lithuanian literary awards are
three prizes granted for Lithuanian
writers in exile--largest settle-
ment of Lithuanians "outside their
ethnographic borders" is the
approximate one million living in
the United States.
   Sources of Information--Letter
from Lithuanian Consulate, U.S.A.
Printed source: "Blue Book of
awards."
LITHUANIAN LITERARY AWARDS
   ADAI PRIZE
   DRAUGUS NOVEL AWARD
   LITHUANIAN WRITERS'
   ASSOCIATION AWARD
                    C-16.
LUXEMBOURG
   The major literary honor is the
Luxembourg Literary Prize,
granted by the National Minister
of Arts and Sciences for works in
Luxembourgese, French, and
German.
   Additional "Official" prizes are
announced from time to time--as
the drama prize offered by the
Minister of Arts and Sciences in
1961: two premiums of 20.000
fr each. The Luxembourg
Association of Writers in French
also offers a triennial award for
writing in French.
   Sources of Information--Letter
from Pierre Gregoire, Minister
of Arts and Sciences, Luxembourg; letter from Bibliothèque

Nationale (14e, Boulevard Royale) giving rules of the two prizes and SELF winners.

LUXEMBOURG LITERARY AWARDS

LUXEMBOURG ASSOCIATION OF WRITERS IN FRENCH PRIZE

LUXEMBOURG LITERARY PRIZE   C-17.

NETHERLANDS

Major Netherlands literary honors are offered by the Netherlands Ministry of Education, Arts and Sciences (Ministerie van Onderwijs, Kunsten en Wetenschappen), and by foundations (Campert Foundation--Essay Prize, Campert Prize, Huygens Prize, Vijverberg Prize) and by professional and book-trade groups, such as the Society of Netherlands Literature (granting the Van der Hoogt Prize, Wijnandts Francken Prize, May Prize) and C.P.N.B. (Comissie voor de Propaganda van het Nederlandse Boek, of the Vereeniging ter Bevordering van de Belangen des Boekhandels-- official Netherlands bookselling organization).

Additional prizes are the ARTISTS RESISTANCE MOVEMENT FOUNDATION LITERATURE PRIZE, granted since 1949; NETHERLANDS LITERARY CRITICS PRIZE, awarded in 1959 to W. L. M. E. van Loeuwen; Karel de GROTER PRIZE, won in 1957 by Jan With with "In den Metalen Stier."

Additional city and regional literary honors are: DEVENTER CULTURAL PRIZE, granted in 1959 to J. A. Rispens for "Voetsporen," collected verse; DRENTE CULTURAL PRIZE, honoring Jan Fabricius in 1957 for his entire literary work; GELDERLAND LITERATURE PRIZE, offered since 1954; LEYDEN CLASSICAL LITERATURE PRIZE, won in 1936 by Jan Fabricius with "Son of Marietta."

An additional award for children's literature is the "LETTERKUNDE" of the Dutch Ministry of Education in collaboration with the Youth Friends Association of New York--presented initially in 1956 to Jean Dulieu for "Francisco," and Cornelie A. Mees for "Demeters dochter."

Sources of Information--Letters and rules from some awarding agencies, especially from Dr. J. Hulsker, Head of Arts Section, Netherlands Ministry of Education, Arts and Sciences. Lists and descriptions of prizes from M. E.'t Hart, Director, Royal Netherlands Academy of Science (Koninklijke Nederlandse Akademie van Wetenschappen); Association for the Advancement of the Interests of the Book Trade (Vereeniging ter Bevordering van Belangen des Boekhandels). 'Winkler Prins Encyclopedie. Boek van het jaar" gives a list each year of major prize winners; two additional sources of Netherlands Literary Awards information (now out of print, and not seen) are: "G. H.'s--Gravesande Letterkundige prijzen in Nederland, 1952;" and "Schrijversalmanak" --last issue 1957. There is incidental mention of literary awards in "Delta," Netherlands' government review in English of arts, life and thought in the Netherlands; and information about early winners of the Japicx and Halbertsma prizes in E. S. de Jong's book.

Details of municipal and private prizes are reported available from: Netherlands Literature Museum and Documentation Centre (Nederlands Letterkundig Museum en Documentatie Centrum, Groenmarkt 1, The Hague, Netherlands).

NETHERLANDS LITERARY AWARDS

AMSTERDAM PRIZES

ARNHEM CULTURAL PRIZE

BAYLE PRIZE
BIJENKORF PRIZE
BOND VAN NEDERLANDSE
PRIZE
BRAND-VAN GENT PRIZE
CAMPERT PRIZE
DE VRIES PRIZE
DUTCH ACADEMY OF LET-
TERS PRIZE
DUTCH LITERATURE PRIZE
DUTCH MASTERSHIP OF
LETTERS PRIZE
DUTCH NOVELLA PRIZE
DUTCH PRIZE FOR THE BEST
CHILDREN'S BOOK
FRANK AWARDS
FRISIAN NOVEL PRIZE
GEERLIGS PRIZE
"GIDS" PRIZE
GOLDEN GOOSE-FEATHER
HALBERTSMA PRIZE
HILVARENBEEK PRIZES
HOLST PRIZE
HOOFT PRIZE
HUYGENS PRIZE
JACOBSON PRIZE
JAPICX PRIZE
K. R. O. POETRY PRIZE
KEMP PRIZE
KUNSTENAARVERZET YOUTH
LITERATURE PRIZE
NIJHOFF PRIZE
ORDER OF THE NETHER-
LANDS LION
PHILIPS PRIZE
"ROTTERDAMSE NUTS"
PRIZE
TOLLENS PRIZE
VAN DEN VONDEL PRIZE
VAN DER HOOGT PRIZE
VAN DER VIES PRIZE
VIJERBERG PRIZE
VISSER-NEERLANDIA PRIZE
WIJNANDTS FRANCKEN
PRIZE   C-18.
NORWAY
Norwegian State Grants for
Writers are the most wide-spread
public recognition for authors in
Norway. Other literary awards
granted by the Ministry of
Church and Education are the
Children- and Youth-Book Award.
Significant literary prizes are

administered by the Norwegian
Association of Writers (Bang
Prize, Stenersen Award), and by
the Literary Council (Osterholt
Prize).

Additional awards are the
Oscar AAGAARD ENDOWMENT
AWARD of N Kr 500, distributed
by the Board of the Norwegian
Association of Writers; and the
NORWEGIAN LIBRARIES' FUND
AWARD, based on use of an
author's books in public and
school libraries. This Norwegian
Public and School Libraries' Fund
for the Benefit of Norwegian
Authors is formed by an annual
contribution of such libraries to a
special fund for the benefit of
writers of Norway. The purpose
of the Fund is "to give living
Norwegian authors and widows of
Norwegian authors compensation
for the books of these authors
which are borrowed," as shown in
the Public and School Libraries
Law, Chapter 3, Compensation
to authors, May 13, 1955 (English
translation).

The KARI MEDAL, a Norwegian
youth book prize recently granted
by the Norsk Kuratorim for barne-
og ungdomsboker (Norwegian
Section of the International Board
on Books for Young People)
initially presented in 1957 to Nils
Slettermark for "Rull, rull, kjerre."

Sources of Information--Letter
from Norwegian Embassy (34th
and Massachusetts Avenue, N.W.,
Washington 7, D.C.) giving infor-
mation about Public Literary
Prizes, and listing the Private
Literary Prizes, as registered
with the Norwegian Association
of Writers, as of September 1960.
NORWEGIAN LITERARY AWARDS
BANG PRIZE
"BASTIAN" PRIZE
DAMM PRIZE
DOUBLOUG ENDOWMENT
PRIZE
NORWEGIAN CHILDREN-
AND YOUTH-BOOK

AWARD
NORWEGIAN LITERARY CRITICS PRIZE
NORWEGIAN STATE GRANTS
FOR WRITERS
OSTERHOLT PRIZE
STENERSEN AWARD
SUNNMØRE PRIZE
TRYSIL AWARD   C-19.
POLAND
Major literary prizes in Poland
are offered by the government
(Polish Prime Minister, and
Polish Minister of National Defense);
by social and cultural groups
(PAX, Polish P.E.N. Club,
Warsaw Student and Youth Clubs,
Marine League of the Friends of
Soldiers). City literary awards
are presented by Lodz, Poznan,
and Warsaw; and literary prizes
are given by the publications:
"Kultura;" "Nowa Kultura;"
"Przeglad Kulturalny;" "Zycie
Literackie."

Older Pre-World War II prizes,
no longer awarded, include the
POLISH NATIONAL PRIZE (1929--
F. Goetel; 1932--Rostworowski;
1933--Strug;1934--Dombrowska;
1935--Illakovics), and the
POLISH ACADEMY OF INDE-
PENDENTS PRIZE, won in 1940
by J. Wittlin with "Salt of the
earth."

Sources of Information--Letter
listing and describing prizes
from Dr. Bogdan Horodyski,
Director, Biblioteka Narodowa
(National Library, ul. Rakowiecka
6, Warsaw 12), and from "Kultura." Also, articles in the
"New York Times," and notes in
"P.E.N. Bulletin."

The Polish Library Associa-
tion annual, "Librarian's and
Bookseller's Guide," (not seen)
is reported to contain a list of
current literary prize winners
in Poland.
POLISH LITERARY AWARDS
KRZYWE KOLO PRIZE
"KULTURA" LITERARY
PRIZE

LODZ POETRY PRIZE
LODZ PRIZE
"NOWA KULTURA" PRIZE
PIETRZAK AWARDS
POLISH MINISTER OF
NATIONAL DEFENSE PRIZE
POLISH P.E.N. CLUB
PRIZES
POLISH PRIME MINISTER'S
AWARD FOR WRITING FOR
CHILDREN AND YOUTH
POLISH UNION OF SOCIALIST
YOUTH PROSE AWARD
POZNAN POETICAL
NOVEMBER PRIZE
"PRZEGLAD KULTURALNY"
PRIZE
WARSAW CITY PRIZE
WARSAW CITY PRIZE FOR
YOUNG POETS
WARSAW STUDENT AND
YOUTH AWARD FOR
YOUNG POETS
ZARUSKI LITERARY PRIZE
"ZYCIE LITERACKIE"
PRIZE   C-20.
PORTUGAL
The largest number of literary
prizes in Portugal are offered by
the government (S.N.I.--Secre-
tariado Nacional da Informacão;
and the Agencia Geral do Ultra-
mar, with four awards to en-
courage Portuguese writing on
overseas topics).

Other prizes are granted by
publishers (Atica Prize, "Livro
do Brasil"), by a newspaper
('Diaria de Noticias'), and by
geographic areas--Castilho Prize
offered by Camara Municipal de
Lisbon, and Costa da Sol Prize.

Additional literary honors
are membership in Academia das
Ciencias de Lisbon--Aquilino
Ribeiro, the novelist, was elected
to membership in 1958; and the
national decoration--Order of St.
James of the Sword, bestowed
upon Australian author Alan J.
Villiers.

Sources of Information--
Letters and award rules from
Secretariado Nacional da In-

formacão; Casa de Portugal
(447 Madison Avenue, New York);
from the Portuguese publishers'
association: Grémio Nacional dos
Editores e Livreiros (Largo de
Andaluz 16 1º, Lisbon 1); and
Instituto de Alta Cultura (Praça do
Principe Real 14, Lisbon 1).
PORTUGUESE LITERARY
AWARDS
 ALMEIDA PRIZE
 ANDRADE PRIZE
 ATICA PRIZE
 BARROS PRIZE
 BRAGANÇA PRIZE
 CASTELO BRANCO PRIZE
 CASTILHO PRIZE
 COSTA DO SOL PRIZE
 "DIARIO DE NOTICIAS"
  PRIZE
 ENES PRIZE
 HERCULANO PRIZE
 LINS DO REGO PRIZE
 MALHEIROS PRIZE
 MENDES PINTO PRIZE
 ORTIGÃO PRIZE
 PESSANHA PRIZE
 PORTUGUESE NATIONAL
  LITERARY PRIZES
 PORTUGUESE WRITERS
  SOCIETY PRIZES
 QUEIROZ PRIZE
 QUENTAL PRIZE
 SALA DE IMPRENSA PRIZE
 SANTOS PRIZE
 VAZ DE CARVALHO PRIZE
 VICENTE PRIZE   C-21.
RUMANIA
  The highest current literary
award in Rumania is the Rumanian
State Prize, an official honor
granted for achievement in many
areas of culture, and including
writers among the creative
workers recognized. The Ruma-
nian Academy Prizes are also
significant contemporary awards
for authors, as are the Rumanian
Ministry of Culture and Education
Prizes.
  Additional prizes are granted
as the LUCEAFARUL AWARDS, of
the bi-monthly magazine "Luceafarul," "which publishes particular-

ly the work of young writers,"
and honors the best works pub-
lished with grants ranging from
1.000 to 4.000 lei.
  Sources of Information--Letters
from the Rumanian Institute for
Cultural Relations with Foreign
Countries (35 Bd, Dacia,
Bucharest); and the Biblioteca
Centrala de Stat (Str. lon Ghica
nr 4, Bucharest 1) give descrip-
tions of prizes, and list winners
of the major awards.
RUMANIAN LITERARY AWARDS
 RUMANIAN ACADEMY
  PRIZES
 RUMANIAN GRAND PRIZE
 RUMANIAN MINISTRY OF
  CULTURE AND EDUCATION
  PRIZES
 RUMANIAN STATE PRIZE
 RUMANIAN-UNITED STATES
  OF AMERICA CULTURAL
  EXCHANGE OF BOOKS
 "VIATA ROMINEASCA"
  AWARDS   C-22.
SPAIN
  Most of the more than 200
literary prizes awarded in Spain
have been established within the
last 15 years. As in France,
many of the major awards are
announced and presented during
the Christmas season. Among
the best-known are the Nadal and
Planeta Prizes for novel; the
Adonais and Boscán Prizes for
poetry; the Calderon de la Barca,
Lope de Vega, and Spanish Crit-
ics' Prizes for drama; Sésamo
Prize for short story; the
Lazarillo Prize for children's
literature; and the Spanish National Prizes and Prizes of the
Spanish Academy. Generally the
literary awards honor works in
Castillian or in Catalan, but
some few prizes mention eligibility
of works in other languages of
Spain. Numerous Festivals with
Floral Games are held each year,
including the MADRID FLORAL
GAMES, revived in 1952 as an
annual event for Spanish and

Spanish-American writers, with awards in 1952 to Jose Ramon Medina (Venezuela) for "Texto sobre el tiempo," and Eduardo Cota (Colombia) for "Salvacion del Recuerdo."

Other prizes are offered for Drama--VALLADOLID DRAMA PRIZE, a premium of 25.000 pts established in 1962 for a "play by a Spanish or Hispano-American writer," offered by La Delegacion del Ministerio de Información y Turismo, Valladolid; VALLE INCLÁN PRIZE, offered by the "Dido" Theatrical group for a "new Spanish-speaking playwright;" for Short Story--Eugenio D'ORS PRIZE for a "social" story, won in 1960 by J.M. García Vaso with "Lance del Negro John y la Gaviota;" for Novel--OVIEDO PRIZE for an "unpublished novel in Castilian," offered by Libreria Universal (Calle Gil de Jaz 11, Oviedo), won in 1961 by Jorge Ferrer Vidal with "Caza Mayor; for Poetry--CAUCE PRIZE, established in 1960 and awarded that year to Guillermo Osorio for "Elaire;" ESCALONA PRIZE, a Madrid poetry award given in 1955 to Ramon de Garciasol for his entire poetry output, especially "Hombre de la Tierra;" Carlos RIBA PRIZE of 10.000 pts won in 1961 by Ramón Bech with "Cants-Terrenals;" for Journalism --two prizes of Secretaria General del Movimiento (Alcala 44, Madrid) offers two 10.000 pts prizes: PRIMERO DE OCTUBRE PRIZE, and VIENTNEUVE DE OCTUBRE PRIZE; Miguel de los SANTOS OLIVER JOURNALISM PRIZE of Ciudad de Palma,won in 1961 by José Salas Guiror.

Sources of Information--Two continuing sources of information give current information about Spanish literary honors and their winners: "Spanish Cultural Index," monthly periodical of the Spanish Cultural Relations De-partment (issued in a Spanish and an English edition); and "El Libro Español," monthly review of the Instituto Nacional del Libro Español (I.N.L.E.--Ferraz 13, Madrid), which includes a section "Concursos y Premios" announcing prizes and their winners in Spain, and also in some non-Spanish countries.

Real Academia Española "Boletin" gives latest information about literary awards and winners of the many Academy prizes.

The most complete listing of Spanish literary prizes examined in a 20-page booklet compiled by Jose Sanchez, "Los Premios Literarios Españoles," describing 160 prizes, and listing winners through 1957. Another current listing of Spanish literary awards is issued by Instituto Nacional del Libro Español: Fernando Cendán Pazos, "Premios Literarios en España," a five-page pamphlet giving facts about 90 prizes periodically awarded in Spain.

Incidental information about Spanish literary honors is found in Willis Knapp Jones, "Recent novels of Spain," a "Hispania" article; in "Spanish writers'prizes and privations," in the "Economist;" and in Maxim Newmark, "Dictionary of Spanish Literature." Other sources are: Anthony Kerrigan, article in "New York Times Book Review," 1957, "A literary letter from Spain;" and in two articles of Jose Sanchez: "Literary awards in present-day Spain," "Books Abroad," Fall 1957, and "'Adonais':" A poetic landmark," in "Hispania."

Publications devoted to specific honors (not examined) are: "Florilege de jeux floraux du Languedoc, 1953;" and "Los premios de novela Ciudad de Barcelona, 1949-1953," a collection of Barcelona prize novels.
SPANISH LITERARY AWARDS
ABARCA PRIZE

ACENTO PRIZE
ADONAIS PRIZE
AEDOS PRIZE
AFRICA PRIZES
ALARCÓN PRIZE
ALAS PRIZE
ALBA PRIZE
ALBACETE PRIZE
ALCOVER PRIZE
ÁLVAREZ QUINTERO PRIZE
ARNICHES PRIZE
ATENEO DE MADRID PRIZE
ATENEO DE VALLADOLID
  PRIZES
BALMES PRIZE
BARCELONA DRAMA CRITICS
  PRIZE
BARCELONA PRIZES
BAROJA PRIZE
BECQUER PRIZE
BOSCÁN PRIZE
BREVE PRIZE
CALDERON DE LA BARCA
  NATIONAL PRIZE
CARTAGENA PRIZE
CATALÁ PRIZE
CAVIA PRIZE
CERRALBO PRIZE
CERVANTES HISPANIC PRIZE
CERVANTES NATIONAL PRIZE
CERVANTES SOCIETY PRIZES
CHIREL PRIZE
CIRCULO DE BELLAS ARTES
  PRIZE
CONDÁL PRIZE
DONCEL PRIZE
DOS ESTRELLAS PRIZE
ESPINA PRIZE
ESPINOSA Y CORTINA PRIZE
FASTENRATH PRIZE
FEMINA PRIZE
FERIA DEL LIBRO PRIZE
FIESTA DEL LIBRO PRIZE
FRANCO NATIONAL PRIZE
FRATERNIDAD HISPANICA
  PRIZE
GIJON PRIZE
HEMINGWAY JOURNALISM
  PRIZE
HISPANIC CULTURAL
  INSTITUTE PRIZE
IBERICO NOVEL PRIZE
INSTITUT D'ESTUDIS CATALANS
  PRIZES

IRVING PRIZE
JULIO PRIZE
JUVENIL CADETE PRIZE
JUVENTUD PRIZES
LARRAGOITI PRIZE
LAUREL DEL LIBRO
LAZARILLO PRIZE
LEÓN PRIZE
LERMA PRIZES
LLORENTE PRIZE
LOPE DE VEGA PRIZE
LUCA DE TENA PRIZE
LUZAN PRIZE
MACHADO POETRY PRIZE
MADRID PRIZE
MALAGA PRIZE
MARAÑON PRIZE
MARCH FOUNDATION PRIZES
MARTORELL PRIZE
MARVA PRIZE
MAURA PRIZE
MENENDEZ PIDAL PRIZE
MENENDEZ Y PELAYO
  NATIONAL PRIZE
MENORCA PRIZE
MIRO PRIZE
MONCADA PRIZE
MORALES PRIZE
NADAL PRIZE
NEBRIJA PRIZE
ONDAS PRIZE
PALMA DE MALLORCA
  PRIZES
PALOMO PRIZE
PAMPLONA PRIZE
PEREZ GALDOS PRIZE
PIQUER PRIZE
PLANETA PRIZE
PLAZA PRIZE
PLAZA Y JANÉS PRIZE
PRIMO DE RIVERA NATIONAL
  PRIZE
PUJOL PRIZE
REAL ACADEMIA ESPAÑOLA
RIBA PRIZE
RIVADENEIRA PRIZE
"SAN GASPAR" PRIZE
SANT JORDI PRIZE
SANTA LUCIA PRIZES
SANTOS OLIVER JOURNALISM
  PRIZE
SESAMO PRIZE
SEVILLE PRIZE

SINERGIA PRIZE
SPANISH CRITICS' PRIZE
SPANISH NATIONAL PRIZES
SPANISH NATIONAL THEATRE
  PRIZE
TIRSO DE MOLINA PRIZE
VALENCIA PRIZES
VIANNA PRIZE
VIERA Y CLAVIJO PRIZE
VIRGEN DEL CARMEN
  PRIZE
YXART PRIZE
ZARAGOZA PRIZE   C-23.

SWEDEN
  About 1,260,000 kroner
($240,000) are currently available
each year in Sweden to authors
in the form of prizes and grants.
Swedish State Awards (such as
ten awards of 10,000 kroner
each; sums distributed by the
Swedish Authors' Fund; and Swedish
Academy Grants) account for a
"considerable part" of the recognition given authors of high literary achievement or promise.
Literary premiums are granted to
writers of children's books (Astrid
Lindgren in 1957; Ake Holmberg
in 1958), and of scientific and
factual works, as well as to
authors of traditional belles lettres.
  Major Swedish literary prizes
are offered by the Swedish Academy, whose cultural activities are
world-famous as the agency awarding the best-known literary honor,
the Nobel Prize for Literature.
As the Académie Française is
composed of "Forty Immortals,"
so the Swedish Academy (founded
by Gustavus III in 1786 with
Académie Française as a model)
is made up of "Eighteen Immortals,"
among whom have been such
famous authors as: Pär Lagerkvist,
and Selma Lagerlöf--the first
woman member.
  Additional Swedish literary
honors are: HELSINGFORS PRIZE,
bringing a premium of $2,100 to

S. Katrina Salminen in 1936;
SWEDISH PRIZE FOR BEST
NOVEL OF THE YEAR, granted
to K. Gorranson-Ljungman in
1941 for "Shining Sea;" VEGA
MEDAL OF SWEDEN, presented
in 1962 to Thor Heyerdahl.
  Sources of Information--Letters
and rules from some awarding
agencies; and letter from the
Swedish Embassy (2249 R Street,
N.W., Washington, D.C.) naming
11 major Swedish literary prizes
currently awarded.
SWEDISH LITERARY AWARDS
  BELLMANN PRIZE
  BONNIERS FUND AND GRANTS
  DOBLOUG ENDOWMENT
    PRIZE
  FRODING STIPEND
  HOLGERSSON MEDAL
  LJUS PRIZE
  THE NINE PRIZE
  SCHUCK AWARD
  SVENSKA AKADEMIEN
    PRIZES
  SVENSKA DAGBLADET
    LITERARY PRIZE
  SWEDISH AUTHORS' FUND
  SWEDISH BOOK LOTTERY
                          C-24.
SWITZERLAND
  According to a recent German
listing of literary prizes and
honors (Trumpf, p. 115-117)
"over 50 'official' prizes are
offered by Swiss states and
municipalities with a total mone-
tary value of 200,000 marks."
Included in these Art and Cultur-
al Awards (Kunst- und Kultur-
preise) are honors of Basel,
Bern, Geneva, Innerschweiz, and
Zurich. In addition, prizes are
offered by foundations (as Buhril
Foundation, Martin Bodmer
Foundation, Schweizerische
Schiller Foundation), and other
professional organizations and
groups.
  Sources of Information--
Letters and rules from some
awarding agencies; letter from
Schweizerischer Schriftsteller-

Verein (Kirchgasse 25, Zurich) listing four prize-awarding agencies. Three German-language sources: Trumpf, "Preise, Praemien, Privilegien," and two serials--"Fischer Weltalmanach," and "Kurschners Deutscher Literatur-Kalender."

SWISS LITERARY AWARDS
  BASEL ARTS PRIZE
  BASEL LIONS CLUB PRIZE
  BASEL LITERATURE PRIZE
  BERN LITERATURE PRIZE
  BUHRIL FOUNDATION AWARD
  GENEVA WRITERS' PRIZE
  GUILDE DU LIVRE PRIZE
  GUTENBERG BOOK GUILD
    PRIZE
  INNERSCHWEIZ PRIZES
  KELLER PRIZE
  LIBERA STAMPA PRIZE
  SWISS TEACHERS' ASSOCIA-
    TIONS YOUTH BOOK PRIZE
  WELTI-STIFTUNG FÜR DAS
    DRAMA PRIZE
  ZURICH LITERATURE PRIZE
                         C-25.

UNION OF SOVIET SOCIALIST REPUBLICS

The major literary honor of the USSR is the Lenin Prize, a general cultural award, which includes prizes in Literature and the Arts. The Stalin prize replaced the Lenin Prize as the official recognition for cultural achievement during the years 1941 through 1953. Other forms of official recognition of accomplishment or potential in the arts, including literature, are the decorations awarded by the government: Order of Lenin, Order of the Hero of Socialist Labor, Order of the Red Banner of Labor, which honor writers as well as other workers.

Many other literary honors are bestowed in the USSR by states of the Union, by professional and labor groups, and by publishers and publications.

Additional honors for writers include: election to the USSR ACADEMY OF SCIENCES

(Mikhail A. Sholokhov was made a member of this group); election to the SUPREME SOVIET OF THE USSR (in 1954 38 writers were so elected, and Mikhail A. Sholokhov has been elected a Supreme Soviet Deputy). Achievement of major posts in the Union of Soviet Writers is a literary honor won by Leonid Leonov, a Praesidium member, and--in 1962--by Eughenny Evtushenko, Andrei Voznesensky, Boris Slutsky, and Robert Rozhdestvnsky.

Sources of Information--The most available English-language source of information about current winners of Soviet literary honors is the "Current Digest of the Soviet Press," which includes a weekly index of "Pravda" and "Izvestia," where honors presented writers are noted, especially the Lenin Prize and other official awards.

Other periodic sources are the encyclopedia yearbooks ("Americana Annual," "Britannica Book of the Year," "New International Yearbook"), and for review articles: Guillebraud's discussion of the "Role of honorary awards in the Soviet economic system;" Simmons' survey of Soviet Literature, 1950-1955 in "Annals of the American Academy;" and books and pamphlets giving systematic or incidental information about Soviet literary awards: Gorchakov, "The theatre in Soviet Russia;" Marc Slonim, "Modern Russian literature from Chekhov to the present;" and "Russian Soviet literature," Library of Congress lecture; Gleb Struve, "Soviet Russian literature, 1917-1950;" Yarmolinsky, "Literature under Communism."

An English-language list of Stalin prize winners in prose and drama, 1941-1952, is found in Rosen's masters' essay from Columbia University.

Other sources include letters

from USSR literary and cultural
groups (USSR Writers' Union,
Foreign Commission; USSR Acad-
emy of Sciences, Division of Lan-
guage and Literature); Annual
Meeting of the USSR Academy of
Sciences, February 2-4, 1961
(U.S. Joint Publications Research
Service Translation); the "Condi-
tions of Lenin Prizes and other
decisions," in "Questions of
Ideological Work," glossary of the
most important decisions of the
Communist Party of the USSR,
1954-1961; and the report of the
1961 Lenin Prizes in the magazine
"USSR," July 1961, by Ozersky
and Grafsky.
RUSSIAN LITERARY AWARDS
  BELINSKY PRIZE
  IZVESTIA COMPETITION
  LENIN PRIZE
  PUSHKIN PRIZES
  STALIN PRIZES
  TOLSTOY MEMORIAL MEDAL
  USSR ORDER OF LENIN
  USSR ORDER OF THE HERO
    OF SOCIALIST LABOR
  USSR ORDER OF THE RED
    BANNER OF LABOR
                  C-26.
WALES
  The single traditional literary
competition in Wales is the Eistedd-
fod Poetic Competition.
  Sources of Information--"New
York Times" articles about compe-
titions and winners.
WELSH LITERARY AWARDS
  EISTEDDFOD POETIC
    COMPETITION   C-27.
YUGOSLAVIA
  The official national recognition
for writers in Yugoslavia is the
Yugoslav Literary Prizes of the
national government. In addition
literary awards are offered by
such Republics of the Federation,
as: Croatia, Macedonia, Montene-
gro, Servia, Slovenia (Presernov
Prize); and by cities, as the
October Prize of Belgrade and the
Zagreb Prize. Other awards are
granted by publishers (Koco Racin

Prize, Levstikov Prize, Nazor
Prize, Ninova Prize, People's
Education Prize, Svjetlost Prize),
by writers' societies, and by
cultural and political groups.
  The Nobel Prize for Literature was won in 1961 by the
Yugoslav author, Ivo Andric, who
had previously received many high
literary awards in Yugoslavia,
including a prize for his most
famous work, "Na Drina Cuprija"
(The bridge on the Drina).
  Sources of Information--Milan
T. Vukovic, "Yugoslav literary
prizes," p.705-715, in his book,
"Mali knjizarski leksikon," which
lists awards representing the
four major language groups of
Yugoslavia: Slovene (Ljubljana);
Croat (Zagreb); Serb (Belgrade);
and Macedonian (Skopje).
YUGOSLAV LITERARY AWARDS
  BOSNIA AND HERZEGOVINA
    WRITERS SOCIETY PRIZES
  BRANKO'S PRIZE
  CROATIAN PEOPLE'S
    REPUBLIC PRIZES
  CROATIAN WRITERS ASSOCIA-
    TION PRIZES
  HRVATSKA PRIZE
  KOCO RACIN PRIZE
  LEVSTIKOV PRIZE
  MACEDONIAN WRITER'S
    SOCIETY PRIZES
  MONTENEGRO PEOPLE'S
    REPUBLIC PRIZES
  NAZOR PRIZE
  "NEVEN" PRIZE
  NINOVA CRITICS PRIZE
  NOVEMBER 13 PRIZE
  OCTOBER PRIZE OF BEL-
    GRADE
  "PEOPLE'S EDUCATION"
    PRIZE
  PRESERNOV AWARD
  SERBIAN PEOPLE'S REPUBLIC
    PRIZES
  SERBIAN WRITERS' ASSOCIA-
    TION PRIZE
  SLOVENE WRITERS' ASSOCIA-
    TION PRIZE
  SVJETLOST PRIZES
  YUGOSLAV CENTRAL COM-

MITTEE OF THE FEDERATION
OF SYNDICATES PRIZE
YUGOSLAV CENTRAL COUN-
CIL OF THE PEOPLE'S YOUTH
PRIZE
YUGOSLAV FEDERATION OF
HUNTING SOCIETIES PRIZE
YUGOSLAV LITERARY
PRIZES
YUGOSLAV SOCIETY FOR
EDUCATION AND CARE OF
CHILDREN PRIZE
YUGOSLAV WRITERS' ASSOCIA-
TION PRIZE
ZAGREB PEOPLE'S PRIZE
ZMAJ PRIZE
                                   C-28.
ALGERIA
    In addition to the Algerian
Grand Prize for Literature,
Algerians writing in French have
won French prizes, such as
Mohammed Dib, who was awarded
the Fénéon Prize in 1953 and the
Laporte Lyric Prize in 1961.
    Sources of Information--"Guide
des Prix Littéraires."
ALGERIAN LITERARY AWARDS
    ALGERIAN GRAND PRIZE
    FOR LITERATURE   C-29.
EGYPT
    The Egyptian government offers
public recognition to writers in
the form of periodic awards for
literary achievement and encour-
agement of young writers. These
are general cultural awards that
include prizes for writers.
    Sources of Information--Dr.
M. A. A. Hafez, Director, United
Arab Republic Cultural and
Educational Bureau, (2215 Wyoming
Avenue, N.W., Washington 8,
D. C.).
EGYPTIAN LITERARY AWARDS
    EGYPTIAN STATE AWARDS
    FOR OUTSTANDING INTEL-
    LECTUAL ACHIEVEMENT
    EGYPTIAN STATE AWARDS
    FOR THE ADVANCEMENT
    OF SCIENCE, SOCIAL SCI-
    ENCES, LITERATURE, AND
    THE FINE ARTS
    JA'IZAT AL-DAULAH   C-30.

GREECE
    Carrying on a long tradition
of the public recognition of excellence in physical and intellectual achievement, literary honors
currently awarded in Greece are
those of the Athens Academy--
prizes with high national prestige
--and of the Greek Ministry of
Education--Greek National Prize.
Cultural and writers' groups such
as the "Group of the Twelve," the
Society of Greek Writers ("Parnassus" Literary Society), and the
Greek Women's Literary Group
also offer prizes for poetry,
children's drama, folklore and
other forms of literature.
    Sources of Information--Letter
from Royal Greek Embassy (2211
Massachusetts Avenue, N.W.,
Washington 8, D.C.) listing seven
major literary awards currently
granted in Greece, with descriptions of prizes and names of
winning authors.
    Incidental listing of prize
winners in "Greek Bibliography,"
the classified and partially annotated list of current Greek publications (March 1959-) issued
by the Greek Ministry to the
Prime Minister's Office, General
Directorate of Press, Research
and Cultural Relations Division,
Athens, National Printing Office
(English language edition).
GREEK LITERARY AWARDS
    ATHENS ACADEMY AWARDS
    FEXIS PRIZE
    GOULDANDRIS PRIZE
    GREEK NATIONAL PRIZE
    GREEK WOMEN'S LITERARY
    GROUP AWARDS
    HATZIPATERA PRIZE
    KALOKAIRINEIOS DRAMA
    CONTEST
    OURANIS PRIZE
    PHILADELPHEA POETRY
    COMPETITION
    POURFINA AWARDS
    SKIARIDEIOS COMPETITION
    FOR CHILDREN'S THEATRE
    TWELVE PRIZES

XANATHOUDIDEIOS FOLKLORE
COMPETITION   C-31.
IRAN
    Major public and official rec-
ognition of writers in Iran is
made by the award of the Iran
Royal Literary Prizes, although
several other awards for literary
works are offered, such as the
IRAN INSURANCE COMPANY
LITERARY PRIZE.
    Sources of Information--Letters
from General Department of Publications and Broadcasting,
Imperial Government of Iran,
Maydan Ark, Teheran; and Commission Nationale Iranienne pour
l'U.N.E.S.C.O., Avenue du
Musée, Teheran.
IRANIAN LITERARY AWARDS
    IRAN ROYAL PRIZES
    SEPASS BADGE   C-32.
IRAQ
    Literary prizes in Iraq are
offered by the Iraqi Academy for
writing in any form, and for
translation by an Iraqui.
    Sources of Information--Letter
from Embassy, Republic of Iraq
(1801 P Street, N.W., Washington 6, D.C.).
IRAQ LITERARY AWARDS
    IRAQI ACADEMY PRIZES
                          C-33.
ISRAEL
    Major literary honors of Israel
are the Israel State Prize, the
Bialik Prize, and a number of
awards of authors' associations
and municipalities, such as the
Holon, Ramat-Gan, Jerusalem,
and Tel-Aviv Prizes.
    Additional literary awards are
the MASSADE PUBLISHING COM-
PANY PRIZE (33 Lilienblum
Street, Tel-Aviv); the ISRAEL
PRIZE FOR CHILDREN'S AND
YOUTH'S LITERATURE, offered
by the American Israel Cultural
Foundation (32 Allenby Road, Tel-
Aviv); and the Yosef AHARONO-
VITZ PRIZE, granted by the
General Federation of Labour in
Israel (93 Arlozoroff Street,

Tel-Aviv).
    Sources of Information--Letter
from Ministry of Education and
Culture of Israel, Jerusalem;
letters and rules from some
awarding agencies.
ISRAEL LITERARY AWARDS
    BIALIK PRIZE
    BRENNER PRIZE
    HANAZIV PRIZE
    HOLON PRIZE FOR LITER-
      ARY AND SCIENTIFIC
      ACHIEVEMENTS
    ISRAEL STATE PRIZE
    LAMDAN PRIZE FOR CHIL-
      DREN'S LITERATURE
    RAMAT-GAN LITERARY
      PRIZE FOR HEBREW
      FICTION
    RAMAT-GAN PRIZE FOR
      STUDIES IN JUDAISM
    RUPPIN PRIZE
    TCHERNICHOFSKY PRIZE
    USSISHKIN PRIZE
    UZIEL PRIZE FOR RELIGIOUS
      LITERATURE
    YAFFE PRIZE   C-34.
LEBANON
    Literary awards in the Lebanese
Republic are judged and, generally,
presented by the "Book Friend
Society" (J Ja'izah Ra'Is Al-
Jumhuriyah), founded in 1959 "to
help and improve the condition of
authors and their production." Dr.
Constantine Zreik, Professor at
the American University, Beirut,
is president of the Society, whose
other literary and book activities
include the establishment of an
annual "Book Week," at the end of
November.   Presentation of the
literary awards is made during
this week--in 1961 at the Literary
Arab Club, whose seventh "Arab
Book Exhibition" coincided with
"Book Week."
    Sources of Information--Letter
from Lebanese Republic National
Commission for UNESCO
(UNESCO Building, Beirut,
Lebanon).
LEBANON LITERARY AWARDS
    BAALBECK ARAB DRAMA

PRIZE
LEBANESE ARAB AUTHORS
PRIZE
LEBANESE DRAMATIC PRIZE
LEBANESE PRIZE FOR MOST
BOOKS IN ARABIC
LEBANESE RESEARCH PRIZE
LEBANESE SCIENCE PRIZE
LEBANESE TRANSLATION
PRIZE   C-35.
TUNIS
    In addition to the Tunisian
Academy of Floral Games Grand
Prize, several other literary
awards are offered in Tunis: Ali
BELHAOUANE AWARD FOR FIC-
TION (500 D premium); TUNISIAN
DRAMA PRIZE (300 D premium
for an original play; 200 D for a
translation or an adaptation);
SFAX LITERARY AWARD, giving
first and second prizes for an
original play (150 D and 75 D),
and for an adaptation or a trans-
lation (75 D and 50 D).
    Sources of Information--Letter
from Cultural Counselor, Embassy
of Tunisia (2408 Massachusetts
Avenue, Washington, D.C.).
Also, the printed source: "Guide
des Prix Littéraires."
TUNISIAN LITERARY AWARDS
TUNISIAN ACADEMY OF
FLORAL GAMES GRAND
PRIZE   C-36.
TURKEY
    Major Turkish literary awards,
announced in such reviews as
"Varlik," "Turk Dil," include
prizes for various literary forms:
Novel, Poetry, Short Story, and
for factual writing and criticism.
    Sources of Information--Millî
Kütüphane, Bibliyografya En-
stitüsü (National Library,
Bibliographic Institute, Yenisehir,
Ankara).
TURKISH LITERARY AWARDS
ATAC CRITICS PRIZE
FAIK SHORT STORY PRIZE
TÖREHAN PRIZE
TURKISH LANGUAGE FOUNDA-
TION SCIENCE AND ART
PRIZE

TURKISH REPUBLICAN
PARTY LITERARY PRIZE
VARLIK NOVEL PRIZE
YEDITEPE POETRY PRIZE
                         C-37.
AFRICA
    The two Pan-African prizes
awarded in Africa are both
granted by agencies in South
Africa: Drum Pan-African Short
Story Contest, of the magazine
"Drum;" and Vilakazi Memorial
Award, offered by Witwatersrand
University, Johannesburg. African
writers have won literary honors
awarded by other nations, including France, Belgium, Sweden,
Switzerland, and the United Kingdom.   Most of these awards are
offered writers without restriction
as to nationality, but several are
directed to African writers. These
prizes, with an indication of
country offering the award, name
of prize, and nationality of the
writer winning the award (further
details usually found under the
name of the prize) are:
FRANCE
    General Honor--
    Prix des Amitiés Françaises
       (Senegal)
    Prix Goncourt (Central Repub-
       lic of Africa)
    Grand Prix de la Société des
       Gens de Lettres (Central
       Republic of Africa)
    Académie Française Prix d'Au-
       male (Central Republic
       of Africa)
    Académie Française Prix de
       Poésie (Central Republic of
       Africa)
    Prix de L'Unanimité (Cameroon)
    For African Writers--
    Grand Prix d'Afrique Occi-
       dental Française (Ivory Coast)
    Prix France-Afrique
    Grand Prix Littéraire d'Afrique
       Noir d'Expression Française
       (Ivory Coast)
BELGIUM
    For African Writers--
    Prix Littéraire de la Foire

Coloniale de Bruxelles
(Congo; Rwanda)
SWEDEN
General Honor--
Nobel Peace Prize (South Africa)
SWITZERLAND
General Honor--
Veillon Prize (Guinea)
UNITED KINGDOM
General Honor--
United Kingdom Royal Society
for Literature Member
(Nigeria)
For African Writers--
Encounter Prize (Nigeria)
Wrong Prize (Cameroon;
Congo; and others)
International Institute of
African Languages and Cultures Prize for Biography
(Nyasaland)
Sources of Information--Rules
and letters from awarding agencies. Several publications, such
as anthologies with biographical
notes: Hughes, "African treasury,"
MacNab, "Poets in South Africa;"
Rutherfoord, "Darkness and light."
Bibliographies by Porter: "Fiction
by African authors," and "Notes
on some African writers." The
periodicals, "Books for Africa;"
"Présence Africaine." For
French-language awards, "Guide
des Prix Littéraires;" and for
English-language prizes, "Cassell's
Directory of Publishing."
AFRICAN LITERARY AWARDS
AFRICAN GRAND PRIZE FOR
LITERATURE IN FRENCH
BRUSSELS COLONIAL FAIR
PRIZE
DRUM PAN-AFRICAN SHORT
STORY CONTEST
FRANCE-AFRICA PRIZE
INTERNATIONAL INSTITUTE
OF AFRICAN LANGUAGES
AND CULTURES PRIZE FOR
BIOGRAPHY
VILAKAZI MEMORIAL AWARD
WRONG MEMORIAL AWARD
C-38.
BURUNDI, KINGDOM OF; and
RWANDA, REPUBLIC OF

(Formerly: Ruanda-Urundi)
Writers of this area have
received a Belgian prize (Prix
Littéraire de la Foire Coloniale
de Bruxelles--1949, J. Saverio
Nagaziki, "Escapade Ruandaise.
Journal d'un clerk en sa Trentième
Année"); and several prizes from
the United Kingdom (Wrong Prize
--1954, M.A. Nsimbi (Uganda);
1956, A. Wandira (Uganda);
1958, Alexis Kagame (Ruanda)).
C-39.
CAMEROON
Literary honors won by
Cameroon authors include two
French prizes:
Prix Sainte-Beuve, 1958,Mongo
Beti, "Mission terminée;"
Prix de l'Unanimité, 2,000 fr
purse in 1959, Ferdinand
Oyono, "Une vie de Boy;"
"Le vieux Nègre et la
médaille"
Also, a Wrong Memorial Prize
from United Kingdom, 1955, S.
Layare. C-40.
CENTRAL AFRICAN REPUBLIC
One writer of this area--
formerly designated Oubangui
Chari, or Ubangi-Shari--received four different French
prizes for his works: René
Maran, Antilles Negro Colonial
Administrator, honored with:
Académie Française Prix d'Aumale, 1953 (40,000 fr);
Académie Française Prix de
Poésie (Prix d'Académie),
1959, for "Le livre du
Souvenir;"
Prix Goncourt, 1921 for
"Batouala;"
Grand Prix de la Société des
Gens de Lettres, 1949,
for his poetical work.
C-41.
CONGO
Information is available concerning only one literary prize
awarded by the Congo: Congo
Literary Prize.
Authors in this area have
also been honored with the

Belgian prize, Prix Littéraire de la Foire Coloniale de Bruxelles (1948, Paul Lomami-Tshibamba, for "Nganda" (The crocodile); and the Wrong Prize of the United Kingdom (1950, G. A. Ngbongbo). Sources of Information--"Books Abroad," 30:283, 1956.

CONGO LITERARY AWARDS
CONGO LITERARY PRIZE
C-42.
GHANA
Literary awards in Ghana, up to the present, are the Medals granted by the Ghana Academy of Sciences.

A Ghana author received a Wrong Prize in 1956: A.W. Kayper Mensah. Sources of Information--Letter from Ghana Academy of Sciences.

GHANAIAN LITERARY AWARDS
GHANA ACADEMY OF
SCIENCES MEDALS   C-43.
GUINEA
The International literary honor, the Charles Veillon Prize, Switzerland, was awarded Camara Laye in 1953 for his book, "L'enfant noir."   C-44.
IVORY COAST
Information was obtained about one award granted by the Ivory Coast: Ivory Coast Republic Literary Prize.

In addition to this award, authors of the area have won three French prizes: Grand Prix Littéraire de l'Afrique Noir d'Expression Française (1960, Aké Loba, "Locoumbo, l'étudiant noir"); Grand Prix de l'Afrique Occidental Française (1932, A. A. Dim Delobsom, "L'Empire du Mogho-Naba"); Prix des Amitiés Françaises (1961, Léopold Sédar Senghor).

Sources of Information--Letter from awarding agency. Printed source: "Guide des Prix Littéraires."

IVORY COAST LITERARY
AWARDS
IVORY COAST REPUBLIC

LITERARY PRIZE
C-45.
NIGERIA
The Nigerian literary awards are offered from time to time for Nigerian writers. Also, United Kingdom literary honors granted to Nigerian authors include: United Kingdom Society for Literature Membership (Raymond Tong, author of "Tunde in trouble"); Margaret Wrong Medal or Prize (1951, D. Nicol; 1955, D. O. Fabunwa, writing in Yoruba; 1956, W. Soyinka; 1959 Albert, Chinua Achebe, "Things fall apart").

Sources of Information--Letter from Librarian, University College, Ibadan. Printed sources --as for Africa as a whole.

NIGERIAN LITERARY AWARDS
ENCOUNTER PRIZE
NIGERIAN FESTIVAL OF THE
ARTS PRIZE
NIGERIAN NATIONAL TROPHY
NIGERIAN NOVEL COMPE-
TITION   C-46.
RHODESIA AND NYASALAND,
FEDERATION OF
The Nyasaland school teacher Samuel Yosia Ntara was awarded the INTERNATIONAL INSTITUTE OF AFRICAN LANGUAGES AND CULTURES PRIZE FOR BIOG-RAPHY in 1933 for his depiction of the life of an African chief, "Man of Africa," arranged and translated from the original Nyanja by T. Cullen Young.
C-47.
SOUTH AFRICA, REPUBLIC OF
Most of the literary prizes noted in the Republic of South Africa are awarded for writing in Afrikaans, with a few prizes for writing in English and for Bantu literature.

The greatest number of literary prizes are awarded by the South African Academy for Science and Art, with other professional and cultural groups granting prizes for Afrikaans children's books (South African Library Association), and in special subject areas, as Music (African Music Society); and in Afrikaans writing (Afrikaans P.E.N. Centre; Nasionale Boekhandel).

Superior writing in both Afrikaans and English is recognized by the awards of the Cape Tercentenary Foundation, Central News Agency, and Advisory Council for Adult Education. The Geerligs Prize is an award for Afrikaans writing as well as for Dutch writing in Holland and Belgium.

In 1961 the Nobel Peace Prize was presented to Albert Luthuli, South African author and public figure, whose recent published writing is, "Let my people go."

Sources of Information--Letters from awarding agencies, especially South African Department of Education, Arts and Sciences, with information about four prizes; University of Capetown Library (Rondebosch, Capetown), with compiled information about ten prize-awarding groups.

A continuing printed source of information is "Cassell's Directory of Publishing," which lists prizes for works in Afrikaans and gives details of awards for works in English.

SOUTH AFRICAN LITERARY AWARDS
    AFRIKAANS CHILDREN'S
        BOOK AWARD
    AFRIKAANS P.E.N. CENTRE
        PRIZE
    AFRICAN PRESS COMBINE
        PRIZE
    CAPE TERCENTENARY
        FOUNDATION MERIT AWARD
    COWELL AWARD
    ENGLISH ASSOCIATION OF
        SOUTH AFRICA LITERARY
        PRIZE FUND
    HERTZOG PRIZE
    HOFMEYR PRIZE
    MARAIS PRIZE
    MQHAGI PRIZE

    SCHEEPERS PRIZE FOR
        YOUTH LITERATURE
    SCHREINER PRIZE
    SOUTH AFRICAN ACADEMY
        FOR SCIENCE AND ART
        PRIZES
    SOUTH AFRICAN BROAD-
        CASTING CORPORATION
        PRIZE FOR RADIO PLAYS
    SOUTH AFRICAN C.N.A.
        LITERARY PRIZE
    SOUTH AFRICAN NATIONAL
        ADVISORY COUNCIL FOR
        ADULT EDUCATION PRIZES
    SOUTH AFRICAN SHORT
        STORY CONTEST

                                         C-48.
AUSTRALIA
    Australian literary honors are numerous, "but almost all of them have been occasional rather than institutional" (Australian Encyclopedia, v 5, p. 327). The government fellowships to writers, granted under the Commonwealth Literary Fund, allow recognized writers to finish or undertake specific projects, and other prizes are directed to recognition of outstanding literary achievement by established writers (Franklin Literary Award, Leven Prize for Poetry), or to the discovery and encouragement of new writers (Adelaide Festival of Arts Awards, Crawford Memorial Short Story Award, Quadrant Literary Award).

Additional commemorative awards are: AUSTRALIAN COMMONWEALTH JUBILEE LITERARY COMPETITION of 1951, bringing a Ŀ1000 novel prize to Tom Ronan in 1953 for "Vision splendid," and a Ŀ1000 nonfiction prize--equally divided --to T. Inglis Moore and J. K. Ewer; MELBOURNE CENTE-NARY NOVEL COMPETITION of 1957 (Vance Palmer shared first prize with his novel, "The Swayne Family"); NEW SOUTH WALES ANNIVERSARY LITERARY COM-PETITIONS (Xavier Herbert won

the Ł250 premium offered for
a novel of Australian life with
"Capricornia").

Significant prizes no longer
offered include: S.H. PRIOR
MEMORIAL PRIZE FOR NOVEL;
SYDNEY MORNING HERALD
LITERARY COMPETITION;
SYDNEY TELEGRAPH AUSTRAL-
IAN NOVEL COMPETITION
(Ł1000 premium won in 1950 by
D. Cusack and F. James with
"Come in spinner"); HODDER &
STOUGHTON PRIZE FOR BEST
WORK ABOUT AUSTRALIA (won
in 1915 by Katharine Prichard
with her first novel, Pioneers");
SYDNEY BULLETIN PRIZE, of-
fering Ł1000 to an Australian
author (won by M.B. Eldershaw--
pseudonym of Marjorie Barnard
and Florence Eldershaw--with "A
house is built" in 1929; and the
following year by Katharine
Prichard, with "Coonardoo").

Sources of Information--Letters
and rules from awarding agencies,
including Australian Journalists'
Association, Fellowship of Aus-
tralian Writers, Commonwealth
Literary Fund; and from the
Mitchell Library (The Public Li-
brary of New South Wales,
Macquarie Street, Sydney); the
National Library of Australia,
Canberra, with a list of 31 major
Australian literary awards.

Printed sources include: "The
Australian Encyclopedia," with a
3-page article on "Literary
Awards;" "Australian Literature,"
reference paper of the Australian
News and Information Bureau;
Children's Book Council of
Victoria, "Australian Children's
Books." Serial publications list-
ing current literary awards, con-
tests, and winners include:
"Bohemia," "Realist Writer,"
"Quadrant," and (not seen) publica-
tions of the Australian Writers'
Professional Service (Box 28,
P.O., Collins Street, Melbourne)
--"Writer's World," bimonthly

news letter; and "Writers'
Marketing Guide," biennial hand-
book listing Australian and New
Zealand literary prizes.
AUSTRALIAN LITERARY AWARDS
  ADELAIDE FESTIVAL OF
  ARTS AWARDS
  ADVERTISER LITERARY
  COMPETITION
  AUSTRALIAN CHILDREN'S
  BOOK OF THE YEAR
  AUSTRALIAN COMMON-
  WEALTH LITERARY FUND
  AUSTRALIAN JOURNALISTS'
  CLUB AWARDS
  AUSTRALIAN LITERATURE
  SOCIETY OF MELBOURNE
  MEDAL
  AUSTRALIAN NATIVES
  ASSOCIATION PRIZE
  AUSTRALIAN POETRY
  SOCIETY COMPETITION
  COFFS HARBOUR ARTS
  COUNCIL PLAY AND SONG
  CONTEST
  CRAWFORD MEMORIAL
  SHORT STORY AWARD
  CROUCH MEMORIAL GOLD
  MEDAL AWARD
  FAR NORTH QUEENSLAND
  PLAY WRITING COMPETI-
  TION
  FRANKLIN LITERARY AWARDS
  GENERAL MOTORS HOLDEN'S
  THEATRE AWARD
  GILMORE PRIZE
  GRENFELL FESTIVAL
  AWARDS
  LEVEN PRIZE FOR POETRY
  LITTLE THEATRE GUILD
  PLAY CONTEST
  PATERSON FESTIVAL
  LITERARY PRIZES
  PRIOR MEMORIAL PRIZE
  QUADRANT LITERARY
  AWARD
  SYDNEY MORNING HERALD
  LITERARY COMPETITION
  WALKLEY NATIONAL
  AWARDS FOR AUSTRALIAN
  JOURNALISTS   C-49.
BURMA
  Most significant literary awards
in Burma are those of the Burma

404 International Literary Awards

Translation Institute--formerly Burma Translation Society. Additional awards are granted by the Burmese UNESCO Commission, and by the Rangoon magazine publisher, Shumawa Company.

Sources of Information--Letter from the Ministry of Culture of Burma (Government of the Union of Burma, Rangoon) describing the three literary awards of Burma and listing winners. A printed source with some information on Burmese literary awards is the article by U On Pe, "Modern Burmese literature" (Atlantic, February 1958).

BURMESE LITERARY AWARDS
  BURMESE UNESCO COMMISSION LITERARY AWARD
  SARPAY BEIKMAN PRIZE
  SHUMAWA PRIZE   C-50.
CAMBODIA

The two literary prizes of Cambodia are offered by the Cambodian Ministry of Education (Sotan Prey Chea En Prize), and by the Association of Kmer Writers (Indradevi Prize), with the patronage of the Cambodian Ministry of Education, and the financial assistance of the Asia Society and private donors.

Sources of Information--Letter from Royal Cambodian Embassy (4500 16th Street, Washington, D.C.) describing Cambodian prizes.

CAMBODIAN LITERARY AWARDS
  INDRADEVI PRIZE
  SOTAN PREY CHEA EN PRIZE   C-51.
CHINA, REPUBLIC OF

A long tradition of literary prizes and honors in China is shown in the Ministry of Education Awards, which are continued under the Republic of China as the Chung Hua (China) Prize for Art and Literature.

An additional traditional honor, granted for outstanding service by the Chinese government, is the ORDER OF JADE, given in

1938 to Kenneth Scott Latourette (U.S.A.).

Sources of Information--Letter from Office of the Cultural Counselor, Embassy of the Republic of China (2311 Massachusetts Avenue, N.W., Washington 8, D.C.). Printed Source: "China Yearbook, 1960-1961."

REPUBLIC OF CHINA LITERARY AWARDS
  CENTRAL DAILY NEWS PRIZE
  CHINA ASSOCIATION OF LITERATURE AND ART PRIZES
  CHUNG HUA PRIZE FOR ART AND LITERATURE   C-52.
CHINA, PEOPLE'S REPUBLIC OF

According to a letter from the Peking Library Reference Section (November 24, 1961), no information is available concerning People's Republic of China prizes in literature "because at the present time our country has not received or given out any prize in literature."

In 1952 a Stalin Prize of the USSR was awarded Ting Ling (Din Lin, pseudonym of CHIANG Ping-Chih) for "The sun shines over the Sankhan River."

Official recognition is given by the government in Peking for outstanding literary work--as that accorded LAO Sheh, who received a car from the government and who "holds offices in government-dominated cultural organizations" (P. Durdin, "Writers in China").

A Stalin Peace Prize continues an award formerly offered in Russia.

Sources of Information--Scattered information in English-language journals: Durdin, article in the "Atlantic;" "New Republic" news note on the Stalin Peace Prize.

PEOPLE'S REPUBLIC OF CHINA LITERARY AWARDS
  STALIN PEACE PRIZE   C-53.
INDIA

The most extensive of the major literary awards currently granted in India are those of the Sahitya Akademi, India's National Academy of Letters, with annual awards (also termed the "President's Prize") for the best work in each of the 14 major languages of India, and additional prizes for Sanskrit writing--creative and critical works. Other significant continuing literary honors are those of the Asiatic Society (Churn, Jones, and Sarkar Medals); Indian Union Ministry of Education awards (India Children's Book Awards, India Hindi Book Prize, UNESCO Indian Prize for the New Reading Public); awards of private foundations (Azad Prizes, Wattumull Awards); and of State and regional governments (such as the Gujurat Book Awards).

Indian writers have also been honored with foreign awards, as the Hawthornden Prize of England (won by Dom Moraes in 1958 with "A beginning"); the USSR Institute of Indian Languages, Moscow (Medal for Novel awarded Shri Amritlal Nagar in 1961 for "Boond Avr Samundar"--"Drop in the Ocean").

Sources of Information--Letters from Information Service of India (2107 Massachusetts Avenue, Washington 8, D.C.); The Asiatic Society (1 Park Street, Calcutta); Indian Council for Cultural Relations (Azad Bhavan, Indraprastha Estates, New Delhi 1).

Printed sources describing Indian literary prizes and listing winners include: "India, A Reference annual," issued by the Indian Ministry of Information and Broadcasting; Sahitya Skademi "Annual Report," with complete list of "Books which have won the Akademi Award;" the collection of prize-winning Marathi literature--All India Library Conference, "Souvenir of Baroda."

Current awards and winners are found in "Times of India Directory;"

"Asian Recorder," "weekly record of outstanding Asian events with index;" and "Cultural News from India."

INDIAN LITERARY AWARDS
AZAD PRIZES
CHURN LAW GOLD MEDAL
GROVE PRESS INDIAN FICTION PRIZE
GUJURAT BOOK AWARDS
INDIA CHILDREN'S BOOK AWARDS
INDIA HINDI BOOK PRIZE
JONES MEMORIAL MEDAL
SAHITYA AKADEMI PRIZES
SARKAR GOLD MEDAL
UNESCO INDIAN PRIZE FOR THE NEW READING PUBLIC
WATTUMULL AWARDS
                              C-54.

JAPAN
Of the many literary awards granted each year in Japan, the most important are those given by the Japanese government (Japanese Education Minister's Prize for Artistic Achievement; Japan Order of Cultural Merit), and by the leading learned societies (Japan Academy of Arts, Japan Academy). Significant prizes are granted by publishers (Akutagawa, Asahi, Bungakukai Shinjin, Chuo Koron, Kodansha, Mainichi, Shinshosha, and Yomiuri Prizes), and by writers' groups--detective story, essay, women writers, poets.

Additional awards are the KOSOAKA TADAYOSHI PRIZE, established in 1952, and two prizes for children's and young people's literature: JAPAN CHILDREN'S LITERATURE PRIZE, created in 1953 by the Japanese Society for Writers of Children's Literature, and the SANKEI JUVENILE LITERATURE AWARD (won in 1952 by Sangyo-Keizai Press).

Sources of Information--Letters from some awarding agencies, especially the Japan Academy, and Japan Academy of Arts; Japanese Ministry of Education;

Japan P.E.N. Club (c/o The Asahi Shimbun, Yurakucho Chiyoda-ku, Tokyo) giving major prize winners since 1957.

Letter from National Diet Library, Tokyo, containing a photostat of "A list of literary prizes" (p. 279-282, "Introduction to Contemporary Japanese Literature," Part II (1935-1955), edited and published by Kokusai Bunka Shinkokai, Tokyo). The most complete listing in English of Japanese literary prizes is that in "Who's Who Among Japanese Writers, 1957," Japanese National Commission for UNESCO and Japan P.E.N. Club, prepared by the P.E.N. Club for the international meeting of the group in Japan.

Other printed sources mentioning Japanese literary prizes are "Japan," issued by Japan Commission for UNESCO, which includes a list of literary awards --public and official prizes and prizes of writers' societies and foundations--under "Encouragement for Good Publications," p. 473-474; "The Japan Annual," 1958, p. 346, which mentions some prominent prizes:Akutagawa, Naoki, Women Writers, and Yomiuri.

A continuing list of Japanese literary awards in Japanese-language text (not seen) is the Bungei nenkan. "Japanese Yearbook of Literature, Drama and the Arts," edited by the Nihon Bungei-ka Kyokai.

JAPANESE LITERARY AWARDS
  AKUTAGAWA PRIZE
  ASAHI CULTURAL PRIZES
  BUNGAKUKAI SHINJIN PRIZE
  CHUO KORON SHINJIN PRIZE
  CUP FOR NEW WRITERS OF
    LIGHT FICTION
  DONON ZASSHI PRIZE
  JAPAN ACADEMY OF ARTS
    PRIZES
  JAPAN ACADEMY PRIZES
  JAPAN DETECTIVE STORY
  WRITERS CLUB PRIZES
  JAPAN ESSAYISTS CLUB
    PRIZE
  JAPAN WOMAN WRITERS
    LITERARY PRIZES
  JAPANESE EDUCATIONAL
    MINISTER'S PRIZE FOR
    ARTISTIC ACHIEVEMENT
  JAPANESE IMPERIAL
    POETRY CONTEST
  JAPANESE ORDER OF CUL-
    TURAL MERIT
  JAPANESE PENSION FOR
    MEN OF CULTURAL
    MERIT
  KIKUCHI PRIZE
  KISHIDA PRIZE FOR DRAMA
  MAINICHI PRIZES
  MR. H'S PRIZE
  NAOKI PRIZE
  NOMA LITERARY PRIZE
  NOMA PRIZE FOR FOSTER-
    ING LITERARY ARTS
  SHINCHO PRIZES
  SHOGAKKAN CHILDREN'S
    CULTURE PRIZE
  SHOSETSU SHINCHO PRIZE
  YOKOMITSU PRIZE
  YOMIURI LITERARY PRIZE
                              C-55.
KOREA

The known literary awards of Korea are offered by the City of Seoul, as part of their cultural prizes, by the Pacific Cement Company (richest prize,with 2,000,000 hwan premium), and by newspapers (Han Kuk Cultural Prize for Publishing, Korean Republic Poetry Prize, Nae Sung Literary Prize), magazines (Dong In Literary Prize), and publishers (Ul Yoo Literary Prize for Translation).

Sources of Information-- Letter from Korean Publishers' Association (Chongno Building, Seoul, Korea).

KOREAN LITERARY AWARDS
  DONG IN LITERARY PRIZE
  HAN KUK CULTURAL PRIZE
    FOR PUBLISHING
  KOREAN REPUBLIC POETRY
    PRIZE FOR ENGLISH

LYRICS
NAE SUNG LITERARY PRIZE
SAMIL LITERARY PRIZE
SEOUL CITY SPECIAL LITER-
ARY PRIZE
UL YOO LITERARY PRIZE
FOR TRANSLATION INTO
KOREAN   C-56.
MALAYA, FEDERATION OF
The single known Malayan
literary award is that of the Dewan
Bahasa Dan Pustaka, the Language
and Literature Agency of the Fed-
eration of Malaya that is a unit
of the National Ministry of Educa-
tion.

In May 1962, the National
Writers' Association requested
the Federation of Malaya, Government to offer annual prizes to
"cover all aspects of literature--
novels, short stories, poems,
essays, and drama," in order
"to encourage Malayan writers to
produce works of high standard"
(The Asian Student, v 10, no
35, May 19, 1962, p. 1).

A prize-winning post-war
Malay novel is "Life at the point
of a sword" by Ahmad Murad Bin
Nasruddin.
Sources of Information--Letter
from Dewan Bahasa Dan Pustaka.
MALAYAN LITERARY AWARDS
DEWAN BAHASA DAN
PUSTAKA LITERARY COM-
PETITIONS   C-57.
MONGOLIAN PEOPLE'S
REPUBLIC
The only known literary award
is the Čoibalsang National Prize.
Sources of Information--Letter
from Union of Mongolian Writers,
Ulan Bator.
MONGOLIAN LITERARY AWARDS
ČOIBALSANG NATIONAL
PRIZE   C-58.
NEW ZEALAND
New Zealand literary prizes in-
clude scholarships and grants for
writers (Burns Fellowship; New
Zealand Department of Internal
Affairs Prizes); and awards rec-
ognizing authors' achievements

from the New Zealand P.E.N.
Club (Church Prose Award, Mac-
Kay Poetry Award); the New
Zealand Women Writers' Society
(Mansfield Memorial Award); and
the New Zealand Library Associa-
tion (Glen Award).
Sources of Information--
Correspondence from awarding
agencies. Printed sources in-
clude: "New Zealand. Official
Yearbook," 1961; "Cassell's
Directory of Publishing," 1960-
1961.
NEW ZEALAND LITERARY
AWARDS
BURNS FELLOWSHIP IN
LITERATURE
CHURCH PROSE AWARD
GLEN AWARD
MACKAY POETRY AWARD
MANSFIELD MEMORIAL
AWARD
NEW ZEALAND AWARD FOR
ACHIEVEMENT
NEW ZEALAND LITERARY
FUND
NEW ZEALAND SCHOLAR-
SHIP IN LETTERS
                        C-59.
PAKISTAN
The official government rec-
ognition of literary achievement
in Pakistan is the Pakistan Presi-
dent's Medal for Pride of Per-
formance, a general cultural
honor, which includes prizes for
literature.
The Adamjee Prize, "among
the richest literary awards in
Southeast Asian Countries," is
administered by the Pakistan
Writers' Guild, which also offers
three other awards for writing
in Bengali and Urdu, major languages of Pakistan, and in four
regional languages.
Sources of Information--Letters
from Cultural and Educational
Attaché, Embassy of Pakistan
(2315 Massachusetts Avenue, N.
W., Washington, D.C.); Pakistan Writers' Guild (Stachan Road,
Karachi 4).

Two written sources sent from the Writers' Guild are: Yusuf Jamal Husain, "World literary awards and the Adamjee Prize for Literature;" and "The cultural scene in Pakistan, 1960-1961, Literature"--English-text excerpts from the four prize-winning works of the Adamjee Prize initial award in 1960.
PAKISTAN LITERARY AWARDS
   ADAMJEE PRIZE FOR
   LITERATURE
   PAKISTAN PRESIDENT'S
   MEDAL FOR PRIDE OF
   PERFORMANCE
   PAKISTAN WRITERS' GUILD
   PRIZES   C-60.
PHILIPPINES, REPUBLIC OF THE
Official national literary honors in the Republic of the Philippines are offered each year by the national government (Philippines Republic Cultural Heritage Awards --also Philippines Republic Pro-Patria Award); and major prizes are granted by private groups and organizations (Magsaysay Awards, Palanca Memorial Awards, Zobel de Ayala Prizes), and publishers (as, Philippines Free Press Annual Short Story Contest).

Other awards take the form of grants allowing a writer to finish work in progress (Stonehill Literary Awards); awards recognizing achievement in a particular form of writing (Stanvac Journalism Awards); and awards given once on specific occasions (Philippines Republic Pro-Patria Award, University of the Philippines Golden Jubilee Short Story Contest).

Sources of Information--Letters from Republic of the Philippines Embassy (1617 Massachusetts Avenue, N.W., Washington D.C.); and from awarding agencies. Letter from the University of the Philippines Library (Quezon City) including a 34-

page typescript describing Republic of the Philippines literary awards and listing winners (prepared by Miss Gloria S. Quiros, Chief, Filipiniana Division). Printed sources are two collections of short stories: Maximo Ramos, "Philippine Cross-Section;" and Carlos Palanca Memorial Awards for Literature, "Prize Stories, 1950-1955." The "Manila Times" lists major awards (as Magsaysay and Palanca) as they are made public.
PHILIPPINE LITERARY AWARDS
   MAGSAYSAY AWARDS FOR
   JOURNALISM AND LITERA-
   TURE
   PALANCA MEMORIAL AWARDS
   FOR LITERATURE
   PHILIPPINES FREE PRESS
   ANNUAL SHORT STORY
   AWARDS
   PHILIPPINES LITERARY
   CONTESTS
   PHILIPPINES REPUBLIC
   CULTURAL HERITAGE
   AWARDS
   PHILIPPINES REPUBLIC
   PRO-PATRIA AWARD
   STANVAC JOURNALISM
   AWARDS
   STONEHILL LITERARY
   AWARDS
   UNIVERSITY OF THE
   PHILIPPINES GOLDEN
   JUBILEE SHORT STORY
   CONTEST
   ZOBEL DE AYALA PRIZE
                       C-61.
THAILAND
The single current literary honor in Thailand is the Thailand Royal Institute of Arts and Sciences Essay Contest.

Several literary prizes formerly awarded on an annual basis in Thailand (NATIONAL LITERARY CLUB POETIC COMPOSITION AWARD; NATIONAL INSTITUTE OF CULTURE PRIZE FOR SHORT STORIES) have been discontinued, as the sponsoring

organizations are no longer
active. Occasional awards are
presently offered by newspapers
and periodicals "For outstanding
short stories and poems."
Sources of Information--
Letter from Thailand Public
Relations Department, Bangkok.
THAI LITERARY AWARDS
THAILAND ROYAL INSTITUTE
OF ARTS AND SCIENCES
ESSAY CONTEST   C-62.

VIET-NAM, SOUTH
The official recognition given
writers in South Viet-Nam is the
Viet-Nam Literary Prize. A
second award, The Revolutionary
Civil Servants' League Literary
Prizes, is granted to encourage
outstanding writing by government
employees.
Sources of Information--Letter
from South Viet-Nam Office of
Cultural Affairs.
VIETNAMESE LITERARY
AWARDS
REVOLUTIONARY CIVIL SER-
VANTS' LEAGUE LITERARY
PRIZES
VIET-NAM LITERARY PRIZE
C-63.

LATIN AMERICA
Of the Latin American literary
honors, few are continuing awards
(except the Cuban Casa De las
Américas Prizes, and the awards
for journalism: Cabot Prizes
and Mergenthaler Prize). The
current Faulkner Foundation's
Latin America Novel Award, and
the previous Life En Español
Prize have been offered one
time, with no definite plans for
subsequent awards.
Additional literary prizes for
Latin American writers are;
Premio LATINOAMERICANO DE
LITERATURE (won in 1954 by
Lautaro Yankas of Chile with "El
vado de la noche"); the SERRA
AWARD of "Americas," presented
in 1961 to Arthur P. Whitaker;
the ESPIRAL PRIZE (won in
1954 by the Colombian writer

Germán Beltrán with "El diablo
sube el telon"); FERNANDEZ
MARTINEZ PRIZE, a 50,000
pesos award founded in Mexico
by José Fernandez Martinez for
articles contributing to better
relations among Hispanic countries (won in 1960 by Enrique
Ruiz Garcia); PAN AMERICAN
NOVEL PRIZE (awarded in 1960
to Alfredo Canton of Panama).
An INTER-AMERICAN LITER-
ARY AWARD planned by the Committee for Cultural Action, Inter-
American Cultural Council of
Pan American Union, as a biennial
honor to be granted on Pan American Day (April 14) has never
been implemented, due to lack of
funds.
Prizes in particular forms of
literature include: INSTITUTO
DE LATINOAMERICANO DEL
TEATRO AWARDS, administered
by UNESCO in Paris; the LIRICA
HISPANA PRIZE, offering prizes
for poetry in Spanish ("Lirica
Hispana," Aptdo 3551, Caracas,
Venezuela); the Fernão MENDES
PINTO PRIZE for fiction, offered
by the Portuguese government
(Agencia Geral do Ultramar,
Lisbon), won in 1955 by Guilher-
mina de Azeredo with "Blanchos
e negros."
Also, the former José TORIBIO
MEDINA PRIZE of the Inter-
American Bibliographical and Li-
brary Association; the SHELL
OIL COMPANY OF CURACAO
LITERARY PRIZE, designed to
reward outstanding writing in
Spanish, English, French, and
Dutch concerning tourism in the
Caribbean, especially in the
Netherlands Antilles.
Spanish prizes are often avail-
able to Latin American writers,
such as the Spanish Academy
Prize, granted for a South Amer-
ican Book in 1928 and won by
Hugo Wast (pseudonym of Gustavo
Martinez Zuviria) with "Valle
Negro" (Black Valley).

Sources of Information--
Letters and rules from some
awarding agencies. In addition
to the encyclopedia yearbooks
which mention prize winners in
annual reviews of "Latin American Literature" ('Americana
Annual," "Britannica Book of the
Year," "New International Yearbook"), the "Spanish Cultural
Index" includes listing of Latin
American prizes and prize winners,
as do "Handbook of Latin American Studies," "Inter-American
Review of Bibliography," and the
periodicals "Americas," and "Hispania."

Members of the 20 Academies
of Latin America (Academias de
la Española),which are associated
with Real Academia Española, are
listed each year in "Almanaque
Mundial."

Older English-language his-
tories of Latin American literature mention prizes incidentally:
Hespelt, Instituto Internacional
de Literatura Iberoamericana.
Periodical articles report or
discuss Spanish American prizes
generally ('Books Abroad," 30:439,
1956), or specific awards (as
"Life en Español", December 12
and 26, 1960).

LATIN AMERICAN LITERARY
AWARDS
    ALBERDI AND SARMIENTO
    AMERICAN FRIENDSHIP
    PRIZE
    AMERICALEE LITERARY
    CONTEST
    BRAZIL THEATRE PRIZE
    CABOT PRIZE
    CASA DE LAS AMÉRICAS
    PRIZE
    CERVANTES PRIZE
    EMECÉ PRIZE
    FAULKNER FOUNDATION
    LATIN AMERICAN NOVEL
    AWARD
    GILDER AWARD
    GREIFF PRIZE
    INTERAMERICAN CULTURAL
    ASSOCIATION PRIZES

    LATIN AMERICAN PRIZE
    NOVEL COMPETITION
    LIFE EN ESPAÑOL PRIZE
    MERGENTHALER PRIZE
    PAN AMERICAN CONGRESS
    OF THE THEATRE
    COMPETITION
    SOUTH AMERICAN PRIZE
    FOR POETRY   C-64.
ARGENTINA
    Major literary prizes of
Argentina are the Official govern-
ment award (Argentina National
Prize); awards of the city of
Buenos Aires (Buenos Aires
Literary Prizes, Ricardo Rojas
Prize); recognition given writers
by Sociedad Argentina de Escri-
tores (Medal of Honor, Bianchi
Essay Prize, Moreno Poetry
Competition, Rojas Pax Prize);
publisher's prizes (such as the
Kraft Prize, Peuser Award);
awards by government agencies
(Casaville Prize of Camara
Argentino del Libro) and private
foundations (as Vaccaro Prize).

Additional literary awards are
the ATENEO PRIZE, formerly
granted and given in 1915 to
Hugo Wast for "La Casa de los
Cuervos" (House of the ravens);
ARGENTINE CRITICS PRIZE--
Premio Nacional de Critica--
presented in 1937 to Arturo
Marasso; Pablo E. CONTI
PRIZE, currently awarded for
publishers newly located in
Buenos Aires; BABEL PRIZE--
Premio de Poesia de la Editorial
Babel--given in 1923 to Conrado
Nalé Roxlo for "El grillo."

Among international literary
honors received by Argentine
writers is the Prix Formentor
of 1961, granted Jorge Luis
Borges, who was cited particularly for his collection of short
stories, "Ficciones."

Additional Argentine prizes
are: ARGENTINE P.E.N.
CLUB BEST NOVEL OF THE
YEAR, given in 1943 to Ernesto
L. Castro for "Los isleros;"

CENTRO GALLEGO PRIZE, won in 1946 by Maria de Vallerino with "Poesia de la saudade y de la tierra;" INSTITUCIÓN MITRE PRIZE, honoring Manuel Galvez in 1928 for "Las caminos de la muerte;" SUR PRIZE-- Premio de la revista Sur-- granted by the Argentine literary review to Roberto Ledesma in 1943.

Sources of Information--Information and rules from some awarding agencies. Printed sources: Latin American sources, and "Diccionario de la Literatura Latinoamericana: Argentina," issued by the Pan American Union; and Juan Torrendell's essay, "Los concursos literarios."

ARGENTINE LITERARY AWARDS
  ARGENTINE AUTHORS
    SOCIETY LITERARY PRIZES
  ARGENTINE NATIONAL
    PRIZE
  ARGENTINE WRITERS'
    SOCIETY PRIZES
  BIANCHI ESSAY PRIZE
  BUENOS AIRES DRAMA
    PRIZE
  BUENOS AIRES INSTITUCIÓN
    CULTURAL ESPAÑOLA
    MEDAL
  BUENOS AIRES LITERARY
    PRIZE
  BUENOS AIRES LITERARY
    PRIZES
  CASAVALLE PRIZE
  GERCHUNOFF PRIZE
  KRAFT PRIZE
  MALINCA DETECTIVE
    NOVEL COMPETITION
  MORENO POETRY COMPE-
    TITION
  PEUSER AWARD
  ROJAS PAZ PRIZE
  ROJAS PRIZE
  SARMIENTO PRIZE
  VACCARO PRIZE
  VEA Y LEA DETECTIVE
    SHORT STORY CONTEST
                              C-65.
BOLIVIA
  Major literary awards of

Bolivia include the government prizes: Bolivian Grand National Prize for Literature, and the Condor of the Andes (a cultural honor awarded for outstanding service to Bolivia).

Bolivian authors have also been honored by receiving such Pan American prizes as the Rubén DARÍO PRIZE--an Inter-American poetry prize won by Javier del Granado; and the SOUTH AMERICAN PRIZE FOR POETRY (Cesar VALLEJO PRIZE), also awarded Javier del Granado.

Sources of Information: Diccionario de la Literatura Latino-americana: Bolivia," issued by Pan American Union

BOLIVIAN LITERARY AWARDS
  BOLIVIAN GRAND NATIONAL
    PRIZE FOR LITERATURE
  BOLIVIAN NATIONAL
    NOVEL CONTEST
  BOLIVIAN SOCIETY OF
    WRITERS AND ARTISTS
    PRIZE
  COCHABAMBA SOCIETY OF
    WRITERS AND ARTISTS
    STORY CONTEST
  CONDOR OF THE ANDES
  LA PAZ PRIZE   C-66.
BRAZIL
  More literary awards are offered each year in Brazil than in any other country of Latin America. Among the more significant awards are the official government honor: Prêmio Nacional; and Prêmios da Academia Brasileira de Letras--which grants a number of prizes most important of which is the Machado de Assis Prize with a premium of Cr$200.000; the P.E.N. Club de Sao Paulo awards; and the prizes of Uniao Brasileira de Escritores de Sao Paulo, P. E.N. Club do Brasil; Câmara Brasileiro do Livro; Universidade do Ceará; and the state and regional prizes, such as those of Guanabara, Sao Paulo, and

Minas Gerais.
Additional literary awards are:
Felipe d'OLIVEIRA AWARD
(granted for the "best novel in
1941 to José Lins do Rêgo for
"Aqua Máe"--Mother Water);
Eduardo PONDAL PRIZE (Buenos
Aires poetry award won in 1954
by José María Álvarez Blázquez);
GABIAO PRIZE (granted in 1959
to five poets including Walmir
Ayala, to the science writer
Helmut Sick, and to the short
story writer Ideu Brandão);
PANDIA CALÓGERAS PRIZE
(granting the initial prize of Cr
$50.000 to Mecenas Dourado in
1957 for "Correio Brasiliense,
an essay on Hipólito da Costa);
Mario de ANDRADE PRIZE (a
poetry award presented in 1955
to Edmir Dominques da Silva for
"Corcel de Espuma").
Also, the title, "Brazilian
LITERARY PERSONALITY OF
THE YEAR," of Camara Brasil-
eira do Livro, given in 1961 to
literary critic Alvaro Lins; the
RECIFE CITY PRIZE (honoring
Francisco Baudeirade Mello in
1955 for "O pássaro narciso");
the Edgar CAVALHEIRO LITER-
ARY PRIZE (won in 1958 by
Nestor de Hollando with "Caminhos
e Fronteiras"); LARROGOITI
PRIZE of Academia Brasileira de
Letras, shared in 1955 by Zoraide
Rocha Freitas and Alberto Silva.
Two additional prizes of
Academia Brasileira de Letras are
the: Augusto de LIMA PRIZE
(awarded in 1960 to Clara Sílvia
Brand Antunes for "Um ateu nos
caminhos de Deus;" Mercês Maria
Moreira Lopes for "Augusto de
Lima;" and Maria Cláudia Cuper-
tino for "Totônio"); and ALCAN-
TARA MACHADO PRIZE (shared
in 1961 by Aída Colares Moreira
and Marília Cardoso Fontes de
Almeida, writing on: "Ensaio e
Conrica--Froenteira dos dois
Generos").
Sources of Information--In-

formation and rules from some
awarding agencies, especially
Academia Brasileira de Letras--
list of winners of Academy prizes
for the past five years; P.E.N.
Club of Sao Paulo, with a list of
13 prize-awarding agencies, and
newspaper reports of literary
awards.
Printed sources: Latin American
sources, and "Anuário da Litera-
tura Brasileira," which describes
major Brazilian literary awards
and lists winners for the year.
BRAZILIAN LITERARY AWARDS
ACADEMIA BRASILEIRA DE
   LETRAS
ALVES PRIZE
ANCHIETA PRIZE
ARANHA PRIZE
ARINOS PRIZE
AZEVEDO PRIZE
BARBAROSA PRIZE
BELO HORIZONTE PRIZE
BRAZIL "DISCOVER THE
   AUTHOR" PRIZE
BRAZILIAN CULTURAL PRIZE
   OF THE ITALIAN CONSUL-
   ATE
BRAZILIAN DRAMA CRITICS
   ASSOCIATION PRIZE
BRAZILIAN NATIONAL
   FEDERATION OF INDUSTRY
   PRIZE
BRAZILIAN NATIONAL PRIZES
BRAZILIAN PRIZE
BRAZILIAN WRITERS' UNION
   OF SAO PAULO PRIZE
BRITO PRIZE
CEARÁ UNIVERSITY PRIZE
CLAUDIO DE SOUSA PRIZE
COELHO NETO PRIZE
DANTAS NOVEL COMPETI-
   TION
DE LAET PRIZE
A GAZETA COMPETITION
   FOR POETRY AND SHORT
   STORIES
GUANABARA STATE PRIZE
JABUTI PRIZE
JORNAL DE LETRAS PRIZE
LINS DO REGO PRIZE
LOPES DE ALMEIDA PRIZE
MACHADO DE ASSIS PRIZE

MINAS GERAIS CULTURAL PRIZE
MOINHO SANTISTA PRIZE
MONTEIRO LOBATO PRIZE
NABUCO PRIZE
NAMI JAFET PRIZE
OLAVO BILAC PRIZE
OTHON LYNCH PRIZE
PAULIST ACADEMY OF
  LETTERS PRIZE
RAMOS PAZ PRIZE
RIBEIRO PRIZE
RIO DE JANEIRO INDEPEND-
  ENT THEATER CRITICS
  AWARD
ROMERO PRIZE
SAO PAULO P.E.N. CLUB
  PRIZE
SAO PAULO PRIZES
SOUTH AMERICAN PRIZE
TARQUINIO DE SOUZA
  PRIZE
VERISSIMO PRIZE   C-67.
CHILE
    Chilean writers are recognized
by several major continuing
literary prizes offered by the
Chilean government (Chilean Na-
tional Prize), the city of Santiago
(Mistral Prize, Santiago Literary
Prizes), by universities (Atenea
Prize, Chilean National Theatre
Prize), and by associations of
professional writers and pub-
lishers (Alerce Prize, Fabry
Prize, Nasimento Prize, Tierra
del Fuego Best Book of the Year).
    Additional prizes are the
SANTIAGO CENTENARY LITER-
ARY PRIZE, offered for the
"most outstanding work dealing
with life in Chile," and won in
the year of award--1941--by
Francisco Coloane with "Cabo
de Horno," a collection of tales;
Juan SAID PRIZE of 35,000
pesos, won in 1953 by Nicano
Parra with "Poemas y antipoemas;"
EL MERCURIO SHORT STORY
COMPETITION, of the Santiago
newspaper, won by Marta Brunet
Caraves in 1929; and awards of
two professional groups:
CHILEAN NATIONAL PRESS
ASSOCIATION PRIZE, granted

by Asociacion Nacional de la
Prensa for an outstanding work
of journalism (1956: Raúl Silva
Castro for "Prensa periodismo
en Chile"); and CHILEAN ACAD-
EMY OF HISTORY MEDAL OF
HONOR, of Academia Chilena de
Historia (presented in 1957 to
Francisco A. Encina for his 20-
volume "Historia de Chile").
    Sources of Infirlation--Infor-
mation from some awarding agen-
cies; letter from Comision
Chilena de Cooperacion Intelec-
tual (Huerfanos 1117, Santiago)
describing six literary honors of
Chile.
    Printed sources: Latin Ameri-
can sources, and Instituto de
Literatura Chilena, "Boletin,"
sent by Biblioteca de la Uni-
versidad de Chile.
CHILEAN LITERARY AWARDS
  ALERCE PRIZE
  ATENEA PRIZE
  CHILEAN NATIONAL PRIZE
    FOR LITERATURE
  CHILEAN NATIONAL
    THEATRE PRIZE
  CHILEAN WRITERS' ASSOCIA-
    TION PRIZES
  CHILEAN WRITERS' UNION
    NOVEL CONTEST
  FABRY PRIZE
  MARTINEZ CUADROS PRIZE
  MISTRAL PRIZE
  NASIMENTO PRIZE
  SANTIAGO LITERARY PRIZE
  TIERRA DEL FUEGO BEST
    BOOK OF THE YEAR
  ZIG-ZAG PRIZE   C-68.
COLOMBIA
    The present major continuing
literary honor in Colombia is
the ESSO "Concurso Nacional."
    Additional prizes, which have
been granted from time to time,
include: Antonio José RE-
STREPO PRIZE for a bio-critical
study to commemorate the cente-
nary of Restrepo's birth, won in
1955 by Alirio Gómez Picón
with "Semblanza de Antonio José
Restrepo; VERGARA Y VER-

GARA PRIZE, awarded Antonio
Curcio Altamar in 1953 for
"Evolución de la novela en
Colombia;" and ESPIRAL PRIZE,
granted Manuel Zapata Olivella
in 1954 for "Hotel de vagabundos."
   Sources of Information--Letters
from Academia Colombiana (Aptdo
815, Bogota); "La Nueva Prensa"
(Carrera 24, no 11-59, Bogota).
Printed sources: Latin American
sources.
COLOMBIAN LITERARY AWARDS
   COLOMBIAN ASSOCIATION
      OF WRITERS AND ARTISTS
      PRIZE
   COLOMBIAN PRESS PRIZE
   ESSO (COLOMBIA) LITERARY
      PRIZE   C-69.
CUBA
   The present major continuing
literary award currently granted
in Cuba is the pan-Latin America:
Casa de las Américas Prize.
   Additional prizes previously
awarded include: CUBAN
TOURIST COMMISSION MEDAL OF
HONOR (granted in 1952 to Ernest
Hemingway for "The Old man and
the sea," and "outstanding contri-
butions to Cuba"); the general
government honor, ORDER OF
CARLOS MANUEL DE CESPEDES
(also presented to Ernest Heming-
way for "The Old man and the sea');
Hernandez CATA SHORT STORY
PRIZE (won in 1954 by Augusto
Mario Ayora of Ecuador with
"Escamas de Culebra," collection
of tales); CUBAN LIBRARY
ASSOCIATION PRIZE (awarded
initially in 1951 to Rodolfo Tro
for his bibliography of Antonio
Bachiller y Morales, 19th century
scholar); TEATRO ADAD THEATRE
CONTEST (among whose first prize
winners is Carlos Felipe with
"Capricho en roja"); and the
former CUBAN NATIONAL PRIZE
(presented in 1943 to Paul Lorenzo
for his book on the life and works
of José Antonio Saco; and to
Federico de Cordova for his
book on the life and works of

Manuel Sangiuly). Cuban authors
honored by foreign literary
awards include Alejo Carpentier,
awarded the Prix du Meilleur
Livre Étranger of France in
1956 for "Le partage des eaux;"
and an earlier French prize--
Reader's Society of France "Best
Book of the Month"--for "Le
Royaume de Ce Monde."
                           C-70.
DOMINICAN REPUBLIC
   A single literary award
granted by the government is the
Dominican Republic National
Literary Prizes. Former liter-
ary awards include those granted
by La Trinitaria, Political Society
of the Dominican Republic.
   Sources of Information--
"Spanish Cultural Index;" and
"Certamen de La Trinitaria,"
of Sociedad Amantes de la Luz.
DOMINICAN LITERARY
AWARDS
   DOMINICAN REPUBLIC
      NATIONAL LITERARY
      PRIZES   C-71.
ECUADOR
   Several prizes in addition to
the Ecuador National Prize are
awarded from time to time.
   Sources of Information-
Printed sources: Latin American
sources.
ECUADORAN LITERARY AWARDS
   CASA DE CULTURA
      ECUATORIANA PRIZE
   ECUADOR NATIONAL PRIZE
   QUITO CENTENNIAL ECUADOR
      PRIZE
   TOBAR PRIZE   C-72.
EL SALVADOR
   The current major literary
honor of El Salvador is the
"Premio Republica de El Salva-
dor," presented winners of the
Certamen Nacional de Cultura.
   Sources of Information--Let-
ters from Biblioteca Nacional
(8a Avenida Norte 228, San
Salvador); Academia Salvadorena
de la Lengua; Departmento
Editorial, Ministerio de Educa-

cion (Pas. Contreras 11, San
Salvador).
SALVADORAN LITERARY
AWARDS
   EL SALVADOR NATIONAL
   CULTURAL AWARDS
   EL SALVADOR NATIONAL
   PRIZES IN SCIENCES AND
   LETTERS   C-73.
GUATEMALA
   No information was obtained
concerning current awards in
Guatemala.
   Sources of Information--
Guatemala (City) Feria Nacional,
"Concurso literario."
GUATEMALA LITERARY
AWARDS
   GUATEMALA (CITY)
   NATIONAL FAIR PRIZE
                       C-74.
HAITI
   No information was obtained
concerning current awards in
Haiti.
   Source of Information--"Books
Abroad," 30:264, 1956.
HAITI LITERARY AWARDS
   HAITI LEGISLATURE PRIZE
   HAITI PRESIDENT'S PRIZE
                       C-75.
HONDURAS
   The single national literary
honor in Honduras is the official
prize of the government: Rosa
Prize.
   Sources of Information--Letter
from Biblioteca Nacional de
Honduras (Av. Salvador
Mendieta 116, Tegucigalpa).
HONDURAN LITERARY AWARDS
   ROSA PRIZE   C-76.
MEXICO
   Highest honors for writers in
Mexico are the Mexican National
Prize for Arts and Sciences; the
Manuel Avila Camacho Prize,
sponsored by Instituto Mexicano
del Libro; the Villaurrutia Prize;
the prizes of geographic areas
(Jalisco State Prize, Mexico City
Prize); and the prizes for
specified forms of writing: Club
España and Lanz Duret Prizes

for novels; Centro Mexicano de
Teatro and Ruiz de Alarcón
Prizes for plays; and Banco de
Mexico prize for writings in
economics.
   Additional significant literary
awards are: Ignacio Manuel
ALTAMIRANO PRIZE, offered by
the State of Guerrero (awarded
in 1947 to Maria Luisa Ocampo
for "Bajo el fuego"); HIDALGO
PRIZE, a special 560,000 fr
prize to commemorate Mexico's
independence, offered by the
Mexican embassy in Paris in
1955 for a writing in French;
MEXICAN BOOK FAIR LITER-
ARY PRIZE (won in 1943 by
Francisco J. Santamaria); "EL
NACIONAL" PRIZE (won by
Sergio Margaña in 1953 with "El
molino del aire"); MEXICAN
BEST FICTION BOOK OF THE
YEAR (awarded to Rosario
Castellanos in 1957;) MEXICAN
ORDER OF THE AZTEC EAGLE,
highest government honor for a
foreigner--granted in six degrees
in recognition of outstanding services to Mexico and to humanity
(won in 1960 by the English
author Betty Ross). The PRE-
MIO SOR JUANA, offered by the
new publisher, was won in 1961
by Rosario Castellanos with the
novel, "Oficio de tinieblas."
   Sources of Information--Let-
ters from awarding agencies;
and from Instituto Nacional de
Bellas Artes y Letras (Palacio de
Bellas Artes, Mexico, D. F.)
describing and listing winners of
seven major literary prizes of
Mexico; and from Fondo de
Cultura Económica (Av de la
Universidad 975, Mexico 12,
D. F.) describing major literary
awards with names of winners
and titles of winning works.
   Printed sources: Latin American sources, and "Estaciones,"
quarterly Mexican literary review; and such periodical
articles as: "Recent Mexican

awards noted," New York Times, April 20, 1950, VII, 26:1; and Yeats, "A study of the Lanz Duret Prize Novels."

MEXICAN LITERARY AWARDS
ACADEMIA MÉXICANA DE LA LENGUA
ATENEO ESPAÑOL DE MÉXICO AWARD
BANCO NATIONAL DE MÉXICO NATIONAL ECONOMICS PRIZE
CAMACHO PRIZE
CERVANTES LITERARY COMPETITIONS
"CLUB ESPAÑA" JOURNALISM PRIZES
ESTACIONES LITERARY PRIZES
JALISCO STATE PRIZE
LANZ DURET PRIZE
MEXICAN DRAMA CENTER PRIZE
MEXICAN NATIONAL DRAMA COMPETITION
MEXICAN NATIONAL PRIZE FOR ARTS AND SCIENCES
MEXICAN WRITERS' CENTER FELLOWSHIPS
MEXICO CITY PRIZE
"NUEVA ESPAÑA" NOVEL PRIZE
PAN AMERICAN ROUND TABLE CONTESTS
RUIZ DE ALARCÓN PRIZE
VILLAURRUTIA PRIZE
C-77.

NICARAGUA
The single literary prize noted in Nicaragua is the Darío Prize.
Sources of Information--Printed sources: Latin American sources.
NICARAGUAN LITERARY AWARDS
DARÍO PRIZE   C-78.
PARAGUAY
No information was obtained concerning literary awards in Paraguay. The Losada Prize, offered for manuscripts in Spanish by the Argentina publisher, was won in 1959 by the Paraguayan writer Augusto Roa Bastos with his novel,"Hijo de

Hombre" (Son of Man).   C-79.
PERU
Major continuing literary honors in Peru are included in the official cultural honor-- Peruvian National Prizes, which were offered in 16 cultural areas in 1961.
Additional awards include the CABOTÍN PRIZE, offered for Peruvian essays. Peruvian writers honored with foreign literary awards include Francisco Garcia Calderon, who won an Académie Française prize (1908) for his cultural study concerning Peru; Ciro Alegría,who won with his novels the Nasimento Prize (1935) with "La serpiento de oro," the Zig-Zag Prize (1939) with "Los perros hambrientos," and the Latin American Novel Contest in 1941 with "El mundo es ancho y ajeno."
Sources of Information--Letters from some awarding agencies. Printed sources: Latin American sources, and two publications (not seen): Alberto Tauro del Pino, "Bibliografia Peruana de Literatura," containing Peruvian prize-winners prior to 1958; and the collection of the Cabotín prize essays, "Los Doce mejores articulos del premio Cabotín 1957."
PERUVIAN LITERARY AWARDS
LIMA SHORT STORY CONTEST
MEJIA BACA FICTION PRIZE
PERUVIAN NATIONAL PRIZE
C-80.
PUERTO RICO
Puerto Rican literary honors appear to be those awarded by the government or subsidized agencies.
Sources of Information-- Printed Sources: Latin American sources, and "Teatro puertorriqueño," of Instituto de Cultura Puertorriqueña.
PUERTO RICAN LITERARY

AWARDS
  PUERTO RICAN THEATRE
    FESTIVAL
  PUERTO RICO POET
    LAUREATE
  PUERTO RICO PRIZE
                          C-81.
URUGUAY
  Official recognition for writers
is given in the Uruguay National
Prize. Writers of Uruguay who
have won foreign literary honors
include Gaston Figueira, awarded
the 1958 Poe Prize by the Maison
de Poésie, Paris, for "Pour ton
Clavecin;" and Jules Superveille,
French poet born in Uruguay,
who received a number of major
French literary honors.
  Sources of Information--
Printed sources: Latin American
sources.
URUGUAYAN LITERARY
AWARDS
  MONTEVIDEO HISTORY
    PRIZE
  URUGUAY NATIONAL
    LITERARY PRIZE
  VAZ FERREIRA PRIZES
                          C-82.
VENEZUELA
  Major official literary award
in Venezuela is the Venezuelan
National Prize for Literature,
granted each year by the Minis-
terio de Educacion, Direccion de
Cultura y Bellas Artes, which
also awards the Venezuelan
National Prize for Journalism and
the Bello Prize.
  Foreign literary honors won
by Venezuelan writers include
the PARIS PRIZE FOR THE
BEST AMERICAN NOVEL (won
in 1924 by Teresa de la Parra
with "Ifigenia"). The Venezuelan
government commissioned the
Spanish writer, resident in
Venezuela, Camillo-José Cela to
write a novel for the sum of
$40,000--the resulting work was
"La Catira" (The Blonde), with
a 900-word glossary of "Vene-
zuelism" as appendix.

  Sources of Information--Letter
describing awards from Direc-
cion General de Cultura y Bellas
Artes.
  Printed sources: Latin American
sources.
VENEZUELAN LITERARY
AWARDS
  ATENEO DE CARACAS
    PRIZE
  BELLO PRIZE
  CARACAS MUNICIPAL COUN-
    CIL PRIZES
  LAZO MARTI PRIZE FOR
    POETRY
  EL NACIONAL SHORT STORY
    CONTEST
  REVERON PRIZE
  ROJAS PRIZE FOR LITERA-
    TURE
  SHEROVER AND JUAN DE
    CASTELLANOS PRIZES
  VENEZUELAN NATIONAL
    PRIZE FOR JOURNALISM
  VENEZUELAN NATIONAL
    PRIZE FOR LITERATURE
  VENEZUELAN WRITERS'
    ASSOCIATION PRIZE
                          C-83.
WEST INDIES
  The Musgrave Medals are the
general cultural honor of Jamaica,
while the French Antilles Prize
and the French Antilles Grand
Prize for Literature recognize
the best writing of the French-
speaking countries of the Carib-
bean: Haiti, Martinique,
Guadeloupe, and French Guiana.
  Writers of the area receiving
foreign literary honors include
the Martinique writer, René
Maran, the first Negro awarded
the Goncourt Prize (1921),
for "Batouala."
  Sources of Information--Letter
from Institute of Jamaica.
  Printed sources include "Handbook
of Jamaica," and "Guide des Prix
Littéraires."
WEST INDIES LITERARY
AWARDS
  CULTURE FRANÇAISE PRIZE
    (formerly FRENCH

ANTILLES PRIZE)
FRENCH ANTILLES GRAND
 PRIZE FOR LITERATURE
MUSGRAVE MEDALS   C-84.

Index

Numbers refer to the serially numbered literary awards described in the main section of the International Dictionary of Literary Awards. The index refers also to the Bibliography (numbers B-1 to B-177) and to Literary Awards by Country (numbers C-1 to C-84). When an author has received one prize two or more times, the number of times the prize has been granted is shown in parentheses after the serial number of the award.

419

Calaferte, L., 327
Caldentey, J., 844
Calder, R., 621
Calderón, F.R., 110
CALDERÓN DE LA BARCA
  NATIONAL PRIZE, 199
Calderón Theatre, 114
Caldwell, J.T., 230
Calef, N., 909
Calendoli, G., 285
Callado, A., 248
Calle Iturrino, E., 21
Callender, R.N., 487
Callovini, C., 447
Pandiá CALÓGERAS PRIZE, 755
Calugaru, I., 960
Calvetti, J., 944
Calvino, I., 103, 972, 1118
Calvo, L., 218
Calvo Sotelo, J., 917, 1029
Calvo y Val, F.B., 389
Calzini, R., 1118
Manuel Avila CAMACHO PRIZE,
  200
Cámara Argentino del Libro, 213
Cámara Brasileira do Livro, 169,
  595
Cámara Cascudo, L. de, 711
Cámara Chilena del Libro, 372
Cámara Leol Tostes, S.M. da, 699
Cámara Municipal de Lisboa, 216
Prêmio CÂMARA MUNICIPAL DE
  SÃO PAULO, 980
Camba, J., 218
Cambó, F., 562
Cambodia. Ministry of Education,
  557, 1020
CAMBODIAN LITERARY
  AWARDS, C-51
Cambours Ocampo, A., 191
Cameroon, C-40
Camilar, E., 960
Premio Adolfo CAMINHA, 614
Cammen, C-4
Camo, P., 8
CAMÕES PRIZE, 201, and 386
Julius C. CAMPE PRIZE, 202
Camón Aznar, J., 744
Camp, L.S. de, 568
Campagne, C., 435
Campaña, A., 977
Campanile, A., 1118
Campards, M., 329
Campe, Verlag Hoffmann und, 202

Campert, R., 51, 203, 412, 449
Jan CAMPERT PRIZE, 203
Jan Campert Stichting, 203,
  547, 1127
Campos de Figueredo, J., 720
Camps y Arboix, J. de, 20
Camus, A., 425, 806, B-93
CANADIAN LITERARY AWARDS,
  B-99, B-100, B-162;
  Children's Books, B-144, B-158
Canabrava, L., 176
Canal Feijóo, B., 64
Canals Frau, C., 64
Canary Islands, 864, 1125
Canavaggia, M., 247
Cancela, A., 191
Candeul, B., 1058
Candio, A., 878
Candoni, L., 246
Cané, L., 191
Canellas Rodriguez, F., 896
Cano, D.M., 21
Cansever, Edip., 1156
Cantaroni, N., 1040
Canto, E., 191
Canton, A., C-64
Canzani, A., 168
Capamy, 1165
Capdevila, A., 64 (2),
  65, 191
CAPE TERCENTENARY FOUNDA-
  TION MERIT AWARD, 204
Cape Town P.E.N. Centre,
  1024A
Cape Verde, 867
Capécia, M., 421
Capek, K. and J., 282
Capitini, A., 972
CAPITOLINE WOLF PRIZE, 205
CAPRI PRIZE, 206
Caprile, M.A., 191
Caprin, G., 782
Capron, M., 399
Caproni, G., 677, 1118
Cara, D., 138, 212
Caracas, Ateneo de, 74
CARACAS MUNICIPAL COUNCIL
  PRIZES, 207
Caraco, A., 882
I.L. CARAGIALE PRIZE FOR
  DRAMA, 957
Carballido, E., 211, 748, 749
Carbonell, L., 618
Carco, F., 9, 852, 1079

Colakovic, B., 1045
Colares Moreira, A., C-67
Coleman, J.G., 1137
Colenda, Editorial, 28, 382
G.J. COLES' PRIZE FOR SHORT
  STORY, 855
Colette, S.G., 46, 490, 858, 918;
  juror--429; about--B-32
Colin, P., 481
Colin, V., 960
Coll, B., 844
Colleville, M., 471
COLLI EUGANEI PRIZE, C-15
Colliander, T., 395
Collin-Delevaud, Mme.,375
Premio COLLODI, C-15
Coloane, F., 977, 1060, C-68
COLOGNE LITERATURE
  PRIZE, 255
Colombi-Guidotti, M., 684
COLOMBIAN ASSOCIATION OF
  WRITERS AND ARTISTS
  PRIZE, 256
COLOMBIAN LITERARY AWARDS,
  C-69
COLOMBIAN PRESS PRIZE, 257
Colombo, R., 1097
COLONIAL FAIR IN BRUSSELS
  PRIZE, 185
Colsen, B., 1024A
Colum, M.M., 1086, C-14
Colum, P., 485, 579
COLUMBIA-CATHERWOOD
  AWARDS, 258
"Columbia Dictionary of
  Modern European Literature",
  B-151
Columbia University, 198, 258,
  612, 701
Columbian Academy, C-15
COLUMBIAN PRIZE, C-15
"Combat", 81, 259
COMBAT PRIZE, 259
"El Comercio," Lima, 746
COMHARTHA AN CHRAOIBHIN,
  445
Comision Chilena de Cooperacion
  Intelectual, C-68
Comisión de Literature
  Juvenile e Infantil, 663
Comisso, G., 103, 1041
Comitato Nazionale per il
  Monumento a Pinocchio, C-15
Comité d'Action de la Résistance,

925
Comité Nacional des Écrivains,
  1079
Commissie voor de Propaganda
  van het Nederlandse Boek,
  334, 335
Communist Party, USSR, 675,
  B-36, B-137, B-150, B-176
Companhia Editora Nacional, 175
Compania Vincola de Saltillo,
  366
Companion of Literature, 1083
Conardy, C., 162
Concepción, Universidad de, 72
Conchon, G.,686
CONCOURS DE POESIE
  VINCULA, 1132
CONCOURS DES FLEURS
  TRADITIONNELLES (Toulouse)
  1067
CONCURSO DE LIBROS SOBRE
  MADRID, 715
CONCURSO DE NOVELA (Club
  España), 250
CONCURSO DE ROMANCES
  ORLANDO DANTAS, 292
CONCURSO DE TEATRO
  (Renata Crespi Prado), 176
CONCURSO FEMININO DE
  POESIAS E CONTOS, 448
CONCURSO INFANTIL FIESTA
  DEL LIBRO, 389
CONCURSO INTERNACIONAL
  DE NARRATIVA, 700
CONCURSO INTERNACIONAL DE
  NOVELAS EDITORIAL
  LOSADA, 700
CONCURSO LITERARIO CER-
  VANTES, 225
CONCURSO LITERARIO DE
  EDICIONES PEUSER, 868
CONCURSO LITERARIO HIS-
  PANOAMERICANO, 211
CONCURSO LITERARIO
  MUNICIPAL (Montevideo), 768A
CONCURSO NACIONAL (Peru),
  866
CONCURSO NACIONAL DE
  LITERATURA (Spain), 1028
CONCURSO NACIONAL DE
  NOVELAS (Bolivia), 152
CONCURSO NACIONAL DE
  TEATRO (Mexico), 749
CONCURSO POETICA ('Il

474 International Literary Awards